1 MONTH OF
FREE
READING

at

www.ForgottenBooks.com

By purchasing this book you are eligible for one month membership to ForgottenBooks.com, giving you unlimited access to our entire collection of over 1,000,000 titles via our web site and mobile apps.

To claim your free month visit:

ISBN 978-0-265-79819-5
PIBN 10891061

This book is a reproduction of an important historical work. Forgotten Books uses
state-of-the-art technology to digitally reconstruct the work, preserving the original format
whilst repairing imperfections present in the aged copy. In rare cases, an imperfection in
the original, such as a blemish or missing page, may be replicated in our edition. We do,
however, repair the vast majority of imperfections successfully; any imperfections that
remain are intentionally left to preserve the state of such historical works.

BULLETINS

AND

OTHER STATE INTELLIGENCE

FOR THE YEAR 1858.

PART III.

BULLETINS

AND

THER STATE INTELLIGENCE

FOR THE YEAR 1858.

IN FOUR PARTS.

COMPILED AND ARRANGED FROM THE OFFICIAL DOCUMENTS
PUBLISHED IN THE LONDON GAZETTE.

BY T. L. BEHAN,

SUPERINTENDENT.

PART III.

PRINTED BY HARRISON AND SONS,
LONDON GAZETTE OFFICE, ST. MARTIN'S LANE.
1860.

*9{ds
Clement's, Lib
10·26·38*

FROM THE

LONDON GAZETTE of JULY 2,
1858.

Admiralty, June 30, 1858.

' DESPATCHES, of which the following are ·
copies, have been received by the Lords Commissioners of the Admiralty from Captain Sotheby,
C.B.; of Her Majesty's ship Pearl, commanding a
Naval Brigade in India :

No. 85.

Camp, Kaptangunge, Goruckpore District,
SIR, *1st May,* 1858.

I HAVE the honour to forward you, for the information of my Lords Commissioners of the Admiralty, a report of the proceedings of a most successful and gallant attack on a body of rebels, posted
at the village of Nuggur on the 29th ultimo, by a
detachment from this force, as per margin*, under
the command of Major Cox, 13th Light Infantry,
at which a portion of the Pearl's Naval Brigade
took a very conspicuous part, under the charge of
Lieutenant Grant, R.N. Having sent an expedition the previous day to drive off a party of
400 rebels within a few miles of our camp, intelligence was shortly afterwards received of another
body of upwards of 1,000 (half of whom were
Sepoys) having crossed the Gogra, and taken up
a very strong position at the above-named place,
about six miles from us. The detachment left at
noon, and arrived at the spot at 2.30 P.M., the

* 92 Naval Brigade; 150 of 13th Light Infantry ; 63
Bengal Yeomaury Cavalry ; 290 Goorkhas and Seikhs.
1858. 7 Y

men principally riding on elephants. They were received by a sharp fire of musketry from the dense jungle that nearly surrounds the village. For the particulars of the attack I beg to forward Lieutenant Grant's account of it.

Major Cox has called my attention to the skilful and quick manner in which that officer, assisted by Mr. C. F. Foot, Midshipman, managed the guns, which were so well directed by their Captains, that only one shell out of 35 failed in striking the object. He has always rendered me most valuable assistance in this very unusual service, and is a most excellent officer.

Lieutenant Pym, R.M., is also reported, to have led the Marines and Seamen most gallantly to the assault, assisted by Mr. J. G. Shearman, Engineer ; as also Mr. Parkins, Gunner, in charge of the rocket ; and I beg most earnestly and humbly that you will be pleased to bring before the notice of my Lords Commissioners of the Admiralty the names of these officers for promotion.

Lieutenant Pym speaks very highly of William Turner and William Bates, Gunners, Royal Marine Artillery.

The dispersion of these rebels was most timely performed, as they were to have been joined the following morning by 3,000 more from Tandak, in concert with another large body in the north, for the invasion of the district, whilst in our front at Belwar there are about 5,000 more, with five guns.

The enemy left everything behind, including a pair of new silk banners, with the Hindoo and Mahomedan colours blended together, apparently just made.

I am sorry to report my men and officers are much suffering from fever, being somewhat unprepared for so long a campaign, and from their late harassing duties. This is the eighth time this field force has been in action, and the Pearl's Brigade guns the only Artillery attached to it, and until very lately the Brigade were the only Europeans. It is most gratifying to report the good behaviour of the men, being now as good artillerymen and soldiers as formerly they were seamen.

I have, &c.,

(Signed)   EDWARD S. SOTHEBY,
Captain R.N., Commanding
Pearl's Naval Brigade.

The Secretary of the Admiralty, London.

SIR,   *Camp, Kaptangunge, May* 1, 1858.

I HAVE the honour to submit for your information, the part taken by a detachment of Her Majesty's ship Pearl's Naval Brigade, with a force under the command of Major Cox, Her Majesty's 13th Light Infantry, in an attack on the town and Fort of Nuggur, on the 29th ult.

The detachment, consisting as per margin,* left camp at noon, and after a hot march of seven miles, approached the west side of the town of Nuggur. A strong body of the 13th Light Infantry and Seikhs, were sent to clear the jungle on that side, while the rest made a detour round to the north side. As we came up we were received by a sharp rifle fire from a thick bamboo jungle, and from what appeared to be a line of works inside.

We opened fire from the guns at a distance of 500 yards on the town, and a tope of trees to the eastward of the place, where an outpost of the

* Royal Marines, 25; Seamen, 67; 2 12-pounder howitzers; 1 24-pounder rocket.

enemy was lodged, who were immediately driven in.

By the direction of Major Cox, I shifted ground about 80 yards to my left front, and directing Mr. Parkins with the rocket to fire steadily at that portion of the town where the enemy seemed in the greatest force. I kept up a steady fire of shell at the different posts held by the enemy.

The marines and seamen, under Lieutenant Pym, were ordered by Major Cox to attack on the right, and by a simultaneous movement with the rest of the force, the town and old fort were carried, the enemy retreating through the bamboo jungle, were pursued to the banks of a large jheel at the back of the place, when all our men were recalled. I believe upwards of 30 dead bodies were counted in the village, but many more must have fallen in the jungle from the rifle practice.

Lieutenant Pym speaks very highly of the forwardness and activity of Mr. J. G. Shearman, Engineer ; Mr. Foot, Midshipman, with the guns, was very zealous ; and Mr. Parkins, Gunner, rendered considerable assistance and made good practice with the rocket.

I beg to enclose a list of casualties.

I have, &c.

(Signed)   HENRY D. GRANT, Lieutenant, in charge of Detachment of the Pearl's Naval Brigade.

Captain Edward S. Sotheby, 'R. N.,
Commanding Her Majesty's ship
Pearl's Naval Brigade.

Return of Casualties of the detachment of the Royal Naval Brigade engaged in the capture of the fort and village of Nuggur, on the 29th April, 1858.

Charles Cloak, A.B., gunshot wound of right thigh, severely wounded.

2 men of Her Majesty's 13th Light Infantry, wounded.

> J. C. DICKENSON, Assistant-Surgeon, Honourable East India Company's Service, in charge of detachment of Naval Brigade.
>
> HY. D. GRANT, Lieutenant, R.N., In charge of detachment of Pearl's Naval Brigade.
>
> ED. S. SOTHEBY, Captain, R.N., Commanding Pearl's Naval Brigade.

Sir,   *Camp, Kaptangugne, April 30, 1858.*

I HAVE much gratification in reporting to you the admirable behaviour of the officers, seamen, and marines of that portion of the Pearl's Naval Brigade under Lieutenant H. D. Grant, R.N., which took part in the engagement at Nuggur yesterday, under my command.

The howitzers and rockets were rapidly and effectually got into action, and were served with the greatest precision under the immediate direction of that very able and efficient officer, Lieutenant Grant. The remainder of the brigade co-operated most effectually in storming the town and fort under Lieutenant F. G. Pym, R.M.L.I., and I was much struck with the gallant and soldierlike manner in which that officer led his men to the assault.

I have, &c.,
J. W. COX,
Major, 13th Light Infantry.

Captain Sotheby, R.N.,
Her Majesty's ship Pearl.

War-Office, Pall-Mall, S.W.,
June 30, 1858.

The Secretary of State for War has received the following Nominal List of Casualties in the Royal Artillery, serving in India.

Calcutta, May 3, 1858.

Gunner Edward Waller, 2 Co. 11 Bat., April 2, killed in action at Beyt Island.

Gunner George Newbourne, 2 Co. 11 Bat., April 2, killed in action at Beyt Island.

Driver Samuel Tims, F. Troop, March 6, severely wounded before Lucknow.

Corporal John Douglas, 5 Co. 12 Bat , March 9, slightly wounded before Lucknow.

Gunner William Sparrow, 5 Co. 12 Bat., March 9, slightly wounded before Lucknow.

Gunner Henry Robbins, 5 Co. 12 Bat., March 9, slightly wounded before Lucknow.

Gunner George Barker, 6 Co. 11 Bat., March 9, severely wounded before Lucknow.

Gunner John Saunders, 5 Co. 12 Bat., March 15, slightly wounded before Lucknow.

Gunner James Sparrow, 5 Co. 12 Bat., March 16, slightly wounded before Lucknow.

Captain N. S. K. Bayly, 2 Co. 11 Bat, April 2, dangerously wounded at Beyt Island.

Gunner Thomas Cavannah, 2 Co. 11 Bat., April 2, severely wounded at Beyt Island.

Gunner Francis Sansom, 2 Co. 11 Bat., April 2, severely wounded at Beyt Island.

Gunner Thomas Oliver, 2 Co. 11 Bat., April 2, severely wounded at Beyt Island.

Gunner Henry Curry, 2 Co. 11 Bat., April 2, very severely wounded at Beyt Island.

Gunner James Adams, 2 Co. 11 Bat., April 2, slightly wounded at Beyt Island.

Gunner Henry Mosse, 5 Co. 3 Bat., drowned whilst bathing at Susseram.

J. E. DUPUIS, Major-General,
Commanding Royal Artillery in India

At the Court at *Buckingham-Palace*, the 5th day of *June*, 1858.

The QUEEN'S Most Excellent Majesty in Council was pleased to confirm a representation duly prepared (as set forth in this Gazette) by the Ecclesiastical Commissioners for England, as to the assignment of a district chapelry to the consecrated church of Saint Philip, situate in Arlington-square, in the parish of Saint Mary, Islington, in the county of Middlesex, and in the diocese of London, to be named " The District chapelry of Saint Philip, Islington."

Also, a representation as to the assignment of a district chapelry to the consecrated church of Saint Paul, situate at Coven, in the parish of Brewood, in the county of Stafford, and in the diocese of Lichfield, to be named " The District Chapely of Saint Paul, Coven."

Crown-Office, July 2, 1858.

MEMBER returned to serve in the present PARLIAMENT.

County of Norfolk.

Eastern Division.

The Honourable Wenman Clarence Walpole Coke, of Holkham, in the county of Norfolk, in the room of Sir Edward North Buxton, Bart., deceased.

Westminster, June 28, 1858.

This day, the Lords being met, a message was sent to the Honourable House of Commons by the Gentleman Usher of the Black Rod, acquainting them, that *The Lords, authorized by virtue of a Commission under the Great Seal, signed by Her Majesty, for declaring Her Royal Assent to an Act agreed upon by both Houses, do desire the immediate attendance of the Honourable House in the House of Peers to hear the Commission read;* and the Commons being come thither. the said Commission, empowering the Lord Archbishop of Canterbury, and several other Lords therein named, to declare and notify the Royal Assent to the said Act, was read accordingly, and the Royal Assent given to

An Act to abolish the property qualifications of Members of Parliament.

An Act to amend the course of procedure in the High Court of Chancery, the Court of Chancery in Ireland, and the Court of Chancery of the county palatine of Lancaster.

An Act to continue " The Peace Preservation (Ireland) Act, 1856."

An Act for confirming a scheme of the Charity Commissioners for Sir Eliab Harvey's Charity in the town of Folkestone.

An Act for confirming a scheme of the Charity Commissioners for certain municipal charities in the city of Bristol.

An Act for confirming a scheme of the Charity Commissioners for certain charities in the parishes of Saint Nicholas and Saint Leonard, in the city of Bristol.

An Act to enable the East Suffolk Railway Company to construct a branch railway near

Lowestoft, to raise further sums of money, and for other purposes.

An Act to confer upon the Waterford and Kilkenny Railway Company facilities for raising money.

An Act for repairing and maintaining the road from Horsham, in the county of Sussex, through Dorking and Leatherhead to Epsom, in the county of Surrey, and from Capel to Stone-street, at Ockley, in the said county of Surrey.

An Act for extending the time for the completion of the works authorized by " The Stokes Bay Railway and Pier Act, 1855," and for other purposes.

An Act to amend the Acts relating to " The East Kent Railway (Extension to Dover.)"

An Act for better supplying with water the inhabitants of the town of Taunton, in the county of Somerset.

An Act to amend " The Tramore Embankment Act, 1852."

An Act for authorising the abandonment of part of the authorised line of the Exeter and Exmouth Railway ; and the making instead of the part so abandoned of an extension of the main line of the railway ; and for reducing and regulating the capital and borrowing powers of the Exeter and Exmouth Railway Company ; and for other purposes.

An Act to confer upon the London, Brighton, and South Coast Railway Company further powers for raising money, and to authorize the purchase and lease by them of the undertakings of certain other railway companies.

An Act to authorize a lease of the Staines, Wokingham and Woking Railway to the London and South Western Railway Company, and for other purposes connected with the Staines, Wokingham and Woking Railway Company.

An Act for enabling the Eastern Steam Navigation Company to extend their powers of trading, to increase their capital, and to alter and amend their Charter and Deed of Settlement.

An Act to enable the Globe Insurance Company to alter and amend some of the provisions of their Deed of Settlement, and to confer further powers on the Company.

An Act to authorize the Cromford and High Peak Railway Company to raise further sums of money, and for other purposes.

An Act providing for the separate incorporation of the overseers of the several townships of Manchester, Ardwick, Chorlton-upon-Medlock, and Hulme, for specific purposes ; for the levying and collection of rates ; for the extinguishing the exemption of gas works from rates.

An Act for enabling the Local Board of Health for the District of Wallasey to construct works and supply their district with water and gas ; for enlarging their powers with respect to the acquisition and maintenance of ferries ; and for other purposes.

An Act to enable the Ballymena, Ballymoney, Coleraine, and Portrush Junction Railway Company to sell their undertaking to the Belfast and Ballymena Railway Company.

An Act to extend the time for the completion of the Salisbury and Yeovil Railway, and to authorise the sale thereof to the London and South Western Railway Company.

An Act to vest the Stirling and Dunfermline Railway in the Edinburgh and Glasgow Railway Company, and for other purposes.

An Act for the formation of a Junction between the Fife and Kinross and Kinross-shire Railways, and the construction of a Joint Station at Kinross.

An Act to repeal "The Blyth Harbour and Dock

Act 1854," and to regulate the Company constituted thereby, and for other purposes.

An Act for the improvement of the parish of Chiswick, in the county of Middlesex, and for other purposes.

An Act to enable the Caledonian Railway Company to make a Branch Railway to the Port Carlisle Railway, and for other purposes.

An Act for enabling the Ayr and Dalmellington Railway Company to raise additional capital; for vesting their undertaking in the Glasgow and South Western Railway Company; and for other purposes.

An Act for extending the limits of the Bradford Waterworks, and for authorising the construction of new and altered works; and for empowering the Corporation of Bradford to borrow a further sum of money; and for other purposes.

An Act for the amalgation of the Hertford and Welwyn Junction Railway Company and the Luton, Dunstable, and Welwyn Junction Railway Company into one Company, to be called the Hertford, Luton, and Dunstable Railway Company, and for regulating the capital of the Company formed by the amalgamation; and for other purposes.

An Act for enabling the Manchester, Sheffield, and Lincolnshire Railway Company to make a Railway from near their Newton and Hyde Station to the township of Marple, in the parish of Stockport, in the county of Chester, to be called the Newton and Compstall Branch; and for other purposes.

An Act to incorporate the Luton Gas and Coke Company; to authorise the adjustment and increase of the present capital; and for other purposes.

An Act to repeal an Act for amending and

maintaining the turnpike road from the northern end of the village of Balby, in the county of York, to Worksop, in the county of Nottingham ;" and to make other provisions in lieu thereof, so far as regards a portion of the said turnpike road.

An Act to alter and amend the Acts for the improvement of the navigation of the rivers Burry, Loughor, and Lliedi, in the counties of Carmarthen and Glamorgan, and to improve the harbour of Llanelly, in the said county of Carmarthen.

An Act for incorporating the City of Waterford Gas Company, and for authorizing them to acquire the existing Gas Works at Waterford, and to supply gas, and for other purposes.

Board of Trade, Whitehall,
July 1, 1858.

The Right Honourable the Lords of the Committee of Privy Council for Trade and Plantations have received, through the Secretary of State for Foreign Affairs, a copy of a Despatch from Her Majesty's Acting Consul at Naples, reporting that henceforth British ships will be permitted to load empty oil casks at any port in the Kingdom of the Two Sicilies, for the purpose of being filled with oil at other ports of that kingdom.

War-Office, Pall-Mall,
2nd July, 1858.

4th Dragoon Guards, Percy Charles Du Cane, Gent., to be Cornet, without purchase, vice Rawlins, appointed to the 8th Light Dragoons. Dated 2nd July, 1858.

1st Dragoons, Cornet J. W. S. Smith to be Lieutenant, without purchase. Dated 2nd July, 1858.

6th Dragoons, Lieutenant Arthur Finch Dawson to be Captain, by purchase, vice Cuthbert, who retires. Dated 2nd July, 1858.

Lieutenant the Hon. C. W. Thesiger to be Captain, by purchase, vice Currie, who retires. Dated 2nd July, 1858.

9th Light Dragoons, Henry John Hall, Gent., to be Cornet, without purchase, in succession to Lieutenant Grant, promoted in the 5th Light Dragoons. Dated 2nd July, 1858.

Military Train. The promotion of Lieutenant Nathaniel Burslem, without purchase, to bear date 26th February, 1858, in lieu of 28th May, 1858, as previously stated.

Royal Artillery. The surname of the Assistant-Surgeon, appointed from the Staff in the Gazette of 22nd June, 1858, as George Ralph *Tait*, M.D , is spelt *Tate*.

Scots Fusilier Guards, Major and Brevet-Colonel E. W. F. Walker, C.B., to be Lieutenant-Colonel, without purchase, vice Brevet-Colonel George Moncrieff, promoted to the rank of Major-General. Dated 14th June, 1858.

Captain and Lieutenant-Colonel and Brevet-Colonel Francis Seymour, C.B., to be Major, without purchase, vice Walker. Dated 14th June, 1858.

Lieutenant and Captain and Brevet-Major the Honourable W. C. W. Coke to be Captain and Lieutenant-Colonel, without purchase, vice Seymour. Dated 14th June, 1858.

1st Foot, Lieutenant Henry S. Bowes Watson has been permitted to retire from the Service by the sale of his Commission. Dated 2nd July, 1858.

4th Foot, Herbert Munro Long Innes, Gent., to be Ensign, without purchase, vice Twentyman, promoted. Dated 2nd July, 1858.

8th Foot.

To be Ensigns, without purchase.

Gentleman Cadet William W. Madden, from the Royal Military College. Dated 2nd July, 1858.

Jeremy Peyton Jones, Gent. Dated 3rd July, 1858.

11th Foot, Brevet-Lieutenant-Colonel John Singleton to be Lieutenant-Colonel, without purchase, vice Brevet-Colonel J. C Harold, who retires upon full-pay. Dated 1st July, 1858.

14th Foot, Charles Henry Jackson, Gent., to be Ensign, without purchase, vice Watson, promoted. Dated 2nd July, 1858.

17th Foot, Edmund Sandilands Savage, Gent., to be Ensign, without purchase, vice Allen, promoted. Dated 2nd July, 1858.

19th Foot.

To be Captains, without purchase.

Captain G. E. L. C. Bissett from half-pay 55th Foot. Dated 2nd July, 1858.

Lieutenant R. Fitz Gibbon Lewis from the 86th Foot. Dated 2nd July, 1858.

Lieutenant W. F. T. Marshall from the 70th Foot. Dated 2nd July, 1858.

Lieutenant Thomas Madden, from the 24th Foot. Dated 2nd July, 1858.

To be Ensigns, without purchase.

Augustus Morant Handley, Gent., vice Rew, promoted. Dated 2nd July, 1858.

James Francis Fraser, Gent., vice Hackett, promoted. Dated 3rd July, 1858.

Francis Herbert Evans, Gent., vice Iles, promoted. Dated 4th July, 1858.

20th Foot.

To be Ensigns, without purchase.

James Smyth, Gent., vice Hoblyn, promoted. Dated 2nd July, 1858.

Clifford Gabourel Gibaut, Gent., vice Blount, promoted. Dated 3rd July, 1858.

21st Foot, Frederick Packman, Gent., to be Ensign, without purchase, vice Pearman, promoted. Dated 2nd July, 1858.

23rd Foot, Lieutenant Charles Cameron Lees, from the 76th Foot, to be Lieutenant and Adjutant. Dated 2nd July, 1858.

George Knox Leet, Esq., late Paymaster of the County Dublin Militia, to be Paymaster. Dated 2nd July, 1858.

24th Foot, Assistant-Surgeon John Colahan, M.D., from the Staff, to be Assistant-Surgeon. Dated 2nd July, 1858.

26th Foot, Gentleman Cadet Henry C. Sharp, from the Royal Military College, to be Ensign, without purchase, vice Bindon, promoted in the 78th Foot. Dated 2nd July, 1858.

31st Foot, Cornet Christopher Kettyles, from half-pay of the late Land Transport Corps, to be Quartermaster, vice Hopkins, appointed to a Depôt Battalion. Dated 2nd July, 1858.

32nd Foot, Gentleman Cadet Frank A. Horridge, from the Royal Military College, to be Ensign, without purchase, vice Gray, promoted. Dated 2nd July, 1858.

37th Foot, Lieutenant John Deering Collum to be Captain, without purchase, vice Atkinson, promoted. Dated 15th June, 1858.

Ensign George John Usil Mason to be Lieutenant, without purchase, vice Collum. Dated 15th June, 1858.

40*th Foot*, Martin Morphy, Gent., to be Ensign, without purchase, vice Dowman, promoted. Dated 2nd July, 1858.

46*th Foot*, Ensign Peter Andrew John Ducrow to be Lieutenant, by purchase, vice Hutton, who retires. Dated 2nd July, 1858.

47*th Foot.* The promotion of Ensign John J. Dunne, as stated in the Gazette of 25th ultimo, has been cancelled.

51*st Foot*, Ensign William Henry Saunders to be Lieutenant, without purchase, vice Swaffield, deceased. Dated 9th May, 1858.

Ensign Henry Chambers to be Lieutenant, without purchase, vice Saunders, whose promotion, on the 20th May, 1858, has been cancelled. Dated 20th May, 1858.

Gentleman Cadet George S. Robertson, from the Royal Military College, to be Ensign, without purchase, vice Chambers, promoted. Dated 2nd July, 1858.

53*rd Foot*, Ensign Hugh R. H. Wilson to be Lieutenant, without purchase, vice Brockhurst, died of his wounds. Dated 20th April, 1858.

Serjeant-Major Charles Pye to be Ensign, without purchase, vice Wilson. Dated 2nd July, 1858.

60*th Foot*, Lieutenant Herbert George Deedes to be Captain, by purchase, vice Steward, who retires. Dated 2nd July, 1858.

Lieutenant John D'Olier George to be Captain, by purchase, vice Cockburn, who retires. Dated 2nd July, 1858.

Ensign J. T. U. Coxen, from the 19th Foot, to be Ensign, vice Mortimer, promoted. Dated 2nd July, 1858.

64*th Foot*, Herbert Grant, Gent., to be Ensign, without purchase. Dated 2nd July, 1858.

65*th Foot*, Richard Oliffe Richmond, Gent., to be Ensign, without purchase. vice Butler, whose appointment, as stated in the Gazette of the 16th March, 1858, has been cancelled. Dated 2nd July, 1858.

66*th Foot*, Ensign W. T. Hody Cox to be Lieutenant, by purchase, vice Dickens, who retires. Dated 2nd July, 1858.

73*rd Foot*, Lieutenant Richard James Hereford to be Captain, by purchase, vice Lucas, who retires. Dated 2nd July, 1858.
Ensign George Pinckney to be Lieutenant, by purchase, vice Hereford. Dated 2nd July, 1858.

76*th Foot*, Ensign Mortimer J. Macdonald to be Lieutenant, without purchase, vice Lees, appointed to the 23rd Foot. Dated 2nd July, 1858.
Gentleman Cadet Albert E. Pearse, from the Royal Military College, to be Ensign, without purchase, vice Macdonald. Dated 2nd July, 1858.

84*th Foot*, Brevet-Major Thomas Lightfoot to be Major, without purchase, vice MacCarthy, who retires upon full-pay. Dated 2nd July, 1858.
Lieutenant Pierce Chute to be Captain, without purchase, vice Lightfoot. Dated 2nd July, 1858.
Ensign George Lambert to be Adjutant, vice Browne, promoted. Dated 2nd July, 1858.
Henry Arkwright, Gent., to be Ensign, without purchase. Dated 2nd July, 1858.

90*th Foot*, Gentleman Cadet Francis Russell, from the Royal Military College, to be Ensign, without purchase, vice Wilmer, promoted. Dated 2nd July, 1858.

Rifle Brigade, Assistant-Surgeon George Baly, from the Staff, to be Assistant-Surgeon, vice Alexander, who exchanges. Dated 2nd July, 1858.

HOSPITAL STAFF.

Assistant-Surgeon William Alexander, from the Rifle Brigade, to be Assistant-Surgeon to the Forces, vice Baly, who exchanges. Dated 2nd July, 1858.

The appointment of Mr. C. B. Mosse to be Staff Assistant-Surgeon, as stated in the Gazette of the 7th May, 1858, has been cancelled.

BREVET.

Brevet-Colonel John Casimir Harold, retired full-pay 11th Foot, to be Major-General, the rank being honorary only. Dated 1st July, 1858.

Lieutenant-Colonel Thomas Williams, C.B., 4th Foot, having completed three years' actual service in the rank of Lieutenant-Colonel, to be promoted to be Colonel in the Army, under the Royal Warrant, 6th October, 1854. Dated 18th June, 1858.

Major William Justin MacCarthy, retired full-pay 84th Foot, to be Lieutenant-Colonel in the Army, the rank being honorary only. Dated 2nd July, 1858.

Captain William Lee, retired full-pay 6th Foot, to be Major in the Army, the rank being honorary only. Dated 2nd July, 1858.

MEMORANDUM.

The transfer of Ensign N. C. Ramsay, from the 25th Foot, to the 23rd Regiment, as stated in the Gazette of the 4th June, 1858, has been cancelled.

Commission signed by the Lord Lieutenant of the County of Southampton.

Hampshire Yeomanry Cavalry.

Walter Jervis Long, Esq., to be Lieutenant, vice James George Boucher, resigned. Dated 26th June, 1858.

Commissions signed by the Lord Lieutenant of the County of Worcester.

Worcestershire Regiment of Militia.

Lieutenant Edward Lyttleton Francis to be Captain, vice W. P. Howell, resigned.

Ensign Christopher H. Hook to be Lieutenant, vice Francis, promoted.

The Committee of Her Majesty's Privy Council on Education certify in this Gazette that the Boys' Home, No. 44, Euston-road, St. Pancras, Middlesex, is an Industrial School within the meaning of the Industrial Schools' Act, 1857.

FROM THE

LONDON GAZETTE of JULY 6, 1858.

War-Office, July 6, 1858.

THE Queen has been graciously pleased to give orders for the appointment of Major-General Sir Hugh Henry Rose, K.C.B., to be an Ordinary Member of the Military Division of the First Class, or Knights Grand Cross, of the Most Honourable Order of the Bath; and of His Highness the Maharajah Jung Bahadoor Koonwar Ranajee,

Commander-in-Chief of the Goorkha Troops lately acting with the British Army in the Field in India, to be an Honorary Member of the Military Division of the First Class, or Knights Grand Cross, of the said Most Honourable Order.

Whitehall, July 6, 1858.

The Queen has been pleased to present the Reverend Robert Kirke to the church and united parishes of Hutton and Fishwick, in the presbytery of Chirnside and county of Berwick, vacant by the death of the Reverend John Edgar.

The Queen has also been pleased to present the Reverend Robert Leitch to the church and parish of Abernyte, in the presbytery of Dundee, and county of Perth, vacant by the transportation of the Reverend Robert Graham, late Minister thereof, to the church of Errol.

Foreign-Office, July 6, 1858.

Notice is hereby given, that the Earl of Malmesbury has appointed B. M. Bradbeer, Esq., to be Agent at Lowestoft for the issue of Foreign-Office Passports.

Whitehall, July 3, 1858.

The Queen, taking into Her Royal consideration that upon the decease of the Most Noble William Spencer Duke of Devonshire, Knight Companion of the Most Noble Order of the Garter, in the month of January last, the Dukedom of Devonshire devolved upon the Most Noble William now Duke of Devonshire, Knight of the Most Noble Order of the Garter, as eldest son and heir of William Cavendish, Esquire, the eldest son of George Augustus Henry, Earl of Burlington, third son of William, fourth Duke of Devonshire, Knight of the Most Noble Order of the Garter, and brother of William, fifth Duke of Devonshire, Knight of the most Noble Order of the Garter, the father of the said William Spencer, late Duke of Devonshire, deceased, whereby, according to the ordinary rules of honour, the brothers and sister of the said William, now Duke of Devonshire, cannot enjoy that place and precedence which would have been due to them had their late father, the said William Cavendish, survived the said William Spencer, late Duke of Devonshire, and had thereby succeeded to the title and dignity of Duke of Devonshire, Her Majesty has been graciously pleased to ordain and declare that the Honourable George Henry Cavendish, Representative in Parliament for the Northern Division of the county of Derby, the Honourable Richard Cavendish, and Fanny, wife of Frederick John Howard, Esquire, shall henceforth have, hold, and enjoy the same title, place, pre-eminence, and precedence, as if their late father, the said William Cavendish, had survived the said William Spencer, late Duke of Devonshire, and had thereby succeeded to the title and dignity of Duke of Devonshire :

And Her Majesty has been further pleased to command that the said Royal Order and Declaration be registered in Her College of Arms.

Commission signed by the Lord Lieutenant of the County of Sussex.

Light Infantry Battalion of the Royal Sussex Militia.

Stewart Paxton Marjoribanks, Gent., to be Ensign, vice Henry Edmund Stanley, appointed to the 23rd Regiment. Dated 26th June, 1858.

*Commission signed by the Lord Lieutenant of the
County of* Radnor.

Royal Radnor Rifles.

Adjutant Edward Rawlings Hannam (late Paymaster 2nd Battalion 60th Rifles) to serve with
the rank of Captain from the 1st day of December, 1856.   Dated 18th June, 1858

*Commission signed by the Lord Lieutenant of the
County of* Middlesex.

1st or Royal East Middlesex Regiment of Militia.

Charles George Norris, Gent., to be Ensign, vice
Wells, resigned.   Dated 30th June, 1858.

*Commission signed by the Lord Lieutenant of the
County Palatine of* Chester.

2nd Regiment of Royal Cheshire Militia.

John Frederick Wilkin, Gent., to be Ensign, vice
Willson, promoted.   Dated 30th June, 1858.

*Commissions signed by the Lord Lieutenant of the
West Riding of the County of* York, *and of the
City and County of the City of* York.

West York Rifle Regiment of Militia.

Lieutenant James Lees Harwar to be Captain,
vice Pollock, resigned.   Dated 12th June, 1858.
Ensign William Monro to be Lieutenant, vice
Harwar promoted.   Dated 12th June, 1858.

*3rd Regiment (Light Infantry) of West York
Militia.*

Ensign Joe Drury Bottomley to be Lieutenant,
vice W. G. Gatliff, resigned.   Dated 23rd
June, 1858.
William Parkin Brown, Gent., to be Ensign, vice
Bottomley, promoted.   Dated 27th June, 1858.

1st West Regiment of Yorkshire Yeomanry Cavalry.

Edward Bury, Gent., to be Cornet, vice James Bury, resigned. Dated 27th June, 1858.

MEMORANDUM.

West York Rifle Regiment of Militia.

Her Majesty has been graciously pleased to accept the resignation of the Commission held in this Regiment by Ensign Edmund Bowyer.

———

The Lords Commissioners of Her Majesty's Treasury having certified to the Commissioners for the Reduction of the National Debt that there was no surplus of Actual Revenue over the Actual Expenditure of the United Kingdom of Great Britain and Ireland for the year ended the 31st day of March, 1858 ;

The Commissioners for the Reduction of the National Debt hereby give notice, that no sum will be applied by them on account of the Sinking Fund under the provisions of the Act 10 Geo. 4, cap. 27, between the 1st day of July, 1858, and the 30th day of September, 1858.

A. Y. Spearman, Comptroller-General.
National Debt Office,
2nd July, 1858.

FROM THE

LONDON GAZETTE of JULY 9,
1858.

War-Office, July 9, 1858.

THE Queen has been graciously pleased to give orders for the appointment of Andrew Smith, Esq., M.D., late Director-General of the Army Medical Department, to be an Ordinary Member of the Civil Division of the Second Class, or Knights Commanders, of the Most Honourable Order of the Bath.

War-Office, July 9, 1858.

The Queen has been pleased to appoint

The Most Honourable the Marquess of Salisbury, K.G., Lord President of the Council and Colonel of the Hertford Militia,

His Grace the Duke of Richmond, K.G., Colonel of the Royal Sussex Artillery Militia, A.D.C. to the Queen,

His Grace the Duke of Buccleuch, K.G., Colonel of the Edinburgh or Queen's Regiment of Light Infantry Militia, A.D.C. to the Queen,

The Most Honourable the Marquess of Downshire, Colonel of the Royal South Down Militia,

The Right Honourable Viscount Palmerston, K.G., G.C.B.,

The Viscount Hardinge, Under Secretary of State for War, Major of the Kent Artillery Militia,

The Lord Methuen, Lieutenant-Colonel of the Royal Wiltshire Militia,

Lieutenant-General Sir Frederick Stovin, K.C.B., K.C.M.G.,

Colonel Robert Percy Douglas, Inspector of Militia,

Colonel James Kennard Pipon, Assistant Adjutant-General to the Forces,

Colonel John Wilson Patten, Colonel of the 3rd Royal Lancashire Militia, A.D.C. to the Queen,

Colonel Richard Thomas Gilpin, Colonel of the Bedford Militia, and

Colonel Robert Alexander Shafto Adair, Lieutenant-Colonel-Commandant of the Suffolk Artillery Militia, A.D.C. to the Queen,

to be Her Majesty's Commissioners for the purpose of enquiring into the Establishment, Organization, Government, and Direction of the Militia Force of the United Kingdom of Great Britain and Ireland.

Crown-Office, July 7, 1858.

MEMBER returned to serve in the present PARLIAMENT.

County of Cornwall.

Western Division.

John Saint Aubyn, of No. 6, Stratford-place, London, Esq., in the room of Michael Williams, Esq., deceased.

Admiralty, 3rd July, 1858.

Corps of Royal Marines.

First Lieutenant Edward Ralph Horsey, of the Artillery Companies, to be Captain, vice Gray, deceased.

Second Lieutenant Clement Winstanley Carlyon, of the Plymouth Division, to be First Lieutenant, vice Horsey, promoted.

Gentleman Cadet William Repton Friend Hopkins to be a Second Lieutenant.

Commissions signed by the Lord Lieutenant of the County of Warwick.

Warwickshire Militia.

2nd Regiment.

Lieutenant Matthew William Furness to be Captain, vice John Wingfield Digby, resigned. Dated 25th June, 1858.

Ensign Malcolm Ronalds to be Lieutenant, vice M. W. Furness, promoted. Dated 25th June, 1858.

Commission signed by the Lord Lieutenant of the County of Dumbarton.

Highland Borderers Light Infantry (Stirlingshire Militia).

Arthur Fawkes, Gent., to be Ensign, vice Thomas Anderson, deceased.

FROM THE

LONDON GAZETTE of JULY 13, 1858.

Whitehall, July 9, 1858.

THE Queen has been pleased to appoint John Inglis, Esq., Her Majesty's Advocate for Scotland, to be Her Majesty's Justice Clerk, and President of the Second Division of the Court of

Session in Scotland, and also one of the Senators of the College of Justice there.

Whitehall, July 10, 1858.

The Queen has been pleased to grant the office of Her Majesty's Advocate for Scotland to Charles Baillie, Esq., Her Majesty's Solicitor-General for Scotland, in the room of John Inglis, Esq., appointed Her Majesty's Justice Clerk, and President of the Second Division of the Court of Session in Scotland.

Whitehall, July 12, 1858.

The Queen has been pleased to grant the office of Solicitor-General for Scotland to David Mure, Esq., Advocate, in the room of Charles Baillie, Esq., appointed Her Majesty's Advocate for Scotland.

Foreign-Office, July 13, 1858.

The Queen has been pleased to approve of Don Carlos Montemar as Consul at Gibraltar for Her Royal Highness the Duchess Regent of Parma.

St. James's Palace, July 9, 1858.

The Queen has been pleased, on the nomination of the Right Honourable the Earl of Shrewsbury and Talbot, to appoint Captain Nathaniel George Philips, late 47th Regiment, one of Her Majesty's Honourable Corps of Gentlemen at Arms, vice Captain C. E. Hopton, resigned.

Westminster, July 12, 1858.

This day the Lords being met a message was sent to the Honourable House of Commons by the Gentleman Usher of the Black Rod, acquainting them, that *The Lords, authorized by virtue of a Commission under the Great Seal, signed by Her Majesty, for declaring Her Royal Assent to several Acts agreed upon by both Houses, do desire the immediate attendance of the Honourable House in the House of Peers to hear the Commission read;* and the Commons being come thither, the said Commission, empowering the Lord Archbishop of Canterbury, and several other Lords therein named, to declare and notify the Royal Assent to the said Acts, was read accordingly, and the Royal Assent given to

An Act to make valid certain Acts of the late Chief Justice of Bombay.

An Act for the better management of County Rates.

An Act for releasing the lands of the commissioners for the exhibition of 1851, upon the repayment of monies granted in aid of their funds.

An Act to continue the Railways Act (Ireland), 1851.

An Act to remove doubts as to the operation of a convention between Her Majesty and the Emperor of the French relative to Portendic and Albreda.

An Act for enabling the Wexford Harbour Embankment Company to alter the number of their shares, and to issue preference shares in lieu of unissued shares and for other purposes.

An Act for enabling the Mayor, Aldermen, and Burgesses of the Borough of Liverpool, to acquire lands for a Post-office and Public Offices, and to make a new, and widen existing streets within the borough, and for other purposes,

An Act for making and maintaining a bridge over the River Yar, in the Isle of Wight, with approaches and roads thereto, and for other purposes.

An Act to extend the time for purchasing certain lands required by the Belfast and County Down Railway Company, and for other purposes connected with the same Company.

An Act for better enabling the British Gas Light Company, limited, to light with gas the City of Norwich, and suburbs thereof, to dissolve the Norwich Gas Light Company, and to repeal the Acts relating thereto.

An Act to authorise the construction of a Railway from Andover to Redbridge in the county of Southampton, and for that purpose to convert the Andover Canal into a railway.

An Act to incorporate and regulate the Oude Railway Company; to enable the Company to construct and maintain railways in the East Indies; and to enter into contracts with the East India Company; and for other purposes.

An Act to enable the London, Brighton, and South Coast Railway Company to complete the communication by Railway between Shoreham, Henfield, and the Mid Sussex Railway, and for other purposes connected with their undertaking.

An Act to amend the Birkenhead Improvement Amendment Act, 1850, especially with respect to the general Mortgage Debt of the Commissioners, and their powers to sell certain lands, and for other purposes.

An Act to repeal the Act relating to the Dean Forest Turnpike Roads, and to make other provisions in lieu thereof, and to authorise the construction of a new road, and for other purposes.

An Act to extend the time for the completion of so much of the Cornwall Railway as lies between Truro and Falmouth, and for other purposes.

An Act for authorising the London and South Western Railway Company to make new works, and to make arrangements with other companies, and for authorising a lease to them of the Salisbury and Yeovil Railway, and for regulating their capital and borrowing powers, and for other purposes.

An Act to enable the Mersey Docks and Harbour Board to construct certain works at Birkenhead, in substitution for, and in addition to those already authorised, and for other purposes.

An Act to consolidate and amend the provisions of the several Acts relating to the Liverpool and Birkenhead Docks and the port and harbour of Liverpool, and for other purposes connected therewith.

An Act for confirming the gift by Francis Crossley, Esquire, to the borough of Halifax, of a park for the benefit of the inhabitants of the borough, and for authorising the mayor, aldermen, and burgesses of the borough to maintain and regulate the park, and to provide, maintain, and regulate public baths in the park, and for making a cemetery ; and for making further provision with respect to the waterworks and the gasworks, and the improvement of the borough, and for other purposes.

An Act for amending the Acts relating to the Manchester Corporation Waterworks.

An Act for making a railway from the Hertford and Ware Branch of the Eastern Counties Railway to Buntingford.

An Act for authorising the raising by the Ulverstone and Lancaster Railway Company of further money, and the selling or leasing of their railway to the Furness Railway Company ; or the making by the two Companies of working arrangements ; and for giving further powers to the two Companies respectively ; and for other purposes.

An Act for making a tramroad from the Aberllefenny Slate Quarries, in the parish of Talyllyn, in the county of Merioneth, to the River Dovey, in the parish of Llanfihangel-Geneu'r-Glyn, in the county of Cardigan, with branches therefrom, and for other purposes.

An Act to enable the Great Northern and Western (of Ireland) Railway Company to make deviations in their authorized railways, and to empower the Midland Great Western Railway of Ireland Company to acquire shares in the undertaking of the Great Northern and Western (of Ireland) Railway Company, and for other purposes.

An Act to afford facilities to the Limerick and Foynes Railway Company for raising the funds necessary to enable them to execute their undertaking.

An Act to enable the Midland Great Western Railway of Ireland Company to make an alteration in the line of their Streamstown and Clara Junction Railway, and for other purposes.

An Act for enabling the Eastern Counties Railway Company to abandon a portion of the Newmarket and Chesterford Railway, and also a railway to the River Thames, at Galleon's Reach.

An Act to enable the Bury and Ratcliffe Waterworks Company to raise further sums of money, and to amend the Act relating to the Company.

An Act for enabling the Portsmouth Railway Company to extend their railway from Havant to Hilsea; to acquire additional lands; to use a portion of the London and South-Western, and London, Brighton, and South Coast Railways; and for other purposes.

An Act to authorise the South Devon and Tavistock Railway Company to lease their railway; to enable them to raise further capital for the completion of their undertaking, and to make arrangements as to their share and borrowed capital ; and for other purposes.

An Act for lighting with gas the town of Northampton and the neighbourhood thereof, in the county of Northampton.

An Act for enabling the Battersea Park Commissioners to sell, and the West End of London and Crystal Palace Railway Company to purchase, pieces of land, situate near the south end of the new bridge, leading from Chelsea to Battersea Park ; for lease of undertaking to the London, Brighton, and South Coast Railway Company ; for extending the time for completing extension to Farnborough ; and for other purposes.

An Act for constructing a market, market-places, and slaughter-houses, with all necessary conveniences, within the hamlet of Canton, in the county of Glamorgan, to be called " The Llandaff and Canton District Markets."

An Act for vesting the undertaking of the Blackburn Railway Company in the Lancashire and Yorkshire and East Lancashire Railway Companies, and for other purposes.

War-Office, Pall-Mall, S.W.,
July 13, 1858.

THE Secretary of State for War has received the following List of Casualties in the Army serving in India.

Nominal Return of Casualties in Action, in Her Majesty's Troops, since date of last Return.

Head Quarters, Camp, Bareilly,
May 9, 1858.

At Kotah, on 30th March, 1858.

72nd Highlanders.

Lieutenant A. S. Cameron, severely wounded.

Private John Elders, killed.

„ Alexander Fraser, slightly wounded.

„ James Gibson, dangerously wounded; since dead.

„ James King, severely wounded.

„ Colin McKenzie, slightly wounded.

„ Robert Risk, slightly wounded.

„ David Roach, slightly wounded.

„ John Steele, slightly wounded.

„ Thomas White, slightly wounded.

At Nuwabgunge, on 13th April, 1858.

7th Hussars.

Lieutenant R. Topham, severely wounded.

Serjeant John Baker, severely wounded.

Private Joseph Carroll, severely wounded.

„ Charles Castle, slightly wounded.

„ John Friel, dangerously wounded.

„ Thomas Maskery, slightly wounded.

„ Richard Parrott, severely wounded.

„ John White, mortally wounded; since .dead.

At Sullanpore, on 23rd February, 1858.

Royal Artillery.

Bombardier G. Winter, 6th Co. 13th Bat., slight contusion of right leg by grape shot.

WM. PAKENHAM, Colonel,
Acting Adjutant-General, Her Majesty's Forces in India.

———

War-Office, Pall-Mall,
13th July, 1858.

2nd Regiment of Dragoon Guards, Cornet H. P. J. Mackenzie has been permitted to resign his Commission. Dated 13th July, 1858.

1858.   8 A

1*st Dragoons*, Ralph William Caldwell, Gent., to be Cornet, by purchase, vice Weaver, appointed to the 5th Light Dragoons. Dated 13th July, 1858.

6*th Dragoons*, Cornet John O'Neill to be Lieutenant, by purchase, vice A. F. Dawson, promoted. Dated 13th July, 1858.

To be Cornets, by purchase.

John Baskerville, Gent., vice the Honourable W. O. B. Annesley, promoted. Dated 13th July, 1858.

Thomas James Williams Bulkeley, Gent., vice the Honourable E. R. Bourke, promoted. Dated 14th July, 1858.

7*th Light Dragoons*, Arthur Hamilton Scrope, Gent., to be Cornet, by purchase, vice Thompson, who retires. Dated 13th July, 1858.

10*th Light Dragoons*, Arthur Barthorp, Gent., to be Cornet, without purchase, vice Dodgson, appointed to the 14th Light Dragoons. Dated 13th July, 1858.

12*th Light Dragoons*, Assistant-Surgeon Samuel Gibson, M.B., from the Staff, to be Assistant-Surgeon, vice Wodsworth, promoted on the Staff. Dated 13th July, 1858.

13*th Light Dragoons*, Lieutenant William Atkinson, from the 52nd Foot, to be Lieutenant paying the difference, vice Keyworth, who exchanges, receiving the difference. Dated the 13th July, 1858.

Military Train, Lieutenant E. B. Bass, from the 67th Foot, to be Lieutenant, vice Burslem, who exchanges. Dated 13th July, 1858.

F. Bullen Morris, Gent., to be Ensign, by purchase, vice Hardy, promoted. Dated 13th July, 1858.

5*th Regiment of Foot*, William Church Ormond,

Gent., to be Ensign, without purchase. Dated 13th July, 1858.

6th *Foot*, Lieutenant Thomas Ffolliott Powell to be Captain, by purchase, vice Taylor, who retires. Dated 13th July, 1858.

Captain Christopher Francis Holmes, from half-pay Unattached, to be Captain, repaying the difference, vice Lee, retired upon full-pay. Dated 13th July, 1858.

Lieutenant Henry Parkinson to be Captain, by purchase, vice Holmes, who retires. Dated 13th July, 1858.

8th *Foot*, Lieutenant W. J. Tarte, from the 31st Foot, to be Lieutenant, without purchase. Dated 13th July, 1858.

11th *Foot*, Brevet-Lieutenant-Colonel Charles Pratt, from half-pay 96th Foot, to be Major, vice Singleton, promoted. Dated 13th July, 1858.

Captain John Walpole D'Oyly to be Major, by purchase, vice Pratt, who retires. Dated 13th July, 1858.

Lieutenant Owen Davies to be Captain, by purchase, vice D'Oyly. Dated 13th July, 1858.

Ensign William Adam Smyth to be Lieutenant, by purchase, vice Davies. Dated 13th July, 1858.

Roper Dacre Tyler, Gent., to be Ensign, by purchase, vice Miers, promoted. Dated 13th July, 1858.

15th *Foot*, De Burgho Edward Hodge, Gent., to be Ensign, by purchase, vice Wintle, promoted. Dated 13th July, 1858.

Walter Lawrence Martin, Gent., to be Ensign, without purchase. Dated 14th July, 1858.

16th *Foot*, Edward Laws, Gent., to be Ensign, by purchase, vice Knox, promoted. Dated 13th July, 1858.

Henry Bowyer Smith, Gent., to be Ensign, without purchase. Dated 14th July, 1858.

17th *Foot*, Ensign Thomas Rochfort Hunt to be Lieutenant, without purchase, vice Disbrówe, deceased. Dated 13th June, 1858.

Ensign James Urquhart Mosse to be Lieutenant, without purchase, vice Hunt, whose promotion on the 15th June, 1858, has been cancelled. Dated 15th June, 1858.

Lieutenant Francis James Berkeley to be Adjutant, vice Disbrowe, deceased. Dated 13th June, 1858.

18th *Foot*, Ensign J. F. Daubeny to be Lieutenant, by purchase, vice Blacker, promoted. Dated 13th July, 1858.

Henry Horace Eden, Gent., to be Ensign, by purchase, vice Daubeny. Dated 13th July, 1858.

19th *Foot*, Lieutenant Thomas Conway Lloyd, from the 4th Foot, to be Captain, by purchase, vice Cochrane, who retires. Dated 13th July, 1858.

The second Christian name of Ensign Handley is *Mourant*, and not *Morant*, as stated in the Gazette of the 2nd instant.

To be Lieutenants, without purchase.

Ensign Beauchamp Colclough, from the 62nd Foot. Dated 13th July, 1858.

Ensign C. J. F. Smith, from the 32nd Foot. Dated 13th July, 1858.

22nd *Foot*, Ensign W. S. Hardinge, from the 89th Foot, to be Lieutenant, without purchase. Dated 13th July, 1858.

23rd *Foot*, Robert Cæsar Bacon, Gent., to be Ensign, without purchase, vice Ramsay, whose appointment, as stated in the Gazette of the 4th of June, 1858, has been cancelled. Dated 18th July, 1858.

24th Foot, Ensign H. C. Marsack, from the 46th
Foot, to be Lieutenant, without purchase, vice
Madden, promoted, in the 19th Foot. Dated
13th July, 1858.

28th Foot, Samuel Forbes Auchmuty, Gent., to
be Ensign, by purchase, vice Fitz-Stubbs, who
has retired. Dated 13th July, 1858.

31st Foot, Ensign W. J. Tarte to be Lieutenant,
by purchase, vice Swettenham, promoted. Dated
13th July, 1858.

34th Foot, Charles Hamilton Webb, Gent., to be
Ensign, without purchase, vice Shiffner, promoted. Dated 13th July, 1858.

35th Foot, Lieutenant John Harris to be Captain, without purchase, vice Le Grand, killed
in action. Dated 24th April, 1858.

Ensign W. H. B. Payn to be Lieutenant, without
purchase, vice Harris. Dated 24th April,
1858.

Ensign Edward Laws, from the 16th Foot, to be
Ensign, vice Payn. Dated 13th July, 1858.

38th Foot, Captain Barnard William Cocker, from
half-pay, Unattached, to be Captain, repaying
the difference, vice Brevet-Major Charles
Frederick Torrens Daniell, whose Brevet Rank
has been converted into Substantive Rank, under
the Royal Warrant of 6th October, 1854. Dated
13th July, 1858.

Lieutenant William K. Elles to be Captain, by
purchase, vice Cocker, who retires. Dated
13th July, 1858.

Dyas Ringrose Lofthouse, Gent., to be Ensign, by
purchase, vice Parry-Jones, promoted. Dated
13th July, 1858.

46th Foot, William Gordon McCrae, Gent., to be
Ensign, by purchase, vice Ducrow, promoted.
Dated 13th July, 1858.

47th Foot, Frederick George Berkeley, Gent., to

be Ensign, by purchase, in succession to Lieutenant Straton, promoted. Dated 13th July, 1858.

John Frederic Bell, Gent, to be Ensign, by purchase, vice Stanley, promoted. Dated 14th July, 1858.

48*th Foot*, Reginald Pennell, Gent., to be Ensign, by purchase, vice Gilling, promoted in 22nd Foot. Dated 13th July, 1858.

49*th Foot*, Herbert John Hill, Gent., to be Ensign by purchase, vice Rogers, promoted in the 19th Foot. Dated 13th July, 1858.

52*nd Foot*, Lieutenant Charles Keyworth, from the 13th Light Dragoons, to be Lieutenant, vice Atkinson, who exchanges. Dated 13th July, 1858.

53*rd Foot*, Lieutenant-Colonel William Payn, from half-pay, Unattached, to be Lieutenant-Colonel, paying the difference, vice Brevet-Colonel W. R. Faber, who exchanges, receiving the difference. Dated 13th July, 1858.

54*th Foot*, Ensign L. K. Edwards to be Lieutenant, by purchase, vice Schlotel, who retires. Dated 13th July, 1858.

Henry Lambard, Gent., to be Ensign by purchase, vice Edwards. Dated 13th July, 1858.

Assistant-Surgeon Alexander Reid, from the Staff, to be Assistant-Surgeon, vice Armstrong, promoted on the Staff. Dated 13th July, 1858.

55*th Foot*, Alfred Hervey Kay, Gent., to be Ensign, by purchase, vice Delano Osborne, promoted. Dated 13th July, 1858.

60*th Foot*, John Alexander Hudson, Gent., to be Ensign, by purchase, vice Ogilvy, promoted. Dated 13th July, 1858.

George Edward Graham Foster Pigott, Gent., to

be Ensign, without purchase, vice Poole, promoted. Dated 14th July, 1858.

62nd *Foot*, Arthur Lake, Gent., to be Ensign, by purchase, vice Carbery, promoted in the 14th Foot. Dated 13th July, 1858.

64th *Foot*, Assistant-Surgeon George Parsons Wall, from the Staff, to be Assistant-Surgeon, vice Carey, promoted on the Staff. Dated 13th July, 1858.

66th *Foot*, Francis Edward Browne, Gent., to be Ensign, by purchase, vice Cox, promoted. Dated 13th July, 1858.

John Tulloch Nash, Gent., to be Ensign, without purchase, vice Bagge, promoted in 10th Foot. Dated 14th July, 1858.

Assistant-Surgeon William Hemphill, M.D., from the 48th Foot, to be Assistant-Surgeon, vice Murray, promoted on the Staff. Dated 13th July, 1858.

67th *Foot*, Lieutenant Nathaniel Burslem, from the Military Train, to be Lieutenant, vice Bass, who exchanges. Dated 13th July, 1858.

William Southby Middleton, Gent., to be Ensign by purchase, vice Cardew, promoted. Dated 13th July, 1858.

68th *Foot*, Charles Clifton Hood, Gent., to be Ensign by purchase, vice Marshall, promoted. Dated 13th July, 1858.

69th *Foot*, Assistant-Surgeon Francis Madden, from the Staff, to be Assistant-Surgeon, vice Gains, promoted on the Staff. Dated 13th July, 1858.

73rd *Foot*, Hugh Francis Hachet Gibsone, Gent., to be Ensign, by purchase, vice Pinckney, promoted. Dated 13th July, 1858.

74th *Foot*, Assistant-Surgeon Arthur Chester, from the Staff, to be Assistant Surgeon, vice

Peacocke, promoted on the Staff. Dated 13th July, 1858.

75th Foot, Assistant-Surgeon Harry Reid, M.D., from the Staff, to be Assistant-Surgeon, vice Fraser, promoted on the Staff. Dated 13th July, 1858.

86th Foot, Richard Jebb Posnett, Gent., to be Ensign, by purchase, vice Jackson, promoted. Dated 13th July, 1858.

Rifle Brigade, Lieutenant Richard Tryon to be Captain, by purchase, vice Brewster, who retires. Dated 13th July, 1858.

UNATTACHED.

Major and Brevet-Lieutenant-Colonel William Payn, of the 53rd Foot, to have his Brevet Rank converted into Substantive' Rank, Unattached, under the Royal Warrant of 6th October, 1854. Dated 13th July, 1858.

HOSPITAL STAFF.

Staff-Surgeon of the First Class William Home, M.D., from half-pay, to be Staff-Surgeon of the First Class, and attached to a Depôt Battalion. Dated 3rd July, 1858.

Staff-Surgeon of the First Class Henry Cooper Reade, from half-pay, to be Staff-Surgeon of the First Class, and attached to a Depôt Battalion. Dated 3rd July, 1858.

William Percy Pickard Mackesy, Gent., to be Assistant-Surgeon to the Forces, vice Preston, appointed to the 22nd Foot. Dated 1st July, 1858.

To be Acting Assistant-Surgeons.

Thomas Lambert Hinton, Gent. Dated 3rd July, 1858.

William Daniel Michell, Gent: Dated 13th July, 1858.

BREVET.

The following Officers having completed three years' actual service in the rank of Lieutenant-Colonel, to be promoted to be Colonels in the Army, under the Royal Warrant of 6th October, 1854:

Lieutenant-Colonel John Clark Kennedy, on half-pay of the 18th Foot (Assistant Quarter-master-General at Aldershott). Dated 22nd June, 1858.

Lieutenant-Colonel Arthur Cyril Goodenough, C.B., commanding a Depot Battalion. Dated 24th June, 1858.

Brevet-Lieutenant-Colonel Charles Pratt, 11th Foot, to be Colonel in the Army. Dated 9th November, 1846.

Captain Barnard William Cocker, 38th Foot, to be Major in the Army. Dated 23rd November, 1841.

Brevet-Major Barnard William Cocker, 38th Foot, to be Lieutenant-Colonel in the Army. , Dated 11th November, 1851.

Captain Christopher Francis Holmes, 6th Foot, to be Major in the Army. Dated 9th November, 1846.

Brevet-Major Christopher Francis Holmes, 6th Foot, to be Lieutenant-Colonel in the Army. Dated 20th June, 1854.

Paymaster Alexander Boyd, on half-pay of the 11th Foot, to be Major in the Army, the rank being honorary only. Dated 15th June, 1858.

The undermentioned Officers having completed three years' actual service in the rank of Lieutenant-Colonel, to be promoted to be Colonels in the Army, under Her Majesty's Order in Council of 13th September, 1854 :

Lieutenant-Colonel John Mitchell, Royal Marines. Dated 22nd June, 1858.

Lieutenant-Colonel George Elliott, Royal Marines. Dated 22nd June, 1858.

Lieutenant-Colonel Thomas Charles Cotton Moore, Royal Marines. Dated 22nd June, 1858.

Commission signed by the Lord Lieutenant of the County of Stirling.

The Right Honourable Charles Adolphus Earl of Dunmore to be Deputy Lieutenant.

Commission signed by the Lord Lieutenant for the Town and County of the Town of Haverfordwest.

Charles Prust, Esq., to be Deputy Lieutenant. Dated 8th July, 1858.

Commissions signed by the Lord Lieutenant of the County of Sussex.

George Weekes, Esq., to be Deputy Lieutenant. Dated 6th July, 1858.

Henry Padwick, Esq., to be Deputy Lieutenant. Dated 6th July, 1858.

Walter Barttelot Barttelot, Esq., to be Deputy Lieutenant. Dated 6th July, 1858.

William Boxall, Esq., to be Deputy Lieutenant. Dated 6th July, 1858.

Commissions signed by the Lord Lieutenant of the Tower Hamlets.

Major Frederick John Parry to be Deputy Lieutenant. Dated 24th June, 1858.

King's Own Light Infantry Regiment of Militia.

William Hadder Heard, Esq., Captain half-pay 86th Regiment, to be Captain, vice Gosling, retired. Dated 28th June, 1858.

Wray Bury Palliser, Esq., late a Captain Tipperary Militia, to be Captain, vice Houlditch, retired. Dated 2nd July, 1858.

Frederick William Best Parry, Gent., to be Ensign, vice Mathews, appointed to 2nd West India Regiment. Dated 2nd July, 1858.

Commissions signed by the Lord Lieutenant of the County of Kent.

The Honourable Henry Frederic Cowper to be Deputy Lieutenant. Dated 8th July, 1858.

Kent Militia Regiment of Militia.

Leonard Strong, Gent., late Lieutenant King's Own Light Infantry Militia, to be First Lieutenant, vice Girardôt, promoted. Dated 7th July, 1858.

East Kent Regiment of Militia.

Ensign Robert Owen Hordern to be Lieutenant, vice Roxburg, resigned. Dated 7th July, 1858.

Commission signed by the Lord Lieutenant of the County of Derby.

1st Regiment of Derbyshire Militia.

Lieutenant Thomas Peach to be Captain, vice Brooke, resigned. Dated 10th July, 1858.

Commission signed by the Lord Lieutenant of the County of Surrey.

1st Regiment of Royal Surrey Militia.

Aubrey de Vere Beanclerk, Gent., to be Ensign. Dated 8th July, 1858.

[Erratum in the Gazette of the 26th of March, 1858.]

Dorset Regiment of Militia.

For Henry Palmer Duncan,

Read, *Francis* Henry Palmer Duncan.

FROM THE

LONDON GAZETTE of JULY 16, 1858.

Whitehall, July 16, 1858.

THE Queen has been pleased to direct letters patent to be passed under the Great Seal, granting the dignity of a Baronet of the United Kingdom of Great Britain and Ireland, unto Alexander Hutchinson Lawrence, Esq., of the Bengal Civil Service (eldest son of the late Sir Henry Montgomery Lawrence, K.C.B.), and to the heirs male of his body lawfully begotten, with remainder, in default of such issue, to Henry Waldemar Lawrence, Esq. (Brother of the said Alexander Hutchinson Lawrence), and the heirs male of his body lawfully begotten.

War-Office, July 16*th*, 1858.

The Queen has been pleased to appoint

Major-General the Right Honourable Jonathan Peel, Secretary of State for War,

General His Royal Highness the Duke of Cambridge, K.G., G.C.B., K.P., G.C.M.G., General Commanding-in-Chief the Forces,

The Right Honourable Lord Stanley, H.M. Commissioner for the Affairs of India,

General the Most Honourable the Marquess of
Tweeddale, K.T., C.B.,
Major-General the Viscount Melville, K.C.B.,
Lieutenant-General Sir H. G. W. Smith, Bart.,
G.C.B.,
Lieutenant-General Sir G. A. Wetherall, K.C.B.,
  ' Adjutant-General of the Forces,
Major-General Patrick Montgomerie, C.B.,
E.I.C.S.,
Major-General Henry Hancock, E.I.C.S.,
Colonel William Burlton, C.B., E.I.C.S.,
Colonel Thomas Forsyth Tait, C.B., E.I.C.S.,
A.D.C. to the Queen,

to be Her Majesty's Commissioners for the purpose of inquiring into the Organization of the Army
at present serving in the pay and under the control and management of the Honourable the East
India Company.

War-Office, July 16, 1858.

The Queen has been pleased to appoint James
Aspinall Turner, Esq., Colonel Henry John
French, and Henry Selfe Selfe, Esq., to be Her
Majesty's Commissioners, for the purpose of en-
quiring into the state of the Store and Clothing
Depôts at Weedon, Woolwich, and the Tower.

Board of Trade, Whitehall,
July 13, 1858.

The Right Honourable the Lords of the Committee of Privy Council for Trade and Plantations
have received, through the Secretary of State for
Foreign Affairs, a copy of a Despatch from Her
Majesty's Chargé d'Affaires at St. Petersburgh,
stating that the following medicinal substances,

published in the Journal de St. Petersbourg, are
prohibited from importation into Russia ; viz. :

Colodium Cantharidale,
Hydrargyrum Zooticum,
Morrison's Pills,
Oleum Harlameuse,
Hydrargyrum Sulphuratum Stibiatum,
Powder of Herbs, known as " Le Roi,"
Ferrum Liniatum Alcoholisatum, and
Revalenta Arabica,
Dragées de Lactale de Fer and Pâte de mou
de Veau,
Essentia Caffeæ.
Extractum Medicinalia,
Extractum filicis maris ætherei Theriaqui.

Board of Trade, Whitehall,
July 13, 1858.

The Right Honourable the Lords of the Committee of Privy Council for Trade and Plantations
have received, through the Secretary of State for
Foreign Affairs, a copy of a Decree of the Sicilian
Government, by which the reduction of the import duties upon Sugar and Coffee, recently granted
by that Government to Spain, is extended to all
other nations.

Board of Trade, Whitehall,
July 13, 1858.

The Right Honourable the Lords of the Committee of Privy Council for Trade and Plantations
have received, through the Secretary of State for
Foreign Affairs, a copy of a Despatch from Her
Majesty's Chargé d'Affaires, at St. Petersburg,
announcing that the Port of St. Nicolas, in the
Black Sea, is now open to trade.

War-Office, Pall-Mall,
16*th July,* 1858.

. GENERAL ORDER.

Horse Guards,
16*th July,* 1858.

IN consideration of the eminent services of
Major-General Sir James Outram, G.C.B., of the
East India Company's Service, in the recent
operations in India, Her Majesty has been graciously pleased to command that he be promoted
to the rank of Lieutenant-General.

By order of His Royal Highness the
General Commanding-in-Chief.

G. A. WETHERALL,
Adjutant-General.

War-Office, Pall-Mall,
16*th July,* 1858.

1st Regiment of Dragoon Guards, Cornet Herbert
Hale Forbes Gifford, from the 3rd Dragoon
Guards, to be Cornet, vice C. Mc D. Moorsom,
appointed to the 100th Foot. Dated 16th July,
1858.

1st Dragoons, Carr Stuart Glyn, Gent., to be
Cornet, by purchase, vice Smith, promoted.
Dated 16th July. 1858

2nd Dragoons, Cornet Percy Charles Du Cane,
from 4th Dragoon Guards, to be Cornet, vice
Blake, promoted in the 6th Dragoon Guards.
Dated 16th July, 1858.

3rd Light Dragoons, Cornet Charles E. Nettles,
to be Quartermaster, vice Crabtree, who retires
upon half-pay. Dated 16th July, 1858.

6th Dragoons, Cornet William J. Shafto Orde to
be Lieutenant, by purchase, vice Thesiger, pro
moted. Dated 16th July, 1858.

7th Light Dragoons, Lieutenant Musgrave Dyne Brisco to be Captain, without purchase, vice Pedder, deceased. Dated 11th May, 1858.

Cornet the Honourable C. Craven Molyneux to be Lieutenant, without purchase, vice Brisco. Dated 11th May, 1858.

Cornet John B. Phillipson to be Lieutenant, by purchase, vice Molyneux, whose promotion, by purchase, on the 4th June, 1858, has been cancelled. Dated 16th July, 1858.

10th Light Dragoons, Edward Alexander Wood, Gent., to be Cornet, without purchase. Dated 16th July, 1858.

Military Train.

To have the rank of Lieutenants.

Ensign and Adjutant John Sweeney. Dated 21st June, 1858.

Ensign and Adjutant William Shackleton. Dated 21st June, 1858.

Ensign and Adjutant William Thompson. Dated 21st June, 1858.

Ensign John Briggs to be Lieutenant, without purchase, vice Thorburn, deceased. Dated 30th June, 1858.

Royal Artillery.

The undermentioned Gentlemen Cadets to be Lieutenants ; viz. :

Robert Smythe Muir Mackenzie. Dated 22nd June, 1858.

Flemyng George Gyll. Dated 22nd June, 1858.

Seymour Hood Toogood. Dated 22nd June, 1858.

Evelyn Baring. Dated 22nd June, 1858.

Henry Norris Jones. Dated 22nd June, 1858.

Henry Bond. Dated 22nd June, 1858.

Arthur Frederick Pickard. Dated 22nd June, 1858.

Thomas Burnett. Dated 22nd June, 1858.

Samuel Holworthy Desborough. Dated 22nd June, 1858.

Royal Engineers.

The undermentioned Gentlemen Cadets to be Lieutenants, with temporary rank ; viz. :

William Innes. Dated 22nd June, 1858.

Robert Mitchell Campbell. Dated 22nd June, 1858.

Hamilton Tovey. Dated 22nd June, 1858.

Richard Nicholas Buckle. Dated 22nd June, 1858.

Robert Athorpe. Dated 22nd June, 1858.

James Fellowes. Dated 22nd June, 1858.

Richard Henry Beaumont Beaumont. Dated 22nd June. 1858.

George Le Breton Simmons. Dated 22nd June, 1858.

6*th Foot,* Major William Albert Stratton to be Lieutenant-Colonel, without purchase, vice Brevet-Colonel Barnes, deceased. Dated 6th May, 1858.

Captain Henry Pratt Gore to be Major, without purchase, vice Stratton. Dated 6th May, 1858.

Lieutenant John L. O'Mansergh to be Captain, without purchase, vice Gore. Dated 6th May, 1858.

Ensign and Adjutant Henry Kitchener to have the rank of Lieutenant. Dated 6th May, 1858.

Lieutenant William Edmondes Harness has been permitted to retire from the Service by the sale of his Commission. Dated 16th July, 1858.

8*th Foot,* Lieutenant Charles Bradford Brown to be Adjutant, vice Ensign Emerson, who resigns the Adjutancy only. Dated 16th July, 1858.

1858.   8 B

The Commission of Lieutenant W. E. Whelan as Adjutant to bear date 30th April, 1858, in lieu of 22nd June, 1858, as previously stated. Dated 16th July, 1858.

15th Foot, Captain Henry Thomas Richmond, from the 98th Foot, to be Captain, vice Scheberras, who exchanges. Dated 16th July, 1858.

Ensign Arthur Heaton to be Lieutenant. by purchase, vice Fry, promoted. Dated 16th July, 1858.

16th Foot, Basil Clifton Westby, Gent., to be Ensign, without purchase, vice Laws, appointed to the 35th Foot. Dated 16th July, 1858.

18th Foot, Lieutenant C. J. Coote to be Captain, without purchase, vice Forster, deceased. Dated 14th May, 1858.

Ensign James Francis Daubeny to be Lieutenant, without purchase, vice Coote. Dated 14th May, 1858.

Charles Crawford Yates Butler, Gent. to be Ensign, without purchase. Dated 16th July, 1858.

19th Foot, Ensign Arthur W. Burton to be Lieutenant, without purchase. Dated 16th July, 1858.

Robert Gayer Traill, Gent., to be Ensign, without purchase, vice Burton, promoted. Dated 16th July, 1858.

21st Foot.

To be Lieutenants, by purchase.

Ensign G. A. Grant, vice Lee, promoted. Dated 16th July, 1858.

Ensign E. E. Digby Boycott, vice Bruce, promoted. Dated 16th July, 1858.

22nd Foot.

To be Lieutenants, without purchase.

Ensign Alexander D. Gilson, from the 49th Foot. Dated 16th July, 1858.

Ensign H. E. Harrison, from the 41st Foot. Dated 16th July, 1858.

23rd *Foot.* The Commission of Ensign Robert Cæsar Bacon to bear date 13th July, 1858, in lieu of 18th July, 1858, as previously stated.

24th *Foot,* Lieutenant Henry James Hitchcock to be Adjutant, vice Munnings, promoted. Dated 16th July, 1858.

34th *Foot.* The promotion of Ensign B. Shiffner to be Lieutenant, without purchase, to bear date 23rd, instead of 22nd, April, 1858.

44th *Foot,* Ensign Henry Garland Matthews has been permitted to retire from the service by the sale of his Commission. Dated 16th July, 1858.

46th *Foot,* Francis Lloyd Priestley, Gent., to be Ensign, without purchase, vice Marsack promoted in the 24th Foot. Dated 16th July, 1858.

47th *Foot,* Ensign Francis Thomas Elwood to be Lieutenant, by purchase, vice Dunne, whose promotion by purchase on the 25th June, 1858, has been cancelled. Dated 16th July, 1858.

51st *Foot,* The Commission of Ensign George S. Robertson, to bear date 26th June, 1858, instead of 2nd July, 1858, as previously stated. Dated 16th July, 1858.

70th *Foot,* Lieutenant George Richard Greaves, to be Adjutant, vice Scheberras, promoted in the 15th Foot. Dated 18th May, 1858.

Ensign Charles G. S. Menteath to be Lieutenant, without purchase, vice Lynch, promoted in 2nd Foot. Dated 18th May, 1858.

71*st Foot*, Ensign W. F. V. Harris to be Lieutenant, without purchase, vice Swainson, deceased. Dated 15th April, 1858.

73*rd Foot*, Lieutenant Richard James Hereford to be Captain, without purchase, vice Williams, deceased. Dated 2nd July, 1858.

To be Lieutenants, without purchase.

Ensign William Bayley, vice Caldwell, deceased. Dated 14th May, 1858.

Ensign Thomas William Shore Miles, vice Bayley, whose promotion on the 21st May, 1858, has been cancelled. Dated 21st May, 1858.

Ensign George Pinckney, vice Miles, whose promotion on the 22nd June, 1858, has been cancelled. Dated 22nd June, 1858.

Ensign Archibald Henry Sharp, vice Hereford, promoted. Dated 2nd July, 1858.

Ensign Hastings D'Oyly Farrington to be Lieutenant, by purchase, vice Pinckney, whose promotion, by purchase, on the 2nd July, 1858, has been cancelled. Dated 16th July, 1858.

75*th Foot*, Lieutenant Frederick Cornwall, from the 84th Foot, to be Lieutenant, vice White, who exchanges. Dated 16th July, 1858.

84*th Foot*, Lieutenant Thomas White, from the 75th Foot, to be Lieutenant, vice Cornwall, who exchanges. Dated 16th July, 1858.

William Frank Wheatley, Gent., to be Ensign, without purchase, vice Cornwall, promoted. Dated 16th July, 1858.

89*th Foot*, Major John Lewes Philipps to be Lieutenant-Colonel, without purchase, vice Skynner, deceased. Dated 9th May, 1858.

Captain Edward Buller Thorp to be Major, without purchase, vice Philipps. Dated 9th May, 1858.

Lieutenant George Harmer Pering to be Captain,

without purchase, vice Nixon, deceased. Dated 27th April, 1858.

Ensign Henry Bishop to be Lieutenant, without purchase, vice Pering. Dated 27th April, 1858.

98*th Foot*, Captain Attilio Scheberras, from the 15th Foot, to be Captain, vice Richmond, who exchanges. Dated 16th July, 1858.

100*th Foot*, Staff-Surgeon of the Second Class William Barrett, M.B., to be Surgeon. Dated 16th July, 1858.

To be Assistant-Surgeons.

Assistant-Surgeon Thomas Liddard, from the Staff. Dated 16th July, 1858.

Assistant-Surgeon Daniel Murray, M.D., from the Staff. Dated 16th July, 1858.

Cape Mounted Riflemen, George Lidwill Harnette, Gent., to be Ensign, by purchase, vice Humphreys, promoted. Dated 16th July, 1858.

VETERINARY MEDICAL DEPARTMENT·

To be Acting Veterinary-Surgeons.

Edwin Thomas Cheesman, Gent. Dated 16th July, 1858.

Joseph Dulley, Gent. Dated 16th July, 1858.

HOSPITAL STAFF.

Assistant-Surgeon Benjamin Tydd, from the 58th Foot, to be Staff-Surgeon of the Second Class, vice Barrett, appointed to the 100th Foot. Dated 16th May, 1858.

To be Acting Assistant-Surgeons.

Bryan Patrick McDonough, M.D. Dated 7th July, 1858.

Richard Robinson Alderson, Gent. Dated 16th July, 1858.

BREVET.

Major-General Sir James Outram, G.C.B., of the service of the East India Company, to be Lieutenant-General in the Army. Dated 16th July, 1858.

The undermentioned Officers, having completed three years' actual service in the rank of Lieutenant-Colonel, to be Colonels in the Army, under the provisions of the Royal Warrant of the 3rd November, 1854, viz.:

Lieutenant-Colonel Peter Pickmore Faddy, of the Royal Artillery. Dated 29th June, 1858.
Lieutenant-Colonel Henry Drury Harness, of the Royal Engineers. Dated 1st July, 1858.
Lieutenant-Colonel Charles E. Law, of the 66th Foot, having completed three years actual service in the rank of Lieutenant-Colonel, to be promoted to be Colonel in the Army, under the Royal Warrant, of the 6th October, 1854. Dated 12th July, 1858.
Quartermaster Abraham Crabtree, on half-pay 3rd Light Dragoons, to be Captain in the Army, the rank being honorary only. Dated 16th July 1858.

MEMORANDUM.

The appointment of Lieutenant-Colonel Robert Sanders, C.B., from half-pay 19th Foot, to be Lieutenant-Colonel of a Depôt Battalion, as stated in the Gazette of the 23rd October, 1857, has been cancelled.

Commission signed by the Lord Lieutenant of the County of Derby.

1st *Regiment of Derbyshire Militia.*

Lieutenant Woolnough to be Captain, vice Bourne, deceased. Dated 13th July, 1858.

FROM THE

SUPPLEMENT

TO THE

LONDON GAZETTE of JULY 16, 1858.

India Board, July 17, 1858.

THE following papers have been received at the East India House :—

No. 1.

GENERAL ORDERS BY THE RIGHT HONORABLE THE GOVERNOR-GENERAL OF INDIA.

Allahabad, April 14, 1858.

No. 73 of 1858.

IN publishing the following despatch, No. 143 A, dated 17th March, 1858, from the Deputy Adjutant-General of the Army, submitting the official report of Brigadier-General T. H. Franks, C.B., regarding the operations of the late Jounpore Field Force, the Right Honorable the Governor-General desires to make known the high satisfaction he has derived from the perusal of its details, evidencing, as they do, no less the military skill of the commander than the gallantry and devotion of the European and Goorkha troops under his command.

R. J. H. BIRCH, Colonel,
Secretary to the Government of India,
with the Governor-General.

No. 2.

The Deputy Adjutant-General of the Army to the Secretary to the Government of India, Military Department, with the Governor-General.

Head-Quarters, Camp, before Lucknow, March 17, 1858.

SIR,   No. 143 A.

I HAVE the honor, by desire of the Commander-in-Chief, to enclose in original a report, with enclosures, as per margin,* dated the 9th instant, from Brigadier-General T. H. Franks, C.B., commanding the late Jounpore Field Force, of the operations of the force, subsequent to its departure from Singramow, which I am to beg you will be so good as to submit to the Right Honorable the Governor-General for favourable consideration.

I have, &c.,
H. W. NORMAN, Major,
Deputy-Adjutant-General of the Army.

---

* Forwards report from Brigadier-General Franks, of the operations of the field force late under his command. Casualty returns. Returns of captured ordnance. Two sketches.

No. 3.

Brigadier-General T. H. Franks, C.B., to the Deputy Adjutant-General of the Army, Head-Quarters Camp.

Camp Dilkoosha, before Lucknow,
March 9, 1858.

SIR,   No. 148.

I HAVE the honor to forward, for submission to his Excellency the Commander-in-Chief, a detailed report of the operations of the field force under my command (strength noted marginally),* from the date of its leaving Singramow, and crossing the Oude frontier on the 19th ultimo, till its junction with the army under his Excellency's command, on the evening of the 4th inst.

2. A report having gained credence in camp, and reached the enemy, that no forward movement would be made before the 20th February, the Nazim Mehundee Hussun had issued his orders for his force, hitherto divided at Waree and Chanda, to be concentrated at the latter place, by the evening of the 19th February.

3. At 6 A.M., however, of that day, the force under my command marched from Singramow, in the following order :—The advance guard composed of the whole of our small party of cavalry, of 240 selected marksmen, of the three British

---

* 6th Company 13th battalion Royal Artillery, 108; 8th Company 2nd battalion Royal Artillery, 52; detachment A Company 3rd battalion Madras Artillery, 66; detachment 4th Company 5th battalion Bengal Artillery, 30; detachment Benares Horse, 38; Her Majesty's 10th Regiment, 730; Her Majesty's 20th Regiment, 717; Her Majesty's 97th Regiment, 661; Allied Goorkha Force, 6 battalions infantry and artillery attached, 3193; Native Artillery detail, 115: total, 5710;—with 2 18-pounder guns, 13 9-pounder guns, 2 42-5-inch mortars, 3 24-pounder howitzers, 2 12-pounder howitzers, 1 12-pounder rocket tube, and 1 6-pounder rocket tube.

regiments and four-horsed guns, under Lieutenant-Colonel Longden, 10th Regiment, was followed by the British brigade, under Brigadier Evelegh, C.B., and by the six battalions of Goorkha Infantry, under Colonel Pulwan Singh, in column of route. The rear and baggage guards, consisting of five companies of the 10th, 20th, and 97th Regiments, and of three companies of Goorkhas, with two-horsed guns, under Major Radcliffe, 20th Regiment, closed the rear.

4. On reaching Koereepore, I learnt, through spies, that the enemy in possession of "Chanda," under the Chuckledar Bunda Hoosain, numbered 8,000 men ; of whom 2,500 were sepoys of the 20th, 28th, 48th, and 71st Regiments Native Infantry, and that the Nazim Mehundee Hussun was still at Waree, eight miles distant in a southerly direction with 10,000 men and 11 guns. The junction of his forces was therefore still incomplete and I determined to attack him before it could be effected.

5. Halting the force out of fire, I reconnoitred the enemy's position.

"Chanda" is a large village, at the south-eastern angle of which are a considerable mud fort and a serai, both of great height, and loopholed for musketry. Round the village, fort, and serai, a breastwork had been thrown up, and a ditch excavated, and six pieces of artillery were placed in position in it and on its left. The principal strength of the position consisted in the close and high cultivation surrounding it on three sides, and rendering approach most difficult.

6. My reconnoissance being complete, at 11 A.M., I attacked in the following order :—The marksmen were extended in skirmishing order out of range of the enemy's artillery ; then, advancing to 700 yards, they opened fire, which was immediately replied to by the guns opposed to us.

Having thus drawn the enemy's fire, and ascertained the position of his artillery, 8 of our light guns were brought up at a gallop, supported as quickly as possible by the two 18-pounders.

Meantime, the main body followed in contiguous quarter distance columns, at deploying distance; the British brigade in the centre, three regiments of Goorkhas on the right, and three on the left; the cavalry divided and covering the flanks; Captain Thring's four 9-pounder bullock guns accompanied the infantry in the centre. As they advanced into the plain, these columns deployed into line.

7. The skirmishers and light guns now gradually moved forward, the enemy retiring before them, the Goorkhas threatening the flanks, and the British brigade advancing in support in the centre.

In this manner the force soon drove the enemy before it, carried the position and captured 6 guns, following the rebels through and past the village.

When the exhausted skirmishers could no longer reach the enemy, two of Major Cotter's guns, and the cavalry,* galloping to the front, acted with great effect; the cavalry charging and cutting up a number of the rebels, and the guns following them with a destructive fire, till the dense thickets which bordered the plain forbade further pursuit.

8. The force was then halted on the right of the road three miles beyond "Chanda."

9. Suspecting the Nazim to be now on the move from Waree on the left, I detached the cavalry under Lieutenant C. N. Tucker, 8th

* A detachment of 25 mounted soldiers of Her Majesty's 10th Foot, and a few of the Benares Horse, under Ressaldar Nuxbund Khan.

Bengal Light Cavalry, and 2 guns of Captain
Middleton's battery to watch that flank; while
the troops, fatigued by great heat and rapid movement, gained time to rest and refresh themselves,
and liquor and cooked provisions were issued to
them. The captured artillery was also meanwhile
collected.

10. When this had been accomplished, we took
ground to the left across the road to the village
of Amereepore, the better to cover the march of
our baggage, and to meet the enemy, should he
advance.

Later in the day, near sunset, when all hopes of
his approach seemed at an end, and while the
ground for encampment was being taken up, the
enemy appeared on our left front.

11. The force immediately changed front, and
attacked in the same order as in the morning.

12. The Nazim having suffered severely on his
right, which was exposed in the open plain to our
artillery and rifle fire, sought shelter in some thick
mangoe groves to his left : thus endeavouring to
work round my right, and bringing an 18-pounder
into action at a distance. But this attempt was
speedily checked by the three battalions of Goorkhas on that flank, who, under Colonel Pulwan
Sing advanced, fired, and charged, driving the
enemy before them.

13. The complete state of preparation in which
the Nazim found us, when he had anticipated
coming unexpectedly on our left rear, took him
by surprise. The heavy fire with which he was
received completed his discomfiture, and caused
his almost immediate retreat in disorder towards
Waree ; his guns having never been closely engaged, with the exception of the 18-pounder
before-mentioned. The lateness of the hour and
his rapid flight alone saved his artillery from capture.

14. Thus terminated the action at an hour after dark : and the force bivouacked on the ground it occupied at the close of the day. I estimate the enemy's loss in these two actions to have been upwards of 800 killed and wounded.

15. On the 20th I remained halted ; as the baggage, delayed by difficult ground, only arrived late on that day.

During this time the enemy remained at Waree ; my flank movement and his defeat at Amereepore having thrown him off his direct line of retreat to Lucknow.

Report, however, tended to show that he contemplated making a wide circuit by our left, and occupying the strong jungle pass, position, and Fort of Budhayan nine miles in our front ; which, if stoutly defended, would have considerably delayed my progress.

But as he was kept in a state of uncertainty as to whether I might not attack him in front at Waree, or in flank if he should march towards Budhayan, to which place I was nearer than he, he deferred this movement till mine should be more distinctly defined, keeping his troops constantly under arms watching mine.

16. At daybreak on the 21st, drawing up my force in order of battle as if to march on Waree, I allowed the whole of my baggage to file away past my right rear towards Lumbooah, —the village of Roostum Suhia, a friendly zemindar, who had shown that he was well affected towards the government by the collection of supplies, and by safely escorting the bridge of boats from Singramow.

17. It having been given out that the force would halt at Lumbooah, the Nazim, whose spies closely watched every movement, thought that he would still be in time to anticipate me at Budhayan.

But I pushed the baggage rapidly through the village of Lumbooah, and, when this had been effected, my advance guard under Lieutenant-Colonel Longden, withdrawing unperceived from Amereepore, overtook and headed the baggage, followed gradually by the whole force, which, by a rapid movement, seized Budhayan and occupied its fort.

18. The Nazim thus missed his opportunity. He had been deceived as to my intentions sufficiently long to allow of the safe progress of my encumbrances through the defile of Budhayan, and had finally been forestalled in the possession of that strong position.

19. Five companies of Goorkhas were thrown into the fort, and six British Companies and two guns, posted on the Nullah which runs under it, assured the main force encamped two miles in advance against attack on left flank or rear.

20. During the 22nd, I remained halted to allow the expected reinforcements of Lahore Light Horse and Pathans to overtake me. In the course of this day, the Nazim with the remnants of his force reached Badshahgunje two miles beyond Sultanpore, where he took up a position in the old cavalry and police lines, and was joined by the fugitives from Chanda, by the whole of the mutined sepoys and Oude Irregulars of this district, and by the remains of the 7th Light and 12th and 15th Irregular Cavalry, the latter under Shaboodeen Khan, late a resaldar in the last named regiment, and who had command in the mutiny at Sultanpore. The infantry was commanded by the Rajah Hussen Ali Khan, of Hussunpore, assisted by his son and by Rhowani Sing, late subadar of infantry. The whole force was under Mirza Guffoor Beg, a general of artillery under the old King of Oude, reinstated in his rank by the present rebel government, and

sent from Lucknow specially to take this command.

21. The rebel force, numbering 25,000 men, of whom 5,000 were sepoys and 1,100 cavalry, with 25 guns, occupied a position, a sketch of which accompanies this report, and which was drawn by Lieutenant Innes, Assistant Field Engineer, from information furnished by Lieutenant Smith, 58th Native Infantry, attached to the Goorkhas, and by Lieutenant Tucker, 8th Bengal Cavalry, who were stationed at Sultanpore at the time of the mutiny. On this plan, drawn up before the action, my operations were based. The position may be described as follows :—

22. A deep and winding ravine runs into the Goomtee, behind which the enemy's line was posted in a plain, his left resting on the Sultanpore Bazar, the centre placed behind the ruined lines of the Police Battalion, and the right covered by a range of low hillocks in advance of the village and strong masonry Serai of Badshahgunje. This position is about a mile and a half in length. The direct road from Sultanpore to Lucknow intersects it at right angles, and on this, at the point where it crosses the Nullah, the enemy's principal battery was directed.

His other guns were distributed along the position, three being posted in the village near the bazar and temple on his extreme left, and six in the Serai and village of Badshahgunje and to its right.

23. Marching at 6 A. M. from my ground in front of Budhayan, in the same order as in the 3rd paragraph of this report, on arriving within a mile of the village of Loramow, my cavalry caught sight of the enemy's outposts: on which I formed my force in order of battle, the front being covered by the 240 selected marksmen of the British Brigade, and eight horsed guns under

Lieutenant-Colonel Longden, 10th foot, the guns being 100 paces in rear of the skirmishers. The two 18-pounders advanced in the centre along the high road which runs through the enemy's position. The British Brigade was formed in contiguous quarter-distance columns at 25 paces interval, supported in second line by the six Battalions of Goorkhas, in quarter-distance columns at deploying distance.

24. Moving through the village in this order, till fully in sight of the enemy's pickets, who thus concluded that our advance would be, as they wished, directly down the high road, I advanced with the Benares Horse under Captain Matheson, and the detachment of 25 mounted men of Her Majesty's 10th Regiment, under Lieutenant Tucker, and drove in the enemy's outposts beyond the Nullah, and through a thick belt of trees which concealed their force from ours.

Having done this, leaving the Benares Horse to prevent their outposts from again reconnoitring us, I moved with the mounted detachment to the left to examine the head of the Nullah which I felt convinced disappeared in the plain; and this proved to be the case, for my search found a point where the road from Allahabad crosses it, where the troops and heavy guns could pass the ravine out of reach of the enemy's fire. Some rising ground here gave me a good view of the rebel position, and, ascertaining that it might be turned by its right, I ordered the whole force to take ground obliquely to its left.

25. My baggage and rear-guards, under Lieutenant-Colonel Turner, C.B., 97th Regiment, were halted in rear of the village of Loramow, where the road to the station of Sultanpore branches off from the road to Lucknow.

The movement of the force, unperceived for a long time by the enemy, brought it round his right completely out of fire; the shot from his heaviest guns, when he at length caught sight of our flank march, falling far short of our columns.

26. The skirmishers, who had been moving in file to flank, covering this movement, now turned to the front, and, with the light guns, closed on the enemy's position, the whole force advancing in two lines in their rear, on the right flank of the enemy, who, disconcerted by being thus turned, was compelled to change the position of his heavy guns, most of which it rendered useless. The left of my force now came on the high road to Lucknow, dividing the enemy's line, a part of which at once retreated along that road, taking with them the 4 guns which had been on their extreme right.

My right now rested on the Nullah, and the left beyond the village of Badshahgunje.

27. The left, circling gradually forward, drove the enemy from the different points of his position placing him with his back to the deep Nullah before described (which here made a bend round his rear), and entirely cutting him off from his line of retreat. Finally, his central battery of 5 heavy guns was captured after an obstinate resistance, the gunners standing by their pieces and serving them to the last.`

The body of Hussum Ali's son was here found amidst the slain, and the State palanquin of the Nazim lay in its neighbourhood.

28. After these guns fell into our hands, the enemy fled in all directions, escaping across the deep ravine in his rear. Three guns and a considerable body, still retaining some formation, retired towards the station of Sultanpore, near which, taking post about a temple and in a thick grove, they continued to fire, till finally driven from their guns by two regiments of Goorkhas.

29. The action was now at an end: the plain

beyond the ravines was everywhere covered with fugitives, whom my want of cavalry precluded my pursuing, and the ravines prevented the further advance of the guns. Two guns of Captain Middleton's Battery, and the small detachment of British Horse, however, continued the pursuit for nearly two miles along a comparatively open strip of land, and overtook and captured in a ravine 2 guns which the enemy had succeeded in withdrawing so far.

30. Halting the main body of the force to cover the collection of the captured ordnance, I pursued that portion of the enemy, which had retired by the Lucknow road, for four miles, with the 20th and 97th Regiments, and four Battalions of Goorkhas; and the mounted soldiers of the 10th, under Lieutenant Tucker, followed these guns for nine miles; but so precipitate had been the enemy's flight, that they were unable to come up with them; but some ammunition waggons and much baggage fell into our possession.

31. Thus ended the battle of Sultanpore, in which, with only 11 casualties on our side, an army of about 25,000 men was driven from a position of great strength, and scattered to the winds, with the loss of 1800 men killed and wounded, and leaving 21 guns, 9 of them of siege calibre, in our hands.

32. I am full of gratitude for the achievement of these great results with so trifling a loss of life.

The effect has been to open the road to Lucknow for the unopposed march of this force, as well as for that of the Maharajah Jung Bahadoor, who has taken this route, instead of that of Fyzabad, as he originally intended.

33. The force halted after the action at Badshahgunje; where it was joined the same evening by the Lahore Light Horse, and Pathan Horse, under Captain Balmain. Next day was employed

in the destruction of the whole of the captured. artillery, for which I had no means of transport,. and of the stores of ammunition and material for gun-carriages, which were found in the town of Badshahgunje, where the Nazim's gun-carriage manufactory appears to have been situated. On the evening of the 24th, the 3rd Seikh Horse, the remaining portion of the cavalry, detached by his Excellency, reached me.

34. On the 25th, in compliance with the telegram from the Chief of the Staff received the previous night, the force resumed its march, reaching the same day Moosafirkhana, 20 miles, and on the 26th Jugdespore, 16 miles, where it was found absolutely necessary to halt on the 27th, to give the cattle rest.

35. By the 28th February, I reached Hydurgurh, 16 miles, and on the 1st March halted at Selimpore, 18 miles from Lucknow: thus arriving as directed by his Excellency, within one march of that city on that date.

36. In this day's march occurred one of the most dashing cavalry combats I have ever heard of.

Captain Aikman, Commanding the 3rd Seikh Cavalry, on the advanced picket with 100 of his men, having obtained information just as the force marched on the morning of the 1st, of the proximity, three miles off the high road, of a body of 500 rebel infantry, and 200 horse, with 2 guns, under Moosahib Ali Chuckledar, attacked and utterly routed them, cutting up more than 100 men, capturing the guns, and driving the survivors into and over the Goomtee.

This feat was performed under every disadvantage of broken ground, and partially under the flanking fire of an adjoining fort.

I regret to add, that Lieutenant Aikman received a severe sabre cut in the face; which will

not, I trust, long deprive me of the services of so
enterprising an officer.

37. On the evening of the 1st, the force having
made a march of eighteen miles, encamped on the
Nullah of Selimpore; with the Goomtee half a
mile on its right. The town of the same name
was abandoned by the enemy at the first sight of
our cavalry, though the strong earth-works surrounding it, which must have been for weeks in
course of construction, might have been expected
to encourage them to withstand our advance.

38. Immediately on my arrival at Selimpore at
7 P. M. on the 1st March, I reported the circumstance by cossid for his Excellency's information,
and solicited further instructions. A duplicate
of this report was despatched by a second runner
in the forenoon of the 2nd.

On the evening of the 3rd a messenger from
Captain Bruce, Deputy Quartermaster-General of
the Army, brought me an order to advance on
Lucknow.

39. Accordingly, on the 4th, at 6 A.M., I marched
from Selimpore, and reached without opposition
a mosque a mile beyond the town of Ameythee,
eight miles from Lucknow.

40. Here intelligence was brought that a large
body of rebels with 2 guns were posted in and
round the fort at Dhowrara, two miles to the
right of the road, and situated in very difficult
ground amongst ravines which run into the
Goomtee.

I had hitherto passed such forts, when situated
at a distance from the road, without taking any
notice of their garrisons, who almost universally
evacuated them when left in rear of our force.

But, being apprehensive that this party, if left
unmolested, might annoy my long train of baggage, I resolved to drive them out.

41. The main column under Brigadier Evelegh,

C.B., moved on a mile further on the road to Goorsaheegunje, where it halted ; while, with the two-Horse Artillery guns of Lieutenant-Colonel D'Aguilar's troop under Lieutenant Arbuthnot, a squadron of 9th Lancers and some Seikh and Pathan Horse, the whole under Captain Coles, 9th Lancers, I examined the fort. About 500 rebels originally occupied it, while nearly 3,000 were collected in its vicinity, most of whom fled down the ravines and escaped over the river when they saw our cavalry circling round their flanks ; 200, however, fell back, and prepared to defend it.

42. The enemy having opened fire on our approach from 2 small guns, the two-Horse Artillery guns were brought into action at 600 yards, the Native Cavalry threatening the enemy's flanks, and the 9th Lancers being held in reserve well out of fire. The guns were subsequently moved up successively to 400, 300, and 200 yards, but, though they silenced the enemy's artillery fire, they failed in putting down that of the matchlockmen securely posted behind the parapet.

43. I therefore ordered up a company of marksmen from each British regiment under Lieutenant-Colonel Longden, 10th Foot, and two 24-pounder howitzers of Major Cotter's Madras Battery ; after a few rounds from which the outer enclosure of the fort and the guns mounted there were abandoned. But a sharp matchlock fire was still kept up from the loopholes which everywhere pierced the keep into which the greater part of the defenders had retired. The Company of the 10th Foot was now extended in a meadow on the river side of the fort, and closed on it in that direction, while the Companies of the 20th and 97th attacked it from the south-east. A few of the assailed, seeing themselves on the point of being surrounded, rushed out of the fort, and attempted

'to escape up one of the ravines, but after a desperate resistance they were despatched by the Native Cavalry posted watching every outlet.

44. The companies of the 20th and 97th now effected an entrance, gallantly headed by Captain Middleton, 29th Regiment, and Ensign Elton, 37th Native Infantry, attached to 10th Foot, and bayonetted about 120 of the occupants.

45. But a report was now brought from Brigadier Evelegh, that considerable bodies of the enemy were hovering on his right front, and that he had disposed the force to meet them.

46. Repeated attempts having failed to break down the door of a house in which the survivors had barricaded themselves, the shot from one of their own guns, which we turned against it, making no impression on the massive gate, a fire kindled against it having no effect, and my only engineer officer, Lieutenant Innes, having been severely wounded while trying to burst open the entrance, I determined to withdraw from the place. The guns having fallen into our hands. I considered it unnecessary to risk a further loss of life and of time, especially as it was now represented that my presence was required with the force. I accordingly drew off the infantry; carrying with us the 2 captured guns, whose removal was accomplished, under the heavy matchlock fire which the enemy continued to pour from the loopholes, principally by the personal labour and exertions of Lieutenant-Colonel Maberly, R.A., and his Quartermaster Lieutenant Strange, R.A., of Captain Middleton, Her Majesty's 29th Regiment, Provost Marshal to the Force, of Major Chichester, and Lieutenants Morgan and Gould, 97th Regiment, and Lieutenant Bradford, Madras Artillery.

47. I regret to add that Lieutenant Percy Smyth, 97th Regiment, a most brave and pro-

mising young officer, here received a musket ball through the abdomen, from the effects of which he died the same night.

48. Galloping to the main body, I found that the alarm of attack had been caused by the appearance of a body of horse, who had, however, fallen back towards the city.

The force, resuming its march, reached his Excellency's camp without further interruption, the same evening.

49. It now becomes my pleasing duty to enumerate the officers to whom I am indebted for their cordial support during the operations above described. Brigadier Evelegh, C.B., commanding the British Brigade, and Lieutenant-Colonel Wroughton, in military charge of the Goorkhas, deserve my warmest acknowledgments of the prompt and able manner in which they have seconded me in the three actions of Chanda, Amereepore, and Sultanpore. The officers on their respective Staff, viz., Captain A. B. Johnson, 5th Regiment Native Infantry, Brigade Major, British Brigade; Ensign Burne, 20th Regiment, Brigade Quartermaster, and Captain Bennett, 20th Foot, Orderly Officer to Brigadier Evelegh, and Captain Steel, 17th Native Infantry, Staff Officer to the Goorkha Force, are mentioned by the officers under whom they serve as having rendered them every support in their several positions.

50. Lieutenant-Colonel E. Maberly, R.A., commanding the artillery of the force, by his unwearied exertions and able performance of the arduous duties of organizing and superintending the Ordnance Park under circumstances of great difficulty, has earned my best thanks; and he has set a brilliant example to the officers of his arm in the field in the different actions in which he has been present. Lieutenant-Colonel Maberly speaks in high terms of the Staff Officers attached

to him,—Lieutenants Smart and Strange of the Royal Artillery.

51. To Lieutenant-Colonels Fenwick, Lys, and Ingram, commanding respectively the 10th, 20th, and 97th Regiments, I have to record my thanks for the skiful and spirited manner in which they invariably led their Regiments.

Lieutenant-Colonel Longden, 10th Foot, is an officer second to few in Her Majesty's service in attainments and experience; and I especially selected him on all occasions to command my advanced guard of marksmen and light guns, a duty invariably performed by him with an intelligence and gallantry not to be surpassed.

52. To Colonel Pulwan Singh, commanding the Goorkha Force, I am under great obligations for his hearty co-operation; and he has been well supported by his Lieutenant-Colonels Shumshere Sing and Indra Sing, and by the Senior Major, Chumpa Sing. The steadiness and intelligence of the Nepaulese troops under these excellent leaders have been the subject of general admiration, and I have had occasion specially to allude to the conduct of the right Brigade in the action of Amereepore.

53. Major Cotter, commanding a battery of Madras Artillery; Captain Middleton, commanding his own battery of Royal Artillery; Captain Thring, commanding a battery of 9-pounders; and Captain Waller, R.A., in charge of two 18-pounders, rendered most efficient service by the masterly way in which they handled their guns. Lieutenant Simeon, Bengal Artillery, commanding two bullock guns, and Lieutenant Percivall, Bengal Artillery, Deputy Commissary of Ordnance, have merited my approbation.

54. Lieutenant J. J. McLeod Innes, Assistant Field Engineer, has been of the greatest assistance to me with his professional aid. I have already

mentioned his distinguished conduct at the attack on the Fort of Dhowrara. It is now his due to relate that, at the action of Sultanpore, far in advance of the leading skirmisher, he was the first to secure a gun which the enemy were abandoning. Retiring from this, they rallied round another gun further back, from which the shot would in another instant have ploughed through our advancing columns, when Lieutenant Innes rode up unsupported, shot the gunner about to apply the match, and, remaining undaunted at his post, the mark for a hundred matchlockmen, sheltered in some adjoining huts, kept the artillerymen at bay until assistance reached him. For this act of gallantry, surpassed by none within my experience, it is my intention to recommend him for the honourable distinction of the Victoria Cross.

55. The cavalry was commanded at Chanda by Lieutenant Tucker, 8th Light Cavalry, at Sultanpore, by Captain Matheson, late 13th Irregular Cavalry, and the excellent services of these officers are duly appreciated by me. The first-named officer made a most dashing charge at Sultanpore with the 25 mounted men of Her Majesty's 10th Regiment, and killed numbers of the enemy.

56. Lieutenant Cary, 37th Regiment Native Infantry, in charge of the treasure chest, and Captain Middleton, Her Majesty's 29th Regiment, Provost Marshal, invariably accompanied me in the field, and were most useful in carrying orders. The latter officer has already been mentioned as actively instrumental in withdrawing the captured guns at Dhowrara, and throughout the time he has been with the force he has displayed in no small degree activity, intelligence, and daring.

57. The medical arrangements of the force under Surgeon C. A. Gordon, M.D., 10th Foot, have met with my entire approval, and the Commissariat Officers, Lieutenant Chalmers, 53rd

Native Infantry; Lieutenant H. R. Wroughton,
40th Native Infantry; and Lieutenant Bolton, 50th
Native Infantry, have been most assiduous and
successful in the discharge of very arduous duties;
as has Lieutenant Rawlins, 17th Madras Native
Infantry, Baggage Master. Messieurs Lind, Jenkinson, and Venables, Civil Service, accompanied
the force in the actions at Chanda and Amereepore.
In the former action Mr. Venables, charging the
flying enemy with the cavalry, with whom he did
good service, received a severe spear wound through
the thigh.

58. Mr. P. Carnegy, Special Commissioner with
the Force, and head of the Intelligence Department, has rendered me most valuable aid. His
information regarding the enemy has proved so
correct, that on it alone the whole of my operations might have been planned : he has always
accompanied me in the field, and assisted in conveying orders under the heaviest fire. To his
knowledge of the locality and skilful guidance, is
to be principally attributed the capture of the
two guns which I have mentioned in the 29th
paragraph of this report as having been overtaken
by Captain Middleton, R.A.

59. To the officers of my personal Staff my best
thanks are due.

Captain Havelock, 18th Royal Irish, late 10th
Foot, Deputy Assistant Adjutant-General, merits
my special acknowledgments. On my appointment to this command in December last, he
hastened to join me, though still suffering from
severe wounds received at Lucknow.

Since then, his great intelligence, unwearied
energy, and devotion to his duties, have won him
the admiration of every one in this force.

60. Lieutenant J. Wall, 87th Royal Irish
Fusiliers, Deputy Assistant Quartermaster-General,
and my Aide-de-camp, Lieutenant H. Henderson,

10th Foot, have afforded me the most zealous and efficient support in their respective positions, and I beg to commend them to the favourable consideration of his Excellency the Commander-in-chief.

61. I should be committing an injustice, were I to omit to mention the officers who commanded the rear and baggage guards of my force ; Lieutenant-Colonels Turner, C.B., Legh, and Burton, of the 97th, Majors Radcliffe and Butler, of the 20th, Chichester, of the 97th Regiment, and Pennycuick, R.A. To the strict performance of most unattractive duties by these officers, not less than the patient endurance of exposure by day and night of fatigue and hunger by the men under their command, do I owe the fact, that not one single article of baggage nor one animal has fallen into the hands of the enemy.

To estimate correctly the value of these services, it must be recollected that a train of upwards of 2,000 carts, drawn in many instances by very inferior cattle, has been safely conducted, most of the time, without any aid from cavalry, over roads often unbridged and nearly impassable, and through a country swarming with a hostile population. Amongst these officers, Lieutenant-Colonel Turner, C.B., 97th Regiment, claims my special commendation, for his masterly disposition of his rear and baggage-guards at the village of Loramow during the battle of Sultanpore.

On the splendid discipline, firm constancy, and dashing courage displayed by this force, both officers and men, it is needless for me to dilate; the results they have gained will speak for themselves. Suffice it to say, that it has marched 130 miles, has beaten an immensely superior enemy in four actions, and has captured thirty-four[*]

, [*] Including 3 captured at Nusutpore, on 23rd January, 1858.

pieces of ordnance, with the loss, in all, of only 37 officers and men killed and wounded.

I beg to record here, before too late, my thanks to the officers who invariably commanded the three companies of selected marksmen (who formed my advanced guards, and were always the first to encounter the enemy); Captain Norman, 10th Foot, Captain Lyons, 20th, and Major Chichester, 97th Regiment.

Returns of Killed, Wounded, and Missing, with Nominal Lists of the Casualties and Returns of captured Ordnance, are inclosed herewith.

I have, &c.

T. H. FRANKS, Brigadier-General,
Commanding 4th Division,
Late commanding Jounpore Field Force.

P.S.—A sketch of the operations at Chanda and Amereepore, and one of the action of Sultanpore, are inclosed.

No. 4.

Return of Casualties in the Field Force, under the Command of Brigadier - General T. H. Franks, C.B., in the Actions at Chanda and Amereepore, on the 19th of February, 1858.

Camp, Amereepore, February 19, 1858.

Attached to 6th Company, 13th Bat. Royal Artillery—1 captain wounded.

Detachment of Mounted Men of H.M.'s 10th Foot —2 rank and file wounded.

Detachment of Benares Horse—3 rank and file wounded.

Batts. of the Allied Goorka Force and Artillery attacked—4 rank and file wounded.

Field Force Staff—Mr. E. F. Venables, C.S., wounded.

Total Casualties, 11 men.

T. H. FRANKS, Brigadier-General,
Commanding Field Force.

No. 5.

From the Nominal List of Casualties in the Field Force, under the Command of Brigadier-General T. H. Franks, C.B., in the Actions at Chanda and Amereepore, on the. 19th of February, 1858.

Camp, Amereepore, February 19, 1858.

Civil Staff — Magistrate E. F. Venables, C.S., severe spear wound of right thigh.

R. A. 9th B.N.I.—Captain J. Angus (Interpreter), slight contusion of right thigh.

No. 6.

Return of Casualties in the Field Force, under the Command of Brigadier-General T. H. Franks, C.B., in the Action at Sultanpore, on the 23rd of February, 1858.

Camp, Badshahgunge, near Sultanpore, February 23, 1858.

6th Co. 3rd Bat. Royal Artillery—1 rank and file wounded.

Detachment A Co. 3rd Bat. Madras Artillery—1 rank and file wounded.

Detachment 4th Co. 5th Bat. Bengal Artillery—3 officers' horses killed ; 1 rank and file, 6 troop horses wounded.

Detachment of Benares Horse—3 rank and file wounded (one since dead).

Her Majesty's 10th Foot—1 rank and file killed ;·
1 serjeant or havildar, 2 rank and file wounded.
6th Battalion of the Allied Goorka Force and
Artillery attached—1 rank and file killed.
Total Casualties—11 men, 9 horses.

T. H. FRANKS, Brigadier-General,
Commanding Field Force.

No. 8.

*Return of Casualties in the Field Force, under the
Command of Brigadier-General T. H. Franks,
C.B., in the Cavalry Combat at Nyapoorwa,
near Hydurgurh, on the 1st of March, 1858.*

Camp, Selimpore, March 1, 1858.

Detachment 3rd Seikh Cavalry—1 troop horse
killed ; 1 subaltern, 3 rank and file, 2 officers'
horses wounded. One of the horses was lost as
well as wounded.
Total Casualties—4 men, 3 horses.

T. H. FRANKS, Brigadier-General,
Commanding Field Force.

No. 9.

*From the Nominal List of Casualties in the Field
Force, under the Command of Brigadier-General
T. H. Franks, C.B., in the Cavalry Combat at
Nyapoorwa, near Hydurgurh, on the 1st of
March, 1858.*

Camp, Selimpore, March 1, 1858.

Lieutenant F. R. Aikman, 3rd Seikh Cavalry,
severe sabre cut in face.

No. 10.

Return of Casualties in the Field Force, under the Command of Brigadier-General T. H. Franks, C.B., in the capture of the Fort of Dhowrara, on the 4th of March, 1858.

Camp Beebeeapore, before Lucknow, March 4, 1858.

Field Force Staff—1 Assistant Field Engineer wounded.

Her Majesty's 10th Regiment—3 rank and file wounded.

Her Majesty's 20th Regiment—1 rank and file killed ; 1 rank and file wounded.

Her Majesty's 97th Regiment - 1 subaltern (since dead), 3 rank and file wounded.

Royal Horse Artillery F. Troop—1 rank and file wounded.

Total Casualties—11 men.

T. H. FRANKS, Brigadier-General, Commanding Field Force.

———

No. 16.

No. 80 of 1858.

Allahabad, April 15, 1858.

THE Right Honorable the Governor-General of India is pleased to publish, for general information, the accompanying despatch from the Deputy Adjutant-General of the Army, forwarding a report from Major-General Sir J. E. W. Inglis, K.C.B., commanding Cawnpore Division, of his recent expedition to Hurra, on the 5th instant.

R. J. H. BIRCH, Colonel, Secretary to the Government of India, Military Department, with the Governor-General.

No. 17.

The Deputy Adjutant-General of the Army to the Secretary to the Government of India, Military Department, with the Governor-General.

Sir,   No. 227 A.

BY desire of the Commander-in-Chief, I have the honor to forward, for submission to the Right Honorable the Governor-General, copy of a report, dated the 6th instant, from Major-General Sir J. E. W. Inglis, K.C.B., commanding Cawnpore Division, of his recent expedition to Hurra, in which the portion of the 8th Irregular Cavalry, engaged under the command of Captain A. M. Mackenzie, behaved with marked gallantry.

I have, &c.
H. W. NORMAN, Major,
Deputy Adjutant-General of the Army.

No. 18.

Major-General Sir J. E. W. Inglis, K.C.B., Commanding Field Force, to the Deputy Adjutant-General of the Army.

Sir,   *Cawnpore, April 6, 1858.*

AGREEABLY to instructions received from his Excellency the Commander in-Chief, through the Chief of the Staff, I assembled the force, noted in the accompanying return, at Oonao, on the evening of the 4th, and marched for Hurra at 3 A.M. on the 5th. On approaching that place, which is surrounded on three sides by an immense mangoe tope, some sowars of the enemy were observed by our advanced cavalry to retire rapidly; as we neared the village, two or three shots were fired, and information received that the enemy, not more than 200 or 300 in number, were escaping to our left front. I immediately

directed Captain Mackenzie, commanding 8th
Irregular Cavalry, to follow and ascertain their
movements; and I have the honor to enclose the
report of that officer, by which it will be perceived that he followed the fugitives, and cut to
pieces the rebel leader and 25 of his men. I then
entered the village of Hurra, which is naturally
an exceedingly strong position, and, having ascertained from Captain Evans, the Deputy-Commissioner, that he considered it would tend more to
the quieting of the district to establish a Thannah
there than to destroy the fort, I placed 200
matchlockmen and Burkundauzes in the post,
which I have no doubt they will hold against
any force that may be brought against them.

In conclusion, I beg to be permitted to bring to
the favorable notice of his Excellency the Commander-in-Chief, the excellent services rendered
by Captain Mackenzie, who, with the faithful
remnant of his corps, most gallantly charged and
destroyed a troublesome enemy (Lultah Sing) and
his body-guard, all of whom rallied around their
leader and fought desperately. The conduct of
the native officers, non-commissioned officers and
men, was admirable, as also was that of Assistant-
Surgeon Currie, who accompanied Captain Mackenzie, and whose care of the wounded afterwards
was unremitting.

Captain Evans was with me the whole time,
and I am much indebted to him for the valuable
imformation his local knowledge enabled him to
afford.

I reached Oonao on my return at 5 15 P.M.
yesterday, and the force marched into Cawnpore
this morning.

I have, &c.,
J. INGLIS, Major-General,
Commanding Field Force.

1858.   8 D

No. 19.

Casualty Return of the 8th Irregular Cavalry.

Camp Hurra, April 5, 1858.

Killed.

One Sowar.

Wounded.

3 Native Commissioned Officers.
Ressaldar Gunga Sing Bahadoor, slightly.
Ressaldar Chubbunath Sing, severely.
Naib Ressaldar Bahadoor Ally Sirdar Bahadoor, dangerously.
3 Non-commissioned officers and men wounded severely.
4 ditto, slightly.
Total, killed 1.
Wounded, 10.

JAMES A. CURRIE, M.A., M.D.
Assistant-Surgeon, 8th Irregular Cavalry.
A. M. MACKENZIE, Captain.
Commanding 8th Irregular Cavalry.

No. 20.

Casualty Return of the 8th Irregular Cavalry.

Camp Hurra, April 5, 1858.

Killed.

1 Sowar,—Four troop horses.

Wounded.

3 Native commissioned officers.
7 Non-commissioned officers, rank and file.
2 European officers' chargers.
6 Troop horses (one since dead).

A. M. MACKENZIE, Captain,
Commanding 8th Irregular Cavalry.

No. 21.

Present State of the Field Force, under Major-General Sir J. E. W. Inglis, K.C.B., Commanding.

April 6, 1858.

8th Regiment Irregular Cavalry — 2 European officers, 10 native officers, 82 non-commissioned officers, rank and file.

17th Regiment Irregular Cavalry—1 European officer, 2 native officers, 35 non-commissioned officers, rank and file.

Royal Horse Artillery (E. troop)—3 European officers, 62 non-commissioned officers, rank and file, two 6-pounder guns, one 12-pounder howitzer.

3rd Co. 5th Bat. Bengal Artillery—1 European officer, 20 non-commissioned officers, rank and file, two 5½-inch mortars.

Naval Brigade—6 European officers, 159 non-commissioned officers, rank and file, three 24-pounders, one 10-inch howitzer.

H.M.'s 78th Highlanders—8 European officers, 241 non-commissioned officers, rank and file.

H.M.'s 80th Regiment — 15 European officers, 255 non-commissioned officers, rank and file.

2nd Regiment Punjaub Infantry—4 European officers, 13 native officers, 354 non-commissioned officers, rank and file.

Total—40 European officers, 25 native officers, 1208 non-commissioned officers, rank and file.

J. E. W. INGLIS, Major-General,
Commanding Field Force.

E. CANNON, Captain,
Officiating Staff Officer, Field Force.

No. 22.

No. 83 of 1858.

THE Right Honourable the Governor-General of India is pleased to publish, for general information, the following despatch from, Brigadier Gordon, commanding at Benares, submitting one from Colonel Milman, commanding at Azimgurh, regarding an affair with the rebels near Atrowlia, on the 21st of March, 1858.

R. J. H. BIRCH, Colonel,
Secretary to the Government of India,
Military Department, with the Governor General.

No. 23.

Brigadier A. Gordon, Commanding at Benares, to the Quartermaster-General of the Army.

Head-Quarters, Camp Benares,
March 23, 1858.

No. 337.

SIR,

I HAVE the honor to forward two letters as per margin,* as also copy of letter No. 336 of this date, addressed by me to Colonel Milman, commanding at Azimgurh, for submission to his Excellency the Commander-in-Chief.

I have, &c.,
A. GORDON, Brigadier,
Commanding at Benares.

* Letter marked A, dated March 1858, from Colonel Milman, Commanding Field Force.
Letter marked B, dated Ghazeepore, 22nd March 1858, from Colonel Dames, Commanding at Azimgurh.

No. 24.

Colonel Milman, Commanding Azimgurh Field Force, to Brigadier Gordon, Commanding at Benares.

Camp, Azimgurh, March 22, 1858.

SIR,

I HAVE the honor to report, for the information of his Excellency the Commander-in-Chief, that, in consequence of a communication received from R. Davies, Esquire, magistrate of Azimgurh, I marched from Camp Koelsa at about 3 a.m., on the 21st instant, and proceeded to Atrowlia, so as to arrive at the latter place at daylight, with detail as per margin.*

Information had been received that a considerable body of mutineers were in the neighbourhood of Atrowlia. I found them posted in several topes of mangoe trees, and advanced with skirmishers thrown out in front, the guns being supported by a party of Her Majesty's 37th Regiment and the Madras Light Cavalry on the flanks under the command of Colonel Cumberlege.

I followed them for some distance as they retired, when shortly afterwards they were driven into the open country. The cavalry were then enabled to act, and cut up a few of the rebels, but the ground was so marshy and unsound for the horses, that the pursuit could not be continued. Lieutenant Welsh, however, opened fire with a 24-pounder howitzer, and, sending a shell right in the midst of them, completed the discomfiture of the rebels, who quickly dispersed amongst the neighbouring trees. After this I continued my march to Lorkha, which place I reached without any further occurrence, and set the village on fire. Having effected the object for which I marched

* Her Majesty's 37th Regiment, 96 rank and file; one 24-pounder howitzer; one 9-pounder Bengal Artillery; 25 European Gunners; 140 Madras Light Cavalry.

from Koelsa, I quietly marched back to Atrowlia. The men were halted in the neighbourhood of this village in a tope of trees, and breakfast was being prepared by the cooks, when news was brought in suddenly that the rebels were advancing in great force. I proceeded with some skirmishers to ascertain their strength and position, and found them strongly posted behind a mud wall in the midst of topes of trees and sugar-cane. I then sent back orders to the troops to advance ; but the number of the rebels increased so fast, and they covered such a large space of ground, that both my flanks were threatened. Accordingly I took up my position on a rising piece of ground slightly in rear. The rebels attempted to turn my left flank, and I withdrew into and through the village of Atrowlia at about 12 p.m., and moved slowly on Koelsa, my flanks and rear being covered by the cavalry. The rebels, though they followed and fired at a distance, the whole way, never once inflicted the slightest damage. Finding on my arrival at Koelsa that the camp was threatened, and that the whole population in the district was disaffected, I despatched a squadron of cavalry, supported by a small infantry picquet, to watch the rebels. They were quickly charged by the cavalry and suffered a heavy loss, twenty-one dead bodies being counted on the field, besides wounded. Information was, however, received that a large body of rebels, estimated at some 5,000, were advancing on the camp. This created such a panic amongst the camp-followers, that many of the hackery drivers left their carts, and all the company's cooks ran away. Under those circumstances, and taking into consideration the position of my camp, which was very untenable in case of a night attack, and that no supplies, or liquor of any kind whatever, could be obtained for the men, I judged it expedient to retire upon Azimgurh, which I reached safely early this morning. In making this movement, I regret to say that, in consequence of many of the hackery drivers having run away, as I previously stated, I was compelled to leave a few tents and some baggage behind.

The loss of the rebels, I judge, must have been some seventy men killed. The casualties on our side were very trifling; two gunners grazed by bullets, one trooper Madras Cavalry severely wounded, and one Sowar mortally, since dead.

Nothing could exceed the steadiness of the troops under my command, and I must particularly mention the able assistance of Colonel Cumberlege, of the 4th Madras Light Cavalry, Commanding, of Captain Pelly, commanding detachment Her Majesty's 37th Regiment, Lieutenant Welsh, Bengal Artillery, for precision in firing, and moving his guns in bad ground. The men marched nearly forty-eight miles by road, exclusive of the ground that was gone over when in action, and upon very scanty fare during the whole time.

Lieutenant Ricketts, 43rd Bengal Native Infantry, acted as staff officer to my force, and he displayed great zeal and activity in his duty.

The rebels consisted chiefly of Sepoys of Koer Singh's force, and on the bodies of the slain were found Sutlej and other medals.

I have, &c.,

EGERTON MILMAN,
Colonel, and Lieutenant-Colonel of Her Majesty's 37th Regiment, Commanding Azimgurh Field Force.

No. 25.

No. 89 of 1858.

Allahabad, April 20, 1858.

THE Right Honorable the Governor-General of India, is pleased to direct the publication of the following despatch from the Deputy Adjutant-General of the -Army, No. 242 A., dated 12th April, 1858, forwarding a report by Brigadier T. Seaton, C.B., commanding the Futtehghur district, of a successful attack on a body of rebels at the village of Khankhur, on the 8th March, 1858. His Lordship fully concurs with his Excellency the Commander-in-Chief in his approval of the excellent arrangements made by Brigadier Seaton, and of the conduct and determination of the troops under his command.

> R. J. H. BIRCH, Colonel, Secretary to the Government of India, Military Department, with the Governor-General.

No. 26.

The Deputy Adjutant-General of the Army to the Secretary to the Government of India, Military Department, with the Governor-General.

, *Head Quarters Camp Lucknow,*
April 12, 1858.

SIR, No 242 A.

I HAVE the honor, by desire of the Commander-in-Chief, to forward copy of a letter, dated the 7th instant, No. 337, from Brigadier T. Seaton, C.B., commanding the Futtehghur District, reporting his successful attack on a body of rebels at the village of Khankhur.

2. In submitting this report to the Right Honorable the Governor-General, I am to request you will express his Excellency's cordial approval of the manner in which this service was conducted by the Brigadier, and his approbation of the patience and determination of the troops as described by the Brigadier.

I have, &c.,

> H. W. NORMAN, Major, Deputy Adjutant-General of the Army.

No. 27.

*Brigadier T. Seaton, C.B., commanding Futteh-
gurh District, to the Chief of the Staff, Head
Quarters.*

Dated *Futtehghur, April* 7, 1858.

SIR,   No. 337.

I HAVE the honor to report, for the information of his Excellency the Commander-in-
Chief, that, as the rebels at Soorujpore Gaut, near
Kumpil, were greatly increasing in numbers, and
were beginning to send parties of horsemen across
the Ganges to plunder the country and collect
revenue, and as I had no sufficient cavalry to oppose them, I deemed it best, under all circumstances, to make a sudden move across the river
on their main body posted near Baugown and its
vicinity.

2. Accordingly, last night, I moved out with
the troops at my disposal, as per margin,* and
taking with me a day's provisions and ammunition
only, and came upon the enemy posted at the
village of Khankhur, and in groves of trees on
the right and left. I formed Her Majesty's 82nd

---

* Artillery—7th Company, 14th Battalion Royal Artillery, with No. 4 field battery ; 6 officers and 74 of other
ranks. Natives—1 non-commissioned officer and 13 syce
drivers. Her Majesty's 82nd Regiment attached to artillery—1 officer and 13 of other ranks. Ordnance—1 24-
pounder howitzer, 2 9-pounder and 2 6-pounder guns ; total,
5 guns, 7 officers, and 101 of other ranks. European Infantry, Her Majesty's 82nd Regiment—33 officers and 677
of other ranks. Punjaub Irregular Infantry, 7th Regiment
—6 European officers and 6 Native officers, and 180 of other
ranks. Irregular Cavalry, Alexander's Horse—1 European
officer, 1 Native officer, and 89 of other ranks. Horsemen
attached to 7th Punjaub Infantry—8 Native officers and 50
of other ranks. Futtehghur Organised Police Battalion—
1 European officer, 6 Native officers, and 165 of other ranks
Total of Native Cavalry—2 European officers, 10 Natives
and 204 of other ranks.

into line with loosened files, and the 7th Punjaub
Infantry in a second line, and with the cavalry on
my left flank, and the artillery on my right front,
I advanced against the enemy's position.

3. The rebel cavalry shewed strongly on my
right and left ; Major Smith opened with his guns
on the cavalry on the right, and a few rounds
drove them back.

4. In the meantime, the large body on the left
advanced towards me, and got into the dry bed of
a nullah, about 700 yards off. As we could see
their heads, I made the 82nd open fire on them,
and in ten minutes they also retreated as hard as
they could. Our artillery now commenced firing
on the enemy's guns on our left ; they replied
feebly, and the shot went mostly over our heads.
I steadily advanced against the village, the rebels
going off in numbers as we approached, and on
getting up to it, the rebels fled precipitately, abandoning 1 gun, a 10-pounder.

5. There were a good many rebels in and about
the village, and in rear of it ; Lieutenant-Colonel
Hale, therefore, at my desire, brought the 82nd
round, and destroyed every one we could find.

6. After gaining the village, I sent the cavalry
in pursuit ; they returned in about an hour, having
killed a number of the fugitives, and captured
several standards, together with a small gun, "a
zumbooruk."

7. I now moved into the groves of trees lately
occupied by the enemy, planted videttes all round,
and bivouacked until the afternoon ; and at half-
past three o'clock commenced my homeward
march. I fully expected that, during the day, the
enemy, collecting their forces from the villages of
Mungla and Patin, distant about two or three
miles, would have attacked me, but their consternation at my unexpected attack was so great,

that they did not, though for some hours their horsemen continued to hover about, when they finally disappeared in the direction of Ala Gunge.

8. The numbers of the enemy are estimated at 800 horse, amongst them 100 of the late Oude Military Police horsemen, and 1,800 infantry, including some sepoys of the 41st and 10th Native Infantry, and Gwalior Contingent. They left as trophies in our hands the 10-pounder gun (native manufacture) already mentioned, and two small guns, several standards, some tents, a heap of papers, the possession of which will afford much useful information, and a large quantity of ammunition, which, for want of sufficient draft cattle, I destroyed.

9. The great enemies we had to encounter, were the long march out and home, full forty miles, the great heat of the weather, and scarcity of water, for all along the road the wells were few and the water foul; but the patience and determination of the troops was worthy of all praise, and enabled me to strike a smart blow (for the loss of the enemy was upward of 250 killed) and bring to a successful termination an operation that will, I trust, have the effect of showing them, that, if they are not safe in their present position between two rivers, it would be dangerous for them to cross to our side. As soon as I learn the effects of this punishment, I will report the result to his Excellency.

10. My best thanks are due to all the troops engaged, officers and men, and I trust that his Excellency will appreciate their services. The officers commanding corps and detachments were :

Brevet-Major C. H. Smith, Royal Artillery, commanding Artillery.

Lieutenant-Colonel E. B. Hale, commanding Her Majesty's 82nd Regiment.

Captain E. L. Stafford, commanding 7th Punjaub Infantry.

Lieutenant M. R. St. John, commanding Detachment Alexander's Horse.

Lieutenant C. Dekantzow, commanding Futtehgurh Organized Police Battalion.

My Staff-Captain W. H. Hawes, Major of Brigade.

. Lieutenant W. Mylne, Deputy-Assistant-Commissary-General.

Lieutenant W. C. Ryves (second in command Futtehgurh Levy), Orderly Officer.

11. Messrs. Vansittart and Power, Civil Service, and Captain Bradford, Assistant-Commissioner, accompanied the troops to render any assistance they could, and I feel very greatly obliged to them. I must not omit to mention Deputy-Magistrate Mirza Abbas Beg, who also accompanied me, and whose services in getting intelligence have been most invaluable ever since I came here. He is a most valuable servant of Government.

12. On my return to Futtehgurh I learnt that the rebel gangs at Ala Gunge and Jerahpore Mow, opposite to Bichpooriyah Ghaut, had broken up their bridge of boats at the first named place. I am just informed, however, now that our force has returned, that they are re-building the same, most probably to enable the beaten troops to pass over the Ramgunga.

13 Enclosed I have the honor to attach a nominal roll of the European officers and men killed. and wounded, and a general casualty return of the force which accompanied me.

I have, &c.,

T. SEATON, Brigadier, Commanding. Futtehgurh District.

No. 28.

Return of Killed, Wounded, and Missing, of the under-mentioned Corps and Detachments, in action at Khankhur, on the 7th of April, 1858.

Brigade Office, Fort Futtehgurh,
April 8, 1858.

7th Co. 14th Bat. Royal Artillery—Missing, 5 syces, grass-cutters, and bullock-drivers, total 5. These are supposed to have been killed.

H. M.'s 82nd Regiment — Killed, 2 privates; wounded, 1 serjeant, 2 privates, total 5. Only one severely wounded.

7th Punjaub Infantry—Killed, 1 sepoy; wounded, 1 subaltern, 4 sepoys, total 6. One dangerously, one severely wounded.

Alexander's Horse—Wounded, 5 sowars, total 5.

Futtehgurh Military Organized Police Horsemen—Killed, 2 sowars; wounded, 4 sowars, one severely, total 6.

Total—1 subaltern, 1 serjeant, 20 privates, sepoys or sowars, 5 syces, grass-cutters, and bullock-drivers.

Grand Total—27.

T. SEATON, Brigadier,
Commanding Futtehgurh District.

No. 29.

From the Nominal Roll of European Officers and Men, Killed and Wounded in action at Khankhur, on the 7th of April, 1858.

Brigade Office, Fort Futtehgurh,
April 8, 1858.

7th Regiment Punjaub Infantry—Lieutenant J. W. H. Johnstone, slightly wounded.

No. 30.

Allahabad, April 20, 1857.

No. 90 of 1858.

THE Right Honorable the Governor-General is pleased to publish, for general information, the following despatch from the Deputy Adjutant-General of the Army, No. 246 A, dated 13th April, 1858, forwarding one from Brigadier St. G. D. Showers, C. B., commanding Agra and Muttra district, reporting the relief of the village of Pinahut, on the 13th March, 1858, and the defeat by him of rebels in the ravines of the Chumbul.

R J. H. BIRCH, Colonel,

Secretary to the Government of India, Military Department with the Governor-General.

No. 31.

The Deputy Adjutant-General of the Army to the Secretary to the Government of India, Military Department, with the Governor-General.

Head-Quarters Camp, Lucknow,
April 13, 1858.

SIR,   No. 246 A.

I HAVE the honor, by direction of the Commander-in-Chief, to inclose copy of a letter, dated 15th ultimo, No. 2 A,* from Brigadier St. G. D. Showers, C.B., Commanding Agra and Muttra district, reporting his relief of the village of Pinahut, and defeat of rebels in the ravines of the Chumbul, which I am to beg you will submit to the Right Honorable the Governor-General.

2. His Excellency desires me to state that

---

* With a report from Brigadier Showers, of the relief of the village of Pinahut, and defeat of a body of rebels in the ravines of the Chumbul.

The Order of Merit has been bestowed on Sepoy Kasee Sing, 72nd Native Infantry, for gallant conduct.

under the provisions of Government General Order, No. 698, of 19th May, 1857, he has directed the bestowal of the 3rd class Order of Merit on Sepoy Kasee Sing, of the 72nd Regiment Native Infantry, for his gallant conduct in this affair.

I have, &c.,
H. W. NORMAN, Major.
Deputy Adjutant-General of the Army.

No. 32.

Brigadier St. G. D. Showers, C.B., Commanding Agra and Muttra District, to the Deputy Assistant Adjutant-General, Meerut Division.

Camp Jeorah, March 15, 1858.

SIR,   No. A 2.

I HAVE the honor to report, for the information of the Major-General commanding the Meerut Division, that, in conformity with the arrangements reported in my letter A 1, of the 11th instant. I moved out with the column noted in the margin,* on the night of the 11th instant. I reached Pinahut on the 13th, just in time, as it appears, to prevent the village from being plundered by the rebels. They had collected there in force two days before, but on hearing of the arrival of my force at Futteahbad, they decamped.

2. The villages inhabited by these rebels are situated within and bordering on the extensive and deep ravines of the River Chumbul, which are formed by the combined action of the drainage of the country on the one side, and by the eddies of the river on the other. They extend to the depth of 120 feet and upwards. There are no direct tracts through them. The sides of the ravines are

---

* 2 9-pounder guns; 1 24-pounder howitzer; 1 8-inch howitzer; 200 rank and file of Her Majesty's 8th (the King's) Regiment; 250 sabres Seikh Police Cavalry; 165 Seikh Police Infantry.

more than usually rugged and irregular, and the ascent and descent among them is difficult even to the inhabitants. The rebels feeling themselves secure in such a position, had issued out and plundered the villages which were loyal and peaceably disposed.

3. On reaching Pinahut, it was considered desirable that these rebel villages should be destroyed. There were no roads to them, and it was necessary to move across the country, over ploughed and cultivated fields ; but Mr. Phillips, the magistrate, having supplied me with 60 bildars to cut through any obstructions I might meet, we succeeded in reaching our present encampment with comparatively little difficulty. On coming up to the first village, Bugrenha, I observed a stream of men behind it, with cattle, moving deeper into the ravines, on which I ordered up 100 rank and file of Her Majesty's 8th (the King's) Regiment, and 100 of the Seikhs, and threw them into the ravines in pursuit. The column was under the command of Major Hennessey, commanding the Agra Police, and the rapidity with which he executed the movement, brought him up with the rebels before the whole had time to cross the Chumbul. He succeeded in killing about 100 of them, among whom was Kuroora Singh, the owner of several villages, and a notorious rebel.

4. After detaching Major Hennessey's force, I moved on with the main body towards Jeorah, where I was led to suppose I should meet with considerable opposition. In advancing with 25 sowars to the right, to attack it from that direction, I was met by a flank fire from some matchlockmen in front of the ravines. These were supported by about a hundred men in their rear, who had taken post at a Hindoo temple, which it seemed they intended to defend. Waiting till the main body reached the opposite flank, I galloped

into the village, which I now found evacuated. I
then directed the guns to be moved forward as far
as the ravines admitted, and some shell to be
thrown into the temple. This dispersed the men
who had assembled there, when I entered the
ravines with another column. We first came on
the village of Khylee, which was deserted as we
approached. In passing further into the ravines,
the column encountered but little opposition. We
met occasionally with parties who had settled
themselves in the recesses, where they evidently
expected they would remain unmolested, as they
had brought out their bedding, clothing, food, &c,
with their women and children.

5. The attack through these ravines was very
laborious, on account of the necessity of keeping
the top of the hills crowned by our skirmishers,
but it was of importance to make these rebels feel
that there are no positions which are inaccessible
to the energy of British troops.

6. It is imposible to estimate the strength of the
enemy, as they never showed themselves together,
but they must have lost about 160 killed; our
own loss was one jemadar, of the Police Battalion,
killed.

7. I cannot conclude this despatch without reporting the gallant conduct of Kasee Singh, a
sepoy of the late 72nd Regiment Native Infantry,
who, in a hand-to-hand encounter with the rebel
chief, Kuroora Singh, showed a dextrous use of the
bayonet and musket against the sword. He par-
ried four successive cuts, and then dashed his
bayonet into his opponent. I beg to recommend
the gallant conduct of this man to the favorable
consideration of the Major-General for promotion
to a Naick.

I have, &c.,
ST. G. D. SHOWERS, Brigadier,
Commanding Agra and Muttra District.

1858. 8 E

No. 33.

Sir R. Hamilton, Bart., Agent to the Governor-General for Central India, to G. F. Edmonston, Esq., Secretary to the Government of India with the Governor-General.

Camp, Jhansi, April 23, 1858.

Sir,   No. 170.

I HAVE the honor to forward, for submission to the Right Honorable the Governor-General, as complete a list as I can obtain of the unfortunate sufferers in the massacre of Jhánsi, on the 8th June, 1857.

2. After the most careful enquiry, I have ascertained that with the exception of Major Dunlop and Lieutenant Taylor, who were murdered on the parade, the whole of the parties in the accompanying list left the Fort of Jhansi on the afternoon of the 8th, under a promise of safety ; that they proceeded towards the cantonment by the Orcha Gate, and had reached the Jhokun Baugh, about 400 yards from the gate, when they were stopped on the roadside, under some trees. They were accompanied by a crowd of mutinous sepoys, irregular sowars, disaffected police, fanatic Musselmen, men in the service of the Ranee, inhabitants of the town, and rabble. Here Bukshis Ali Jail Darogah called out, "It is the Ressaldar's order that all should be killed," and immediately cut down Captain Skene, to whom he was indebted for his situation under Government. An indiscriminate slaughter of the men, women, and children then commenced, all were mercilessly destroyed, and their bodies left strewn about the road, where they remained until the third day, when, by permission of the same Ressaldar, they were all buried in two general pits close by. The place having been marked out, and cleared with a view to the construction of an enclosing wall, the

funeral service was read over the remains by the Reverend Mr. Schwabe, Chaplain to the Force, in the presence of the Major-General commanding himself, the Staff, and the British troops.

3. Subsequently a service was performed by Mr. Strickland, the Roman Catholic Chaplain attached to the Force.

4. I have requested the European Officer to submit a plan and estimate of an enclosing wall and obelisk, which will be hereafter submitted for his Lordship's orders.

I have, &c.,

R. N. C. HAMILTON, Agent,

Governor-General for Central India.

No. 34.

List of Europeans and Anglo-Indians murdered at Jhansi on the occasion of the Mutiny.

4 { Captain Skene, Superintendent
Mrs. Skene
2 Female children

2 { Mrs. Browne, wife of Lieutenant Browne, Deputy Commissioner, Jalom
Miss Browne, his sister

1 Captain Gordon, Deputy Commissioner of Jhansi

1 Lieutenant Burgess, Revenue Surveyor

1 Lieutenant Tumbrill, Assistant Surveyor

3 { Lieutenant Powis, Assistant Surveyor for Irrigation
Mrs. Powis
1 Female child

2 { Dr. MacEgan
Mrs. MacEgan

1 Captain Dunlop, 12th Bengal Native Infantry

1 Lieutenant Campbell, commanding 14th Irregular Cavalry

1   Lieutenant Taylor, 12th Bengal Native Infantry

{ Mr. Newton, Quartermaster-Serjeant
4 { Mrs. Newton
{ 2 children

1   Mr. Andrews, Principal Sudder Ameen

{ Mr. R. Andrews, Dep. Col. and Magistrate
{ Mrs. Andrews
6 { 2 Male children
{ 2 Female children   "

{ Mr. W. S. Carshore, Collector of Customs
6 { Mrs. Carshore
{ 4 children

{ Mr. T. C. Wilton, Patrol
{ Mrs. Wilton
5 { Child
{ 2 sisters of Mrs. Wilton

{ Mr. D. T. Blyth, Assist. Revenue Surveyor
{ Mrs. Blyth and her mother
7 { 1 Female child
{ 3 Male children

{ Serjeant Millard, Sub-Assistant Revenue Surveyor
5 { Mrs. Millard
{ 3 children

1   Mr. Bunnett, Sub-Assistant Revenue Surveyor

2 { Mr. J. Young, Sub-Assist. Revenue Surveyor
{ Mrs. Young

1   Mr. G. Young, Apprentice
1   Mr. Palpheryman, Apprentice
1   Mr. Munrowed, Sub-Assistant Revenue Surveyor
1   Mr. Scott, Clerk in Deputy Commissioner's Office
1   Mr. Purcell, Clerk in Superintendent's Office
1   Mr. Purcell (2nd), Clerk in Deputy Commissioner's Office
1   Mr. Mutlow, Clerk in Superintendent's Office
1   Mr. Mutlow (2nd), unemployed

1   Mr. Elliot, Clerk in Deputy Commissioner's
    Office
2 { Mr. Elliot } Parents of the above
  { Mrs. Elliot }
1   Mr. Flemming, unemployed
1   Mr. Crawford
___
67

F. W. PINKNEY, Captain,
Superintendent.

___

No. 35.

GENERAL ORDERS BY THE GOVERNOR-GENERAL OF INDIA.

Allahabad, April 26, 1858.

·   No. 101 of 1858.

THE Right Honorable the Governor-General of India is pleased to publish the following account from Colonel F. Rowcroft, Commanding Sarun Field Force, of his engagement with the rebels on the 17th instant.

R. J. H. BIRCH, Colonel,
Secretary to the Government of India,
Military Department, with the
Governor-General.

___

No. 36.

Colonel Rowcroft to Colonel R. J. H. Birch, C.B., Secretary to the Government of India, Military Department, with the Governor-General, Allahabad.

*Camp, Amorah, Goruckpore District,
April* 19, 1858.

SIR,   No. 241.

I HAVE the honor to acquaint you, for the information of the Right Honorable the Governor-

General, that about 7½ o'clock on the morning of
the 17th instant, several villagers came into camp,
stating that parties of the rebels from Belwa,
Horse and Foot, were out plundering the villages
between this place and Belwa. I ordered out detachments of cavalry and infantry to drive them
back and cut them off, and afterwards reinforced
them with fresh detachments and 2 guns. From
other reports received, that the enemy were getting
up reinforcements from Belwa, and hearing our own
guns and those of the enemy, and it appearing as
if the insurgents were holding their ground, I
moved out of camp with the Head Quarters of the
Field Force between 10 and 11 o'clock A.M. Near
the village of Jahmoulee, about three miles from
camp, on the Belwa road, I found the troops first
sent out with Major Cox, Her Majesty's 13th
Light Infantry, and Captain Sotheby, R.N., of Her
Majesty's ship Pearl, judiciously drawn up with
their centre and guns in a small wood, to which
they had retired, in hopes of bringing the enemy
into the plain from the woods and villages, but the
rebels would not venture into the open. Major
Cox joined me with a portion of the 13th Light
Infantry; and hearing from him how matters
stood, and that a large body of the enemy was also
on our extreme right, it was determined to make a
move round to the right, and leaving Captain
Sotheby on the left, I moved, with the remaining
troops which I had brought up, and the two small
Mountain Train howitzers, and with Major Cox
and a portion of the 13th Light Infantry, well to
the right, and advanced The sowars and rebels
on our right soon retired with a gun, which they
only fired two or three times, and, bringing up our
right shoulders, the enemy on the left, in front of
Captain Sotheby, finding we had turned their left
and rear, ceased firing, and soon gave way and
retired, getting a few shells from the small how-

itzers, assisted by the skirmishers with their Enfields and Minies. We continued to advance and press the enemy till near Belwa, when a favorable opportunity appeared to charge a body of the insurgents retreating, as I suspected, with one or two of their guns. After giving them four rounds of shell, I ordered Major Richardson, in command of the 2nd Troop right Squadron Bengal Yeomanry Cavalry, with my portion of the force to move from my right flank, and charge this body of the enemy. The 2nd troop, under its gallant leader, made a noble home charge, and though they came upon a larger body of the enemy behind a village, and the sepoys made a desperate resistance, nothing stopped this brave cavalry, and they cut down and killed full sixty of the rebels, and captured a 6-pounder gun, with limber, and the enemy were completely dispersed.

The day, unfortunately, was very unfavorable, the hot weather blowing half a gale, with a blinding dust, or the enemy would have suffered more severely in this action. Major Cox, and Captain Sotheby on the left, with his two guns, the Naval Rifles, and the Enfields of Her Majesty's 13th Light Infantry, early in the day, did good execution among the enemy. From all the reports I have received, the enemy must have lost, killed and wounded, between 200 and 300, and one of the Gonda Rajah's Chief Pundits was killed. Although the enemy had removed several of the killed from the ground where the cavalry charged, 46 dead bodies were counted there yesterday by one of our best spies. The enemy were reported to be about 2,000 sepoys, some Golundauze, 1,000 irregulars, 100 sowars, with 4 guns. The Rajah of Gonda was not present, but his karinda or head agent was on the ground on an elephant. When the cavalry charged, as soon as I could get a party of cavalry from the rear or the left, I moved them

up in support, under Captain Chapman, and some
Infantry, to assist also in bringing away the gun.
As soon as the wounded had been cared for and
the gun brought away, we returned to camp,
reaching it at 4 P.M.

My best thanks are due to Captain Morgan,
22nd Regiment Native Infantry, Field Force Staff,
and my Acting Aide-de-camp, the Honorable
V. A. Montague, R.N., for their zealous readiness
and activity in carrying out my orders. To
Major Cox, commanding left wing Her Majesty's
13th Light Infantry, who was ever active and
ready for any duty required of him; to Captain
Sotheby, R.N., of Her Majesty's ship Pearl, commanding the Naval Brigade; to Major Richardson,
commanding Bengal Yeomanry Cavalry; to Captain Barclay, 68th Native Infantry, in military
charge of Gorucknath Goorkha Regiment; to Captain Brooks, 1st Regiment Light Cavalry, attached
to Goorkhas, which active and zealous officer I
sent forward with the 2nd detachment of Her
Majesty's 13th Light Infantry, as a guide and
interpreter; to the Goorkha Commandant Colonel
Byroop Singh Koor, and Major Captain Sewukram
Thappa, and to Lieutenant Burlton, 40th Regiment
Native Infantry, in charge of the detachment of
Seikhs. Also to Drs. Shore and Dickinson, Naval
Brigade, Dr. Kirwan, Her Majesty's 13th Light
Infantry, and Dr. Eteson, attached to Goorkhas,
all ready, active, and present in the field. Major
Richardson brings to my notice the prompt, ready,
and careful aid afforded by Dr. J. W. R. Ames-
bury, Bengal Yeomanry Cavalry, to those who fell
in the charge of the 2nd troop, ably and readily
assisted by Dr. Dickinson, doing duty with the
Naval Brigade. Also my thanks are due to
the troops of all arms engaged, for the zealous and
cheerful manner they went through a fatiguing day
under a burning sun. My best thanks are espe-

cially due to the officers and men of the 2nd Troop
Bengal Yeomanry Cavalry, and their gallant
leader, Major Richardson, who himself, in the
charge, killed six of the enemy, Supernumerary
Cornet Copland killed three, Cornet and Quartermaster Kloer killed three, Cornet Scott killed
several.   Major Richardson also brings to my
notice, that Lieutenants Davis, 2nd troop, and
Percival, 1st troop, distinguished themselves, as
also Serjéant Bulmore, Corporal Craven, his orderly,
Ridingmaster-Serjeant W. Curran, Troopers G.
Smith and Williams, and Trumpeter O'Donnell.
Trooper Kindred, 3rd troop, defended Cornet
Troup while on the ground, wounded, shooting
four of the rebels.   Lieutenant de Hoxar, 3rd
troop, wounded early in the action, and Captain
Chapman, severely hurt by his horse falling, re-
mained in the field till the close of the action.

I was obliged to leave our camp standing, and
could afford to leave but small detachments to
guard it, under the charge of Captain MacGregor,
9th Light Cavalry, attached to the Goorkha Force.
I felt somewhat anxious about it, receiving a
report, as I joined the force in advance, that there
was a body of the rebels in our rear on the left;
nearly all the sick were left in the small fort and
entrenchment.

My best thanks are due to Mr. Wingfield, Commissioner, who accompanied me to the field, and
for his obliging readiness to convey any orders;
and to Deputy Magistrate Sheikh Khairoodeen,
for his ready attention in the field.

I beg to recommend to the most favorable notice
of the Right Honorable the Governor-General, all
the officers and men of the different arms engaged
in the action.

I have the honor to annex a casualty roll.

I have, &c.,

F. ROWCROFT, Colonel,
Commanding Sarun Field Force.

Left Wing Her Majesty's 13th Light Infantry.

ABSTRACT.

Wounded severely 1 private, wounded slightly 1 private, total 2.

Bengal Yeomanry Cavalry.

Supy. Cornet H. B. Troup, killed.

General Abstract.

Killed—1 officer, 1 rank and file.
Wounded—4 officers, 7 non-commissioned officers, 6 rank and file.

No. 38.

No. 102 of 1858.

THE Right Honorable the Governor-General of India is pleased to direct the publication of the following despatch, from the Deputy Adjutant-General of the Army, No. 257 A, dated 20th April, 1858, forwarding copy of a report from Brigadier-General R. Walpole, Commanding Field Force, detailing his operations against and capture of the fort of Rooya, on the 15th instant.

His Lordship participates in the grief expressed by his Excellency the Commander-in-Chief, at the heavy loss which the British army has sustained in the death of that most admirable officer, Brigadier the Honourable A. Hope, whose very brilliant services he had had the gratification of publicly recognizing in all the operations for the relief and the final capture of Lucknow. No more mournful duty has fallen upon the Governor-General in the course of the present contest than that of recording the premature death of this distinguished young commander.

The Governor-General shares also in the regret of the Commander-in-Chief, at the severe loss of valuable lives which has attended the operations against the fort of Rooya.

R. J. H. BIRCH, Colonel,
Secretary Government of India, Military
Department, with the Governor-General.

No. 39.

The Deputy Adjutant-General of the Army to the Secretary to the Government of India, Military Department, with the Governor-General.

Head Quarters Camp, Poorah,
April 20, 1858.

Sir,   No. 257 A.

I HAVE the honor, by order of the Commander-in-Chief, to enclose copy of a despatch from Brigadier-General R. Walpole, dated the 16th instant, which I am to beg you will submit to the Right Honorable the Governor-General.

2. In this despatch the capture of the fort of Rooya is described, an operation which, to the great regret of his Excellency, has been attended with considerable loss.

3. Among the names of those who have fallen, appears that of Brigadier the Honorable A. Hope. The death of this most distinguished and gallant officer causes the deepest grief to the Commander-in-Chief. Still young in years, he had risen to high command, and by his undaunted courage, combined as it was with extreme kindness and charm of manner, had secured the confidence of his brigade to no ordinary degree.

4. This brigade he had led in several assaults, of which the last was in the attack on the Begum Kotee, at the late siege of Lucknow.

5. The service of Her Majesty could, in Sir

Colin Campbell's opinion, hardly have sustained a greater loss.

I have, &c.

H. W. NORMAN, Major,
Deputy Adjutant-General of the Army.

No. 40.

*Brigadier General R. Walpole, Commanding Field
Force, to the Chief of the Staff.*

Camp Madhogunge, April 16, 1858.

SIR,

I HAVE the honor to acquaint you, for the information of his Excellency the Commander-in-Chief, that yesterday morning I marched to this place (which almost joins Roodamow) from Gosegunge.

Nurput Sing, who, I stated in my despatch of yesterday, was at Rooya Fort, which is about one mile to the north of this place, did not come in or send any satisfactory reply to the message of Captain Thurburn, the magistrate who accompanies this force. I therefore thought it advisable to attack him, particularly as Captain Thurburn informed me that he understood this man had received only the day before yesterday a letter from the Begum, and that his intentions were certainly hostile to the Government; and under these circumstances it would have had the worst effect to have passed this fort without taking it.

I accordingly directed my baggage to be massed in the open plain, near Madhogunge, under a strong guard of cavalry, infantry, and two field guns, and proceeded with the remainder of the force towards Rooya, turning off from the road, about two miles from Madhogunge, for the purpose of getting round to the north side of the fort, which was stated to be the weakest part of it, where there was a gate, and where there were very few guns.

The fort on the east and north side is almost surrounded with jungle, and at these two sides, the only two gates were stated to be, which information proved correct. It is a large oblong, with numerous circular bastions all round it, pierced for guns, and loopholed for musketry, and surrounded by a broad and deep ditch; there is an inner fort or citadel, surrounded in like manner by a deep ditch, and with a high wall considerably elevated above the rest of the work. On the west and part of the south side, there was a large piece of water, which was partially dried up.

On arriving before the north side, I sent forward some infantry in extended order, to enable the place to be reconnoitred, when a heavy fire of musketry was immediately opened upon them, and an occasional gun; the cavalry at the same time swept entirely round to the west side, to cut off all communication with the fort.

A tolerable view of the fort having been obtained from the road which leads into it from the north, the heavy guns were brought up; the two 18-pounders were placed on it; the two 8-inch mortars behind a wood still further to the right.

After a short time, a great many of the infantry were killed and wounded from having crept up too near the fort, from which the fire of rifles and matchlocks was very heavy. These men had gone much nearer to the fort than I wished or intended them to go, and some of the Punjaub Rifles, with great courage, but without orders, jumped into the ditch and were killed in endeavouring to get up the scarp. I therefore gave directions that they should be withdrawn from their forward and exposed situation, and here it was that I regret to say the gallant and able soldier Brigadier Hope was killed by a rifle or musket ball fired by a man from a high tree within the walls of the place.

By half-past 2 o'clock the fire of our heavy guns appeared to have made little or no impression upon the place, and as no gun could be brought to bear upon the gate, the passage to which was not straight, and it could not be approached with out the men being exposed to a very heavy fire from the bastion and loopholed walls that commanded it, I considered it better not to attempt an assault until more impression had been made upon the walls of the place, and as it was getting late, to withdraw from the north side and commence operations against the south-east angle, on the following morning, which had been reconnoitred by the engineers, and where they thought it would be easier to effect a breach, as it could be better seen and more direct fire could be brought to bear.

I therefore directed the camp to be pitched on the south side, about a mile from the fort, and withdrew from the north side, where it would have been dangerous to have passed the night, as it was surrounded by thick jungle.

This morning at day-light, Major Brind, Bengal Artillery, and Captain Lennox, Royal Engineers, proceeded again to reconnoitre the place thorough-ly before recommencing operations, and found that the enemy had evacuated it, leaving their guns behind them, five in number, ammunition, a large quantity of attah, and some tents. As some of the carriages were found without their guns, and the track of a gun-carriage could be traced to a well, where the water is very deep, I have no doubt other guns have been thrown down it. I had information that there were more in the place, and it is certain none were carried out.

The reports as to the numbers of the enemy vary so much, that it is impossible to arrive at

any certainty upon that point ; but I am inclined
to think the number stated in my despatch yesterday, viz., about fifteen hundred, to be nearly
correct; but the strength of the garrison consisted
in the nature and situation of the fort, not in their
numbers.

I regret to say that this operation has cost us
above one hundred officers and men killed and
wounded, and I have deeply to deplore the loss of
Brigadier the Honorable A. Hope, from whom I
had received the greatest assistance.

The loss of the enemy it is impossible to ascertain ; it must have been heavy from the fire of our
guns, and especially from our howitzers and mortars. A few bodies which seem to have been
overlooked, and three large funeral fires with the
remains of the bodies smouldering, was all that
remained of their dead on our entering the place
this morning.

The fort which has over-awed this part of the
country for the last year, is being destroyed under
the superintendence of Captain Lennox, Royal
Engineers, and I am in hopes that its destruction
will be of the greatest advantage.

I have received the most willing support from
all under my command during this operation ; and
I beg particularly to offer my best thanks to Brigadier Hagart, commanding the cavalry, and to
Major Brind, commanding the artillery, for their
most able and valuable assistance ; also to Captain
Lennox, the senior engineer officer, to Lieutenant-
Colonel Hay, commanding the 93rd Regiment, who
succeeded to the command of the infantry brigade
on the death of Brigadier Hope, to Lieutenant-
Colonel Cameron, commanding 42nd Regiment,
Lieutenant-Colonel Taylor, commanding 79th Regiment; to Captain Cape, commanding 4th Punjaub Infantry, who, I regret to say, was severely
wounded ; to Lieutenant-Colonel Tombs, and

Major Remmington, commanding troops of horse artillery ; to Captain Francis, commanding heavy guns ; to Captain Coles, commanding 9th Lancers, and Captain Browne, commanding 2nd Punjaub Cavalry.

I beg also to return my best thanks to the officers of my staff, Captain Barwell, Deputy Assistant Adjutant-General ; Captain Carey, Deputy Assistant Quartermaster-General, Captain Warner, aide-de-camp, and Lieutenant Eccles, Rifle Brigade, my extra aide-de-camp.

Enclosed I beg to forward a list of the casualties, and likewise a sketch of the fort, which has been made in a hurry, but will afford information of the nature of the work.

I have, &c.,

R. WALPOLE, Brigadier-General,
Commanding Field Force.

No. 41.

Numerical Return of Casualties in the Field Force under Command of Brigadier-General R. Walpole, on the 15th of April, 1858.

Camp, Roodamow, April 16, 1858.

Staff Infantry Brigade—1 European officer killed.

Artillery—2 horses killed ; 1 European officer, 3 non-commissioned officers, 3 drummers, rank and file, wounded ; 1 native rank and file, 2 horses, 5 bullocks, wounded.

2nd Punjaub Cavalry—1 native rank and file, wounded.

Bengal Sappers and Miners—2 native non-commissioned officers, 1 rank and file, wounded.

Punjaub Pioneers—1 European non-commissioned officer, wounded.

42nd Royal Highlanders — 1 non-commissioned officer, 6 drummers, rank and file, killed ; 3

officers, (2 officers since dead), 3 non-commissioned officers, 28 drummers, rank and file, wounded.

79th Royal Highlanders — 1 rank and file, wounded.

93rd Royal Highlanders — 1 non-commissioned officer, 4 drummers, rank and file, wounded.

4th Punjaub Rifles—1 European officer, killed ; 1 native officer, 1 non-commissioned officer, 7 drummers, rank and file, killed ; 2 European officers, 3 native non-commissioned officers, 31 drummers, rank and file, wounded.

Total—2 European officers, 1 non-commissioned officer, 6 drummers, rank and file ; 1 native officer, 1 non-commissioned officer, 7 drummers, rank and file, killed ; 6 European officers, 8 non-commissioned officers, 36 drummers, rank and file, 5 native non-commissioned officers, 34 drummers, rank and file, wounded.

Grand Total—18 European and native officers and men, and 2 horses, killed ; 89 European and native officers and men, 2 horses, and 5 bullocks, wounded.

R. WALPOLE, Brigadier-General, Commanding Field Force.

No. 42.

From the Nominal Roll of Casualties in Brigadier-General Walpole's Field Force on the 15th of April, 1858.

Dated Camp, Roodamow, April 17, 1858.

Brigade Staff—Brigadier the Honourable A. Hope, killed in action.

1858.   8 F

1st Lieutenant H. E. Harington, Artillery, wounded severely.

Serjeant John Knox, Artillery, wounded severely.

Lieutenant Charles Douglas, 42nd Royal Highlanders, wounded dangerously, since dead.

Lieutenant A. J. Bramly, 42nd Royal Highlanders, wounded dangerously.

Lieutenant G. W. Cockburn, 42nd Royal Highlanders, wounded severely.

Colour-Serjeant Thomas Ridley, 42nd Royal Highlanders, wounded severely.

Colour-Serjeant John Stephen, 42nd Royal Highlanders, wounded slightly.

L. Serjeant Josh. Hartley, 42nd Royal Highlanders, wounded severely.

Serjeant James Fraser, 42nd Royal Highlanders killed in action.

Serjeant David Sim, 93rd Highlanders, wounded severely.

Lieutenant E. C. P. Willoughby, 4th Punjaub Rifles killed in action.

Captain A. McCafe, 4th Punjaub Rifles, wounded severely.

Lieutenant F. V. H. Sperling, 4th Punjaub Rifles. wounded slightly.

No. 43.

No. 103 of 1858.

THE Right Honorable the Governor-General of India is pleased to direct the publication of the following reports from Brigadier-General Sir E. Lugard, K.C.B., Commanding Azimghur Field Force, dated 12th and 16th April, 1858, detailing the particulars of his operations during his march to Azimghur, and after his arrival there.

It is with deep regret that his Lordship has to

announce the subsequent death of Mr. Venables, of Azimghur, from the wound received by him while gallantly assisting in the pursuit of the rebels under Kooer Sing.

Mr. Venables, although bound to the service of the State by no tie, save his courageous and patriotic spirit, had rendered the most valuable assistance to Government from the commencement of the mutinies, and had been greatly distinguished by his intrepidity and energy, tempered with a singularly calm and sound judgment.

The Governor-General records, with much sorrow, his sincere respect for the memory of Mr. Venables.

R. J. H. BIRCH, Colonel,

Sec. Gov. of India, Mily. Dept.,

with the Governor-General.

No. 44.

Brigadier-General Sir E. Lugard, K.C.B., to the Chief of the Staff.

SIR, *Camp, Tigra, April 12, 1858.*

IN my communication of the 10th instant from Jounpore, I reported my arrival at that station on the previous day, and that I had been compelled to halt there, from the exhausted conditon of my cattle, which had marched over bad roads for twelve days continuously, without a halt ; also that I intended proceeding towards Azimghur by the direct road the following day.

2. I have now the honour to report to you, for the information of his Excellency the Commander-in-Chief, that in consequence of intelligence received during the 10th, that a party of insurgents under Golam Hossain, Chuckledar, had advanced to within twelve miles of Jounpore, destroyed the village of Selaidapore, and actually threatened

the city of Jounpore, I decided, late on the evening of the 10th, to change my route to the one through Tigra and Deedar Gunge, which would enable me, I hoped, to punish Golam Hossain and his party, whilst my arrival at Azimghur would only be delayed one or two days.

3. Independently of the safety of Jounpore, in my opinion, requiring this movement, I was further induced to change my route in consequence of its having been proclaimed to the people of Oude, by these rebel Chuckledars, that the force under my command was the remnant of the British army which had been destroyed at Lucknow, and was flying for safety to the Lower Provinces.

4. On my arrival at Tigra, where I proposed encamping, I found that the rebel force had moved back some six miles, after destroying the village and house of Selaidapore, and as the morning had been unusually oppressive, and the troops much distressed by the march of nearly sixteen miles, I considered it unadvisable to proceed, and therefore halted for the day, scouts being sent out to reconnoitre the enemy's position.

5. Towards evening, I received intelligence that there was a movement amongst the rebels as if they intended to march. This was about 4 P.M., and fearing they would make off, I at once ordered out all the cavalry off duty, consisting of 293 sabres, with three Horse Artillery guns, and proceeded with them in pursuit, requesting Brigadier Douglas, to bring up a portion of the infantry in support.

6. The enemy were, I understood, in groves of trees on the other side of the village Munnihar, numbering altogether 3,000, of whom 500 or 600 were sepoys, and 200 cavalry, (said to have been

the volunteer regiment, probably 37th Native Infantry), and the 12th Irregular Cavalry, and two guns.

We came upon the cavalry picquets of the rebels within three or four miles from our camp; but they rode off as we advanced, and finding that the whole were in full retreat, I at one pushed on at a rapid pace, the 3rd Irregular Cavalry under Captain Pearse, and a party of the 12th Irregulars, under Lieutenant C. Havelock, supported by a squadron of the Military Train under Major Robertson. The guns, also, in command of Major Michell, Royal Artillery, followed in support; but the evening was too far advanced, and the country too close, for them to act with any effect.

7. The pursuit was continued for more than three miles, and at least eighty of the rebels killed and their two guns captured; one a very large iron eight-pounder, and the other a two and three fourths-pounder (also a large iron gun, though of small bore).

They are both of native manufacture, and being pronounced unfit for our service, I had them burst, and the massive carriages broken up for their material.

The force did not return until 10 o'clock, and the captured guns were not brought into camp until 4 o'clock this morning.

I have therefore been obliged to halt for this day.

8. The cavalry could not certainly have marched yesterday less than thirty-two miles, and the infantry twenty-eight miles. The exertion in such weather was very great, but I considered the object required it; for had Golam Hossain's force gone away unpunished and with their guns, there would have been no limit to their falsehoods and boastings. As it is, the fact of their flight,

punishment, and loss of their guns, must become patent to the district.

9. Although our loss is trifling as to numbers, it is, from its nature, I regret to say, most severe, and deeply felt and deplored by all.

Lieutenant Havelock was shot through the head when gallantly leading his men, and he expired before we returned to camp.

He was an intelligent, brave, and gallant soldier, well worthy of the name he bore, and as I before stated, his loss is deplored by every one in this force.

10. In conclusion, I beg you will bring to the notice of his Excellency the high spirit of the troops, European and native, and the obligations I am under to all ranks for the great exertions they have made, and the cheerfulness with which they have endured the fatigues of the long marches.

11. Mr. Forbes, C. S., has accompanied my force from Lucknow, and rendered me much assistance in the intelligence department. Mr. Jenkinson, C. S., and Mr. P. Carnegy, Deputy Commissioner, also accompanied me from Jounpore, and by their local knowledge, assisted me greatly.

I proceed to Azimghur, *viâ* Deedargunge to-morrow.

F. LUGARD, Brigadier-General,
Commanding Azimghur Field Force.

No. 45.

Return of Casualties in the Azimghur Field Force, under command of Brigadier-General Sir Edward Lugard, K.C.B., in the Action of Munnihar, Oude, on the 11th April, 1858.

3rd Seikh Cavalry—3 troop horses killed; 5 rank and file, 7 troop horses, wounded.

12th Irregular Cavalry—1 subaltern, killed; 1 native officer, 1 rank and file, wounded; 1 troop horse missing.

Total—1 subaltern, 3 troop horses, killed; 1 native officer, 6 rank and file, 7 troop horses, wounded; 1 troop horse missing.

EDWARD LUGARD, Brigadier-General,
Commanding Azimghur Field Force.

No. 46.

From the Nominal Return of Casualties in the Azimghur Field Force, under Command of Brigadier-General Sir Edward Lugard, K.C.B. in the Action at Munnihar, Oude, on the 11th of April, 1858.

12TH IRREGULAR CAVALRY.

Lieutenant C. W. Havelock, Commanding, April 11, gunshot wound through the head; died one hour after being wounded

Total casualties—1 killed, 7 wounded.

EDWARD LUGARD, Brigadier-General,
Commanding Azimghur Field Force.

No. 48.

Brigadier-General Sir E. Lugard, K.C.B., Commanding Azimghur Field Force, to the Chief of the Staff.

Camp, Azimghur, April 16, 1858.

SIR,

I HAVE the honor to report to you, for his Excellency's information, that the field force under my command marched from Tigra to Deedargunge, 13 miles, on the 13th instant, and the following morning, learning from Azimghur that the bulk of the garrisom had been sent towards Mhow, in order to cover Ghazeepore, which was threatened by a large body of the enemy with 2 guns, which had quitted Azimghur the previous night, I moved on 24 miles to Ranee-ka-Serai ; and the same evening sent forward a squadron of cavalry, 3 guns, and 4 companies of the 10th Foot, under Lieutenant-Colonel Fenwick, of that regiment, to reconnoitre the bridge, which the enemy had thrown over the Tonse, to the west of the city, with instructions to seize it if possible, as from the plan of the entrenchments and town (annexed), which had been furnished me from Azimghur by Lieutenant-Colonel Longden, Chief of the Staff, Azimghur Field Force, it occurred to me that by crossing a portion of my force over this bridge, I should be able to turn the enemy's position, and attack it in the front and rear at the same time.

2. On nearing the Jounpore masonry bridge, Lieutenant-Colonel Fenwick found the enemy, who had crossed over the westward bridge in force, commencing an attack upon a picquet of the 37th Foot, posted in the Judge's house there. It appeared from subsequent intelligence, that, unacquainted with my immediate vicinity, and aware of the departure of most of the garrison, they had contemplated a general attack upon the entrenchments that night.

3. The consternation of the rebels was great on finding themselves opposed by this fresh party, and after exchanging a few shots, they retired over the broken ground towards their bridge, where our troops could not follow them in the dark. Lieutenant-Colonel Fenwick, therefore, bivouacked for the night.

4. At daybreak of the 15th, I advanced with my whole force on Azimghur, having heard during the night that Kooer Singh, with a considerable

body, was still in position. The reconnoitring party before mentioned, under the guidance of Lieutenant-Colonel Longden and Mr. Venables, proceeded at the same time to the enemy's bridge, which, after a sharp skirmish, they succeeded in carrying, and driving the rebels from the factory house on the left bank.

5. The position was a very strong one, and was held with much determination by a party of about 300 rebel sepoys of the late 7th, 8th, and 40th Regiments Native Infantry, as shown by the uniforms upon the bodies of those found slain on the field.

6. The bridge had been partially destroyed, but was speedily repaired by a party of Punjaub Sappers under Lieutenant Keith, Royal Engineers, whom I had sent with Lieutenant-Colonel Fenwick's party, and I at once crossed over 3 guns of Royal Horse Artillery, a squadron of the Military Train, and all the available Seikh Cavalry.

7. In the meantime, the main column under Brigadier Douglas, C.B., had advanced over the Jounpore bridge direct upon the city, and learning that the whole of the rebels remaining in Azimghur had fled on losing their bridge, I directed the Horse Artillery and Cavalry, under Major Michell, Royal Artillery, to pursue, and use their utmost endeavours to capture Kooer Singh. In this, I regret to say, they failed, owing to the regularity and devoted courage with which the retreat was covered by a band of the rebels; 3 guns, however, and nearly all their ammunition and baggage fell into our hands. The pursuit was continued up to the vicinity of the village of Jewunpoor, where the road turns off to Azimghur, and ascertaining that the rebels had thrown themselves into a small fort there,

and had been joined by the strong body with 2 Horse Artillery guns (said to be of the Neemuch troops), who had quitted Azimghur about the 12th and 13th instant, I directed the pursuing party to halt, until reinforced by infantry, and heavier guns and mortars. These are now proceeding thither under Brigadier Douglas, when the fort will be attacked, should the rebels remain in it, and the pursuit continued. In the meantime, I have sent an express to Colonel Cumberlege, whose force is at Mhow, covering Ghazeepore, to patrol in strength towards Ghasee, where a portion of the rebels, it is expected, will proceed. My loss at the western bridge amounted to one killed and six wounded of the 10th Foot and Madras Artillery. In the pursuit I regret that the casualties were heavier. Mr. Venables was wounded in the left arm by a musket shot ; Lieutenant Hamilton, Adjutant 3rd Seikh Cavalry, was badly wounded, and died during the night. Twenty-five casualties are reported, killed and wounded, details of which will be sent hereafter.

8. The loss of the enemy at the bridge could not be exactly ascertained ; bodies of sepoys in the uniform of the 7th, 8th and 40th Regiments Native Infantry, were found on the ground. The rapid rush of the 10th Foot, after crossing the bridge, prevented their being removed ; but those killed by the artillery and rifle fire before the bridge was taken, were seen to be carried away. In the pursuit, it is supposed that about 70 of the enemy were killed.

9. As this is but one of many skirmishes, it is more than probable the Azimghur Field Force may be engaged in, during the very arduous operations upon which it is at present employed, I shall refrain, until its conclusion, from bringing to his Excellency's notice such officers as I deem

worthy of special mention. In the meantime, I beg to express my grateful obligations to all officers and men, for their cheerful endurance of fatigue and exposure, and to those who have engaged the enemy for their undeviating gallantry.

I have, &c.,
EDWARD LUGARD, Brigadier-
General, Commanding Azimghur
Field Force.

No. 49.

No. 105 of 1858.

THE Right Honorable the Governor-General of India, is pleased to direct the publication of the following report, by Colonel Lord Mark Kerr, detailing the result of an engagement with the rebels by the detachment under his command on the 6th instant, while in progress to join the force at Azimghur.

R. J. H. BIRCH, Colonel, Secretary
Government of India, Military Department, with the Governor General.

No. 50.

Colonel W. L. Dames, Commanding at Azimghur, to Brigadier P. Gordon, Commanding at Benares.

Dated Azimghur, April 16, 1858.

SIR, No. 108.

I HAVE the honor herewith to enclose, for submission to his Excellency the Commander-in-Chief, an additional report furnished by Colonel Lord Mark Kerr, commanding Her Majesty's 13th

Light Infantry, regarding his engagement with the rebels on the morning of the 6th April.

In forwarding this report, I beg to state that Colonel Lord Mark Kerr has informed me that the previous report which he sent to me was drawn up in a most hurried manner, and, owing to the very little time he had at his disposal, he was unable to fill in many details, and mention the names of various officers who distinguished themselves, as he would have desired.

Lieutenant Collum, of Her Majesty's 37th Regiment, at that time doing duty with Her Majesty's 13th Light Infantry, very much distinguished himself in the engagement of the 6th instant, by his coolness and bravery. Colonel Lord Mark Kerr states that, not knowing his name, he was unable to mention it in his report; but desires that it may be forwarded in this transmitting letter.

I have, &c.,

W. L. DAMES, Colonel, Commanding at Azimghur.

No. 51.

Colonel Lord Mark Kerr, Commanding Field Force, to the Chief of the Staff.

Dated Azimghur, April 6, 1858.

SIR,

I HAVE the honor to announce, for the information of his Excellency the Commander-in-Chief that I have succeeded this day in joining the besieged Azimghur Garrison.

I left Benares at 10 P.M. on the 2nd instant, to proceed to Azimghur by forced marches, with the troops as per margin*. At Sursana, 10 miles

* 2nd Dragoon Guards (Bays), 2 officers 55 men; Royal Artillery (two 6 pounder guns, two 5½ inch mortars), 1 officer, 17 men; 13th Light Infantry, 19 officers, 372 men.

from Azimghur, where I arrived on the 5th instant, I received pressing letters, at different hours till midnight, from the Staff Officer at Azimghur, to come on without delay; but thinking it imprudent to risk anything by a night march, I did not start till 4 A.M. on the 6th. There was a bright moon at that hour, and I moved on with a reconnoitring party of the Bays. At 6 A.M. I observed a mangoe tope and buildings to the left of the road, and also the banked ditches of the fields to the right of it to be crowded with sepoys. After returning to the column, and waiting till half-past seven o'clock to allow our train of elephants, camels, and carts to close up, Captain Boyd's company advanced in skirmishing order to the right of the road, and opened fire on the enemy, hoping to turn their left flank, and so clear the ground for the advance of the convoy, and succeeded at once in driving the enemy to a further line of ditches. But by this time a heavy fire came from the mangoe tope and buildings, and well back on our left flank, and also on the right, where our skirmishers had driven on the enemy; large bodies of them were firing from enclosures to our rear. Captain H. Jones, 13th, with his own, Lieutenant Everett's, and Lieutenant Gilbert's companies threw out skirmishers, with their left thrown back to the left of the road, taking advantage of any cover at hand, and Lieutenant Robertson, Royal Artillery, and two guns, threw shrapnel into the enclosures to the right, at a distance of 500 yards, Lieutenant Hall, 13th, who was soon dangerously wounded, being sent with a sub-division in support also of Captain Boyd. This continued for some time without producing any effect on the strong defensive point of the enemy, the buildings and tope, from the branches of which latter a severe fire was kept up for some time.

We were now in a serious position ; but such
precautions had been taken for our large convoy
that I had no fears for it. When I discovered
that it had gone back some distance, I sent Lieutenant Stewart, 13th, an excellent officer and horseman, with 25 of the Bays, to the rear. I heard from
him, that immediately on the fire opening, every
driver and mahout had fled, the former having first
turned their cattle to the rear, and then, after
getting them into confusion, absconded. At this
time, in rear of the enemy's skirmishers on our
flanks, were seen their reserves in quarter-distance columns, and between my small force and
the rear guards and baggage, appeared also large
bodies of the enemy. It was necessary to advance,
however ; the slightest change of position to the
rear caused the enemy to rise up, and with loud
shouts show their numbers all around. I wished
to try the effect of the $5\frac{1}{2}$-inch mortars on the
buildings so necessary to seize ; but for this, it
was requisite to retire the gunners and their
supports, who would have been struck by the
shells. But I at once saw that I must give up
the attempt. A party of volunteers attempted an
assault, after a slight breach had been made by
one of the 6-pounder guns at a distance of about
60 yards, which the soldiers were manfully enlarging, when an inner wall appeared, and I recalled the party, and tried the gun again. One
gun was constantly engaged throwing shrapnel at the
enemy in rear of our right flank. The buildings had
been fired at the first ; but the sepoys held them
with desperation. Just as I had determined on
another assault, they evacuated the place. A pile
of dead bodies inside covered the ground to the
height of three feet. Lieutenant Ormsby, commanding the Bays, came to the front in pursuit ;
our whole line advanced ; the skirmishers, thrown
back on the left, wheeled rapidly up, and the

fight was won.   It was now nearly ten o'clock
A.M.

Immediately in our rear there was a high embankment crossing the road.   The enemy had seized on this in great numbers.   Captain Wilson Jones, a most gallant young man, commanding the company of the rear guard, was killed while leading his men in the successful attack of it.   I had just before sent Major Tyler, 13th, to take command of the rear and baggage guards, with orders to stand firm, relying on his cool judgment, and I resolved to force my way to Azimghur, about two miles distant, and return, with Madras Riflemen, whom I knew to be capable, as European soldiers are not, of driving the bullocks.

But, by the blessing of God, it was unnecessary for me to leave my convoy, for on our advance the enemy fled with extreme rapidity, and when I came upon a village a quarter of a mile to the front, a very strong position, I found scarcely any opposition, and at the same time saw our rear advancing, the drivers, on our success, having returned.   On ariving at the bridge leading across the Nullah towards the intrenchment of Azimghur, I sent a request to Colonel Dames, Commanding Garrison. for assistance in bringing in our convoy, and one of my companies to take temporarily the place of any men he might spare.   Two companies of the 37th and Madras Rifles were sent and proved of service.   At the bridge there was firing from the high ground, the other side of the Nullah, well answered by Lieutenant Welsh, Bengal Artillery, with 2 guns from the fort and a few skirmishers from the 13th.

I regret to say that my casualties are severe, 1 officer and 7 men killed, and 1 officer and 33 men wounded, mostly severely or dangerously. But I am certain the enemy did not number less than 4,000, the 7th, 8th, and 40th, so called fighting regiments of the sepoy army among them. Deducting the large number required for the safety of our large convoy, consisting of 312 carts, 11 elephants, 20 camels, our whole strength in front was about 300 combatants. I am truly thankful to say that all the officers under my command behaved with daring courage and resolution. Non-commissioned officers and private soldiers the same. I owe my best thanks to Lieutenant Honorable James Dormer, Staff Officer of my force, and to Ensign Yardley, my Orderly Officer, who both behaved with great coolness under heavy fire. To Lieutenant-Colonel Longden and Mr. Venables, who accompanied me throughout the day, I am most deeply indebted for their cordial and constant advice and assistance. Major Tyler speaks of invaluable assistance from Quartermaster Hoban, 13th, in many difficulties and dangers with the convoy.

I have, &c.,

MARK KERR, Colonel,

Lieutenant-Colonel 13th, Prince Albert's Light Infantry, Commanding Field Force.

No. 52.

From a Nominal Return of Killed and Wounded in the 1st Battalion Head Quarters, Her Majesty's 13th Light Infantry, in Action at Azimghur, on the 6th of April, 1858.

Captain W. H. Jones, killed.

Lieutenant H. E. Hall, wounded dangerously through the back.

No. 53.

Return of Killed and Wounded of the Force under the command of Colonel Lord Mark Kerr, in Action with the Enemy near Azimghur, on the 6th of April, 1858.

Azimghur, April 7th, 1858.

Head Quarters H.M.'s 13th Light Infantry—1 captain (Captain Wilson Jones), 7 privates killed; 1 subaltern (Lieutenant H. Edward Hall), 8 privates, wounded dangerously; 1 serjeant, 7 privates, wounded severely; 1 serjeant, 11 privates wounded slightly.

Detachment 2nd Dragoon Guards—8 horses killed and missing; 3 privates severely wounded; 2 privates slightly wounded.

Total killed and wounded—1 captain, 1 subaltern, 2 serjeants, 38 privates. 8 horses killed and missing.

MARK KERR, Colonel 13th Light Infantry, Commanding Field Force.

No. 54.

No. 106 of 1858.

THE Right Honorable the Governor-General is pleased to publish for general information, the following letter from Brigadier-General R. Walpole, commanding Field Force, reporting further successes in his operations against the rebels.

No. 55.

Brigadier-General R. Walpole, Commanding Field Force, to the Chief of the Staff.

SIR, *Camp, Allahgunge, April* 22, 1858.

I HAVE the honor to acquaint you, for the information of his Excellency the Commander-in-

Chief, that I marched at daylight this morning from Sewajpore.* Just before we arrived at Sirsie, where I had intended to encamp, the advanced guard came on the enemy, who were in great force, both cavalry and infantry. I brought up the field guns and some infantry to the front, and sent the cavalry to our right, the enemy retreated to a village, from which they opened fire on us with 4 guns. We advanced, and our horse artillery opened with great effect upon it, and in a short time they retreated, taking off their guns. We advanced, took their 4 guns, the cavalry pressing their left and rear. We followed them about 6 miles to this place, killing a great many the whole way, and got possession of the bridge here, where I halted, and have pitched my camp. We have killed certainly as many as 500 or 600, have taken a great quantity of ammunition, hackeries, grain, and their camp. Our loss, as far as I can learn, is 1 man killed, and 3 or 4 wounded. I will send particulars to-morrow.

I have, &c.
R. WALPOLE, Brigadier-General,
Commanding Field Force.

No. 56.
Allahabad, April 29, 1858.
No. 110 of 1858.

THE Right Honorable the Governor-General of India is pleased to direct the publication of the following letter from the Deputy Adjutant-General of the Army, No. 266 A, dated April 26, 1858, forwarding a despatch from Major-General Sir Hugh Rose, K.C.B., commanding Central India Field Force, reporting the opera-

* Called in my route Mahabadpore.

tions of the 2nd Brigade of the force subsequent to the capture of the Fort of Garakota.

No. 57.

The Deputy Adjutant-General of the Army, to the Secretary to the Government of India, Military Department, with the Governor-General.

Head-Quarters, Camp, Futtehgurh,
April 26, 1858.

Sir,   No. 266 A.

I HAVE the honor, by desire of the Commander-in-Chief, to transmit for submission to the Right Honorable the Governor-General, a despatch dated 26th ultimo, from Major-General Sir H. Rose, K.C.B., commanding Central India Field Force, reporting the operations of the 2nd Brigade of the force, subsequent to the capture . of the Fort of Garrakota, embracing the forcing of the pass of Mudinpore, and capture of the Forts of Serai and Marowra.

2. His Excellency considers that these operations were most skilfully conducted.

I have, &c.
H. W. NORMAN, Major,
Deputy Adjutant-General of the Army.

No. 58.

Major-General Sir Hugh Rose, K.C.B., to Major-General Mansfield, Chief of the Staff.

Cawnpore, Camp before Jhansi,
Sir,   .   March 26, 1858.

I HAVE the honor to report to you, for the information of his Excellency the Commander-in-Chief, the operations of the 2nd Brigade of the Central India Field Force, under my orders, since the capture of the fort of Garrakota.

8 G 2

A halt of four days at Saugor was necessary for the repair of my siege guns ; I therefore marched back to Saugor, in two days, leaving Major Boileau, with the Sappers and Miners, at Garrakota, to demolish all he could of its defences.

The rebels had held a steep and thickly wooded hill, a few miles to the north of Garrakota, which gave them the command of the road to Dumoh ; after the fall of Garrakota they then abandoned it, leaving open the communication between Saugor and Dumoh.

My siege artillery was ready in four days, on the 18th instant ; but want of supplies, caused by the devastation of the Saugor and the neighbouring districts, by the rebels and other circumstances, did now allow me to leave Saugor till the 27th instant.

This delay did away very much with the good effects of the speedy fall of Garrakota. The rebels not seeing any further operations or movements to the front against them, regained courage, and occupied again in force the strong positions in the Shaghur and adjoining districts, such as the forts of Serai and Marowra, and the difficult passes in the mountainous ridges which separate the Shaghur and Saugor districts.

These passes are three in number. The pass of Narut and the fort of Carnelgurh, near Malthone, of Mudinpore, and of Dhamooney.

My object was to reach Jhansi, against which I was ordered to move as quickly as I could ; but on my road there I wished to take up my 1st Brigade, which I had marched from Mhow and Indore to Goonah, for the purpose, as previously stated, of clearing and opening the Grand Trunk road from Bombay to Agra, in obedience to my instructions.

I anticipated resistance to my advance on Jhansi at the passes, the forts of Serai, Murowra, and Thal-Behut, at which latter place it was said that the Rajah of Banpore intended to make his last stand.

It was also affirmed by some, but denied by others, that the fort of Chundeyree, to the west of the River Betwa, formerly a family possession of the Rajah of Banpore, would be defended.

It was necessary that the 1st Brigade, on the west, and the 2nd Brigade on the east of the Betwa, should be concentrated for the attack of Jhansi.

I determined to force these obstacles to the forward movement of my force, and to the union of my 1st and 2nd Brigade ; and accordingly gave orders to Brigadier Stuart, commanding my 1st brigade, to move from Goonah westwards, and take Chundeyree, whilst I forced my way northwards, and, crossing the Betwa, march with both brigades against Jhansi.

An operation against the passes was more than usually difficult on account of the great length of my line of march ; for, knowing the danger of a want of ammunition, I took with me abundant reserves of it, having besides to take care of a convoy of 15 days' supplies for my force and its camp followers.

The pass of Narut was by far the most difficult, and the enemy, having taken it into their head that I must pass through it, had increased its natural difficulties, by barricading the road with abatis and parapets made of large boulders of rock, 15 feet thick, all passage by the sides of the road being made impracticable by the almost precipitous hills, covered with jungle, which came down to the edge of the road. The Rajah of Banpore, who is both enterprising and courageous, defended this pass with 8,000 or 10,000 men.

The next most difficult pass was Dhamooney ; very little was known about the third, Mudinpore, except that in the Ordnance Map it was described as "good for guns."

Under these circumstances, I requested Major Orr to reconnoitre these passes, whilst I was detained at Saugor for supplies.

Supplies for my force having come into Saugor, I marched from that place on the 27th instant to Rijwass, a central point from which I could move againt any one of these passes. Major Orr's force joined me at Rijwass ; with his usual intelligence, he had collected information which made me select the pass of Mudinpore for my point of attack.

In order to deceive the enemy as to my intention, and prevent the Rajah of Banpore from coming from the pass of Narut to the assistance of the Rajah of Shahgur, who defended Mudinpore, I made a serious feint against Narut by sending Major Scudamore, commanding Her Majesty's 14th Light Dragoons, with the force stated in the margin*, with their tents and baggage, to the fort and town of Malthone, just above the pass of Narut, whilst I made the real attack on the pass of Mudinpore. Having taken the ruined little fort of Barodia, and left a small garrison in it to keep up my communications, I marched on the 3rd instant against the pass of Mudinpore, with the force stated in the margin†.

* Major Scudamore's Force.—2 troops H.M.'s 14th Light Dragoons; 1 troop 3rd Light Cavalry; 100 Irregular Cavalry ; one 24-pounder howitzer ; 3 Bhopal 9-pounders; 24th Regiment Bombay Native Infantry.

† Sir H. Rose's Force.—Advanced Guard : 500 Hydrabad Cavalry; 200 Hydrabad Infantry; 4 Guns Artillery; 1 company 3rd Bombay Europeaus. Centre : 1 troop H.M.'s

As the column approached the pass, the enemy's skirmishers fired on the advanced guard from a ridge of hills on our right, near the village of Noonee. I sent up a party of the Salt Customs, under Mr. Bartie, who, advancing, drove them back.

At about 800 yards from the entrance of the pass, we saw the enemy in force on the hills, on the left of the pass. Major Orr made some good practice at them with round shot and spherical case.

The pass was formed by a sudden descent of the road into a deep glen, thickly wooded. To the right further on, the road ran along the side of a lake. The left of the road was lined by rocky and precipitous hills.

The ardour of an excellent officer induced him at this time, to make an incautious movement with his guns to his right front, with the view to pour an enfilading fire into the enemy. But he had not taken into consideration that this movement brought him to within fifty or sixty yards of the edge of the glen, in which lay concealed some hundred sepoys, who, before he could unlimber, opened a very heavy fire on his guns, which he was unable to depress on them. The sepoys fortunately fired too quick, and too high, and the officer retired his guns out of the range of their musketry, with only a few casualties. The sepoys hailed this little reverse with shouts. But their success had only brought on their more rapid

14th Light Dragoons; Sappers and Miners; 4 Guns Horse Artillery; Right Wing 3rd Bombay Europeans; 3 9-pounder Guns, Captain Lightfoot's Battery; 2 5½-inch mortars; 1 8-inch mortar; 1 1-inch howitzer; Left Wing 3rd Bombay Europeans; Siege Train; 3rd Bombay Light Cavalry; baggage and convoy. Rear Guard: 125 Hydrabad Infantry; 1 howitzer and Gun Horse Artillery; 1 troop H.M.'s Light Dragoons; 50 Hydrabad Cavalry.

defeat. For knowing now their exact position, and seeing the necessity of showing them that a calm retreat was only the prelude of a rapid offensive, I advanced 100 of the Hydrabad Contingent Infantry under Captain Sinclair, at double time, and made them charge into the glen, bring their right shoulders forward, and sweep it down towards the road, following this up by a movement of a company of the 3rd Europeans, against the front of the sepoys, and of the Salt Customs, from the extreme right, against their rear. To still further discomfit them, I sent a troop of Her Majesty's 14th Light Dragoons to a knoll, quite in rear of the glen, and commanding a view of the lake and the other end of the pass. The rebels were driven with loss from the glen, and crossing, the road ascended the hill on its left, for the purpose of joining the large body of rebels, who occupied the hills divided by ravines on the left of the road. The troop of Horse Artillery would have swept them away with grape, had not the officer commanding it mistaken the rebels, on account of the similarity of dress, for men of the Salt Customs.

Not giving the rebels time to breathe, I directed Captain Macdonald, my Assistant-Quartermaster-General, to storm the hill to the left of the road, with two companies of the 3rd Europeans. Captain Macdonald conducted them ably and gallantly up the almost precipitous height, and extending the Grenadier Company from the right, and supporting them with the other company, drove them from the first to the second line of hills. As soon as Lieutenant-Colonel Liddell had come up, with the rest of the 3rd Europeans, I moved him up the hill, in support of his two companies, directing him to advance and drive the enemy successively from all the hills commanding the pass.

He performed this movement entirely to my satisfaction.

The glens and hills which protected the pass having been taken, I sent Captain Abbott, with the 4th Hydrabad Cavalry, to clear the pass, and drive in the enemy's front; this he did effectually.

The enemy, repulsed in flank and front, retired to the village of Mudinpore, in rear of the end of the lake. The village was fortified by a formidable work, in the shape of a bund of great thickness of earth and solid masonry, which dammed up the lake. The enemy had placed the few guns they had in rear of the bund, and had been firing with them on the 3rd Europeans on the hill.

The pass having been gained, I sent directions to Brigadier Steuart, whom I had halted in rear of the pass, with the reserve and siege train to advance through it, and occupy the head of the lake. As soon as they had arrived, I opened with the 8-inch howitzer, and the 9-pounders in advance of it, a fire on the rebel guns.

At this time I received a message from the officer commanding the rear guard, that the enemy had fired, from the range of hills running to the pass of Narut, on him and his long line of baggage. I had all along thought it likely, that the Rajah of Banpore might come to the aid of the rebels at Mudinpore as soon as he discovered that the move of Major Scudamore was a feint and my attack the real one. I therefore sent a troop of Her Majesty's 14th Light Dragoons and a Regiment of Hydrabad Cavalry, to cover the Rear Guard.

A few rounds drove the enemy from their position in rear of the bund, and they retired from

Mudinpore, through the jungle, towards the Fort of Serai.

I directed Major Orr to pursue with the remainder of the Hydrabad Cavalry.

The cavalry which I had detached with Major Scudamore, and to assist the rear guard, rendered the force available for the pursuit small.

Major Orr, and Captain Abbott under him, pursuing along the road through the jungle, came up with the rear of the rebels, consisting principally of the 52nd Bengal Native Infantry, and killed a good many of them, amongst the number the notorious mutineer, Lall Turbadio, who, as Havildar Major of the 52nd, was instigator of the mutiny in that regiment, and whom they made their commanding officer.

I owe my acknowledgments to Major Orr and Captain Abbott for their conduct on this occasion. Captain Pinkney, who accompanied my force as Political Agent at Jhansie, distinguished himself in the pursuit.

I marched the force several miles beyond the pass into an open and level country. The line of baggage was so long that it did not come up till the next day ; but owing to the precautions I had taken, it did not sustain the slightest loss.

The results of the success at Mudinpore were as numerous as they were favorable. My force had got into the rear of the passes, and the enemy's line of defences, of which they thought so much. The pass of Narut considered by them to be impregnable was turned.

· Mudinpore, it is true, was the weakest of the passes ; but, on the other hand, it had been defended by the sepoys of the 52nd and other regiments, and by 7000 picked Bundeelas. The sepoys and the Bundeelas quarrelled, the former declaring that the latter had run away, and left them to fight at the pass ; general mistrust and a panic ensue in the rebel camp.

The fort of Serai, or Soyrage, a fortified palace of the Rajah of Shahghur, perfect in architecture, now used as an arsenal for the manufacture of powder and shot, fell the next day into the hands of my troops. The dyes of the old Saugor Mint, from which the rebels were making balls, were found here in quantities.

The day after, I took possession of Marowra, an ancient fort with a double line of defences, in an important position, on the road from Saugor to Jhansi, and from Shaghur to Malthone.

The Shaghur territory was attached to the British possessions by Sir Robert Hamilton, and in consequence, the British flag was hoisted on the fort of Marowra in presence of my brigade.

The passes of Narut and Dhamooney were abandoned, and Sir Robert Hamilton established a police station at Malthone.

In fact, the whole country between Saugor and Jhansi, to the east of the River Betwa, which, since the outbreak of the rebellion, had been in the hands of the insurgents, was now, with the exception of Thal-Behut, restored to the Government.

I beg leave to recommend to your Excellency, for their conduct at the forcing of the pass of Mudinpore, Lieutenant-Colonel Liddell ; Major Scudamore, for the skilful manner in which he conducted the feint against Malthone, which neutralized the force of the Rajah of Banpore ; Major Orr ; Captain Abbott ; Captain Sinclair ; Captain Macdonald, Assistant Quartermaster-General; and Mr. Bartie, commanding the Salt Customs Police, who had a short time before been strongly

recommended for his gallant conduct in attacking
the rebel's position at Dhamooney.

I have the honor to enclose a list of casualties in forcing the pass.

I have, &c.,
HUGH ROSE, Major-General,
Commanding Central India
Field Force.

No. 59.

*From the Return of Killed and Wounded of the
2nd Brigade, Central India Field Force, and
Hydrabad Contingent Field Force, during the
Action with the Rebels, on the 3rd March, 1858,
in the pass of Mudinpore.*

Camp Jhansi, April 8, 1858.

Serjeant Dickenson, Artillery, 1st Troop, wounded
severely below left knee.

Captain Prettejohn, 14th Light Dragoons, contusion by a spent ball.

No. 60.

No. 111 of 1858.

THE Right Honorable the Governor-General
of India is pleased to publish for general information, the following despatch from the Deputy
Adjutant-General of the Army, No. 267, dated
April 26, 1858, forwarding a detailed report from
Brigadier-General R. Walpole, commanding Field
Force, of his successful affair with the rebels near
Allahgunge, on the 22nd instant.

No. 61.

The Deputy Adjutant-General of the Army, to the Secretary to the Government of India.

Military Department,
with the Governor-General.

Head-Quarters Futtehghur,
April 26, 1858.

SIR,   No. 267.

I HAVE now the honor, by desire of the Commander-in-Chief, to transmit for the information of the Right Honorable the Governor-General, a detailed report from Brigadier-General R. Walpole, dated 23rd instant, of his successful affair near Allahgunge on the previous day, when 4 guns were captured and considerable loss inflicted on the enemy.

2. The action was one of horse artillery and cavalry, and both these arms appear to his Excellency to have highly distinguished themselves.

I have, &c.
H. W. NORMAN, Deputy
Adjutant-General of the Army.

No. 62.

Brigadier-General R. Walpole, Commanding Field Force, to the Chief of the Staff.

Camp Allahgunge, April 23rd, 1858.

SIR,

I TRANSMITTED yesterday a short account of the defeat of that portion of the rebel force which occupied the villages on the left bank of the Ram Gunga. from Allahgunge to Hoolapore. I have now the honor to forward for the information of his Excellency the Commander-in-Chief a more detailed report of that operation.

I marched at daylight on the 22nd instant, from Sewajpore, intending to encamp in the neighbourhood of Sirsie, and to proceed to this place the following day. However, on the advanced guard approaching Sirsie, the enemy was discovered in our front. I rode forward to reconnoitre and ordered up Major Remmington's troop of horse artillery and the infantry, desiring the heavy guns to follow, and made the following dispositions. Four guns of Lieutenant-Colonel Tombs's troop of horse artillery, (two being on the rear guard) supported by a squadron of 9th Lancers and 100 infantry, all which troops had formed the advanced guard, occupied the left. Major Remmington's 9-pounder troop was directed to its right, and the main body of the cavalry, consisting of 9th Lancers and 2nd Punjaub Irregulars, under Brigadier Hagart, was placed on the extreme right to protect that flank from the numerous cavalry of the enemy, and with instructions to sweep round the enemy's left and rear the moment they retired, with the hope of getting any guns they might endeavour to save.

I knew, from having occupied the right bank of the Ram Gunga during the winter, that our left was covered by that river, and that from the great bend it takes beyond the villages of Mow and Jerapore, our cavalry would be useless on our left flank.

We advanced in the above order some distance, crossing the Sende Nuddee, when the enemy opened fire upon us with their guns, which were placed in the village of Hoolapoor, upon which they had retired, and where they made their stand. Their fire was rapid and good, the shot plunging among our artillery, but doing little damage. Lieutenant-Colonel Tombs's troop advanced rapidly to within six or seven hundred yards of the village and opened upon it ; Major Remmington's troop soon after followed, taking ground to its right. The guns of these two troops were so well served that, in about twenty minutes, those of the enemy appeared to be silenced.

I now perceived the enemy streaming in large numbers from the rear of the village ; our whole line advanced, Lieutenant-Colonel Tombs's Troop on one side of the village, Major Remmington's on the other. On the extreme right, just at this place, there was a thick jungle which prevented Brigadier Hagart turning their left flank at this point ; but Major Remmington's guns having been ordered to accompany him, the jungle was soon cleared, and he advanced between it and Hoolapoor, and, as the enemy's guns, which had been withdrawn from that village, were being carried off, three of them were gallantly captured by Captain Wilkinson's troop of the 9th Lancers, he being supported by Lieutenant Richardes with a troop of 2nd Punjaub Cavalry, and every man with the guns was killed. A fourth gun was taken by the cavalry during the rout that followed.

We now advanced with an extended front, one squadron 9th Lancers, Lieutenant-Colonel Tombs' guns, and the infantry which had formed the advanced guard on the left, Major Remmington's guns, and the cavalry under Brigadier Hagart, to the right rather in advance, and swept the whole country, driving the enemy through the villages of Nebonuggra and Jerapoor, at the latter of which their camp was captured, and then through Chumputteapoor and Saibgunge as far as Allahgunge, where they had a bridge of boats protected by a breast-work pierced for guns. Having secured this town, and the pursuit having continued for six miles, I considered it advisable to halt, and I sent for my baggage and pitched my camp.

Nizam Ali Khan, who commanded, was killed in the action, and some documents were found in his tent, one describing the preparations he had made for stopping the advance of the English.

The loss of the enemy must have amounted in the whole to between five and six hundred, and we captured four guns, the enemy's camp, ammunition, stores and grain in large quantities.

Our loss, I am happy to say, was small, very small, considering the results obtained ; it consisted of one man killed and six wounded.

I am particularly indebted to Brigadier Hagart, for the admirable manner in which he conducted the operations of the cavalry on the right. I beg also to return my best thanks to Major Brind, Bengal Artillery, for his exertions, and the able manner in which he commanded the artillery, and to Lieutenant-Colonel Tombs, and Major Remmington, commanding troops of horse artillery, for the excellent management of their guns which drove the enemy from their position at Hoolapoor with great loss. Brigadier Hagart speaks in great praise of Captain Coles, commanding 9th Lancers, and Captain Browne, commanding 2nd Punjaub irregular cavalry. I have on all occasions experienced great assistance from these officers. The Brigadier also expresses his obligations to Captain Sarel, 17th Lancers, brigade-major to the cavalry brigade, and to Lieutenant Gore, 7th Hussars, who acted as his orderly officer ; and Major Brind speaks in high terms of Lieutenant Bunny, Bengal Artillery, his staff officer.

I beg to record the assistance I received from my staff, Captain Barwell, Deputy Assistant Adjutant General, Captain Carey, Deputy Assistant Quarter-Master General, Captain Warner, Aide-de-camp, and Lieutenant Eccles, Extra Aide-de-camp.

The action was fought with artillery and cavalry and the pursuit was so rapid, there was no chance for the infantry taking a part in it.

I have learnt to-day, that the enemy who were posted at Jelalabad, on the fugitives reaching that place, and on their hearing of the death of Nizam Ali Khan, evacuated the fort there the same evening, and have proceeded, it is supposed, towards Bareilly.

I have, &c.,

R. WALPOLE, Brigadier-General, Commanding Field Force.

No. 64.

No. 113 of 1858.

THE Right Honorable the Governor-General of India is pleased to publish the following account, from Major-General G. Whitlock, commanding Saugor Field Division, of his engagement with the rebels at Jheeghun, on April 10, 1858.

No. 65.

Major-General G. Whitlock, Commanding Saugor Field Division, to Major-General Mansfield, Chief of the Staff.

Camp, Logassie, April 12, 1858.

SIR, No. 121.

I HAVE the honor to report, for the information of his Excellency the Commander-in-Chief of India, that Major Ellis, Political Assistant in Bundlecund, having acquainted me that 2000 rebels had collected at Jheeghun, one of their strongholds and the depôt for their plunder, distant about 17 miles from Chutterpore, I decided on making a night march, with the view of surprising them.

The force marched at 8 P.M., on the 9th instant, but from the intricacies of the road, and ignorance of the guides, it was still 4 miles from Jheeghun, at 5 A.M. on the following morning. The only chance now of a surprise was by a rapid advance of mounted troops, and I immediately moved with the A Troop Horse Artillery, two squadrons of Lancers, and detachment of Ressalah Hydrabad Contingent. The result was satisfactory; the rebels, leisurely evacuating their position, were unprepared for our sudden appearance.

The artillery opened, and the cavalry, gallantly dashing amongst them, committed much havoc.

A portion of cavalry and guns were moved to intercept their flight; this was successful.

Under a fire of matchlocks, and through jungle which had been set on fire to impede pursuit, but unavailing, our troops came up with the rebels, and the slaughter was heavy.

To follow further without infantry (for the jungle was becoming dense) would have been as useless as imprudent, and the force returned to camp, leaving 97 rebels dead on the field, and bringing with them 39 prisoners.

Dassput, the rebel chief, long the terror of the district, narrowly escaped capture; he had just returned from Jhansi.

His two nephews, named Beenijao and Jheet Sing, equally notorious for their villanies, fell into our hands, and with seven other prisoners, were hanged on the evening. A large portion of baggage, cattle, grain, matchlock, ammunition, and some percussion caps, were found; the latter, with articles of uniform stamped Bengal Artillery, led me to believe that some of the mutineers must have been present.

The conduct of all the troops employed gave me much satisfaction, and I only regretted that the infantry, after a toilsome and wandering night's march, had not an opportunity of being brought into contact with the rebels.

The village and stronghold has been completely destroyed under the superintendence of our field engineer, and the Thakoor of Logassie has expressed his gratification at such a horde of budmashes being driven from his neighbourhood. Our casualties were two of the Ressalah wounded, and one horse missing.

I have, &c.

G. WHITLOCK, Major-General,
Commanding Saugor Field
Division.

No. 66.

No. 668 of 1858.

Fort William, April 29, 1858.

THE Honorable the President of the Council of India in Council directs the publication of the following letter from Brigadier-General Sir J. Hope Grant, K.C.B., in continuation of his report on the cavalry operations, published in Government General Order, No. 315 of the 22nd February, 1858.*

No. 67.

Brigadier-General Sir J. H. Grant, K.C.B., Commanding Cavalry Division, to the Deputy Adjutant-General of the Army.

Dated Camp Lucknow Cantonments,

SIR,   No. 54.   *March* 8, 1858.

I BEG to state, for the information of his Excellency the Commander-in-chief, that, through inadvertence, I omitted to mention Lieutenant-Colonel W. N. Custance, 6th Dragoon Guards, in my report of the operations of the cavalry force during the present campaign.

Lieutenant-Colonel Custance commanded a wing

---

* Horse Artillery, 6 guns; 325 R. and F. 14th Light Dragoons; 140 Light Cavalry; 476 sabres Hydrabad Cavalry.

of his regiment throughout the whole of the operations before Delhi, and on the 14th September, the day of the assault, I gave him charge of the second line of cavalry.

I regret very much my having omitted to mention the zealous support which I received from Colonel Custance during the arduous duties required of the cavalry throughout the siege, and my approval of the judicious manner in which he carried out my orders on the day of the assault, on which occasion he was attended by Major Richardson, 3rd Light Cavalry, and Lieutenant G. S. Davies, 6th Dragoon Guards, both most zealous and gallant officers.

I have, &c.,

J. HOPE GRANT, Brigadier-General, Commanding Division.

———

No. 68.

Major-General Sir Hugh Rose, K.C.B., Commanding Central India Field Force, to Colonel Green, Adjutant-General of the Army, Bombay.

SIR,   *Camp Mote, April* 30, 1858.

I HAVE the honor to report to you, for the information of his Excellency the Commander-in-Chief, the operations of my force, against the fortress and fortified city of Jhansi.

On the 20th ultimo, the 2nd Brigade under my command arrived at Simra, one day's march from Jhansi. My 1st Brigade had not yet joined me from Chundeerie.

The same day I sent Brigadier Steuart with the cavalry and artillery, noted in the margin,* to invest Jhansi.

The 20th ultimo was the day which, when at Saugor, I had named for my arrival before Jhansi.

* See London Gazette, April 23, 1858.

I should have reached it some days sooner but for the delay occasioned by my waiting to see whether the 2nd Brigade would be required to assist in taking Chundeerie.

I arrived the following day, the 21st ultimo, with the remainder of my brigade before Jhansi.

The pickets of the cavalry sent on the day before had sabered about 100 armed men, bundeelas, endeavouring to enter Jhansi, having been summoned by the Ranee to defend it.

Having no plan, or even correct description of the fortress and city, I had, together with the officers commanding the artillery and engineers, to make long and repeated reconnoissances, in order to ascertain the nature of the enemy's defences; this delayed for some days the commencement of the siege operations.

The great strength of the fort, natural as well as artificial, and its extent, entitles it to a place amongst fortresses. It stands on an elevated rock, rising out of a plain, and commands the city and surrounding country. It is built of excellent and most massive masonry. The fort is difficult to breach, because, composed of granite, its walls vary in thickness from sixteen to twenty feet.

The fort has extensive and elaborate outworks, of the same solid construction, with front and flanking embrasures for artillery fire, and loopholes, of which in some places there were five tiers for musketry. Guns placed on the high towers of the fort commanded the country all around.

One tower, called the "White Turret," had been raised lately in height by the rebels, and armed with heavy ordnance.

The fortress is surrounded by the city of Jhansi on all sides except the west and part of the south face.

The steepness of the rock protects the west; the fortified city wall, with bastions, springing from the centre of its south face, running south, and ending in a high mound, or mamelon, protects, by a flanking fire, its south face. The mound was fortified by a strong circular bastion for five guns, round part of which was drawn a ditch 12 feet deep and 15 feet broad, of solid masonry. Quantities of men were always at work in the mound.

The city of Jhansi is about 4½ miles in circumference, and is surrounded by a fortified and massive wall, from 6 to 12 feet thick, and varying in height from 18 to 30 feet, with numerous flanking bastions armed as batteries with ordnance, and loop-holes, with a banquette for infantry.

Outside the walls the city is girt with wood, except part of its east and south fronts; on the former is a picturesque lake and water palace; to the south are the ruined cantonments and residences of the English, temples with their gardens; one, the Jockun Bagh, the scene of the massacre of our lamented countrymen; and two, rocky ridges, the easternmost called "Kafoo Tekri," both important positions, facing and threatening the south face of the city wall and fort.

I established seven flying camps of cavalry, as an investing force round Jhansi, giving to Major Scudamore half a troop of horse artillery, and later, to Major Gall two 9-pounders. These camps detached to the front outposts and videttes, which watched and prevented all issue from the city, day and night, each camp, on any attempt being made to force its line, was to call on the others for help. I gave directions also that the roads from the city should be obstruced by trenches and abatis.

The attack of Jhansi offered serious difficulties.

There were no means of breaching the fort, except from the south ; but the south was flanked by the fortified city wall and mound just described

The rocky ridge was excellent for a breaching battery, except that it was too far off, 640 yards, and that the fire from it would have been oblique.

The mound enfiladed two walls of the city, and commanded the whole of the south quarter of it, including the palace.

It was evident that the capture of the mound was the first and most important operation, because its occupation ensured, in all probability, that of the south of the city and of the palace, affording also the means of constructing, by approaches, an advanced breaching battery.

The desideratum, therefore, was to concentrate a heavy fire on the mound, and on the south of the city, in order to drive the enemy out of them and facilitate their capture; to breach the wall close to the mound, and to dismantle the enemy's defences, which protected the mound, and opposed an attack. This was effected :—

Firstly—By occupying and placing batteries on a rocky knoll, the right attack, which I had found in my reconnoissance, to the south of the lake, opposite the Aorcha gate and south-east wall of the town, which took in reverse the mound and two walls running from it.

Secondly—On the rocky ridge the left attack.

These batteries could not be completed till the arrival of the 1st Brigade with its siege-guns on the 25th ultimo.

In the meantime, the right attack opened fire from an 8-inch howitzer and two 8-inch mortars, on the rear of the mound and the south of the city, with the exception of the palace, which I wished to preserve for the use of the troops.

A remarkable feature in the defence was, that the enemy had no works or posts outside the city.

Sir Robert Hamilton estimated the number of the garrison at 10,000 bundeelas and valartees, and 1,500 sepoys, of whom 400 were cavalry; and the number of guns in the city and fort at thirty or forty.

The fire of the right attack, on the first day of the opening of the fire, the 23rd ultimo, cleared the mound of the workmen and the enemy. The mortars, in consequence of information I had received, shelled and set on fire long rows of hay-ricks in the south of the city, which created an almost general conflagration in that quarter.

The enemy had been firing actively from the White Turret, the Two tower Battery in the fort, and the Wheel Tower, Saugor, and Sutehmen, gate batteries, in the town. About mid-day their fire ceased almost completely, but recommenced the next day with increased vigour.

The chief of the rebel artillery was a first-rate artilleryman; he had under him two companies of Golundauze. The manner in which the rebels served their guns, repaired their defences, and reopened fire from batteries and guns repeatedly shut up, was remarkable. From some batteries they returned shot for shot. The women were seen working in the batteries and carrying ammunition. The Garden Battery was fought under the black flag of the Fakeers.

Everything indicated a general and determined resistance; this was not surprising, as the inhabitants, from the Ranee downwards, were more or less, concerned in the murder and plunder of the English. There was hardly a house in Jhansi which did not contain some article of English plunder, and, politically speaking, the rebel confederacy knew well, that if Jhansi, the richest Hindoo city and most important fortress in Central India, fell, the cause of the insurgents in this part of India fell also.

To relieve this city, wall batteries to the south-
and cannonade more effectually the town, two 24,
pounder guns were placed in battery, between the
8-inch howitzer and the two 8-inch mortars; and
opened fire on the 25th ultimo. They produced
a good effect, but not to the extent of silencing
the town batteries. Unfortunately on this day
the 8-inch howitzer was disabled by the breaking
of its trunnion.

On the 24th ultimo, I caused the rocky ridge,
the left attack, to be occupied by a strong picket,
under Captain Hare, with two 5½-inch mortars,
which played on the mound and the houses adjacent to it.

On the 25th ultimo, the siege-train of the 1st
Brigade having arrived, batteries were constructed
and opened fire from the 26th to the 29th ultimo
on the rocky ridge, as follows, forming the left
attack.

Two 18-pounders, to dismantle the defences of
the fort.

Two 10-inch mortars, to destroy the fort.

Two 8-inch mortars and one 8-inch howitzer, to
act on the mound and adjacent wall and city.

One 18-pounder, to breach the wall near the
bastion of the mound, which was thus exposed to
a vertical and horizontal fire, on its right face and
left rear. The 18-pounders were changed from
travelling to garrison carriages.

In order to prevent delay and confusion, I gave
names to all the enemy's batteries in the town as
well as in the fort; they were thirteen in number.

The fire of the two 18-pounders was so efficient
that towards sunset the parapets of the White
Turret, the Black Tower, and the Tree Tower,
which faced our attack, were nearly destroyed.

The two 10-inch mortars created great havoc in
the fort, and having pointed out to Lieutenant
Pittman, Bombay Horse Artillery, the position of

a powder magazine, respecting which I had information, he blew it up the third shot, keeping up a well-directed fire on the fort; for which good service I beg to recommend him to your Excellency.

The breaching gun, so solid was the wall, and so hard the masonry, did not produce the result contemplated on the first, or indeed on the second day, but on the 30th, the breach was practicable. The enemy retrenched the breach with a double row of palisades filled with earth, on which I ordered every description of fire, including red-hot shot, to be directed upon it, and the result was that a considerable portion of the stockade was destroyed by fire.

Riflemen, to fire at the parapets and the embrasures and loop-holes, were placed in all the batteries, with sand bag loop-holes, and posts of riflemen were distributed in the temples and gardens on the east and south sides of the city. I occupied also the Jokun Bagh, nearly opposite the mound, with a picket of riflemen. The riflemen caused numerous casualties amongst the rebels in the town as well as on the parapets.

Two of the enemy's defences which annoyed the left attack the most, were the Wheel Tower on the south, and the Garden Battery on a rock, in rear of the west wall of the city. To silence the former a new battery, called the Kapoo Tekree, or "E." Battery, was established on a ridge to the east of the rocky ridge, with two 5½-inch mortars, which not proving sufficient, I substituted for them two 8-inch mortars and a 9-pounder; I afterwards added a 24-pound howitzer to enfilade the wall running eastwards from the mound.

Before the sand-bag battery could be made for the 9-pounder, acting Bombardier Brenna, of Captain Ommanney's Company, Royal Artillery, quite a lad, commanded and pointed the 9-pounder in the open, and silenced the enemy's gun in battery in the bastion, destroying, besides, its defences.

I praised him for his good service, on the ground, and promoted him.

The two 8-inch mortars, and occasionally the two 10-inch mortars of the left attack, answered the Garden Battery, shelling also the Nia Bustia, and five wells, where the sepoys had taken up their quarters, on account of the good water.

After the capture of Jhansi, we had proof of the havoc caused by the shelling and cannonade in the fort and city. Beside the damage done to the houses and buildings, the rebels acknowledge to have lost from 60 to 70 men a day killed.

Our batteries had, by the 30th, dismantled the defences of the fort and city, or disabled their guns. It is true that the rebels had made, on the white turret, an excellent parapet of large sand bags, which they kept always wet, and still ran up fresh in lieu of disabled guns; but their best guns had been disabled, and their best artillery men killed. Their fire was therefore no longer serious.

However, the obstinate defence of the enemy, the breach, and the extent fired on, had caused a great consumption of ammunition; so much so, that it was evident that there would not be sufficient to multiply breaches in the town wall, or to establish a main breach in the south double wall of the fort.

Under these circumstances, the officer commanding the artillery and engineers called to my notice the necessity of having recourse to escalade, to which I gave my consent, requiring, however, that the breach should form an important and principal point of attack. Both of these officers entertained a mistrust of the breach, thinking that it was mined or not practicable.

Knowing the risk which generally attend escalades, I had recourse to every means in my power for facilitating an entry by the breach. In order to widen it, and destroy still more effectually the entrenchment and stockade which the enemy had constructed in rear of the breach, I kept up a fire day and night on it from the 18-pounder and the 8-inch howitzer, and with the view to prevent the enemy working, and to render the mound too hot for them, I shelled it and the adjoining houses day and night from the mortar batteries in the centre and left attacks. Lieutenant Strutt, Bombay Artillery, made excellent practice, throwing the shells on the spots occupied by the guards of the city walls.

I had made arrangements on the 30th for storming, but the general action on the 1st instant, with the so-called army of the Peshwa, which advanced across the Betwa to relieve it, caused the assault to be deferred.

With the view to acquire rapid information respecting the enemy's movements, I established a telegraph on a hill commanding Jhansi and the surrounding country. It was of great use telegraphing the Ranee's flight, the approach of the enemy from the Betwa, &c.

On the 2nd instant, Major Boileau reported to me that he had made all the necessary preparations for the escalade, and that a 24-pound howitzer had been placed in battery in front of the Jokun Bagh, for the purpose of enfilading and clearing, during the night, the wall from the mound to the fort, and the Rocket Bastion, which is on it. I issued a division order for the assault of the defences of the city wall, of which a copy with a plan of the attack was furnished to the officers in command.

I have the honour to enclose copies of reports, from Brigadier Stuart commanding my 1st, and

Brigadier Steuart commanding my 2nd brigade, of the operations of their respective columns against Jhansi.

The left attack, ably and gallantly conducted by Brigadier Stuart, succeeded perfectly,—its right column passing without loss or difficulty through the breach, which turned out as well as I thought it would; and the left effecting, with some casualties, the escalade of the Rocket Bastion. Colonel Lowth, commanding Her Majesty's 86th Regiment, acted with cool judgment, and I witnessed with lively pleasure the devotion and gallantry of his regiment.

The 3rd Europeans, under Lieutenant-Colonel Liddell, did their duty, as they always have done; but they could not control adverse circumstances, arising from bad ladders and a mistake in the road; they returned to the assault with alacrity, and fought their way through the town manfully.

I beg leave to support earnestly the recommendations of officers contained in these reports of the Brigadier's, particularly of Captain Darby, wounded; Lieutenant Dartnell, severely wounded in three places, who led the assault of the Rocket Bastion; and Lieutenant Fox, severely wounded. It will be a gratification also to the relatives of Lieutenants Meiklejohn and Dick, of the Bombay Engineers, to know that these two young officers had gained my esteem by the intelligence and coolness which they evinced, as engineer officers, during the siege. I should have recommended both for promotion, if they had not died in their country's cause, for conspicuous gallantry in leading the way up two scaling ladders.

The 86th, on their road to the palace from the mound, sustained many casualties, from their left flank being exposed, as they passed through an open space, to a flanking musketry fire from an outwork of the fort, and from houses and the palace itself to their front. I directed loopholes for riflemen to be made through houses which brought a fire to bear on the outwork of the fort, a large house to be occupied close to the palace, and covered communication to be made to the mound.

The skirmishers of the regiment penetrated gallantly into the palace; the few men who still held it made an obstinate resistance, setting fire to trains of gunpowder, from which several of the 86th received fatal injuries.

Having received no reports from the right attack, composed of the 3rd Europeans and Hydrabad Contingent, I made my way to them in the south-east quarter of the city. I found them engaged with the enemy, and making their way to the palace. The rebels were firing at them from the houses, which the troops were breaking open and clearing of their defenders. I found Lieutenant-Colonel Turnbull, commanding the Artillery, here, wounded mortally, I deeply regret to say, by a musket-shot from a house. He had followed me through the breach into the streets, and having received directions from me to bring guns into the city, to batter houses in which rebels held out, he had gone round by the right, to the east quarter of the city, to fix the road by which they were to enter. The Archa Gate was the best for guns, but it was so barricaded by masses of stones, that it could not be opened for several hours.

In the despatches I have recorded, the excellent service performed by Lieutenant-Colonel Turnbull, particularly in the general action of the Betwa, always exposing himself to the fire of the enemy, in order to choose the best position for his guns. This devoted officer was as useful to me as Commandant of Artillery, as Captain of a troop of Horse Artillery. His premature fall prevented his receiving the reward which was his due. I can now only earnestly recommend that his numerous family may inherit their father's claims on his country.

The right and left attacks being now concentrated in the palace, I gained possession of a large portion of the city by advancing the 3rd Europeans to the north-east, and occupying the Burrah Goug Gate, on which I rested, their right flank forming an oblique line from the gate to the palace with the 3rd Europeans and the 86th in the palace, the two regiments occupying with pickets commanding houses to their front. This line was in prolongation of the second line, leading from the mound under the fort to the palace. This done, it was necessary to clear the large portion of the city, in rear of this oblique line, of the numerous armed rebels who remained in the houses, and who were firing on the troops. This was not effected without bloody, often hand-to-hand, combats. One of the most remarkable of them was between detachments of Her Majesty's 86th Regiment and 3rd Europeans, and 30 or 40 Valaitee sowars, the body-guard of the Ranee, in the palace stables, under the fire of the fort. The sowars, full of opium, defended their stables, firing with matchlocks and pistols from the windows and loopholes, and cutting with their tulwars, and from behind the doors. When driven in, they retreated behind their horses, still firing, or fighting with their swords in both hands, till they were shot or bayoneted, struggling even when dying on the ground, to strike again. A party of them remained in a room off the stables, which was on fire till they were half burnt, their clothes in flames, they rushed out, hacking at their assailants, and guarding their heads with their shields.

Captain Rose, my aide-de-camp, saved the life of a man of the 86th, who was down, by bayoneting his assailant.

All the sowars were killed, but not without
several casualties on our side. The gallant soldiers
captured, in the quarters of the sowars, the Ranee's standards, three standards of the body-guard,
three kettle-drums, and horses, and an English
union-jack of silk, which Sir Robert Hamilton
tells me Lord William Bentinck had given the
grandfather of the husband of the Ranee, with
the permission to have it carried before him, as a
reward for his fidelity,—a privilege granted to no
other Indian prince. I granted the soldiers their
request, to hoist on the place the flag of their
country, which they had so bravely won. Captain
Sandwith, who was wounded, commanded with
spirit the Europeans on this occasion ; and Serjeant Brown, of the Commissariat Department,
was the first to dash boldly into the stables.

Numerous incidents marked the desperate feeling which animated the defenders. A retainer of
the Ranee tried to blow up himself and his wife ;
failing in the attempt, he endeavoured to cut her
to pieces, and then killed himself. Two Valaitees
attacked by the videttes, threw a woman who
was with them into a well, and then jumped
down it themselves.

Whilst engaged in the town, I received a
report from the officer commanding one of the
Hydrabad Cavalry flying camps, that a large body
of the enemy, flying from the town, had tried to
force his picket, that a few had succeeded, but
that the main body, from 350 to 500 strong, had
been driven back, and had occupied a high and
rocky hill to the west of the fort ; that he had
surrounded the hill with cavalry, till reinforcements were sent. I immediately ordered out
from the camps of the two brigades the available
troops of all arms against the hill. A report
received from Major Gall shows how satisfactorily
these rebels were disposed of. Lieutenant Park·

was killed whilst gallantly leading on a party of the 24th Bombay Native Infantry along the ridge of the hill. The Ranee's father, Mamoo Saheb, was amongst the rebels ; he was wounded on the hill, and captured some days afterwards, and hanged at the Joken Bagh.

After having cleared the quarter of the town in our possession of the enemy, I had intended attacking the remainder of it, but deferred doing so till the next day, on Brigadier Stuart's representation that the men were too much exhausted for any further operations that day.

Towards sunset, it was telegraphed from the observatory, that the enemy were approaching from the east. I had therefore to re-occupy, with all the force I could collect, the field of action of the Betwa, the devoted troops marching to a fresh combat, after thirteen hours' fighting in a burning sun, with as much spirit as if they had not been engaged at all.

The alarm proved to be a false one, troops from Tehree having been mistaken for the enemy.

The next day Brigadier Stuart and myself occupied the rest of the city by a combined movement, assisted by Major Gall, who spiritedly scaled the bastion at the Onou Gate, from his flying camp, and capturing the gun which was there, threw it down the rampart.

The following morning a wounded Mahratta retainer of the Ranee was sent in to me from Captain Abbott's flying camp. He stated that the Ranee, accompanied by 300 Valaitees and 25 sowars, fled that night from the fort ; that after leaving it, they had been headed back by one of the pickets, where the Ranee and her party separated, she herself taking to the right, with a few sowars, in the direction of her intended flight to Bundere. The Observatory also telegraphed, " enemy escaping to the north-east." immediately sent off

strong detachment of Her Majesty's 14th Light
Dragoons, 3rd Light Cavalry, and Hydrabad
Cavalry, to pursue, with guns to support them, as
it was said that Tantia Topee had sent a force to
meet her. I also sent Brigadier Steuart with
cavalry, to watch the fords of the Betwa.

In the meantime, detachments of the 86th and
3rd Europeans, took possession of the fortress.

In sight of Bundere, 21 miles from Jhansi, the
cavalry came in sight of the Irregular Horse, sent
to meet the Ranee, which separated, probably
with the view to mislead her pursuers as to her
real course.

Lieutenant Dowker, Hydrabad Cavalry, was
sent by Captain Forbes through the town of
Bundere, whilst he, with the 3rd Light Cavalry
and 14th Light Dragoons, passed it by the left.
In the town, Lieutenant Dowker saw traces of
the Ranee's hasty flight, and her tent, in which
was an unfinished breakfast. On the other side
of the town he came up with, and cut up, 40 of
the enemy, consisting of Rohillas and Bengal Irregular Cavalry. Lieutenant Dowker was gaining
fast on the Ranee, who, with four attendants, was
seen escaping on a grey horse, when he was dismounted by a severe wound, and obliged to give
up the pursuit.

From the time the troops took the palace, the
rebels lost heart, and began to leave the town and
fort. Nothing could prove more the efficiency of
the investment than the number of them cut up
by the pickets of the flying camps; the woods,
gardens, and roads round the town were strewed
with the corpses of fugitive rebels. The Ranee's
flight was the signal for a general retreat. Early
in the morning I caused the outskirts of the city
to be scoured with cavalry and infantry; it will
give some idea of the destruction of insurgents
which ensued, when a party of the 14th Dragoons

alone killed 200 in one patro'. The rebels, who were chiefly Valaitees and Pathans, generally sold their lives as dearly as they could, fighting to the last with their usual dexterity and firmness. A band of forty of these desperadoes barricaded themselves in a spacious house, with a court-yard, vaults, &c.; before they were aware of its strength, it was attacked by a detachment of Hydrabad Infantry, under Captain Hare, with the loss of Captain Sinclair, of whose conduct it is my duty again to make honorable mention. Reinforcements and several pieces of siege artillery were brought up by Major Orr, who commanded the attack against this house, but even when it had been breached and knocked to pieces the rebels continued to resist in the ruined passages and vaults. They were all as usual destroyed, but not without several casualties on our part. Major Orr expresses his obligations to Captains Woolcombe and Douglas of the Bombay and Bengal Artillery; Lieutenant Lewis, and Ensign Fowler, of Her Majesty's 86th Regiment,—the first very severely wounded, who led the men; and also Lieutenant Simpson, 23rd Regiment, Bengal Native Infantry, wounded.

Captain Abbott, Hydrabad Contingent, speaks highly of the gallantry with which Lieutenant Dun, and detachments of the 1st and 4th Hydrabad Contingent, stormed, dismounted, a house and garden, held obstinately by fugitives, and he recommends, as I beg to do also, the officers, whose names follow, for promotion, and for the Order of Merit, for gallantry in the field.

Recommended for promotion :—

1st CAVALRY, HYDRABAD CONTINGENT.

Russaidar, Allaoodeen Khan, 3rd troop.
Jemadar, Mahomedeen Khan, (wounded).

TROOPERS.

Kerreem Ali Khan, (wounded).
Tigmalsing   (wounded).
Meer Amzed Ali.
Train Sing.

4th CAVALRY, HYDRABAD CONTINGENT.

Jemadar, Hunooman Sing, (wounded).
Duffadar, Himmut Khan.

TROOPERS.

Bugwan Sing.
Khair Mahomed Khan, (wounded).
Khairoolah Khan.
Takoob Khan.
Syad Shireef (2nd Cavalry), doing duty with

4th CAVALRY, HYDRABAD CONTINGENT.

Recommended for the Order of Merit :—

1st CAVALRY, HYDRABAD CONTINGENT.

Russaidar, Allaoodeen Khan, 3rd troop.
Jemadar, Mahomedeen Khan, 3rd troop (wounded).

4th CAVALRY, HYDRABAD CONTINGENT.

Jemadar, Hunooman Sing, (wounded).

It was not till Jhansi was taken that its great strength was known.

There was only one part of the fortress, the south curtain, which was considered practicable for breaching ; but, when inside, we saw that this was a mistake, there being at some distance, in rear of the curtain, a massive wall, fifteen or twenty feet thick ; and immediately in rear of this, a deep tank, cut out of the lime rock.

I beg leave to bring to the favorable notice of the Commander-in-Chief, the conduct of the troops under my command in the siege, investment, and capture of Jhansi. They had to contend against an enemy more than double their numbers, (behind formidable fortifications), who defended themselves, afterwards, from house to house, in a spacious city, often under the fire of the fort; afterwards in suburbs, and in very difficult ground, outside of the walls. The investing cavalry force were day and night, for seventeen days, on arduous duty, the men not taking their clothes off, the horses saddled and bridled up at night. The nature of the defence, and the strictness of the investment, gave rise to continued and fierce combats, for the rebels, having no hope, either for quarter or escape, sought to sell their lives as dearly as they could; but the discipline and gallant spirit of the troops enabled them to overcome difficulties and opposition of every sort, to take the fortified city of Jhansi by storm, subduing the strongest fortress in Central India, and killing 5000 of its rebel garrison.

According to the first reports which I received, only 3000 rebels were killed, but those received since the withdrawal of the seven flying camps, make the loss of the enemy amount to above 5000 killed; native accounts, received by Brigadier Wheeler, at Saugor, make the loss of the rebels to amount to more than 5000.

I beg to recommend to his Excellency, for gallant and good service in investing the fortress of Jhansi,—Major Scudamore, Her Majesty's 14th Light Dragoons, the senior officer in command of the flying camps; Major Gale, Her Majesty's 14th Light Dragoons; Major Forbes, C.B., commanding 3rd Bombay Light Cavalry; Captain Abbott, and Lieutenant Dowker, Hydrabad Cavalry.

The Commander-in-Chief will learn with pleasure that the troops under my command treated with great humanity the women and children of

Jhansi. Neither the desperate resistance of the rebels, nor the recollections of Jhansi of last year, could make them forget, that, in an English soldier's eye, women and children are sacred; so far from hurting, the troops were seen sharing their rations with them. I gave orders also that the destitute women and children of Jhansi should be fed out of the prize grain.

I have the honour to enclose a list of the guns and ordnance stores captured in the city and fort of Jhansi, and of the casualties of the force during the siege. I regret much that our loss should have been so considerable, but it was caused, in a great measure, by the strict investment which proved so fatal to the enemy, and the loss of my force is, out of all proportion, smaller than that of the enemy. They lost fifty to my one killed, not counting the wounded on our side.

I beg leave to state the obligations I am under to the following officers, for the services which they have rendered to me during the siege operations and capture of Jhansi :—

Brigadier Stuart, Commanding 1st Brigade.

Brigadier Steuart, C.B., Commanding, 2nd Brigade.

Lieutenant-Colonel Lowth, Commanding Her Majesty's 86th Regiment.

Lieutenant-Colonel Liddell, Commanding 3rd Bombay European Regiment.

Major Scudamore, Commanding Her Majesty's 14th Light Dragoons.

Major Orr, Commanding Hydrabad Field Force.

Major Forbes, C.B., Commanding 3rd Bombay Light Cavalry.

Major Robertson, Commanding 25th Regiment Bombay Native Infantry.

Captain Lightfoot, Commanding Battery Bombay Artillery.

Captain Woollcombe, Commanding Battery Bombay Artillery.

Captain Fenwick, Commanding Company Royal Engineers.

Captain Hare, Commanding 5th Regiment Hydrabad Infantry.

Captain Brown, Commanding Company Madras Engineers.

Lieutenant Goodfellow, Commanding Company Bombay Engineers.

Lieutenant Lowry, Commanding Battery Royal Artillery.

Lieutenant Pittman, Commanding Troop Bombay Horse Artillery.

GENERAL STAFF.

Captain Wood, Assistant Adjutant-General.

Captain Macdonald, Assistant Quartermaster-General.

Major Boileau, Commanding Engineers.

Captain Ommanney, Commanding Artillery.

Lieutenant Haggard, Commanding Ordnance.

Doctor Arnott, Superintending Surgeon.

Doctor Vaughan, Staff Surgeon.

Captain Rose, Aide-de-camp.

Lieutenant Lyster, Interpreter.

I have much gratification in bringing to the notice of his Excellency the officers mentioned in the Brigade despatches:—

FIRST BRIGADE.

Major Stuart, Her Majesty's 86th Regiment.

Lieutenant Dartnell, Her Majesty's 86th Regiment.

Lieutenant Fowler, Her Majesty's 86th Regiment.

Lieutenant Jerome, Her Majesty's 86th Regiment.

Lieutenant Webber, Royal Engineers.

Ensign Sewell, Her Majesty's 86th Regiment.

Brigade Staff.

Captain Coley, Major of Brigade.
Captain Bacon, Deputy Assistant Quartermaster-
General.

Second Brigade.

Captain Sandwith, 3rd Bombay European Regi-
ment.
Captain Robison, 3rd Bombay European Regiment.
Lieutenant Fox, Madras Engineers.
Lieutenant Bonus, Bombay Engineers.
Lieutenant Goodfellow, Bombay Engineers.
Lieutenant Park, 3rd Bombay European Regiment.
Ensign Newport, 3rd Bombay European Regiment.

Brigade Staff.

Captain Todd, Major of Brigade.
Captain Leckie, Deputy Assistant Quartermaster-
General.

> HUGH ROSE, Major-General,
> Commanding Central India Force.

No. 69.

*Brigadier Stuart, Commanding First Brigade,
C.I.F.F., to the Assistant Adjutant-General
Central India Field Force.*

SIR,   *Camp Jhansi, April* 13, 1858.

IN compliance with Field Force Order, No. 7,
of yesterday's date, I have the honor to transmit
herewith a return of casualties in the 1st Brigade
Central India Field Force during the siege and
storm of Jhansi, and with reference to the latter
beg to place on record the part taken in it by the
brigade under my command.

2. As directed in Field Force Orders, dated the
2nd April, the assaulting column of the 1st Brigade was formed up at daybreak of the 3rd April
ready to move on the two points of attack which had

been indicated, viz., the breach at the monur and the rocket tower, and the low curtain immediately to the right of it. Lieutenant-Colonel Lowth, Her Majesty's 86th Regiment, commanded the former, and Major Stuart, Her Majesty's 86th Regiment, the latter attack. On the signal being given, both parties moved steadily to the front, under a smart fire from the enemy. Captain Darby, Her Majesty's 86th Regiment, led the stormers up the breach in the most gallant manner, and the enemy were driven before them at all points, while at the same time Major Stuart's attack by escalade at the rocket tower succeeded admirably, though hotly opposed. On gaining the town, Lieutenant-Colonel Lowth, with great judgment, moved part of his men to his right, and thus took the enemy in flank and rear, when they were meeting the right attack of the 2nd Brigade with great vigour. All the troops of the 1st Brigade then concentrated on the Ranee's palace, which was taken possession of by Lieutenant-Colonel Lowth and his men in the most gallant manner. As the Major-General was himself a witness of the greater part of the operations at this and at a subsequent period, I do not enter into further details.

3. I beg in conclusion to bring to the notice of the Major-General, the excellent and gallant behaviour of both officers and men of the 1st Brigade on this occasion, the energy and judgment displayed by Lieutenant-Colonel Lowth, Her Majesty's 86th Regiment, proved of the greatest service, and much contributed to the success of our attack. Major Stuart, Her Majesty's 86th Regiment, carried out the duties confided to him in the most satisfactory manner, and led the escalading party with the greatest gallantry. He was assisted by Lieutenant Dartnell and Ensigns Sewell and Fowler, of Her Majesty's 86th Regi-

ment, who were all wounded, the first two officers severely; also by Lieutenant Webber, Royal Engineers, commanding the ladder party of the Royal Sappers, who most ably performed their duty. On this occasion Lieutenant Dartnell greatly distinguished himself, as also Sergeant Alleyn Walfe and Private Roger Matthews, both Her Majesty's 86th Regiment; the conduct of Lieutenant Jerome and Private Burns, Her Majesty's 86th Regiment, has also been brought to my notice. Under a murderous fire, they carried off Ensign Sewell, who had fallen severely wounded, and who would otherwise have been cut up. I lament to say that Assistant-Surgeon Stack, Her Majesty's 86th Regiment, was killed near the palace, whilst most nobly and courageously attending to the wounded under a hot fire. I beg also to record an act of daring on the part of Havildar Shaik Dawood, Light Company, 25th Regiment Native Infantry, brought to my notice by Captain Little, commanding that regiment. After an entrance had been effected into the city, a number of rebels were found to have taken refuge in the recesses of a large well, the only approach to which was by narrow and steep stairs, having a sharp turning, at which one resolute man could have kept off any number; whilst measures were being arranged for seizing these rebels, Havildar Shaik Dawood volunteered to capture them; so, fixing his bayonet he boldly descended the well, and being followed by others, brought up thirteen of the enemy.

I have, &c.,
C. S. STUART, Brigadier,
Commanding 1st Brigade, C.I.F.F.

No. 70.

Brigadier C. Steuart, C.B., commanding 2nd Brigade, C.I.F.F., to the Assistant Adjutant-General, Central India Field Force.

SIR,   *Camp Jhansi, April 29,* 1858.

IN obedience to orders received through you, the brigade under my command moved in two columns on the morning of the 3rd of April, to the assault of the town of Jhansi.

The left column led by Captain Robison, 3rd Bombay European Regiment, the right by Lieutenant-Colonel Liddell, advanced with great steadiness through a very heavy fire of musketry and wall pieces towards the ladders, on reaching which they were assailed with rockets, earthen pots filled with powder, and, in fact, every sort of missile.

On arriving at the temple where the reserve of which I was in command was to take up its position, Major Boileau, Madras Engineers, came to me, and reported that the ladders were without protection, and requested me to give him some Europeans to protect them. I therefore gave him the hundred men of the 3rd Bombay European Regiment that were with the reserve.

Lieutenants Meiklejohn and Dick, of the Bombay Engineers, led the way up the ladders of the right column, both of whom were unfortunately killed. Lieutenant Bonus, Bombay Engineers, Lieutenant Fox, Madras Sappers, led up the ladders of the left column, both of whom were wounded—the latter severely.

The ladders were found in some instances too short, in others too weak, breaking under the men, who were withdrawn from the heavy fire to which they were thus unnecessarily exposed, and the movement was made with great precision and coolness.

Shortly after this, Captain Robison, 3rd Bombay European Regiment, was informed by Captain Baily, executive engineer, that some of the 86th Regiment had entered by the breach to his left, and he doubled some of his party round to that point, at which he effected an entry and cleared the ramparts, so as to enable the remainder to mount the ladders unopposed. Lieutenant-Colonel Liddell, on finding his ladders of no use, ordered Lieutenant Goodfellow, of the Bombay Engineers, to try a bag of powder at a postern, but from being built up inside, no entry could be effected ; however, by this time, Captain Robison had made good his lodgment, and was followed by the right column, when all proceeded towards the palace, which, as the Major-General is aware, was taken after a desperate resistance.

Both columns behaved with great coolness and gallantry, and I trust I may be pardoned for bringing their leaders to the notice of the Major-General, as also Captain Sandwith and Lieutenant Park, 3rd Bombay European Regiment, Lieutenant Goodfellow, Bombay Engineers, and also Privates Fen and Whirlpool, 3rd Bombay European Regiment, of whom Lieutenant-Colonel Liddell speaks in the highest terms. Captain Robison's conduct, in doubling round with some of his men to the breach, speaks for itself, but he has brought to my notice Corporal Hard, Privates Roger and Archibald, all of the Grenadier Company, and Private Drummond, No. 1, and Private Doran, No. 3 Company of the 3rd Bombay European Regiment, all of whom fought most gallantly at the head of the ladders, till they gave way. Ensign Newport and Private Gillman, of No. 1 Company, 3rd Bombay European Regiment, assisted by Corporal Hard, of the Grenadiers, carried off the body of Lieutenant Fox, of the Madras Sappers and Miners, through the hottest of the fire, after Captain Robison had ordered the troops to retire. Lieutenant Bonus, Bombay Engineers, has also been especially brought to my notice for the gallant manner in which he led up and maintained his position on the ladders, until disabled and knocked over by the blow of a stone.

Captain Tod, Brigade Major, and Captain Leckie, Deputy Assistant Quartermaster-General of the 2nd Brigade, on this, as on every previous opportunity, have afforded me every assistance; and it is only to the circumstance of all former operations in which they have been engaged, being conducted so entirely under the Major-General, as to render any special report from me unnecessary that I have failed in earlier bringing my sense of their worth to his notice, a circumstance which I feel sure will not act to their detriment.

I have, &c.,

C. STEUART, Brigadier,
Commanding 2nd Brigade,
Central India Field Force.

No. 71.

From the Return of Casualties of the Central India Field Force and Hydrabad Contingent Field Force, during the Siege and Storm of Jhansi, exclusive of those Killed and Wounded on the 1st of April, at the Action of the Betwa.

Camp Jhansi, April 16, 1858.

1ST BRIGADE.

Lieutenant G. Simpson, $\frac{4}{}$ Artillery, severely wounded.

Assistant-Surgeon John Cruickshank, 21st Co. Royal Engineers, severely wounded.

Sapper Hempell Ramsay, 21st Co. Royal Engineers, severely wounded.

Sapper George Moore, 21st Co. Royal Engineers, slightly wounded.

Sapper James Smith, 21st Co. Royal Engineers, severely wounded.

Captain Charles Darby, H.M.'s 86th Regiment. severely wounded.

Lieutenant J. G. Dartnell, H.M.'s 86th Regiment, severely wounded.

Lieutenant W. R. M. Holroyd, H.M.'s 86th Regiment, severely wounded.

Ensign S. W. Sewell, H.M.'s 86th Regiment, severely wounded.

Surgeon Thomas Stack, H.M.'s 86th Regiment, killed.

Serjeant Thomas Pickaring, H.M.'s 86th Regiment, severely wounded.

Serjeant Dennis Connors, H.M.'s 86th Regiment, severely wounded.

Lieutenant R. F. Lewis, H.M.'s 86th Regiment, dangerously wounded.

Ensign George Fowler, H.M.'s 86th Regiment, slightly wounded.

Lieutenant P. P. P. Fenwick, 25th Regiment Bombay N.I., slightly wounded.

2ND BRIGADE.

Lieutenant-Colonel Sydney Turnbull, 1st Troop Horse Artillery, dangerously wounded. Died 4th April.

Serjeant F. Cooper, H.M.'s 14th Light Dragoons, severely wounded.

Lieutenant F. R. Fox, B. Company Madras Sappers and Miners, very dangerously wounded.

First Lieutenant W. G. Dick, Bombay Sappers and Miners, killed in action.

Second Lieutenant J. Bonus, Bombay Sappers and Miners, slightly wounded.

Captain Sandwith, 3rd Bombay European Regiment, slightly wounded.

Assistant-Surgeon Miller, 3rd Bombay European Regiment, severely wounded.

Colour-Serjeant Robert Steavens, 3rd Bombay European Regiment, slightly wounded.

Serjeant John Walsh, 3rd Bombay European Regiment, slightly wounded.

Lieutenant A. A. Park, 24th Regiment Bombay N.I., killed in action.

HYDERABAD CONTINGENT FIELD FORCE.

Captain Commanding, H. D. Abbott, 1st Cavalry, contusion from musket ball.

Lieutenant H. C. Dowker, 1st Cavalry, severely wounded.

Captain Commanding W. Murray, 4th Cavalry, contusion from musket ball.

Captain John Sinclair, Left Wing 3rd Infantry, dangerously wounded, died soon after admission.

Serjeant-Major Dixon, 5th Infantry, severely wounded.

ABSTRACT.

1ST BRIGADE.

$\frac{4}{2}$ Artillery—2 wounded.

21st Company, Royal Engineers—6 wounded.

Her Majesty's 86th Regiment—8 killed, 60 wounded, 6 since dead.

25th Regiment Bengal Native Infantry—5 killed, 25 wounded, 1 since dead.

Total—13 killed, 93 wounded.

2ND BRIGADE.

1st Troop, Horse Artillery—1 wounded, since dead.

Her Majesty's 14th Light Dragoons—3 wounded.

B Company, Madras Sappers and Miners—2 killed, 11 wounded, 2 since dead.

Detachment Bombay Sappers and Miners—2 killed, 6 wounded, 1 since dead.

3rd Bombay European Regiment—7 killed, 47 wounded, 5 since dead.

24th Regiment Native Infantry — 5 killed, 10 wounded, 1 since dead.

Total—16 killed, 78 wounded.

Hydrabad Contingent Field Force—9 killed, 44 wounded, 5 since dead; 16 horses killed, dead and missing.

Grand Total—38 killed, 215 wounded.

3rd Light Cavalry—1 horse killed, 3 horses wounded.

H. H. A. WOOD, Captain,
Assistant Adjutant-General, C.I.F.F.

No. 74.

. GENERAL ORDERS by the GOVERNOR-GENERAL of INDIA.

Allahabad, May 1, 1858.

No. 121 of 1858.

THE Right Honorable the Governor-General is pleased to publish, for general information, the following correspondence, relative to the defence of the bridge and Bithoor road, at Cawnpore, by Brigadier Carthew, on the 28th of November, 1857.

No. 75.

Brigadier M. Carthew, Commanding Madras Troops in Bengal, to the Deputy Assistant Adjutant-General, Cawnpore Division.

Cawnpore, December 1, 1857.

SIR,

. IN reply to your letter of this day's date, I have the honor to submit, for the information of Major-General Windham, commanding the Cawnpore Division, the following report on my defence of the bridge and Bithoor road on the 28th ultimo.

At daylight, on the 28th of November, I proceeded, according to instructions, with her Majesty's 34th Regiment, two companies of Her Majesty's 82nd Regiment, and four guns of Madras Native Artillery, to take up a position at the Racket Court, two companies of Her Majesty's 64th Regiment having been placed in the Baptist chapel to keep up communication with me. When within a few hundred yards of the Racket Court, I received instructions, through the late Captain McCrea, that General Windham preferred the position of the previous evening being taken up on the bridge, and the Bithoor road defended. I consequently retired, leaving a company of Her Majesty's 34th Regiment, to occupy the front line of broken down Native Infantry huts, and another company in their support in a brick building, about 100 yards to their rear. I then detached a company of Her Majesty's 34th to the opposite side of the road across the plain, in a line with the above support, to occupy a vacant house, to man the garden walls, and the upstairs verandah. These companies formed a strong position, and quite commanded the whole road towards the bridge. I halted at the bridge with the remainder of the 34th, and four guns, and barricaded the road, and placed two guns on the bridge. I then sent two companies of the 34th, under Lieutenant-Colonel Simpson, to occupy the position he held the previous evening, to prevent the egress of the enemy from the town towards the entrenchment, as also to defend the road from Allahabad. This picquet I subsequently strengthened with two of my guns, which could not be worked on the bridge.

A brisk fire was kept up by the enemy from their position amongst the native lines on the advanced skirmishers and picquet, and upon the bridge, by their guns (18-pounders), throughout the whole day. About mid-day, Captain McCrea conveyed instructions to me to proceed to the front to attack the enemy's infantry and guns,—that he was to convey the same instructions to Her Majesty's 64th Regiment, and both parties to advance at the same time.

Captain McCrea took with him to strengthen the 64th, 40 men of a company of Her Majesty's 82nd, which I had placed as a picquet at the old Commissariat compound, for the protection of the road leading from that direction to the entrenchment. I advanced with my two guns and a company of the 34th from the bridge, taking, as I advanced, the company stationed to my right in the upstair house, and the company occupying the broken huts (with its support) on my left. On advancing and clearing the front line of huts, I was desirous, and endeavoured to push the whole of my party across the plain in front to charge the enemy's guns ; but as their infantry still occupied the broken ground of other huts, and my force without support, it could not be done. The enemy's guns were driven far to the rear by the fire of my two guns, after which, my skirmishers, support, and right picquet, took up their original positions, and I returned with the guns to the bridge. Shortly after this, the enemy's infantry were seen to be skirting along the edge of the town, with the evident intention of turning our flank, and of pouring a fire upon us from the houses on our left. Both piquet and skirmishers applied for reinforcements which I could not afford, but desired them to hold their positions as long as possible, and then fall back to the head of the bridge, which they did about 5 o clock.

The enemy were now increasing in large numbers on our left, occupying houses, garden walls, and the church. A company was sent through the gardens to dislodge the enemy and drive them from the church, but the enemy were strong enough to maintain, or rather to return to, their position. I then concentrated all my force on both flanks of the bridge, and with the guns kept up a heavy fire. The enemy now brought up a gun into the churchyard, which enfiladed the bridge, at a distance not exceeding 150 yards, my own guns not being able to bear on their position.

The enemy were still increasing and working round to my rear by my left flank. I retired the guns about 100 yards, so as to command the bridge and the road leading from the town. Officers and men were at this time falling fast around me, I applied for a reinforcement, but by the time they arrived, night had set in, and I now considered it prudent to retire with the remainder of my force into the entrenchment, which was done with perfect regularity, the reinforcement of Rifles protecting the rear.

Although for some time earnestly advised to retire, I refrained from doing so, until I felt convinced, that, from the increasing numbers of the enemy, the fatigue of the men after three days' hard fighting, and my own troops firing in the dark into each other, the position was no longer tenable, and that consequently it became my painful duty to retire.

I beg to forward a return of the killed and wounded during the day.

Return of the Killed, Wounded and Missing, in the Force under Brigadier Carthew, employed in defending the Bridge on the Bithoor-road, 28th November, 1857.

Staff ... ... 2 Captains wounded.

Madras Artillery C. Company, 5th Battalion, Golundauze } 1 havildar, 8 privates and 1 havildar gun Lascar, wounded.

Iajesty's 34th ziment ... { 3 officers, 2 serjeants, 8 rank and file, killed ; 7 officers, 1 serjeant, and 50 rank and file, wounded.

idierCompany r Majesty's id Regiment } 2 rank and file, killed ; 1 officer, 5 rank and file, wounded.

Abstract.

	Officers.	Serjeants.	Havildars.	Rank and File.	Havildar Gun Lascars.	Horses.
...	3	2	0	10	0	1
ded ...	10	1	1	63	1	0
g ...	0	0	0	1	0	0

3.—Killed and wounded of light company, Iajesty's 82nd Regiment not included, that iny having been taken on by Captain a, and engaged in the right attack with Iajesty's 64th Regiment.

I have, &c.,
M. CARTHEW, Brigadier,
Comdg. Madras Troops.

No. 76.

*Memorandum by the Chief of the Staff, upon Briga-
dier Carthew's retreat from his post, on the 28th
November, 1857.*

*Head-Quarters Camp, Cawnpore,
December 9, 1857.*

THE Commander-in-Chief has had under con-
sideration, Brigadier Carthew's despatch, dated
Cawnpore, 3rd December, 1857, addressed to the
Deputy Assistant Adjutant-General, Cawnpore
Division.

Although his Excellency fully admits the
arduous nature of the service on which Brigadier
Carthew had been engaged during the 28th
November, he cannot record his approval of that
officer's retreat, on the evening of that day.

Under the instructions of Major-General Windham, his commanding officer, Brigadier Carthew
had been placed in position. No discretion of retiring was allowed to him. When he was pressed
hard, he sent for re-inforcements, which, as the
Commander-in-Chief happened to be present
when the request arrived, his Excellency is
aware were immediately conducted to his relief
by Major-General Windham in person.

It would appear from Brigadier Carthew's letter
of explanation, that he did not wait to see the
effect of the re-inforcements which had been
brought to him ; but to the great astonishment of
Major-General Windham and his Excellency, retired almost immediately after.

With respect to these occurrences his Excellency feels it necessary to make two remarks :—

In the first place, no subordinate officer, when
possessing easy means of communication with his
immediate superior, is permitted, according to the
principles and usages of war, to give up a post
which has been entrusted to his charge, without a
previous request for orders, after representation

might have been made that the post had become no longer tenable.

It might have occurred to Brigadier Carthew that when Major-General Windham proceeded to reinforce the post according to his first request, instead of ordering the garrison to retire, it was the opinion of the Major-General, that to hold it was an absolute necessity.

His Excellency refrains from remarking on the very serious consequences which ensued on the abandonment of the post in question.

The night which had arrived was more favorable to the Brigadier for the purpose of strengthening his position than it was to an enemy advancing on him in the dark; at all events there were many hours during which a decision could have been taken by the highest authority in the entrenchment whether the post should be abandoned or not, without much other inconvenience than the mere fatigue of the garrison.

The Commander-in-Chief must make one more remark.

Brigadier Carthew, in the last paragraph of his letter, talks about his men firing into one another in the dark. His Excellency does not see how this could occur if the men were properly posted, and the officers in command of them duly instructed as to their respective positions.

No. 77.

The Deputy Adjutant-General of the Army to the Secretary to the Government of India, Military Department.

Head-Quarters Camp, Cawnpore,
December 22, 1857.

SIR.   No. 34 A.

WITH reference to my despatch of the 10th instant, No. 20 A. and its enclosures, relative to Brigadier M. Carthew's defence of the bridge and

Bithoor road at Cawnpore, on the 28th ultimo, I have now the honor, by direction of the Commander-in-Chief, to forward, for submission to the Right Honorable the Governor-General in Council, copies of letters as per margin,* marked A, B, and C.

2. When the memorandum, dated 9th instant, was written, copy of which was transmitted in my letter No. 20 A, and in which the conduct of Brigadier Carthew was commented on by his Excellency, the Commander-in-Chief was under the strongest impression, that Brigadier Carthew had retired from his post, on the 28th November, without orders, and that no discretionary power had been given to him.

Sir Colin Campbell conceived it to be an imperative duty to mark what he considered to be a violation of one of the first principles of war.

3. It appears now, however, that his Excellency's impression was erroneous, and it is a matter of the sincerest regret to him, that his having acted under such erroneous impression should have been detrimental to Brigadier Carthew, and give pain to that meritorious officer.

4. The Commander-in-Chief directs me to request that you will solicit the permission of his Lordship in Council, that his memorandum of the 9th instant, may be considered null and void, and, if it should have been sent forward to the Government of Madras, he begs that this further correspondence may be despatched to the destination in justice to Brigadier Carthew.

I have, &c.
H. W. NORMAN, Major,
Deputy Adjutant-General of the Army.

* A—From Brigadier M. Carthew to the Chief of the Staff, dated 15th December, 1857.

B—From the Chief of the Staff. to Major-General C. Windham, C.B., dated 19th December, 1857.

C—From Major-General C. Windham, C.B., to the Chief of the Staff, dated 19th December, 1857.

No. 78.

A.

Brigadier M. Carthew, commanding Madras Troops, to Major-General Mansfield, Chief of the Staff.

SIR,   *Cawnpore, December* 15, 1857.

WITH reference to your communication to me of the 9th December, conveying the remarks of his Excellency the Commander-in-Chief, regarding my retreat from the position I had been directed to defend by Major-General Windham, commanding the force, on the evening of the 28th November, I beg I may be permitted most respectfully to state, that I was under the full impression, that I had due authority from the Major-General to retire when the post became no longer tenable.

I received a verbal message during that day, either from the late Captain McCrea, or Lieutenant Budgeon (I cannot recollect which), that, when I could hold out no longer, I was to retire to the entrenchment, where Her Majesty's 64th Regiment was located.

I cannot call to mind receiving any express instructions to that effect from Major-General Windham himself, but I am under the impression that the Major-General, on the previous evening, made some such remark as, " Well, gentlemen, when we can hold out no longer, we must retire to the entrenchment."

Under that impression I acted during the day, and made my retrograde movement into the entrenchment in the evening, and I trust his Excellency will be able on this explanation, to exonerate me from blame and censure in that particular respect.

I have, &c.,
M. CARTHEW, Brigadier,
Commanding Madras Troops.

No. 79.

B.

*Major-General W. R. Mansfield, Chief of the Staff,
to Major-General Wyndham, C.B., commanding 5th Brigade.*

       Head-Quarters Camp, near Cawnpore,
SIR,   *December* 19, 1857.

I HAVE the honor to enclose, for your remarks, a letter received from Brigadier Carthew,
in answer to a memorandum written by order of
the Commander-in-Chief, and forwarded through
you by the Assistant Adjutant-General of the
Army, conveying his Excellency's opinions on the
retreat of that officer from the post entrusted to
his charge, on the 28th November, 1857, without,
as his Excellency conceived, any discretion having been left to him for such a movement on his
part.

His Excellency would be much obliged to you
to communicate to me, for his information, your
opinion as to whether Brigadier Carthew had reason to imagine, that a discretionary power was left
to him in the exercise of his command of the post
in question, which could be interpreted in the
sense implied in the enclosed letter.

His Excellency's impressions on this subject
were founded on the fact of the general surprise
displayed by yourself and others, at the abandonment of the post in question, after you had proceeded with the reinforcements demanded some
short time before, almost immediately after his
Excellency's arrival in the entrenchment.

           I have, &c.,

    W. R. MANSFIELD, Major-General,
           Chief of the Staff.

No. 80.

C.

Major-General C. A. Windham, C.B., to Major-General Mansfield, Chief of the Staff.

SIR, *Cawnpore, December* 19, 1857.

IN answer to your communication of to-day, I have the honor to state, for the information of his Excellency, that I think Brigadier Carthew has made a fair representation of my views.

On the night of the 27th, at a general meeting of the superior officers, I thought it my duty to hold as much of the town as I could, as we might expect a large number of women and children, sick and wounded, to arrive shortly, and that it would be cruel to shut them all up in the fort, even if it were possible.

Therefore I was resolved, that every one should hold on as long as possible; and, if obliged to fall back, they could but come to the fort at last.

In the plan of defence, we abandoned the centre of the city, thinking it too cramped and narrow in its streets for the enemy to enter with his big guns.

When I took down the detachment of Rifles to Brigadier Carthew's assistance, I observed it was a sharp fight, and immediately went and ordered Lieutenant-Colonel Watson and two companies 82nd to go to him, and saw him on the road there.

I was in hopes this force would have prevented the necessity of his retiring, which was the cause of my being surprised at it.

I have, &c.,

C. A. WINDHAM, Major-General.

No. 81.
GENERAL ORDERS by the GOVERNOR-GENERAL of INDIA.

Allahabad, May 5, 1858.

No. 124 of 1858.

THE Right Honorable the Governor-General is pleased to direct the publication of the following despatch, from the Deputy Adjutant-General of the Army, No. 285 A, dated 1st May, 1858, forwarding copy of one from Brigadier-General J. Jones, C.B., Commanding Roorkee Field Force, detailing the operations of the force under his command against rebels from the 13th to the 19th April, 1858.

No. 82.

The Deputy Adjutant-General of the Army, to the Secretary to the Government of India, Military Department, with the Governor-General.

Head-Quarters Camp, Shahjehanpore,
May 1, 1858.

SIR, No. 285 A.

I HAVE the honor, by direction of the Commander-in-Chief, to forward, for submission to the Right Honorable the Governor-General, copy of a despatch dated 20th ultimo, from Brigadier-General J. Jones, C.B., Commanding Roorkee Field Force, detailing the successful operations of the force under his command from the 13th to the 19th idem.

I have, &c.,
H. W. NORMAN, Major,
Deputy Adjutant-General of the Army.

No. 83.

Brigadier-General J. Jones, C.B., Commanding Roorkee Field Force, to the Assistant Adjutant-General of the Army.

Camp, Nujeebabd,
April 20, 1858.

SIR,

I HAVE the honor to forward a detailed statement of my operations, of which his Excellency has been informed by telegram.

On the 13th instant I arrived at Roorkee, and assumed command of the field force. On that evening I despatched a party, as per margin,* under Major Churchill, 60th Rifles, to Kunkhul, for the protection of the bridge which the engineers were there throwing over the Ganges. The head-quarters 60th Rifles arrived on the 14th by forced marches, and on the 15th the column encamped by the bridge-of-boats. The heavy guns and stores had been sent to the ford opposite Nagul, and Major Smyth was ordered to divert the enemy's attention by making a show of crossing there.

On the 17th, I crossed the river, and moved into the forest in the following order :—

Advance Guard.

One company 60th Rifles, in skirmishing order.
One company 60th Rifles, in support two guns.
Sappers and Miners and a troop of Cavalry.

Main Body.

One troop Cavalry, Captain Austin's Battery.
60th Rifles, Punjaub Infantry Brigade.
Ammunition and treasure, the Mooltanee Regiment of Cavalry.

* Artillery, 2 guns. Cavalry, 1 squadron. Infantry—60th Rifles, 2 companies; 17th Punjaub Native Infantry, wing.

Rear Guard.

One Company Punjaub Infantry ; a troop of Cavalry.

On each flank of the main body was a patrol of a company Native Infantry, and a half troop of Cavalry.

The force had moved about four miles into the forest, when the advance guard discovered the enemy. The thick jungle rendered it difficult to make out his position, and impossible to tell his strength.

Major Muter, (Deputy Assistant Adjutant-General), in command of the advance guard, judiciously seized on an adjoining height, on which he posted a company of the Rifles, and bringing up the cavalry and guns of the guard, commenced the action.

I ordered Captain Cureton's horse, and Captain Austin's guns, to the front at the gallop, and, forming the infantry into line with their proper supports, and the flanks covered by skirmishers, advanced on the enemy, making out his position by the fire of his artillery.

The rebels, defeated in their intention of effecting a surprise, and disconcerted by the destructive fire of the artillery and rifles, and the charge of a troop of the Mooltanee Regiment of Cavalry led by Lieutenant Gostling, 5th Cavalry, on his left-flank, drew back his guns and retired before the imposing force advancing upon him.

I seized the opportunity, and at once pushed on the cavalry and artillery. No time was given the enemy to take up another position. He was charged by Captain Cureton, wherever he attempted to stand, and the guns, unlimbering as they came up, opened with shrapnell. The enemy, thus pushed over positions of great natural strength, and unable to show front even on the bank of a stream where he had erected stockades, and behind which his camp was pitched, fell more and more into confusion. His retreat became a flight; gun after gun was abandoned, and in utter rout the rebels fled through the forest, leaving the ground covered with their arms, and throwing off even their clothes to facilitate their escape. Fully two hundred of their dead were left in the Terai, and four pieces of their artillery were taken on the road, with all their ammunition and camp equipage.

When clear of the Perai, I pitched my camp about five miles from Nagul, from which place information soon reached me, that the enemy had retreated, leaving his camp standing. I gave immediate orders for the passage of the river by the heavy guns and stores.

On the 18th, the force moved in the same order as on the preceding day to Nujeebabad.

When near the town, I sent forward a party to reconnoitre under Brigadier Coke, C.B., and halted the column in the concealment of a tope of trees. The town was deserted, and the Brigadier found, on pushing on to the Fort of Phutteeghur, that it had also been evacuated by the enemy. The cavalry, following in pursuit, came up with their infantry, and cut up about thirty of their number.

Two guns were taken in the town and six in the fort, besides large quantities of grain, hammered shot, and ammunition, a return of which I enclose.

I am happy to say that the casualties attending these operations, have been trifling. I annex a return.

The behaviour of the troops in the action of the 17th, was all his Excellency could wish. Young regiments acted like veteran soldiers, and the difficult nature of the ground (a jungle, the residence of wild beasts only), applied no mean test to their discipline and drill.

I beg to bring to the notice of the Commander-in-Chief, the very able assistance afforded me by Brigadier Coke, C.B., in the field, in council, and in his intimate knowledge of the native character.

The Mooltanee regiment of cavalry was led by Captain Cureton and his officers, in the most gallant and dashing style, and I trust his Excellency will notice this.

The manner in which Captain Austin brought his guns into action, notwithstanding the difficulty of the ground, and the thickness of the jungle, afforded me the highest satisfaction.

Much praise is due to Major Palmer, commanding 1st Battalion 60th Rifles, for bringing his men so steadily and rapidly to the front. Also to Major Gordon, commanding 1st Seikh Reigment; to Captain Larkins, 17th Regiment Punjaub Infantry; and to Captain Lambert, of the 1st Punjaub Regiment, for the able way in which they moved their corps.

My thanks are due to Captain H. Drummond, commanding, Field Engineer, who afforded me much assistance; to Captain Carter also, Officiating Deputy Commissary-General; and to Surgeon Innes, Field Surgeon, for their unfailing zeal.

I have received every assistance from my personal Staff, and I am much indebted for their exertions.

To Major Muter, Deputy Assistant Adjutant-General; to Captain Tedlie, Deputy Assistant Quartermaster-General; and to Lieutenant H Deedes, Aide-de-camp, these acknowledgments are due.

I have, &c.

JOHN JONES, Brigadier-General,
Commanding Roorkee Field Force.

No. 84.

STRENGTH OF THE ROORKEE FIELD FORCE.

Artillery, 1st Company 1st Battalion, 6 guns.

Heavy Guns, two 18-pounders, two 8-inch mortars, two 8-inch howitzers, two 5-inch mortars (not joined).

Cavalry, Mooltanee Regiment of Cavalry, 600 sabres.

Cavalry attached to 1st Punjaub Infantry, 70 sabres.

Infantry, 60th Rifles, 1st Battalion, 568 rank and file.

Infantry, 1st Punjaub Regiment (Rifles), 692 rank and file.

Infantry, 1st Seikh Regiment, 444 rank and file.

Infantry, 17th Punjaub Infantry, 704 rank and file.

Sappers and Miners, 103 rank and file.

No. 85.

Casualty Return of the Roorkee Field Force in Action near Bhagowla, on the 17th of April, 1858.

Camp Nujeebabad, April 20, 1858.

1st Battalion 60th Rifles—1 non-commissioned officer wounded.

Mooltanee Regiment of Cavalry—1 sowar and 1 horse killed; 1 jemadar. 2 duffadars, 1 naib duffadar, 12 sowars, and 19 horses, wounded; 4 horses missing.

    Total—1 non-commissioned officer wounded; 1 sowar and 1 horse killed; 1 jemadar, 2 duffadars, 1 naib duffadar, 12 sowars, and 19 horses, wounded, 4 horses missing.

        JOHN JONES, Brigadier-General.

        Commanding Field Force.

No. 87.

List of Casualties by Death, among the European Commissioned Officers of the Honourable Company's Army, in consequence of the Mutinies in Northern India, that have been reported to this Department, from the 27th of April, 1858, up to this date.

Captain John Sinclair, 39th Regiment Native Infantry, killed in action at Jhansi, April 5, 1858.

Lieutenant Henry Clerk, 8th Regiment Native Infantry, severely wounded, 1st April, 1858, in action at the Betwah river, before Jhansi.

G. A. ARBUTHNOT,
Acting Second Assistant-Adjutant-General
of the Army.

Adjutant-General's Office,
Fort Saint George, May 8, 1858.

No. 88.

Casualty by Death, among the European Commissioned Officers of the Honourable Company's Army, in consequence of the Mutinies in Northern India, reported since the 9th of May, 1858.

Lieutenant Clarence Harry Colbeck, 3rd European Regiment, died 20th April, 1858, at Bandah, of wounds received in action on the 19th April, 1858.

F. S. GABB, Major,
Deputy Adjutant-General of the Army.

Adjutant-General's Office,
Fort Saint George, May 20, 1858.
1858.   8 L

No. 89.

From the List of Casualties among the Military and Naval Officers of the Bombay Establishment, known up to this date.

Bombay Castle, June 4, 1858.

Lieutenant Hafed Lamont, Her Majesty's 89th Regiment, May 22, 1858, Camp Ahmedabad, from fever.

Lieutenant E. Willoughby, of the 10th Regiment Native Infantry, and Quartermaster 1st Belooch Battalion, April 15, killed in action in the fort of Roodanow.

H. L. ANDERSON,
Secretary to Government.

FROM THE

LONDON GAZETTE of JULY 20, 1858.

Whitehall, July 19, 1858.

THE Queen has been pleased to present the Reverend Frederic Southgate, B.A., to the Vicarage of Northfleet, in the county of Kent, and diocese of Rochester, void by the death of the Reverend Richard Keats.

Whitehall, July 20, 1858.

The Queen has been pleased to give and grant unto Major William Gilly Andrews, of the Royal Artillery, Her Majesty's royal licence and permission that he may accept and wear the Insignia of the Imperial Order of the Legion of

Honour of the Fifth Class, which His Majesty the Emperor of the French hath been pleased to confer upon him, as a mark of His Imperial Majesty's approbation of his distinguished services before the enemy during the late war.

Downing-Street, July 17, 1858.

The Queen has been pleased to appoint Richard Cornwall Legh, Esq., to be Auditor-General for the Island of Malta.

Crown-Office, July 19, 1858.

MEMBER returned to serve in this present
PARLIAMENT.
Borough of Stamford.

Sir Stafford Henry Northcote, Bart., of Pynes, in the county of Devon, in the room of John Inglis, Esq., who has accepted the office of Her Majesty's Lord Justice Clerk in Scotland.

Whitehall, July 10, 1858.

The Queen has been pleased to grant unto John-Borlase Maunsell, of Thorpe Malsor and of Barton Seagrave, both in the county of Northampton, Esquire, late a Captain in Her Majesty's 12th (Prince of Wales's Royal) Regiment of Lancers, Her royal license and authority that he may, in compliance with a proviso contained in the last will and testament of Charles Tibbits, late of Barton Seagrave aforesaid, Esquire, deceased, take and henceforth use the surname of Tibbits only, and bear the arms of Tibbits quarterly with the arms of his family, such arms being first duly exemplified according to the laws of arms, and accorded in the Herald's Office,

otherwise the said royal licence and permission to
be void and of none effect :

And also to command that the said royal concession and declaration be recorded in Her
Majesty's College of Arms.

Board of Trade, Whitehall,
July 14, 1858.

The Right Honourable the Lords of the Committee of Privy Council for Trade and Plantations have received, through the Secretary of
State for Foreign Affairs, a copy of a Despatch
from Her Majesty's Acting Consul at Marseilles,
reporting that a malignant fever had broken out
at Bengazi, and that in consequence all vessels
arriving from that port will have to undergo a quarantine at Marseilles of ten days, and that vessels
arriving at that port from Alexandria and Tripoli,
will only be admitted to free pratique, provided
they have been 8 or 10 days on their passage, and
according as they have a medical man on board
or not.

Board of Trade, Whitehall,
July 16, 1858.

The Right Honourable the Lords of the Committee of Privy Council for Trade and Plantations
have received, through the Secretary of State for
Foreign Affairs, an extract from the Moniteur, of
which the following is a translation :

" The Department of Marine and Colonies had
directed, with the view of encouraging the cultivation of long stapled Cotton in the Colonies, the
purchase from planters of cotton of this description in 1857 at a remunerative price.

" In execution of this measure, an agent of the
local government has collected and assorted at

Guadaloupe eighty bales of long stapled blanc couronné indigène from Siam, and from the Sea Island of the Isle of Edisto.

"These cottons have arrived at Havre, where they have been officially classified by a broker. They are chiefly of extra fine quality, particularly the specimens from the Ile Désirade.

"His Imperial Highness Prince Napoleon, anxious to encourage this interesting production, as well for the benefit of the Colonies as for industry and the maritime commerce of the country, has ordered a public sale of seventy-seven bales of long stapled Edisto cotton, from Guadaloupe, to take place at the Bourse of Havre, on the 31st July, in presence of an agent of the Department, through the Commissary-General of Marine, by Mr. Ch. Gallois, Broker.

"The bales are to be seen in the magazines of the Marine Department, and the specimens may be inspected at the brokers, at Havre, Lille, Mulhouse Chambers of Commerce, at the Exposition of the French Colonies, No. 244, Rue de Rivoli, Paris."

NOTICE TO MARINERS.

Pilotage—Port of Vigo.

A representation having been made to the Board of Trade by Her Majesty's Consul at Vigo, that the pilots there are in the habit of imposing on masters of British vessels by boarding their ships, for the purpose of claiming pilotage, although their services are not required, shipmasters are informed that pilotage is not obligatory on vessels entering the Bay of Vigo, and that the Captain of that Port has made it known to all pilots of the district, that unless they see the usual pilot signal (Union Jack with a white border,) flying on board British ships, they need not offer their services.

Shipmasters are recommended, in order to avoid claims on the part of the pilots when their services have not been required, to dismiss the boats from alongside at once, and not to hoist the pilot signal at the pilots' bidding, or even take their boats in tow.

Board of Trade, 19*th July,* 1858.

War-Office, Pall-Mall,
20*th July,* 1858.

GENERAL ORDER.

Horse Guards,
20*th July,* 1858.

THE Queen has been graciously pleased to command that Brevet-Colonel Thomas Harte Franks, C.B., of the 10th Foot, be promoted to the rank of Major-General in the Army, in consideration of his distinguished services in the command of a column during the operations in India, prior to, and at, the capture of Lucknow.

By order of His Royal Highness the General Commanding-in-Chief,

G. A. WETHERALL,
Adjutant-General.

War-Office, Pall-Mall,
20*th July,* 1858.

BREVET.

Brevet-Colonel Thomas Harte Franks, C.B., 10th Foot, to be Major-General in the Army. Dated 20th July, 1858.

To be COLONEL in the Army.

Lieutenant-Colonel Alexander Macdonell, C.B., Rifle Brigade. Dated 20th July, 1858.

To be LIEUTENANT-COLONELS.

Major Arthur Scudamore, 14th Light Dragoons. Dated 20th July, 1858.

Brevet-Major William Campbell Mollan, 75th Foot. Dated 20th July, 1858.

Brevet-Major John Richard Anderson, C.B., Royal Artillery. Dated 20th July, 1858.'

Major Richard George Amherst Luard, half-pay Unattached. Dated 20th July, 1858.

Brevet-Major Lothian Nicholson, Royal Engineers. Dated 20th July, 1858.

Brevet-Major Francis Cornwallis Maude, Royal Artillery. Dated 20th July, 1858.

Brevet-Major Lawrence Pleydell Bouverie, 78th Foot. Dated 20th July, 1858.

To be MAJORS.

Captain Josias Rogers John Coles, 9th Light Dragoons. Dated 20th July, 1858.

Captain Stephen Francis Charles Annesley, 10th Foot. Dated 20th July, 1858.

Captain James Robert Gibbon, Royal Artillery. Dated 20th July, 1858.

Captain Henry Rudford Norman, 10th Foot. Dated 20th July, 1858.

Captain Chardin Philip Johnson, 9th Light Dragoons. Dated 20th July, 1858.

Captain Mawdistly Gaussen Best, 34th Foot. Dated 20th July, 1858.

Captain Frederick Dobson Middleton, 29th Foot. Dated 20th July, 1858.

Captain Keith Ramsay Maitland, 79th Foot, Dated 20th July, 1858.

Captain Alexander Mackenzie, 78th Foot. Dated 20th July, 1858.

Captain John Everett Thring, Royal Artillery. Dated 20th July, 1858.

Captain Septimus Moore Hawkins, 97th Foot. Dated 20th July, 1858.

Captain Francis Henry Atherley, Rifle Brigade. Dated 20th July, 1858.

Captain Alexander Cockburn M'Barnet, 79th Foot. Dated 20th July, 1858.

Captain Archibald Richard Harenc, 97th Foot. Dated 20th July, 1858,

Captain Henry Edward Bale, 34th Foot. Dated 20th July, 1858.

Captain William Gustavus Alexander Middleton, 93rd Foot. Dated 20th July, 1858.

Captain Horatio Page Vance, 38th Foot. Dated 20th July, 1858.

Captain Jervoise Clarke Jervoise, 23rd Foot. Dated 20th July, 1858.

Captain Frederick William Burroughs, 93rd Foot. Dated 20th July, 1858.

Captain George Bennett, 20th Foot. Dated 20th July, 1858.

Captain William Henry Seymour, 2nd Dragoon Guards. Dated 20th July, 1858.

Captain Honourable Charles J. Addington, 38th Foot. Dated 20th July, 1858.

Captain Henry Holford Stevenson, 79th Foot. Dated 20th July, 1858.

Captain James Duff, 23rd Foot. Dated 20th July, 1858.

Captain John Drysdale, 42nd Foot. Dated 20th July, 1858.

Captain James Herne Wade, 90th Foot. Dated 20th July, 1858.

Captain Robert Crosse Stewart, 35th Foot. Dated 20th July, 1858.

Captain William Drummond Scrase Dickins, 20th Foot. Dated 20th July, 1858.

Captain Richard Henry Magenis, 90th Foot. Dated 20th July, 1858.

Captain William Hicks Slade, 5th Light Dragoons. Dated 20th July, 1858.

Captain Henry Richard Legge Newdigate, Rifle Brigade. Dated 20th July, 1858.

Captain Henry Lynch Talbot, Royal Artillery. Dated 20th July, 1858.

Captain Henry Wilmot, Rifle Brigade. Dated 20th July, 1858.

Captain Coote Synge Hutchinson, 2nd Dragoon Guards. Dated 20th July, 1858.

Captain William Howley Goodenough, Royal Artillery. Dated 20th July, 1858.

Captain Honourable J. de V. T. W. Fiennes, 7th Light Dragoons. Dated 20th July, 1858.

Captain Henry Buck, 53rd Foot. Dated 20th July, 1858.

Captain H. Taylor Macpherson, 78th Foot. Dated 20th July, 1858.

To be COLONEL in the Army.

Lieutenant-Colonel Henry Tombs, C.B., Bengal Artillery. Dated 20th July, 1858.

To be LIEUTENANT-COLONELS.

Major George Sackville Cotter, Madras Artillery. Dated 20th July, 1858.

Major Henry Alexander Carleton, Bengal Artillery. Dated 20th July, 1858.

Major Alfred Thomas Wilde, Madras Native Infantry. Dated 20th July, 1858.

Major Henry Daly, C.B., Bombay European Fusiliers. Dated 20th July, 1858.

Major Alexander Taylor, Bengal Engineers. Dated 20th July, 1858.

Major Jeremiah Brasyer, C.B., Unattached, Bengal Army. Dated 20th July, 1858.

To be MAJORS.

Captain John Hood, Bengal Native Infantry. Dated 20th July, 1858.

Captain John Gordon, 6th Bengal Native Infantry. Dated 20th July, 1858.

Captain Alexander Hume, Bengal European Fusiliers. Dated 20th July, 1858.

Captain George Moir, Bengal Artillery. Dated 20th July, 1858.

Captain Ennis Cunliffe, Bengal European Fusiliers. Dated 20th July, 1858.

Captain Thomas Raikes, Madras European Fusiliers. Dated 20th July, 1858.

Captain Samuel James Browne, Bengal Native Infantry. Dated 20th July, 1858.

Captain William Alexander Mackinnon, Bengal Artillery. Dated 20th July, 1858.

Captain Richard Lloyd Thompson, 10th Bengal Native Infantry. Dated 20th July, 1858.

Captain John Blick Spurgin, 1st Madras European Fusiliers. Dated 20th July, 1858.

Captain Hamilton Forbes, Bengal Native Cavalry. 20th July, 1858.

Captain Charles John Stanley Gough, Bengal Native Cavalry. Dated 20th July, 1858.

Captain Allen Bayard Johnson, Bengal Native Infantry. Dated 20th July, 1858.

Captain Alfred Pearson, Bengal Artillery. Dated 20th July, 1858.

HOSPITAL STAFF.

The appointment of Assistant-Surgeon Benjamin Tydd, from the 58th Foot, to be Staff-Surgeon of the Second Class, to bear date 16th *July*, 1858, instead of 16th *May*, 1858, as previously stated.

Admiralty, 14th July, 1858.

Corps of Royal Marines.

Captain and Brevet-Major William Henry March to be Lieutenant-Colonel, vice Elliot, retired on full pay.

First Lieutenant and Adjutant Arthur Ellis to be Captain, vice March, promoted.

Second Lieutenant William Stirling to be First Lieutenant, vice Ellis, promoted.

Commission signed by the Queen.

Royal Sussex Light Infantry Regiment of Militia.

Thomas Buckner Henry Valintine, Esq., to be Paymaster, from 8th June, 1858. Dated 2nd July, 1858.

Commission signed by the Vice Lieutenant of the County of Perth.

Colonel Robert Richardson Robertson to be Deputy Lieutenant. Dated 30th June, 1858.

Commissions signed by the Lord Lieutenant of the County of Sussex.

Patrick Francis Robertson, Esq., to be Deputy Lieutenant. Dated 13th July, 1858.

Light Infantry Battalion of the Royal Sussex Militia.

Thomas Carr Foster, Gent., to be Ensign. Dated 7th July, 1858.

Commission signed by the Vice Lieutenant of the County of Lincoln.

Royal South Lincoln Militia.

Tom Hewitt, Gent., to be Assistant-Surgeon, vice William Dymock, resigned. Dated 7th July, 1858.

Commissions signed by the Lord Lieutenant of the County of Edinburgh.

Royal Mid-Lothian or Edinburgh Yeomanry Cavalry.

John Inglis, Esq., to be Captain vice Maitland, resigned. Dated 29th June, 1858.

Cornet John Crawford Tait to be Lieutenant, vice Forbes, resigned. Dated 29th June, 1858.

Cornet Archibald David Cockburn to be Lieutenant, vice James Forman, promoted. Dated 29th June, 1858.

John Turnbull, Gent., to be Cornet, vice, Cockburn, promoted. Dated 29th June, 1858.

Commissions signed by the Lord Lieutenant of the County of Northumberland.

Northumberland Light Infantry Regiment of Militia.

Fenton John Aylmer, Esq., late of the 97th Regiment, to be Captain. Dated 13th July, 1858.

Northumberland Regiment of Militia Artillery.

Thomas Forsyth Forrest, Gent., to be Lieutenant. Dated 13th July, 1858.

FROM THE

LONDON GAZETTE of JULY 23, 1858.

Master of the Horse's Office, July 1, 1858.

THE Queen has been graciously pleased to appoint Colonel Francis Hugh George Seymour, Unattached, to be Equerry in Ordinary to Her Majesty, in the room of Major-General E. W. Bouverie, resigned.

Buckingham Palace, July 1, 1858.

His Royal Highness the Prince Consort has been pleased to appoint Colonel the Honourable Arthur Edward Hardinge, C.B., to be Equerry to His Royal Highness, vice Colonel Francis Hugh George Seymour, appointed Equerry to The Queen.

NOTICE TO SHIPOWNERS AND MASTERS.

DELIVERY OF SHIPS' MANIFESTS IN FRENCH PORTS.

A representation having been made to the Board of Trade that Ship-Masters trading to the Port of Dunkirk are in the habit of disregarding the imperial law which requires that the Master of every vessel trading to a French port shall have a manifest of cargo ready for delivery at the Custom House on arrival in port.

It is hereby notified to Masters and Owners of vessels trading to French Ports generally that the strictest attention is necessary to the above regulation, the neglect to comply with which may in future subject them to serious inconvenience.

Board of Trade, 20th July, 1858.

War-Office, Pall-Mall,
2*3rd July,* 1858.

2*nd Regiment of Dragoon Guards,* Edward Vandeleur, Gent., to be Cornet, without purchase, vice De Montmorency, promoted. Dated 23rd July, 1858,

Alexander Frederick Stewart, Gent., to be Cornet, without purchase, vice Mackenzie, resigned. Dated 24th July, 1858.

3rd Dragoon Guards, Lieutenant James Charles Still to be Captain, by purchase, vice Mulville, who retires. Dated 23rd July, 1858.

Cornet Edward Maunder to be Lieutenant, by purchase, vice Still. Dated 23rd July, 1858.

9th Light Dragoons, Cornet Thomas Stanton Starkey to be Lieutenant, by purchase, vice Rich, promoted. Dated 13th July, 1858.

10th Light Dragoons, William Morgan Maunder, Gent., to be Cornet, by purchase, vice Lovell, promoted. Dated 23rd July, 1858.

11th Light Dragoons, Lieutenant Daniel Shaw Stewart to be Captain, by purchase, vice Vansittart, who retires. Dated 23rd July, 1858.

Cornet Paget Peploe Mosley to be Lieutenant, by purchase, vice Stewart. Dated 23rd July, 1858.

12th Light Dragoons, Cornet Frederick Swindley to be Lieutenant, without purchase, vice Hancocke, deceased. Dated 9th May, 1858.

Military Train, Robert Warner Stone, Gent., to be Ensign, by purchase, vice Lane, promoted. Dated 23rd July, 1858.

The promotion of Ensign B. H. Burke to a Lieutenancy, without purchase, vice Murphy, appointed to the 5th Light Dragoons, to bear date 17th March, 1858, in lieu of 15th June, 1858, as previously stated.

1st Regiment of Foot, Staff-Surgeon of the Second Class Charles William Woodroffe to be Surgeon, vice Crocker, appointed to the Staff. Dated 23rd July, 1858.

2nd Foot, Assistant-Surgeon Henry Cole Peppin, from the Staff, to be Assistant-Surgeon. Dated 23rd July, 1858.

4th Foot.

To be Captains, without purchase.

Lieutenant A. J. D. Smith, from the Ceylon Rifle Regiment. Dated 23rd July, 1858.

Lieutenant William Congreve, from 29th Foot. Dated 23rd July, 1858.

Lieutenant J. W. Madden, from 70th Foot. Dated 23rd July, 1858.

Lieutenant John McDowell Elliot. Dated 23rd July, 1858.

Ensign David Smith to be Lieutenant, without purchase, vice Elliot. Dated 23rd July, 1858.

6th Foot.

To be Lieutenants, by purchase.

Ensign George Gandy, from the Ceylon Rifle Regiment, vice Powell, promoted. Dated 23rd July, 1858.

Ensign D. C. Campbell, vice Parkinson, promoted. Dated 23rd July, 1858.

Ensign William Neal, vice Harness, who has retired. Dated 23rd July, 1858.

8th Foot, Lieutenant Henry Leeson, from the 31st Foot, to be Lieutenant. Dated 23rd July, 1858.

9th Foot.

To be Captains, without purchase.

Lieutenant C. C. Grantham, from the Ceylon Rifle Regiment. Dated 23rd July, 1858.

Lieutenant Whiteford John Bell, from 74th Foot. Dated 23rd July, 1858.

Lieutenant B. C. W. C. Bloxsome. Dated 23rd July, 1858.

To be Lieutenants without purchase.

Lieutenant Charles Masterman Smyth, from 3rd

West India Regiment, vice Plumridge, who exchanges. Dated 23rd July, 1858.
Ensign G. M. Cadwick, vice Bloxsome. Dated 23rd July, 1858.
Ensign John Aplin. Dated 23rd July, 1858.
Ensign J. S. Jeffares. Dated 23rd July, 1858.

13*th Foot.* The surname of Junior Quartermaster, is *Landrey,* and not *Landry,* as previously stated.

15*th Foot.*

To be Captains, without purchase.

Lieutenant Charles Crawley, from the 70th Foot. Dated 23rd July, 1858.
Lieutenant John Hudson, from the 64th Foot. Dated 23rd July, 1858.

18*th Foot,* Ensign W. Albert Le Motteé, to be Lieutenant, by purchase, vice Daubeny, whose promotion, by purchase, as stated in the Gazette of the 13th July, 1858, has been cancelled. Dated 23rd July, 1858.
Wright Sherlock, Gent., to be Ensign, without purchase, vice Daubeny, promoted. Dated 23rd July, 1858.

19*th Foot,* Lieutenant H. E. Jerome, from the 86th Foot, to Captain, without purchase, vice Lewis, appointed to 86th Foot. Dated 23rd July, 1858.

20*th Foot,* Quartermaster-Serjeant William Unwin to be Ensign, without purchase, vice Burne, promoted. Dated 10th April, 1858.

21*st Foot,* Ensign Ernest Lewis, from the 2nd West India Regiment, to be Lieutenant, without purchase. Dated 23rd July 1858.

22nd Foot.

To be Captains, without purchase.

Lieutenant W. J. Lutman, from the 3rd West India Regiment. Dated 23rd July, 1858.

Lieutenant J. F. Trydell, from 43rd Foot. Dated 23rd July, 1858.

Lieutenant W. H. Rowland, from 45th Foot. Dated 23rd July, 1858.

Lieutenant Robert Richardson Ellis. Dated 23rd July, 1858.

To be Lieutenant.

Lieutenant E. M. Cookesley, from the 97th Foot. Dated 23rd July, 1858.

29th Foot, Ensign John North Bomford to be Lieutenant, without purchase, vice Congreve, promoted in the 4th Foot. Dated 23rd July, 1858.

31st Foot, Ensign Henry Leeson to be Lieutenant, by purchase, vice Litton, promoted. Dated 23rd July, 1858.

John Michael Bradley Wood, Gent., to be Ensign, by purchase, vice Tarte, promoted. Dated 23rd July, 1858.

45th Foot, Ensign Edward O'Neill to be Lieutenant, without purchase, vice W. H. Rowland, promoted in 22nd Foot. Dated 23rd July, 1858.

48th Foot, Major J. G. R. Aplin, from Depôt Battalion, to be Major, vice West, who exchanges. Dated 23rd July, 1858.

58th Foot, Ensign William Bolton to be Adjutant, vice Lieutenant Wynyard, promoted. Dated 6th April, 1858.

Quartermaster-Serjeant Mathew Slattery to be Quartermaster, vice Moir, who retires upon half-pay. Dated 23rd July, 1858.

1858.   8 M

70th Foot, Ensign G. A. Hilton to be Lieutenant, without purchase, vice Madden, promoted in 4th Foot. Dated 23rd July, 1858.

Ensign Herbert J. Hill, from 49th Foot, to be Ensign, vice Menteath, promoted. Dated 23rd July, 1858.

73rd Foot, Ensign James Fraser, from the 22nd Foot, to be Ensign, vice Farrington, promoted. Dated 23rd July, 1858.

75th Foot, Ensign F. Bullen Morris, from the Military Train, to be Ensign, vice Streets, promoted. Dated 23rd July, 1858.

86th Foot, Captain R. FitzGibbon Lewis, from the 19th Foot, to be Captain, vice Robinson, deceased. Dated 8th July, 1858.

91st Foot, Lieutenant Henry Wood to be Captain, by purchase, vice Kerr, who retires. Dated 23rd July, 1858.

Ensign John Macleod Tingcombe to be Lieutenant, by purchase, vice Wood. Dated 23rd July, 1858.

97th Foot, Assistant-Surgeon Thomas Sharkey, from the Staff, to be Assistant-Surgeon, vice Dumbreck, deceased. Dated 23rd July, 1858.

100th Foot, Brown Wallis, Gent., to be Lieutenant, without purchase. Dated 23rd July, 1858.

To be Ensigns, without purchase.

Charles Arkoll Boulton, Gent. Dated 23rd July, 1858.

Thomas Henry Baldwin, Gent. Dated 24th July, 1858.

3rd West India Regiment, Lieutenant James John Plumridge, from the 9th Foot, to be Lieutenant, vice C. M. Smyth, who exchanges. Dated 23rd July, 1858.

Ensign C. F. Lloyd to be Lieutenant, without purchase, vice Lutman, promoted in 22nd Foot. Dated 23rd July, 1858.

Ceylon Rifle Regiment.
To be Lieutenants, without purchase.

Ensign Orby Montgomery Hunter, vice A. J. D. Smith, promoted in 4th Foot. Dated 23rd July, 1858.

Ensign A. M. Walker, vice Grantham, promoted in 9th Foot. Dated 23rd July, 1858.

DEPOT BATTALION.

Major Frederick West, from the 48th Foot, to be Major, vice Aplin, who exchanges. Dated 23rd July, 1858.

HOSPITAL STAFF.

Surgeon Alfred Crocker, from the 1st Foot, to be Staff-Surgeon of the Second Class, vice Woodroffe, appointed to the 1st Foot. Dated 23rd July, 1858.

To be Assistant-Surgeons to the Forces.

John Alexander Lamb, Gent., vice Curran, appointed to the 73rd Foot. Dated 22nd June, 1858.

William White, Gent., vice John, appointed to the 29th Foot. Dated 22nd June, 1858.

John Mahon, Gent., vice Davis, appointed to the 57th Foot. Dated 22nd June, 1858.

Richard Beresford Carson, M.B., vice Cuppage, appointed to the 17th Foot. Dated 22nd June, 1858.

William Langworthy Baker, Gent., vice Atkinson, appointed to the 5th Light Dragoons. Dated 22nd June, 1858.

George Harman Harris, Gent., vice Sly, appointed to the 16th Foot. Dated 22nd June, 1858.

Henry William Delvin, Gent., vice Spencer, appointed to the 18th Foot. Dated 22nd June, 1858.

Hugh Mackay Macbeth, Gent., vice Berkeley, appointed to the 23rd Foot. Dated 22nd June, 1858.

Thomas Michael O'Brien, Gent, vice Knaggs, appointed to the 59th Foot. Dated 22nd June, 1858.

Horatio Scott, Gent., vice O'Grady, appointed to 1st Foot. Dated 22nd June, 1858.

John Henry Halked Tothill, Gent., vice Maclean, appointed to be 6th Foot. Dated 22nd June, 1858.

To be Acting Assistant-Surgeons.

Alfred Bowden, Gent. Dated 15th July, 1858.

James Bell Jardine, Gent. Dated 23rd July, 1858.

BREVET.

Lieutenant-Colonel Caledon Richard Egerton, Depôt Battalion, having completed three years actual service in the rank of Lieutenant-Colonel, to be promoted to be Colonel in the Army, under the Royal Warrant of 6th October, 1854. Dated 18th April, 1858.

Major John Butler Wheatstone, retired full-pay 8th Foot, to be Lieutenant-Colonel in the Army, the rank being honorary only. Dated 23rd July, 1858.

The undermentioned promotion to take place in the East India Company's Army consequent on the death of Major-General Nicholas Penny, C.B., Bengal Infantry, 30th April, 1858 :—

Colonel Richard James Holwell Birch, C.B.,

Bengal Infantry, to be Major-General. Dated 1st May, 1858.

The undermentioned Officers of the East India Company's Service, retired upon full-pay, to have a step of honorary rank, as follows, viz. :—

To be Major-Generals.

Colonel John Brownrigg Bellasis, Bombay Infantry. Dated 23rd July, 1858.

Colonel James Allardyce, Madras Infantry. Dated 23rd July, 1858.

Colonel George Bruce Michell, Bengal Infantry. Dated 23rd July, 1858.

To be Colonel.

Lieutenant-Colonel Thomas Plumbe, Bengal Infantry. Dated 23rd July, 1858.

To be Lieutenant-Colonels.

Major William John Morris, Bombay Infantry. Dated 23rd July, 1858.

Major John Davies Leckie, Bombay Infantry. Dated 23rd July, 1858.

Major Ralph Smyth, Bengal Artillery. Dated 23rd July, 1858.

Major William L. Walker, Madras Cavalry. Dated 23rd July, 1858.

Major Charles Swinton, Bengal Infantry. Dated 23rd July, 1858.

Major John Mann, Madras Infantry. Dated 23rd July, 1858.

To be Majors.

Captain Joseph Chilcott, Bengal Infantry. Dated 23rd July, 1858.

Captain Frederick Fanning, Bombay Infantry. Dated 23rd July, 1858.

[Erratum in Supplement to London Gazette, 24th March, 1858.]

To be Major.

For Captain John *Cunningham* Anderson, Madras Engineers,

Read, Captain John *Cumming* Anderson, Madras Engineers.

Admiralty, 14th July, 1858.

Corps of Royal Marines.

Gentleman Cadet Alfred Emanuel Otter to be Second Lieutenant.

Commission signed by the Lord Lieutenant of the County of Lancaster.

5th Regiment of Royal Lancashire Militia.

George Smirthwaite, Gent., to be Assistant-Surgeon, vice Henry Hancox, resigned. Dated 8th July, 1858.

Commission signed by the Lord Lieutenant of the County of Somerset.

North Somerset Regiment of Yeomanry Cavalry.

Cornet Lionel Helbert to be Captain, vice Langton, resigned. Dated 15th July, 1858.

Commission signed by the Lord Lieutenant of the County of Wilts.

Royal Wiltshire Militia.

Edward John Hayward, Gent., to be Ensign, vice Glascott, resigned. Dated 3rd July, 1858.

LONDON GAZETTE of JULY 27, 1858.

War-Office, July 27, 1858.

THE Queen has been graciously pleased to give orders for the appointment of Major-General Thomas Harte Franks, C.B., to be an Ordinary Member of the Military Division of the Second Class, or Knights Commanders of the Most Honourable Order of the Bath.

Her Majesty has also been graciously pleased to make and ordain a Special Statute of the said Most Honourable Order, for appointing Colonel Robert Napier, C.B., of the Bengal Engineers, to be an Extra Member of the Military Division of the Second Class, or Knights Commanders of the said Order, and also for appointing the under-mentioned Officers in the Service of Her Majesty and of the East India Company, to be Extra Members of the Military Division of the Third Class, or Companions of the said Order, viz.:

Colonel Charles Franklyn, 84th Regiment.
Colonel William Campbell, 2nd Dragoon Guards.
Colonel Charles Hagart, 7th Hussars.
Colonel Percy Hill, 2nd Battalion, Rifle Brigade.
Colonel Richard Denis Kelly, 34th Regiment.
Colonel Henry Drury Harness, Royal Engineers.
Lieutenant-Colonel Alexander Cameron, 42nd Regiment.
Lieutenant-Colonel George Mowbray Lys, 20th Regiment.
Lieutenant-Colonel William Fenwick, 10th Regiment.

Lieutenant-Colonel Charles James Buchanan Riddell, Royal Artillery.

Lieutenant-Colonel Edmund Cornwall Legh, 97th Regiment.

Lieutenant Colonel Evan Maberly, Royal Artillery.

Lieutenant-Colonel James Macaul Hagart, 7th Hussars.

Lieutenant-Colonel James Peter Robertson, Military Train.

Major William George Le Mesurier, Royal Artillery.

Major William Chester Master, 5th Regiment.

Major William Alexander Middleton, Royal Artillery.

Dr. John McAndrew, Inspector-General of Hospitals.

———

Lieutenant-Colonel James Duncan Macpherson, 22nd Regiment of Bengal Native Infantry.

Lieutenant-Colonel Edwin Beaumont Johnson, Bengal Artillery.

Lieutenant-Colonel Michael Galwey, 1st Regiment of Madras European Fusiliers.

Lieutenant-Colonel William Olpherts, Bengal Artillery.

Lieutenant-Colonel George Wade Guy Green, 2nd Regiment of Bengal Fusiliers.

Lieutenant-Colonel Henry Alexander Carleton, Bengal Artillery.

Major Lousada Barrow, 5th Regiment of Madras Native Cavalry.

Major Herbert Bruce, 2nd Bombay European Regiment.

Major William Arden Crommelin, Bengal Engineers.

Whitehall, July 24, 1858.

The Queen has been pleased to direct letters patent to be passed under the Great Seal, appointing James Major, Esq., Barrister-at-Law, and Christopher Copinger, Esq., Barrister-at-Law, to be Her Majesty's Commissioners, for the purpose of inquiring into the state of the municipal affairs of the borough of Belfast.

Whitehall, July 26, 1858.

The Queen has been pleased to present the Reverend William Millner, M.A., to the Rectory of the United Parishes of Saint Antholin and Saint John the Baptist, in the city and diocese of London, void by the cession of the Reverend William Calvert.

Whitehall, July 26, 1858.

The Queen has been pleased to appoint Edward Strathearn Gordon, Esq., Advocate, to be Sheriff of the shire or sheriffdom of Perth.

Whitehall, July 27, 1858.

The Queen has been pleased to direct letters patent to be passed under the Great Seal, granting the dignity of a Baron of the United Kingdom of Great Britain and Ireland, unto Sir John Buller Yarde Buller, Bart., and to the heirs male of his body lawfully begotten, by the name, style, and title of Baron Churston, of Churston Ferrers, and Lupton, in the county of Devon.

Foreign-Office, July 24, 1858.

The Queen has been graciously pleased to appoint William Garrow Lettsom, Esq., now Secretary to Her Majesty's Legation to the

Mexican Republic, to be Her Majesty's Chargé d'Affaires and Consul-General to the Republic of Bolivia.

The Queen has also been graciously pleased to appoint George Benvenuto Mathew, Esq., now Her Majesty's Consul-General for the Russian Ports in the Black Sea and in the Sea of Azoff, to be Secretary to Her Majesty's Legation to the Mexican Republic.

The Queen has also been graciously pleased to appoint Edwin Corbett, Esq., now Paid Attaché to Her Majesty's Legation at Copenhagen, to be Secretary to Her Majesty's Legation at Florence.

The Queen has also been graciously pleased to appoint Eustace Clare Grenville Murray, Esq., now Third Paid Attaché to Her Majesty's Legation at the Court of Persia, to be Her Majesty's Consul-General for the Russian Ports in the Black Sea and in the Sea of Azoff.

The Queen has also been graciously pleased to appoint George Payne Rainsford James, Esq., now Her Majesty's Consul in the State of Virginia, to be Her Majesty's Consul-General for the Austrian Coasts of the Adriatic Sea.

The Queen has also been graciously pleased to appoint Lewis John Barbar, now British Vice-Consul at Alexandretta (Acting Consul at Naples), to be Her Majesty's Consul in the State of Virginia.

Westminster, July 23, 1858.

This day the Lords being met a message was sent to the Honourable House of Commons by the Gentleman Usher of the Black Rod, acquainting them, that *The Lords, authorized by virtue of a Commission under the Great Seal, signed by Her Majesty, for declaring Her Royal Assent to several*

*Acts agreed upon by both Houses, do desire the
immediate attendance of the Honourable House in
the House of Peers to hear the Commission read;*
and the Commons being come thither, the said
Commission, empowering the Lord Archbishop of
Canterbury, and several other Lords therein named,
to declare and notify the Royal Assent to the said
Acts, was read accordingly, and the Royal Assent
given to

An Act to repeal certain provisions for the issue
out of the Consolidated Fund of fixed amounts
for the reduction of the Funded Debt.

An Act to provide for the allotment of the
Commonable Lands within the boundaries of the
late Forest of Hainault, in the county of Essex.

An Act to amend the provisions of an Act of
the sixth year of King William the Fourth, for
separating the Palatine Jurisdiction of the county
palatine of Durham from the Bishoprick of Durham ; and to make further provision with respect
to the Jura Regalia of the said county.

An Act to confer powers on the Commissioners
of Her Majesty's Works and Public Buildings to
acquire the Theatre Royal, Edinburgh, and adjacent property, for the erection of a new General
Post Office, and for other purposes.

An Act to extend the time for making advances
towards Navigations in Ireland, under the provisions of an Act of the nineteenth and twentieth
Victoria, chapter sixty-two.

An Act for shortening the time of prescription
in certain cases in Ireland.

An Act to amend the Municipal Franchise in
certain cases.

An Act to give to the Universities of Oxford,
Cambridge, and Durham, and the colleges in
those Universities, and to the colleges of Saint
Mary of Winchester near Winchester, and of

King Henry the Sixth at Eton, power to sell, enfranchise, and exchange lands under certain conditions, and also to grant leases for agricultural, building, and mining purposes, and to deal with the interests of their lessees under proper reservations and restrictions.

An Act to suspend the making of Lists and the Ballots for the Militia of the United Kingdom.

An Act further to amend the law relating to the erection and endowment of Churches, Chapels, and Perpetual Curacies in Ireland.

An Act to amend the law relating to the Confirmation of Executors in Scotland, and to extend over all parts of the United Kingdom the effect of such confirmation, and of grants of Probate and Administration.

An Act to amend the Act of the fifth and sixth years of Her present Majesty, for enabling Ecclesiastical Corporations, aggregate and sole, to grant leases for long terms of years.

An Act to appoint a Clerk of *Nisi Prius* for the consolidated *Nisi Prius* Court in Ireland, and to make provision for the appointment of Tipstaffs in the Superior Courts of Common Law and Equity in Ireland.

An Act for the future appropriation of the Tithe or Tenth of Lead Ores in the parishes of Stanhope and Wolsingham, in the county of Durham, belonging to the respective rectors thereof, subject to the existing incumbencies, and for making other provisions for the endowment of the said rectories in lieu thereof, and for other purposes connected therewith.

An Act to amend the law of False Pretences.

An Act to provide for the relief of Her Majesty's subjects professing the Jewish Religion.

An Act to substitute one Oath for the Oaths of Allegiance, Supremacy, and Abjuration ; and for the relief of Her Majesty's subjects professing the Jewish Religion.

An Act to remove doubts as to the validity of certain Marriages of British subjects abroad.

An Act to amend the Joint Stock Companies Acts, 1856 and 1857, and the Joint Stock Banking Companies Act, 1857.

An Act to continue certain temporary provisions concerning Ecclesiastical Jurisdiction in England.

An Act further to continue the exemption of certain Charities from the operation of the Charitable Trusts Acts.

An Act to continue appointments under the Act for consolidating the Copyhold and Inclosure Commissions, and for completing proceedings under the Tithe Commutation Acts.

An Act to indemnify such persons in the United Kingdom as have omitted to qualify themselves for offices and employments, and to extend the time limited for those purposes respectively.

An Act to revive and continue an Act amending the Act for limiting the time of service in the Army.

An Act for making a railway from Athenry to Tuam, in the county of Galway, and for other purposes.

An Act to authorize the Great Northern and and for transferring the undertaking of the Birkenhead and Claughton Gas and Water Company, the Manchester, Sheffield, and Lincolnshire Railway Companies to work in common, and for certain other purposes relating to the Great Northern Railway.

An Act for enabling the East Kent Railway Company to extend their railway from Strood to join the Mid-Kent Railway (Bromley to Saint Mary's Cray) ; and for other purposes connected with their undertaking.

An Act for making a railway from the Great North of Scotland Railway, to Old Deer, and thence to Peterhead and Fraserburgh, with a branch to Ellon, all in the county of Aberdeen, to be called " The Formartine and Buchan Railway."

An Act for extending the powers of the Shrewsbury and Welchpool Railway Company, for purchasing lands and completing their railway, and for other purposes.

An Act for the amalgamation of the undertakings of the East Suffolk Railway Company, the Yarmouth and Haddiscoe Railway Company, and the Lowestoft and Beccles Railway Company ; for leasing the same ; and for other purposes.

An Act for making a railway from or near Guisbrough to or near to Skinningrove, all in Cleveland, in the North Riding of the county of York ; and for other purposes.

An Act for enabling the Stockton and Darlington Railway Company to make a new railway in the county of Durham, in connection with the Wear Valley and Stockton and Darlington Railways ; to acquire additional lands ; and for other purposes.

An Act for enabling the Stockton and Darlington Railway Company to make new railways in the North Riding of the county of York, and for other purposes.

An Act for the amalgamation of the Stockton and Darlington, the Wear Valley, the Middlesbrough and Redcar, the Middlesbrough and Guisbrough, and the Darlington and Barnard Castle Railway Companies, and for regulating the capital and borrowing powers of the Stockton and Darlington Railway Company formed by the amalgamation, and for other purposes.

An Act to authorise the construction of a Station near Victoria-street, Pimlico, in the county of Middlesex, and of a railway to connect the same with the West London and Crystal Palace Railway at Battersea, in the county of Surrey, in order to afford improved communication between certain of the railways south of the Thames and the western districts and the metropolis, and for other purposes.

An Act for the improvement of the western parts of the parish of Hove, in the county of Sussex, and for establishing more efficient Police Regulations within the whole of the said parish.

An Act for consolidating and amending the Acts of the North British Railway Company, and for authorising alterations in the Leith and Fisherrow or Musselburgh branches thereof, and for other purposes.

An Act for making a Railway Communication between Dublin and Meath.

An Act for carrying into effect an agreement between the Ribble Navigation Company and Sir Thomas George Hesketh, Baronet.

An Act for making a railway from the Tillicoultry station of the Stirling and Dunfermline Railway, to the Fife and Kinross Railway at Hopefield, to be called "The Devon Valley Railway;" and for other purposes in relation thereto.

An Act to make provision for better supplying Birkenhead and Claughton with Gas and Water, to the Birkenhead Improvement Commissioners, and for other purposes.

An Act to confer further powers upon the Oxford, Worcester, and Wolverhampton Railway

Company, with respect to the completion, alteration, or abandonment of certain of their branch
railways, and to authorise certain arrangements
with respect to their share capital and the purchase of the Stratford-upon-Avon Canal, and to
amend the Acts relating to the Company, and for
other purposes.

. An Act to authorise the making of a turnpike
road from Thames-street, in the parish of Clewer,
in the borough of New Windsor, in the county
of Berks, to Oxford-road, in the said parish, and
for other purposes.

An Act to enable the Newport, Abergavenny,
and Hereford Railway Company to divert their
railway in the parish of Aberdare, in Glamorgan-
shire, and to confer upon them other powers.

An Act to incorporate the Crystal Palace District Gas Company; to enable the said Company
to raise further money; to authorise the Company
to contract for and purchase the undertaking,
land, and premises of the Sydenham Gas and Coke
Company; and for other purposes connected
therewith.

An Act to enable the Whitehaven Junction Railway Company to construct new branches; to
widen their line; to erect shipping places, and
other works; to raise a further sum of money;
and for other purposes.

An Act to empower the Lancaster and Carlisle Railway Company to abandon a part of the
Lancaster and Carlisle and Ingleton Railway,
and to alter and divert certain roads in connection with their railway; to acquire additional
lands; and for other purposes.

An Act to authorise arrangements between the
Chester and Holyhead Railway Company, and
London and North Western Railway Company,

and to authorise the Chester and Holyhead Railway Company to raise a further sum of money, and for other purposes.

An Act for enabling the London and North Western Railway Company to construct works and to acquire additional lands in the counties of Salop, Middlesex, Hertford, Buckingham, Warwick, Chester, Stafford, Northampton, Leicester, and Lancaster; for authorising arrangements in reference to " The Improved Postal and Passenger Communication between England and Ireland Act, 1855," and for other purposes.

An Act for the establishment of a Board of Guardians of the Poor in the parish of St. Leonard, Shoreditch, in the county of Middlesex; and for other purposes with respect to the parish.

An Act to consolidate and amend the Acts relating to the Stockton, Middlesbrough, and Yarm Water Company; to change the name of the Company, and authorize the construction of additional works, and the raising of further monies; and for other purposes.

An Act to enable the North Yorkshire and Cleveland Railway Company to construct a new branch from their railway, to make a deviation in the main line and other works, to alter and amend the Acts relating to the Company, and for other purposes.

An Act for making further provision with respect to the Severn Valley Railway, in order to the completion thereof; and for other purposes.

An Act to improve the management of the Manchester South Junction and Altrincham Railway.

An Act to authorize the construction of a railway from Redditch, to the Midland Railway.

Board of Trade,
July 21, 1858.

PILOTAGE—NORWAY AND SWEDEN.

THE Right Honourable the Lords of the Committee of Privy Council for Trade and Plantations have received, through Her Majesty's Consul-General at Christiania Copies of two Royal Rescripts relating to Pilotage in Norway and Sweden.

1. Respecting the Rates of Pilotage on Ships.
2. Respecting Exemptions from Compulsory Pilotage.

Translations of these Rescripts are subjoined.

(Copy.)

1. PILOTAGE RATES.

Law respecting the payment of Pilotage in Norway,
which came into operation on the 1st January,
1858.

WE, Oscar, by the Grace of God, King of Norway and Sweden, the Goths and Vandals, make known, that the Resolution of the at present assembled Storthing, of the 22nd September this year, as follows, has been laid before us:

SECTION 1.

Instead of the pilot rates in the 16th section of the Pilot Regulations of the 6th August, 1824, the following have been determined on :

For piloting into harbour, when the distance from the outermost Skerries to the anchorage, according to the sailing channel, does not exceed one mile (4 English), shall be paid,

During the Summer Months, from the 1st April to the 30th of September, inclusive.

	Vessels Sharp built.			Vessels with Lee Boards.		
When the ship or vessel draws 6 feet or less than that ...	Sp.2	0	16	Sp.3	1	0
Between 6 feet and 7 feet ...	2	3	8	4	0	0
,, 7 ,, 8 ,, ...	3	1	0	4	4	0
,, 8 ,, 9 ,, ...	3	8	16	5	3	0
,, 9 ,, 10 ,, ...	4	1	8	6	2	0
,, 10 ,, 11 ,, ...	4	4	0	7	1	0
,, 11 ,, 12 ,, ...	5	1	16	8	0	0
,, 12 ,, 13 ,, ...	5	4	8	8	4	0
,, 13 ,, 14 ,, ...	6	2	0	9	3	0
,, 14 ,, 15 ,, ...	6	4	12	10	2	0
,, 15 ,, 16 ,, ...	7	2	8	11	1	0
,, 16 ,, 17 ,, ...	8	0	21	12	1	8
,, 17 ,, 18 ,, ...	9	0	8	13	3	0
,, 18 ,, 19 ,, ...	10	0	16	15	1	0
and for every foot the vessel draws above 19 feet ...	1	0	8	1	3	0

During the Winter Months, from the 1st October to the 31st March, inclusive.

	Vessels Sharp built.			Vessels with Lee Boards.		
	Sp. 2	3	8	Sp. 4	0	0
When the vessel draws 6 feet or under that ...	3	1	16	5	0	0
Between 6 feet and 7 feet ...	4	0	0	6	0	0
,, 7 ,, 8 feet ...	4	3	8	7	0	0
,, 8 ,, 9 ,, ...	5	1	16	8	0	0
,, 9 ,, 10 ,, ...	6	0	0	9	0	0
,, 10 ,, 11 ,, ...	6	3	8	10	0	0
,, 11 ,, 12 ,, ...	7	1	16	11	0	0
,, 12 ,, 13 ,, ...	8	0	0	12	0	0
,, 13 ,, 14 ,, ...	8	3	8	13	0	0
,, 14 ,, 15 ,, ...	9	1	16	14	0	0
,, 15 ,, 16 ,, ...	10	1	2	15	1	6
,, 16 ,, 17 ,, ...	11	1	16	17	0	0
,, 17 ,, 18 ,, ...	12	3	8	19	0	0
,, 18 ,, 19 ,, ...						
And for every foot the vessel draws above 19 feet ...	1	1	16	2	0	0

For piloting outwards, when the distance to the outermost skerries, according to the sailing channel, does not exceed one mile (4 English).

From the 1st April to the 30th September, inclusive.

	Sharp built Vessels.			Vessels with Lee Boards.		
When the vessel draws 6 feet and under that ...	Sp.1	1	0	Sp.1	4	14½
Between 6 feet and 7 feet ...	1	3	0	2	2	0
" 7 " 8 " ...	1	4	14½	2	4	10
" 8 " 9 " ...	2	1	5	3	1	19
" 9 " 10 " ...	2	2	21	3	4	5
" 10 " 11 " ...	2	4	10	4	1	16½
" 11 " 12 " ...	8	1	0	4	0	0
" 12 " 13 " ...	8	2	14	5	1	10
" 13 " 14 " ...	8	4	5	5	3	19
" 14 " 15 " ...	4	0	19	6	1	5
" 15 " 16 " ...	4	2	20	6	3	14½
" 16 " 17 " ...	4	4	12	7	1	18
" 17 " 18 " ...	5	2	5	8	0	19
" 18 " 19 " ...	6	0	10	9	0	14½
And for every foot the vessel draws above 19 feet ...	0	3	5	0	4	19½

From the 1st October to 31st March, inclusive.

	Sharp built Vessels.			Vessels with Lee Boards.		
When the vessel draws 6 feet or under that	Sp. 1	3	0	Sp. 2	2	0
Between 6 feet and 7 feet	2	0	0	8	0	0
" 7 " 8 "	2	2	0	3	3	0
" 8 " 9 "	2	4	0	4	1	0
" 9 " 10 "	3	1	0	4	4	0
" 10 " 11 "	3	8	0	5	2	0
" 11 " 12 "	4	0	0	6	0	0
" 12 " 13 "	4	2	0	6	8	0
" 13 " 14 "	4	4	0	7	1	0
" 14 " 15 "	5	1	0	7	4	0
" 15 " 16 "	5	8	0	8	2	0
" 16 " 17 "	6	1	0	9	1	12
" 17 " 18 "	6	4	0	10	1	0
" 18 " 19 "	7	8	0	11	2	0
And for every foot the vessel draws above 19 feet...	0	4	0	1	1	0

SECTION 2.

The mileage rate according to section 17 in the above law, when the pilot distance does not exceed 10 miles (40 English), is to be computed according to the following table :—

From the 1st April to the 30th September, inclusive.

	Vessels Sharp Built.			Vessels with Lee Boards.		
	Sp.			Sp.		
When the vessel draws 6 feet, or under that	0	1	21	0	2	19½
Between 6 feet and 7 feet	0	2	2	0	3	3
„ 7 „ 8 feet	0	2	7	0	3	10¼
„ 8 „ 9 „	0	2	12	0	3	18
„ 9 „ 10 „	0	2	17	0	4	1¼
„ 10 „ 11 „	0	2	22	0	4	9
„ 11 „ 12 „	0	3	3	0	4	16¼
„ 12 „ 13 „	0	3	8	1	0	0
„ 13 „ 14 „	0	3	13	1	0	7¼
„ 14 „ 15 „	0	3	18	1	0	15
„ 15 „ 16 „	0	3	21	1	0	22¼
„ 16 „ 17 „	0	4	4	1	1	6
Any depth exceeding the above, for every mile	1	0	0	1	2	12

From the 1st October to the 31st March, inclusive.

	Vessels Sharp Built.			Vessels with Lee Boards.		
When a vessel draws 6 feet and under that	Sp.	0	2 8	Sp.	0	3 12¾
Between 6 feet and 7 feet		0	2 14½		0	3 22
„ 7 „ 8 „		0	2 21		0	4 7½
„ 8 „ 9 „		0	3 3		0	4 16⅓
„ 9 „ 10 „		0	3 9¼		1	0 2
„ 10 „ 11 „		0	3 15⅓		1	0 11¼
„ 11 „ 12 „		0	3 22		1	0 21
„ 12 „ 13 „		0	4 4		1	1 6
„ 13 „ 14 „		0	4 10		1	1 15¾
„ 14 „ 15 „		0	4 16½		1	2 1
„ 15 „ 16 „		0	4 22¾		1	2 10¼
„ 16 „ 17 „		1	0 5		1	2 19½
And exceeding the above, for every mile... ...		1	1 6		1	4 9

For any number of miles exceeding the 10 miles (40 English) the rates fixed in Section 17 of the Pilot Law are to be in force.

Section 3.

The regulated diet money of 48 skillings, according to Section 20 of the above-named Law, is to be raised to 60 skillings.

The present Law is to come into operation from the 1st January next year.

As we have approved and confirmed, we do herewith approve and confirm this Resolution as Law.

Given in Christiania, 12th October, 1857.

Under the Seal of State.

Under His Majesty's, my gracious King and Master's, illness.

(Signed)   CARL.
VOGT.
SCHOUBOE.

(Copy.)

2. Exemptions from Compulsory Pilotage.

Law containing Changes in the Law respecting the Pilot Establishment of the 6th August, 1824.

WE, Oscar, by the grace of God, King of Norway and Sweden, the Goths and Vandals, make known ; that the resolution of the Ordinary Storthing at present assembled, made on the 21st March this year, has been laid before us as follows :

Section I.

Section V. in the law regarding the Pilot Establishment of the 6th August, 1824, is altered, so that every ship or vessel going from one place to another, either *between* Norway and Sweden, or *between* one port of Norway and another, shall be exempt from taking a pilot, if the Master venture to go without a pilot ; on the *other hand*, every ship or vessel, coming from, or going to any place *beyond* the United Kingdom, shall be obliged to take a pilot, should the vessel be of five commercial lasts burden or over.

SECTION II.

Steamers going as regular mail or passenger vessels, shall be exempt from the obligation to take a pilot. Whereas we have approved and ratified this resolution as a law; we do hereby approve and ratify it.

Given at the Palace of Stockholm, the 13th April, 1848.

Under our hand and the seal of the State.

(Signed.) OSCAR.

     FREDR. DUE.

     J. C. BLIX.

Board of Trade, Whitehall,

July 23, 1858.

The Right Honourable the Lords of the Committee of Privy Council for Trade and Plantations have received, through the Secretary of State for the Colonies, a copy of a Despatch from the Governor of Malta, reporting that a Quarantine of ten days had been established on vessels arriving at Valetta from Bengazi, in consequence of the prevalence of a disease of a malignant character at that place.

War-Office, Pall-Mall,

27th July, 1858.

Royal Artillery, Captain and Brevet-Major Henry Rogers, from temporary half-pay, to be a Supernumerary Captain. Dated 7th July, 1858.

Acting Veterinary-Surgeon James Lambert to be Veterinary-Surgeon, vice W. Stockley, retired on half-pay. Dated 1st July, 1858.

6th Dragoons, Major Frederick Wellington John FitzWygram to be Lieutenant-Colonel, without purchase. Dated 26th July, 1858.

To be Majors, without purchase.

Captain Edmund D'Arcy Hunt, vice FitzWygram, Dated 26th July, 1858.

Captain James D. Cowell, from the 10th Light Dragoons. Dated 26th July, 1858.

To be Captains, without purchase.

Captain William Mavor Julius, from half-pay 13th Light Dragoons. Dated 26th July, 1858.

Lieutenant T. E. Anderson, vice Hunt. Dated 26th July, 1858.

Lieutenant Joseph Thomas Wetherall to be Captain, by purchase, vice Julius, who retires. Dated 26th July, 1858.

Lieutenant James Leith, from the 14th Light Dragoons, to be Captain, without purchase. Dated 27th July, 1858.

Cornet Edward Napier to be Lieutenant, without purchase, vice Anderson. Dated 26th July, 1858.

Lieutenant George M. Billington, from the 4th Foot, to be Lieutenant, paying the difference. Dated 27th July, 1858.

Cornet Burton John Daveney, from the 3rd Dragoon Guards, to be Lieutenant, without purchase. Dated 27th July, 1858.

To be Cornets, without purchase.

Cornet John Augustus Beaumont, from the 4th Dragoon Guards. Dated 26th July, 1858.

Cornet Arthur James Billing, from the 13th Light Dragoons. Dated 26th July, 1858.

Cornet Robert Davies, from the 4th Light Dragoons. Dated 26th July, 1858.

Cornet Thomas Joseph Fitz-Simon. from the 5th Light Dragoons. Dated 26th July, 1858.

Cornet Alexander Frederick Stewart, from the 2nd Dragoon Guards, vice Chapman, promoted. Dated 26th July, 1858.

BREVET.

Captain William Mavor Julius, 6th Dragoons, to be Major in the Army. Dated 11th November, 1851.

Admiralty, 21st July, 1858.

Corps of Royal Marines.

First Lieutenant James Conway Travers to be Adjutant, vice Ellis, promoted.

Commission signed by the Queen.

4th or Royal South Middlesex Regiment of Militia.

Mathews Copplestone, Esq., to be Paymaster, from 5th April, 1858, vice Frend, appointed to 36th Foot. Dated 7th June, 1858.

Commission signed by the Lord Lieutenant of the County of Middlesex.

5th or Royal Elthorne Light Infantry Regiment of Middlesex Militia.

Ensign Henry Milward Nash to be Lieutenant, vice Coote, resigned. Dated 17th July, 1858.

Commissions signed by the Lord Lieutenant of the County of Warwick.

Warwickshire Militia.

2nd Regiment.

Lieutenant Henry Leftwich Freer to be Captain, vice Captain George Woodyatt, resigned. Dated 19th July, 1858.

Ensign Richard James to be Lieutenant, vice Freer, promoted. Dated 19th July, 1858.

Commission signed by the Lord Lieutenant of the County of Lancaster.

1*st Regiment of the Duke of Lancaster's Own Militia.*

Edmund Geoffrey Stanley Hornby, Esq., to be Captain. Dated 17th July, 1858.

Spalding Union — Spalding Parish.

An order of the Poor Law Board, to the Churchwardens and Overseers of the poor of the parish of Spalding, in the county of Lincoln, and to all others whom it may concern ; dated the 12th July, 1858, directs that so much of the Act 13th and 14th Vict., cap. 57, as relates to the providing of a room or suitable buildings for the purpose of holding vestry or other meetings for the transaction of any business of or relating to the said parish of Spalding, shall forthwith be applied to and put in force within such parish.

FROM THE

SUPPLEMENT

TO THE

LONDON GAZETTE of JULY 7, 1858.

India Board, July 28, 1858.

THE following papers have been received at the East India House :—

No. 1.

GENERAL ORDERS BY THE GOVERNOR-GENERAL.

Allahabad, May 10, 1858.

No. 130 of 1858.—The Right Honorable the Governor-General of India is pleased to direct the

publication of the following letter from Brigadier
F. Rowcroft, commanding Sarun Field Force,
No. 260, dated 1st May, 1858, forwarding a
report from Major Cox, commanding left wing,
Her Majesty's 13th Light Infantry, of an action
with the rebels, at Nuggur, on the 29th
ultimo :—

No. 2.

*Brigadier F. Rowcroft, Commanding Sarun Field
Force, to Colonel Birch, C. B., Secretary to the
Government of India, Military Department,
with the Governor-General, Allahabad.*

> Camp Captaingunge, Goruckpore District,
> May 1, 1858.

SIR,   No. 260.

I HAVE the honor to forward to you, for
submission to the Right Honorable the Governor-
General, the accompanying report, dated 30th
April, from Major Cox, commanding left wing
Her Majesty's 13th Light Infantry, reporting to
me the complete success of the detachment I sent
out under his command, on the 29th ultimo,
to dislodge and disperse about 1000 sepoys and
other rebels who had assembled at Nuggur, six
or seven miles south-east from camp, but without guns, and about the same distance from Bustee. It was necessary this should be done without delay, as, from the reports received by the
Commissioner, Mr. Wingfield, there was great
probability of the rebels at Nuggur being joined
by a considerable force, with guns, from Tanda.
We learnt yesterday morning, that this was intended, and that the rebels from Tanda were to
have joined those at Nuggur on the night of the
29th April. A karinda or agent of the Nuggur
rajah, was at the head of the body of rebels at
Nuggur.

2. The two silk colours captured by the Sikhs, are partly native, but the pike heads and tassels appear to be regimental. One native colour was taken by the men of the Naval Brigade, and another by Deputy-Magistrate Shekh Kairoodeen, who shot the rebel with his pistol who was carrying it away. A quantity of powder and ammunition and a number of ponies and other property were captured. About 100 of the enemy were killed and wounded. I am very glad to say we have only three men wounded.

3. The expedition has been very ably and most successfully carried out by Major Cox, commanding the detachment, and the Officers and men of all arms behaved admirably, and with great zeal and gallantry.

4. The Commissioner, Mr. Wingfield, accompanied the detachment, and afforded Major Cox valuable assistance.

5. I beg to recommend all engaged to the most favorable notice of the Right Honorable the Governor-General, Viscount Canning.

I have, &c.,

F. ROWCROFT, Brigadier,

Commanding Sarun Field Force.

No. 3.

Major J. W. Cox, 13th Light Infantry, to Brigadier Rowcroft, Commanding Field Force.

Camp, Captaingunge, April 30, 1858.

SIR,

AUTHENTIC information having yesterday morning been received, that a body of the enemy, about 1000 strong (half of them being sepoys), were posted at and about the town of Nuggur, seven miles from our camp; I have the honor to report that, in compliance with your orders, I started to dislodge them at 1 P.M., with a force as per margin.*

The intelligence procured from villagers on the road, corroborated our information both as to the numbers and position of the enemy ; and, on approaching, we found them in occupation of the town, and partially ruined fort of Nuggur, which is situated at the extremity of a dense bamboo jungle, about two miles in length, the jungle being bordered by a large lake with swampy ground about it ; on the further extremity of the town there are thick groves of trees, which, as well as the bamboo jungle, were occupied by the enemy.

By making a slight detour, we kept the jungle about half a mile on our right as we advanced, covered by a flanking party of the 13th, and the Sikhs, who skirmished with the enemy, and kept them back until the column came opposite the town and fort.

I then halted, and wheeled into line to the right, while I directed the two guns and rocket to take up a position on a slight rise of ground 500 yards from the town, and sent the cavalry round beyond the groves, to intercept any force which might escape in that direction.

* Left Wing, Her Majesty's 13th Light Infantry.—5 officers and 151 men, under command of Captain Kerr, 13th Light Infantry.

"Pearl" Naval Brigade.— 5 officers and 91 men, with 2 12-pounder howitzers and 1 24-pounder rocket, under Lieutenant Grant, Royal Navy.

Bengal Yeomanry Cavalry.— 9 officers and 58 men, under command of Captain Jenkins, Bengal Yeomanry Cavalry.

Gorucknath Regiment of Goorkhas.—11 officers and 281 men, in charge of Captain Barclay, 68th Regiment Native Infantry.

Sikhs of the Bengal Police Battalion.—1 officer and 46 men, under Lieutenant Burlton, Honorable East India Company's Service.

The guns and rocket under Lieutenant Grant, Royal Navy, then opened, with precision and effect, and, after about 40 shells and rockets had been thrown, the enemy's fire began to slacken ; I then sent orders for the guns to cease firing, directed Captain Kerr's Company of the 13th and the Sikhs to clear the groves beyond the town, wheel to their right and enter from that side, while the remainder of the Naval Column, gallantly led by Lieutenant Pym, Royal Marines, Light Infantry, and the Goorkhas by Captain Barclay, having arrived within 100 yards, we made a simultaneous advance on the town and fort which was completely successful ; the enemy were driven through both town and fort, some of them being killed in houses which they ineffectually attempted to defend, and were pursued for a considerable distance into the swamps and jungle, leaving 40 or 50 dead on the field.

As soon as we had got possession of the town, I sent orders for the cavalry to pass round to the rear, and endeavour to intercept the enemy in their retreat ; this was promptly done by Captain Jenkins, but the extremely unfavorable nature of the ground prevented him from cutting off many of the fugitives.

Four standards were captured during the day, two of them being handsome silk colours; we also found a quantity of powder and ammunition, and a large number of baggage animals, with other property.

The conduct of the whole of the troops was excellent, and they were ably and gallantly led by their respective commanding officers.

Mr. Wingfield (the Civil Commissioner) accompanied me during the action, and I feel much indebted for the valuable and accurate information he afforded me ; he was also good enough to convey my orders to the cavalry, and guide them to the position I wished them to take up.

Lieutenant Leet, 13th Light Infantry, acted as Staff Officer on the occasion, to my entire satisfaction.

I beg to inclose a return of casualties which, I am glad to say, are not of a serious nature.

I have, &c.,
J. W. COX, Major,
13th Light Infantry.

No 5.

No. 131 of 1858.

IN publishing the accompanying despatches regarding the pursuit of the insurgents under Koer Sing, the Right Honorable the Governor-General desires to record his thanks to Brigadier-General Sir E. Lugard, K. C. B., for the judgment and energy with which his operations have been conducted ; to Brigadier Douglas, C.B., for the very able and active manner in which he carried on the pursuit of the rebels ; and to the officers named in the despatches ; and, generally, to the whole force employed, for the courage, endurance, and gallantry shown by them during these operations.

Mr. Davies. Civil Service, Collector of Azimghur, is also entitled to the acknowledgments of the Governor-General, for the valuable services rendered by him during these operations.

R. J. H. BIRCH, Colonel.
Secretary to the Government of India,
Military Department, with the Governor-General.

No. 6.

The Deputy Adjutant-General of the Army, to the Secretary to the Government of India, Military Department, with the Governor-General.

Head Quarters Camp, Furreedpore,
May 4, 1858.

No. 295 A.

SIR,

I HAVE the honor, by desire of the Commander-in-Chief, to forward, for submission to the Right Honorable the Governor-General, copy of a despatch from Brigadier-General Sir E. Lugard, K.C.B., commanding Azimghur Field Force, dated 25th ultimo, enclosing report from Brigadier J. Douglas, C. B., of his pursuit of Koer Sing to the banks of the Ganges.

2. The vigour and closeness of this pursuit are considered by his Excellency, to reflect the highest credit upon the Brigadier, and upon the troops under his command.

I have, &c.

H. W. NORMAN, Major,
Deputy Adjutant-General of the Army.

No. 7.

Brigadier-General Sir E. Lugard, K.C.B., Commanding Azimghur Field Force, to the Chief of the Staff.

Camp Mhow, April 25, 1858.

SIR,

IN my report of the 16th instant, I had the honor to acquaint you, for the information of his Excellency the Commander-in-Chief, that, in consequence of the rebels under Koer Sing having taken up a strong position at Azimutghur, I had reinforced the pursuing column, and placed the whole under the command of Brigadier Douglas, C. B.

2. This force then consisted of the details as per margin,* which, equipped as lightly as my means permitted, I deemed quite sufficient to accomplish the object in view.

3. The remainder of the Field Force, including the heavy guns, park, &c., I retained under my immediate command in Camp at Azimghur, which place I considered it was necessary to hold strongly for the present, and to remain there myself, as a strong body of rebels under the Rajahs of Nuhurpoor and Naneejor (who formed a portion of Koer Sing's Force before Azimgurh,) had gone in a northerly direction towards Oude ; scattered portions also of Gholam Hossein's force, which I had dispersed at Tigra, were known to be near Sandah ; and other parties of rebels were reported to be collecting in the vicinity of Mundoree and Koelser, whilst Benares had been denuded of troops to assist in the operations against Koer Sing. Thus the central situation of Azimghur enabled me to watch the proceedings of the rebels north of it. to cover Benares and Ghazeepore, and to direct and control the combined movements in pursuit of Koer Sing.

4. At daybreak on the 17th instant, Brigadier Douglas, in obedience to my instructions, attacked the rebels near Azimutghur, drove them from their position with much slaughter, and followed them to Ghosee, whence they fled to Nugra, and thence to Secunderpore, closely pursued by the Brigadier.

5 On reaching Secunderpore on the 19th, it was found that the rebels had proceeded but a few hours, with the intention of crossing the Gogra ;

---

* 3 guns E troop, Royal Horse Artillery ; 4 guns Major Cotter's Battery ; 2 5½-inch mortars ; 1 Squadron Military Train ; 2 Squadrons Seikh Cavalry ; 1 Wing 37th Foot ; 84th Regiment ; Detachment Punjaub Sappers.

as soon as he possibly could, the Brigadier followed, and at daybreak of the 20th instant, came up with them at Muneer Khass, and, taking them by surprise, killed 'and wounded a great many, captured a brass 9-pounder gun, complete with limber, horses, &c., two ammunition waggons, several elephants, horses and bullocks, with 20 carts laden with stores, harness, &c., and dispersed the main body, the bulk of which fled towards Bulliah and Beyreah.

6. Nineteen elephants were separated from the rebel force during this attack, and, making their way to Ghazeepore, were handed over to the magistrate there by the native in charge.

7. Colonel Cumberlege, who had been posted at Mhow to cover Ghazeepore, and co-operate with the pursuing force, was duly warned and directed to move towards Bulliah, and endeavour to intercept the fugitives.*

8. No time was lost by Brigadier Douglas in renewing the pursuit, but, on reaching Sheopore on the 21st, it was found that Koer Sing had effected the passage of the river in boats, which had been prepared by his adherents, and were in readiness for him! The other 9-pounder brass gun which Koer Sing was known to have here, fell into our hands, together with several elephants, and much ammunition.

9. A party of rebels is reported to have crossed near Bulliah, but I have not yet learnt what steps were taken to intercept them by Colonel Cumberlege, who was placed there for that purpose.

10. Having left a sufficient force in Azimghur, I am now *en route* with provisions to effect a junction with my scattered troops, who have been directed to meet me, when I shall be in a position

* 2 guns, 6-pounder; 2 battery guns; 50 men 2nd Dragoon Guards; 180 men 4th Madras Cavalry; 300 men Her Majesty's 13th Light Infantry; 100 men 10th and 97th Foot; and 100 men Madras Rifles.

to operate, as may be necessary, against any bands of rebels, either of Koer Sing's force, who, unable to cross, may still remain in the district, or against those to the northward of Azimghur, who may again venture to collect in strength.

11. I regret extremely that, after the very great exertions which have been made to capture Koer Sing, he should have evaded our pursuit; he returns however to his own district a fugitive, hunted and nearly worn out with fatigue, and dispirited by the loss of nearly all his warlike munition.

12. Since the rebels quitted Azimghur, we have deprived them of five guns (two of which belonged to the Government), about 30 elephants, all their ammunition, and most of their stores and plunder; a large number of the rebel Sepoys have been killed, and every report agrees that the remainder are much dispirited.

13. I beg you will do me the favor to bring to the especial notice of his Excellency the Commander-in-Chief the very extraordinary exertions made by Brigadier Douglas, and the troops under his command, and the judgment and untiring energy with which this officer has conducted the pursuit. I consider that all has been done that it was possible for a military force to do under the circumstances; and that, but for the unforeseen event of boats being in readiness on the river, the whole of the rebels must have been captured or annihilated. Brigadier Douglas was just in time to fire a few rounds from his guns at the rearmost boats, and to sink one of them.

14. Much credit is also due to Mr. Davies, Civil Service, magistrate of Azimghur, who accompanied the Brigadier, and aided him with his local knowledge, and the correct intelligence of the movements of the rebels.

I have, &c.

EDWARD LUGARD, Brigadier-General,
Commanding Azimghur Field Force.

P.S.—Since writing this, I have received from Brigadier Douglas, a more full and connected despatch than his daily reports; copy of this, together with returns of casualties and captured ordnance, stores, &c., I beg to enclose.

No. 8.

Brigadier John Douglas, C.B., Commanding Brigade of the Azimghur Field Force, to Brigadier-General Sir E. Lugard, K.C.B., Commanding Azimghur Field Force.

Camp Sheopoor Ghaut, April 22, 1858.

SIR,

I HAVE the honor to forward, for the information of Brigadier-General Sir E. Lugard, K.C.B., a detailed account of the operations of the force under my command, from the 17th to the 21st April inclusive, the object being to press the rebels as much as possible, and to force them to give up their guns.

On the 17th, according to instructions, I marched at 3 A.M. from Nuthoopoor, with a force as per margin,* and found the enemy strougly posted at Nughai, near Azimutghur; I sent the cavalry and horse artillery of the advanced guard through the village by the road, the infantry cutting across the fields; the guns became immediately engaged, but the enemy stood well behind their breastworks. At the edges of topes of trees, it was now certain that a large force was opposed to us with artillery, as they came round on almost every side, and made several attempts to charge the

* 3 guns, E. Troop Royal Horse Artillery; 4 guns, Major Cotter's battery, Madras Artillery; 2 5½-inch mortars; Detachment Punjaub Sappers; one squadron Military Train; two squadrons, 3rd Seikh Cavalry; one wing Her Majesty's 37th Regiment; Her Majesty's 84th Regiment; one company, Madras Rifles.

guns. I threw part of the 37th, 84th, and the Company of Madras Rifles, into skirmishing order with supports, who rapidly advanced under a very heavy fire, carried the enemy's positions, and drove them off: they retired in good order from tope to tope, followed by the infantry, a number were bayoneted in their trenches, and a colour was taken by the 37th. Whilst the infantry were clearing our front, the enemy appeared in great force on our left, and were kept in check by the horse artillery and Major Cotter's Battery, supported by the cavalry, who made several charges. I followed the enemy for some distance, and a number were cut up; they were very determined, and evidently trained soldiers: in their retreat they divided into two bodies, and I halted for some time, till I could ascertain which was the main body; I then started in pursuit along the lower Ghoosee road, passing through Chuprah and Etawah, at which latter place the enemy seemed to have united; our force bivouacked at Ghoosee, within four miles of the enemy, after a march of twenty miles; from information afterwards received, the enemy, on our arrival, moved six miles further on.

On the 18th, we marched within three miles of Nugra, a distance of about 24 miles, the Cavalry and Horse Artillery going on in advance, and following the enemy till they took up their position in the town of Nugra: during the evening, information was received that the enemy, hearing of our approach, had rapidly left the town, but the spies could not inform us which road they had taken; about midnight we heard that the enemy had retired towards Secunderpore, and intended to cross the Gogra there: at 2 A.M. on the 19th, we followed in pursuit, and bivouacked four miles beyond Secunderpore, and within four miles of the enemy at Munuhur in the Ghazeepore District:

during this long march we picked up several of the enemy's stragglers : we here heard that the enemy were in much distress by the rapid pursuit, not having had time during the last two days either to cook or sleep. On the 20th, we started so as to arrive at Munnuhur at daylight, and found the enemy posted in some very thick woods to the right of the village. I ordered a few rounds of grape to be fired, and then advanced part of the 37th and 84th, and Madras Rifles, in skirmishing order through the wood, the cavalry, and Horse and Madras Artillery moving round by the right. The enemy were quickly driven from their position, broken, and pursued for six miles by the cavalry and artillery ; the Horse Artillery and two of Major Cotter's guns, supported by the greater portion of the Military Train, proceeding along the bank of the Gogra, where a few of the enemy crossed in boats, but under a heavy fire. Two of Major Cotter's guns, with a small portion of the Military Train, and the 3rd Seikh Cavalry, followed to the right, in pursuit of a large body of about 1,500 ; unfortunately, one of the guns broke down in consequence of the rough nature of the ground, and they were obliged to be withdrawn, the Seikhs having continued the pursuit for several miles, cutting up a great number, and dispersing the remainder.

Captain Pearse, commanding the Seikh Cavalry, desires particularly to mention the gallant conduct of Sepoy No. 1772, Furradun, Madras Rifles, who kept up with the cavalry, killing several of the enemy. In the hasty retreat of the enemy, they abandoned a brass 9-pounder gun belonging to the Honorable East India Company's service, complete in horses and ammunition, several limbers and waggons, and immense quantity of ammunition and a large quantity of treasure, a number of bullocks and hackeries, and four elephants ; and the regimental colours of the 28th Bengal Native Infantry were found wrapped round the body of a subadar who was shot. The enemy on this occcasion were completely dispersed. Having collected my force, I proceeded to Bansdeh, where the roads diverge to Bulliah and Beyreah, and then halted till I could ascertain which road the rebels had taken. Koor Sing was reported first to have gone to a village named Rajogaon, and afterwards to Taintwar, where the dispersed rebels had their rendezvous. I proceeded in that direction, and found several bodies of the enemy on my left, and I also understood that they were holding the village; it being nearly dark, and the country thickly wooded, I did not consider it advisable to advance further, and bivouacked within two miles of Taintwar. During this night no spies came in; we were under arms at 2 A.M., on the 21st; but at this time a spy came in, saying that the enemy had collected all their forces in a dry tank close to the village, and our reconnoitring party made the same statement, which prevented my moving off till daylight. On advancing, I found that the enemy had moved off, and I am led to believe that they went at a very early hour. I immediately pushed the cavalry and Horse Artillery on, as quickly as possible, to the ghaut here, where it was reported the enemy intended to cross the Ganges, but from all information I was led to believe that they had no boats, and must ford on elephants, in which case I should have been up in time to have prevented their crossing; the information, however, on this head, proved false, as they were provided with boats, and the cavalry and Horse Artillery arrived only in time to cut up about 200, and sink one of the last boats that crossed; on this march, we took another Horse Artillery brass 9-pounder gun, belonging to the Honorable East India Company's service, complete in every respect, and several elephants. I enclose a return of the killed and wounded in the two actions, which must be considered very small, in comparison with that of the enemy, which I believe could not have been less than 1,000 men. I believe the original number of the enemy to have been between 4,000 and 5,000 men, nearly all sepoys; a good many of them are still on this side of the river. I beg to bring to your notice the admirable manner in which the troops performed this rapid and arduous march of nearly 120 miles in five days, many hours in each day under a burning sun, and never under canvass. I beg to thank Colonel Riddell, Royal Artillery, for the assistance hé rendered me during the action of the 17th, and whose orders were to return to Azimgurh; I have also to thank Major Cotter, Madras Artillery; Captain Lightfoot, commanding the 84th Regiment; Captain Harrison, commanding 37th Regiment; Captain Wyatt, commanding Military Train; Captain Pearse, commanding 3rd Seikh Cavalry; Captain Broome, commanding detachment Madras Rifles; Lieutenant Fulford, commanding Punjab Sappers, —for their able co-operation during the two actions; also Major Mitchell, Royal Horse Artillery, who was several times detached in command of cavalry and artillery; also Lieutenants Jennings and Beadon, 3rd Seikh Cavalry, for the assistance they gave in reconnoitring and collecting information. I also beg most particularly to mention Captain Stevenson, 79th Highlanders, Major of Brigade, and Major Turner, Royal Artillery, who acted as artillery staff officer, and who both rendered me valuable assistance. In conclusion, I beg to return my best acknowledgments to Mr. R. A. Davies, the collector of Azimgurh, who accompanied me throughout the operations, and gave me the greatest assistance by his valuable information;

he also carried orders for me during the actions, and behaved in the most gallant manner,

I have, &c.

JOHN DOUGLAS, Brigadier,
Commanding Brigade of the Azimgur
Field Force.

P.S.—It has just been reported by the magistrate at Chuprah, that Koer Sing is wounded in the thigh and arm.

————————

No. 9.

Numerical Return of Casualties in a portion of the Azimgurh Field Force, detached under Command of Brigadier J. Douglas, C.B., in the pursuit of the Rebels from Azimgurh, in the Engagements at Azimgurh on the 17th, at Munnihur on the 20th, and at Sheopore Ghat on the 21st of April, 1858.

E. Troop Royal Horse Artillery—1 rank and file wounded.

2nd Battalion Military Train—1 troop horse killed.

Her Majesty's 37th Regiment—1 rank and file, killed; 1 subaltern, 7 rank and file, wounded.

Her Majesty's 84th Regiment—8 rank and file, wounded.

3rd Seikh Cavalry—1 troop horse killed; 1* havildar, 4 rank and file, and 3 troop horses, wounded.

Total—1 rank and file, 2 troop horses, killed; 1 subaltern, 1 havildar, 20 rank and file, and 3 troop horses, wounded.

Total Casualties.

1 man killed, 22 wounded.
1 follower wounded.
2 horses killed, 3 wounded.

E. LUGARD, Brigadier-General,
Commanding Azimghur Field Force.

No. 10.

From Return of Casualties of a portion of the Azimgurh Field Force, detached under Command of Brigadier J. Douglas, C.B., in the pursuit of the Rebels from Azimgurh, in the Engagements at Azimutgurh on the 17th, at Munnuhur, on the 20th, and at Sheopore Ghat on the 21st of April, 1858.

Lieutenant H. P. Lasage, H.M.'s 37th Regiment, April 17.

No. 12.

No. 133 of 1858.

Allahabad, May 11, 1858.

IN continuation of General Order No. 103, dated 25th April, 1858, the Right Honourable the Governor General directs the publication of the following Return. of Casualties in the Field Force, under command of Brigadier-General Sir E. Lugard, K.C.B., at the passage of the bridge over the Tonse river, and subsequent pursuit of the enemy to Azimgurh, on the 15th April, 1858 :

No. 13.

Return of Casualties in the Azimgurh Field Force under Command of Brigadier-General Sir E. Lugard, K.C.B., at the passage of the Bridge over the Tonse River, at Azimgurh, and the subsequent pursuit of the Enemy to Azimutgurh, on the 15th of April, 1858.

A Company 3rd Battalion Madras Artillery, with No. 2, Light Field Battery attached—1 rank and file, wounded.

Native Establishment attached to the above—1 rank and file, wounded.

24th Punjaub Pioneers—2 rank and file, wounded.

Her Majesty's 10th Regiment—1 serjeant killed ; 1 serjeant and 2 rank and file, wounded.

Her Majesty's 2nd Battalion Military Train—1 serjeant, 3 rank and file, 2 troop horses, killed ; 1 serjeant, 6 rank and file, 3 troop horses, wounded.

3rd Seikh Cavalry—1 subaltern, 1 native officer, 1 rank and file, 4 troop horses, killed ; 2 native officers, 4 rank and file, 17 troop horses, wounded.

> Total—1 subaltern, 1 native officer, 2 serjeants, 4 rank and file, 6 troop horses, killed ; 2 native officers, 2 serjeants, 16 rank and file, 20 troop horses, wounded.

> E. LUGARD, Brigadier-General, Commanding Azimgurh Field Force.

No. 14.

From the Nominal Return of Casualties in Azimgurh Field Force under Sir Edward Lugard, K.C.B., at the passage of the Bridge over the Tonse River at Azimgurh, and the subsequent pursuit of the Enemy to Azimutgurh, on the 15th of April, 1858.

Serjeant George Wragg, Her Majesty's 10th Foot, April 15, 1858, killed.

Colour-Serjeant William Hamell, Her Majesty's 10th Foot, April 15, slightly wounded.

Serjeant James Tucker Wilkins, 2nd Battalion Military Train, April 15, killed.

Serjeant William McQuestion, 2nd Battalion Military Train, April 15, wounded.

Lieutenant and Adjutant R. A. Hamilton, 3rd Seikh Cavalry, April 15, killed.

Total Casualties—7 killed, 21 wounded.

E. LUGARD, Brigadier-General,
Commanding Azimgurh Field Force.

No. 15.

Allahabad, May 17, 1858.

No. 144 of 1858.

THE Right Honorable the Governor-General is pleased to direct the publication of the following despatch, from Brigadier-General J. Jones, C.B., commanding Roorkee Field Force, dated the 28th April 1858, reporting his proceedings at Moradabad :—

No. 16.

Brigadier-General J. Jones, C.B., Commanding Roorkee Field Force, to the Deputy Adjutant-General of the Army.

SIR,   *Camp Moradabad, April 28, 1858.*

THE day following the action of Nugeenah (on the 22nd), the column moved to Dhampoor, and on the 23rd, I struck into the high road from Nozuffurnuggur to Moradabad at Noorpoor, with the view of nearing the Ganges, in case the enemy should halt in their flight, and attempt to pass my right flank, and get into the Bijnoor district. I found the people on this road much more friendly ; some of the villages had turned out against the enemy's cavalry, and cut up about thirty, taking a gun also which had broken down. Directions were forwarded to the officer commanding the troops watching the ford at Duranuggur to cross and occupy Bijnoor. Mr. A. Shakespear, the collector of the district, left my camp at Noorpoor for Bijnoor : I must here record my thanks to Mr. Shakespear for the able assistance he has rendered me : his knowledge of the country is considerable, and the exertion he has made to obtain intelligence and supplies indefatigable. The column marched to Chujlite on the 24th ; intelligence reached me on the road that Moradabad had been occupied by Feroze Shah, son of the late Emperor of Delhi, with 2,500 followers. It appeared that he had defeated the troops of Ram pore, on the 22nd instant, under the Nawab's nephew, taking his guns : some of tho Nawab's troops had acted treacherously and gone over to the enemy.

On the morning of the 25th, I marched for Moradabad :.on nearing the town, I was met by the brother of the Nawab of Rampoor. He had marched a body of troops from Rampoor on Moradabad, and defeated Feroz Shah, who, hearing of our approach, evacuated Moradabad and retreated on Bareilly, taking his own and the guns captured with him. I encamped on the race course. Under the direction of Brigadier Coke, the town was occupied by infantry and cavalry, and a diligent search made for the rebel chiefs about whom he had obtained information. This search under that most indefatigable officer was attended with unlooked-for success, and I have much pleasure in enclosing his report, and a list of the persons taken.

I would beg to draw the attention of his Excellency to the gallant conduct, as related in this report, of Lieutenant Richard Fisher Angelo 1st Punjaub Infantry, and the loyal and faithful service of Willayut Hoosein Khan, deputy collector.

From Mr. J. F. D. Inglis, Civil Service, I have received most valuable assistance, and I am happy in having an officer of this service in my camp, on whose knowledge and discretion· I can so much rely.

From all the information I can gather, I am led to believe that the rebels who have escaped, are all making towards Bareilly, and I believe I have fully carried out his Excellency's directions to clear the enemy from this portion of Rohilcund.

I have, &c.,

JOHN JONES, Brigadier-General,
Commanding Roorkee Field Force.

P.S—I must not omit to mention an excellent young officer of the Civil Service accompanying my camp, Mr. Lowe, from whom I have received much assistance.

No. 17.

Lieutenant-Colonel John Coke, Commanding Infantry of the Force, to Major Muter, Assistant Adjutant-General, Field Force.

Moradabad, April 26, 1858.

SIR,

ON the arrival of the force at this place yesterday, I obtained information from Mr. Inglis, Civil Service, in charge of the civil department with this force, that it was probable that a number of the chief rebels were concealed in the city ; this was confirmed by the information of Willayut Hoosein, deputy collector of Moradabad.

I accordingly made an inspection of the city with Mr. Inglis, and, having settled the different points to be held during the search, I obtained the Major-General's sanction to take a sufficient force into the city to carry out this object. I had previously placed parties of the Mooltanee Cavalry round the city to prevent the escape of the rebels. About 12 o'clock I proceeded with 2 guns of Captain Austin's Battery, a party of Sappers and the 1st Punjaub Infantry, to search the Mohulla of Nawab Mujjoo Khan, the chief of the rebels in this district, who had caused himself to be proclaimed Nawab of Moradabad, and had instigated the people to murder and plunder the Europeans at this place.

After a long search, I succeeded in capturing Nawab Mujjoo Khan : one of his sons and his nephew were shot on the spot, as resistance was made by the soldiers of the Nawab's Guard.

The capture of the Nawab was effected by Lieutenant Angelo, doing duty with the 1st Punjaub Infantry, who deserves great credit for his spirited conduct on this occasion. This officer, having burst open the door of the room in which the Nawab and his sons were concealed, and having captured them, was fired on by the guard of the Nawab, who were in a room on an upper story, commanding the house in which the Nawab was concealed. Lieutenant Angelo rushed up the narrow stairs leading to this room, burst open the door, and single-handed, entered the room, shot three men with his revolver, and, on being joined by some of his men, captured the rest of the guard.

A quantity of property and some horses were, with my sanction, taken by the troops, and an elephant belonging to the Nawab, was made over to the Commissariat.

I enclose herewith a list of the chief rebels, captured on this occasion, furnished by Mr. Inglis.

I am much indebted to Willayut Hoosein Khan, deputy collector, for the information afforded by him : he has proved the correctness of the opinion formed of him by Mr. Wilson, "that he was a loyal subject and might be fully trusted." I hope he may be rewarded for the excellent service he has rendered.

Having effected the capture of the rebel leaders, and as Mr. Inglis considered his police able to effect the capture of the followers of the Nawab and the other rebels in the city, I brought the force back to camp.

The energy displayed by officers and men in carrying out my orders after the long march in the five hours' laborious work in the city, was very creditable to them.

I have, &c.,

JOHN COKE, Lieutenant-Colonel,
Commanding Infantry of the Force.

List of Rebels Captured in the City of Moradabad on the 26th April 1858.

Mujjo Khan.
Shaik Eneautoollah Vakeel.
Abid Ali Khan.
Sayud Allie Khan.
Niaz Allie Khan.
Jhubbur Ali Khan.
Abdul Kurreem Khan.
Ala Ali Khan.
Shaik Goolam Hussein.
Nusuroodeen.
Mirza Yakoob Beg.
Mirza Jahangeen Beg.
Hoosain Bux.
Kurreemoolah,

Elahie Bux.
Jafur Hoosein.
Rugwedeen Sha.
Muddut Khan.
Shuffaoodeen.
Ahmud Hussein.
Looman.

Killed in the City during the capture.

Nugeemoodeem, son of Mujjoo.
Noobarik Allie Khan, grandson of Mujjoo.
Emaum Sha, } Servants of Mujjoo.
Moona,

No. 18.

No. 145 of 1858.

THE Right Honorable the Governor-General is pleased to publish, for general information, the following letter from the Deputy Adjutant-General of the Army No. 297, A, dated the 6th of May 1858, and the despatch which accompanied it, from Brigadier H. R. Jones, of her Majesty's 6th Carabineers, giving an account of an affair which took place at Kukerowlee, on the 30th ultimo, between the rebels and the force under Major-General N. Penny, C.B., who lost his life on the occasion.

The Governor-General shares the deep regret expressed by his Excellency the Commander-in-Chief, at the loss which the service has suffered, in the death of that distinguished officer.

No. 19.

The Deputy Adjutant-General of the Army to the Secretary to the Government of India, Military Department, with the Governor-General.

Head Quarters Camp, Bareilly, May 6, 1858.

SIR, No. 297 A.

I HAVE the honor, by desire of the Commander-in-Chief, to forward, for submission to the Right Honorable the Governor-General, a despatch from Brigadier H. R. Jones, of her Majesty's 6th Carabineers, in which that officer gives an account of an affair which lately took place at Kukerowlee, in the Budaon district of Rohilcund.

2. His Excellency desires to express the deep regret he feels at having to announce to his lordship, the death of the lamented Major-General Penny, C.B. This old and very deserving officer had remained patiently in the district for the last six weeks, at the head of his moveable column, performing a most important service in the safeguard of the communications, while the country was much denuded of troops in consequence of the operations in Oudh. With all the anxiety of a young man for military distinction, he rode a very long distance to confer with his Excellency, prior to his passage of the Ganges, notwithstanding the intense heat of the weather.

3. As shown in the despatch of Brigadier Jones, it would appear, that the lamented Major-General lost his life, in consequence of having been blinded by false intelligence, which caused him, probably for the sake of sparing his troops, to neglect some common military precautions.

I have, &c.,

H. W. NORMAN, Major,
Deputy Adjutant-General of the Army.

No. 20.

Colonel H. R. Jones, Carabineers, Commanding
Field Force, to the Chief of the Staff.

Camp Kukerowlee, April 30th, 1858.

SIR,

I HAVE the honor to report, for the information of his Excellency the Commander-in-Chief, that, under the orders of Major-General Penny, C. B., commanding the force, a column, strength as per margin,* was held in readiness to move from the village of Nerolee, upon the town of Oosait, at 8 o'clock P.M., on the evening of the 29th April. At the latter place, it was supposed that the rebels were in considerable force, with one or more guns, and the object of the movement was to surprise and cut them up. The column moved off at about 9 o'clock, but owing to one delay or another did not reach Oosait, a distance of about seven miles, till 12 o'clock that night. The column, up to this point, moved in military formation with an advanced guard, followed by artillery, duly supported by cavalry, with the infantry in rear, the heavy guns and baggage having been sent with a sufficient escort straight to Kukerowlee.

When within a short distance of Oosait, Mr. Wilson, the Commissioner, informed General Penny, that the rebels had entirely evacuated the place, and with their guns had retired to Datagunge. The column, however, still moved forward, and on reaching Oosait, the information given to Mr. Wilson by the town people appeared to satisfy him of the correctness of the above report. From this point military precautions were

* Her Majesty's Carabineers, 200 men; 4 guns Light Field Battery; Her Majesty's 64th Regiment, 350 men; Mooltan Horse, 250 men; Wing Belooch Battalion, 360 men; 2nd Punjaub Infantry, 299 men.

somewhat neglected, the mounted portion of the column being allowed very considerably to out-march the infantry, and eventually, though an advanced guard was kept up, it was held back immediately in front of the artillery, and such was the confidence placed in native reports, that Major-General Penny and his staff, under the guid-ance of Mr. Wilson, the Commissioner, were riding at the head of the advanced guard, at about 4 o'clock on the morning of the 30th of April, leading it to Kukerowlee, where it had been pre-viously determined that our camp should be pitched, and the force halted for the day. When within one or two hundred yards of Kukerowlee, some horsemen were indistinctly seen in front, and some inquiries were made as to what they could be; it was supposed they must be a portion of our own force, that had marched by the direct route to Kukerowlee, and the advance was con-tinued without any extra precaution being taken, till we found ourselves close to the town of Kuke-rowlee, in a regularly prepared ambuscade, with guns opening on us from the right, with grape and round shot at not more than forty yards distance, while the horsemen charged down from the left, and infantry opened on us with musketry from the front. As far as can be ascertained, it was at this moment that the much-lamented Major-General Penny fell disabled by a grape shot ; he was at any rate not seen alive afterwards.

The 4 guns of Captain Hammond's Light Field Battery were now ordered to the front, and nobly did this officer and his men respond to the call. The ground, however, where the enemy had taken up their position, was, to our left, nothing but a mass of sand hills, while, to our right, they were protected by thick groves. of trees, and immedi-ately in their rear, they had the town of Kuke--rowlee to fall back upon. Owing to these circumstances, and to the want of light, the execution done by the fire of our Artillery, was less severe than it would have been under more favorable circumstances, and the same causes operated against an effective advance of our cavalry. The enemy's numbers and real position could not be seen, and, under these circumstances, it was deemed best merely to hold our ground till daylight might enable us to determine the particular point for our attack, and the infantry could be brought up and made available. On the arrival of Lieutenant-Colonel Bingham, with Her Majesty's 64th Foot, he was ordered to advance upon and dislodge the enemy from his front and right ; this was done in the most gallant style, and the enemy were speedily driven into the town. Not feeling myself stong enough to follow them there, the Artillery was directed to fire the town by shelling, and this they speedily accomplished. Some time after this, information was brought that the rebels were evacuating Kukerowlee at the opposite end of the town. The force was accordingly put in pursuit, but it soon became evident that nothing but a rapid advance of cavalry would enable us to come up with them. Major Bickerstaff, in command of the two squadrons of Her Majesty's Carabineers, and Lieutenant Lind, in command of the Mooltan Horse, were accordingly ordered forward at a gallop to endeavour to overtake them ; this duty was performed by both, thoroughly and zealously : they drove the enemy in confusion with them, and succeeded in cutting up many, capturing one of his guns, and two carts containing powder. The enemy being no longer in sight, the force returned to Kukerowlee, and encamped there for the day, after having marched fully 25 miles. I have now to return my thanks to the officers of Major-General Penny's Staff, who, on his death, volunteered their ser-

vices to me, and rendered me much assistance
during the day ; viz., to Major Harriott, Deputy
Judge Advocate-General ; Captain Simeon, Assistant Adjutant-General ; Captain Briggs, Commissariat Officer with the Force; Lieutenant Eckford,
Assistant Quartermaster-General ; this officer, I
regret to say, was severely wounded. Also, Captain Dudgeon, of Her Majesty's 61st Regiment,
and Lieutenant Warde, of the late 11th Native
Infantry, both Aides-de-Camp to Major-General
Penny. A return of casualties will be forwarded
as soon as made out.

I have, &c.,

HY. R. JONES, Colonel, Carabineers.

Commanding Field Force.

No. 21.

*General Return of Killed and Wounded of
the Moveable Column under the Command of
Colonel Henry Richmond Jones, 6th Dragoon
Guards, in Action at Kukerowlie, on the 30th
of April, 1858.*

General Staff—Major-General N. Penny, C.B.,
Commanding Meerut Division and Moveable
Column, killed ; Lieutenant A. H. Eckford,
Deputy Assistant-Quartermaster-General, se-
verely wounded.*

Artillery Division—1 gunner, 2 horses, killed ;
3 gunners, 1 syce driver, 4 horses, wounded ;
2 horses, heat and exhaustion.

Total—4 gunners, 1 syce driver, 8 horses.

6th Dragoon Guards—1 rank and file, 7 horses,
killed ; 1 serjeant, 17 rank and file, 12 horses,
wounded ; 3 horses, missing.

Total—2 Captains, 2 subalterns, 1 serjeant,
18 rank and file, 22 horses.†

* Lieutenant Eckford's charger killed.
† Major Bickerstaff's and Captain Betty's chargers
wounded.

H.M.'s 64th Regiment—2 rank and file, wounded.
Mooltanee Horse—1 rank and file, 2 troopers,
killed ; 3 native officers, 5 rank and file, 2
officers' chargers, 8 troopers, wounded ; 2
troopers, missing.
  Total – 3 native officers, 6 rank and file, 2
  officers' chargers, 12 troopers.

H. RICHMOND JONES, Colonel,
Commanding Moveable Column.

No. 22.

From Nominal Return of Casualties with the
Moveable Column under the Command of
Colonel H. R. Jones, in Action on the 30th of
April, 1858.

6th Dragoon Guards.

Captain John Forster, wounded severely.
Captain William Thomas Betty, wounded se-
verely.
Lieutenant G. S. Davies, contused wound.
Lieutenant and Adjutant William Graham,
wounded slightly.
Troop Serjeant-Major Henry Bouchier, wounded
slightly.

No. 24.

No. 146 of 1858.

THE Right Honorable the Governor-General
is pleased to direct the publication of the following
despatch from his Excellency the Commander-in-
Chief, dated 8th May, 1858, reporting operations
against the rebels in Rohilcund.

His Lordship desires that his Excellency will accept his hearty congratulations and thanks upon the complete accomplishment of all the operations projected for Rohilcund.

The small cost of life at which success has been secured to the forces under his Excellency's command, is again a source of the highest satisfaction to the Governor-General; while the cheerful endurance by the troops of the fatigue and exposure to which they have necessarily been subjected of late, is quite admirable.

The whole of Brigadier-General Jones's progress from Roorkee to Bareilly, has, in the Governor-General's opinion, been marked with a happy combination of energy and prudence.

No. 25.

The Commander-in-Chief to the Governor-General.

Camp Bareilly, May 8, 1858.

MY LORD,

I HAVE the honor to report to your Lordship that, according to my intentions already announced, my Head-Quarters were transferred to General Walpole's Division in Rohilcund on the 27th ultimo. The siege train, &c., having joined him on the previous day.

The time had now arrived for General Walpole's Division to advance on Bareilly on the one side, while directions were sent to Brigadier-General Jones, Her Majesty's 60th Rifles, with whose movements your Lordship has already been made acquainted, to move forward from Moradabad in a like direction.

The late lamented General Penny, C.B., was instructed to cross the Ganges with the troops as per margin,* at the same time at Nudowlee, to advance through the Budaon District, and unite himself to the column under my immediate orders at Meranpore Kutra, on the end of the 6th March, from Futtyghur.

Although this officer unhappily lost his life in a trifling skirmish, the orders were literally obeyed, and the junction was effected as designed, under the orders of Brigadier Jones, Her Majesty's 6th Dragoon Guards; the rebels who had so long occupied the ghats of the Ganges above Futtyghur, and the District of Budaon, having retired before him, and swelled the mass of the insurgents at Bareilly. During my advance from Futtyghur towards Bareilly, the detached parties of the enemy which had previously occupied Shahjehanpore and the various large villages along the line of road, did not venture in a single instance to offer resistance. Accordingly every town and village was spared, and I advanced by the regular marches, having halted one day at Shahjehanpore to form a military post at that place.

On the 5th instant, a movement was made on Bareilly. The information which had been furnished me from various quarters was most conflicting, and to place reliance on it was utterly impossible. In short, in spite of the assumed friendship of the Hindoo portion of the population, I have not found it easier to obtain information in Rohilcund on which trust could be put, than has been the case in dealing with the insurrection in other parts of the empire.

Very early on the morning of the 5th, the advance having been made from Furreedpore, the

* Detail of General Penny's force.—Light Field Battery, Heavy Field Battery, under Major Hammond; Head-Quarters and 2 squadrons 6th Dragoon Guards (Carabineers); detachment Moultanee Horse; Head-Quarters Her Majesty's 64th Foot 7 companies; Wing 1st Belooch Battalion; 22nd Punjaub Infantry.

force consisting of as per margin,* was formed in
line of battle about 6 o'clock, A.M. The first line
consisted of the Highland Brigade, supported by
the 4th Seikhs and Belooch Battalion, with a heavy
field battery in the centre, with Horse Artillery
and Cavalry on both flanks, under the respective
Brigadiers and Commandants.

The second line was wholly employed for the
protection of the baggage and siege train, this precaution appearing to be necessary owing to the
very numerous rebel cavalry. The enemy, who
had come out from the city with much boldness,
and taken position on the left bank of the Nuttea

* Detail of the force on the 5th May.—Cavalry—1st
Brigade, under Brigadier Jones, 6th Dragoon Guards;
Head-Quarters and 2 squadrons 6th Dragoon Guards, un-
der Captain Bickerstaff; Captain Lind's Mooltanee Horse;
2nd Brigade, under Brigadier Hagart, 7th Hussars; Her
Majesty's 9th Lancers, under Major Coles; 2nd Punjaub
Cavalry, under Major S. Browne; Detachments Lahore
Light Horse, 1st Punjaub Cavalry, 5th Punjaub Cavalry,
17th Irregular Cavalry. Artillery—Under Lieutenant-Co-
lonel Brind, C.B., B.A.; Lieutenant-Colonel Tomb's Troop,
B.H.A.; Lieutenant-Colonel Remmington's Troop, B.H.A.;
Major Hammond's Light Field Battery, B.A., 4 guns;
2 Heavy Field Batteries, Captain Francis, B.A.; Siege
Train, with Major LeMesurier's Company R.A., under Cap-
tain Cookworthy's Detachment, B.A.; Detachment R.E.,
Bengal and Punjaub Sappers and Miners, under Lieutenant-
Colonel Harness, R.E,. Chief Engineer to the force. Infantry
—Highland Brigade, under Lieutenant-Colonel Leith Hay,
C.B., Her Majesty's 93rd Highlanders; Her Majesty's
42nd Highlanders, under Lieutenant-Colonel Cameron;
Her Majesty's 79th Highlanders, under Lieutenant-Colonel
Taylor, C.B.; Her Majesty's 93rd Highlanders, under
Lieutenant-Colonel Ross; 4th Punjaub Rifles, Lieutenant
McQueen; Belooch Battalion, Captain Beville; Brigadier
Ststed's (78th) Brigade; 7 Companies Her Majesty's 64th
Foot, Lieutenant-Colonel Brigham, C.B.; Her Majesty's
78th Highlanders, Colonel Hamilton; 4 Companies Her
Majesty's 82nd Foot, Colonel the Honourable P. Herbert,
C.B.; 2nd Punjaub Infantry, Lieutenant-Colonel Greene;
22nd Punjaub Infantry, Captain Stafford.

Nuddee, having that stream in his rear, fired his first guns about 7 o'clock A.M.

His guns were well placed, advantage having been taken of the road along which we were advancing, and of certain sand hills. The Horse Artillery and Cavalry advanced at the trot from both flanks, while the heavy field battery, with infantry in line, pressed up along the centre.

In a short time the enemy was driven from his guns, the left part of our line taking position on the river, while the right crossed the bridge and advanced about three quarters of a mile towards the town. The heavy guns were rapidly passed over in succession, and placed in a position from which they raked the centre of the enemy's second. line, which he had taken up in the suburbs. A considerable distance had now been traversed by the troops, and it became necessary to check the advance to allow time for the siege train and baggage to close up.

About 11 A.M., great activity was observed in the enemy's ranks ; and, while the attention of my right was occupied by a considerable body in the suburbs, the most determined effort that I have seen made in this war to turn and break through the left, was executed at this time by the enemy.

Some old cavalry lines had been occupied by a Seikh regiment. Such was the vigor with which this regiment, a most distinguished one (Major Wilde's), under command of Lieutenant McQueen, was attacked by a large body of fanatical Ghazees, that they gave way for a few minutes. The Ghazees, pursuing their advantage, rushed like madmen on the 42nd Highlanders, who had been formed in line in rear of the village to support the Seikhs as soon as the hostile movement was described. These men were all killed in the very ranks of the 42nd Highlanders in a most desperate hand-to-hand encounter.

The 42nd, supported by the 4th Seikhs and a part of the 79th Highlanders then advanced, sweeping through the various lines for about a mile and a half, into the cantonments where they were placed in position for the day.

Whilst the Ghazee attack had been going on the the left of the first line, a very large body of the enemy's cavalry, some 600 or 700 in number, coming round our extreme left, attacked the baggage. They were quickly encountered by Lieutenant-Colonel Tombs's Horse Artillery troop, which, after the first advance across the river, had been left to meet such a contingency, by Her Majesty's Carabineers (6th Dragoon Guards), the Moultanee Horse and infantry of the rear guard; their instant dispersion took place.

This was the last effort made by the enemy. A short time afterwards, the 79th and 93rd were directed to seize all the suburbs in their front, and the troops were put under shade as far as possible, the action having lasted for about six hours, and the troops having been under arms from 2 A.M.

Early on the next morning, on the 6th instant, the whole force advanced into the cantonment. At the same time I had the pleasure to hear Brigadier-General Jones's guns on the Moradabad side of Bareilly. This officer had obeyed his instructions with great judgment and spirit, defeated a portion of the enemy on the 5th instant, taking 3 guns, and, finding himself resisted in his approach to the town on the 6th, took three more which were in position against him, entered the town, and took three advanced positions without delay.

On the morning of the 7th, the town was finally reduced, and the Mussulman portion of it, where there were still detached bodies of Ghazees remaining with the intention to sell their lives as dearly as possible, was cleared.

When I passed through Shahjehanpore, I was

informed that the Fyzabad Moulvie and the Nawab
of the former place were at Mohumdee, with a considerable body of men who had retired from Shahjehanpore. I thought it would be impolitic to
leave the district of that name without evidence of
our presence; a post was therefore formed consisting of 500 of Her Majesty's 82nd Foot, a detachment of artillery, with 2 24-pounders and 2 9-
pounders and DeKantzow's Horse, under the command of Lieutenant-Colonel Hale, C.B., Her Majesty's 82nd Foot. He was directed to hold the
large enclosure of the gaol. I anticipated that, as
soon as my back was turned, the Moulvie and the
Nawab would annoy him. This expectation turned
out to be correct, and on the 3rd instant he was
attacked and invested by immense bodies and
cavalry. The guns brought against him were of
very insignificant calibre, and he writes that he had
no casualties within his entrenchments.

Brigadier-General Jones marched this morning
with a force as per margin,* to his relief. The
Brigadier-General has a discretionary power to
attack Mohumdee after the relief has been effected,
I have not as yet received Brigadier-General
Jones's despatch of his own operations on the
5th and 6th instant, but it will be forwarded to
the Secretary of Government for submission to
your Lordship in due course. In the meantime,
I beg to recommend most favourably to your
Lordship, the Brigadier-General and the officers
to whom he is indebted since his passage of the
Ganges, to take part in the general contribu-
tion arranged for reduction of Rohilcund. I have

* Detail of troops under Brigadier-General Jones.—The
Shajehanpore Brigade, consisting of 2 squadrons 6th Dra-
goon Guards; Cureton's Horse; No. 7 Light Battery,
B.A.; detachment of heavy guns and Sappers; Her Ma-
jesty's 60th Rifles; Her Majesty's 79th Highlanders; Her
Majesty's 82nd Foot left wing; 22nd Punjaub Infantry.

the greatest reason to be satisfied with all the troops under my own immediate command. Their alacrity to meet the enemy on all occasions is of course what your Lordship expects from them; but I must not lose this opportunity of bearing my testimony to the constancy displayed by all ranks of the force in the performance of their duty during the great and incessant heat of the season of the year. It is difficult to speak too highly of that cheerful endurance of intense fatigue, to which we are indebted for the victories gained at comparatively trifling loss on the day of battle.

I beg to return my thanks to the officers of the Staff and officers commanding regiments and corps employed during the campaign of Rohilcund, and to append a list of their names.

I have, &c,

C. CAMPBELL, General,
Commander-in-Chief, East Indies.

No. 27.

Numerical Return of Killed, Wounded, and Missing, of the Field Force under Command of his Excellency the Commander-in-Chief, in Action with the Enemy near Bareilly, on the 5th May, 1858.

General Staff—1 European officer, wounded.
Divisional Staff—1 European officer wounded.

ARTILLERY.

2nd Troop 1st Brigade Horse Artillery—2 non-commissioned officers, rank and file, 1 horse, killed ; 1 non-commissioned officer, rank and file, wounded.
3rd Troop 3rd Brigade Horse Artillery—1 non-commissioned officer, rank and file, 1 horse, wounded.

ENGINEERS.

23rd Company Royal Engineers—2 non-commissioned officers, rank and file, died from sunstroke.

CAVALRY BRIGADE.

H.M.'s 6th Dragoon Guards — 1 horse, killed.

H.M.'s 9th Lancers—1 non-commissioned officer, rank and file, wounded.

17th Irregular Cavalry—1 horse, wounded.

2nd Punjaub Cavalry—2 non-commissioned officers, rank and file, 1 horse, killed ; 6 non-commissioned officers, rank and file, wounded.

Mooltanee Horse—2 horses, killed.

INFANTRY.

H.M.'s 42nd Royal Highlanders — 1 non-commissioned officer, rank and file, killed ; 2 European officers, 12 non-commissioned officers, rank and file, wounded.

H.M.'s 79th Highlanders—2 rank and file, died of sun-stroke ; 2 rank and file wounded.

H.M.'s 93rd Highlanders—1 rank and file died from sun-stroke.

H.M.'s 82nd Regiment—3 non-commissioned officers, rank and file, died from sun-stroke.

4th Punjaub Infantry—5 non-commissioned officers, rank and file, killed ; 13 non-commissioned officers, rank and file, wounded.

Total—18 non-commissioned officers, rank and file, 5 horses, killed ; 4 European officers, 36 non-commissioned officers, rank and file, 2 horses, wounded.

H. W. NORMAN, Major,
Deputy Adjutant-General of the Army.

Adjutant-General's Office, Head Quarters,
Camp Bareilly, May 8, 1858.

No. 28.

From the Nominal Roll of the Europeans Killed, Wounded, and Missing, of the Force under command of his Excellency the Commander-in-Chief, in Action with the Enemy near Bareilly, on the 5th of May, 1858.

Major H. W. Norman, Deputy Adjutant-General of the Army, General Staff, wounded, severe contusion by round shot.

Brigadier-General R. Walpole, C.B., commanding Field Force, Divisional Staff, wounded, sword cut on right hand.

Lieutenant-Colonel A. Cameron, Her Majesty's 42nd Royal Highlanders, wounded slightly, sword cut on wrist.

Assistant-Surgeon A. T. Thornhill, Her Majesty's 42nd Royal Highlanders, wounded slightly, sword cut on foot.

Colour-Serjeant William Garden, Her Majesty's 42nd Royal Highlanders, wounded slightly, sword cut on thigh.

No. 29.

Roll of Officers of the Staff, and Officers commanding Regiments and Corps, employed during the Campaign in Rohilcund.

General Staff.

Major-General Sir W. R. Mansfield, K.C.B., Chief of the Staff.

Colonel the Honourable W. L. Pakenham, C.B., Acting Adjutant-General H.M.'s Forces in India.

Major H. W. Norman, Deputy Adjutant-General of the Army.

Major D. M. Stewart, 2nd Assistant Adjutant-General of the Army.

Lieutenant-Colonel J. D. Macpherson, Acting Quartermaster-General of the Army.

Captain G. Allgood, Officiating Assistant Quartermaster-General of the Army.

Personal Staff of the Commander-in-Chief.

Colonel A. C. Sterling, C.B., Military Secretary.
Major Sir D. Baird, Bart., Aide-de-Camp.
Lieutenant F. M. Alison, Aide-de-Camp.
Major J. Metcalfe, Interpreter.
Assistant-Surgeon W. A. Mackinnon, Surgeon.

Personal Staff of the Chief of the Staff.

Lieutenant R. G. Hope Johnstone, Deputy Assistant Adjutant-General.
Major H. H. Crealock, Acting Aide-de-Camp.

Divisional Staff.

Brigadier-General R. Walpole, C.B., commanding Field Force.
Major C. A. Barwell, Deputy Assistant Adjutant-General.
Major T. A. Carey, Deputy Assistant Quartermaster-General.
Captain A. C. Warner, Aide-de-Camp.
Lieutenant W. H. Eccles, Extra Aide-de-Camp.
Captain W. H Earle, Deputy Judge-Advocate-General.
Captain R. G. Simeon, Deputy Assistant Adjutant General, Meerut Division.
Major F. J. Harriott, Deputy Judge Advocate-General, Meerut Division.
Captain R. Ouseley, Officiating Deputy Assistant Quartermaster-General, Meerut Division.
Lieutenant J. Morland, Baggage Master.
1st Class Staff-Surgeon J. C. G. Tice, M.D., Superintending Surgeon.

Artillery.

Lieutenant-Colonel James Brind, C.B., commanding Artillery.

Captain A. Bunny, Staff Officer of Artillery.

Major W. G. Le Mesurier, commanding 3rd Co., 14th Bat. Royal Artillery.

Lieutenant-Colonel H. Tombs, C.B., commanding 2nd Troop, 1st Brigade, Bengal Horse Artillery.

Lieutenant-Colonel F. F. Remmington, commanding 3rd Troop, 3rd Brigade, Bengal Horse Artillery.

Captain H. Hammond, commanding No. 14 Light Field Battery.

Captain H. Francis, commanding Heavy Field Battery.

Lieutenant W. Tod Brown, Commissary of Ordnance.

Lieutenant J. R. Pearson, Deputy Commissary of Ordnance.

Captain C. Cookworthy, commanding Bengal Artillery attached to Siege Train.

Engineers.

Lieutenant-Colonel H. D. Harness, commanding Engineers.

Captain F. E. Cox, Staff Officer of Engineers.

Major W. O. Lennox, commanding Royal Engineers.

Lieutenant F. R. Maunsell, commanding Bengal Sappers and Miners.

Lieutenant J. St. J. Hovenden, commanding 24th Punjaub Infantry (Pioneers).

1st Cavalry Brigade.

Brigadier C. Hagart, Commanding.

Major H. A. Sarel, Major of Brigade.

Lieutenant A. F. W. Gore, Orderly Officer.

Captain J. R. J. Coles, commanding Her Majesty's 9th Lancers.

Captain J. H. Balmain, commanding Lahore Light Horse.

Lieutenant G. C. Thomson, commanding Detachment 17th Irregular Cavalry.

Lieutenant A. K. J. C. Mackenzie, commanding Detachment 1st Punjaub Cavalry.

Captain S. Browne, commanding 2nd Punjaub Cavalry.

Lieutenant W. F. Fergusson, commanding Detachment Punjaub Cavalry.

Lieutenant S. G. Warde, doing duty 2nd Punjaub Cavalry, commanded a detachment in pursuit on the 6th.

2nd Cavalry Brigade.

Brigadier R. Jones, Commanding.

Captain C. H. Nicholetts, Major of Brigade.

Major R. Bickerstaff, commanding 6th Dragoon Guards.

Lieutenant J. B. Lind, commanding Mooltanee Horse.

1st Infantry Brigade.

Lieutenant-Colonel A. S. L. Hay, C.B., commanding.

Major J. H. Cox, Major of Brigade.

Lieutenant-Colonel A. Cameron, commanding Her Majesty's 42nd Highlanders.

Lieutenant-Colonel R. C. H. Taylor, commanding Her Majesty's 79th Highlanders.

Lieutenant-Colonel R. L. Ross, commanding Her Majesty's 93rd Highlanders.

Lieutenant J. W. McQueen, commanding 4th Punjaub Infantry.

Lieutenant H. Beville, commanding Wing Beloch Battalion.

2nd *Infantry Brigade.*

Brigadier H. W. Stisted, C.B., commanding.

Lieutenant A. Cassidy, Major of Brigade.

Lieutenant-Colonel G. W. P. Bingham, C.B., commanding Her Majesty's 64th Regiment.

Lieutenant-Colonel H. Hamilton, C.B., commanding Her Majesty's 78th Regiment.

Colonel the Honourable P. E. Herbert, C.B., commanding Detachment H.M.'s 82nd Regiment.

Lieutenant-Colonel G. W. G. Green, commanding 2nd Punjaub Infantry.

Captain W. J. F. Stafford, commanding 22nd Punjaub Infantry.

Commissariat Department.

Major G. S, Macbean, in principal Commissariat charge.

Lieutenant F. Goldsworthy, in Commissariat charge, Army Head-Quarters.

Captain R. Bridge, Officiating Sub-Assistant Commissary-General. In attendance on the Commander-in-Chief on the field, and of great use from his local knowledge.

H. W. NORMAN, Major,
Deputy Adjutant-General of the Army.

No. 30.

No. 150 of 1858.

THE Right Honorable the Governor-General is pleased to direct the publication of the following despatch from Major-General Sir J. H. Grant, K.C.B., commanding Lucknow Field Force, No, 85, dated the 24th of April, 1858, reporting operations at Barree against a rebel force assembled there.

No. 31.

Major-General Sir J. H. Grant, K.C.B., Commanding Lucknow Field Force, to the Deputy-Adjutant-General of the Army.

Lucknow, April 24th, 1858.

SIR,   No. 85.

I HAVE the honor to report, for the information of his Excellency the Commander-in-Chief, that, agreeably to the instructions I received from his Excellency, I marched with the force detailed in the margin* on the 11th instant towards Barree, where a rebel force was reported to be assembled under the Fyzabad Moulvie. Early on the morning of the 13th, when about a mile from Camp Uttereah, my advance guard, consisting of one troop Irregular Cavalry, one squadron 7th Hussars, two Horse Artillery Guns, pioneers of regiments, and 100 infantry, came upon an advance force of the enemy. The advanced guard, under the orders of Lieutenant-Colonel J. M. Hagart, was immediately formed to the front. The enemy's cavalry charged two Horse Artillery guns under the command of Lieutenant Hunter, opened a well-directed and rapid fire upon them, and a detachment of the 1st Seikh Cavalry, under command of Lieutenant Prendergast, met them in a very gallant style, and had a hand-to-hand encounter with them, in which Lieutenant Prendergast was wounded. A squadron of the 7th Hussars was covering the guns and in support. The enemy's cavalry was

* DETAIL.—Cavalry: Her Majesty's 7th Hussars; Her Majesty's 2nd Dragoon Guards (1 squadron); 1st Seikh Cavalry (Wale's); Hodson's Horse (1 squadron). Artillery: 1 troop Horse Artillery; 1 Light Field Battery; 1 Heavy Field Battery. Infantry: Brigadier Horsford's Brigade, consisting of Her Majesty's 38th Regiment, Her Majesty's 2nd Battalion Rifle Brigade, 1st Bengal Fusiliers, a wing 5th Punjaub Rifles; Detail of Sappers and Miners.

soon driven off with loss. In the meantime, I had ordered the column to be formed to the front, the cavalry to the right. The 2nd Battalion of the Rifle Brigade in the first line, on the left, supported by the wing of the 5th Punjaub Infantry, the 38th in the second line. The enemy's cavalry, which had retired to my right, moved round towards the rear, and made an attack upon the baggage, but they were repulsed and driven off by a troop of the 7th Hussars, under Lieutenant Topham, supported by a squadron of that regiment under Major Horne, and the 1st European Bengal Fusiliers, which I had ordered to cover the right rear. I then advanced against the main body of the enemy's infantry, which was posted in a strong position in my front and towards the left. The battalion of the Rifle Brigade soon drove them off, and they retired in disorder towards Barree. On this occasion the rapidity and steadiness with which the cavalry under Lieutenant-Colonel Hagart was manœuvred on my right and right rear, when the enemy attempted to attack the long line of baggage, is deserving of great praise. The Horse Artillery and the Field Battery also did good service here : whenever the enemy showed himself, there was a detachment to meet and repulse him ; on one occasion two companies of the 1st Bengal Fusiliers in line defeating a charge of cavalry.

I would also bring to the notice of his Excellency the steadiness of the Rifles in the general advance, reserving their fire until it was really wanted.

The enemy showed no guns on the field, but a tumbril full of ammunition was found deserted.

My acknowledgments are due to the following officers for the support they rendered me on this occasion :—

Brigadier Horsford, C.B., commanding the in fantry, whose coolness and ability in manœuvring his brigade I wish to bring to his Excellency's notice.

Lieutenant-Colonel Hagart, commanding the cavalry, who had also the superintendence of the out-post duty on this as on former occasions, was most active and energetic.

Lieutenant-Colonel Maberly, commanding the Artillery, who, though suffering from bad health, was most active in the discharge of his duties.

Lieutenant-Colonel Kelly, commanding 38th Regiment; Lieutenant-Colonel Hill, commanding 2nd Battalion Rifle Brigade; Major Sir W. Russell, commanding 7th Hussars; Major Horne, 7th Hussars, who had command of the detachment covering the rear.

Major Nicholson, Royal Engineers, commanding Engineers and Sappers and Miners. who was most energetic and active; Captain Hume, commanding 1st European Bengal Fusiliers; Captain Middleton, commanding Battery, Royal Artillery; Captain Mackinon, commanding troop Bengal Horse Artillery; Captain Talbot, Royal Artillery, commanding Heavy Battery; Captain Hutchinson, commanding squadron, 2nd Dragoon Guards; Lieutenant Stewart, commanding 1st Seikh Cavalry; Lieutanant Lawford, commanding squadron Hodson's Horse; Lieutenants Hunter and McLeod, Bengal Artillery; Lieutenant Prendergast, 1st Seikh Cavalry, who was wounded in the charge on the advanced guard; Lieutenant Topham, 7th Hussars; the troop under this officer's command met the enemy's cavalry at the charge, when one man of the 7th was killed, and Lieutenant Topham and six men wounded.

Major Mollan, 75th Regiment Major of Brigade of Infantry, and Captain the Honourable J. Fiennes, Major of Brigade of Cavalry.

Captain Reid, Deputy Commissioner, and who had charge of the Intelligence Department, rendered important service.

To my personal staff—Captain the Honourable A. Anson, 84th Regiment, aide-de-camp, Captain Wolseley, 90th Light Infantry, Deputy-Assistant-Quartermaster-General, and Major W. Hamilton, 9th Lancers, Deputy-Assistant-Adjutant-General, my acknowledgments are also due.

On arrival at Barree, it was found to be evacuated by the rebels ; a quantity of military stores were found in it, which were destroyed.

I arrived at Mamadabad on the 15th instant, there had been a large body of rebels here, but on the approach of the column they dispersed. In the fort was found one brass gun and a quantity of gunpowder. The Nawab's house, a large building in the fort, was blown up and completely destroyed by the Engineers in the course of the afternoon.

The force arrived at Ramnugger on the 19th. The Rajah's house here I had also destroyed, as he was assisting the rebels.

At Ramnugger I received intelligence that the large force which was assembled at Bitowlee had dispersed on the approach of the column.

On the 22nd, on the march from Munsowlee to Nawabgunge, three native iron guns were found in the fort of Jungerabad, which was given up without resistance, and a 24-pounder native iron gun was found at a village about three miles from Nawabgunge. The four guns were all destroyed.

On the 23rd instant I made over command of the column to Brigadier Horsford, C.B., and it will be encamped to-morrow at Chenuote, four miles from the iron bridge.

I have, &c.,

J. HOPE GRANT, Major-General,
Commanding Lucknow Field Force.

No. 32.

No. 153 of 1858.

Allahabad, May 20, 1858.

THE Right Honorable the Governor-General is pleased to direct the publication of the following despatches from Major-General G. C. Whitlock, commanding Saugor and Nerbudda Field Division, dated 24th and 30th April, 1858 ; the former reporting the particulars of a general action with the troops of the Nawab of Banda on the 19th April, and the latter bringing to notice the valuable service of Major Ellis, Political Assistant for Bundlekund.

No. 33.

Major-General G. C. Whitlock, Commanding Saugor Field Division, to Major-General Mansfield, Chief of the Staff, Bengal.

Camp, Banda, April 24, 1858.

SIR,   No. 130.

I HAVE the honor to report, for the information of his Excellency the Commander-in-Chief of India, that the force under my command, as per margin,* fought a general action with the troops of the Nawab of Banda, on the 19th instant.

Nawab Ali Bahadoor, determined on opposing my advance on Banda, took up, during the 18th instant, a position about five miles from the left bank of the River Kane, selected with consummate judgment, and in every respect well adapted for the protection of his capital.

* A Troop H. A. European, 110; E. Troop H. A. Native, 176 ; H. M.'s 12th Lancers, 227, 1 Squadron Hyd. Cavalry, 136 ; Detachment Royal Artillery, 111 ; Detachment Madras Foot Artillery, 75 ; No. 1 Horse Battery, 84 ; Detachment Sappers and Miners, 101; 3rd Madras European Regiment, 538; 1st Regiment Native Infantry, 255; Detachment 50th Native Infantry, 156. Total of all arms, 1,899.

His artillery commanded the main road on which my force was moving, enabling him to withdraw his guns if hard pressed—broken ground, with numerous ravines and nullahs covered his whole front, affording excellent cover to a swarm of skirmishers, who not only knew their value, but most skilfully availed themselves of them, whilst every desired movement on my part on the enemy's flanks, was impeded by ground most difficult for the combined operations of artillery and cavalry.

The enemy, 6,000 in number, with 3,000 in reserve, were under the personal command of the Nawab, and principally composed of mutineers of the three arms, the infantry with percussion muskets. Videttes on our flanks and front watched our advance, and a near approach to reconnoitre disclosed the enemy's position, from which a sharp fire of artillery was opened.

An advanced party under Colonel Apthorp, 3rd Madras Europeans, first encountered their infantry, and soon found themselves under a heavy fire ; every nullah was vigorously disputed, and the judgment and decision with which that officer conducted his movements, thus avoiding much severe loss, called forth my highest commendations.

It now became necessary to dislodge a battery on our right flank, which would have swept through our skirmishers had they further advanced, and no men ever charged more nobly than the squadron of the 2nd Hydrabad Contingent Cavalry, under their gallant leader, Captain Macintire ; one gun was captured ; the other in the *melée* escaped for a time, but the object was effected.

The main body of my force had now come up, and I directed its movement to the left, thus cooperating with the advanced guard, which was hardly pressed. A flanking fire soon relieved them, and the desperate resistance and continued struggle of the enemy to maintain his ground, led to many a hand-to-hand conflict, where the bayonet did great execution.

By the most persevering efforts, my artillery and cavalry flanked the enemy, causing heavy loss, and capturing three guns, and the gallantry of Her Majesty's 12th Lancers and the Rissalah, were most conspicuous on these occasions.

The Horse Artillery and Horse Battery did their work with an alacrity, spirit, and precision of fire not to be surpassed, and each man of the native troop vied with the European soldier in his vigorous pursuit of the enemy.

The 18-pounders served by the Royal Artillery, made some excellent practice ; it was work of much labour to bring them into position, but it was cheerfully and well executed by officers and men.

Although the enemy now began to retire, it was four hours before the firing ceased ; they fell back, occupying every available ground for opposition, and our guns were in constant employment to dislodge them.

The Nawab at length fled, leaving on the field (from information I have since received) more than 1,000 of his men, 800 of whom were amongst the killed ; several men of note were slain, and, within a few hours, many notorious vagabonds have been hanged.

A fort commanding the ford was reported to be occupied by the enemy, and it was necessary to bring up some heavy guns previous to advancing : this retarded our movement, and enabled the enemy to cross the river, and get so far ahead as to escape further pursuit.

A flag of truce now approached ; it was borne by some of the principal inhabitants of the city, who informed me that the Nawab had fled, the town been evacuated, and the mutineers had set fire to their lines. So great indeed was the panic, and so sudden, that on occupying the palace, we found food preparing for the Nawab.

My troops are now in possession of the palace and town, 13 large brass guns, besides several of small calibre — a large quantity of ammunition, much valuable property belonging to the Nawab, some 40,000 rupees in specie — four elephants, 50 camels, with other cattle,—and about 2,000 rupees, worth of grain of sorts.

The British flag was hoisted under a general salute in the presence of the troops, and the Commissioner is busily employed in establishing order.

The contest was a lengthened one, but Europeans and natives fought well and manfully against their disciplined enemy, and merit my warmest praise for their conduct.

It was the first time the 3rd Madras European Regiment were under fire. I noticed their steadiness and good discipline with pride, as well as the gallantry of the Hydrabad Company, who charged, and, with great slaughter, drove a large party from their stronghold.

Our own loss is extraordinarily small, considering the fire to which the troops were so long exposed. Amongst the killed I have to lament a promising young officer, Lieutenant Colbeck, of the 3rd Europeans.

I beg to attach copies of the reports from Brigadier Miller, commanding the Artillery, and Major Oakes, commanding the Cavalry Brigade, and it is most gratifying to me to add my testimony to the distinguished gallantry of those officers whose names they have brought to notice, and the dashing style in which they led their guns. and troops into action.

Brigadier Miller, a most able and energetic officer, disposed of his artillery with a skill and intelligence most praiseworthy, and I cordially thank him. I regret to add he was severely wounded, and that I am thereby deprived for a time of his valuable services. Major Lavie assumed command, and I have special satisfaction in recording the steadiness and intelligence with which he conducted his important duties.

Major Oakes displayed the zeal and activity of an excellent cavalry officer throughout the day.

Brigadier Carpenter brought his infantry into action, with a steady precision with which I was perfectly satisfied.

Colonel Apthorp's management of the troops placed at his disposal, was what I expected from an officer of his high character. I beg to annex his report.

It is a pleasing duty to bring to the special notice of his Excellency the Commander-in-Chief, a favour which I beg to solicit at your hands, the name of Captain Macintire, of the Madras Artillery, commanding a squadron of the 2nd Hydrabad Contingent Cavalry, always distinguished for his zeal, a soldier's spirit, and a judgment well fitting him for his command; his charge on the enemy's guns (I had no infantry at hand for that purpose), was the admiration of all who witnessed the affair, and his men followed their leader with an order with which his high bearing has inspired them, and I cannot express myself in too high terms of their spirit and their gallantry. Lieutenant Ryall, the Adjutant of the regiment, accompanied the troop on its attack, and with his commanding officer, cut down several of the enemy in hand-to-hand combat.

I received much assistance from my Assistant Adjutant-General, Major R. Hamilton, an able, intelligent, and worthy officer, as well as from·

my Assistant Quartermaster-General, Captain Law-der, both were by my side during the whole of the action; also Major Mayne, Deputy-Judge-Advocate-General to the Force.

Lieutenant Homan, 50th Regiment Native Infantry, my Aide-de-Camp, was very useful to me.

Major Brett, 3rd Madras European Regiment, an experienced and able officer, who was attached as orderly officer to me during the day, was very active in carrying my orders.

The officers of the Engineers' Department were with me on the field, and Major Ludlow, Field Engineer, received the flag of truce.

The Commissariat Department, under Lieutenant Barrow, has been admirably conducted for the many months the force has been marching, and, from the excellent system of this able officer, the troops were furnished without delay with all their customary supplies at the conclusion of the contest.

I am very much indebted to Major Barrow, Commissary of Ordnance, whose duties have been most arduous, but who has performed them with the utmost efficiency; he was with me throughout the day, and of much service to me.

To Major Abbot, of the Bengal Infantry, who, with the troops of the Chirkarree Rajah, protected my baggage and a lengthened siege train, and brought all safely into camp, my best thanks are due.

The arrangements of the Medical Department were excellent, and my thanks are due to Super-intending-Surgeon Davidson, and Field-Surgeon Macfarlane.

I inclose a list of killed and wounded.

I have, &c.,

G. C. WHITLOCK, Major-General, Commanding Saugor Field Division.

No. 34.

Colonel E. Apthorp, Commanding 3rd Madras European Regiment, to Major-General Whitlock, Commanding Saugor Division.

Camp Banda, April 20, 1858.

SIR,

I BEG leave prominently to bring to your notice the gallant conduct of Captain Macintire, and his squadron of Hydrabad Cavalry, which formed part of the advanced guard I had the honor to command in the action which took place yesterday morning.

On approaching within six hundred yards of the enemy's position, I formed my troops into line, and placed Captain Macintire's Ressallah on the right. After advancing a short distance, I found that one or two of the enemy's guns were posted so as to enfilade the infantry as they advanced. I therefore ordered Captain Macintire to charge the guns, which was done in most gallant style. The ground to be got over was most difficult for cavalry, being intersected with deep nullahs filled with the enemy's infantry.

I consider this charge enabled the infantry to reach the enemy, who were at least 6,000 strong, with comparatively trifling loss.

The whole of the guard behaved with the greatest gallantry on this occasion.

I remain, &c.,

E. APTHORP, Colonel,
Commanding 3rd Madras European
Regiment.

,No. 35.

Brigadier W. H. Miller, Commanding Artillery Brigade Saugor Field Force, to the Assistant Adjutant-General, Saugor Field Division.

Camp Banda, April 20, 1858.

SIR,   No. 50.

I HAVE the honor to forward herewith a return of casualties in the Artillery Brigade under my command, at the battle of Banda yesterday.

2. It will be observed, that these are providentially very small, a subject both of astonishment and congratulation, considering the length of time we were under fire, and the obstinate resistance of the enemy, whilst defending their first position, where their artillery was chiefly brought into play against us, and which was both well and rapidly served, although, fortunately for us, their range was generally short, probably owing to the inferiority of their powder.

3. It is a source of no slight gratification to me, to bring particularly to the Major-General's notice, the admirable conduct of the whole of the native portion of the artillery, affording as it did the most ample proof of their attachment to the service and fidelity to the state. Nothing could be finer than the way in which the native troop of Horse Artillery, under Major Brice, emulated the cheerfulness, alacrity and cool courage of the gallant comrades of the European troop under Major Mein.

4. It is not very often, I believe, that opportunities offer to artillerymen of distinguishing themselves in any line other than their own, but some such, having presented themselves yesterday, were eagerly laid hold of by officers and men. Major Lavie cut down one gunner, and disarmed another flying from one of the enemy's guns taken ; Major Barrow and Lieutenant Hennegan, gallantly supported by Lieutenant Blunt, of Her

8 R 2

Majesty's 12th Royal Lancers, with a few of his
men, captured another gun : Serjeant-Major Din-
widdie, F. Troop ; and Serjeant Alford, D. Troop
Horse Artillery (my orderly serjeant) cut down
several of the enemy during the action, and the
Major-General himself, I believe, witnessed the
daring manner in which a gunner of the A. Troop
Horse Artillery (Michael Carroll, General No.
4054) went in on a mutineer, who was fighting
with the resolution of despair, and had for some
time kept several men, both Europeans and natives, at bay.

5. I cannot help wishing, that Captain Palmer's
fine Company of the Royal Artillery, had had
more opportunity of distinguishing themselves, but
the effect on the enemy of the fire they did open
from the 18-pounders and 8-inch howitzers, was
most marked, and did them much credit.

6. The conduct during the action of every
officer and man under my order, merits my unqualified approval and highest admiration ; but I
would beg leave to bring more prominently to the
favourable notice of Major-General Whitlock,
the names of the following officers, viz. :— Major
Lavie, commanding Madras Artillery Division ;
Major Brice, commanding F. Troop, and Major
Mein, commanding A. Troop, Madras Horse Artillery ; Captain Palmer, commanding Royal Artillery ; Lieutenant Pope, commanding No. 1
Madras Horse Field Battery; Brevet-Captain
Holmes, and Lieutenant Hennegan, commanding detachments of their respective troops of
Horse Artillery with the advance ; Major Barrow,
Commissary of Ordnance, and Brevet-Captain
Harrison, acting as my Brigade Major for that
excellent officer Captain Gosling, unfortunately
laid up at present with small-pox.

7. The zeal, kindness, and attention, of the
different medical officers of the Brigade, Doctor

Macfarlane, Field Surgeon, Assistant-Surgeons, Allan and Dunman, of the Madras Horse Artillery, and Assistant-Surgeon Webb, of the Royal Artillery, were most conspicuous, and, as such, well deserve especial mention being made of them,

I have, &c.,

W. H. MILLER, Brigadier,
Commanding Artillery Brigade
Saugor Field Force.

No. 36.

Major T. Oakes, Commanding Cavalry Brigade, Saugor Field Division, to the Assistant-Adjutant General, Saugor and Nerbudda Field Force.

Camp, Banda, April 20, 1858.

SIR,   No. 7.

I HAVE the honour to inform you, for the information of the Major-General commanding the division, that the Ressallah and a troop of the 12th Lancers were detached with the advanced guard, the remainder of the Brigade forming the main column, when the enemy's artillery opened fire (after crossing the dry bed of a river). I advanced the remainder of the Lancers in column of troops, when I saw the Rissallah charging the left flank of the enemy's position. Owing to the bad ground, which was greatly intersected by deep nullahs, the Lancers had to cross in single files, the Ressallah having been temporarily checked by an unexpected fire of grape and musketry from a nullah 20 yards off; before I could bring the Lancers up to support them, they suffered severely. I immediately formed line, and charged the enemy, who did not stand, but dispersed all over the country. The Lancers followed them up for about four miles to the River Kane, cutting up about 300 of them. I then deemed it advisable to re-assemble them, and bring them back to the main column. The troop of Lancers attached to the advanced guard, charged the enemy's right flank, and took a gun.

When we advanced upon the enemy's second position, I detached a troop of Lancers to protect the Artillery on our left flank, and a troop of the Ressallah, the Artillery on the right flank. When the heights were gained, the 12th Lancers advanced, and took a large brass gun pursuing the enemy, who were in full retreat (here Brigadier Miller was cut down, whose life was saved by private Thomas Elliss, 12th Lancers, who speared the rebel.) The retreat of the enemy was covered by some heavy guns on the left of the fort.

I then, in concert with the officer commanding the European Horse Artillery (the fire of the enemy being very heavy, and our guns not being able to tell upon them,) deemed it advisable to retire out of range, and wait until the heavy guns and main column came up.

I beg to bring to the favourable notice of the Major-General, Captain Prior, commanding the 12th Lancers, and Captain Macintire, commanding the 2nd Hydrabad Irregular Horse, who gave me every assistance by strictly carrying out my orders : also my Brigade-Major, Lieutenant Roe, 12th Lancers, who afforded me every help in conveying orders with rapidity.

A nominal roll of killed and wounded is transmitted herewith.'

I have, &c.

T. OAKES, Major, Commanding Cavalry
Brigade Saugor Field Division.

No. 37.

General Return of Killed and Wounded in the Saugor Field Division, under Command of Major-General G. C. Whitlock, Commanding Saugor Field Division, on the 19th of April, 1858.

Camp Banda, April 20, 1858.

Staff—1 field officer, wounded.

A Troop Horse Artillery—1 rank and file, wounded.

F Troop Horse Artillery—1 rank and file, wounded.

Left Wing H.M.'s 12th Lancers—1 subaltern, 1 troop serjeant-major, 1 serjeant, 1 trumpeter, 3 rank and file, 3 troop horses, wounded; 1 European officer's charger killed; 1 troop horse missing.

Squadron Hyderabad Contingent Cavalry—1 native officer, 3 rank and file, 1 native officer's charger, 4 troop horses, killed; 1 subaltern, 1 native officer, 2 serjeants, 11 rank and file, (3 of the wounded since dead), 1 European officer's charger, 6 troop horses, wounded.

3rd Madras European Regiment—1 rank and file, killed; 1 subaltern, 3 rank and file, wounded.

1st Regiment Madras Native Infantry—1 rank and file, wounded.

    Total—1 native officer, 4 rank and file, 1 European officer's charger, 1 native officer's charger, 4 troop horses, killed; 1 field officer, 3 subalterns, 1 native officer, 1 troop serjeant-major, 3 serjeants, 21 rank and file, 1 European officer's charger, 9 troop horses, wounded; 1 troop horse missing.

    G. C. WHITLOCK, Major-General,
      Commanding Saugor Field Division.

No. 38.

Major-General G. C. Whitelock, Commanding Saugor Field Division, to Major-General J. Mansfield, Chief of the Staff, Bengal.

Camp Banda, *April* 30, 1858.

SIR, No. 135.

I MUCH regret I omitted to mention, in my despatch of the 24th instant, the name of the Political Agent for Bundlecund, Major Ellis, who accompanied the force from Punnah, and his services have been most useful to me; he was on the field during the action of the 19th instant, and it was through his valuable intelligence, I became acquainted with the position of the rebels.

I have, &c.

G. C. WHITLOCK, Major-General
Commanding Saugor Field Division.

No. 39.

Allahabad, May 22, 1858.

No. 159 of 1858.

THE Right Honorable the Governor-General is pleased to direct the publication of the following despatch from Brigadier Rowcroft, commanding Sarun Field Force, No. 258, dated 30th April, 1858, forwarding a report from Captain Clerk, commanding detachment at Bustee, of an action with the rebels in that neighbourhood on the 25th April 1858.

No. 40.

Brigadier H. Rowcroft, Commanding Sarun Field Force to Colonel Birch, C.B., Secretary to Government of India, in the Military Department, Allahabad.

Camp Captaingunge, District of Goruckpore,
April 30, 1858.

SIR, No. 258.

I HAVE the honor to submit, for the information of the Right Honorable the Governor-General, a report in original, from Captain Clerk, of the 4th Madras Cavalry, commanding a small detachment at Bustee, of an encounter which he had with a party of rebels in that neighbourhood on the 25th instant, and which appears to have been very ably carried out by Captain Clerk.

2. Mr. Wilson, deputy magistrate, gallantly lead the small detachment of Goorkhas to the attack, and received a bullet through his hat, close over the head.

3. Sheogholam Singh, the leader of the insurgents, who was killed, was a man of considerable influence, and the Commissioner was about to offer a reward of rupees 3,000 for his capture.

4. Captain Clerk has since reported to me, that the loss of the enemy killed and dead of their wounds, has been ascertained to be sixty.

I have, &c ,
H. ROWCROFT, Brigadier,
Commanding Sarun Field Force.

No. 41.

Captain E. Clerk, Commanding Detachment 4th Regiment Madras Light Cavalry, to Captain Morgan, Brigadier Major, Goruckpore Field Force, Amorah.

SIR, *Camp Captaingunge, April 26, 1858.*

I HAVE the honor to report, for the information of Brigadier Rowcroft, commanding the

Goruckpore Field Force, that, having received intelligence yesterday, that a party of rebels, under Sheogholam Sing, had taken up a position at Pyrah, about six miles north of Bustee, on the road to Rudowlee, I proceeded with the force noted in the margin* to attack them.

2. I found the rebels in a large grove of mangoe trees, terminating in a small village surrounded with bamboos, and separated by small spaces of open country from numerous other groves which extended to a considerable distance. Directing the Goorkhas to form line and advance straight on the enemy, I rode round with my troop to intercept their retreat from the further side of the village. At first the enemy formed line at the edge of the grove of trees, but, as the Goorkhas advanced, he retired, keeping up a sharp but ill-directed fire, under the shelter of the bamboos, where he, for some time, made a stout resistance, till driven out by a party of Goorkhas led on by Mr. Wilson, the assistant magistrate. As soon as the rebels appeared in the open, I charged them with my troop, cutting down and wounding several, and driving them till they were completely dispersed in the surrounding groves.

3. As intelligence had been received, that another party of rebels were about five miles from Bustee on the north-west, I did not consider it advisable to follow Sheogholam Sing's party further, and accordingly returned to camp.

4. Our loss is two killed and five wounded, six horses wounded and one missing.

5. I herewith forward a casualty list.

6. The enemy must have numbered from four to five hundred, half of whom however retreated, on the opposite side of the village which I took, without taking any part in the fight. Twenty-

* 49 Sabres; 4th Madras Cavalry; 150 Goorkhas, Barruck Regiment.

four bodies were found lying on the field, and amongst them that of Sheogholam Singh.

I have, &c.,

E. CLERK, Captain,
Commanding Detachment 4th Regiment
Madras Light Cavalry.

No. 43.

Allahabad, May 24, 1858.

No. 162 of 1858.

THE Right Honorable the Governor-General is pleased to direct the publication of the following despatch from the Deputy Adjutant-General of the Army, No. 330 A, dated 19th May 1858, forwarding a report from Brigadier-General J. Jones, C.B., of the relief of the garrison of Shahjehanpore on the 11th May 1858 :—

No. 44.

The Deputy Adjutant-General of the Army to the Secretary to the Government of India, Military Department, with the Governor-General.

Head Quarters, Camp Shahjehanpore,
May 19, 1858.

SIR.   No. 330 A.

I HAVE the honor, by desire of the Commander-in-Chief, to forward copy of a despatch, dated the 16th instant, from Brigadier-General J. Jones, C.B., reporting his relief of the garrison of Shahjehanpore, on the 11th idem ; and I am to beg that, in submitting it to the Right Honorable the Governor-General, you will express to his lordship, his Excellency's entire approval of the

manner in which the duty entrusted to the Brigadier-General has been carried out.

I have, &c.,

H. W. NORMAN, Major,
Deputy Adjutant-General of the Army.

No. 45.

*Brigadier-General John Jones, C.B., Commanding
Shahjehanpore Brigade, to the Deputy Adjutant-
General of the Army.*

Camp Shahjehanpore, May 16*th,* 1858.

SIR,

BY daylight of the morning of the 11th, I
reached the ford, which I was to cross to relieve
the garrison in the jail of Shahjehanpore.

To cover the crossing of the main body, the
cavalry and No. 7 Light Field Battery crossed
over; but, on attempting the passage of the heavy
guns, the ford was found impracticable, on account
of quicksand.

A large body of the enemy's cavalry, crossing
from the city by the bridge of boats, appeared on
my right flank, and threatened the baggage in
the rear.

Under these circumstance, I changed the plan
suggested, and advanced upon the jail, over the
bridge of boats, and through the city.

I therefore withdrew the guns and cavalry,
which had passed the ford, and formed line with
the Infantry, the 60th Rifles and 79th Highlanders being in advance, with the Light Field
Battery, and Mooltanee Cavalry on the right, and
the heavy guns and Carabineers on the left; the
whole supported by the wing of Her Majesty's
82nd, and the 22nd Punjaub Infantry.

When within range, the heavy guns opened on
the enemy's cavalry, which though, led by the

Moulvie in person, was scattered by a few well-directed rounds from the 8-inch howitzers.

The field guns, pushing rapidly on, opened with effect as the enemy retreated across the bridge.

Having swept this bank clear, the heavy guns were moved close to the head of the bridge, and the town I shelled for two hours.

The fire was principally directed on the fort, and it had the effect of setting the city on fire in several places.

When I had reason to believe that the place was abandoned by the enemy, I directed Colonel the Honorable Percy Herbert, with the wing of the 82nd Regiment, and two guns, to advance up the street, and occupy the fort and the head of the stone bridge on the other side of the town, which was effected without opposition.

These points being secured, and the troops refreshed by the halt under a tope of trees, I advanced with the 60th and 79th, the four light guns and the Carabineers.

I had previously detached Captain Cureton, with the Mooltanee Cavalry across by the ford I attempted in the morning, for the purpose of occupying the attention of the enemy, while I passed through the town, and came up in their rear.

He found, on approaching the jail, that the enemy had moved, and was able to open a communication with Colonel Hale.

No opposition was made to my passage through the streets, but, on debouching into the open country, the enemy's cavalry was seen in swarms. They were dispersed by the fire of the skirmishers, and retreated towards Mohumdee.

Major Bickerstaff led the wing he commands of the Carabineers in pursuit; and, crossing the nullah, he succeeded in capturing one of the enemy's guns, and cutting up a few of their cavalry.

On my approach, the enemy abandoned his position around the jail, and having effected the relief, I pitched my camp on the parade ground in the vicinity.

I regret to say that the troops suffered very severely from the exposure in accomplishing these important operations.

The brigade marched at 2 o'clock, A.M., and the tents were not pitched till 7 o'clock that evening.

Some men were struck dead by the sun, and several carried into hospital.

The energy with which this trying work was done, and the patience with which the suffering was borne, elicited my highest admiration, and I feel much indebted to the officers, non-commissioned officers, and men of this force.

To Colonel the Honorable Percy Herbert, C.B., 82nd Regiment; Lieutenant-Colonel Taylor, 79th Highlanders; Major Palmer, 60th Rifles; and to Captain Ouseley, 22nd Punjaub Infantry, my thanks are due. Also to Major Bickerstaff, commanding a wing of the Carabineers; and Captain Cureton, of the Mooltanee Cavalry; Captain Austin, Artillery; and to Lieutenant Stubbs, in charge of the heavy guns.

The members of my Staff, whom I have, on several occasions, mentioned individually, showed their usual energy and cheerful endurance, and I am much indebted to them all.

I enclose a list of the casualties, and a statement of the gun captured.

I have, &c.,

JOHN JONES, Brigadier-General,

Commanding Shahjehanpore Brigade.

No. 46.

Return of Killed and Wounded which took pl ce in the Shahjehanpore Brigade, in action with the Enemy, on the 11th of May, 1858, at Shahjehanpore.

Camp Shahjehanpore, May 16, 1858.

1st Battalion 60th Royal Rifles—1 non-commissioned officer, 1 rank and file, killed.

Left Wing H.M.'s 6th Dragoon Guards—1 horse wounded.

Mooltanee Regiment of Cavalry—1 non-commissioned officer, 1 rank and file, 2 horses, wounded.

Total—1 European non-commissioned officer, 1 rank and file, killed ; 1 native non-commissioned officer, 1 rank and file, and 3 horses, wounded.

JOHN JONES, Brigadier-General,
Commanding Shahjehanpore Brigade.

No. 48.

Allahabad, May 25, 1858.

No. 164 of 1858.

THE Right Honorable the Governor-General is pleased to publish, for general information, the following despatch from the Deputy-Adjutant-General of the Army, dated 13th May, 1858, forwarding a report of the operations of the column under the command of Brigadier-General J. Jones, C.B., commanding Roorkee Field Force, against a body of rebels, on the 21st April, 1858, near Nuggeenah.

The Governor-General offers his best thanks to General Jones, and his acknowledgments to the officers and men engaged, for the good service rendered in these operations.

No. 49.

Brigadier-General J. Jones, C.B., commanding Roorkee Field Force, to the Deputy-Adjutant-General of the Army.

Camp, Noorpoor, April 23, 1858.

SIR,

ON the 20th instant, I forwarded from Nujee-babad, a statement of the operations of the column under my command to the 19th April, and I now proceed from that date to inform his Excellency of the subsequent events.

On the 20th instant the heavy guns arrived at camp, and information reached me that the rebels from Durranuggur, 6,000 strong, had marched to Nuggeenah, and there been joined by the nephews of the Nujeebabad Nawab, with their followers and guns.

I moved early on the 21st, and crossed the canal which fronts the town of Nuggeenah by half-past eight A.M. The enemy was then taking up his position. He was late on the ground, and lost the site I conclude he would have chosen. His left thrown forward rested on the canal communicating with the other bank by a bridge, and his line, running at an inclined angle to the canal for between two and three miles, reached a tope of trees which covered his right. He had two brass guns on his left, besides some iron pieces, five opposite the bridge by which I crossed, and others distributed along his front. I observed considerable bodies of cavalry in his line, and I am of opinion from what I saw, and have since heard, that the numbers given by the spies (10,000 infantry and 2,000 cavalry) were not exaggerated.

The squadron 6th Dragoon Guards I placed on the right flank with two guns, and the skirmishers of the advanced guard; the Mooltanee regiment of cavalry were on the left, and the remainder of the field guns were pushed to the front and opened fire ; the infantry were rapidly formed in line, the 60th Rifles and 1st Punjaub in advance, the 17th Punjaub in support ; the 1st Seikh Regiment swept the other bank of the canal ; the enemy having poured a body of troops into our rear by means of the bridge they held.

In this formation, I advanced with the utmost speed : no time was given the enemy to get our range. The 60th rifles and 1st Punjaub Regiment charged the 5 guns, and instantly carried them, while the squadron carabineers, under Captain Bott, captured at the gallop the guns on the enemy's left, one of which had burst on the field.

The rebels, driven from their guns, attempted to retreat into the city, but I rapidly changed front to the right, throwing the left forward at the double, and cutting off their line of retreat, drove them to the left of the town. I afterwards found it had been prepared for defence, barricades having been erected in the streets. Bodies of the rebels sought shelter in walled enclosures, and were there cut to pieces : in one of these nearly two hundred were shot ; and, the town being afterwards entered by the 17th Punjaub Regiment, numbers were there killed and many taken prisoners. I passed round Nuggeenah by the right, and halted in rear of the town ; nothing of the enemy 'was to be seen, they had been scattered in every direction.

The Mooltanee Regiment of cavalry swept round the town by the left, and, moving rapidly in pursuit of the enemy's horse, headed the main body of the fugitives on the principal line of the retreat. Captain Cureton, with great judgment, drew his men together and concealed them in a tope of trees. Six elephants carrying officers of importance among the rebels, accompanied by 13 guns and a body of cavalry and infantry, soon came by; the Mooltanee Regiment charged this body, cutting up the Sowars, and capturing the elephants and guns. The telegraph signaller taken some time ago by the enemy was re-taken here, and was the only person carried by the elephants that escaped death. Captain Cureton led his regiment some miles in pursuit of other parties of fugitives, and left the ground covered with their bodies. In this action the force captured 10 brass guns and 5 of iron, a return of which I have the honor to enclose. It is difficult to estimate accurately the enemy's loss in men, but it could be little less if not quite 800 killed. I am happy to add, that our loss in obtaining such results is trifling. Annexed is a list of the casualties, Lieutenant Gostling being the only officer or British soldier killed.

I forward also a despatch from Brigadier Coke, C.B., and I concur most heartily in what he says of his brigade, and the officers he mentions; my best thanks are due to himself. His gallantry is always conspicuous, and his energy indefatigable. I have to thank Captain Bott for the manner in which he led his squadron 6th Dragoon Guards. To that able and most gallant officer Captain Cureton, commanding the Mooltanee Regiment of Cavalry, I consider some acknowledgment due and I would especially recommend him to the notice of his Excellency, for the manner in which his regiment has behaved on this occasion, and on the 17th instant, for the way in which he led it, and for the capture of the 3 guns and the 6 elephants. I have again to thank Captain Austen, for the style he brought his guns into action, and the admirable fire he kept up.

Brigadier Coke, C.B., has mentioned the gallant manner in which Major Palmer brought the 60th Rifles in their charge up to the guns, and the admirable conduct of that battalion. My best thanks are due to him, and to Major Gordon, commanding the 1st Seikhs, who swept the canal clear of a large body of the enemy ; to Captain Lambert, commanding the 1st Punjaub Regiment for his charge on the guns : and to Captain Larkins, commanding the 17th regiment, who did good service in the town. I have received much assistance from Captain Drummond, commanding Field Engineer, and his subordinates ; also from Surgeon Innes, Field Surgeon, and Captain Carter, Officiating Deputy Commissary General.

I am much indebted to Major Muter, Deputy Assistant Adjutant-General ; to Captain Tedlie, Deputy Assistant Quarter-Master-General ; to Lieutenant Deedes, Aide-de-Camp ; and to Lieutenant Tyler, 20th Native Infantry, Orderly Officer, for their untiring zeal and ability. I have much pleasure in forwarding Captain Cureton's report of the gallant conduct of Mr. Hannah, of the Roorkee College ; and in seconding the application of Brigadier Coke, that this brave young gentleman may obtain a commission for his conduct in the field.

I have, &c.,
JOHN JONES, Brigadier-General,
Commanding Roorkee Field Force.

No. 50.

Lieutenant-Colonel J. Coke, C.B. Commanding Infantry Brigade, to the Deputy Assistant Adjutant-General, Roorkee Field Force.

Camp Dhanpore, April 22, 1858.

SIR,

WITH reference to the attack yesterday, on the rebel force posted in front of the town of Nuggeenah, I have the honor to report, for the information of the Brigadier-General commanding, that, while the force was passing the bridge over the canal, the advanced guard of the 60th Royal Rifles, reported the enemy advancing in our front. I sent an order to the rear, to bring up the Infantry. The Mooltanee Cavalry, Captain Austen's Battery, and the 60th Royal Rifles, had already crossed the above-mentioned bridge.

The artillery, under Captain Austen, moved rapidly to the front, and opened fire in reply to the enemy's advance guns, which were in a grove of trees about nine hundred yards to our front. The 60th Royal Rifles formed line, and advanced steadily to the front. The 1st Punjaub Infantry were formed to their left, and the Mooltanee Cavalry on the left front of the 1st Punjaub Infantry.

Observing the rebel cavalry advance to turn our left, I directed Captain Cureton, commanding the Mooltanee Cavalry, to attack them, and after driving them back to turn the right of the enemy's infantry. The 1st Punjaub Infantry were ordered by me to advance, and take the guns in flank, while the 60th Royal Rifles moved to the front.

These orders were well and rapidly carried out ; the rebels finding their flank completely turned, retreated hastily, abandoning their guns. and were followed up for nearly two miles by the artillery, 60th Royal Rifles, and 1st Punjaub Infantry.

Simultaneously with this move on the left, I sent directions to Major Gordon, commanding 1st Sikh Infantry on the right, to move down both banks of the canal, which were thickly wooded, and full of the rebel infantry. This was carried out in a most satisfactory manner ; and the enemy, defeated at all points, fled rapidly.

The 17th Punjaub Infantry were held in reserve. Soon after our arrival at Nuggeenah, when the pursuit of the infantry had ceased, Captain Larkins was ordered with his corps to clear the city of the rebels. Numbers were killed and taken prisoners; numbers in their retreat threw themselves into large walled gardens near the town, from which but few escaped alive.

It is quite unnecessary for me to say anything in praise of the 60th Royal Rifles, who have always distinguished themselves. On the 17th and 22nd instant they proved themselves to be the perfection of light infantry.

My thanks are due to Major Palmer, commanding the 60th Royal Rifles; Major Gordon, commanding 1st Sikh Infantry; Captain Lambert, commanding 1st Punjaub Infantry; and Captain Larkins, commanding the 17th Punjaub Infantry; who carried out their orders most efficiently.

Captain Anderson, Major of Brigade, has shown himself on this and all other occasions a most efficient staff officer.

Captain Parrott, of the Haupper Stud, attached to the camp, and Captain Smith, of the Pathan Horse, acted as my orderly officers; I am much obliged to them for their exertions.

I beg to forward herewith a report from Captain Cureton, which was forwarded at my request, of the conduct of a young student of the Roorkee College, in the hopes that his gallant conduct may lead to his advancement, or to his obtaining a commission, of which he appears most deserving.

I have, &c.,

JOHN COKE, Lieutenant-Colonel,
Commanding Infantry Brigade.

No. 51.

Captain Charles Cureton, commanding the Mooltanee Regiment of Cavalry, to Brigadier Coke, C.B., commanding the Infantry Brigade.

SIR,   *Camp, Dhanpore, April 22, 1858.*

WHEN ordered by you to advance and outflank the enemy yesterday morning, I was joined by a young gentleman, who I thought was a young officer, but who I have since learnt was Mr. Hannah, of the Roorkee College. He begged permission to join my regiment as a volunteer, which I gladly assented to.

During the charge and pursuit, Mr. Hannah behaved with great gallantry; but I regret exceedingly to say that he has received two dangerous wounds. I trust he will soon recover from these, and that he will not be ultimately a sufferer for his distinguished conduct.

I have, &c.,
CHARLES CURETON, Captain,
Commanding the Mooltanee Regiment
of Cavalry.

No. 52.

Return of Killed and Wounded which took place in the Roorkee Field Force, in action with the Enemy, on the 21st of April, 1858, at Nuggeenah.

Camp Noorpore, April 23, 1858.

Detachment of 6th Carabineers—1 rank and file, 6 horses, wounded; 2 horses, killed; 1 horse, missing.

Mooltanee Horse—1 European commissioned officer, killed; 1 European commissioned officer, 4 native commissioned officers, 3 native non-commissioned officers, 23 rank and file, and 38 horses, wounded; 20 horses, missing.

Cavalry attached to 1st Punjaub Infantry—1 rank and file, killed; 1 rank and file, wounded; 2 rank and file, missing; 2 horses, killed.

1st Battalion 60th Royal Rifles—4 rank and file, wounded.

1st Regiment Seikh Infantry—3 rank and file, wounded.

1st Regiment Paunjaub Infantry—1 native non-
commissioned officer, missing.

Total—1 European commissioned officer,
killed ; 1 European commissioned officer, 5
. rank and file, wounded ; 1 native rank and
file, killed ; 4 native commissioned officers,
3 non commissioned officers, 27 rank and
file, wounded ; 1 non-commissioned officer,
2 rank and file, missing ; 4 horses, killed ;
44 wounded ; 21 missing.

> JOHN JONES, Brigadier-General,
> Commanding Roorkee Field Force.

No. 53.

Names of Officers Killed or Wounded.

Lieutenant Gostling, 5th Cavalry, attached to
Mooltanee Regiment of Cavalry, killed.
Lieutenant Williams, Mooltanee Regiment of
Cavalry, contusion.

No. 55.

Allahabad, May 26, 1858.

No 166 of 1858.

THE Right Honorable the Governor-General
is pleased to direct the publication of the following despatch from the Deputy Adjutant-
General of the Army, dated 18th May, 1858, forwarding a report of the operations of the Shahjehanpore Brigade, under the command of Brigadier-
General Jones, C.B., against the enemy, on the
15th instant :—

No. 56.

Major D. D. Muter, Deputy Assistant Adjutant-General, Shahjehanpore Brigade, to the Chief of the Staff.

Camp, Shahjehanpore, May 15, 1858.

SIR,

I AM directed by Brigadier-General Jones, commanding Shahjehanpore Brigade, to inform you that the enemy, led by the Moulvie, attacked his position, at Shahjehanpore, at 12 o'clock this day.

The intelligence was, that the rebels in great force would attack us at daylight, and in three columns. The Brigadier-General therefore took up his position at 2 o'clock, A.M. The enemy did not attack till 12 o'clock, when he opened fire from the ridge that runs along the left bank of the nullah on the Mohumdee side of Shahjehanpore. His guns were too far to produce any effect, but his cavalry, of which he had a very large force, crossed this nullah a few miles up, and charged on our guns with considerable loss to themselves, but none to us. The troops will bivouac to-night on the ground they occupy.

The enemy have not all withdrawn, and the Brigadier-General remains out in the field. He has directed me to write and forward this express.

Had the information been positive, something might have been done to capture the rebels' guns, but an attack on the city and on the left flank was looked for, and cautious measures adopted.

A strong patrol of Mooltanee cavalry have crossed the nullah, and the Brigadier-General awaits intelligence of the enemy's movements.

I have, &c.,

D. D. MUTER, Major,
Deputy Assistant Adjutant-General,
Shahjehanpore Brigade.

No. 57.

Brigadier-General John Jones, C.B., Commanding Shahjehanpore Brigade, to the Chief of the Staff.

Camp, Shahjehanpore, May 16, 1858.

SIR,

IN continuation of the express of yesterday, I have to inform you, that the troops have this morning been withdrawn to camp.

The enemy is said to have retreated to Mohumdee. His loss is reported as considerable. A chief of importance is among the killed, but it has not yet been ascertained who he is.

There can be no doubt that several of the chief rebels led the attack yesterday, and it is the general opinion that they have been much disheartened by the result.

Further intelligence will be sent express when it is received by me, and I have considerable bodies of cavalry out.

As far as I can make out, the enemy opened with 8 guns.

I have, &c.,

JOHN JONES, Brigadier-General,
Commanding Shahjehanpore Brigade.

No. 58.

Brigadier Stuart, Commanding 1st Brigade Central India Field Force, to the Assistant Adjutant-General Central India Field Force.

Camp Musjed Ghat, en route to Jhansi, March 21, 1858.

No. 85.

FOR the information of the Major-General commanding Central India Field Force, I have the honour to forward documents, and to report the proceedings of his brigade in connection with the capture of the fort of Chandairee.

2. The 1st Brigade Central India Field Force, strength as per margin,* reached Khoorassa on the left bank of the river Our, about eight miles distant from the Fort of Chandairee on the 5th March, and, having crossed the river without opposition, encamped there; in the course of that afternoon Major Gall, commanding Left Wing Her Majesty's 14th Light Dragoons, accompanied by Captain Fenwick, Field Engineer, and Captain Keatinge, Political Assistant, having proceeded on a reconnoissance, ¦was fired on by a picket of the enemy at the Khooshee Ka Mahall, an old palace, about a mile distant from the Fort of Chandairee; on the morning of the 6th March the brigade marched, and, on arriving at the palace in question, found that the picket which occupied it the preceding day had fallen back upon a strong line of masonry defences which cover the Futtiabad outskirt of the town, and, having been reinforced, held the same in strength; I immediately attacked them, having previously detached two bodies of infantry to turn both flanks of their works. The left flank attack, though made over most difficult ground, succeeded admirably, and the enemy commenced to retreat. On moving up the main body of the brigade to the Futtiabad gate, which was about the centre of the position, I found that the enemy had all fled precipitately to

* Left wing Her Majesty's 14th Light Dragoons, 110 rank and file; 3rd Regiment C. H. C., 183 do.; No. 6 Field Battery Royal Artillery, 109 do.; No. 4 Light Field Battery, 40 do.; 21st Company Royal Engineers, 103 do.; 2nd Company Bombay Sappers and Miners, 50 do.; Her Majesty's 86th Regiment, 517 do. Of these 318 joined with head-quarters on the 16th March; detachment 3rd European' Regiment, 64 do.; 25th Regiment Native Infantry, 818 do., including 150 recruits; total 1,989 rank and file.

the fort; accordingly I encamped the brigade near to the gate in question, until a plan of operations against the fort should be determined on. On the afternoon of that day Captain Fenwick, Field Engineer, in company with Captain Keatinge, Political Assistant, made a reconnoissance, and their report determined me on moving the brigade the next morning near to the village of Ramnuggur, possession of which they had already secured. On the morning of the 7th March, the brigade marched in two columns, dislodging the Kutty-ghatty outpost of the enemy and clearing the whole approach to that part of the fort against which the Field Engineer recommended that breaching operations should be commenced. The description of the Fort of Chandairee and the Field Engineer's journal of the siege herewith transmitted, will explain to the Major-General the difficulties we had to encounter, not the least of which was experienced in conveying the siege pieces to the batteries. From the 8th to the 16th March, siege operations were steadily carried on, particulars of which will be found in the journal already referred to. These operations extended over a longer period than was at first anticipated; but I beg to assure the Major-General that the delay in bringing matters to an issue was quite unavoidable. On the afternoon of the 16th March, I received a favourable report of the breach from the Field Engineer, and immediately ordered that the assault should take place at daybreak the following morning, 17th March, and that the troops should attack in the order named in the margin.*

* Advance Party—50 rank and file Her Majesty's 86th Regiment, under an officer; 50 rank and file 25th Regiment Native Infantry, under an officer, the senior to command the whole. Column of Assault—50 rank and file 21st Company Royal Engineers, under an officer, carrying ladders and various implements; Her Majesty's 86th Regi-

I also arranged that another attack to our left by escalade should be at the same time made by the troops marginally noted under command of Captain Little, 25th Regiment Native Infantry, at the re-entering angle of the fort opposite to the Khutty-ghetty pass. Captain Little, I should mention, had been in command of an outpost at this pass from the time of our arrival before the fort, and had therefore had good opportunities of studying the ground and making his arrangements. I also caused another diversion in our favour to be made by a small body of cavalry under command of Lieutenant Gowan, Her Majesty's 14th Light Dragoons, who moved out to the eastward of the fort, and opened a brisk fire when the assault took place, shortly after 5 A.M. of the 17th March, the troops having formed up near the breaching battery with a steadiness and silence which no one could fail to appreciate. I gave the precon-certed signal for the assault, viz.: a salvo from all the siege pieces in position, which had been care-fully laid for the head of the breach and the enemy's bastions. The storming party, com-manded by Lieutenant Jerome, Her Majesty's 86th Regiment, and accompanied by Lieutenant Forbes, 25th Regiment Native Infantry; Lieu-tenant Gossett, Assistant Field Engineer; and Cap-tain Keatinge, Political Assistant, moved steadily to the front, received a volley at the foot of the

ment and 25th Regiment Native Infantry, column of sec-tions right in front. Reserve—50 rank and file 21st Com-pany Royal Engineers; 2nd Company Bombay Sappers and Miners; 30 rank and file Her Majesty's 86th Regiment, under an officer; 70 rank and file 25th Regiment, under an officer, the senior to command. Captain Little's Column.—100 rank and file Her Majesty's 86th Regiment, under Lieu-tenant Jerome; 100 rank and file 25th Regiment Native Infantry, under Lieutenant Mills; 13 rank and file 2nd Company Bombay Sappers and Miners, under Lieutenant Gordon, Assistant Field Engineer.

breach, and with a cheer only for a reply, dashed gallantly up it. They were warmly received by the enemy, but, resolutely driving all before them at the point of the bayonet, they made good the assault, and their cheers soon told the whole brigade how their brave conduct had been rewarded. The column of assault quickly followed them, and, moving steadily across the fort, completely cleared that part of it of the enemy who fled most precipitately, throwing themselves headlong from the walls in many instances. Line was then formed to the left, and with three companies of Her Majesty's 86th Regiment in skirmishing order, their line being prolonged to the right flank by skirmishers, 25th Regiment Native Infantry; also three companies, Her Majesty's 86th Regiment, as supports, and the 25th Regiment Native Infantry as reserve. The brigade swept down the plateau of the fort, which is of some extent. On nearing the palace, where it was expected some stand would be made, a gun opened on the line, but the Grenadiers of Her Majesty's 86th Regiment rushed to the front and instantly took it. The remainder of the enemy then retreated from the fort in precipitate flight, in the direction by which I had every reason to believe they would encounter Captain Abbott's cavalry. The miscarriage, however, of my letter to Captain Abbott on the previous evening admitted of their escape by that road, to my very great regret. As the Major-General is aware, the small body of cavalry at my disposal, and the difficult nature of the country round Chandairee for cavalry, enabled me only to hold them in readiness to pursue as might be practicable. As, however, the enemy scattered in every direction, mostly by twos and threes, into thick jungle and hilly ground, except in the direction by which I anticipated Captain Abbott would fall in with them, I had no opportunity of using my cavalry in pursuit.

3. I am happy to be able to state that the left attack on the fort of Chandairee, under the command of Captain Little, 25th Regiment Native Infantry, supported by Lieutenant Lewis, Her Majesty's 16th Regiment, Lieutenant Mills, 25th Regiment Native Infantry, and Lieutenant Gordon, Assistant Engineer, was admirably carried out, and I beg to forward Captain Little's report, by which the Major-General will be able to see how gallantly it was conducted, and how well all the troops concerned in it behaved.

4. I regret to have to report the death of Lieutenant Moresby, Royal Artillery, a most promising young officer, who was killed at the breaching battery on the 11th March, whilst most gallantly performing his duty; the loss in Her Majesty's 86th Regiment, as the Major-General will perceive, has been severe; 7 men of this regiment were unfortunately killed or wounded by the enemy exploding a magazine, regardless of their own fate. It has not been in my power to ascertain the loss of the enemy during these operations; after the fort came into our possession, 87 of their bodies were found and buried ; many newly made graves were also observable. I am therefore of opinion that their losses were much heavier than I at first anticipated.

5. According to instruction received, the fort of Chandairee has been, as much as possible, dismantled, the guns and munitions of war have been disposed of as directed, also the stores of grain, &c., and I have made over the fort to the charge of the Sir-Sooba of H. H. Scindia.

6. I beg, in conclusion, to place on record how much I have been indebted to Captain Keatinge, Bombay Artillery, and Assistant to the Agent of

the Governor-General for Central India, throughout these operations. This officer joined me at Ragooghur, and proved of the very greatest assistance to me in gaining information as to the enemy's movements, and also in making me acquainted with all particulars as to the defences of the fort of Chandairee; so anxious was he to verify his information that, on two occasions, immediately before the assault, he examined the intermediate ground, which is of a very difficult nature, from the breaching battery to the very foot of the breach. The knowledge thus gained led him to volunteer to assist in guiding the storming-party, and I deeply grieve to add that he fell dangerously wounded at the head of the breach, foremost amongst the foremost of the stormers.

7. To the officers of my staff my best thanks are due. Captain Fenwick, Field Engineer, carried out the onerous duties entrusted to him with the greatest skill and with the most untiring zeal and energy; he was ably seconded by his assistants, Lieutenants Gossett, Webber, Festing, and Gordon; Captain Coley, Major of Brigade; Captain Bacon, Deputy Assistant Quartermaster-General; Lieutenant Loury, Deputy Commissary of Ordnance, and Lieutenant Henry, Sub-Assistant Commissary-General, were most unremitting in their exertions in their several departments. Surgeon Mackenzie, Staff Surgeon, displayed his usual care and attention in the arrangements as to the Field Hospital, and with the greatest success, for the prompt and ready aid afforded to the wounded was remarked by all; the Rev. W. H. Schwabe, Field Chaplain, also availed himself of every opportunity most earnestly to discharge his duties. I beg also to bring to the notice of the Major-General the excellent and gallant conduct of all the officers and men of this brigade. Captain Ommanney, Royal Artillery, Commandant of

Artillery, and Captain Woollcombe, commanding ⅘ Artillery, distinguished themselves on all occasions by the capital artillery practice directed against the fort; these officers and the officers and men under their command were most unwearied in their exertions, which extended over a protracted period. Lieutenant Edwards, commanding 21st Company Royal Engineers, and Lieutenant Meiklejohn, commanding 2nd Company Bombay Sappers and Minèrs, and their men, carried out the works intrusted to them in the most indefatigable manner. Major Gall, commanding left wing of Her Majesty's 14th Light Dragoons, and his officers and men, were continually employed in reconnoissances in the neighbourhood of Chandairee, during the time this brigade was before the fort. These were most ably conducted by Major Gall, with whom Lieutenant Clerk, commanding 3rd Regiment C. H. C. and his men most zealously co-operated. On the occasion of the assault on the fort of Chandairee nothing could exceed the brilliant courage displayed by both officers and men of Her Majesty's 86th Regiment and 25th Regiment Native Infantry. Colonel Louth, commanding the former, and Major Robertson the latter regiment, led their men in the most gallant manner, and I felt that, with such troops and so commanded, success, however we might be opposed, was certain. I cannot conclude this despatch without bringing to the notice of the Major-General how much I am indebted to Captain Little, 25th Regiment Native Infantry, and the officers and men who accompanied him, for the very spirited and successful assault by escalade on the fort of Chandairee, which I have called the left attack. On this occasion, Lieutenant Lewis reports that Private Sheahan, Her Majesty's 86th Regiment, saved his life, by bayonnetting one of the enemy, who took the Lieutenant at a disadvantage. Captain Little also reports that Havildar Rambaz Khan and Private Shaik Lall, of the 25th Regiment of Native Infantry, accompanied him on a reconnoissance on the evening preceding the assault, and, behaving with great coolness and daring, greatly assisted him in discovering the best point at which to make his attack.

I have, &c.

C. S. STUART, Brigadier,
Commanding 1st Brigade, Central India
Field Force.

P.S. I beg to be allowed to add to my report that, on the morning of the assault on the fort, Captain Daun, commanding detachment, 3rd European Regiment, with his men, was placed in charge of the Kattee Ghatty outpost, and performed the duty entrusted to him in a most satisfactory manner.

C. S. STUART; Brigadier,
Commanding 1st Brigade Central India
Field Force.

No. 59.

Captain A. B. Little, 25th Regiment Native Infantry, Commanding left Attack on Fort of Chandairee, to the Brigade Major, 1st Brigade, Central India Field Force.

Camp before Chandairee, March 17, 1858.

SIR,

I DO myself the honor to report, for the information of the Brigadier commanding 1st Brigade Central India Field Force, that, agreeably to his instructions, I proceeded with my detachment as

per margin,* through the Kattee Ghatee. Shortly
after the brigade had moved past my post this
morning, I led my men as quietly as possible towards the point I had decided on attacking, but
had not reached the lower wall between the round
bastion and the "corner" one, opposite our mortar
battery, when we were challenged by the sentry of
the enemy on the round bastion, and fire immediately opened from their guns and matchlocks; we,
however, continued to advance steadily, and had
just reached the wall, when the signal for assault
was fired. I saw, to my joy, that the wall was
broken down, and no impediment except very rugged and bushy ground was between us and the
wall of the fort itself, and, hearing the cheers of
the column assaulting at the breach, with a yell,
we charged, and in a few minutes many of us had,
with each other's assistance, and without the aid
of ladders, scaled the wall; the ladders were however soon up, and the remainder of my detachment also gained the fort. The round bastion
having been taken on our left, we swept to our
right, and, driving the enemy before us, carried
with slight opposition the next (square) bastion.
We here fell in with some of the enemy (who
were flying before our troops, who had entered at
the breach), many of whom were killed. Seeing
the next or "corner" bastion, as I have above
designated it, had not been taken by our men,
I could not resist the temptation of taking it also,
though exceeding the orders I had received. In
getting some men together with a rush, the object
was soon gained. We then advanced towards the

* 100 rank and file Her Majesty's 86th Regiment, under
command of Lieutenant Lewis ; 13 Bombay Sappers and
Miners, under Lieutenant Gordon, Assistant Field Engineer; 100 Rank and File, 25th Regiment Native Infantry,
under Lieutenant Miles.

palace (taking the gate-way on our left), and were then joined by the whole assaulting column, &c.

The conduct of all under my command, both Europeans and Natives, was admirable, and, where all behaved so well, it would be difficult to bring any one prominently to notice. I cannot, however, conclude my report without saying I consider Havildar Rambaz Khan and Private Shaikh Loll, Light Company 25th Regiment Native Infantry, are deserving of much praise, as by their aid I was in a great measure guided to the point I was anxious to gain ; these two men had, on the night of the 15th instant, attended me on a reconnoissance in the same direction, and did good service. I trust they will meet with some mark of approval of the good service done by them.

Our loss this morning was, I am sorry to say, 1 private 86th killed, and 8 wounded.

I have, &c.,

A. B. LITTLE, Captain, 25th Regiment Native Infantry, Commanding Left Assault on Fort Chandairee.

No. 61.

From the Nominal Roll of Officers and Men of the 1st Brigade Central India Field Force Killed and Wounded in the Operations before and during the day of Assault and Capture of the Fort of Chandairee.

Political Agent, and Captain Bombay Artillery, R. H. Keating, Staff, March 17, 1858, dangerously wounded.

Lieutenant Richard Moresby, Royal Artillery, March 11, killed.

Lieutenant and Adjutant H. S. Cochrane, H.M.'s 86th Regiment, March 17, slightly wounded.

Lieutenant R. F. Lewis, H.M.'s 86th Regiment, March 17, slightly wounded.

Serjeant-Major Jerome Murphy, H.M.'s 86th Regiment, March 17, slightly wounded.

Lieutenant John Forbes, 25th Bombay Native Infantry, March 17, slightly wounded.

Abstract.

Staff—1 wounded.

Royal Artillery—1 killed ; 1 wounded.

Royal Engineers—1 wounded.

¼ Bombay Artillery—1 wounded.

Details attached to the Siege Train—2 wounded.

2nd Company Bombay Sappers and Miners—1 wounded.

Her Majesty's 86th Regiment—1 killed, 18 wounded, 2 since dead.

25th Regiment Bombay Native Infantry—3 wounded.

Total—2 killed, 28 wounded.

W. MACKENZIE, M.D.,
Staff-Surgeon, 1st Brigade, C.I. Field Force.
Camp, Chandairee, March 18, 1858.

No. 62.

Major-General Sir Hugh Rose, K.C.B., to the Adjutant-General of the Bombay Army.

SIR,   Camp, *Goolowlie, May* 17, 1858.

WHILST I was detained at Jhansie by the necessity of protecting it against the Kotah rebels and the late Chandairee garrison, who made an incursion on the road from Jhansie to Goonah, I sent Major Orr, as I have already had the honor to report, across the Betwa to clear Mhow, on the road from Jhansie to Chirkaree, where rebels were said to have reassembled, with orders to proceed northwards to Goorseraie, of which district the chief is our ally, gain all possible information from him, and move against Kotra, an important ford across the Betwa, said to be occupied by rebels, co-operating with Major Gall, 14th Light Dragoons, whom I had sent along the road from Jhansie to Calpee, with the force detailed in the margin,* to gain information respecting the enemy, the most contradictory accounts existing as to their movements and number. When I moved from Calpee, I was to take up Major Orr's and Major Gall's force.

I wished to clear Kotra and the circumjacent line of the Betwa, because I apprehended that the rajahs of Banpore and Shahgur would either hurry on and annoy my right flank or rear as I advanced to Calpee, or double back across the Betwa and again create troubles and disorders in the south of Bundlecund, the Chandairee, and Shahgur districts. Major Orr found no enemy in Mhow, but between Goorserai and the Betwa he came upon a fort occupied by the rebels; some of them escaped, the remainder, 40 in number, surrendered, with 3 guns. He found that Kotra at that time was occupied by Goorserai troops, not by rebels. Major Orr marched to the ford of Erich, across the Betwa, to the west of Kotra, and entered into communication with Major Gall, who advanced as far as Poorh, and ascertained that the enemy in force in that town intended to oppose my advance to Calpee.

Major Gall, in order better to observe the enemy, had a jemadar's party of Hydrabad Cavalry at Lohare, a village and mud-fort, about 8 miles from Poorh, garrisoned by some 70 or 80 men of the rajah of Sumbter, who is said to be our ally. These men betrayed the party of Hydrabad cavalry to the rebel cavalry, in Koonch, in the basest way, and the former with great difficulty cut their way through

* 3 guns, Bengal Artillery; 1 squadron, 14th Light Dragoons; 3rd Hydrabad Cavalry.

their assailants, with the loss of a man killed, all their baggage, and 3 or 4 camp followers.

I sent Major Gall, on my arrival at Poorh, with the party detailed in the margin.* to punish the treacherous garrison of Lohare, who, it turned out afterwards, were, if not all, the greater part, disguised sepoys of the 12th Regiment Bengal Native Infantry, quantities of their accoutrements' being found in the fort.

I have the honor to enclose copy of the report of Major Gall of the capture of Lohare ; and, in seconding strongly the recommendation of the officers and men who behaved with so much gallantry, I beg to bring to the notice of his Excellency the Commander-in-Chief, that this is not the first occasion on which Major Gall has done good service. His daring, combined with great intelligence, and indefatigable zeal, have induced me to employ him frequently on reconnoissances and duties belonging especially to light cavalry. On all these occasions Major Gall has shown how important are the duties of this arm, and how thoroughly he understands them.

I have, &c,

HUGH ROSE, Major-General,

Commanding Central India Field Force.

No. 63.

Major R. H. Gall, Commanding Field Force Detachment, to the Chief of the Staff, Central India Field Force.

SIR,   *Camp, Poorh, May 5, 1858.*

I HAVE the honor to report, for the information of the Major-General, commanding Central

---

* 4 guns Royal Artillery; 1 squadron 14th Light Dragoons; 100 sabres Hydrabad Cavalry; left wing 3rd Bengal European Regiment; left wing 25th Regiment Native Infantry; 50 Bombay Sappers.

India Field Force, that, in pursuance of his instructions, I marched with the force, as per margin,* at 2 A.M. on the 2nd instant, upon the fort of Loharee, about nine miles distant from, and to the north-west of, Poorh.

My cavalry, rapidly pushed forward, had completed the investment of the place soon after daybreak, and my main body was halted on the plain to the east of the fort, and within cannon-shot of it, at half-past 6 o'clock.

As I passed Girsa, I sent a party of the 3rd Regiment Hydrabad Cavalry, under a Duffedar, to Khullea, a fort reported to be be occupied by the enemy, and to my right, as I advanced, with orders to watch any hostile movement that might be made from that quarter.

When the force halted, I rode, accompanied by Captain Baigill, Deputy Assistant Quartermaster General, Central India Field Force, and Guneshe Lall, a native official in the service of the Governor-General's agent for Central India, through the village of Loharee, up to the walls of the fort, and sent Guneshee Lall to the main gateway with directions to summon the killedar of the place to surrender at discretion. A man soon after made his appearance, whom I supposed to be the killedar, but he was not, though he did by my orders summon the garrison to surrender; they paid no attention to him.

Discovering, however, that Munshur Sing was himself in the fort, I sent Guneshee Lall to summon him.

Munshur Sing delayed obeying my summons for a long time, but at last he came out with a small

* 1 squadron 14th Light Dragoons, 120; Hydrabad Cavalry, 100; 4 guns, Royal Artillery, under Captain Field; left wing 3rd Europeans; left wing 25th Bombay Native Infantry; 20 Sappers, Bombay.

retinue and gave up his sword, and his retinue laid down their arms.

To Munshur Sing I returned his sword at his own urgent request; at the same time, I called upon him to order out his garrison and direct them to lay down their arms. To the best of my belief he endeavoured to induce them to do so, but they refused. Munshur Sing had clearly no control over them whatever.

All my own efforts failing to induce the garrison to give themselves up, I proceeded to make my dispositions for attack, my skirmishers advancing through the village until they had reached some low mud enclosures, beyond which was an open space between it and the fort, about 150 yards in extent. I placed two guns on the Khullea road, and a howitzer and one gun opposite a guardhouse that stands outside of, and on the eastern side of, the fort.

The fort and village of Loharee are situated in an extensive level plain; the village being separated from the fort by the clear space of ground above alluded to.

The little fort itself is square, and built of mud and sun-burnt bricks. The square is flanked by round towers at the corners; it has a ditch and a second line of works outside the ditch, and the length of the interior side is about 100 yards.

A company of the 3rd Europeans (Bombay) crossed the open space between the village and fort without opposition, and established themselves in the guard-house close to the ditch.

Two of the fort-gates were opened for us by Lieutenant Armstrong, commanding the left wing of the Europeans. They were undefended, the garrison having retired within a third which was closed, the enemy taking post behind it.

The last of several summonses, accompanied by a threat that, if not obeyed, I would destroy the fort and the garrison too, having failed to cause a single man to come out and lay down his arms, I directed Captain Field, Royal Artillery, to open fire with two 9-pounders and a 24-pounder howitzer on a building at the summit, whence the men of the 3rd Bombay Europeans might have been seriously annoyed by the sepoys, who were collecting there.

Captain Field continued firing on various parts of the work, wherever the enemy showed themselves in any numbers; and the enemy replied to my fire with matchlocks, and with a 9-pounder brass gun, that fired grape and round shot alternately upon the dragoons in the plain and all who came near a well, commanded by the bastion on which it stood.

Lieutenant Bonus, of the Bombay Engineers, after a very close reconnoissance, had reported to me the extreme difficulty of taking the place by escalade. Nothing then remained, in my opinon, but to blow open the third gate with a bag of gunpower, and carry the fort by storm. By good luck a gunsmith's shop had been discovered in the village, and in it an old pair of forge bellows. Lieutenant Bonus borrowing fifty pounds of powder from the artillery, soon converted this into a very efficient powder-bag.

The distribution for the assault was as follows.

Twenty-five files of the 3rd Europeans, under Lieutenants Armstrong and Donne and Ensign Newport, were told off as a storming party; an equal number of the 25th Bombay Native Infantry, under Lieutenant Rose of that regiment, was formed in support.

The storming party and support occupied the gateways that were already in our possession; twenty-five files of the Bombay Europeans and fifty files of the 25th were in reserve behind the guard-house.

The remainder of both detachments were so disposed as to afford support to the guns, and also to meet any attempt at escape from the fort into the village.

A false attack with three scaling ladders, under the superintendence of Lieutenant Fenwick, drew off the attention of a few of the garrison for a short time to the south side, and was not without its use.

When the powder-bag was filled, Lieutenant Bonus, under the cover of a sharp fire from the 3rd Europeans, placed it in front of the closed gate—a strong wooden one with iron spikes,—the small piece of portfire was lighted, and the firing party withdrew. After about a minute and a half the explosion took place. The gate was demolished, and the stormers under Lieutenants Armstrong and Donne and Ensign Newport, whom I accompanied, rushed in through the smoke, and almost immediately met the enemy face to face at a fourth gateway at right angles to the third, and from which a very narrow curved passage with a wall of seven feet in height on either side led to where the garrison was assembled, and whence they rushed, getting down sword in hand and firing matchlocks.

A desperate combat commenced, and as the stormers, so well led, advanced, they were assailed by a shower of stones and brickbats from above, as well as by men who cut, and stabbed, and shot at them from the walls on either side as they went by; the enemy were giving way when a cloth full of loose powder, and burning, was dropped from above into the midst of the crowded stormers who, thrown into some confusion, fell back to avoid the explosion, which not taking place immediately, was harmless; the enemy following their advantage, came close up to the bayonets of the Europeans and dealt sword-cuts at them, but were repulsed.

A third time Lieutenant Donne and Ensign Newport led on their men with daring valour into the very midst of the enemy, from whom, I regret to say, these noble young men received some very severe wounds whilst fighting hand to hand, yet, wounded as they were, they beat off their assailants, and their retreat was protected by the bayonets of their men. Lieutenant Armstrong could give them no assistance, as he had just been knocked down by a blow on the head from a brickbat, which stunned him for a time. Matters were becoming serious, as the enemy pressed boldly down to the fourth gateway, in which, however, they were not permitted to gain a footing.

Lieutenant Rose now came opportunely to the front, and the fight was continued in the narrow lane until, with a final shout and charge, the Europeans with some of the 25th Native Infantry, fairly broke and drove their foe before them to our right, along what I can only describe as an uncovered way passing round the walls of the fort, but, at less than fifty yards beyond the first corner, turned the fugitives, rallied behind two trees, and firing off their matchlocks actually advanced again; beneath the trees a bloody melée took place, and in this spot ten of the garrison were cut, or shot down; the regiment, now reduced to about five-and-twenty, fled.

Some vainly sought refuge in a mud guard-house below the south wall, some in the interior of the place itself; they were followed up and slain.

A last stand was made by a few desperate men to the immediate left of the gateway near which the conflict had commenced, and here the last man of the garrison of Loharee fell.

Fifty-seven bodies were counted by an officer within the gateways of the fort.

Previous to forming the column of assault, I had

made over the command of the cavalry on the plain to Captain Thompson, 14th Dragoons; he reports that several of the enemy, being observed letting themselves down from the bastion at the north-west angle of the fort. he moved forward a division of his Dragoons, intercepted and cut them down.

All who endeavoured to escape on the south side into the village were met and shot by a company of the 25th under Lieutenant Fenwick.

I can safely assert that none of the garrison (which must have numbered, including Munsheet Sing and his retinue, at least ninety men) escaped.

During the assault Captain Blyth, of the 14th Dragoons, rode within a very short distance of Khuleea and observed a great many men assembling on the bastions of that fort, and some in the "topes" that surround it, but seeing our cavalry drawn upon the plain between them and Loharee, they did not attempt to make a forward movement.

I would here observe that many indications of the presence of the mutineer sepoys amongst the garrison met my eye; for instance, an European drum and bugle were found in the fort; also many brass cap plates, belonging to the 12th Regiment Bengal Native Infantry, which garrisoned Jhansie at the period of the mutiny there, and several red dootees with yellow facings. Many of the slain had the appearance of sepoys of the Bengal army, —tall, broad shouldered, narrow waisted men.

In conclusion, I trust I may be permitted to bring to the notice of the Major-General the gallantry and steadiness displayed by the officers and men of all arms composing the field force, which I had the honor and the pleasure of commanding on this occasion. I feel much indebted to Captain Little, commanding the left wing of the 25th Bombay Native Infantry, for the manner in which

he brought up a support consisting of 25 files of
his detachment which followed close upon the
heels of the storming party, when the place was
carried, and subsequently aided them in several
combats with the remnant of the garrison before
it was completely destroyed. Captain Field, commanding the battery, I have to thank for rendering
untenable by his fire the strongest position the
enemy could have occupied to annoy me, and Captain Thompson, 14th Light Dragoons, for his dispositions outside the fort during the assault, and
for the vigilance with which he intercepted the
fugitives.

Captain Baigrie, Deputy-Assistant Quarter-
Master-General deserves my best acknowledge-
ments for making himself generally useful to me
throughout the day.

I beg also to thank Assistant-Surgeon O'Brien
attached to 3rd Europeans, and Assistant-Surgeon
Skipton 78th Highlanders, attached to 14th Light
Dragoons, for their prompt attention to the
wounded; but the following officers and men I
beg especially to recommend to the protection of
the Major-General, as having under my own eyes
greatly distinguished themselves in the conflict at
the gates—one of unusual severity :—

Lieutenant Armstrong, 3rd Bombay Europeans,
who commanded the storming party.

Lieutenant Donne, 3rd Bombay Europeans ;

Ensign Newport of the same regiment ; who both
fell severely wounded.

Lieutenant Rose, of the 25th Bombay Native Infantry, who joined me from the rear, and when
the two former officers were struck down ably
supplied their place.

Also :—

Regimental No. 1031, Private Frederick Whirlpool*, No. 5 Company, 3rd Bombay Europeans.

Regimental No. 223, Private Robert Howard, No. 8 Company, 3rd Bombay Europeans.

Regimental No. 153, Private Patrick Fitzgerald, 3rd Bombay Europeans.

Private Bhola Gudurya, 9th Company 25th Regiment Bombay Native Infantry.

The readiness of resource evinced by Lieutenant Bonus will, I feel, be appreciated by the Major-General. I can further bear witness to the coolness with which, under fire, Lieutenant Bonus adjusted the powder-bag to the gate, and enabled us to effect an entrance into the fort.

I subjoin a list of casualties in the F. detachment under command.

On the wall of the fort a brass 9-pounder gun was captured and brought into camp. I had the carriage, which was perfectly new, destroyed.

Upwards of 150 stand of arms were taken from the enemy—swords, matchlocks, and spears, which I caused to be broken up. One of the garrison used a double-barrelled gun.

I have, &c.,

R. H. GALL, Major,

Commanding Field Force Detachment.

No. 64.

From Return of Casualties during the Attack and Capture of the Fort of Lahore, on the 2nd of May, 1858.

Lieutenant W. A. Armstrong, 3rd Bombay European Regiment, contused wound.

Lieutenant F. C. Donne, 3rd Bombay European Regiment, severely wounded.

---

* This gallant man fell covered with wounds at the final charge, in which he was one of the very foremost.

Ensign W. H. Newport, 3rd Bombay European Regiment, severely wounded.

Lieutenant W. Rose, 25th Regiment, N.I., slightly wounded.

Abstract.

3rd Bombay European Regiment—1 killed, 17 wounded.

25th Regiment, N.I., 5 wounded.

H. H. A. WOOD, Captain,
Assistant Adjutant-General.

————

Admiralty, 2ʔth *July,* 1858.

A DESPATCH, of which the following is an extract, has been received by the Lords Commissioners of the Admiralty, from Rear-Admiral Sir Michael Seymour, K.C.B., the Commander-in-Chief of Her Majesty's ships and vessels on the East India Station, dated 21st May, 1858:—

I accordingly lost no time in consulting with Rear-Admiral Rigault de Genouilly, and making the necessary arrangements, and the same afternoon we proceeded with all the English gun-boats across the bar to the mouth of the river, where the gun-vessels and French gun-boats named in the margin* had been previously stationed, to give weight to the negotiations. The Slaney, Firm, Staunch, and Bustard, conveyed our landing parties, and the Leven and Opossum those of the French.

From the arrival of the Ambassadors on the 14th April, the Chinese have used every exertion to strengthen the forts at the entrance of the Pei-Ho; earthworks, sand-bag batteries, and parapets for the heavy gingalls, have been erected on both sides for a distance of nearly a mile in length,

* Nimrod, Cormorant. Mitraille, Fusée, Dragonne, Avalanche.

upon which, 37 guns in position were visible, and the whole shore had been piled to oppose a landing. As the channel is only about 200 yards wide, and runs within 400 yards of the shore, these defences presented a formidable appearance. Two strong mud batteries, mounting respectively 33 and 16 guns had been also constructed about 1000 yards up the river, in a position to command our advance. In the rear, several entrenched camps were visible, defended by flanking bastions, and it was known that large bodies of troops had arrived from Pekin. All the forts and the camps were covered with the various coloured flags under which the "troops of the eight banners," as the Tartar soldiers are styled, range themselves.

At 8 A.M. yesterday, the notification to the Imperial Commissioner Tan, and the summons to deliver up the forts within two hours, were delivered by Captain Hall, my Flag Captain, and Capitaine Reynaud, Flag Captain of the French Admiral, and accompanied by my gallant colleague, and attended by our respective secretaries and Flag Lieutenants, we embarked in the Slaney, to direct the movements of the squadron. ·

I beg to enclose a copy of the plan of attack, which was arranged in concert with Admiral Rigault.

No answer having been returned to the summons by 10 o'clock, the signal agreed upon was made, and the gun-boats advanced in the prescribed order, led by the Cormorant. The Chinese opened fire immediately, and the signal to engage was made a few minutes afterwards from the Slaney. By the time all the vessels had anchored in their respective stations, the effects of our well-directed fire had become very apparent. The first fort was entirely dismantled and abandoned, and the second partially so, whilst those on the north side had been completely subdued by the Cormorant and two French gun-boats. At the short range within which we engaged, every shot told, and many of the massive embrasures of mud were levelled by shells. At the end of an hour and a quarter, the enemy's fire ceased. The landing parties were then pushed on shore, the one for the north forts, under the orders of Captain Sir F. Nicholson and Captain Leveque, and that for the south forts, under Captains Hall and Reynaud, Flag Captains, the Royal Marines on each side being commanded by Major Robert Boyle and 1st Lieutenant McCallum.

Owing to the destructive fire from the gun boats, but little opposition was made to our landing, and the Chinese troops were observed moving off in masses, whilst our people were in the boats. The flags of the Allied Powers soon replaced those of the Chinese. On the south side 200 large gingalls were found in position near the landing place, on an embankment.

Having obtained possession, the dismantling of the works was commenced, and field pieces landed for the protection of the forces against the possible attacks of the Chinese. Shortly after the landing, our gallant allies sustained a melancholy and heavy loss of men, killed and wounded, by the accidental explosion of a magazine.

When all the vessels had taken up their positions, a bold attempt was made to send down upon them a long array of junks, filled with straw in flames, and drawn across the river; but they fortunately grounded, and though the people, guiding them down the river with ropes, made great efforts to get them off, a few shells from the Bustard drove them away, and the vessels burnt out without doing any damage.

1858.   8 U

Much skill and labour had been expended in the construction of these forts. The guns were much better cast, and not so unwieldly, as those in the Canton River, and were better equipped in every respect. They had good canister shot, and the hollow 8-inch shot appeared imitations from our own. There were several English guns in the batteries.

Directions were now sent to Captain Sir F. Nicolson and Capitaine Leveque to advance and capture the two forts up the river, which had kept up a smart fire.

This movement was successfully executed, under the supporting fire from the Bustard, Staunch, and Opossum. Several entrenched camps were also destroyed.

The Chinese stood well to their guns, notwithstanding shot, shell, and rockets were flying thickly around them. Most of the gunboats were hulled, some several times, whilst boats, spars, and rigging were cut by round shot, grape, and gingall balls. This signal success, after the Chinese had ample time to fortify their position, and were confident of their strength, may probably have a greater moral effect on the Chinese Government than if we had attacked them in the first instance, when they were less prepared.

The necessary arrangements at the entrance of the river having been completed, a further advance was made to the village of Takoo, where we found a barrier of junks filled with combustible matter, moored by chains right across the river, whilst seven similar obstructions to our progress were observed within a mile higher up. Captain Hall, with my Flag Lieutenant and a party of men, landed, and took possession of 18 field pieces in front of an abandoned encampment at Takoo. Whilst on shore, the residence of the High Commissioner

Tan was visited, and found deserted, though a significant proof of his recent presence was found in a beheaded Chinaman near his gate. It was ascertained here that the main body of the Chinese troops had retired with Tan to a position about 8 miles up the river.

The barrier at Takoo offering good security to our vessels below, it was made our advanced position for the night, in charge of Sir F. Nicolson and Capitaine Thoyon.

I enclose a list of our casualties, amounting to 1 warrant officer and 4 men killed, and 2 officers and 15 men wounded. That of our gallant allies is, I regret to state, much heavier; amounting to 4 officers and 2 men killed, and 5 officers and 56 men wounded. Many of these wounded were taken on board the Coromandel, Flag tender, where arrangements had been made for the purpose, under the able supervision of Dr. C. A. Anderson, Staff Surgeon, whose services on this occasion, and on all former occasions where we have been employed on active service, I feel bound to bring to their Lordships' favourable notice.

It now becomes my pleasing duty to mention to their Lordships, the laudable conduct of both officers and men under my orders. From Captains Sir Frederick Nicholson, Hall, and Osborn, I have received the greatest assistance, as well as from Commanders Leckie, Saumarez, and Cresswell. Commander Saumarez excited the admiration of the whole force by the noble manner in which he led the attack, and for some time sustained the heavy fire from the north forts.

I can bear witness also to the zeal and gallantry of the officers commanding the gun-boats, and beg to recommend Lieutenants Hoskins, Nicolas, Hudson, Wildman, and Hallowes, to their Lordships' favourable notice, as well as the second masters, particularly Mr. C. Prickett, of the Opossum, who has been severely wounded. I also beg strongly to recommend Lieutenant A. Bland, of the Pique, an old and meritorious officer. The names of Lieutenant R. P. Cator, of the Calcutta ; Lieutenant A. T. Thrupp, of the Nimrod ; Lieutenant H. K. Leet, of the Cormorant ; and Lieutenant C. Parry, of the Surprise, have been also brought to my notice. Commander Saumarez has brought to my knowledge the gallant conduct of Mr. W. H. Fawckner, master of the Elk, lent from the Hesper, and of Mr. H. H. Burniston, Paymaster ; Mr. Webster, Master's Assistant ; and Mr. Campbell, Midshipman of the Cormorant, who worked a 24-pounder howitzer, and kept up a continued fire from that gun on the south forts. I beg to call their Lordships' attention to the list of the officers engaged.

Mr. W. D. Jeans, my Secretary, has accompanied me in this, as on other expeditions ; also Mr. W. H. M. Arnold, Chief Clerk in my office, whom I would beg to recommend for promotion for his arduous duties during the progress of the operations in China.

In conclusion, I have much gratification in recording the cordial co-operation of my gallant colleague, and of the forces under his command. We have been actuated by the sole desire to carry into effect the orders of our respective Governments, in a spirit of the most perfect friendship.

Arrangements are making for a further advance up the river towards Tientsin.

I have the honour to enclose two sketches of the forts, made by Lieutenant A. T. Thrupp, of the Nimrod, and Mr. F. C. B. Bedwell, Secretary's Clerk.   I have, &c.

        M. SEYMOUR, Rear-Admiral and
                Commander-in-Chief.

List of Casualties at the Capture of the Forts at the Mouth of the Pei Ho, on the 20th May, 1858.

KILLED.

Fury—Mr. John Colley, carpenter.
Calcutta—Thomas Halloran, A.B.
Nimrod—Henry Love, A.B.
Bustard—William Potter, private Royal Marines.
Furious—John Cunningham, A.B.

WOUNDED.

Calcutta — Henry Calvert, ordinary, slightly; Thomas Collings, ordinary, slightly; William Smith, A.B., slightly.
Nimrod—E. A. T. Stubbs, Lieutenant, slightly; John Sutton, stoker, severely; James Martin, A.B., slightly.
Fury—Michael Parker, A.B., slightly.
Coromandel—Richard White, ordinary, slightly.
Cormorant—George Stevens, boatswain's mate, slightly.
Slaney—G. G. Dunlop, gunner, 3rd class, slightly.
Opossum—Mr. C. Prickett, second master, severely.
Staunch—G. Davis, A.B., slightly; J. Blair, A.B., slightly; J. Palmer, ordinary, slightly.
Bustard—James Parsons, quartermaster, slightly; Patrick Nevin, A.B., severely.

Abstract.

Number killed and since dead	...	5
Number wounded ...	...	... 16
Total	...	... 21

CHAS. A. ANDERSON, M.D.,
Staff-Surgeon on Detached Service.

French Loss.

Killed	...	...	...	... 6
Wounded	...	...	...	... 61
		Total	...	... 67
	Grand Total	...	...	88

Return of Officers, Seamen, and Marines, of Her Majesty's Ships employed on shore at the Capture of the Forts at the Mouth of the Pei Ho, on the 20th May, 1858.

Commander-in-Chief and Staff.

Rear Admiral Sir Michael Seymour, K.C.B.
Mr. W. D. Jeans, Secretary.
Lieutenant M. C. Seymour, Flag Lieutenant.
Lieutenant Sholto Douglas.
Mr. W. H. M. Arnold, Assistant-Paymaster.
Mr. F. Le B. Bedwell, Secretary's Clerk.
Mr. A. T. Dale, Midshipman.

Barge's Crew, 13 Seamen.

FIRST DIVISION.

Pique.

Captain Sir F. Nicholson, Bart.
Lieutenant A. Bland.
Lieutenant G. Robinson.
Lientenant E. H. Stuart, Acting.
Lieutenant A. C. May, Acting, Volunteer.
Mr. L. Chichester, Acting Mate.
Mr. J. Hanmer, Acting Mate.
1st Lieutenant E G. McCallum, R.M.
1st Lieutenant W. H. Clements, R.M.
Mr. W. H. Cruice, Assisting-Surgeon

Mr. Mitchell, Acting Gunner, 3rd Class (lent from Fury.)

> Total—11 officers, 136 petty officers and seamen, 37 marines.

Furious.

Captain S. Osborne.
Lieutenant P. Brock.
Lieutenant D. G. Davidson.,
Mr. Ommaney, Acting Mate.
Mr. Allfry, Midshipman.
Mr. Harvey, Midshipman.
Mr. Vincent, Midshipman.
Mr. Older, Midshipman.
Mr. Chapman, Midshipman.
Mr. Bridges, Master's Assistant.
1st Lieutenant H. H. Nott, R.M.A.
Mr. H. G. Ruby, Assistant-Surgeon.

> Total—12 officers, 103 petty officers and seamen, 24 marines.

Surprise.

Commander S. G. Cresswell.
Lieutenant C. Parry.
Lieutenant John Patton.
Mr. H. P. Gilbert, Mate.
Mr. King, Midshipman.
Mr. Bagge, Naval Cadet.
Mr. Purchase, Chief Engineer.

> Total—7 officers, 40 petty officers and seamen, 14 marines.

Hesper.

Mr. W. H. Fawckner, Master Commanding.
Mr. Webster, Master's Assistant.

> Total—2 officers, 14 petty officers and seamen.

Nimrod.

Dr. Jno. Rose, Surgeon.

Cormorant.

Dr. A. Watson, Surgeon.

Afforded assistance on shore, particularly to the French, after the explosion.

SECOND DIVISION.

Calcutta.

Captain W. K. Hall, C.B.
Commander J. G. Goodenough.
Commander H. H. Beamish.
Lieutenant Ralph P. Cator.
Lieutenant G. S. Bosanquet.
Lieutenant W. R. Kennedy (Acting).
Mr. J. B. Murphy, Assistant-Surgeon.
Mr. N. B. Smith, Acting Mate.
Mr. C. E. Buckle, Acting Mate.
Mr. H. Brand, Midshipman.
Mr. P. B. Nind, Midshipman.
Mr. E. H. Seymour, Midshipman.
Mr. H. McHardy, Midshipman.
Mr. H. H. A'Court, Midshipman.
Mr. C. H. Russell, Midshipman.
Honourable H. Meade, Midshipman.
Mr. A. K. Wilson, Midshipman.
Mr. H. B. Cobb, Midshipman.
Mr. T. S. Jackson, Midshipman, Aide-de-Camp, accompanied Captain Hall on this and every other expedition.
Mr. S. S. Swan, Master's Assistant.
Mr. H. H. Rawson, Naval Cadet.
Mr. J. Dinham, Acting Gunner.
Mr. C. Blackador, Acting Boatswain.

Total—23 offices, 312 petty officers and seamen

Major R. Boyle, R.M.
Second Lieutenant W. W. Allnutt, R.M.

Second Lieutenant H. T. M. Cooper, R.M.
Mr. C. B. Lamb, Assistant-Surgeon.
  Total—4 officers and 130 marines.

First Lieutenant H. Savage, R.M.A., (lent from
Sampson) with 19 marines.

Fury.

Commander C. T. Leckie.
Lieutenant C. C. Robinson.
Lieutenant J. E. Evered.
Mr. R. C. Scott, Surgeon.
Mr. P. J. Murray, Mate.
Mr. G. F. Lyon, Acting Mate.
Mr. F. L. Graham, Assistant-Surgeon.
Mr. C. A. Hayes, Midshipman.
Mr. J. M. Lloyd, Master's Assistant.
Mr. T. Bertram, Assistant Engineer.
Mr. Valser, Clerk.
Mr. W. Chambers, Boatswain.
Mr. John Colley, Carpenter.

Calcutta.

Lieutenant W. A. Cambier,* lent to Her Majesty's
gun-boat Slaney.
Lent to H.M.'s ship Cormorant, 10 petty officers
and seamen.
Lent to H.M.'s ship Nimrod, 10 petty officers and
seamen.
Lent to H.M.'s gun-boat Opossum, 10 petty
officers and seamen.
Lent to H.M.'s gun-boat Firm, 6 petty officers and
seamen.

Attending wounded on board the Coromandel.

Calcutta—Dr. C. A. Anderson, Staff-Surgeon.
Surprise—Mr. J. F. Pritchard, Surgeon.

* Gunnery Lieutenant, and made admirable practice
against the Fort.

Hesper—Mr. E. Mortimer, Assistant-Surgeon.
Calcutta—Rev. J. W. Bussell, Chaplain.

Commander-in-Chief and Staff, 7 officers, 13 petty officers and seamen.
    Grand Total—87 officers, 721 petty officers and seamen, 224 marines.
French force landed 700.
        (Signed)   M. SEYMOUR,
    Rear-Admiral and Commander-in-Chief.

FROM THE

LONDON GAZETTE of *JULY* 30, 1858.

Whitehall, July 24, 1858.

THE Queen has been pleased to grant unto Israel Lewis, of Gloucester-terrace, Regent's Park, in the county of Middlesex, formerly of Great Ormond-street, Queen-square, in the same county, Gentleman, Her royal licence and authority that he may, in compliance with a condition contained in the last will and testament of Israel Barned, late of Gloucester-terrace aforesaid, Esquire, deceased, take and henceforth use the surname of Barned, in addition to and after that of Lewis, and bear the arms of Barned quarterly with those of Lewis, and that such surnames and arms may in like manner be taken, borne, and used by his issue, such arms being first duly exemplified, according to the laws of arms, and recorded in the Herald's Office, otherwise the said Royal licence and permission to be void and of none effect :

And also to command that the said Royal concession and declaration be recorded in Her Majesty's College of Arms.

PASSPORTS.

Foreign-Office, July 30, 1858.

Persons requiring Passports from the Foreign-Office must address their letters to the *Chief Clerk of the Foreign-Office, London*, with the word " *Passport* " conspicuously written upon the cover : if sent addressed to the Secretary of State much time is lost.

PASSPORTS.

Foreign-Office, July 30, 1858.

Notice is hereby given, that the Earl of Malmesbury has appointed the following persons to be Agents for the issue of Foreign Office Passports, at the undermentioned places :

Birmingham . .	George A. Everitt, Esq.
Dover	Samuel Metcalfe Latham, Esq.
Devonport . . .	Thomas H. Hawker, Esq.
Folkestone . . .	Francis M. Faulkner, Esq.
Hull	John England, Esq.
Liverpool . . .	Nathan Litherland, Esq.
Lowestoft . . .	B. M. Bradbeer, Esq.
Newcastle-on-Tyne	Edward Glynn, Esq.
Newhaven . . .	F. G Turner, Esq.
Southampton . .	W. J. Le Feuvre, Esq,
Weymouth . . .	Richard Hare, Esq.

Board of Trade, Whitehall,
July 27, 1858.

THE Right Honourable the Lords of the Committee of Privy Council for Trade and Plantations have received, through the Secretary of State for Foreign Affairs, a copy of a Despatch from Her Majesty's Chargé d'Affaires at the Hague, inclosing copies of two Decrees published in the Netherlands Official Gazette, respecting the exhibition and use of Lights and Fog Signals on board ships.

1. On board all sea-going vessels.
2. On board vessels (not sea-going) trading on the rivers and inland waters of the Netherlands.

The regulations for sea-going vessels are the same as those recently prescribed by the British Admiralty, and are, like them, to take effect on and after the 1st October next.

War-Office, Pall-Mall,
30th July, 1858.

45th Regiment of Foot.

Major-General Sir Hugh Henry Rose, G.C.B., to be Colonel, vice General Thomas Brabazon Aylmer, deceased. Dated 20th July, 1858.

War-Office, Pall-Mall,
30th July, 1858.

2nd Regiment of Life Guards, Hamilton Sandford Pakenham, Gent., to be Cornet and Sub-Lieutenant, by purchase, vice Cunninghame, promoted. Dated 30th July, 1858.

1st Dragoons, George Lake Harvey, Gent., to be Cornet, without purchase. Dated 30th July, 1858.

2nd Dragoons, Cornet George Campbell Ross to be Lieutenant, by purchase, vice Handley, who retires. Dated 30th July, 1858.

Acting Veterinary Surgeon Thornton Hart to be Veterinary Surgeon, vice Opie Smith, who retires upon half-pay. Dated 30th July, 1858.

3rd Light Dragoons, Cornet George Shippen Willes, from the 13th Light Dragoons, to be Cornet, vice John Unett, promoted. Dated 30th July, 1858.

5th Dragoons, Theodore William Rathbone, Gent., to be Cornet, by purchase, vice O'Neill, promoted. Dated 30th July, 1858.

Assistant-Surgeon Robert Graves Burton, from the Staff, to be Assistant-Surgeon. Dated 30th July, 1858.

10th Light Dragoons, Cornet Thomas James William Bulkeley, from the 6th Dragoons, to be Cornet, vice Lord R. D. Kerr, promoted. Dated 30th July, 1858.

12th Light Dragoons, Troop-Serjeant-Major Joseph Devonsber Jackson, from the 5th Light Dragoons, to be Cornet, without purchase, vice Swindley, promoted. Dated 30th July, 1858.

16th Light Dragoons, Lieutenant Hugh d'Arcy P. Burnell to be Captain, by purchase, vice Burnand, who retires. Dated 30th July, 1858.

Cornet Arthur Gooch, from the 17th Light Dragoons, to be Lieutenant, by purchase, vice Burnell, promoted. Dated 30th July, 1858.

Military Train, Captain Thomas Rice Hamilton, from the 3rd Foot, to be Captain, vice Cater, who exchanges. Dated 30th July, 1858.

To be Lieutenants, without purchase.

Ensign and Adjutant John Sweeny, vice Dawson, killed in action. Dated 21st May, 1858.

Ensign Henry Keogh. Dated 30th July, 1858.

Ensign Ruben Hill Powell. Dated 30th July, 1858.

To be Ensigns, without purchase.

Cornet Henry David James Macleod, from half-pay of the late Land Transport Corps, vice Briggs, promoted. Dated 30th July, 1858.

Cornet Andrew Munro, from half-pay of the late Land Transport Corps, vice Keogh, promoted. Dated 30th July, 1858.

Cornet William Laughton, from half-pay of the late Land Transport Corps, vice Powell, promoted. Dated 30th July, 1858.

The promotion of Ensign and Adjutant J. Sweeney, as stated in the Gazette of the 16th July, 1858, has been cancelled.

Grenadier Guards, Captain William Earle to be Instructor of Musketry, in succession to Captain the Honourable J. Dormer, removed to the 74th Foot. Dated 16th July, 1858.

1st Regiment of Foot.
To be Lieutenants, by purchase.

Ensign Charles Atkinson Logan, vice White, promoted. Dated 30th July, 1858.

Ensign William John Shanly, vice Curtois, promoted. Dated 30th July, 1858.

3rd Foot, Captain William Edmund Cater, from the Military Train, to be Captain, vice Hamilton, who exchanges. Dated 30th July, 1858.

4th Foot, Ensign Charles Edward Billing to be Lieutenant, by purchase, vice Davies, who has retired. Dated 30th July, 1858.

Ensign Edward Chinn to be Instructor of Musketry. Dated 19th July, 1858.

5th Foot, Quartermaster Edward Henry Drake, from a Depôt Battalion, to be Quartermaster, vice Webster, who retires upon half-pay. Dated 30th July, 1858.

Assistant-Surgeon Peter Frederick Newland, from the Staff, to be Assistant-Surgeon. Dated 30th July, 1858.

6th Foot, Captain Charles Parker Catty to be Major, by purchase, vice Brevet-Lieutenant-Colonel Lowndes, who retires. Dated 30th July, 1858.

To be Ensigns, by purchase.

Thomas Kent Neild, Gent., vice D. C. Campbell, promoted. Dated 30th July, 1858.

William Grant, Gent., vice Neal, promoted. Dated 31st July, 1858.

7th Foot, Lieutenant Adrian Bennett to be Captain, without purchase, vice Coney deceased. Dated 1st May, 1858.

Ensign William Lloyd Browne to be Lieutenant, without purchase, vice Bennett. Dated 1st May, 1858.

Ensign Edmund Waller to be Lieutenant, by purchase, vice Browne, whose promotion by purchase on the 4th June, 1858, has been cancelled. Dated 30th July, 1858.

8th Foot, Ensign J. E. Winchester Black to be Lieutenant, without purchase. Dated 30th July, 1858.

9th Foot, Captain Patrick McCarthy, from half-pay, Unattached, to be Captain, without purchase. Dated 30th July, 1858.

Lieutenant Henry Marcus Beresford to be Captain, by purchase, vice McCarthy, who retires. Dated 30th July, 1858.

Ensign James Lewis Bradshaw to be Lieutenant, by purchase, vice Beresford. Dated 30th July, 1858.

10th Foot, Brevet-Lieutenant-Colonel H. E. Longden to be Lieutenant-Colonel, without purchase, vice Brevet-Colonel Sir T. Harte Franks, K.C.B., promoted to the rank of Major-General. Dated 20th July, 1858.

Brevet-Major H. R. Norman to be Major, without purchase, vice Longden. Dated 20th July, 1858.

Lieutenant J. L. S. Aldersey to be Captain, without purchase, vice Norman. Dated 20th July, 1858.

11th Foot.

To be Ensigns, by purchase.

David Halliday, Gent., vice Corrie, promoted. Dated 30th July, 1858.

Hugh Montil Toller, vice Smyth, promoted. Dated 31st July, 1858.

14th Foot, Captain J. Mackay McKenzie, from the 70th Foot, to be Captain, vice de Quincey, who exchanges. Dated 30th July, 1858.

Lieutenant Henry Theodore Vernede to be Captain, by purchase, vice Bond, who retires. Dated 30th July, 1858.

Lieutenant James Anderson to be Instructor of Musketry. Dated 19th July, 1858.

17th Foot, Captain Charles Edward Johns, from the 38th Foot, to be Captain, vice McNair, who exchanges. Dated 30th July, 1858.

21st Foot, John Dudley Edwar Crosse, Gent., to be Ensign, by purchase, vice Grant, promoted. Dated 30th July, 1858.

23rd Foot, Ensign Charles James Wrench to be Lieutenant, without purchase, vice H. J. Richards, deceased. Dated 29th May, 1858.

Ensign Harry Charles Willes to be Lieutenant, without purchase, vice Wrench, whose promotion, on the 4th June, 1858, has been cancelled. Dated 4th June, 1858.

Quartermaster-Serjeant James Clayton to be Ensign, without purchase, vice Willes, promoted. Dated 30th July, 1858.

27th Foot, Assistant-Surgeon Alexander Stevenson Russell, M.D., from the Staff, to be Assistant-Surgeon, vice Teevan, appointed to the Staff. Dated 30th July, 1858.

28th Foot. The third Christian name of Ensign Auchmuty, appointed by purchase on the 13th July, 1858, is Frederic.

31st Foot, Isaac Parsons, Gent., to be Ensign, by purchase, vice Leeson, promoted. Dated 30th July, 1858.

37th Foot, Henry Bullen, Gent., to be Ensign, by purchase, vice Bell, deceased. Dated 30th July, 1858.

38th Foot, Captain George Augustus McNair, from the 17th Foot, to be Captain, vice Johns, who exchanges. Dated 30th July, 1858.

47th Foot.

The undermentioned Officers have been superseded, being absent without leave :

Ensign Crosbie Kidd. Dated 30th July, 1858.
Ensign Edmund Gray. Dated 30th July, 1858.

53rd Foot, Ensign William Lamb Barr to be Lieutenant, without purchase, vice Munro, deceased. Dated 11th May, 1858.

70th Foot, Captain Paul F. de Quincey, from the 14th Foot, to be Captain, vice McKenzie, who exchanges. Dated 30th July, 1858.

Ensign Henry Leake, from the 44th Foot, to be Lieutenant, without purchase, vice Crawley, promoted in the 15th Foot. Dated 30th July, 1858.

Charles Hamilton Prior, Gent., to be Ensign, without purchase, vice Hilton, promoted. Dated 30th July, 1858.

73rd *Foot*, St. John Dupond Galwey, Gent., to be Ensign, by purchase, vice Sharp, promoted. Dated 30th July, 1858.

The third Christian name of Ensign Gibson is *Hacket*, and not *Hachet* as previously stated.

75th *Foot*, The Commission of Surgeon Dr. Domenichetti to be antedated to the 10th June, 1857.

89th *Foot*, Lieutenant Barnes Slyfield Robinson to be Captain, without purchase, vice Thorp, promoted. Dated 9th May, 1858.

91st *Foot*, William Gamul Edwards, Gent., to be Ensign, by purchase, vice Tingcombe, promoted. Dated 30th July, 1858.

Rifle Brigade, Hugh William Reid, Gent., to be Ensign, without purchase. Dated 30th July, 1858.

2nd *West India Regiment*, Lieutenant James Franklin to be Instructor of Musketry. Dated 17th July, 1858.

Gold Coast Artillery Corps, John James Mathew, Gent., to be Ensign, without purchase, vice Gwillim, whose appointment, as stated in the Gazette of the 22nd June, 1858, has been cancelled. Dated 30th July, 1858.

DEPOT BATTALION.

Cornet R. P. Brooks, from half-pay of the late Land Transport Corps, to be Quartermaster, vice Drake, appointed to the 5th Foot. Dated 30th July, 1858.

To be Instructors of Musketry.

Captain Thomas Biggs, 60th Foot, in succession to Captain Cunninghame, resigned. Dated 15th July, 1858.

Captain Edward William Bray, 83rd Foot. Dated 22nd July, 1858.

HOSPITAL STAFF.

Assistant-Surgeon George Pain, from the Royal Artillery, to be Staff-Surgeon of the Second Class, vice Willocks, deceased. Dated 30th July, 1858.

Assistant-Surgeon Thomas Stephenson Teevan, from the 27th Foot, to be Assistant-Surgeon to the Forces, vice Russell, appointed to the Staff. Dated 30th July, 1858.

Christopher Thompson, M.B., to be Acting Assistant-Surgeon. Dated 21st July, 1858.

Staff-Assistant-Surgeon Walter Johnstone has been permitted to resign his Commission. Dated 30th July, 1858.

The surname of the Assistant-Surgeon appointed in the Gazette of 23rd instant, is *Devlin*, and not *Delvin*, as previously stated.

BREVET.

The undermentioned promotion to take place, consequent on the decease of the following Generals :

Sir R. Darling, died 2nd April, 1858 ;

Sir T. Hawker, died 13th June, 1858 ;

T. B. Aylmer, died 19th July, 1858 ;—

General Sir Colin Campbell, G.C.B., the senior supernumerary of his rank, to be placed on the Fixed Establishment of Generals. Dated 20th July, 1858.

Major-General Benjamin Orlando Jones, being supernumerary of his rank, to be placed on the

Fixed Establishment of Major-Generals. Dated 20th July, 1858.

Lieutenant-Colonel G. W. Francklyn, Depot Battalion, to be Colonel. Dated 20th July, 1858.

Major James Cockburn, Unattached, Staff-Officer of Pensioners, to be Lieutenant-Colonel. Dated 20th July, 1858.

Captain James Holt Freeth, Royal Engineers, to be Major. Dated 20th July, 1858.

Major and Brevet-Lieutenant-Colonel R. H. R. Howard Vyse, of the Royal Regiment of Horse Guards, having completed three years' actual service in the rank of Lieutenant-Colonel, to be promoted to be Colonel in the Army, under the Royal Warrant of 6th October, 1854. Dated 10th July, 1858.

Quartermaster Robert Webster, late of the 5th Foot, having retired upon half-pay, to have the honorary rank of Captain, agreeably to the provisions of the Royal Warrant of 17th December, 1855. Dated 30th July, 1855.

The undermentioned Gentlemen Cadets of the East India Company's Service, to have the local and temporary rank of Lieutenant, whilst doing duty at the Royal Engineer Establishment at Chatham.

William Maxwell Campbell. Dated 30th July, 1858.

James Henry Robert Cruickshank. Dated 30th July, 1858.

George Wingate Oldham. Dated 30th July, 1858.

Charles William Ingleby Harrison. Dated 30th July, 1858.

Frederick Jervis Horne. Dated 30th July, 1858.

Louis D'Aguilar Jackson. Dated 30th July, 1858.

Henry Wathen Watson. Dated 30th July, 1858.
Beresford Lovett. Dated 30th July, 1858.
Gray Townsend Skipwith. Dated 30th July, 1858.
Henry McVeagh Crichton. Dated 30th July, 1858.
Edward Andrew Trevor. Dated 30th July, 1858.
Ross Thompson. Dated 30th July, 1858.
Philip Samuel Marindin. Dated 30th July, 1858.
Alexander Thomas Fraser. Dated 30th July, 1858.

War-Office, Pall-Mall,
30th July, 1858.

MEMORANDUM.

The undermentioned Officers of the Militia, having obtained first class certificates at the School of Musketry at Hythe, have been appointed by His Royal Highness the General Commanding-in-Chief, with the concurrence of the Secretary of State for War, to act as Instructors of Musketry to the Regiments to which they belong :

Lieutenant F. F. R. M. Morgan, Bedford. Dated 12th April, 1858.
Lieutenant James Broft Byers, 2nd Cheshire. Dated 20th April, 1858.
Lieutenant James Sisson Cooper, North Lincoln. Dated 12th February, 1858.
Lieutenant William E. Smith, Nottingham. Dated 2nd February, 1858.
Lieutenant Carrington Jones, 1st Stafford. Dated 30th April, 1858.
Lieutenant Isaac De L. Wilson, 2nd Stafford. Dated 1st February, 1858.
Lieutenant Frank Paul Matthews, Sussex. Dated 21st April, 1858.

Lieutenant Elijah Littlewood, King's Own Light Infantry. Dated 19th April, 1858.

Lieutenant John George S. Willcocks, 3rd West York. Dated 8th January, 1858.

Lieutenant Robert Pollok, 2nd Lanark. Dated 29th April, 1858.

Lieutenant William Magee Hunter, Antrim. Dated 15th January, 1858.

Lieutenant John Quarry, North Cork. Dated 10th April, 1858.

Captain Robert Patterson Elliot, Donegal. Dated 26th April, 1858.

Lieutenant John Hooker Vowell, Dublin City. Dated 28th February, 1858.

Lieutenant Frederick Tottenham, Fermanagh. Dated 11th May, 1858.

Admiralty, 29th July, 1858.

Corps of Royal Marines.

Second Lieutenant William Winkworth Allnutt to be First Lieutenant, vice George Gill, to the Half-pay List.

Commissions signed by the Lord Lieutenant of the County of Essex.

John Wardlaw, Esq., to be Deputy Lieutenant. Dated 23rd July, 1858.

Sir Bridges Powell Henniker, Bart., to be Deputy Lieutenant. Dated 23rd July, 1858.

Gordon Maynard Ives, Esq., to be Deputy Lieutenant. Dated 23rd July, 1858.

Commission signed by the Lord Lieutenant of the County of Cumberland.

Royal Cumberland Regiment of Militia.

William Gaitskill, Gent., to be Lieutenant, vice Brooksbank, resigned. Dated 16th July, 1858.

Commission signed by the Lord Lieutenant of the County Palatine of Chester.

The Earl of Chester's Yeomanry Cavalry.

George Fairbairn, Gent., to be Cornet, vice Edward Hyde Greg, promoted. Dated 15th July, 1858.

Commission signed by the Lord Lieutenant of the County of Kent.

West Kent Light Infantry Regiment of Militia.

Morgan Dalrymple Treherne, Gent., to be Lieutenant, vice Waldo, resigned. Dated 26th July, 1858.

Commissions signed by the Lord Lieutenant of the County of Sussex.

Light Infantry Battalion of the Royal Sussex Militia.

Lieutenant John Kincaid Smith to be Captain, vice Bates, resigned. Dated 21st July, 1858.

Ensign William Orme to be Lieutenant, vice Smith, promoted. Dated 21st July, 1858.

Ensign Pargiter Malvoisie Dickenson to be Lieutenant, vice Walmesley, resigned. Dated 21st July, 1858.

Ensign John Charles William Lever to be Lieutenant, vice James John Pickford, resigned. Dated 21st July, 1858.

Commissions signed by the Lord Lieutenant of the County of Lanark.

1st Royal Lanarkshire Militia.

David Blair Lockhart, Esq., to be Captain, vice Douglas Hamilton, appointed to the South Down Militia. Dated 2nd July, 1858.

FROM THE

SUPPLEMENT

TO THE

LONDON GAZETTE of JULY 30, 1858.

AT the Court at *Osborne House, Isle of Wight,* the 31st day of *July,* 1858.

PRESENT,

The QUEEN's Most Excellent Majesty in Council

WHEREAS by the " West Indian Encumbered Estates Act, 1854," provision was made to facilitate the sale and transfer of Encumbered Estates in the several West India Colonies, named in a schedule to the said Act (among which is the colony of Tobago,) and it was enacted that Her Majesty might from time to time, by Order in Council, direct the said Act to come into operation in any of the said colonies, but that no such Order in Council should be made in respect of any colony until the legislature thereof should have presented an address to Her Majesty, praying Her Majesty to issue such order, and should also have made provision to the satisfaction of Her Majesty's Principal Secretary of State for the Colonies, for payment of the salaries of the Local Commissioners in the said Act mentioned, and of all such assistant secretaries, clerks, messengers, and officers, as might be appointed under the said Act in such colony, and of such other expenses of carrying the said Act into execution as were therein directed to be provided for by the said legislature.

And whereas the legislature of Tobago, by an address dated the 22nd December, 1857, has prayed Her Majesty to issue such Order as aforesaid, and by an Act passed on the 13th January, 1858, entitled "An Act for carrying into execution in Tobago the West Indian Encumbered Estates Act, 1854," has made provision for the payment of such salaries and other expenses as aforesaid, to the satisfaction of Her Majesty's Principal Secretary of State for the Colonies.

It is, therefore, hereby ordered by the Queen's most Excellent Majesty, by and with the advice of Her Privy Council, that the said "West Indian Encumbered Estates Act, 1854," shall, from the date of this Order in Council, come into operation in the colony of Tobago.

And the Right Honourable Sir Edward Bulwer Lytton, Bart., one of Her Majesty's Principal Secretaries of State, is to give the necessary directions herein accordingly.

Wm. L. Bathurst.

At the Court at *Osborne House, Isle of Wight,* the 31st day of *July,* 1858.

The QUEEN'S Most Excellent Majesty in Council was pleased to order, upon the petition of the Justices of the Peace for the county of Northumberland, in quarter sessions assembled, that Felton, Warkworth, Whittingham, Lowick, Cornhill, Hartburn, and Widdrington, shall be polling places for the Northern Division of the said county of Northumberland.

Also upon the petition of the Justices of the Peace for the county of Gloucester, in quarter sessions assembled, in Gloucester, that Bilson Woodside, in the township of East Dean, shall be a polling place for the western division of the said county of Gloucester.

Also upon the petition of the Justices of the Peace for the North Riding of the county of York, in general quarter sessions assembled, that the town of Easingwold shall be a polling place for the said North Riding of the county of York.

Also upon the petition of the Justices of the Peace for the county of Buckingham, in general quarter sessions assembled, that the towns or places of Amersham, Bletchley, Brill, High Wycombe, and Slough shall be polling places for the said county of Buckingham, in lieu of the polling place of Beaconsfield, and, further, that the town or place of Beaconsfield shall cease to be a polling place for the said county.

Also upon a petition of the Justices of the Peace for the county of Wilts, in general quarter sessions assembled, that the town of Downton shall be a polling place for the southern division of the said county of Wilts.

Also upon the petition of the Justices of the Peace for the county of Northumberland, in quarter sessions assembled, that the towns and places of Blyth, Bywell, Falstone, Haydon Bridge, Humshaugh, Kirkwhelpington, Ponteland, Slaley, and Stannington, shall be polling places for the southern division of the said county of Northumberland.

At the Court at *Osborne House, Isle of Wight,* the 31st day of *July,* 1858.

The QUEEN'S Most Excellent Majesty in Council was pleased to approve of the representations duly prepared (as set forth in this Gazette) by the Ecclesiastical Commissioners for England, as to the assignment of district chapelries to—

The consecrated church of Saint Paul, situate at Skelmersdale, in the parish of Ormskirk, in the county of Lancaster, and diocese of Chester, to be called "The District Chapelry of Saint Paul, Skelmersdale."

The consecrated church of Saint John, situate at Canton, in the parish of Llandaff, in the county of Glamorgan, and diocese of Llandaff, to be called "The District Chapelry of St. John, Canton."

The consecrated church called Christ Church, situate at Eaton, in the parish of Astbury, in the county and diocese of Chester, to be called "The District Chapelry of Christ Church, Eaton."

At the Court at *Osborne House, Isle of Wight,* the 31st day of *July,* 1858.

The QUEEN'S Most Excellent Majesty in Council was pleased to approve and ratify a scheme duly prepared (as set forth in this Gazette) by the Ecclesiastical Commissioners for England—

For effecting an exchange of certain estates belonging to the Bishop of Lincoln in right of his See, and the said Commissioners respectively.

Also a representation duly prepared by the said Commissioners (as set forth in this Gazette), as to the assignment of a district chapelry to the consecrated church of Saint John the Baptist, situate at Purbrook, in the parish of Farlington, in the county of Southampton, and in the diocese of Winchester, to be called "The District Chapelry of Purbrook."

Also the schemes duly prepared by the said Commissioners (as set forth in this Gazette)—

For authorizing the sale of certain property formerly belonging to the Prebend of Chute and Chisenbury, in the Cathedral Church of Salisbury, and now vested in them.

And for authorizing the sale of certain property formerly belonging to the Prebend of Highworth, in the cathedral church of Salisbury, and now vested in them.

Also representations duly prepared as aforesaid, as to the assignment of a district chapelry to the consecrated church of Saint Catherine, situate at Blackrod, in the parish of Bolton-le-Moors, in the county of Lancaster, and in the diocese of Manchester, to be named " The District Chapelry of Saint Catherine, Blackrod."

And as to the assignment of a consolidated chapelry to the consecrated church of Saint Philip, situate at Earl's-court, in the new parish of Saint Barnabas, Kensington, in the county of Middle· sex and diocese of London, to be named " The Consolidated Chapelry of Saint Philip, Earl's-court, Kensington."

Also a scheme duly prepared as aforesaid, making better provision for the cure of souls in the chapelry district of Haverthwaite, in the county of Lancaster, and in the diocese of Carlisle.

Also the representations, duly prepared as aforesaid, as to the assignment of consolidated chapelries to—

The consecrated church of Saint Stephen, situate at Old Ford, in the parish of Saint Mary, Stratford, Bow, in the county of Middlesex, and in the diocese of London, to be named " The District Chapelry of Saint Stephen, Old Ford."

And to the consecrated church of Saint Andrew, situate at North Horton, in the parish of Bradford, in the county of York, and diocese of Ripon, to be named " The Consolidated Chapelry of Saint Andrew, Bradford."

Also the schemes duly prepared by the said Commissioners—

For authorizing the sale of certain property, formerly belonging to the prebend of Fridaythorpe, in the cathedral and metropolitical church of York, and now vested in them.

For authorizing the sale of certain property, formerly belonging to the Dean and Chapter of the collegiate church of Westminster, and now vested in them.

For authorizing the sale of certain property formerly belonging to the Prebend of Waltham, in the cathedral church of Chichester, and now vested in them.

At the Court at *Osborne House, Isle of Wight*, the 31st day of *July*, 1858.

The QUEEN'S Most Excellent Majesty in Council was pleased to order, with reference to the representations made (as set forth in this Gazette), by the Right Honourable Spencer Horatio Walpole, one of Her Majesty's Principal Secretaries of State, that no new burial-ground shall be opened in any of the undermentioned parishes without the previous approval of one of Her Majesty's Principal Secretaries of State, and that burials in the said parishes shall be discontinued with the following modifications, from and after the twelfth of August next (except as is herein otherwise directed), as follows; viz. :—

BLACKBURN.—Beneath the *parish church* of Blackburn; and it is also ordered that (except in vaults and walled graves, existing on the sixth day of March, one thousand eight hundred and fifty-eight in which each body shall be embedded in charcoal and entombed in an air-tight manner) interment of the inhabitants of Blackburn Township be discontinued in the *churchyards* of *St. Mary* and *St. Peter*, on the first day of August, one thousand eight hundred and fifty-eight, and for the inhabitants of other places on the first day of August, one thousand eight hundred and fifty-nine. BIRSTAL, YORKSHIRE.—In the *parish church* of Birstal, and, with the exception of now existing vaults and family graves, in the ancient part of the *churchyard*, and also in the part added in the year one thousand seven hundred and eighty ; that from and after the first day of March, one thousand eight hundred and fifty-nine, in *St. James's Churchyard, Heckmondwike*, with the exception of now existing vaults and brick graves which can be opened without disturbing soil that has been already buried in, and in which each coffin shall be separately entombed in an air-tight manner. In the vaults under *Christ Church, Liversedge.* In the *chapel* of the ecclesiastical district of *Whitechapel, Cleckheaton*, and, from and after the first day of March, one thousand eight hundred and fifty-nine, in the *chapelyard*, with the exception of now existing brick graves which can be opened without disturbing soil that has been already buried in, and in which each coffin shall be separately entombed in an air-tight manner ; and forthwith in *Tong* Church. HALIFAX.—Beneath *Coley Church*, in the parish of Halifax ; and also within three yards of all dwelling-houses in the burial-grounds of the *Methodist New Connexion Chapel, Wesleyan Chapel*, and *Independent Chapel, North Owram*, in *Coley.* Beneath *Luddenden Church*, in the parish of Halifax, and from and after the first day of February, one thousand eight hundred and fifty-nine, in the *churchyard*, with the exception of vaults and walled graves which were in existence on the first of January, one thousand eight hundred and fifty-eight, which can be opened without disturbing soil that has been already buried in, and in which each coffin shall be separately entombed in an air-tight manner; and it is ordered that in the burial-ground of the *Wesleyan Methodist Chapel, Ludden-den*, burials be forthwith discontinued within three yards of all dwelling-houses; also that burials be forthwith discontinued in the *churchyard* of *Illingworth*, in the parish of Halifax, within three yards of all dwelling-houses, and from and after the first day of January, one thousand eight hundred and sixty-one, in the whole of the churchyard, except in now existing vaults and walled graves, which can be opened without disturbing soil that has been already buried in, and in which each coffin shall be entombed in an air-tight manner; that burials be discontinued forthwith in *Moor End Independent Chapel*, and in *Mount Tabor Wesleyan Chapel Burial-ground*, Illingworth, within three yards of the Sunday School; also, that burials be discontinued in the *parish church* of *Elland-cum-Greetland*, in the *Wesleyan Methodist Chapel* and *Unitarian Chapel, Elland*, and from and after the first day of January, one thousand eight hundred and sixty, with the exception of now existing vaults and brick graves, which can be opened without disturbing soil that has been already buried in, and in which each coffin shall be entombed in an air-tight manner, in the *parish churchyard* of *Elland-cum-Greetland*, and in the burial-grounds of the *Wesleyan Methodist Chapel, Independent Chapel*, and *Unitarian Chapel, Elland*. That burials be forthwith discontinued in the *church* of *Stainland*, in the parish of Halifax, and also in the *churchyard* and *Wesleyan Chapel Burial-ground, Stainland*, within three yards of all dwelling-houses.

Also Ecclesfield, Yorkshire.—In the *Parish*

Church of Ecclesfield, in the county of York, also in the *churchyard* within three yards of all dwelling-houses, and in the ancient part of the churchyard, except in family vaults and graves, and in ground which can be opened without disturbing human remains; also under the *Independent Chapel, Loxley,* and the school adjoining, and in *Bradfield Church,* both in the parish of Ecclesfield, and that from and after the thirty-first day of December, one thousand eight hundred and sixty, in *Bradfield Church-yard,* with the exception of now existing family vaults and brick graves, which can be opened without disturbing ground that has been already buried in, and in which each coffin shall be entombed in brick or stonework, properly cemented ; and also, with the exception of re-served earthen grave spaces, in which no body shall be buried within four feet of the surface, measuring from the upper part of the coffin to the ordinary level of the ground. ECCLES, LAN-CASHIRE.—In the Burial-grounds of the *Bruns-wick, Bethesda,* and *Windsor Chapels,* in the township of Pendleton, also in the old part of the *parish churchyard* of *Eccles,* except in the vaults and walled graves existing on the first day of March, one thousand eight hundred and fifty-eight, in which each coffin shall be embedded in charcoal, and be separately entombed in an air-tight manner, or in now existing family graves which can be opened to the depth of five feet without the exposure of remains; and it is also ordered, that in the rest of the churchyard, and in the detached churchyard, and in the *Wesleyan* and *Roman Catholic Burial-grounds at Barton,* and in the *Churchyard* and *Wesleyan Burial-ground* at *Swinton* (except in vaults and walled graves, used with the above

precautions), one body only be buried in a grave,
not less than five feet deep, and no grave reopened within fourteen years, except to bury
another member of the same family, in which
case a foot of earth shall be left undisturbed
above the previously buried coffin; also, that
in the *Independent Burial-grounds* at *Patricroft*
and at *Pendlebury*, no grave be reopened except
to bury another member of the same family, no
grave to be less than five feet deep, or dug in
soil which is not free from water and remains;
also, that interments be wholly discontinued in
the vaults beneath *Pendleton Church*.

Also ALVINGTON, GLOUCESTERSHIRE.—Wholly in
the *Parish Church* of Alvington, and within
three yards of the walls thereof. WHALLEY,
LANCASHIRE.—Wholly in the *Wesleyan Association Burial-ground, Rawtenstall*; in the
churchyard, and in the *Wesleyan* and *Unitarian
Burial-grounds, Rawtenstall*, and also in the
churchyard and in the *Wesleyan*, the *Wesleyan
Association* and *Unitarian Burial-grounds* of
New Church, in Rossendale, except so far as
is compatible with the official regulations for new
Burial-grounds, omitting No. 3. HAMBLE,
HANTS.—Beneath the *Parish Church* of Hamble.
ROSS.—Beneath the *Parish Church* of Ross;
and also in the *additional parish churchyard*,
except so far as is compatible with the Regulations for new burial-grounds; and in the
Baptist Burial-ground, except in vaults and
walled graves, in which each coffin shall be
embedded in charcoal, and separately entombed
in an airtight manner, and except in graves
never previously buried in. FOREST OF DEAN,
GLOUCESTERSHIRE.—Beneath the churches of
Christ Church Berry Hill, St. Paul's Park End,
and in the *Burial-grounds of Christ Church*,

within five yards of the parsonage and the school-room ; and in the *Burial-ground* of *St. Paul's,* except so far as is compatible with the following regulations; viz. : that the ground be drained, so that no water accumulate in any grave, that no coffin be buried within a foot of any other coffin, or less than four feet below the surface of the ground, unless deposited in a vault or walled grave, and separately entombed in an air-tight manner.

Also MONMOUTH.—Beneath the several *churches* and *chapels* in the parish of Monmouth, and also in *St. Thomas's Churchyard,* and the *Baptist Burial-ground;* and in the *cemetery* or *additional churchyard of St. Mary's,* Monmouth, except so far as is compatible with the Official Regulations for new burial-grounds, omitting No. 3 :—and that in the *Independent Burial-ground* except in graves not less than five feet deep which are free from water and remains. FINCHLEY, MIDDLESEX. - From and after the first day of June, one thousand eight hundred and fifty-nine, in the *parish churchyard* of Finchley, with the exception of now existing vaults and brick graves, which can be opened without disturbing soil that has been already buried in, and in which each body shall be separately entombed in brick or stone work properly cemented, and that the only bodies interred be those of the husband, wife, parents, unmarried children, and brothers and sisters of persons already buried therein ; and it is ordered that in *Holy Trinity Churchyard,* in the parish of Finchley, except in family vaults and graves, only one body be buried in each grave. LLANDAFF. — In the *Cathedral* of Llandaff, and within three yards thereof, also except in now existing vaults and walled graves, in which each coffin shall be embedded in charcoal and separately entombed in an airtight manner in that part of the *churchyard* which is to the south of the cathedral, and from and after the first of May, one thousand eight hundred and sixty, in the rest of the churchyard. TITCH-FIELD, HANTS.—In the *parish church* of Titch-field ; and from and after the first day of January, one thousand eight hundred and sixty-one, in the *parish churchyard*, with the exception of family vaults and brick graves, which can be opened without disturbing soil that has been already buried in, and in which each coffin shall be separately entombed in brick or stone work properly cemented. WEST-BOURNE, SUSSEX. — In the *parish church* of Westbourne; and from and after the first day of May, one thousand eight hundred and fifty-nine, in the *churchyard*, with the exception of vaults and brick graves which were in existence on April thirtieth, one thousand eight hundred and fifty-eight, and which shall be used on the following conditions, —that they are free from water, that, when required, they be opened without disturbing soil that has been recently buried in, and that each coffin be entombed in brick or stone work properly cemented. GREAT WARLEY, ESSEX.— In the *parish church;* and from and after the first day of May, one thousand eight hundred and fifty-nine, in the *churchyard* of Great Warley, Essex.

———

At the Court at *Osborne House, Isle of Wight,* the 31st day of *July*, 1858.

The QUEEN'S Most Excellent Majesty in Council was pleased to order that the time for the discontinuance of burials in the churchyards and burial-grounds undermentioned be postponed as follows, viz.:

In All Saints' Churchyard, in Christ Churchyard, in Holy Trinity Churchyard, and in the burial-grounds of the Ebenezer and Mares Green Independent Chapels, and of the Wesleyan Chapel, all in WEST BROMWICH, from the first of July to the first of October, one thousand eight hundred and fifty-eight; in the parish churchyard, in the burial-grounds of the Baptist Chapel, Townfields, of the Lower Baptist Chapel, and of the Independent Chapel, and in the old burial-ground of the General Baptist Chapel, all in the parish of CHESHAM, Bucks, from the twenty-fourth of June to the twenty-ninth of September, one thousand eight hundred and fifty-eight; in the churchyard of the parish of EGHAM, Surrey, from the first of July to the first of October, one thousand eight hundred and fifty-eight; in the parish churchyard of GLOSSOP, in the Independent Chapel Burial-ground, in the township of *Whitfield*, and in the Wesleyan Chapel Burial-ground, in the township of *Hadfield*, both in Glossop, from the first of July, one thousand eight hundred and fifty-eight, to the first of July, one thousand eight hundred and fifty-nine; in the churchyard of HAVERFORDWEST, from the first of July to the first of September, one thousand eight hundred and fifty-eight; in the parish churchyard, and in the Baptist Chapel Burial-ground, HUSBAND's BOSWORTH, from the first of August to the first of September, one thousand eight hundred and fifty-eight; in the churchyard of KIMBOLTON, Hunts, from the first of September to the first of November, one thousand eight hundred and fifty-eight; in Christ Church Burial-ground, Every-street, *Ancoats*, in MANCHESTER, from the first of September to the 31st of December, one thousand eight hundred and fifty-eight, on condition that all the regulations prescribed by certain Orders in Council of the seventh of December, one thousand eight hundred and fifty-five, and twenty-second of October, one thousand eight hundred and fifty-six, in reference to this burial-ground, be strictly observed; in the new portion of the churchyard at All Saints, NEWMARKET, and in the new burial-ground in St. Mary's Parish in that town, from the first of July to the first of August, one thousand eight hundred and fifty-eight; in the parish churchyard of NEWPORT, Salop, from the first of July, one thousand eight hundred and fifty-eight, to the first of January, one thousand eight hundred and fifty-nine; in the churchyard of Christ Church, OLDBURY, in the parish of Halesowen, from the first of July to the first of August, one thousand eight hundred and fifty-eight; in the new parish burial-ground, and in Bechen Grove Chapel Burial-ground, WATFORD, Herts, from the first of August to the first of November, one thousand eight hundred and fifty-eight; in the churchyards of St. Peter, St. Helen, St. Andrew, St. Alban, St. Swithin, All Saints, St. Martin, and St. Nicholas, in St. George's Churchyard, in the parish of CLAINES, and in the Independent Burial-ground in All Saints' Parish, all in the city of WORCESTER, from the first of August to the first of October, one thousand eight hundred and fifty-eight.

And whereas by an Order in Council of the thirty-first of March, one thousand eight hundred and fifty-five, burials were directed to be discontinued, as therein mentioned, in the parish churchyard, and in the burial-grounds of the Baptist and Independent Chapels, LYMINGTON, and it seems fit that the said Order be varied; now therefore Her Majesty, by and with the advice of Her Privy Council, is pleased to order, and it is hereby ordered, that permission be granted to use now existing vaults and brick graves in the said churchyard and burial-grounds, in the parish of Lymington, upon the following conditions, viz.: that no interment take place within three yards of any dwelling-house or public institution; that each grave, when required, be opened without the disturbance of soil that has been already buried in; that each coffin be embedded in a layer of powdered charcoal four inches thick, and be separately entombed in an airtight manner; and that the only bodies interred be those of the husband, wife, unmarried children, brothers and sisters of persons already buried therein.

And whereas by an Order in Council of the eighteenth of October, one thousand eight hundred and fifty-four, burials were directed to be discontinued in the churchyard of St. Gregory, SUDBURY, in Suffolk, from and after the first of August, one thousand eight hundred and fifty-five, which period has since been extended in respect of part of such churchyard, to the first of June last; and whereas by an Order of the fifth of that month, burials were permitted in the said churchyard, subject to certain provisions and exceptions, and it seems fit that such Orders be varied; now, therefore, Her Majesty, by and with the advice aforesaid, is pleased to order, and it is hereby ordered, that the said churchyard of St. Gregory, Sudbury, be closed on and after the first of January, one thousand eight hundred and sixty, with the exception of now existing family vaults and brick graves; and it is further ordered that the said family vaults and brick graves be used on condition that they be opened without disturbing soil that has been already buried in, and that each coffin be embedded in a layer of powdered charcoal, four inches thick, and be separately entombed in an airtight manner.

___

At the Court at *Osborne House, Isle of Wight,* the 31st day of *July,* 1858.

The QUEEN'S Most Excellent Majesty in Council was pleased to order that the representations made by the Right Honourable Spencer Horatio Walpole, one of Her Majesty's Principal Secretaries of State (as set forth in this Gazette), stating that for the protection of the public health, no new burial-ground should be opened in any of the undermentioned parishes without the previous approval of one of Her Majesty's Principal Secretaries of State, and that interments in the same should be discontinued, with the following modifications:

KELLOE, DURHAM.—On and after the first day of June, one thousand eight hundred and fifty-nine, in the *parish churchyard* of Kelloe, except in family graves that are free from water and remains to the depth of five feet. ALSTON, CUMBERLAND.—Forthwith in the *parish church* of Alston, and within three yards of any dwelling in the *parish churchyard.* And from and after the first day of June, one thousand eight hundred and fifty-nine, in the rest of the *churchyard*; also, that the earth now piled up against the walls of houses be removed to the level of the room floors. WANSTEAD, ESSEX.—Forthwith in the *vaults* and *crypts* underneath the *parish church* of Wanstead ; and from and after the first day of June, one thousand eight hundred and fifty-nine, in the *churchyard*, with the exception of now existing vaults and brick graves, which can be opened without disturbing soil that has been already buried in, and in which each coffin shall be separately entombed in brick or stone-work properly cemented ; and also with the exception of reserved grave spaces, provided that no coffin be buried without a covering of four feet of soil. BECKINGTON, SOMERSETSHIRE. — Forthwith in Beckington *Church* and in the *Baptist Chapel*, and from and after the first day of June, one thousand eight hundred and fifty-nine in the *churchyard* and *Baptist Burial ground*, except in now existing vaults and walled graves, in which each coffin shall be embedded in charcoal and separately entombed in an air tight manner, and except in other graves not less than five feet deep, to be used only for the burial of members of the same family, and which can be opened without the exposure of remains. STOCKTON-ON-TEES.— Forthwith in the several *churches* and *chapels* in the parish of Stockton-on-Tees ; and that the *churchyard* of *Holy Trinity*, Stockton, be so drained that water may not accumulate in any vault or grave to be buried in, and that no grave be dug within a foot of any other grave, or so as to expose any coffin or remains ; and that interment in the Roman Catholic burial-ground be discontinued. BOWDON. —Forthwith in the *parish church* of Bowdon, and also in the ancient part of the *churchyard*, except in vaults and walled graves, and that in the rest of the churchyard the Official Regulations for new burial-grounds Nos. 4, 5, 6, 7, and 8, be observed ; and that in *St. George's Churchyard* one body only be buried in a grave, and no grave previously buried in be reopened unless to bury another of the same family ; no coffin to be placed within a foot of another coffin, or less than four feet below the surface of the ground. Also STANHOPE, DURHAM. — Forthwith in the *parish church* of Stanhope ; and in that part of the *churchyard* which is south of the *church*, except in family graves, and that no grave be reopened in any part of the churchyard within fourteen years after the previous burial. BISHOPS-AUCKLAND.—Forthwith in the *church of St. Andrew*, Bishops - Auckland, and in the old part of the *churchyard*, except in family graves, and that coffins buried in vaults and walled graves be separately entombed in an airtight manner. EARSDON, NORTHUMBERLAND. – Forthwith in the several *churches* and *chapels* within the parish of Earsdon, and in *Seghill Churchyard*, except so far as is compatible with the Regulations for New Burial-grounds, omitting No. 3 ; and from and after the first day of June, one thousand eight hundred and fifty - nine, in *Earsdon Parish Churchyard*, except in graves not less than five feet deep which can be opened without disturbance of remains ; and from and after the first day of June, one thousand eight hundred and fifty-nine, in the *burial-ground* of *Blyth Chapel*. HALTWHISTLE, NORTHUMBERLAND.—Forthwith wholly in the *Parish Church;* and from and after the first day of July, one thousand eight hundred and fifty-nine, in the *churchyard*, except in family graves which can be opened to the depth of five feet without the disturbance of remains. BURY, LANCASHIRE.—Forthwith in that part of the *Burial-ground* of *Bamford Chapel* which is before the parsonage and within four yards of the chapel or school-room, and also in the rest of the burial-ground, except so far as is compatible with the observance of the Regulations for New Burial-grounds, omitting No. 3. CHESTER-LE-STREET, DURHAM.—Forthwith in *Birtley Churchyard*, except so far as is compatible with the observance of the Regulations for New Burial-grounds. GAINFORD, YORKSHIRE.—From and after the first day of June, one thousand eight hundred and fifty-nine, in the *church* and *churchyard* of *Barnard Castle*. CHEPSTOW. Forthwith in the *Independent Burial-ground*, except in graves never before buried in, and in which actual members of the congregation only and their children shall be interred. CHARING, KENT. —Forthwith in the *parish church* of Charing; and from and after the first day of June, one thousand eight hundred and fifty-nine, in the *churchyard*, with the exception of now existing vaults and brick graves which can be opened without disturbing soil that has been already buried in, and in which each coffin shall be entombed in brick or stonework properly cemented; also with the exception of reserved earthen grave spaces, in which the only bodies to be interred shall be those of the husbands and wives of persons already buried.

should be taken into consideration by a Committee of the Lords of Her Majesty's Most Honourable Privy Council, on the thirteenth day of September next.

At the Court at *Osborne House, Isle of Wight,*
the 31st day of *July,* 1858.

The QUEEN'S Most Excellent Majesty in
Council was pleased to order that the churchwardens or such other person as may have the
care of the vaults under the churches of Saint
Dunstan's in the West, Saint Bride's Fleet-street,
Saint Sepulchre's, Skinner-street, Saint Magnus
Martyr, and Saint Andrew, Holborn, do respectively adopt, or cause to be adopted, the following
measures in respect of such vaults, viz.—

Saint Dunstan's in the West.

1. That the coffins in the two public vaults
underneath the church be deposited in one of the
angular vaults, and be covered with earth and
powdered charcoal.

2. That the entrance to the vault selected be
bricked up, and a ventilating tube be carried from
the vault to the roof of the church.

3. That those crypts in the public catacombs
which are at present open be bricked up.

4. That the works, so far as relates to sanitary precautions for the protection of the workmen and otherwise, be effected under the superintendence of the medical officer of health of the
city of London, and that McDougall's powder,
chloride of lime, or other disinfectants, be employed whenever requisite.

Saint Bride's, Fleet-street.

1. That, where accessible, the vaults under the
church of St. Bride's, Fleet-street, the vestry, and
the churchyard, be freely limewashed.

2. That in those vaults the coffins be covered
with earth and powdered charcoal.

3. That the existing ventilating openings in
these vaults and the entrance be bricked up, and

that two ventilating tubes at the west end and two at the east end be carried from these vaults above the roof of the church.

4. That the work, so far as relates to the sanitary precautions for the protection of the workmen and otherwise, be effected under the superintendence of the medical officer of health for the city of London, and that McDougall's powder, chloride of lime, or other disinfectants, be employed whenever requisite.

Saint Sepulchre's, Skinner-street.

1. That, where accessible, the vaults under the church of Saint Sepulchre's, Skinner-street, be freely limewashed.

2. That the coffins in the vaults under the vestries be covered with earth and powdered charcoal, and that the opening from the aisle of the church be bricked up. That the coffins in the vaults under the entrance of the church at the south-west angles, and in the vault entered from the churchyard at the north-west angle of the church be laid down and covered with earth and powdered charcoal, and that the entrances be bricked up.

3. That the existing ventilating openings from the above vaults be closed, and ventilating tubes be carried from them to the roof of the church. That a ventilating tube be carried to the roof from the vault under the south aisle.

4. That the works, so far as relates to sanitary precautions for the protection of the workmen and otherwise, be effected under the superintendence of the Medical Officer of Health of the city of London ; and that McDougall's powder, chloride of lime or other disinfectants, be employed, whenever requisite.

Saint Magnus Martyr.

1. That the vaults under the churchyard of
Saint Magnus Martyr be freely limewashed, where
accessible.

2. That the coffins at present contained in the
vault under the churchyard, be deposited in the
vault under the church.

3. That the coffins in this vault be covered
with earth and powdered charcoal.

4. That the existing entrances be closed with
brickwork ; and that the ventilation in the large
vault under the church be closed, and a ventilating
tube or tubes provided to carry off any foul air
which may escape above the roof of the church.

5. That the works, so far as relates to sanitary
precautions for the protection of the workmen
and otherwise, be effected under the superintendence of the Medical Officer of Health of the city
of London, and McDougall's powder, chloride of
lime, or other disinfectants be employed whenever
requisite.

Saint Andrew, Holborn.

1. That, where accessible, the vaults under
the church of Saint Andrew, Holborn, be freely
limewashed

2. That the coffins be covered with earth and
powdered charcoal.

3. That the existing ventilating openings in
the east end of the church, and on the north and
south sides, be closed, together with the entrance ;
and that ventilating tubes be carried above the
roof on the north and south sides of the church.

4. That the works, so far as relates to sanitary
precautions for the protection of the workmen
and otherwise, be effected under the superintendence of the Medical Officer of Health of the city
of London, and that McDougall's powder, chloride

of lime, or other disinfectants be employed whenever requisite.

At the Court at *Osborne House, Isle of Wight,*
the 31st day of *July,* 1858.

The QUEEN'S Most Excellent Majesty in
Council was pleased to order, with reference to a
Petition of the Local Board of Health for the
district of Sowerby Bridge, in the West Riding of
the county of York, established under "The
Public Health Supplemental Act, 1856," that the
said Local Board shall be a burial board for the
district of such local board, in accordance with the
provisions of the Act passed in the last session of
Parliament, intituled "An Act to amend the
Burial Acts."

At the Court at *Osborne House, Isle of Wight,*
the 31st day of *July,* 1858.

The QUEEN'S Most Excellent Majesty in
Council was pleased to order, with reference to
an Order in Council of the fifth day of June last,
vesting powers in the town council of the city of
Hereford, for providing requisite places of burial,
under the provisions of the Act passed in the
session of Parliament held in the seventeenth and
eighteenth years of Her Majesty's reign, intituled
"An Act to make further provision for the burial
of the dead in England beyond the limits of the
metropolis," or of any other Act of Parliament
relating to burials, for the inhabitants of the
parishes of All Saints, Saint Peter, Saint Owen,
Saint Nicholas, and Saint John the Baptist, in the
said city, that the parish of All Saints, in the said
city of Hereford, be exempted from the operation
of the aforesaid Order in Council.

This Gazette contains an ordinance, framed by
the Commissioners appointed for the purposes of
the Act of the 17th and 18th Vict. cap. 81, intituled " An Act to make further provision for the
good government and extension of the University
of Oxford, of the colleges therein, and of the College of Saint Mary, Winchester," in relation to the
exhibitions of the foundation of the Lady Elizabeth .
Hastings, within the Queen's College, in the University of Oxford.

Also an ordinance in relation to the exhibitions
or scholarships of the foundations of Frederick
Tylney, Esq., and others, within the Queen's
College aforesaid.

Also an ordinance in relation to the exhibitions
of Dame Elizabeth Holford's foundation at Christ
Church, in the said University.

At the Court at *Osborne House, Isle of Wight,*
the 31st day of *July,* 1858.

PRESENT,

The QUEEN's Most Excellent Majesty in Council.

WHEREAS by an Act passed in the session
of Parliament holden in the fifty-seventh year
of the reign of his late Majesty King George
the Third, intituled " An Act to empower His
" Majesty to suspend training, and to regulate
" quotas of the Militia," it is, amongst other things,
enacted, " That it shall be lawful for His Majesty,
" by any Order or Orders in Council, to suspend
" the calling out of the Militia of the United
" Kingdom, or any part of the United Kingdom,
" or of any county, riding, shire, stewartry, city,
" town, or place, for the purpose of being trained
" and exercised in any year, and to order and
" direct that no training or exercising of the

" Militia of the United Kingdom, or of any part
" of the United Kingdom, or of any county or
" counties, riding or ridings, shire or shires,
" stewartry or stewartries, city or cities, town or
" towns, or place or places, specified in any such
" Order or Orders in Council shall take place in
" any year, anything contained in any Act or
" Acts of Parliament to the contrary notwith-
" standing."

And whereas it has seemed fit to Her Majesty,
by and with the advice of Her Privy Council, to
suspend the calling out of the Militia of certain
parts of the United Kingdom hereinafter mentioned for the purpose of being trained and
exercised in the year one thousand eight hundred
and fifty-eight.

Now, therefore, Her Majesty, by the advice of
Her Privy Council, doth hereby suspend the
calling out of the regiments of Militia specified in
the schedule annexed to this Order for the purpose of being trained and exercised in the year
one thousand eight hundred and fifty-eight, which
schedule is hereby directed to be taken as part of
this Order ; and it is further ordered, that this
Order and the said schedule be published in the
London Gazette.

Wm. L. Bathurst.

———

Schedule of Militia Regiments referred to in the
foregoing Order.

Argyll and Bute Rifles.
The Edinburgh, or Queen's, Regiment of
Light Infantry.
Edinburgh Artillery.
Fifeshire Artillery.
Perthshire Rifles.
Renfrewshire.

India Board, August 2, 1858.

THE following General Order has been this day received at the East India House:—

GENERAL ORDER BY THE GOVERNOR-GENERAL OF INDIA.

No. 1855.—Foreign Department.

Allahabad, June 24, 1858.

THE Right Honourable the Governor-General has the highest gratification in announcing that the town and fort of Gwalior were recovered by Major-General Sir H. Rose, on the 19th instant, after a general action, in which the rebels, who had usurped the authority of Maha Rajah Scindia, were totally defeated.

On the 20th June, the Maha Rajah Scindia, attended by the Governor-General's Agent for Central India and Sir Hugh Rose, and escorted by British troops, was restored to the palace of his ancestors, and was welcomed by his subjects with every mark of loyalty and attachment.

It was on the 1st June that the rebels, aided by the treachery of some of Maha Rajah Scindia's troops, seized the capital of His Highness's kingdom, and hoped to establish a new Government under a Pretender in His Highness's territory. Eighteen days had not elapsed before they were compelled to evacuate the fort and town of Gwalior, and to relinquish the authority which they had endeavoured to usurp.

The promptitude and success with which the strength of the British Government has been put forth for the restoration of its faithful ally to the capital of his territory, and the continued presence of British troops at Gwalior to support His Highness in the re-establishment of his administration, will afford to all a convincing proof that the British Government has the will and the power to befriend those, who, like Maha Rajah Scindia, do not shrink from their obligation, or hesitate to avow their loyalty.

The Right Honourable the Governor-General, in order to mark his appreciation of the Maha Rajah Scindia's friendship, and his gratification at the re-establishment of His Highness's authority in his ancestral dominions, is pleased to direct that a royal salute shall be fired at every principal station in India.

By order of the Right Honourable the Governor-General of India.

G. F. EDMONSTONE,
Secretary to the Government of India, with the Governor-General.

Osborne House, July 31, 1858.

This day had audience of Her Majesty;

Don José de Marcoleta, Envoy Extraordinary and Minister Plenipotentiary from the Republick of Nicaragua, and Minister Plenipotentiary from the Republick of Costa Rica, to deliver his credentials:

To which audience he was introduced by the Earl of Malmesbury, Her Majesty's Principal Secretary of State for Foreign Affairs.

Foreign-Office, June 26, 1858.

The Queen has been graciously pleased to appoint David Erskine, Esq., to be Her Majesty's Consul in the Island of Madeira.

Westminster, August 2, 1858.

This day the Lords being met a message was sent to the Honourable House of Commons by the Gentleman Usher of the Black Rod, acquainting them, that *The Lords, authorized by virtue of a Commission under the Great Seal, signed by Her Majesty, for declaring Her Royal Assent to several Acts agreed upon by both Houses, do desire the immediate attendance of the Honourable House in the House of Peers to hear the Commission read;* and the Commons being come thither, the said Commission, empowering the Lord Archbishop of Canterbury, and several other Lords therein named, to declare and notify the Royal Assent to the said Acts, was read accordingly, and the Royal Assent given to

An Act to apply a sum out of the Consolidated Fund and the surplus of Ways and Means to the service of the year one thousand eight hundred and fifty-eight, and to appropriate the supplies granted in this session of Parliament.

An Act to amend the Act of the fifth and sixth years of Her present Majesty, to consolidate and amend the laws relating to the copyright of designs for ornamenting articles of manufacture.

An Act to authorize the inclosure of certain lands in pursuance of a special report of the Inclosure Commissioners of England and Wales.

An Act to continue certain Acts to prevent the spreading of contagious or infectious diseases among sheep, cattle, and other animals.

An Act to continue certain Turnpike Acts in Great Britain.

An Act to amend an Act of the last Session, to render more effectual the police in counties and burghs in Scotland.

An Act to substitute in certain cases the Bishop

of one diocese for the Bishop of another as a trustee of certain trusts.

An Act to simplify the forms and diminish the expense of completing titles to land in Scotland.

An Act to facilitate the sale and transfer of land in Ireland.

An Act to amend the law concerning the powers of Stipendiary Magistrates and Justices of the Peace in certain cases.

An Act for the re-arrangement of the districts of the County Courts among the Judges thereof.

An Act to amend the Act of the ninth and tenth years of Her present Majesty, chapter thirty-nine, and to abolish foot passenger tolls on Chelsea Bridge after payment of the sum of eighty thousand pounds and interest.

An Act to repeal certain enactments requiring returns to be made to one of the Secretaries of State.

An Act to amend the law concerning detached parts of counties.

An Act to impose fees on the branding of barrels under the Acts concerning the herring fisheries in Scotland.

An Act for confirming a scheme as amended of the Charity Commissioners for Cowley's Charity in the parish of Swineshead, in the county of Lincoln.

An Act to amend and extend the Settled Estates Act of 1856.

An Act to enable the Committees of both Houses of Parliament to administer oaths to witnesses in certain cases.

An Act for enabling the Commissioners of Public Works in Ireland to acquire certain lands and houses for the site of a new courts or courts, and other offices and buildings required for the public service, in extension of the Four Courts in the city of Dublin ; and for other purposes.

An Act to amend the law relating to cheap trains, and to restrain the exercise of certain powers by Canal Companies being also Railway Companies.

An Act to amend an Act of the last session, for the regulation of the care and treatment of lunatics, and for the provision, maintenance, and regulation of Lunatic Asylums, in Scotland.

An Act to regulate the qualifications of practitioners in Medicine and Surgery.

An Act to enable Joint Stock Banking Companies to be formed on the principle of limited liability.

An Act to provide for the conveyance of county property to the Clerk of the Peace of the County.

An Act to enable persons to establish legitimacy and the validity of marriages, and the right to be deemed natural-born subjects.

An Act to amend the Copyhold Acts.

An Act to make provision for the better Government and discipline of the Universities of Scotland, and improving and regulating the course of study therein ; and for the union of the two Universities and Colleges of Aberdeen.

An Act to amend the Act of the twentieth and twenty-first Victoria, chapter seventy-seven.

An Act to confirm certain provisional orders made under an Act of the fifteenth year of Her present Majesty, to facilitate arrangements for the relief of turnpike trusts.

An Act to make further provision for the practice of vaccination in Ireland.

An Act to amend the law relating to cheques or drafts on bankers.

An Act to amend "The West Indian Incumbered Estates Act, 1854."

An Act to defray the charge of the pay, clothing, and contingent and other expenses of the disembodied Militia in Great Britain and Ireland ; to grant allowances in certain cases to Subaltern Officers, Adjutants, Paymasters, Quartermasters, Surgeons, Assistant-Surgeons, and Surgeons, Mates of the Militia ; and to authorize the employment of the non-commissioned officers.

An Act to continue an Act to enable Her Majesty to accept the services of the Militia out of the United Kingdom.

An Act further to continue an Act to authorize the embodying of the Militia.

An Act to continue and amend the Corrupt Practices Prevention Act, 1854.

An Act for vesting in the Privy Council certain powers for the protection of the public health.

An Act to amend the Public Health Act, 1848, and to make further provision for the local government of towns and populous districts.

An Act to provide for the Government of British Columbia.

An Act to regulate the office of Clerk of Petty Sessions in Ireland.

An Act to amend the Act of the eighteenth and nineteenth years of Her present Majesty, chapter sixty-three, relating to Friendly Societies.

An Act to indemnify certain persons who have formed a voluntary association for the disposal of works of utility and ornament by chance or otherwise as prizes.

An Act to promote and regulate reformatory schools for juvenile offenders in Ireland.

An Act to alter and amend the Metropolis Local Management Act (1855), and to extend the powers of the Metropolitan Board of Works for the purification of the Thames and the main drainage of the Metropolis.

An Act to extend the Act of the twenty-fourth year of King George the Third, chapter twenty-six, for issuing writs during any recess of the House of Commons, whether by prorogation or adjournment.

An Act to amend an Act of the fourteenth and fifteenth years of Her present Majesty, to consolidate and amend the laws relating to Civil Bills and the Courts of Quarter Sessions in Ireland, and to transfer to the Assistant Barristers certain jurisdicton as to Insolvent Debtors.

An Act to amend an Act of the thirteenth and fourteenth years of Her present Majesty, to amend the laws concerning judgments in Ireland.

An Act for the better government of India.

An Act to amend the Act of the twentieth and twenty-first Victoria, chapter eighty-five.

An Act to declare and define the respective rights of Her Majesty and of His Royal Highness the Prince of Wales and Duke of Cornwall to the mines and minerals in or under land lying below high-water mark, within and adjacent to the county of Cornwall, and for other purposes.

An Act to incorporate and regulate the Great Southern of India Railway Company, and for other purposes connected therewith.

An Act to alter and improve the boundaries of the Municipal Borough and District of Middlesbrough; to enable the Local Board of Health of the District to enlarge the Market-place, to enable the Corporation to construct landing-places on the north side of the River Tees, and to establish a public passage up and over the said river; to transfer the powers of the Burial Board to the Local Board; and to confer other powers on the Local Board and the Corporation; and for other purposes.

An Act to confer additional powers on the Tees Conservancy Commissioners; to regulate the Fisheries in the River Tees; to vest the anchorage

and plankage dues in the said Commissioners; to
alter and amend their existing Acts; and for other
purposes.

An Act to extend the time for making the
Worcester and Hereford Railway, and for granting
further powers with respect to that undertaking.

An Act for extending the powers of the Plymouth Great Western Dock Company, and for
other purposes.

An Act to make further provisions for vesting
the Sheffield, Rotherham, Barnsley, Wakefield,
Huddersfield, and Goole Railway, in the Lancashire
and Yorkshire Railway Company, and for other
purposes.

An Act for enabling the Limerick and Castle
Connell Railway Company to extend their railway
from Castle Connell to Killaloe; to issue preference shares, and for other purposes.

An Act for the abandonment of the West End
of London and Clapham and Norwood Junction
Railway, and for other purposes.

An Act to enable the South Wales Railway
Company to acquire additional lands at Newport,
and for other purposes.

An Act for authorizing a lease of the Vale of
Towy Railway to the Llanelly Railway and Dock
Company.

An Act for enabling the Atlantic Telegraph
Company to create and issue preference capital;
for the extension of borrowing powers, and
amendment of Act.

An Act to consolidate and amend the Acts
relating to the River Clyde and Harbour of
Glasgow.

An Act for limiting, defining, and regulating
the capital and debt of the Warrington and Stockport Railway Company; for amending the Acts

relating to the Company, and conferring on them further powers, and for other purposes relating to the Company.

(1193.)

Board of Trade, Whitehall,
July 30, 1858.

The Right Honourable the Lords of the Committee of Privy Council for Trade and Plantations have received, through the Secretary of State for Foreign Affairs, a copy of a Despatch from the Lord High Commissioner of the Ionian Islands, reporting the establishment of a quarantine of 30 days' duration upon all vessels arriving in those islands from the northern coast of Africa (including Egypt).

(1203.)

Board of Trade, Whitehall,
July 31, 1858.

The Right Honourable the Lords of the Committee of Privy Council for Trade and Plantations, have received, through the Secretary of State for Foreign Affairs, a copy of a Despatch from Her Majesty's Consul-General at Tunis, reporting the establishment of a quarantine of fifteen days on vessels arriving from the Province of Tripoli.

(84.)

Board of Trade, Whitehall,
August 3, 1858.

The Right Honourable the Lords of the Com-Committee of Privy Council for Trade and Plantations have received, through the Secretary of State for Foreign Affairs, information that the articles exempted from payment of duties of any kind on their being landed at the Port of Salvador, by a decree of that Republic, published in the Gazette of 21st January last, are not to be so exempted if introduced into the interior for sale, in which case they will be liable to the duties previously established.

War-Office, Pall-Mall, S.W., 3rd August, 1858.

The Secretary of State for War has received the following Lists of Casualties in the Army serving in India.

Numerical Return of Casualties in Action in Her Majesty's Troops at Bareilly, on the 5th, 6th, and 7th May, 1858.

> *Head-Quarters, Camp Futtyghur,*
> *June* 1, 1858.

May 5, 1858—1 drummer or rank and file, killed ; 3 officers, 1 serjeant, 13 drummers and rank and file, wounded.

May 6—1 serjeant, killed ; 2 drummers and rank and file, wounded.

May 7—1 serjeant, killed ; 1 serjeant, 3 drummers and rank and file, wounded.

Total—2 serjeants, 1 drummer or rank and file, killed ; 3 officers, 2 serjeants, 18 drummers and rank and file, wounded.

> W. L. PAKENHAM, Colonel,
> Acting Adjutant-General,
> Her Majesty's Forces in India.

From the Nominal Return of Casualties, in Action, in Her Majesty's Troops at Bareilly, on the 5th, 6th, and 7th of May, 1858.

Head-Quarters, Camp, Futtyghur,
June 1, 1858.

Staff—Brigadier-General R. Walpole, slightly wounded.

42nd Highlanders – Lieutenant-Colonel A. Cameron, slightly wounded.

42nd Highlanders — Assistant-Surgeon T. A. Thornhill, slightly wounded.

42nd Highlanders—Colour-Serjeant W. Gardiner, slightly wounded.

1st Battalion, 60th Rifles—Colour-Serjeant Henry Baillie, killed.

1st Battalion 60th Rifles — Serjeant Patrick O'Shaugnessy, severely wounded.

From the Nominal List of Casualties in Action at Jugderpore, on the 23rd April, 1858.

Head-Quarters, Camp, Futtyghur,
June 1, 1858.

35th Regiment, Killed in Action at Jugderpore.

Captain A. J. LeGrand, Lieutenant W. G. Massey, Assistant-Surgeon Clarke, Colour-Serjeant Richard Bush, Colour-Serjeant William Russell, Serjeant Will Britton, Serjeant William Johnson, Serjeant Thomas Morton, Corporal George Barnes, Corporal William Barrett, Corporal David Heard.

W. L. PAKENHAM, Colonel,
Acting Adjutant-General,
Her Majesty's Forces in India.

From the Nominal Return of Casualties in Action, in Her Majesty's Troops, since date of last Return.

Head Quarters, Camp, Futtyghur, June 1, 1858.

1st Battalion 60th Rifles—Colour-Serjeant James Roper, Bhagawalla, April 17, 1858, dangerously wounded.

9th Lancers—Serjeant Charles May, Allegunge, April 22, slightly wounded.

1st Battalion, 60th Rifles—Serjeant John Woodgate, Shajeehanpore, May 11, severely wounded, since dead.

NOTICE TO MARINERS.

Board of Trade, Whitehall, August 2, 1858.

The Right Honourable the Lords of the Committee of Privy Council for Trade and Plantations have received, through the Secretary of State for Foreign Affairs, a copy of a Despatch from Her Majesty's Consul at Dunkirk, stating that owing to the neglect of Shipmasters to comply with the Police Regulations at that Port, issued in August, 1857, the authorities have republished an Extract of the same, of which a translation is subjoined.

(Translation.)

PORT OF DUNKIRK.

Police Regulations of the 18th August, 1857.

Extract Notice for Continual Guidance of Captains.

N.B.—For all that is not inserted in this extract notice, captains must conform themselves to the general rules, which they will find at the Harbour Master's office.

Captains frequenting the harbour are urgently requested to keep a copy of this extract notice.

CHAPTER THE 1ST.

ART. II. All vessels coming in or going out, must hoist their national flag.

ART. III. All Captains, on their arrival in port, must have their jib booms rigged in, anchors stowed on the forecastle, all sails furled, and their lower yards picked.

ART. VII. Captains must report their arrival at the Harbour Master's office within 24 hours of their coming in. This report regulates the turn to obtain a quay berth.

CHAPTER THE 3RD.

ART. II. No movement can take place in port unless with leave, and according to the Harbour Master's orders.

ART. VI. Harbour Masters have the power of putting on board of vessels sufficient hands according to what they think necessary to insure the execution of the movements they order, at the expense of the captains, consignees, or owners of the vessels.

ART. VII. It is forbidden to unfurl sails during the night. During a gale captains or shipkeepers must double their hawsers, &c.

ART. VIII. Captains are obliged every evening to have the quay opposite to their vessels swept, and as far as half the distance which separates them from the next vessels.

ART. IX. All vessels must hoist their national flags on Sundays and Holy days.

CHAPTER THE 4th.

ART. V. and VI. Appointed time for loading and unloading of vessels, Sundays and Holy days included.

(This time counts from the day on which the vessel has been placed in a position to commence her loading or unloading,) viz. :

A vessel of 50 tons measurement and under, 3 days.

A vessel above 50 tons, and not exceeding 75 tons, 4 days.

A vessel above 75 tons and not exceeding 100 tons, 5 days.

A vessel above 100 tons and not exceeding 125 tons, 6 days.

A vessel above 125 tons and not exceeding 150 tons, 7 days.

A vessel above 150 tons and not exceeding 175 tons, 8 days.

A vessel above 175 tons and not exceeding 200 tons, 9 days.

A vessel above 200 tons and not exceeding 250 tons, 10 days.

A vessel above 250 tons and not exceeding 300 tons, 11 days.

A vessel above 300 tons and not exceeding 350 tons, 12 days.

A vessel above 350 tons and not exceeding 400 tons, 13 days.

A vessel above 400 tons and not exceeding 450 tons, 14 days.

A vessel above 450 tons and not exceeding 500 tons, 15 days.

A vessel above 500 tons and not exceeding 575 tons, 16 days.

A vessel above 575 tons and not exceeding 650 tons, 17 days.

A vessel above 650 tons and not exceeding 725 tons, 18 days.

A vessel above 725 tons and not exceeding 800 tons, 19 days.

A vessel above 800 tons and not exceeding 875 tons, 20 days.

A vessel above 875 tons and not exceeding 950 tons, 21 days.

48 hours are allowed beyond the time of unloading, to finish to take away the goods.

24 hours are allowed beyond the time of unloading, to vessels which will be in want of taking ballast to stiffen them, after they are discharged.

In case of a force put (*sic. in orig.*) sufficiently verified, which should have prevented the entire loading or unloading within the time allowed, the Harbour Masters will have the power of granting an extension.

ART. VII. All vessels unloading on the quay are obliged to make use of spars, planks, or tarpaulins for heavy goods or others, specially appointed by the regulations.

CHAPTER THE 7TH.

ART. III. It is forbidden to have any fire or light on board, unless in a ship's lantern, also to smoke, unless on deck and during the daytime.

It can only be derogated to those rules by special orders from the Harbour Masters, and by having a watch when fire is allowed.

By order of the Prefecture of Lille, the 18th August, 1857.

The Prefet,
COLLET-MEYGRET.

N.B. According to article 5 of chapter 10 of the rules, the Harbour Masters give notice to captains that, as a measure of order, all vessels in the docks must lay bows up, and outside the belvederes bows out.

Whitehall, July 27, 1858.

The Queen has been pleased to grant unto George Stucley Buck, of Hartland Abbey and of Affton Castle, both in the county of Devon,

Esquire, sometime representative in Parliament for the borough of Barnstaple, only son of Lewis William Buck, of Affton aforesaid, Esquire, sometime representative in Parliament for the Northern Division of the County of Devon, deceased, Her Royal licence and authority, that he and his issue may take and use the surname of Stucley only, and also bear the arms of Stucley quarterly with his and their own paternal arms ; such arms being first duly exemplified according to the laws of arms, and recorded in the Heralds' office, otherwise the said Royal licence and permission to be void and of none effect :

And also to command that the said Royal concession and declaration be registered in Her Majesty's College of Arms.

——— ——

Whitehall, August 2, 1858,

The Queen, taking into Her royal consideration that on the 24th day of June last it was resolved, by the Lords Spiritual and Temporal, in Parliament assembled, that William Constable Maxwell, of Nithsdale, in the county of Dumfries, and of Everingham, in the county of York, Esquire, was entitled to the honour, title, and dignity of Lord Herries, of Terregles, in the Peerage of Scotland ; and whereas, according to the ordinary rules of honour, his brothers and sister cannot hold and enjoy that title, place, and precedence which would have been due to them had their late father, Marmaduke Constable Maxwell, lived to have been restored in blood, by virtue of an Act of Parliament passed in 1848, whereby their said brother, William Constable Maxwell, and all the descendants of the body of William Earl of Nithsdale, attainted in 1716, were fully restored in blood, to the effect of enabling them to prefer any claim which they might have of right, but for such bar,

to all honours, dignities, and titles, will all rights
and privileges thereunto belonging, and to which
they would have been entitled as heir or heirs of
the body of the said Earl of Nithsdale; Her
Majesty has been graciously pleased to ordain and
declare that Marmaduke Constable Maxwell, of
Terregles, in the stewartry of Kirkcudbright,
Esquire, Henry Constable Maxwell, of Scarthing-
well, in the county of York, Esquire, Joseph
Constable Maxwell, Clerk, and Theresa, wife of
the Honourable Charles Thomas Clifford, brothers
and sister of the said William Lord Herries, of
Terregles, shall henceforth have, hold, and enjoy
the same title, place, and precedence which they
would have had and enjoyed in case their late
father had survived and received the Grace of the
Crown, and been adjudged entitled to and admitted
as of right to the said dignity of Lord Herries of
Terregles :

And Her Majesty has been further pleased to
command that the said Royal order and declaration
be registered in Her College of Arms.

---

*Commissions signed by the Lord Lieutenant of the
county of Sussex.*

The Honourable Walter John Pelham, commonly
called Lord Pelham, to be Deputy Lieutenant.
Dated 27th July, 1858.
Henry Peter Crofts, Esq., to be Deputy Lieutenant. Dated 27th July, 1858.

*Commission signed by the Lord Lieutenant and
Sheriff Principal of the County of Ayr.*

Lieutenant-Colonel John Ferrier Hamilton to be
Vice-Lieutenant, vice Sir David Hunter Blair,
Bart., deceased. Dated 27th July, 1858.
1858.   9 A

Commission signed by the Lord Lieutenant of the County of Edinburgh *or* Mid-Lothian.

Royal Mid-Lothian or Edinburgh Yeomanry Cavalry.

William Roy, Gent., to be Cornet, vice Tait promoted. Dated 27th July, 1858.

Commission signed by the Lord Lieutenant of the County of Lancaster.

Royal Lancashire Militia Artillery Regiment.

John Betham, Gent., to be Assistant-Surgeon, vice Samuel Shepherd, resigned. Dated 9th July, 1858.

FROM THE

LONDON GAZETTE of AUGUST 6, 1858.

The Speech of the Lords Commissioners to both Houses of Parliament, on Monday, August 2, 1858.

My Lords and Gentlemen,

WE are commanded by Her Majesty to express Her satisfaction at being enabled to release you from the duties of a session, which, though interrupted, has, by your unremitting assiduity, been productive of many important measures.

Her Majesty is happy to believe that Her relations with Foreign Powers are such as to enable Her Majesty to look with confidence to the preservation of general peace.

Her Majesty trusts that the labours of the Plenipotentiaries now sitting in Conference at Paris may lead to a satisfactory solution of the various questions which have been referred to them.

The efforts, the gallantry, and devotedness displayed in India by Her Majesty's Forces, and those of the East India Company, have been above all praise; and Her Majesty hopes that those efforts have already been so far crowned with success, that the formidable revolt which has raged throughout a large portion of Her Indian Possessions may now, under the blessing of Almighty God, be speedily suppressed, and peace be restored to those important Provinces.

In this hope Her Majesty has given Her willing assent to the Act which you have passed for transferring to Her direct authority the Government of Her Indian Dominions; and Her Majesty hopes to be enabled so to discharge the high functions which She has assumed, as, by a just and impartial adminstration of the law, to secure its advantages alike to Her subjects of every race and creed, and, by promoting their welfare, to establish and strengthen Her Empire in India.

Gentlemen of the House of Commons,

Her Majesty commands us to thank you for the judicious liberality with which you have made provision for the exigencies of the public service.

The present state of the revenue authorizes Her Majesty to entertain a confident hope that the supplies which you have granted will be found fully adequate to the demands upon them.

My Lords and Gentlemen,

The sanitary condition of the Metropolis must always be a subject of deep interest to Her Majesty, and Her Majesty has readily sanctioned the Act which you have passed for the purification of that noble river, the present state of which is little creditable to a great country, and seriously prejudicial to the health and comfort of the inhabitants of the Metropolis.

Her Majesty has also willingly assented to an Act, whereby greater facilities are given for the acquisition by towns and districts of such powers as may be requisite for promoting works of local improvement, and thus extending more widely the advantages of municipal self-government

Her Majesty trusts that the Act which you have passed 'for the future government of the Scotch Universities, will be found highly advantageous to those venerable institutions, and will greatly promote and extend a system of sound moral and religious education in Scotland.

The Transfer of Land Bill, which extends the powers hitherto exercised by the Incumbered Estates Commissioners, and facilitates the acquisition of an indefeasible title by purchasers of land in Ireland, cannot fail to be highly beneficial to the landed proprietors, and to advance the prosperity of that part . of Her Majesty's dominions

The Act to which Her Majesty has assented for the establishment of the colony of British Columbia was urgently required, in consequence of the recent discoveries of gold in that district; but Her Majesty hopes that this new colony on the Pacific may be but one step in the career of steady progress, by which Her Majesty's dominions in North America may ultimately be peopled, in an unbroken chain, from the Atlantic to the Pacific, by a loyal and industrious population of subjects of the British crown.

Her Majesty thankfully acknowledges the diligence and perseverance which has enabled you in a comparatively short time to pass these and other measures of inferior but not insignificant importance.

Many of you, in returning to your respective

counties, have extensive influence to exercise, and
duties to perform of hardly less value to the Com-
munity than those from the labours of which you
are about to be released ; and Her Majesty enter-
tains a confident assurance that, under the guidance
of Providence, that influence will be so employed,
and those duties so performed, as to redound to
your own honour, and to promote the general
welfare and the happiness of a loyal and contented
people.

———

Then a Commission for proroguing the Parliament was read ; after which the Lord
Chancellor said,

My Lords and Gentlemen,
By virtue of Her Majesty's Commission, under
the Great Seal, to us and other Lords directed,
and now read, we do, in Her Majesty's name,
and in obedience to Her commands, prorogue this
Parliament to Tuesday the nineteenth day of
October next, to be then here holden ; and this
Parliament is accordingly prorogued to Tuesday
the nineteenth day of October next.

———

At the Court at *Osborne House, Isle of Wight,*
the 31st day of *July,* 1858.

The QUEEN'S Most Excellent Majesty in
Council was pleased to order that all the " Common Law Procedure Act, 1852," and the provisions of the " Common Law Procedure Act,
1854," and the rules made and to be made in pursuance thereof, shall extend and apply to the
Court of Record, holden in and for the Borough
of Poole.

Also that all the provisions of the said " Summary Procedure on Bills of Exchange Act, 1855,"

shall apply to the said Court of Record, holden in and for the said borough of Poole.

Whitehall, August 2, 1858.

The Queen has been pleased to direct letters patent to be passed under the Great Seal, granting the dignity of a Baron of the United Kingdom of Great Britain and Ireland, unto John Charles, Earl of Seafield, and the heirs male of his body lawfully begotten, by the name, style and title of Baron Strathspey, of Strathspey, in the counties of Inverness and Moray.

Whitehall, August 3, 1858.

The Queen has been pleased to direct letters patent to be passed under the Great Seal, granting the dignity of a Baron of the United Kingdom of Great Britain and Ireland unto General Sir Colin Campbell, G.C.B., Commander-in-Chief in the East Indies, and the heirs male of his body lawfully begotten, by the name, style, and title of Baron Clyde, of Clydesdale, in that part of the said United Kingdom called Scotland.

The Queen has also been pleased to direct letters patent to be passed under the Great Seal, granting the dignity of a Baronet of the United Kingdom of Great Britain and Ireland unto Sir John Laird Mair Lawrence, G.C.B., Chief Commissioner and Agent to the Governor-General of India for the Affairs of the Punjab, and the heirs male of his body lawfully begotten.

Whitehall, July 29, 1858.

The Queen has been pleased to grant unto Edward Roberts, of the city of Chester, only child and heir of Edward Roberts, of the city of Chester, aforesaid, Esquire, in the Commission of.

the Peace for the said city of Chester, by Frances Catherine, his wife, only child and heir of George Stoakes, late of Oswestry, in the county of Salop, Gentleman, all deceased, Her Royal licence and authority that he and his issue may take and henceforth use the surname of Stoakes, in lieu of that of Roberts :

And to command that the said Royal concession and declaration be recorded in Her Majesty's College of Arms, otherwise to be void and of none effect.

War-Office, Pall-Mall,
6th August, 1858.

1st *Regiment of Dragoon Guards,* Lieutenant Walter Clopton Wingfield to be Captain, by purchase, vice Bridge, who retires. Dated 6th August, 1858.

Cornet Richard Harpur Crewe to be Lieutenant, by purchase, vice Wingfield. Dated 6th August, 1858.

2nd *Dragoon Guards,* John Taylor Marshall, Gent., to be Cornet, without purchase, vice Alexander Frederick Stewart, appointed to the 6th Dragoons. Dated 6th August, 1858.

3rd *Dragoon Guards,* Winship Percival Roche, Gent., to be Cornet, without purchase, vice Daveney, promoted in 6th Dragoons. Dated 6th August, 1858.

5th *Dragoon Guards,* St. John Cland Paulet, Gent., to be Cornet, without purchase vice Heyworth, promoted. Dated 6th August, 1858.

7th *Dragoon Guards.*

The Commissions of the undermentiond Officers to be antedated as follows :

Lieutenant C. Barton, to 15th September, 1857.

Lieutenant W. D. Wentworth, to 15th September, 1857.

Lieutenant G. R. Caldwell, to 16th September, 1857.

5th Light Dragoons, Serjeant-Major William Rant, to be Riding Master, vice Greatrex, appointed to the 18th Light Dragoons. Dated 6th August, 1858.

The appointment of Paymaster John Atkin Dyer, to bear date 15th March, 1858, instead of 4th June, 1858, as previously stated.

6th Dragoons. The transfer of Cornet John Augustus Beaumont, from the 4th Dragoon Guards, as stated in the Gazette of 27th July, 1858, has been cancelled.

8th Light Dragoons, Lieutenant Robert Cooper Sawbridge to be Captain, by purchase, vice Mayne, promoted, by purchase, to an Unattached Majority. Dated 6th August, 1858.

13th Light Dragoons, Cornet Richard Harold Bush to be Lieutenant, by purchase, vice Toulmin, who retires. Dated 6th August, 1858.

14th Light Dragoons, Henry Richard Abadie, Gent., to be Cornet, without purchase. Dated 6th August, 1858.

Military Train. The promotion of Ensign and Adjutant W. Shacketon and Ensign and Adjutant W. Thompson to be antedated to 21st May, 1858.

Ensign John Briggs to be Lieutenant, without purchase, vice Dawson, killed in action. Dated 21st May, 1858.

Ensign H. Keogh to be Lieutenant, without purchase, vice Briggs, whose promotion on 30th June, 1858, has been cancelled. Dated 30th June, 1858.

The promotion of Ensign and Adjutant J. Sweeny was on the Establishment, and not vice Lieutenant Dawson, killed in action, as stated in Gazette of 30th July, 1858.

The promotion of Ensign H. Keogh, on 30th July, 1858, has been cancelled.

1st *Regiment of Foot*, Percy Bingham Schreiber, Gent., to be Ensign, without purchase, vice F. W. Thompson, deceased. Dated 6th August, 1858.

4th *Foot*, Ensign Edward Chinn to be Lieutenant, by purchase, vice T. C. Lloyd, promoted in 19th Foot. Dated 6th August, 1858.

Ensign Stephen Weston Bent, from the 66th Foot, to be Lieutenant, without purchase, vice Billington, appointed to the 6th Dragoons. Dated 7th August, 1858.

7th *Foot*, Henry Wadham Locke Paddon, Gent., to be Ensign, without purchase, vice Waller, promoted. Dated 6th August, 1858.

10th *Foot*, Lieutenant Spencer Edward Orr to be Instructor of Musketry. Dated 17th July, 1858.

11th *Foot*, Frederick Dudley Walker, Gent., to be Ensign, without purchase. Dated 6th August, 1858.

13th *Foot*, Lieutenant Cornwallis H. Chichester to be Captain, without purchase, vice William Henry Jones, killed in action. Dated 7th April, 1858.

Ensign E. L. England to be Lieutenant, without purchase, vice Chichester. Dated 7th April, 1858.

Ensign Aubrey Henzell to be Lieutenant, without purchase, vice England, whose promotion, on the 30th April, 1858, has been cancelled. Dated 30th April, 1858.

14th *Foot*, Denis Creagh, Gent., to be Ensign,

without purchase, vice Wilson, promoted. Dated 6th August, 1858.

15*th Foot*, Frederick Bowdler Gipps, Gent., to be Ensign, without purchase. Dated 6th August, 1858.

16*th Foot*, Edward Logan Stehelin, Gent., to be Ensign, without purchase, vice Stockwell, appointed to the 10th Foot. Dated 6th August, 1858.

Lieutenant Alexander Gibson to be Instructor of Musketry. Dated 23rd July, 1858.

17*th Foot*, Lieutenant James Urquhart Mosse, to be Instructor of Musketry. Dated 20th July, 1858.

19*th Foot*, Cortlandt Skinner, Gent., to be Ensign, without purchase, vice Coxen, appointed to the 60th Foot. Dated 6th August, 1858.

20*th Foot*, Edward Alexander Hawtrey Parks, Gent., to be Ensign, without purchase, vice Chatfield promoted. Dated 6th August, 1858.

21*st Foot*, Walter Noyell Carey, Gent., to be Ensign, by purchase, vice Boycott, promoted. Dated 6th August, 1858.

22nd Foot.

To be Ensigns, without purchase.

William Pilsworth, Gent., vice Fraser, appointed to the 73rd Foot. Dated 6th August, 1858.
Frederick William Best Parry, Gent. Dated 7th August, 1858.

23*rd Foot*, William Robert Murray, Gent., to be Ensign, without purchase. Dated 6th August, 1858.

40*th Foot*, Major Arthur Leslie to be Lieutenant-Colonel, without purchase, vice Brevet-Colonel

Valiant, who retires upon full-pay. Dated 6th August, 1858.

Captain and Brevet-Major R. Carey to be Major, without purchase, vice Leslie. Dated 6th August, 1858.

Lieutenant and Adjutant T. B. Richards to be Captain, without purchase, vice Carey. Dated 6th August, 1858.

43rd *Foot*, Ensign D'Urban W. Farrer Blyth to be Lieutenant, without purchase, vice Elmes, deceased. Dated 24th May, 1858.

45th *Foot*, Serjeant-Major Forbes William Guernsey to be Ensign, with purchase, vice O'Neill, promoted. Dated 6th August, 1858.

53rd *Foot*, Captain Thomas Moubray to be Major, without purchase, vice Brevet-Lieutenant-Colonel William Payn, whose Brevet Rank has been converted into Substantive Rank, under the Royal Warrant of 6th October, 1854. Dated 6th August, 1858.

Lieutenant Graham Taylor to be Captain, without purchase, vice Moubray. Dated 6th August, 1858.

55th *Foot*, Lieutenant Arthur Sibley Young has been permitted to resign his Commission. Dated 6th August, 1858.

60th *Foot*, Ensign James Walker King to be Lieutenant, by purchase, vice Deedes, promoted. Dated 6th August, 1858.

73rd *Foot*, Lieutenant Bryan George Davies Cooke to be Captain, by purchase, vice Hereford, whose promotion, by purchase, on the 2nd of July, has been cancelled. Dated 6th August, 1858.

77th *Foot*, Major the Honourable Augustus George Charles Chichester, to be Lieutenant-Colonel, without purchase, vice Brevet-Colonel

Straton, C.B., deceased. Dated 16th June, 1858.

Brevet-Lieutenant-Colonel Henry Robert Carden, to be Major, without purchase, vice Chichester. Dated 16th June, 1858.

Lieutenant William Thomas Exham Fosbery to be Captain, without purchase, vice Carden. Dated 16th June, 1858.

84th *Foot*, Quartermaster Henry Donelan to be Paymaster, vice Eddy deceased. Dated 6th August, 1858.

97th *Foot*, Ensign and Adjutant Robert Smith to be Lieutenant, without purchase, vice Cookesley, appointed to the 22nd Foot. Dated 6th August, 1858.

98th *Foot*, Lieutenant Edward Frank Gregory to be Adjutant, vice Quin, promoted, in the 22nd Foot. Dated 6th August, 1858.

100th *Foot*, The removal of Cornet C. McD. Moorsom from the 1st Dragoon Guards to bear date 27th June, 1858, instead of 29th of that month, as previously stated.

Serjeant-Major Frederick Morris, from the School of Musketry, at Hythe, to be Ensign, without purchase. Dated 28th June, 1858.

Rifle Brigade, Ensign John Charles Stephen Fremantle, from the 5th Fusiliers, to be Ensign, without purchase. Dated 6th August, 1858.

Assistant-Surgeon Charles Seward, from the Staff, to be Assistant-Surgeon. Dated 6th August, 1858.

3rd *West India Regiment*, Serjeant-Major John Moore to be Ensign, without purchase, vice Lloyd, promoted. Dated 6th August, 1858.

Ceylon Rifle Regiment, Francis Pearson Murray, Gent., to be Ensign, by purchase, vice Gandy, promoted in the 6th Foot. Dated 6th August, 1858.

Gold Coast Artillery Corps, Lieutenant Edward N. Robert Gatehouse to be Instructor of Musketry. Dated 24th July, 1858.

DEPOT BATTALION.

Brevet-Lieutenant-Colonel Edward W. C. Wright, from 91st Foot, to be Major, without purchase, vice Maydwell, appointed to the Staff in Ceylon. Dated 6th August, 1858.

STAFF.

Major Henry Law Maydwell, from Depôt Battalion, to be Deputy Adjutant-General to the Forces, serving in Ceylon, with the rank of Lieutenant-Colonel in the Army, vice Brevet-Colonel Brunker, whose term of service in that situation has expired. Dated 6th August, 1858.

UNATTACHED.

Captain Taylor Lambard Mayne, from the 8th Light Dragoons, to be Major, by purchase. Dated 6th August, 1858.

HOSPITAL STAFF.

Surgeon Robert Lewins, M.D., from half-pay, 63rd Foot, to be Staff-Surgeon of the 2nd Class. Dated 30th July, 1858.

To be Acting Assistant-Surgeons.

Thomas Henry Burgess, M.D. Dated 22nd July, 1858.

George Alexander Moorhead, Gent. Dated 22nd July, 1858.

Francis Potter Beamish, Gent. Dated 24th July, 1858.

BREVET.

Brevet-Colonel Thomas James Valiant, retired full-pay 40th Foot, to be Major-General, the rank being honorary only. Dated 6th August, 1858.

The undermentioned Officers having completed three years' actual serevice in the rank of Lieutenant-Colonel, to be promoted to be Colonels in the Army, under the Royal Warrants of 13th September, 1854, and 6th October, 1854:

Lieutenant-Colonel George Dixon, C.B., Depôt Battalion. Dated 20th May, 1858.

Lieutenant-Colonel Henry William Bunbury, C.B., half-pay 23rd Foot, Assistant Adjutant-General, Shorncliffe. Dated 1st July, 1858.

Lieutenant-Colonel Augustus Flemyng, Royal Marines. Dated 10th July, 1858.

Lieutenant-Colonel William Bookey Langford, Royal Marines. Dated 14th July, 1858.

MEMORANDUM.

Brevet-Lieutenant-Colonel J. H. Trevelyan, upon half-pay as Major Unattached, has been permitted to retire from the Service by the sale of his Commission, he being about to become a Settler in Canada. Dated 6th August, 1858.

Admiralty, S.W., 29th July, 1858.

Corps of Royal Marines.

Gentleman Cadet Frederic Amelius Ogle to be Second Lieutenant.

Commissions signed by the Lord Lieutenant of the County of Nottingham.

Royal Sherwood Foresters, or Nottinghamshire Regiment of Militia.

Ensign Frederick Francis Wall to be Lieutenant, vice Clements, resigned. Dated 3rd August, 1858.

George Wood, Gent., to be Ensign, vice Wall, promoted. Dated 3rd August, 1858.

Commissions signed by the Lord Lieutenant of the County of Lancaster.

The Squadron of the Duke of Lancaster's Own Regiment of Yeomanry Cavalry, called the Lancashire Hussars

William John Legh, Esq., to be Captain, vice Loch, resigned. Dated 26th July, 1858.

Cornet Joscelyn Tate Westby to be Lieutenant, vice Suffield, resigned. Dated 26th July, 1858.

The Right Honourable Edward Bootle Wilbraham, Lord Skelmersdale, to be Cornet, vice Westby, promoted. Dated 26th July, 1858.

Commissions signed by the Lord Lieutenant of the West Riding of the County of York *and of the City and County of the City of* York.

5th Regiment of West York Militia.

Robert Morrison, Gent., to be Ensign. Dated 20th July, 1858.

MEMORANDUM.

West York Rifle Regiment of Militia.

Her Majesty has been graciously pleased to accept the resignation of the Commission held by Captain Henry W. Stansfeld.

2nd Regiment (Light Infantry) of West York Militia.

The Commission of Ensign Eugene Thomas Curzon Whittell is dated 1st January, 1858, and not 23rd February, as previously gazetted.

3rd Regiment (Light Infantry) of West York Militia.

Her Majesty has been graciously pleased to accept the resignation of the Commission held by Ensign Adolphus William Murray.

Festiniog Union.—Parish of Festiniog.

An Order of the Poor Law Board to the Churchwardens and Overseers of the poor of the parish of Festiniog, in the county of Merioneth, and to all others whom it may concern ; dated 10th July, 1858, directs that so much of the Act passed in the fourteenth year of the reign of Her Majesty, 13th and 14th, cap. 57, as relates to the appointment of a Vestry Clerk, shall forthwith be applied to, and be put in force within the said parish of Festiniog.

FROM THE

LONDON GAZETTE of AUGUST 10, 1858.

Whitehall, August 9, 1858.

THE Right Honourable Spencer Horatio Walpole has received the following Despatch from the Earl of Malmesbury, dated Cherbourg, August 5, 1858.

SIR, *Cherbourg, August* 5, 1858.

I HAVE the honour to inform you that Her Majesty, the Prince Consort, and His Royal

Highness the Prince of Wales arrived here, at 6·30 yesterday evening, in the royal yacht, after a passage of five hours from Osborne. Her Majesty was attended by the Earl of Delawarr, Sir John Pakington, myself, and by the Countess of Desart and Miss Bulteel. The escorting squadron met the yacht five miles from Cherbourg, and entered the harbour in two lines, the royal yacht leading the centre. Her Majesty was received by a general salute from nine line-of-battle ships and a heavy frigate, ranged in line within the breakwater, and from all the batteries. This was returned by the English ships, and the roar of two thousand pieces of cannon produced a most striking effect. The royal yacht anchored within the French line of battle, surrounded by the escort, at 8·30. The Emperor Napoleon and the Empress came on board, under a general salute. Their Majesties were attended by the Maritime Prefect, the Admiral of the Fleet, the Minister of Marine, Marshals Pelissier and Baraguay d'Hilliers, Generals Niel and McMahon, and the Princess d'Essling. Their Majesties retired at 9·30, under a general salute and illumination of the British men-of-war. This day Her Majesty will breakfast with the Emperor, at the Prefecture, and dine with His Majesty on board the Bretagne, four-decker.

To-morrow Her Majesty proposes to return to Osborne, at twelve o'clock.

Her Majesty and the Royal Family are in perfect health, and appear much pleased with their reception.

I have, &c.,
MALMESBURY.

The Right Hon. S. H. Walpole, M.P.,
&c, &c., &c.

1858. 9 B

India Board, August 10, 1858.

THE following papers have been received at the East India House :

No. 1.

Major-General Sir Hugh Rose, K.C.B., Commanding Central India Field Force, to the Adjutant-General, Bombay Army.

Camp Pooch, April 30, 1858.

SIR,

I HAVE the honor to report to you, for the information of his Excellency the Commander-in Chief in India, that on the 1st of April the force under my orders, fought a general action with the so-called Army of the Peishwa, which attempted to relieve Jhansi while I was besieging it, and gained a complete victory over it, pursuing him two miles beyond the river Betwa, taking 18 guns, of which one was an eighteen pounder, one an eight-inch mortar, two twelve pounders, and two English nine pounders, and killing upwards of 1500 rebels.

For some time past Sir Robert Hamilton had given me information that Tantia Topee, a relative and the agent of Nana Sahib, had been collecting and organizing a large body of troops in the neighbourhood of Mhow and Nowgong, in Bundelcund, which was called "The Army of the Peishwa," and displayed the standard of that abolished authority. After the fall of Chicharee, this army was reinforced by the numerous rebel troops, Sepoys from Calpee and Bundelas, who had besieged and taken it. Towards the end of last month I received constantly reports that this force, estimated at 20,000 or 25,000 men, with 20 or 30 guns, was advancing against me. On the 30th ultimo, Sir Robert Hamilton informed me, that its main body had arrived at Burra-Saugor, about three miles from the Betwa, would cross that river during the night, and attack me next morning.

In hopes of forcing the enemy to engage with the river in his rear, I left the parks and heavy baggage of the second brigade, with which I was, with the 1st brigade, and marched at 9 P.M. on the 30th ultimo from Jhansi to the village of Bussoba, six miles from Jhansi, which commands the two fords of Rajpore and Kolwar, by which the enemy coming from Burra-Saugor must cross the Betwa.

At Bussoba I received reports from the two outposts which I had sent to watch the fords, that they had been and heard nothing of the enemy. The next morning they made a similar report

I came to the conclusion that the enemy would not cross the river whilst I was so close to it, and that nothing would be more likely to encourage them to do so, than a retrograde movement on my part, which they would construe into a retreat. I returned, therefore, to camp, leaving the outposts to watch the fords. I was not mistaken ; that same day the enemy crossed the upper ford, the Rajpore, in great numbers, preceded by an advanced guard of Vilaities, and took up, after sunset, a position in order of battle, opposite the rear of the camp of the second brigade.

At sunset the enemy lit an immense bonfire on a rising ground on the side of the Betwa, as a signal to Jhansi of their arrival ; it was answered by salutes from all the batteries of the fort and city, and shouts of joy from their defenders.

It was evident that the enemy sought a battle with my force ; this self-confidence was explained afterwards by prisoners, who stated that Tantia Topee had been informed by his spies, that nearly all my force was scattered, and engaged in the siege and investment, and that he could easily destroy the few who guarded the camp.

The fact is, that Jhansi had proved so strong,

and the ground to be watched by cavalry was so extensive, that my force had actually enough on its hands. But I relied on the spirit of British soldiers, which rises with difficulties, and resolved, whilst I fought a general action with the enemy, not to relax either the siege or the investment.

The details in the margin* show how weak I was when compared with the enemy. My first brigade had only a little more than 200 European infantry; my 2nd brigade about the same. On the first news of the approach of the enemy, I had sent Major Orr, with a party of his cavalry, along the road to the Betwa, to watch their movements.

I drew up my force across the road from the Betwa, half-a-mile from my camp. On the right flank of my 1st line, the 2nd brigade, I placed Lieutenant Clark's Hydrabad horse, a troop 14th Light Dragoons, and 4 guns Horse Artillery; in the centre, detachments of the 24th Regiment Bombay Native Infantry, and 3rd Europeans, three heavy guns, and detachments Hydrabad Infantry; on the left flank, Captain Lightfoot's Battery and two troops 14th Light Dragoons.

The second line was in contiguous columns at quarter distance; a weak troop 14th Light Dragoons on the right, and Hydrabad Cavalry on the left flank; in the centre Her Majesty's 86th Regiment, Captain Woolcombe's Battery of six, and Captain Ommaney's Battery of nine pounders, and detachments 25th Regiment Bombay Native Infantry.

I threw out pickets and lines of videttes of the 14th Light Dragoons and Hydrabad Cavalry, well to my front and flanks. The Vilaities' out-

* Artillery, 3 siege guns, 16 light field guns; 14th Dragoons, 243 rank and file; Hydrabad Cavalry, 207 sabres; 86th Regiment, 208 rank and file; 3rd Bombay European Regiment, 226 rank and file; 24th Bombay Native Infantry, 298 rank and file; and 25th Bombay Native Infantry.

posts called out during the night, that they were very numerous, that we were very few, that in the morning they would finish us, &c.

In consequence of the lateness of the enemy's advance, and the distance of my first brigade, my force was not in position till long after dark. The silent regularity with which it was effected did credit to their discipline.

Both ourselves and the enemy slept on our arms opposite each other.

A little after midnight one of the Hydrabad cavalry left at the lower, the Kolwar ford, came in as hard as he could, and reported that the enemy were crossing in great numbers. I thought it probable that they would make this move, of which the object was to turn my left flank, and force their way along the Burragong road, through Major Scudamore's Flying Camp into Jhansi. I had, therefore, ordered the outpost at the Kolwar ford to watch it with the utmost vigilance.

I detached Brigadier Stuart at once with the first brigade along the Burragong road to the village of the same name, about eight miles from Jhansi, close to the river Betwa, from whence he could oppose and out-flank the enemy, who had crossed by the ford above Burragong.

The accompanying report from Brigadier Stuart shows how well he executed my instructions, and how much he contributed to the success of the day. I beg to record my acknowledgement of the service he did, and to second warmly his recommendation of the officers and men of his gallant brigade.

The departure of the First Brigade left me without a second line, I was therefore obliged to withdraw the detachment of the 24th Native Infantry from the 1st, and make a second line of them.

The best way with Indians, for making up for numerical inferiority, is a determined attack on their weak point. I had therefore intended to commence the attack at daylight, advance in line, pour into the rebels the fire of all my guns, and then double up their left flank. But the enemy, before daybreak, covered by a cloud of skirmishers, advanced against me.

My pickets and videttes retired steadily, closing to each flank, in order that I might open upon them the fire of my guns, and then turn his left flank from my right.

Before my line was uncovered, the enemy took ground to his right. I conformed, to prevent his outflanking my left, but very cautiously, lest he should draw me away too much to the left, and then fall on my right flank. This was probably his intention, for a body of horse was seen towards my right. I halted and fronted ; the enemy did the same, and instantly opened a very heavy artillery, musket, and matchlock fire on my line from the whole of his front, to which my batteries answered steadily.

The enemy had taken up an excellent position, a little in rear of a rising ground, which made it difficult to bring an effective fire on him. I ordered my front line of infantry to lie down, the troop of Horse Artillery to take ground diagonally to the right, and enfilade the enemy's left flank. In this movement a round shot broke the wheel of a Horse Artillery gun.

Captain Lightfoot took up an advanced position to his left front, which made the fire of his battery much more efficacious. Whilst the enemy were suffering from the fire of the troop and battery, I directed Captain Prettejohn, 14th Light Dragoons, to charge with his troop, supported by Captain M'Mahon, 14th Light Dragoons, the enemy's right flank, and I charged myself their left with Captain Need's troop, 14th Light Dragoons, supported by a strong troop of Hydrabad cavalry.

Both attacks succeeded, throwing the whole of

the enemy's first line into confusion, and forcing them to retire.

I beg to do justice to Captain Need s troop; they charged, with steady gallantry, the left, composed of the rebels' best troops, Vilaities and Sepoys, who, throwing themselves back on the right, and resting the flanks of their new line, four or five deep, on the rocky knolls, received the charge with a heavy fire of musketry.

We broke through this dense line, which flung itself amongst the rocks, and, bringing our right shoulders forward, took the front line in reverse, and routed it.

I believe I may say, that what Captain Need's troop did on this occasion was equal to breaking a square of infantry; and the result was most successful, because the charge turned the enemy's position, and decided in a great measure the fate of the day.

I have the honor to recommend to his Excellency's favorable consideration, Captain Need and his devoted troop, and Lieutenant Leith, who saved Captain Need's life, for which I have ventured to recommend him for the Victoria Cross.

The enemy's right gave way, before the squadron of the 14th Light Dragoons, under Captain Prettejohn, reached them; he pursued and cut up several of them.

In order to follow up rapidly this success, I ordered a general advance of the whole line, when the retreat of the rebels became a rout.

I moved forward the whole of the artillery and cavalry in pursuit, the Horse Artillery following the road to the Betwa, from which it had enfiladed the enemy's position, the field battery going across country. We soon came up with six guns and the ammunition waggons, which we left for the infantry, and passed on to the main body of the rebels, broken into knots, and scattered in every direction.

Severe combats occurred between the pursuing cavalry and the fugitives, who singly, or standing back to back, always took up, like most Indians, the best position the ground admitted, and fought with the desperation which I have described on other occasions. The body wedged themselves so dexterously into the banks of a nullah, that neither musketry nor artillery fire could destroy them. Lieutenant Armstrong. of the 3rd Bombay European Regiment, coming up with a few skirmishers, dashed at them and bayonetted them all, but not without some loss. This officer is postmaster of the force, but his zeal always leads him into action, where he does good service on those occasions which require bold decision.

The pursuit had now penetrated and cleared away the first line. A cloud of dust, about a mile and a half to our right, pointed out the line of retreat of another large body, the second line of the rebels, which, by a singular arrangement of the rebel general, Tantia Topee, must have been three miles in rear of his first line.

The whole force again went in immediate pursuit, and came up with the skirmishers in rocky and difficult ground, covering the retreat of the second line: driven in, they closed to their right, and uncovered the main body which cannonaded the troops in pursuit with an 18-pounder, an 8-inch mortar and other guns.

Colonel Turnbull answered with a few rounds, which told. Captain Lightfoot, who had come up, thinking that he could bring his guns to ground from which he could enfilade the enemy's left, I directed him to join the Hydrabad Cavalry, and a troop of the 14th Light Dragoons, whom I had sent to turn their left flank, and take, if possible, their guns.

The enemy did not wait for this attack, but retired with precipitation by the high road to the Rajpore ford.

Neither the jungle, which was set on fire to stop the pursuit, nor difficult ground, could check the ardour of the pursuing troops, who saw within their reach the great prize, the enemy's heavy artillery.

Once on the road, guns and cavalry galloped without a check, till they came within gun shot of the village of Rajpore, where the enemy made their last and third stand.

The troop and battery, advantageously placed on two rising grounds, crossed their fire on the enemy, who rapidly left this, but kept up a heavy fire with musketry, and with a 12-pounder from the opposite bank of the river; the 12-pounder hit by a round shot retired disabled.

I ordered two troops of the 14th Light Dragoons and the Hydrabad Cavalry across the Betwa.

On going down the road to the river, we saw the stream crowded with the enemy's artillery, ordnance park, and quantities of stores, the 18-pounder and the 8-inch mortar, drawn by two elephants, ammunition waggons, and carts full of ammunition of the Gwalior Contingent.

The enemy kept up a heavy fire on us as we crossed the ford, and ascended the steep road leading up the opposite bank; the 14th Light Dragoons and Hydrabad Cavalry gallantly surmounted all opposition, and sabred the rebels, who still held their ground.

I detached parties in pursuit of the numerous fugitives who took across country; another body followed the road and captured, a mile and a half from the Betwa, the disabled 12-pounder, being the eighteenth and last gun of the rebel army.

Two standards were also captured.

The infantry who had followed in skirmishing order, to prevent the escape of any of the enemy, gave proof of their zeal by the rapidity with which they marched up to the front.

Horses and men being completely exhausted by

incessant marching and fighting during the last 48 hours, and being now 9 miles from Jhansi, I marched the troops back to camp.

I beg leave to bring to the favourable notice of the Commander-in-Chief, the conduct of the force under my command, which, without relaxing in the least the arduous siege and investment of a very strong fort and fortified city, garrisoned by 10,000 desperate men, fought, with the few numbers left in camp, a grand action with a relieving army, beat. and pursued them nine miles, killing 1,500 of them, and taking from them all their artillery, stores, and ammunition.

The officers whom circumstances called prominently into action, and who, profiting by the opportunity, did valuable service, were Brigadier Stuart, and the officers whom he mentions, Lieutenant-Colonel Turnbull, Bombay Horse Artillery; Captain Lightfoot, Bombay Artillery; Captain Need, 14th Light Dragoons; Lieutenant Leith, 14th Light Dragoons; Lieutenant Armstrong, 3rd Bombay European Regiment; and Lieutenant Prendergast, Madras Sappers and Miners, who, on various occasions, under my eye, has distinguished himself by his merit and gallantry, as devoted as they were unostentatious.

Serjeant Gardiner, 14th Light Dragoons, attacked and killed a cavalry soldier, as well as two armed men on foot; his gallant conduct at Dhar had been previously honourably mentioned. The conduct of the men of the 14th Light Dragoons was so uniformly good, that their Commanding Officer finds it difficult to bring any particular case of good conduct to my notice.

I am much indebted for their zeal and assistance to me during the action, to Major Orr, Commanding Hydrabad Contingent Field Force; Captain Prettejohn, Commanding 14th Light Dragoons; Captain Hare, Commanding regiment Hydrabad

Force, and Lieutenant Haggard, Commissary of Ordnance, in command of the siege train ; as also to my staff Captain Macdonald, Assistant Quartermaster General ; Captain Wood, Assistant Adjutant-General ; Captain Rose, Rifle Brigade, my Aide-de-Camp ; and Lieutenant Lyster, 72nd Bengal Native Infantry, my Interpreter.

I have, &c ,

HUGH ROSE, Major-General,
Commanding C. I. Field Force.

No. 2.

Brigadier Stuart, Commanding 1st Brigade Central India Field Force, to the Assistant Adjutant General Central India Field Force.

Camp, Jhansi, April 6, 1858.

SIR,

FOR the information of the Major-General Commanding Central India Field Force, I have the honor to report the proceedings of the 1st Brigade Central India Field Force, strength as per margin,* on the morning of the 1st April last.

2. In compliance with the instructions conveyed to me by the Major-General, I marched my Brigade from its position as support to the 2nd Brigade, about 1 o'clock, A.M., on the 1st instant, and proceeded by the Calpee road to another ford of the Betwa River, by which the rebels were expected to pass : the village of Boregaum, about half a mile from the ford in question, was reached

* Left Wing, Her Majesty's 14th Light Dragoons, 40 rank and file, under command of Lieutenant Giles ; two Troops Cavalry, Hydrabad Contingent, one of 1st Regiment, one of 3rd Regiment, both commanded by Lieutenant Johnstone, 107 sabres ; two Guns, Captain Ommaney's Battery ; Captain Woolcombe's Battery ; Her Majesty's 86th Regiment under Colonel Lowth, 208 rank and file ; 25th Regiment Native Infantry, under Major Robertson, 400 rank and file.

about daybreak, when I heard heavy firing from
the direction of the 2nd Brigade; accordingly, I
halted the column and pushed on the cavalry to
the ford, with orders to reconnoitre and return
with all despatch. In a very short time I received
information that none of the enemy were to be
seen or heard of in the vicinity of the river, so I
counter-marched my force and proceeded to join
the 2nd Brigade as quickly as possible: after
about an hour's march, some fugitive rebels were
observed on our left front. I sent the detachment
Her Majesty's 14th Light Dragoons in pursuit,
and many of them were cut up; the brigade was
now approaching the village of Kooshabhore, and
I found that a large body of the enemy, upwards
of two thousand in number, and consisting of
artillery, cavalry, and infantry, were prepared to
oppose our progress. Having placed some guns in
position, in and about the village, I immediately
threw all my infantry into skirmishing order,
placing my cavalry on either flank, and moving
my guns on the main road until within about six
hundred yards of the enemy's position; fire was
then opened with the artillery with most excellent
effect, the enemy were soon shaken, and, the
moment our guns ceased firing, the skirmishers of
Her Majesty's 86th Regiment, and 25th Regiment
Native Infantry dashed forward, carried the
village at the point of the bayonet, capturing all
the enemy's artillery, consisting of six pieces,
together with supply of ammunition, &c.; the
line then steadily advanced, drove the enemy over
some difficult ground in rear of the village, until
a second village was reached, on the outskirts of
which the enemy made another stand; from this
the men of Her Majesty's 86th Regiment immediately dislodged them, and they retired in good
order, leaving a strong rear guard to cover their
retreat, which was effected in so compact a

manner, that though the small body of Her Majesty's 14th Light Dragoons, and the squadron of the cavalry, Hydrabad Contingent, charged them as opportunity offered, they could do little more than cut up the stragglers; the ground over which the enemy were now passing, was, I regret to say, of such a nature that I could only with the greatest difficulty bring up my artillery; otherwise their loss would have been more severe. About two hundred and fifty of their number were, I compute, killed; and, in addition to their guns and ammunition, two elephants and some camels were captured. Had not the troops of my Brigade been in such an exhausted state from the exertions of the previous thirty-six hours, during which, as the Major-general is aware, they were under arms or marching with but little intermission, I should have continued the pursuit. I felt however that as the enemy were rapidly moving off away from the vicinity of Jhansi, nothing further could be done, so returned to camp.

3. I have now in conclusion the pleasure of placing on record how much I was indebted on this occasion to the Officers of my Staff, to Commanding Officers of Regiments, and to all officers and men under their command: all ranks both European and Native were called upon to exert themselves to the utmost and they responded to the call most nobly: Lieutenant and Adjutant Cochrane, Her Majesty's 86th Regiment, behaved in the most gallant manner during this engagement; he was ever to the front, and had three horses shot under him. I beg to support the recommendation of Colonel Lowth, Commanding Her Majesty's 86th Regiment, that some mark of distinction may be awarded to this deserving officer; Lieutenant Mills, 25th Regiment Native Infantry, also did good service in surrounding and destroying, with a small number of his men, some

rebels who had taken up a difficult position amongst rocks; the .conduct of Ressalder Allahoodeen, Khan of the 1st, and Ressalder Trumder Ali Beg, of the 3rd Regiment, C.H.C., was also marked by great bravery; the latter officer, I regret to say, has received two very severe and dangerous wounds.

4. I have already transmitted a casualty roll of the men who suffered in this engagement, and I beg to report that all the guns and ammunition taken from the enemy, have been made over to the Commissary of Ordnance, Central India Field Force.

I have, &c.,

C. S. STUART, Brigadier,

Commanding 1st Brigade, Central India Field Force.

P. S. I have forwarded herewith a duplicate roll of killed and wounded.

No. 5.

From the Return of Killed and Wounded of the Central India Field Force during the Engagement with the enemy on the 1st April, 1858, on the Betwa.

1ST DIVISION.

Reg. Serjeant-Major Thomas, H.M.'s 14th Light Dragoons, April 1, 1858, slightly wounded.

Serjeant John Myers, H.M.'s 14th Light Dragoons, April 1, slightly wounded.

Lieutenant Commanding, Henry Clerk, 3rd Cavalry Hyderabad Contingent, April 1, severely wounded.

Serjeant William Coirns, H.M.'s 86th Regiment, April 1, dangerously wounded.

2ND BRIGADE.

Lieutenant-Colonel S. Turnbull, 1st Tr. Horse Artillery, April 1, contusion of right shoulder, caused by musket ball.

Quartermaster-Serjeant Richard Hiles, 1st Tr. Horse Artillery, April 1, dangerously wounded.

Serjeant William Bright, 1st Tr. Horse Artillery, April 1, mortally wounded (since dead).

Captain J. G. Lightfoot, 2nd Co., Reserve Artillery, April 1, sword cut in right hand.

Lance-Serjeant William Crosby, H. M.'s 14th Light Dragoons, April 1, killed.

Serjeant Thomas Bowen, H.M.'s 14th Light Dragoons, April 1, slightly wounded.

Serjeant William Parkins, H.M.'s 14th Light Dragoons, April 1, severely wounded.

Serjeant James Saine, 3rd Bombay European Regiment, April 1, slightly wounded.

Abstract.

1ST BRIGADE.

Her Majesty's 14th Light Dragoons—Killed 1; wounded 5.

3rd Cavalry Hyderabad Contingent—Killed 2; wounded 4.

Her Majesty's 86th Regiment—Wounded 2.

25th Regiment Bombay Native Infantry—Killed 2; wounded 3, one since dead.

2ND BRIGADE.

1st Troop Horse Artillery—Wounded 5, one since dead.

Her Majesty's 14th Light Dragoons—Killed 4; wounded 19.

2nd Company Reserve Artillery—Wounded 1.

3rd Bombay European Regiment— Killed 2; wounded 3, two since dead.

24th Regiment Bombay Native Infantry—Killed
1; wounded 8, two since dead.

1st Cavalry Hyderabad Contingent — Killed 1;
wounded 4.

4th Cavalry Hyderabad Contingent—Killed 2;
wounded 2.

3rd Infantry Contingent—Wounded 4.

5th Infantry Contingent—Wounded 6, one since
dead.

Total—Killed 15; wounded 66.

No. 6.

GENERAL ORDERS BY THE GOVERNOR-GENERAL.

Allahabad, May 29, 1858.

No. 172 of 1858.—The Right Honorable the
Governor-General is pleased to direct the publica-
tion of the following despatch, from the Deputy
Adjutant-General of the Army, dated 23rd May,
1858, forwarding a communication from Brigadier-
General Jones, C.B., commanding the Roorkee Field
Force, detailing his operations since leaving Mo-
radabad on the 3rd, and his actions with the
Rebels on the 5th and 6th of May, near and at
Bareilly :—

No. 7.

*Brigadier-General Jones, C.B., Commanding
the Roorkee Field Force, to the Chief of the Staff.*

Camp Shahjehanpore, May 13, 1858.

SIR,

ON the 3rd instant, the Field Force left Moradabad for Bareilly, and on the morning of the 5th
approached Meragunge, where a strong picquet of
the rebel army was entrenched.

The force that had been detached under Major

Gordon was recalled and joined near the village of Moollick.

I placed 4 guns of No. 7 Light Field Battery on the right, supported by the squadron of Carabineers and the Affghan Horse.

To the left I sent 2 guns, and the Mooltanee Cavalry.

In the centre of the road were the heavy guns, the 1st Sikhs on the right, and the Royal Rifles on the left, supported by the 17th Punjaub Infantry. The 1st Punjaub Rifles were on the left of the 60th. In this formation I passed through the enemy's entrenchments, which he abandoned as I approached, retreating towards the River Dojoora. As I saw it was not his intention to stand on this side of the stream, I determined to push him rapidly, and endeavour to capture his guns, before they could be got into position on the other bank.

The cavalry and artillery on the right, were ordered to pass rapidly round a village, and come down on the enemy's flank.

This order was admirably carried out by Captain Smith in command, who, moving swiftly, came up with the rebels, and charging with the Affghan horse, cut down a considerable number.

Finding it now impossible to get his 3 guns over the ford, with this body in such close pursuit, the enemy halted, formed up his cavalry, and opened fire with his guns.

Captain Austin instantly replied with shrapnell, and the destructive nature of this fire, and the imposing advance of the Carabiniers, disconcerted these horsemen, who turned and fled, leaving the guns in Captain Smith's hands.

The enemy attempted no further opposition: his well-mounted cavalry retreated rapidly to Bareilly, with the General who had been sent from that city with reinforcements to check my advance.

The field force crossed the Dojoora, and encamped on the left bank.

I enclose Captain Smith's report, and also a detailed statement of the captured ordnance.

Early the next morning I struck my camp, and drew up the force close to the city of Bareilly. I failed in gaining positive intelligence of his Excellency's movements, as the country was swarming with fugitive Sowars, but my information led me to believe that Khan Bahadoor had been defeated the day before, and that the Commander-in-Chief's camp was pitched in the cantonment.

I detached Captain Cureton with the Mooltanee cavalry to the left, which appeared to be the enemy's principal line of retreat, and this excellent officer cut up about 100 of their cavalry and infantry, among whom was the General who had been sent out to oppose me.

Brigadier Coke led a party of cavalry to the bridge, by which Bareilly is entered on this side, where he was informed some guns had been abandoned; but he found them in position, and they opened on him with grape.

On this being reported to me by Major Muter, I ordered up the heavy guns, and threw strong parties of the Royal Rifles into the gardens through which the road leads.

Brigadier Coke, having reconnoitred and obtained a most correct idea of the position of those guns, suggested that our heavy artillery should be moved to the right. Lieutenant Stubbs, in charge, got his guns into position at about 1200 yards, and made some excellent practice.

By this fire, and that of the Rifles from the gardens, the enemy were quickly silenced, when the Royal Rifles advanced, supported by the 17th

Punjaub infantry, and rushing up the street, captured at the point of the bayonet the guns the enemy were endeavouring to withdraw.

Some Ghazies threw themselves on these soldiers, and were killed in the streets and adjoining houses; but a most valuable colour serjeant of the. Rifles was slain, and some men received severe sword cuts.

Under the direction of Brigadier Coke, the captured portion of the city was secured, the principal points being occupied, and barricades erected in the streets.

While these operations were being performed, Captain Lambert with the 1st Punjaub Rifles, 2 guns, and the squadron of Carabiniers, made corresponding advance on the left, and bringing their left shoulders forward, swept the gardens clear of the enemy, and advanced upon the bridge.

Entering the city with a portion of the Punjaub Rifles, he took part in the operations already described.

Captain Cureton was detached with a squadron, and accompanied by my Aide-de-Camp, Lieutenant H. Deedes, passed round this city and entered his Excellency's camp, whom I met the next morning in the centre of the city.

In these, the last operations of the Roorkee Field Force, 3 more guns were captured, making in all since crossing into Rohilcund on the 17th instant, 36 pieces of artillery.

The reputation borne by Brigadier Coke, C. B., led me to expect most valuable assistance from that officer, and in this I have in no instance been disappointed. His high courage, energy, and judgment, render him an ornament to the service to which he belongs.

I am much indebted also to the officers of his brigade; to Major Palmer, who has so well commanded the 1st battalion 60th Rifles; to Major

Gordon, commanding the 1st Sikhs; Captain Larkins, of the 17th Punjaub Infantry; and Captain Lambert, of the 1st Punjaub Rifles.

I have before expressed the high estimation in which I hold Captain Cureton, of the Mooltanee Cavalry, who has shown himself so admirable a leader of irregular cavalry; and I am happy in bringing to his Excellency's notice, the distinguished part taken by Captain Smith, of the Affghan Horse, in the operations of the 5th.

I am much indebted to both Captain Austin, of the Artillery, and Captain Bott, of the Carabiniers, for the steady support which they have always rendered.

I have also to notice three officers of the 60th Rifles, whose companies did such excellent and gallant service in the city; Captain Bowles, Captain M'Queen, and Lieutenant Ashburnham.

I have received every assistance from Major Muter, Deputy Assistant Adjutant-General; also from Captain Tedlie, Deputy Assistant Quarter-Master General; Lieutenant H. Deedes, Aide-de-Camp; and Lieutenant Tyler, Orderly Officer. I am much indebted to that most valuable officer, Captain Drummond, of the Engineers, and Lieutenant Brownlow, of the same corps, and also Lieutenant W. Jeffreys, who commanded the Sappers and Miners.

Surgeon Innes, Field Force Surgeon, has always exerted his excellent judgment and great skill to the utmost; and I am indebted to Captain Carter, Deputy Commissary General, for his untiring zeal.

I have, &c.

JOHN JONES, Brigadier General,
Commanding Roorkee Field Force.

No. 8.

Captain A. Smith, Commanding Affghan Horse, to Major D. D. Muter, Assistant Adjutant General, Roorkee Field Force.

SIR,   *Camp Bareilly, May* 7, 185.

I HAVE the honor to report, for the information of Brigadier-General J. Jones, C. B., Commanding the Roorkee Field Force, that on the 5th instant, agreeably to orders, I followed in pursuit of the retreating enemy from the village of Meergunge, with the Affghan Horse and Cock's Rissalah, the latter under Lieutenant R. F. Angelo, 1st Punjaub Infantry ; strength together about 150.

During the pursuit, several fugitive horsemen were overtaken and immediately cut down. After about 3 miles' chase, we came upon a horsed gun which had been abandoned by the flying enemy ; having secured which, we had advanced but a short distance in continuance of the pursuit, when the rebels opened on us with grape and round shot. Observing that their fire swept down the road, I made a movement to the right, intending to charge their left flank ; as, however, there was a very large force of cavalry in support of their position, and as my men had become much scattered, owing to the rapidity of the pursuit, I deemed it necessary to wait till I should get a larger body collected.

The enemy perceived our flank movement, and kept turning their guns on us, thus removing their fire from the road, and leaving it clear for advance of artillery of the advanced guard, which now came up, and taking up their position on our left opened fire.

During our gradual movement to the right, we were under a heavy fire as the enemy had our range exactly. My own horse was killed under me by a round shot, as was also that of a Sowar, and some were wounded with grape.

As soon as our artillery ceased firing, we galloped forward, and got possession of 2 more guns, cutting down the few men who were just abandoning them, and continued the pursuit as far as the nullah at Dojoora. Here observing the enemy assembled, about 700 strong, on the opposite bank, and most of our own party being very much behind, owing to the length of the pursuit and rapidity of the rebels' flight, I drew up in a tope on this side to get my men together, deeming that I carried out the orders I received in capturing the 3 guns, which were all the enemy were reported to have possessed. I should consider the enemy's loss to be about 60 killed. Our own casualties were of the Affghan horse:—men wounded 3, missing 1, supposed to be killed; horses, 1 killed and 2 wounded. In Coke's Rissalah, men wounded 2, horses killed 1, and wounded 1.

The enemy's force consisted almost entirely of cavalry, and those well mounted.

I have, &c.

ANDREW SMITH, Captain,
Commanding Affghan Horse.

No. 9.

Return of Killed and Wounded which took place in the Roorkee Field Force in action with the Enemy, on the 5th and 6th of May, 1858, near and at Bareilly.

Camp Shahjehanpore, May 13, 1858.

Mooltanee Regiment of Cavalry—1 rank and file killed; 1 native non-commissioned officer, 4 rank and file, wounded; 6 horses killed; 8 horses wounded; 1 horse missing.

Cavalry attached to 1st Punjaub Infantry—2 rank and file, wounded ; 1 horse killed ; 3 horses wounded.

1st Battalion 60th Royal Rifles—1 non-commissioned officer, killed ; 1 non-commissioned officer, 4 rank and file, wounded.

1st Punjaub Infantry—1 rank and file, wounded.

17th Punjaub Infantry—3 rank and file, wounded.

Affghan Horse—1 rank and file, killed ; 1 native commissioned officer, 5 rank and file, wounded ; 1 rank and file, missing ; 2 horses killed ; 3 horses wounded.

Total—1 European non-commissioned officer, killed ; 1 European non-commissioned officer, 4 European rank and file, wounded ; 2 native rank and file, killed ; 1 native commissioned officer, 1 native non-commissioned officer, 15 native rank and file, wounded ; 1 native rank and file, missing ; 9 horses killed i 14 horses wounded ; 1 horse missing.

JOHN JONES, Brigadier-General,
Commanding Roorkee Field Force.
D. D. MUTTER, Major,
Deputy Assistant Adjutant-General,
Roorkee Field Force.

No. 10.

Return of Ordnance captured from the Rebels by the Force under Command of Brigadier-General J. Jones, C.B., in action near Meergunge, on the 5th May, 1858.

No 1. Brass 3-pounder, native made, with carriage and limber.

No. 2. Brass 6-pounder, native made, with carriage and limber.

No. 3. Brass 6¼-pounder, native made, with carriage and limber.

Total – Guns 3, carriages 3, and limbers 3.

F. W. STUBBS, Lieut., Bengal Artillery,
Comdg. Heavy Ord., Roorkee Field Force.
Camp Bareilly, May 6, 1858.

Return of Ordnance captured by the Force under Command of Brigadier-General J. Jones, C.B., in action at Bareilly, on the 6th May, 1858.

No. 1. Brass 1½-pounder, native made, with carriage, brought in by the Sappers.

No. 2. Brass 6¼-pounder, native made, carriage and limber.

No. 3. Iron 1-pounder, native made, with carriage.

One cart laden with shot and grape.

} Taken at the bridge.

The powder was blown up at the bridge leading into the city.

Total—Brass guns	... ...	2
Iron do	... ...	1
Ammunition cart	...	1
Carriages	... ...	3
Limber	... ...	1

F. W. STUBBS, Lieut.,
Commanding Heavy Ordnance Roorkee
Field Force.
Camp Bareilly, May 6, 1858.

No. 11.

Allahabad, May 31, 1858.

No. 174 of 1858.

THE Right Honorable the Governor-General of India is pleased to direct the publication of the following despatch from the Deputy Adjutant-

General of the Army, No. 342 A, dated 23rd May, 1858, forwarding a communication from Major-General Sir Hugh Rose, K.C.B., Commanding Central India Field Force, detailing his operations against, and the capture of, the fortress and town of Jhansie.

His Lordship entirely concurs with the Commander-in-Chief in the satisfaction his Excellency has expressed at the manner in which this fortress has been captured by Major-General Sir Hugh Rose, and in his Excellency's high estimation of the services of the Major-General, and of the officers and men under his command.

No. 12.

The Deputy Adjutant-General of the Army, to the Secretary to the Government of India, Military Department, with the Governor-General.

Head Quarters Camp, Shahjehanpore,
May 23, 1858.

SIR, No. 342 A.

I HAVE the honor, by direction of the Commander-in-Chief to enclose, for submission to the Right Honorable the Governor-General, copy of a despatch,* dated the 30th ultimo, from Major-General Sir H. Rose, K.C.B., commanding Central India Field Force, detailing the operations of the troops under his command, against the fortress and town of Jhansie.

2. His Excellency desires to express his cordial satisfaction with the manner in which the capture of this important place was effected, and his perfect appreciation of the services of Sir H. Rose and those under his command, and he begs to recommend all to the favorable consideration of

* See London Gazette, July 17, 1858.

his Lordship, especially those who have been more prominently mentioned by the Major-General.

I have, &c.

H. W. NORMAN, Major,
Deputy Adjutant-General of the Army.

———

No. 13.

No. 176 of 1858.

THE Right Honorable the Governor-General is pleased to publish, for general information, the following despatch from the Deputy Adjutant-General of the Army, dated 24th May, 1858, forwarding copy of one from Major-General Sir J. Hope Grant, K.C.B., reporting his operations between the 10th and 13th instant, with returns of casualties and of ordnance captured.

———

No. 14.

Major-General J. H. Grant, Commanding Lucknow Field Force, to the Chief of the Staff, Head Quarters.

Camp, Nugger, May 14, 1858.

SIR,   No. 9858.

I HAVE the honor to report that, on the morning of the 10th instant, the column under my command arrived at Doundea Keira, which is a strong mud fort in the midst of jungle, belonging to the rebel Ram Buksh. On my arrival at this fort, I found it deserted. Three guns were found concealed in wells, one a brass 32-pounder howitzer. I had the fort destroyed as much as possible, and the principal buildings in the town belonging to Ram Buksh burnt. On the 12th, the column marched to Nuggur, and hearing there that Bene Madho and Shewrutten Singh had assembled an army of 15,000 infantry, 1,600 cavalry; and 11 guns at Sirsee, a village with a fort in it five miles off, I determined that afternoon to proceed to attack them, leaving all the baggage, supplies, &c., with tents struck, in a safe position, with a force of cavalry, infantry, and artillery for its protection.

It is very difficult in this country to get good information, though there are several excellent civil officers with the column for that purpose; the consequence was, on arriving at the ground, I found it much stronger than I had reason to expect. The enemy were placed along a difficult nullah with a very strong and large jungle in their rear. The village and fort of Towrie also lay in this jungle. The enemy's first gun began to open about 5 o'clock, but, as soon as our column was formed with the cavalry and horse artillery covering our right flank, they were attacked with such boldness and vigour, that they gave way and were driven into the jungle, leaving two iron guns behind them, a 9-pounder and 8-pounder.

Our column was almost surrounded at one time, but the cavalry and artillery, the former commanded by Lieutenant-Colonel Hagart, a very superior officer, and the latter by Captain Gibbon, succeeded in clearing our right flank. Brigadier Horsford, with the Rifles and Seikhs, supported by the 90th Regiment, in the most admirable manner drove them away from our left flank; the 38th Regiment supported the heavy guns. The enemy suffered a considerable loss, and it is reported and I believe with truth, that Shewrutten Singh and his brother are both killed.

I did not think it advisable to allow the troops to enter the jungle, and I directed them to bivouac for the night on the ground where the fight had taken place, and returned on the morning of the 13th to the camp at Nugger.

I have, &c.,

J. H. GRANT, Major-General,
Commanding Lucknow Field Force.

No. 15.

Return of Casualties of the Field Force under the Command of Major - General Sir J. Hope Grant, K.C.B., on the 12th of May, 1858, at Sirsee.

Camp Nuggur, May 13, 1858.

Artillery.

2nd Troop, 3rd Brigade, B.H.A.—1 troop horse, killed ; 1 serjeant or havildar, 1 troop horse, wounded.

Q. Field Battery, R.A.—3 trumpeters, drummers, rank and file, 1 troop horse. killed ; 1 captain, 3 trumpeters, drummers, rank and file, wounded.

Cavalry.

H.M.'s 7th Hussars—1 trumpeter, rank and file, 1 officer's horse, 1 troop horse, wounded.

1st Seikh Cavalry—1 trumpeter, rank and file, and lascar, and 1 troop horse, wounded.

Infantry.

H.M.'s 38th Regiment—13 trumpeters, drummers, rank and file, killed ; 2 trumpeters, drummers, rank and file, wounded.

H.M.'s 90th Light Infantry—3 trumpeters, drummers, rank and file, killed.

2nd Battalion Rifle Brigade—2 trumpeters, rank and file, killed ; 5 trumpeters, rank and file, wounded.

6th Punjaub Rifles—1 trumpeter, rank and file, or lascar, killed ; 1 native officer, 6 trumpeters, rank and file, and lascars, wounded.

> Total—22 trumpeters, drummers, rank and file, and lascars, 2 troop horses, killed ; 1 captain, 1 native officer, 1 serjeant or havildar, 18 trumpeters, drummers, rank

and file, and lascars, 1 officer's horse, 3
troop horses, wounded.

> J. HOPE GRANT, Major-General,
>   Commanding Lucknow Field Force.

> W. HAMILTON, Major,
>   Deputy-Asst.-Adjt.-General,
>   Lucknow Field Force.

No. 16.

List of Officers Wounded.

Captain J. R. Gibbon, Royal Artillery, severely,
accidental.

No. 18.

No. 178 of 1858.

The Right Honorable the Governor-General is
pleased to direct the publication of the following
letter from the Deputy Adjutant-General of the
Army, No. 356 A, dated 28th May, 1858, forwarding two despatches from Brigadier-General
Jones, C.B., announcing his advance on Mohumdee,
and his capture of that place.

No. 19.

*The Deputy Adjutant-General of the Army to the
Secretary to the Government of India, Military
Department, with the Governor-General.*

> *Head Quarters Camp, Futtehgurh,*
> *May* 28, 1858.

(No. 356 A.)

SIR,

BY desire of the Commander-in-Chief, I have
the honor to forward, for the information of the
Right Honorable the Governor-General, two de-

spatches, dated the 24th and 25th instant, from
Brigadier-General J. Jones, C.B., announcing his
advance on and capture of Mohumdee.

2. The Brigadier-General's operations were, his
Excellency considers, pressed with their usual
vigour, but the retreat of the enemy was so rapid
that he was not able to inflict heavy loss on the
fugitives.

3. The Commander-in-Chief had himself arrived
at Shahjehanpore with a weak escort on the 18th
instant. On the afternoon of that day, the enemy
showed in considerable force, and there was a prolonged skirmish. The arrangements of the force
did not permit of an advance, and his Excellency
restricted the efforts of the troops. The enemy
suffered from the effects of our cannonade. A
return of the casualties on this occasion is annexed.

4. The Commander-in-Chief thought it advisable to remain at Shahjehanpore till a sufficient
force had been assembled at that place to admit
of the Brigadier-General's forward movement
being made with perfect safety. His Excellency's
presence being much needed on the line of the
telegraph communication, owing to the numerous
references from the Commanders of the various
columns still in the field, he returned to Futtehgurh on the 25th instant, very exact instructions
having been given to Brigadier-General Jones for
his guidance.

5. Head-Quarters are still at Futtehgurh.

I have, &c.

H. W. NORMAN, Major,
Deputy Adjutant-General of the Army.

No. 20.

Brigadier-General J. Jones, C.B., Commanding Shahjehanpore Field Force, to the Chief of the Staff.

Camp, 11 *miles from Mohumdee,*
SIR,   May 24, 1858.

I ATTACKED the enemy at day-light this morning. The fort was taken quickly, and without loss; but the enemy retired with such speed that I could not come up with him. The carriage of one of his heaviest guns was broken to pieces by a 24-pounder shot; but the gun has not been found. One only was taken in the fort, a gun that had burst.

The enemy were very strong on their own right, and large bodies of their cavalry out-flanking us, checked the advance of Brigadier Hagart with a large portion of the cavalry, and Tombs' troop, horse artillery, on our left. The rebel cavalry charged the Mooltanee cavalry, thirty of them riding through the regiment; five or six of Cureton's men were wounded, but all the rebels that broke through his regiment were killed. A waggon of Major Hammond's battery exploded while moving with the Carabiniers at the gallop, and two Europeans and one native were killed. I advanced about nine miles with great rapidity, but I could not come up with the enemy. The cavalry and light guns were pushed on a few miles further in pursuit. The guns they (the enemy) principally used were drawn by horses, and with these he covered the retreat of those drawn by bullocks, withdrawing the latter at the first round from our artillery.

The country greatly favoured the retreat of the enemy, being everywhere open and unbroken, so that they could scatter, and sufficiently wooded to conceal their principal line of retreat.

The force will reach Mohumdee early to-morrow; it is about eleven miles from my camp. A few fatal cases of sun-stroke occurred.

I have, &c

JOHN JONES, Brigadier-General,
Commanding Shahjehanpore Field Force.

No. 21.

Brigadier-General J. Jones, C.B., Commanding Shahjehanpore Field Force, to the Chief of the Staff.

Camp, Mohumdee,
Sir, May 25, 1858, 4 P.M.

I ARRIVED at Mohumdee this morning. I found some of the enemy's cavalry in position in front of the town; but on driving them away, the town was discovered to be abandoned. One damaged gun was taken in the fort. The rebels retreated over the River Goomtee and into the jungles.

The town is now occupied by some of Coke's Infantry, and arrangements are being carried out for blowing up the fort.

I am in hopes of capturing some guns still, for information has reached me that the enemy did not succeed in bringing them all away from Bunnye.

I regret to say that these operations have cost, and are likly to cost, the lives of a considerable number of European soldiers struck down by the sun.

The main body of the rebels under their leaders retreated yesterday into the jungles, carrying their families with them.

I have, &c.
J. JONES, Brigadier-General,
Commanding Shahjehanpore Field Force.

No. 22.

Return of Wounded which took place in the Shahjehanpore Brigade, in Action with the Enemy on the 18th of May, 1858, at Shahjehanpore.

Camp, Shahjehanpore, May, 16, 1858.

2nd Troop 1st Brigade Horse Artillery—2 rank and file.

No. 7 Light Field Battery—1 rank and file, and 1 horse.

DeKantzow's Horse—2 rank and file.

H.M.'s 79th Highlanders—2 rank and file.

Total—5 European rank and file, 2 native rank and file, and 1 horse.

JOHN JONES, Brigadier-General,
Commanding at Shahjehanpore.

No. 23.

Allahabad, June 2, 1858

No. 182 of 1858.

THE Right Honorable the Governor-General is pleased to publish for general information the following despatch from the Deputy-Adjutant-General of the Army, dated 26th May, 1858, forwarding a report by Brigadier-General Sir E. Lugard, K.C.B., of the operations of the Azimgurh Field Force, with returns of casualties, and ordnance captured in the skirmish at Judgespore, on the 9th ultimo :—

No. 24.

Brigadier-General Sir Edward Lugard, K.C.B., Commanding Azimghur Field Force, to the Chief of the Staff.

SIR,   Camp, Judgespore, May 10, 1858.

I HAVE the honor to make the following report of the operations of the Azimgurh Field

1858.   9 D

Force under my command, for the information o?
his Excellency the Commander-in-Chief.

My last despatch, dated the 25th ultimo, will
have informed you of the result of the pursuit of
Koer Sing's force, which I had directed under
Brigadier Douglas, C.B., and of my having marched
from Azimgurh on the 23rd idem to join the Brigadier in furtherance of the operations against the
fugitives.

On the 30th ultimo, learning that alarm was
felt for the safety of Arrah, I directed Brigadier
Douglas, who had already crossed his troops over
to the right bank, to move the 84th Foot, Seikh
Cavalry, and two 9-pounder guns to that station
without delay ; and by making forced marches I
reached Synha Ghat on the 2nd instant, and at mid-
day of the 4th the whole of my force was crossed to
the right bank, notwithstanding the prevalence
of a strong easterly gale, which continually prevented the boats leaving the bank, and on the
5th instant I reached Arrah.

As my troops had not halted since quitting
Azimgurh, and the marches had been of great
length, I remained at Arrah on the 6th, to give
them rest and to enable me to have an interview
with the Commissioner of Patna and Brigadier
Christie, who had come over on purpose to afford
me all the assistance in their power in making
my arrangements.

On the 7th I moved from Arrah by the railroad to Beheea, with the force as per margin,*
leaving my heavy baggage, sick, &c., behind, with
eight Infantry and 145 dismounted Sikh Cavalry

---

* Artillery.—3 Royal Horse Artillery; 6 Cotter's Bat-
tery ; 2 8-inch howitzers (R. A.); 2 5½-inch mortars (R.A.)
Cavalry.—Military Train, 188 ; 4th Madras Cavalry, 100 ;
3rd Sikhs, 275 : 12th Irregulars, 35 ; total, 598. Infantry.
—Punjaub Sappers, 57 ; 10th Foot, 582 ; 84th Foot, 585 ;
Madras Rifles, 69 ; Rattray's Seikhs, 114. Total, 1407.

for their protection, in addition to the party of the 35th Foot and Naval Brigade already holding the entrenched position, and taking nothing but provisions and tents, which in this season are absolutely necessary for the protection of the lives of Europeans, many having already fallen a sacrifice to coup-de-soleil.

So far as I could learn from the extremely scanty information procurable (every soul in the district being apparently against us), the rebels confidently calculated upon my moving upon them east by the direct road from Arrah, viâ Deena, or due south from Beheea, both of which led through dense jungle, and had been strongly entrenched. I therefore decided upon attacking from the west ; but to provide against any attempt upon Arrah, I detached from Beheea on the morning of the 8th a moveable force, composed of a party of Seikh sowars, two 9-pounder guns, two companies 84th Foot, and one company Madras Rifles, under Major Carr, (M.R.), with instructions to take post a few miles from the town of Arrah on the Jugdespore road, and to be prepared to move as circumstances required. At the same time I despatched a patrol of cavalry and horse artillery towards Domnaon under Lieutenant-Colonel Robertson, Military Train, to distract the attention of the enemy, and to conceal my ultimate plans, whilst I remained at Beheea threatening that road. A body of rebels made an attempt during the day to cross the line of railroad to my rear, but were driven back into the jungle with some loss.

On the 9th I moved through the belt of jungle beyond Beheea, and circling due south came upon the west side of Jugdespore, where the country is pretty open, by the village of Hatumpore. Sowars had given timely notice of my approach to the parties posted at the entrenchments of Deleea and Duwa ; so on my arrival opposite Jugdespore I found the whole rebel force prepared to defend their position. This decided me upon attacking the place at once, and as soon as the troops were formed, I advanced upon it in line ; the 10th Foot and one company of Sikhs, with two 9-pounder guns on the right, the two 8-inch howitzers in the centre, and the 84th Foot, with a company of Madras Rifles and two 9-pounder guns on the left, the cavalry and horse artillery protecting my flanks and rear.

The rebels made a determined stand, first at the high embankments of a large tank ; and, when driven back by the artillery fire, they held with much obstinacy the village and house of Jugdespore, but were speedily dislodged and driven through the jungle by the infantry. Some of the 84th Foot arrived first at Koer Singh's house, and turned a gun they found inside the enclosure, charged with grape, upon the enemy. This gun (with two others unfinished) had been recently constructed for the purpose of defending the position ; it was formed of wood, with a copper tube, most skilfully made, and although unfit for much service, would have answered effectually for a short defence. A good deal of ammunition, tents, &c., were captured, with some store of grain. . The rebels fled south through the jungle.

After posting four companies of European Infantry and one company of Seikhs, under Captain Norman, 10th Foot, to hold Jugdespore for the night, I encamped the remainder of my force on the plain between Hatumpore and Jugdespore.

My casualties, I am happy to say, amounted to only two men slightly wounded.

I have much pleasure in expressing my great approbation of the conduct of all the troops engaged.   I have, &c.,

EDWARD LUGARD, Brigadier-General,
Commanding Azimgurh Field Force.

No. 25.

Numerical Return of Casualties in Head Quarters of the Azimgurh Field Force, under Command of Brigadier-General Sir Edward Lugard, K.C,B., in the Skirmish at Jugdespore, on the 9th May, 1858.

Camp, Jugdespore.

H.M.'s 84th Regiment—1 rank and file, slightly wounded.

4th Madras Light Cavalry — 1 rank and file, slightly wounded.

Total—2 rank and file.

E. LUGARD, Brigadier-General,
Commanding Azimgurh Field Force.

No. 28.

Allahabad, June 3, 1858.

No. 183 of 1858.

THE Right Honorable the Governor-General is pleased to direct the publication of the following despatch from the Deputy-Adjutant-General of the Army, No. 352 A, dated 27th May, 1858, forwarding a report from Major W. Middleton, 17th Madras Native Infantry, of the successful operations of the column under his command, on the banks of the Jumna; near the village of Ghurrah, on the 9th ultimo. His Lordship concurs with his Excellency the Commander-in-Chief in viewing the whole affair as most creditable to Major Middleton and the troops under his command.

No. 29.

The Deputy-Adjutant-General of the Army to the Secretary of the Government of India, Military Department, with the Governor-General,

Head Quarters Camp, Futtehgurh,
May 27, 1858.

SIR, No. 352 A.

BY desire of the Commander-in-Chief, I have the honor to forward, for submission to the Right Honorable the Governor-General, the enclosed copy of a report from Major W. Middleton, 17th Madras Native Infantry, relating the operations of the column under his command on the banks of the Jumna, near the village of Ghurrah, where a party of rebels was successfully surprised and destroyed.

2. The whole affair appears to his Excellency to be creditable to Major Middleton and the troops under his command.

I have, &c.,
H. W. NORMAN, Major,
Deputy-Adjutant-General of the Army.

No. 30.

Major W. Middleton, Commanding Moveable Column, to the Brigade-Major, Madras Troops, Futtehpore.

Camp, Ghatumpore, May 10, 1858.

SIR,

AGREEABLE to instructions received through Brigadier Carthew, from the Assistant-Adjutant-General's Office, Cawnpore, I have the honor to report that not being able to obtain any certain information regarding the movements of a large body of rebels that were threatening this place,

I advanced the moveable column under my command to this station on the 8th instant, and upon inquiry I ascertained that about 200 rebel sepoys and a large body of villagers had, after plundering Lallpore, retired to the village of Ghurrah, on the bank of the Jumna, distant from here 12 miles, and were encamped there ; and as they appeared to be the dread of this neighbourhood, I determined (with the assistance of a detachment of Her Majesty's 80th Regiment, kindly placed at my disposal by Colonel Maxwell) to drive them across the Jumna.

2. On the morning of the 9th instant, I advanced with the force as per margin* towards the village of Ghurrah. On approaching the village I ordered H.M.'s 80th Regiment detachment and Madras Rifles to advance in skirmishing order with supports. The detachment 17th Regiment Madras Native Infantry forming the reserve, the detachment 8th Bengal Irregular Cavalry forming on the right of the skirmishers ; the guns moving in rear of the skirmishers. While moving forward in this order, a number of men were seen escaping to the right, with the intention of crossing by a ford, but they were intercepted by the cavalry (the rebels opened fire upon them) and driven back. On the skirmishers approaching the bank of the river the rebels, after firing a few shots, fled, throwing their muskets and matchlocks into the river. Between three and four hundred precipitated themselves into the water, aud tried to reach the opposite bank ; the guns had by this time got into position aud opened fire, which, together with the deadly fire of the infantry, proved so severe that very few reached the

* Detachment of 8th Irregular Cavalry, in all 60 ; two guns Madras Horse Artillery ; 2 do. do. Foot do. ; 150 of H M.'s 80th Regiment ; 160 17th Regiment Madras Native Infantry ; 68th Madras Rifles.

opposite shore. Three boats succeeded in escaping before the force came up; these, filled with rebels, opened fire upon us, but were soon silenced by guns and Enfields. They took refuge in the bottom of their boats until a favourable opportunity occurred of escape.

After clearing the river I ordered the retreat to be sounded. We remained under some trees during the remainder of the day, and at 5 P.M. marched for our encampment. It is quite impossible to make any estimate of the loss of the rebels, but I should suppose at the least there were 200 killed and wounded, while the loss on our side only amounted to one private of the 80th Regiment wounded (contusion), and one private, 80th Regiment, missing. I cannot conclude without bringing to the notice of the Brigadier commanding the valuable services rendered by Lieutenant Woodcock, 8th Irregular Bengal Cavalry; by Lieutenant Bridge, commanding Madras Artillery; by Captain Browne, commanding detachment Her Majesty's 80th Regiment; by Lieutenant Obbard, commanding detachment 17th Regiment Madras Native Infantry; by Captain Doveton, commanding Madras Detachment Rifles; and to all other officers and men under their command, to all of whom I tender my best thanks; as also to Lieutenant R. Stuart, 17th Regiment Madras Native Infantry, Staff Officer; and Assistant-Surgeon Busteed.

I have, &c.,
WM. MIDDLETON, Major,
Commanding Moveable Column.

No. 31.

No. 184 of 1858.

THE Right Honorable the Governor-General is pleased to direct the publication of the following despatch, from the Deputy Adjutant-General of the Army, No. 353 A, dated 27th May, 1858, forwarding one from Major-General Sir S. Cotton, K.C.B., commanding the Peshawur division, detailing the operations of the force under his immediate command, recently employed on the Eusuffzai border.

The Governor-General fully appreciates the ability and judgment of Sir S. Cotton, in the conduct of the expedition, and it will afford his Lordship great satisfaction to bring to the favorable notice of the home authorities the eminent merits of the Major-General, and the excellent services of the officers and troops under his command :—

No. 32.

The Deputy Adjutant-General of the Army to the Secretary to the Government of India, Military Department, with the Governor-General.

Head Quarters, Camp Futtehgurh,
May 29, 1858.

SIR,   No. 353 A.

I AM directed by the Commander-in-Chief to transmit a despatch dated the 6th instant, (received this day) from Major-General Sir Sydney Cotton, K.C.B., Commanding the Peshawur Division detailing the operations of a force under the Major-General's immediate command, recently employed on the Eusuffzai border, and in submitting it to the Right Honorable the Governor General, I am to request you will draw the attention of his Lordship to the skill and judgment displayed by the Major-General in conducting the service, and in attaining the objects of the expedition.

2. Sir Colin Campbell recommends the officers

and troops employed to the favorable notice of
his Lordship.

I have, &c.
H. W. NORMAN, Major,
Deputy Adjutant General of the Army.

No. 33.

*Major-General Sir S. Cotton, K.C.B., to Major
H. W. Norman, Deputy Adjutant-General of
the Army.*

Camp Kubbull, May 6, 1858.

SIR,

IN continuation of the report made by me to
the Quarter master General of the Army, (copy of
which is enclosed) announcing the assembly of a
field force under my personal command, for service
on the Eusuffzai frontier; I have the honor to
state, for the information of his Excellency the
Commander-in-Chief, that, having been joined by
the Commissioner, Lieutenant-Colonel Edwardes,
C.B., the force marched from Nowshera on the
23rd ultimo.

2. On the morning of the 25th ultimo, the force
reached the Eusuffzai frontier, village of Selim
Khan (distant from Punjtar about 5 miles) and
at the mouth of a pass by which the Punjtar
valley is entered.

3. Reconnoitring parties, one under Captain
Wright, Chief Staff Officer of the Force, and the
other under Lieutenant-Colonel Edwardes, C.B.,
Commissioner, were at once sent forward, when it
was found that the fortified town of Punjtar was
only occupied by Mookurrub Khan, the Chief of
the Khoodookheil tribe, with about 60 Sowars,
the inhabitants having previously wholly evacuated
the place.

4. Mookurrub Khan, apparently under the
impression that the reconnoitring parties were

closely followed up by our column, fled, leaving the town entirely unoccupied.

5. It was now determined to enter the Punjtar district ; on the following morning, the force being told off for that purpose into three columns,* as shown in the margin, and making Selim Khan the base of operations, where our camp remained standing, I proceeded, in company with Lieutenant-Colonel Edwardes, with No. 1 Column, furnished with two days' provisions, so as to enter the Punjtar district by the Durrund Pass ; whilst Colonel Renny, Her Majesty's 81st Regiment, proceeded in command of No. 2. Column, direct to Punjtar, with orders to destroy that place ; No. 3 Column, under Major Allan, Her Majesty's 81st Regiment, remaining in charge of our standing camp at Sel m Khan.

6. At one o'clock on the morning of 26th April,

* No. 1 Column.—Artillery : 2 9-pounder guns, and 2 24-pounder howitzers, of Captain Stallard's Light Field Battery ; 1 3-pounder gun, and 1 12-pounder howitzer. of the Peshawur Military Train Battery. Cavalry : 100 sabres, 7th Irregular Cavalry ; 200 sabres, Guide Cavalry ; 30 sabres, Peshawur Light Horse. Infantry : 100 Sappers, under Captain Hyde ; 260 rank and file, Her Majesty's 98th. under Major Peyton ; 300 rank and file, 21st Native Infantry, under Major Milne ; 400 rank and file. 9th Punjaub Infantry, under Captain Thelwall ; 400 rank and file. 18th Punjaub Infantry, under Lieutenant Williamson ; 300 rank and file. Guide Infantry, under Lieutenant Kennedy.

No. 2 Column.—Cavalry : 100 Sabres, 18th Irregular Cavalry, under Major Ryves. Infantry : 47 Sappers, under Lieutenant Tovey ; 200 rank and file, Her Majesty's 81st, under Captain Brown ; 200 rank and file. Kelat-i Gi'zie Regiment. under Lieutenant Rowcroft ; 450 rank and fi e, 8th Punjaub Infantry, under Lieutenant Brownlow.

No. 3 Column.—Cavalry : 25 sabres, 7th Irregular Cavalry ; 25 sabres, 18th Irregular Cavalry ; 60 sabres, Guide Cavalry. Infantry : 105 Her Majesty's 81st Regiment ; 10 Her Majesty's 98th Regiment : 155 of 21st Regiment, Native Infantry ; 254 Kelat-i-Gilzie Regiment ; 54 of 8th Punjaub Infantry ; 137 of 9th Punjaub Infantry ; 185 of 18th Punjaub Infantry ; 76 Guide Infantry.

No. 1 Column under my command left camp for Chinglee, and at daylight entered the Durrund Pass which is a remarkably narrow defile of about 2 miles, between two hills. It is not formidable to disciplined troops, because the heights on either side have only to be crowned to cover the safe passage of the force ; and the length of the pass is so limited that, if stoutly contested, it could not resist for more than a couple of hours. The enemy did well, therefore, to abandon it, and allow us to ascend unmolested into the elevated valley of Chinglee, or Upper Punjtar.

7. It may be as well to record here, that there is a well of spring water in the pass, at the foot of the last steep.

8. As soon as the column had reached the top of the Durrund Pass, it proceeded at once by the most direct route towards the village of Chinglee, which is the chief place in the Punjtar country. Chinglee contains about 1000 houses, very substantially built, and is an emporium for the wood trade with the plains of Eusuffzai. Here resided Moobarus Khan, uncle of Mookurrub Khan, of Punjtar, who had a substantial littlefort of wood and stone. But no resistance was attempted. During the day it was observed that some of the village people with their property had endeavoured to secrete themselves in ravines in the mountain side overlooking the town of Chinglee, and the 9th Punjaub Infantry, under Captain Thelwall, was ordered by a circuitous route to ascend the mountain with a view to cutting off their retreat into the Chumla territory, whilst a party of the 98th Foot under Captain Cotton, my Aide-de-Camp, proceeded straight up the hill to dislodge them from their position. A few shots only were however exchanged, and the enemy hastily escaped, leaving a few killed by the 9th Punjaub Infantry.

During the day the troops were employed under

the direction of Captain Hyde, Engineers, in destroying the fort, town, and crops, and at night were bivouacked on a ridge near Chinglee.

9. On the 27th April, the force having completed its work at Chinglee returned to Selim Khan, not by the Durrund Pass through which it came, but through the heart of the country by Swawai and Punjtar, for the importance of adding on this expedition to our knowledge of the independent hills was not lost sight of. On the formation of the force, I attached Lieutenant Taylor. of the engineers, a very able officer, to the staff of the field force, for the express purpose of making a survey of the country through which we passed, a copy of whose map I beg to forward with this report.

10. The direct road by which we returned from Chinglee to Selim Khan, proved to be of about equal length with the road viâ the Durrund Pass, but there can be no question that the Durrund line is the easiest for an army. From Selim Khan to Chinglee viâ Durrund, is an open plain, with one difficulty in it, viz., the Pass itself, which can be soon surmounted. From Selim Khan to Chinglee viâ Punjtar is chiefly through a broken country, winding among ups and downs of jungle and ravine, very embarrassing to a column, and at one point passing through a rocky defile called Turrulee (the bed of the stream which flows under Punjtar, which would be infinitely more formidable than the Durrund Pass, if disputed by the enemy.

11. Mookurrub Khan's horsemen and footmen were seen lurking about our line of march this day, but, apparently, only in the hopes of preying on stragglers from the force. On our return to Punjtar we found scarcely a vestige left of the five villages from which it took its name, so thoroughly had its demolition been completed by the troops of the 2nd column, employed under the

direction of Lieutenant Tovey, Assistant Field Engineer.

. 12. We had now destroyed both Punjtar and Chinglee, and might have moved on to Suttana, but there was a stronghold in Mookurrub Khan's country which he had made over to the Syuds, and Hindustanees, and only resorted to it himself in the last extremity. The name of this place is Mungul Thanna. It stands on one of the chief spurs of the Mahabun mountain, and it was the head quarters of that Moulvie Enayut Allee, who so perseveringly endeavoured at Narinjee and other places, to raise Eusuffzai in rebellion during 1857. This Moulvie died about the beginning of April 1858, and his followers were said to have gone off from Mungul Thanna to Suttana, to place themselves under another Hindustanee Moulvie there. But Mookurrub Khan's family and property were reported to have been removed for safety to the vacant fort of Moulvie Enayut Allee at Mungul Thanna. It would therefore render the chastisement of the Khan more complete and memorable, if we could also destroy this last remaining fastness. By all accounts the road from Punjtar to Mungul Thanna was practicable, though difficult. The Totallye people were our allies, and would show us the road. The troops we had, were well suited to such an expedition. I therefore fully concurred with Colonel Edwardes, C.B., in the expediency of attacking Mungul Thanna.

13. On the 28th ultimo, the force was again divided into three columns as per margin,* the 1st

---

* 1st COLUMN.

Artillery—2 guns Mountain Train Battery; 2 24-pounder howitzers of Captain Stallard's Light Field Battery. Infantry—Sappers; 250 men of Her Majesty's 81st Regiment; 8th Punjaub Infantry; 250 men of Her Majesty's 18th Regiment; Kelat-i-Gilzie Regiment; Guide Infantry.

column to act against Mungul Thanna; the 2nd
column to proceed and halt at Punjtar, as a support to the 1st column; and the 3rd column to
remain in reserve at Selim Khan, and to protect
the camp which was left standing.

14. At 11 P.M., on the 28th April, the 1st column, under my own personal command, left the
camp at Selim Khan, and pushed on by moonlight
towards Mungul Thanna. The ascent of the hills
was very arduous and toilsome, and half the
column was ultimately left as an intermediate
support at Dhukara, which is midway between
Punjtar and Mungul Thanna. The advance
reached the heights about 11 A.M., not a shot had
been fired at us, as we laboured up the steep and
wooded road, and on entering Mungul Thanna we
found the fort abandoned, and every sign of a
hasty and recent flight.

15. Mungul Thanna consists of two villages,
Upper and Lower. The Lower contains 30 or 40
houses, and is occupied by Syuds, who are peace-
able and inoffensive. Upper Mungul Thanna
stands on a plateau in the midst of three crests,
which are themselves outworks while held by the
garrison, but, as soon as carried by an enemy, command the place. On this plateau stood first, the
fortified house of Enayut Allee, with enclosures
for Hindustanee followers; secondly, the fortified
residence of Syud Abbas; and thirdly, Syud
Abbas's citadel, a white masonry tower, the whole
having about 30 or 40 houses clustered round

2nd Column.

Infantry.— 260 men, Her Majesty's 98th; 450 men 9th
Punjaub Infantry. Cavalry—250 Guide Cavalry.

3rd Column.

Artillery.—2 9-pounder guns. Cavalry.—125 sabres, 7th
Irregular Cavalry; 125 sabres, 18th Irregular Cavalry.
Infantry.—21st Regiment Native Infantry; Detachments
of all Corps over the Regimental Baggage.

them. These fortifications had been laboriously constructed of large stones and fine timber, and the Hindustanee fanatics and thieves who flocked around Syud Abbas, must have lived here in great enjoyment and security, and it was easy to understand the prestige that surrounded them.

16. The advanced troops bivouacked at Mungul Thanna for the night ; the Sappers being engaged all night under Captain Hyde's instructions in mining the buildings. At daylight of the 30th April, the troops being drawn off, the mines were fired, and when the dust and smoke had cleared away, Mungul Thanna existed no longer.

17. Mungul Thanna is probably between 5000 and 6000 feet above the level of the sea. The trees grow thickly about it, and the scenery about it is much like that of Murree.

18. It would be possible to cross Mahabun from this point and descend upon Suttana in two marches; but all accounts agree that the road is more difficult even than that to Mungul Thanna,

19. On the 30th April, the whole of the troops at Mungul Thanna, Dhukara, and Punjtar, returned to their camp at Selim Khan, and there halted on the 1st May.

20. It now only remained to deal with the fanatic colony of Suttana, for which purpose the force under my command proceeded towards Kubbul, distant from Suttana about four miles. The force emcamped at Kubbul on the morning of 3rd May.

21. By previous arrangements, Major Becher, the Deputy Commissioner of Hazara, moved down simultaneously to the left bank of the Indus with the troops as per margin,* with a view to crossing the river so as to co-operate with the force under

* 2 12-pounder howitzers and 1 3-pounder gun, Hazara Mountain Train ; 300 of 2nd Sikhs ; 450 of 6th Punjaub Infantry; 300 of 12th Punjaub Infantry.

my command, in making a general attack on the enemy's villages at Suttana, and on their Ghurree, or defensive enclosure near the village of Mundee.

22. Having on the evening of 3rd May reconnoitered the hills and towns of the enemy, and fixed on the following morning to make the general attack, Major Becher with his troops crossed the Indus early in the day, whilst the force under my command marched out of its encampment at Kubbul, towards the enemy's position, thus coming upon him from the eastward and southward simultaneously, the chief of the Umb territory, Jehandad Khan our ally, having occupied the hills northward of Upper Suttana, and by so doing completed the general co-operation.

23. As we approached the Lower Suttana, the column of skirmishers detached as per margin* were directed to crown and hold the heights above the several villages of the enemy. These with other troops, hereafter mentioned, moved up the mountain at no less than six different points.

24. During the progress of these troops up the steep and rugged sides of the mountain, I proceeded with Lieutenant-Colonel Edwardes, C. B., towards Upper Suttana, and was there joined by Major Becher, with the 6th Punjaub Infantry under Lieutenant Quin, and 2nd Sikhs, under Captain Harding, which had just crossed the river. These corps with the Guide Infantry, under Lieutenant Kennedy, proceeded to assist in holding the heights above the town. The Sappers and Miners, under Captain Hyde, of the Engineers, were set to work to destroy all the towns. A wing of Her Majesty's 81st Regiment, under Colonel Renny, was, during these operations, placed in the town of Upper Suttana.

I could from this spot observe the several

* 150 men of Her Majesty's 98th; 400 men of 9th Punjaub Infantry; 300 men of 18th Punjaub Infantry.

columns on the hills, and was enabled from thence to direct the operations generally.

25. The 18th Punjaub Infantry, under Lieutenant Williamson having, without opposition, succeeded in reaching the crest of the mountain above Lower Suttana, and having moved northward along the same, and also on a pathway on the side of the mountain in two divisions, came in contact with the enemy (the fanatics) on the height called Shah Noorkee Lurree, where they were strongly posted in a small village, and in a stockade, which position was very desperately defended. Lieutenant Williamson and his gallant corps, the 18th Punjaub Infantry, drove the enemy from this height, having killed 36 on the hill top, and wounded many more. Lieutenant Vandergucht, of that corps, was wounded in a hand-to-hand encounter, in the thigh; a subadar and 4 sepoys being killed, and 15 wounded. The 18th Punjaub Infantry, for the first time in action with the enemy since being embodied, thus highly distinguished itself, under its gallant Commander, Lieutenant Williamson, who reports most favorably on the spirited conduct of the European Officers of his corps, viz., Lieutenant Vandergucht, Lieutenant O'Malley and Lieutenant Green, Her Majesty's 70th Regiment, temporarily attached to the corps. The 19th Punjaub Infantry, under Captain Thelwall, ably supported the attack of the 18th Punjaub Infantry, on the enemy's position. The 6th Punjaub Infantry, under Lieutenant Quin, having ascended the northern spur of the range, took the enemy's position in rear, and thus co-operating with the 18th Punjaub Infantry drove the Hindustanee fanatics towards the latter regiment. The conduct of this regiment, under Lieutenant Quin, was also admirable. The attack was unhesitating and vigorous, and speedily completed the defeat of the enemy. The Detachments,

Her Majesty's 98th Regiment, under Major Peyton, 2nd Seikhs, under Captain Harding, also Captain Brougham's Mountain Train Battery, which had several opportunities of making very successful practice in the various positions of the enemy, were all most useful, and efficiently performed the duties allotted to them respectively, during the operations.

26. The position of the enemy having been carried at all points; the fanatics compelled to retreat precipitately in the hills, with very severe loss; and the whole of their villages being destroyed; the Commissioner, Colonel Edwardes, C.B., considered that adequate punishment had been inflicted on them, and called upon me to withdraw the troops, not deeming it expedient to raise against the British Government, by further pursuit of the enemy into the hills, the Judoon and other independent hill tribes who had naturally become excited by the presence of so large a British force in and amongst their mountains.

27. In the general withdrawal of the troops, the detachments, Her Majesty's 98th, under Major Peyton, and Guide Infantry, under Lieutenant Kennedy, rendered excellent service in covering the retirement, in presence of the hill tribes, who, during the day, had assembled in considerable number, and had assumed a threatening attitude on the surrounding heights; and here the practice of the Enfield rifles of the 98th Regiment was most effective, leaving, I am informed, a lasting impression, on the minds of the hill people, as to the vast superiority of this weapon over their own matchlocks.

28. The hill tribes, with some few of the Hindustanee fanatics, having closely followed up the troops during their descent from the hills, I employed with very great advantage two 5½-inch

mortars, under Captain Stallard, to assist in covering the retirement of the troops. The practice of these mortars was very effective, and thoroughly arrested the further progress of the enemy.

29. The whole of the force, it being late in the day, returned to camp, and on the following morning, 5th May, on the requisition of the Commissioner, marched to Kubbul.

30. These operations, having been so completely successful, enabled the civil authorities to come to a most satisfactory settlement with the Judoon tribes, whose Chiefs ratified a treaty, by which they were bound to expel from their territories any of the remaining Hindustanee fanatics who attempted to re-establish themselves among them, as also to protect the allies of the British Government, viz., the inhabitants of the villages of Kyr and Kubbul, and Jehundad Khan, the Chief of Umb, who had rendered us great and valuable assistance during the above operations.

31. Lieutenant-Colonel Edwardes, C.B., having notified to me that the objects of the campaign having been fully attained, and that the services of the troops were no longer required, I forthwith directed the return of the force to Nowshera, where, on arrival, the troops will be sent to their respective quarters.

32. It now becomes my pleasing duty to record, for the information of his Excellency the Commander-in-Chief, and of the Government, my acknowledgment of the valuable services rendered by the various civil and military officers who have accompanied the force under my command.

I am deeply indebted to Lieutenant-Colonel Edwardes, C.B., Commissioner of Peshawur, for his very able co operations and advice, which have enabled me to bring the operations of this short campaign to such a satisfactory termination. I beg specially to recommend this officer's most important services to the favourable consideration of his Excellency the Commander-in-Chief, and of Government.

I also desire to bring to notice the excellent service performed by Major Becher, Deputy Commissioner of Hazara, who commanded the Hazara field force, during the recent action at Suttana. The disposition made by Major Becher of his troops was indeed admirable, and contributed in no small degree to the success of the general attack made on the enemy's position. My warmest thanks are due to Major Becher, for the very able manner in which he commanded the Hazara force in the operations against Suttana.

To Colonel Renny, Her Majesty's 81st, who commanded the 1st Brigade; and to Major Allen, Her Majesty's 81st, who commanded the 2nd Brigade of Infantry; to Lieutenant-Colonel Mulcaster, 7th Irregular Cavalry, who commanded the cavalry force in camp; and to Captain Brougham, who commanded the artillery, my cordial thanks are particularly due, for the able and energetic support they rendered me in their respective commands.

To the regimental Commanders, Major Peyton, commanding detatchment Her Majesty's 98th; Captain Brown, commanding Her Majesty's 81st; Captain Stallard, commanding Light Field Battery; Captain Pulman, in charge of the mortars; Lieutenant Butt, commanding Hazara Mountain Train Battery; Lieutenant Cordner, commanding detachment Peshawur Mountain Train Battery; Major Ryves, commanding detachment 18th Irregular Cavalry; Major Milne, and subsequently, on that officer's illness, Lieutenant Brown, commanding Head-Quarter Detachment 21st Regiment Native Infantry; Lieutenant Rowcroft, commanding Head-Quarter Detachment Kelat-i-Gilzie Regiment; Lieutenant Quin, Lieutenant Brownlow, Captain Thelwall, Captain Blagrave, and Lieutenant Williamson, commanding respectively 6th, 8th, 9th, 12th, and 18th Punjaub Infantry; Lieutenant Kennedy, commanding corps of Guides; Lieutenant Lockwood, commanding detachment of Peshawur Light Horse; I have to offer my best thanks, for the efficient manner in which they commanded their respective corps: the same are due to the officers and men of the whole force, whose excellent conduct and discipline in the field deserve my most unqualified approbation.

To the Engineer Officers, Captain Hyde, commanding detachment of Sappers and Miners; Lieutenant Tovey, Her Majesty's 24th Regiment, Assistant Engineer, Peshawur, doing duty with the same; Lieutenant Henderson and Lieutenant Taylor, whose valuable survey of the country through which the force proceeded, is herewith forwarded, I feel particularly indebted for the ability and zeal which they have displayed in the performance of their professional duties.

I beg to return my best thanks to the Staff Officers of the Force, Captain Wright, Deputy Assistant Adjutant-General, Chief Staff Officer of the Force; Lieutenant Greaves, Her Majesty's 70th Regiment, who acted as Deputy Assistant Adjutant-General to the Field Force; Captain Cooper, Deputy Assistant Quartermaster-General; Lieutenant Whigham, Adjutant, Peshawur Light Horse, who officiated in the Quartermaster-General's Department; Captain Jones, Deputy Judge Advocate-General; Captain L. S. Cotton, my Aide-de-Camp; Captain Fane, Peshawur Light Horse, my Orderly Officer; Captain Tonnochy, Her Majesty's 81st Regiment, and Captain Ellerman, Her Majesty's 98th Regiment, who officiated as Brigade Major to the 1st and 2nd Infantry Brigades respectively; Lieutenant Tierney, Staff Officer of Artillery; Lieutenant Osborne, 7th Irregular Cavalry, Staff Officer of Cavalry; Lieutenant White, 12th Punjaub Infantry, Staff Officer to the Hazara Field Force, under Major Becher; all of whom performed the Staff duties of the force with much zeal and efficiency.

To Surgeon Mann, 5th Light Cavalry, who accompanied the force as field surgeon, my especial obligations are due for the skilful arrangements made by him for the care and comfort of the sick.

I have also to state that Mr. Sub-Conductor Cooper conducted the duties of the Commissariat Department much to my satisfaction.

33. In conclusion, I beg to submit for the information of his Excellency the Commander-in-Chief, and of Government, a map of the country. in which the operations above detailed have taken place; and also a return showing the number of casualties in the field force in the action of Suttana.

I have, &c.
SYDNEY COTTON, Major-General,
Commanding Peshawur Division.

P.S.—I have the honor to annex for submission to his Excellency the Commander-in-Chief, a copy of an order which I issued to the field force before breaking it up, and which was called for by the excellent conduct of the whole of the troops during the period they were in the field.

No. 34.

Return of Casualties in the Field Force under the Command of Major-General Sir Sydney Cotton, K.C.B., in the action of Suttana, on the right bank of the Indus, on the 4th May, 1858.

Corps.	Killed.				Wounded			
	European Officers.	Native Officers.	Havildars.	Rank and File.	European Officers.	Native Officers.	Havildars.	Rank and File.
21st Regiment N. I.	..	..	..	..	..	..	..	1
6th Punjaub Infantry	..	..	..	1	..	..	..	5
9th ditto	..	..	..	1	..	1	..	6
18th ditto	..	1	..	3	*1	..	..	15
Total	..	1	..	5	1	1	..	27

Abstract.

Killed	....	....	....	6
Wounded....	....	....	....	29
Total	....	....	35

SYDNEY COTTON, Major-General,
Commanding Peshawur Division.

* Lieutenant Vandergucht, sabre cut on the leg.

No. 35.

Major General Sir Sydney Cotton, K.C.B., Commanding Peshawur Division, to Colonel Macpherson, Officiating Quartermaster-General of the Army.

Division Head Quarters,
Camp Nowshera, April 23, 1858.

SIR,

I HAVE the honour to report for the information of his Excellency the Commander-in-Chief that, on the requisition of the Commissioner of Peshawur, Colonel Edwardes, C.B., and under the sanction of Government, an expeditionary force, composed as per annexed statement, has been concentrated on the left bank of the Cabool River, opposite to Nowshera. The force under my personal command will march to-morrow morning towards the Eusuffzai frontier.

It is proposed by the civil authorities to enter the Punjtar valley in view to destroying certain villages which have afforded shelter to a fanatical Moulvie, who caused much annoyance to our frontier villages during the last hot season. Having effected this object, and overcome any opposition which may offer itself in that valley, the force will return to Eusuffzai, and proceed, viâ Topi, to attack and destroy the fort and village of Suttana, a nest of fanatic Hindoostanees, situate on the right bank of the Indus opposite Hazara.

I have, &c.
SYDNEY COTTON, Major-General,
Commanding Peshawur Division.

No. 36.

DETAIL OF THE FIELD FORCE.

Artillery.

2 24-pounder howitzers.
2 9 „ guns.
2 12 „ howitzers.
2 3 „ guns.

Cavalry.

125 sabres, 7th Irregular Cavalry.
125 „ 18th „

Sappers.

100 sappers of 5th and 6th companies.

Infantry.

250 rank and file, with head-quarters and band
   H.M. 81st Regiment
250 ditto H.M.'s 98th Regiment.
400 ditto with band, 21st Regt. N.I.
400 ditto Kelat-i-Gilzie Regiment.
450 ditto 6th Punjaub Infantry.
450 ditto 8th ditto.
450 ditto 9th ditto.
450 ditto 18th ditto.

Guide Corps.

250 Cavalry.
350 Infantry.

T. WRIGHT, Captain,
Deputy Assistant Adjutant-General.

No. 37.

Extract from Division Orders issued by Major-General Sir Sydney Cotton, K.C.B., Commanding Division, Head Quarters, Camp Yar Hossain, May 13, 1858.

No. 272.

THE services of the force under the command of Major-General Sir Sydney Cotton, K.C.B., being no longer required in the district, the troops will return to their quarters under orders which will be communicated to corps respectively.

In bidding adieu to the officers, non-commissioned officers and soldiers, European and Native of this highly disciplined column, the Major-General offers to all his unqualified thanks for the ready and cheerful obedience to his wishes in the discharge of duties frequently under difficult and trying circumstances of fatigue and exposure.

To the orderly and steady conduct of the soldiers, mainly, must be attributed their efficiency for work and healthiness in a very considerable heat of climate : the absence of crime in this force has been most remarkable; and, when an enemy had to be encountered, the troops displayed their wonted gallantry.

The force now returns to its quarters under the assurance of Lieutenant-Colonel Edwardes, C.B., Commissioner, (to whom the Major-General offers his best thanks for his very valuable co-operation at all times,) that the objects of Government in assembling it, have been most fully and satisfactorily accomplished. Taking ample guarantee for the future from the border tribes, the Eusuffzai district has now been placed in an unprecedented state of security, and it is gratifying to think that whilst this all-important object has been gained by the chastisement of the real enemies of the British Government, the well-disposed and inoffensive have, by a wise discrimination on the part of the civil authorities, been permitted to remain in the undisturbed enjoyment of their ancient rights and privileges.

No. 38.
No. 185 of 1858.

THE Right Honorable the Governor-General is pleased to direct the publication of the following despatch, from the Deputy Adjutant General of the army, No. 362 A, dated 29th May, 1858, forwarding one from Lieutenant-Colonel Hale, C.B., of Her Majesty's 82nd Regiment, reporting the circumstances attending the investment of the jail of Shahjehanpore by the rebels on the 3rd ultimo, and his successful and very skilful defence of that post.

No. 39.

The Deputy Adjutant-General of the Army to the Secretary of the Government of India, Military Department, with the Governor General.

Head Quarters, Camp, Futtehgurh
May 29, 1858.

SIR,   No. 362 A.

IN forwarding, for the information of the Right Honorable the Governor-General, a copy of a despatch, dated the 25th instant, from Lieutenant-Colonel E. B. Hale, C.B., of Her Majesty's 82nd Regiment, reporting the circumstances attending the investment of the jail of Shahjehanpore by the enemy on the 3rd idem, and his successful defence of that post, I am directed by the Commander-in-Chief to beg you will inform his Lordship, that the Lieutenant-Colonel hardly does justice to himself in his report of this defence, which was conducted by him with prudence and skill, and consequently with trifling loss.

I am to add that Lieutenant-Colonel Hale, although he makes no mention of the fact, was himself wounded by a musket bullet in the leg, from the effects of which he has not yet recovered.

I have, &c.

H. W. NORMAN, Major,
Deputy Adjutant-General of the Army.

No. 40.

Lieutenant Colonel E. B. Hale, C.B., Her Majesty 82nd Regiment, Commanding Shahjehanpore, to the Deputy Adjutant General of the Army.

Camp Shahjehanpore,
SIR, May 25, 1858.

I HAVE the honor to report, for the information of his Excellency the Commander-in-Chief, that agreeably to instructions received from the chief of the staff, I marched on the morning of the 2nd with the force detailed in general order of the 1st instant, from the camp Azeezgunge, for the purpose of occupying the jail in cantonments at this place as a military post. I pitched my camp in a tope of trees adjoining the jail, as there was no shade inside the walls, and immediately proceeded to put the jail in a state of defence by placing the guns (two 24-pounders and two 9-pounders) in position and digging a ditch along the south wall which was much broken, and at the same time storing my ammunition and commissariat stores inside the entrenchment. On the morning of the 3rd, I was informed by Mr. Money, of the civil service, that a spy had come in to say, the enemy were within four miles of this on the Mohumdee road. I immediately directed the

camp to be struck and every thing taken inside
the intrenchment, at the same time ordering out
four companies of the 82nd Regiment, with a view
to protect the camp, while it was being moved.
After proceeding about 200 yards, I ordered the
men to halt while I went on to reconnoitre, when
I perceived the enemy's cavalry appearing on the
brow of the hill across the Kunhout river. After
a time they moved to my left, and, crossing the
river, came down in great force, when, being informed that the whole of my camp or nearly so
was inside the intrenchment, I retired the 82nd
inside also. Lieutenant De Kantzow, who was
posted with his cavalry on my right flank,
gallantly charged the enemy, but, seeing him
greatly out-numbered, and my orders being to act
strictly on the defensive, I ordered him in also.
The enemy quickly brought guns to bear upon
the jail, but fortunately did very little damage;
they kept up a constant fire upon us night and
day with their guns and matchlock men, while
their cavalry patrolled all round, until the arrival
of Brigadier-General Jones with his force on the
11th, when they were quickly dispersed.

I have, &c.

E. B. HALE, Lieutenant-Colonel,
82nd Regiment,
Commanding Shahjehanpore.

No. 41.

Allahabad, June 7, 1858.

No. 195 of 1858.—The Right Honorable the
Governor-General is pleased to direct the publica-
tion of the following Despatch from the Deputy
Adjutant-General of the Army, No. 359 A, dated
29th May, 1858, forwarding one from Brigadier-
General Sir E. Lugard, K. C. B., Commanding

Azimghur Field Force, detailing further operations of the troops under his command.

The Governor-General offers his best acknowledgments to Sir Edward Lugard, for the ability and energy displayed in his operations, and his Lordship cordially concurs in the praise bestowed by his Excellency the Commander-in-Chief, on the troops employed.

No. 42.

The Deputy Adjutant-General of the Army, to the Secretary to the Government of India, Military Department, with the Governor-General.

Head Quarters' Camp, Futteghur,
May 29th, 1858.

SIR,   No. 359 A.

I HAVE the honor, by direction of the Commander-in- Chief, to forward, for the information of the Right Honorable the Governor-General, copy of a Despatch, dated the 14th instant, from Brigadier-General Sir E. Lugard, K. C. B., Commanding Azimghur Field Force, detailing further operations of the troops under his orders.

2. His Excellency desires to record his thanks to the Brigadier-General for the skill he has displayed in the conduct of this, as well as of preceding operations, and to express his admiration of the manner in which the troops have undergone the great exposure and fatigue to which they have been subjected.

I have, &c.,
H. W. NORMAN, Major,
Deputy Adjutant-General of the Army.

No. 43.

Brigadier-General Sir E. Lugard, K.C.B., Commanding Azimghur Field Force, to the Chief of the Staff.

Camp, Jugdespore, May 14th, 1858.

SIR,

IN continuation of my Despatch, dated 10th instant, I have the honor to report, for his Excellency's information, that, in consequence of intelligence reaching me that evening of the probable arrival, at Peeroo, of Colonel Corfield with troops from Sasseram, to co-operate with me, I directed Lieutenant-Colonel Longden, Chief of the Staff, to proceed the following morning across the open country, west of the jungle, with horse artillery and cavalry, under Lieutenant-Colonel Robertson, Military Train, to reconnoitre the country in that direction, and endeavour to communicate with Colonel Corfield, to whom I had written on the 4th instant. after crossing the Ganges, but of whose movements, up to this time, I had only heard indirectly and vaguely.

During the morning of the 11th, the special Commissioner with my camp, Mr. Macdonald, Civil Service, received what he conceived trustworthy intelligence, that the rebels who had been strongly entrenching themselves near Duleepore, and at the Bungalow at Chitoura, were preparing to decamp; and as I deemed it highly important that a blow should be struck before they separated, I immediately advanced through the jungle with the force as per margin,* carrying nothing but spare ammunition and soldier's rations; elephants

* Artillery.—4 9-pounder guns; Cotter's Battery; 2 5½-inch Mortars, Royal Artillery.
Cavalry.—Military Train, 80; 3rd Sikh Cavalry, 75; total. 155.
Infantry.—10th Foot, 570; 1st Company Madras Rifles, 85; total 655.

laden with puckalls of water accompanied the party; and to this arrangement I mainly ascribe the success of the operation, and the safety of the troops; for the heat was beyond all description, scarcely a breath of wind penetrated the dense jungle, and many old and tried soldiers sank exhausted.

At the same time, I communicated, by express, my intentions to Lieutenant-Colonel Longden, who, receiving my letter at Peeroo, to which place he had pushed on, leaving Lieutenant-Colonel Robertson and his party to guard the west, at once applied to Colonel Corfield for 2 9-pounder guns under Lieutenant Franklin, Royal Artillery, and 100 of Rattray's Sikh Sowars, and proceeded to watch the south-western portion of the jungle; whilst Colonel Corfield got the remainder of his force under arms, consisting of about 750 European Infantry, 110 Naval Brigade, with 2 9-pounder guns, 1 5½-inch mortar, and 60 Sikh Battalion, as per copy of report annexed.

At Duleepore, the rebels first attempted to oppose our progress, and, after being routed by the line of skirmishers, which extended well into the jungle, and a few discharges of grape, they spread round, right and left, through the thickest part of the jungle, where our soldiers could scarcely penetrate, and attacked the rear flanks of the column, but the steadiness and quick fire of the companies of the 10th Foot in support, speedily drove them back, and we pushed on to the Bungalow, where another and more determined stand was made, with, however, the same result, except that the loss of the enemy was more severe. About this time firing was heard to the south, which we subsequently ascertained was caused by an attack made by the troops under Colonel Corfield, upon a party of the rebels who had established themselves in the villages at the southern limit of the jungle. Colonel Corfield, after driving the enemy from the villages and setting them on fire, returned to his camp at Peeroo, and it was not until the following day that I learnt of his co-operation, when I moved my party to the vicinity of his camp, as the heat in the jungle was unbearable.

The rebels suffered severely, as shown by several masses of their dead lying about, the extensive cordon of pickets, with which I surrounded our position during the night, preventing their being removed.

My casualties amounted to one officer, 10th Foot (Lieutenant St. John), shot through the left arm; one soldier of the same regiment killed, and five wounded; also three men of the Madras Artillery wounded. After driving the enemy from their position at Duleepore, I sent the Seikh Cavalry, under Lieutenant Jennings, through the jungle, by a path to the east, to cut off any fugitives that might attempt to escape in that direction; this party re-joined me at the Bungalow late in the evening.

A strong body of the rebels, said to be under Ummur Sing, broke from the jungle after our forcing their position at Duleepore, and attacked the cavalry and horse artillery, under Lieutenant-Colonel Robertson, but were driven back with severe loss; another body of about 300 showed themselves at the edge of the jungle to the south-west, but retired on Lieutenant-Colonel Longden moving up his guns.

On the 13th, I halted at Peeroo, having previously sent back to Jugdespore, for provisions, but, learning on that evening that the rebels had again shown themselves in force at Jugdespore, attacked our position, and threatened our camp, I marched back on the morning of the 14th, since when I learned that the main bodies of the rebels lie concealed in the thickest parts of the extensive jungle, whence, in consequence of the extreme heat of the weather, and the exhaustion experienced by the troops as soon as they enter the thick jungle, I fear it will be most difficult for me to expel them with the means at my disposal.

I am of opinion that the only measure to be adopted for clearing this district of the rebels, or indeed for getting at them in the jungle, is to cut broad roads through it in several directions. I have already communicated with the civil authorities on the subject.

I beg you will assure his Excellency, that the exertions made by the force under my command, to ensure the success of our operations, have been of no ordinary kind; without tents, or anything but the clothes on their backs, they (one and all) have been exposed to the inclemency of the weather, in the several attempts to accomplish the object in view, viz., the destruction of the rebel force. No troops but the two seasoned regiments now with me could, I feel confident, have gone through all the fatigue and exposure to which they have been subjected; indeed the Casualty Return of Colonel Corfield's Force, which simply operated for a few hours before sunset, will prove my assertion, seven (7) men having died of coup-de-soleil in that time; and further, that out of a party of 110 men of the 6th Foot, which left their camp with Lieutenant-Colonel Longden on the 13th instant, to meet the convoy already mentioned, as ordered from Jugdespore, full sixty (60) men fell out, most of whom had to be carried into their camp.

Lieutenant-Colonel Fenwick, commanding 10th Foot, fell, I regret to say, from the effects of a sun-stoke, near Duleepore,* and the immediate

* When Captain Orme assumed command of the Regiment.

presence of the Doctor alone prevented a fatal result. This officer will not be able to resume his duties again without a change to Europe.

I have, &c.

EDWARD LUGARD, Brigadier-General, Commanding Azimgurh Field Force.

No. 44.

Colonel T. B. Corfield, Commanding S. P. Shahabad, to the Chief of the Staff, with Brigadier-General Sir E. Lugard.

SIR,   Camp Peeroo, *May* 12, 1858.

I HAVE the honor to report, for the information of Brigadier-General Sir Edward Lugard, K.C.B., that yesterday, after I had detached my cavalry, and two 9-pounder guns of the Royal Artillery with you, on hearing firing in the direction of Juttowra, I immediately proceeded with the force noted in the margin,* towards the jungle. After advancing about two miles, and just at the entrance of the jungle, the enemy opened fire upon me, on which I advanced three companies of infantry in skirmishing order, and opened fire with my guns.

After considerable opposition, I brought up my right shoulder, driving the rebels towards my left, in the direction you had proceeded in with the cavalry and artillery: all firing on my right then ceased, as I had arranged with you that I should not advance into the jungle, unless I heard long continued firing in the Juttowra direction. I then halted to watch the outlets of the jungle on this side; about half an hour afterwards, the rebels again appeared in force, moving from our

* Her Majesty's 6th Regiment, with drafts, 750 strong.

Indian Naval Brigade, two pounders, one 5½ 9-inch mortar, 110 men.

Sikh Battalion, 60 men.

left front towards the position they first occupied. On this I advanced, and reinforcing the skirmishers, closed round the village and stormed it. The rebels then retreated into other villages close at hand. I pursued them steadily, burning each village as I took it.

At sunset I recalled my skirmishers, and was returning to camp, when the Brigadier-General's message to advance on Juttowra reached me. As night was coming on, and my men had had no food all day, I was unable to comply with his orders.

I have the honor to inclose a return of my casualties; it is impossible to estimate correctly the loss of the rebels, but I have every reason to believe it must have been heavy, more particularly on my left.

I beg to state, that I have every reason to be satisfied with the conduct of the officers and men engaged, both with the Infantry under Major Stratton, Her Majesty's 6th Regiment, and the Indian Naval Brigade, under Lieutenant Carew, who worked their guns admirably. The small detachment of Seikhs under Lieutenant Earle behaved with their usual gallantry.

The Deputy Magistrate of Sasseram, Mr. E. Baker, accompanied me, and was of the greatest assistance; and Lieutenant Staunton, Engineers, who, in the absence of my Staff Officer, kindly consented to officiate as my Orderly Officer, was of the greatest use to me.

I have, &c.

T. B. CORFIELD, Colonel,

Commanding S. P. Shahabad.

No. 45.

RETURN OF CASUALTIES.

Killed by Coup-de-soleil.

1 Corporal, 5 Privates, Her Majesty's 6th Regiment.
1 Private, 24th Regiment.

Wounded.

1 Serjeant, 13th Light Infantry.
2 Privates, 6th Regiment.
1 Private, Seikh Battalion.

T. B. CORFIELD, Colonel,
Commanding S. P. Shahabad.

No. 46.

Numerical Return of Casualties in the Azimghur Field Force, under the Command of Brigadier-General Sir Edward Lagard, K.C.B., in the Skirmishes detailed in the accompanying Report.

Camp Jugdespore, May 14, 1858.

E. Troop Royal Horse Artillery—1 serjeant, 1 rank and file, 1 troop horse, wounded.
A. Company 3rd Battalion Madras Artilley—1 troop horse, killed; 1 havildar, 2 rank and file, wounded.
H.M.'s 10th Regiment—1 rank and file, killed; 1 subaltern, 5 rank and file, wounded.
H.M.'s 84th Regiment—1 rank and file, wounded.
4th Madras Light Cavalry—5 troop horses, killed.
    Total—1 rank and file, 6 troop horses, killed; 1 subaltern, 1 serjeant, 1 havildar, 9 rank and file, 1 troop horse, wounded.
    Total Casualties—13 men, 7 horses.

E. LUGARD, Brigadier-General,
Commanding Azimghur Field Force.

No. 47.

From the Nominal Return of Casualties in the Azimghur Field Force, under Command of Brigadier- General Sir Edward Lugard, K.C.B., in the Skirmishes detailed in the accompanying Report.

Camp Jugdespore, May 14, 1858.

Serjeant Robert Campbell, E. Troop Royal Horse Artillery, May 11, wounded slightly.

Serjeant Peter Murray, A. Company, 3rd Battalion Madras Artillery, May 11, wounded severely.

Lieutenant St. A: B. St. John, H.M.'s 10th Regiment, May 11, severe gunshot wound, with fracture of left arm

No. 48.

The Brigadier General Commanding the Northern Division of the Bombay Army, to the Adjutant General of the Army.

SIR,   *Camp near Baroda, 5 June, 1858.*

I BEG you will lay before his Excellency the Commander-in-Chief, the accompanying report by Major Grimes, of his operations against the Kolies of a village named Dubbora, belonging to the Guickwar.

2. These men, when called on to surrender their arms, quitted their village, and, having taken up strong positions in the Hills, sent a threatening letter to the Political Agent, Major Whitelock.

3. A Guickwar's horseman proceeding on service with a note, was shot by these Kolies, and it became absolutely necessary to attack them.

4. Major Grimes' report will show how strong was the country, and how gallantly all obstacles were overcome by the officers and men.

5. Dubbora is a notoriously turbulent village, and the severe punishment inflicted on its inhabitants, when sheltered in their mountain fastnesses, will have an immense effect throughout the country.

6. I beg to be allowed to bring to the favorable notice of his Excellency the valuable service performed on this occasion by Major Grimes and the officers and men under his command.

I have, &c.

R. SHAKESPEAR.

No. 49.

Major Grimes, Commanding Mahee Kanta Field Force, to the Assistant Adjutant-General, Northern Division of the Bombay Army.

SIR,   *Camp Dubbora*, 1st *June*, 1858.

I HAVE the honor to report, for the information of the Brigadier-General Commanding the Division, that, about mid-day on the 28th ultimo, at Edur (where I had proceeded at the request of Major Whitelock to confer with him on our future operations, having left the two columns under my command at Walassna Kheraloo), I was informed by that officer, that the inhabitants of Dubbora were in rebellion, and it was necessary for me to proceed against them. I immediately sent orders to both columns to march on this place that night, so as to arrive here at daylight, in hopes by this sudden move to have been in time to prevent them taking to the jungle and hills. I joined the Head-Quarter column that evening, and reached this place at daylight, on the morning of the 29th, having been joined by the Kheraloo column on the march, and found the town completely deserted; but Lieutenant Le Geyt reported that the Kolies were posted in the jungles at the foot of the Taringa hills, about two miles to the right of my position, and had fired on his party, whom I had detached to reconnoitre. A similar party of the Guzerat Horse had gone round to the left, under Captain Anderson, 11th Regiment, who kindly volunteered his services, and which were placed at my disposal by Major Whitelock. The day being by this time advanced, and the men fatigued by a long march, I did not deem it expedient with the little information I had as to their whereabouts, to attempt to enter the jungle and hills at that time, and therefore encamped for the day, during which I got all the information I could regarding the hills, and the probable place the Kolies would locate themselves in ; it was supposed that they would go into these strongholds of Taringa, a fortified position on the top of the hills, and about 4 miles from my camp, and having during the evening examined the nature of the hills and jungle, in company with Major Whitelock, as far as practicable, and during which we came on the body of one of his sowars whom he had despatched in the morning with a note to the Tymba Chief, and who had been cruelly murdered by the Kolies. I determined to attack them the following morning. I accordingly started at half-past four, A.M., on the 30th, with my whole force, excepting double guards left for the protection of the camp, and advanced through the jungles towards the hills, with four companies, 2nd Grenadiers, under Lieutenants Law and Macdonnell in skirmishing order. Finding on this side, that the jungles were clear of the rebels, though we came to a large encampment lately vacated by them, the four companies, under Lieutenant Law, advanced over the hill. I ordered Captain Conybeare's Battery and one Company 2nd Grenadiers to return to camp, and proceeded myself with the Mountain Train, the company of Her Majesty's 89th Regiment, and 3 companies, 2nd

Grenadiers, round the left of the hills, and advanced up the direct road to the Dubbora gate of the Taringa strongholds, and here detached Lieutenant Bell to skirmish to the left, with two companies. The road soon became so steep that I had to leave our horses and the mountain train under the protection of a portion of Her Majesty's 89th Regiment, and a company 2nd Grenadiers. I pushed up the hill, hearing Lieutenants Law and Macdonnell's parties engaged on my right front. On reaching the top of the first range, I met Lieutenant Law, and found the Kolies had been surprised, and were strongly posted in a deep ravine underneath, and to the left of the Dubbora gate of Taringa, which was now plainly visible, and within range of our rifles; and, the road up to it being in many parts completely commanded by us, the retreat of the main body of them into it was cut off, though the gateway was still held by some of them. Lieutenant Bell's party came upon them from the west, and the only retreat for them was round a large and almost inaccessible hill, and here it was that the greatest loss was inflicted on them. The three parties under Lieutenants Law, Macdonell, and Bell followed them up closely, over immensely difficult ground, and under a very heavy fire, and through a dense jungle, in a manner that excited the admiration of myself and Major Whitelock, who accompanied me through the whole of the operations, and to whom I am much indebted for the assistance and information, which, from his local knowledge of the place, and his position, he was enabled to afford me. At this time, finding the day fast advancing, and that some hours would be required to get up the mountain mortars to shell Taringa, and as there did not appear to be any great number of the enemy in it, I advanced on the gateway with a section of the Company, Her Majesty's 89th Regiment, and a few Grenadiers I had with me. The Enfield Rifles having cleared the gateway, as the first shot from them brought down a man standing sentry on the top of it, at a distance of about 800 yards, which must have astonished them, and made them shy of letting us too near them, we reached the gate in about 20 minutes, and took possession of it; but, finding the interior of the Fort was still occupied by a party of Kolies, we held that, until we were joined by a Company of the Grenadiers which I had sent for; and on their arrival Major Whitelock and myself advanced through the stronghold, driving the Kolies before us, until we arrived at the famous temples of Taringa, the Head Quarters of the Force. The day was now far advanced, and the heat very great, and the men done up, and to pursue was impossible. I had previously desired Lieutenants Law and Macdonnell to return, and therefore sounded the assembly, and returned to camp, having, I hope, taught the Kolies a lesson, and proved to them that they are not safe from us even in their wildest fastnesses, and we effected this with only two rank and file 2nd Grenadiers severely wounded, and one Guzerat and Irregular Horseman slightly, whereas the loss inflicted on the enemy could not, I think, from the reports of the officers in command, have been less than 80 killed and wounded, and of them, 25 or 30 were certainly killed, ten were taken prisoners, two of them wounded, and are now in my camp, but will be sent to Major Whitelock, in a day or two. I beg to annex the reports of the officers in separate commands, for, after we were once in the hills, communication of orders was impossible, and each officer was left to himself in a great measure; and I have great gratification in reporting my entire approval of the manner in which they carried out my plans. Nothing could have exceeded the zeal and courage of all ranks, and their steadiness under.

fire, and noble exertions over almost inaccessible country, deserve my warmest thanks.

I beg you will do me the favour to bring prominently to the notice of the Brigadier-General the names of Lieutenants Law, Macdonnell, and Bell, of the 2nd Grenadiers, to whose exertions I am in a great measure indebted for the success that has attended us. My staff officer, Lieutenant Browning, Her Majesty's 89th Regiment, was a great assistance to me ; and my thanks are also due to Assistant-Surgeon McAlister, for the prompt assistance he rendered, and the arrangements he made in his department in every way.

The Casualty Roll is herewith enclosed.

By desire of Major Whitelock, I have destroyed the town of Dubbora, and propose marching on Oondinee to-morrow morning, unless I get further information where the Kolies have gone to. They have I believe left the Taringa hills entirely, and gone to the North East, but it is very difficult to get any information regarding them.

I have, &c.

G. R. GRIMES, Major,
Commanding Mahee Kanta
Field Force.

No. 50.

Lieutenant J. C. Law, Commanding Head Quarters 2nd Grenadier Regiment N.I. to the Brigade-Major of the Mahee Kanta Field Force.

Sir,   *Camp Dubbora*, 31st *May*, 1858.

I HAVE the honor to submit the following report for the information of the officer commanding the field force.

2. On the arrival yesterday morning of the force at the edge of the jungle round the Taringa hills, I received the instructions of the commanding officer to extend two companies in skirmishing

order, to upport them with two companies, and, leaving the remainder of the regiment under Lieutenants Bell and Blair as a guard to the guns, to take the jungle and hills which lay before us. I requested Lieutenant Macdonell, the Adjutant, ot 'lead the right skirmishers, taking the left myself, there being no other European officers present. We advanced through dense jungle, and. after crossing the first and lowest of the ranges of hills, called the Talinge, we were fired on by the enemy. We still advanced, driving them before us, and firing with good effect, whenever a man showed himself. I learnt from the smart firing on my right that Lieutenant Macdonell was also engaged and advancing. On our progress we passed two or three deserted camps of the Bheels, the cattle wandering about; clothes, food, cooking pots, hookahs, &c. &c., strewed on the ground; showing how they had been taken by surprise. My left was here prolonged by a company of skirmishers under Lieutenant Bell.

3. The jungle was so dense and the ground so oroken that it was often times impossible to see more than 10 or 12 of the men at a time and some men of the supports being too eager to get forward became mixed up with the skirmishers in front. On the second range of hills the fire became hotter and here I lost private Lyenac Luknac, No. 5 company, shot through the chest. Still advancing, we took a very steep hill, on which the retiring enemy kept up a smart fire, by which an excellent non-commissioned officer Naik, Kurrum Sing was shot through the body. Advancing from this position, we climbed the highest and steepest hill in the range; the ascent of which was extremely difficult, and could not have been accomplished but for the mutual aid which officers and men gave each other. On the summit I found Lieutenant Macdonell and his skirmishers, and we ob-

served together the enemy in flight far away and down the hill.

4. Our men being now thoroughly tired, and blown by the steep ascent, and there remaining no chance of coming up with the Bheels, we retraced our steps.

5. The whole position chosen by those Bheels was immensely strong, and if held by men capable of offering an organized resistance, such a weak force as ours could not have advanced 500 yards, our whole line of skirmishers not numbering 150 men.

6. Once in the dense jungle, each officer was obliged to act somewhat independently, as sometimes a thick jungle, and at others a precipitous hill, separated his men from those on his right or left, and I therefore beg to forward for the commanding officer's information the reports of Lieutenants Macdonell and Bell; the former places the loss of the enemy at 20, Mr. Bell reports 12, and in my immediate front perhaps 8 or 10 fell, making their total loss at about 60 killed and wounded by the line of skirmishers, but accuracy on this point and on such ground is impossible; three prisoners, of whom one was wounded, were brought in by Lieutenant Bell. On our side, a naik and a private are, I fear, mortally wounded ; these were of my party, but I am happy to have to report no casualties amongst the skirmishers on my right and left, on whom a sharp fire was kept up, and the ground they advanced on was well contested from every favorable spot, and these were not few.

7. I trust that I may not be considered presuming (commanding the regiment as I did under fortuitous circumstances only) in wishing to bring to notice the admirable manner in which Lieutenant Macdonell led his men ; so quickly and steadily as to press close on the heels of the retreating Bheels, four of whom during this advance fell to

his own rifle, and a fifth subsequently. Mr. Bell, too, was ever to the front, leading and encouraging his men. To the capital leading of these officers may be attributed the really excellent conduct of the men ; these were cool and eager, and managed to climb over places and push through jungle which, under other circumstances and to men less willing, might be called inaccessible.

8. Lieutenants Macdonell and Bell particularize Jemadars Nagoo Chowhan and Paharsing. I also noticed the good behaviour of these two native officers, and would add, for the notice of the commanding officer, the names of Soobedar Sirdar Bahadoor Gunga Sing, Jemadar Nowmactur, and Havildar Peearee Lall, as setting examples of coolness and zeal.

I have. &c.
J. C. LAW, Lieutenant,
Commanding Head Quarters,
2nd Grenadier Regiment N.I.

No. 51.

Captain Anderson, 11th Regiment Native Infantry, to the Major of Brigade, Mahee Kan:a Field Force.

SIR, *Camp at Dubbora, May 30, 1858.*

I HAVE the honor to report, for the information of Major Grimes, commanding field force, that agreeably to his orders, I marched shortly after daylight with the squadron of the Guzerat Irregular Horse under my command, and took up a position clear of the jungle, to the west of the Taringa Hills, with a small hill in my rear, from which I obtained a view of the country round.

Shortly after the firing commenced, I saw a horseman, accompanied by a man on foot, making for the hill when the firing was going on. I sent a jemadar and ten sowars to intercept them and bring them to me. On seeing the party approaching they tried to make their escape, and succeeded in getting into some thick jungle, &c. Some of the sowars coming up, attacked them; the man on foot was killed, and the other wounded and made a prisoner, but not before they had wounded one sowar and one horse. I saw no people from the hills trying to make their escape, and returned to camp with the prisoner at 1 P.M.

I have, &c.

W. F. ANDERSON, Captain,
11th Regiment Native Infantry.

No. 52.

Lieutenant Stanley Bell, 2nd Grenadiers, to the Adjutant, 2nd Grenadiers.

SIR,   *Camp Dubbora, May 30, 1858.*

I HAVE the honor to report that, according to the orders I received from Major Grimes, I threw out No. 7 Company in skirmishing order, supported by No. 8 Company, and advanced towards the base of the hills on the left of our position. On arriving at these hills, having met with no opposition, I heard heavy firing on my right, and at once ordered the men under my command to skirmish over the hills so as to join the centre skirmishers. The ascent was most arduous, and in several places almost impassable, the men being dragged up one after another. On reaching the top of the hill the enemy were discovered in a ravine below me, and, hastily forming up a few men, I advanced to drive them from this position, which was done after a short but determined resistance. The enemy kept up a heavy fire of matchlocks, and, from the loudness of the reports, I fancy that they must have had one or two gingalls. Every rock and tree was most obstinately defended, but in every case the enemy were utterly routed. I took three prisoners armed with swords, one of which I could have shot with my revolver, but preferred taking him alive, in hopes of gaining some valuable information from him. At this period I joined the left of the centre skirmishers under Lieutenant S. C. Law, 2nd Grenadiers, and advancing together, we drove the enemy before us.

The loss of the men opposed to me must at least have been from ten to twelve killed, and from twenty to twenty-five wounded, which result was accomplished with no loss on my side. Two men were severely contused from falling down rocks.

I cannot conclude without bringing to the Commanding Officer's notice the very gallant way in which the men under my command behaved; and I would particularly mention Subadar Pahar Sing, who joined me with the left of the centre skirmishers.

I have, &c.
STANLEY BELL, Lieutenant,
2nd Grenadiers.

No. 53.

Lieutenant Le Geyt, Commanding Detachment of the Guzerat Irregular Horse, to the Major of Brigade Field Force.

SIR, *Dubbora, June 1, 1858.*

I HAVE the honor to report, for the information of the officer commanding the field force, that, in accordance with orders received on the 29th ultimo, I marched from camp with a squadron of the Guzerat Irregular Horse on the 30th at daylight, and took up a position to the south of the Taringa Hills, on the skirts of the thick jungle which surrounds them. I placed my videttes and sent out patrols in the directions I thought it probable the Kolies might attempt to escape; but none were seen by us the whole morning, the firing and entire operations of the force being on the other side of the hills. I returned into camp with my men at half-past 1 P.M.

I have, &c.

P. H. LE GEYT, Lieutenant, Commanding Detachment Guzerat Irregular Horse.

No. 54.

Lieutenant and Adjutant D. J. Macdonell, 2nd Grenadier Regiment Native Infantry, to Lieutenant S. C. Law, Commanding, Head-Quarters, 2nd Grenadier Regiment, Native Infantry.

SIR,   *Dubbora, May 30,* 1858.

I HAVE the honor to report that, agreeably to your instructions, I took command of the right skirmishers (Right Flank Company), supported by No. 1 Company, in the attack made this morning on the insurgent Kolies, for the purpose of driving them from their positions in the Taringa Hills.

2. Shortly after crossing the first range of hills nearest the village of Dubbora, I came in sight of several parties of Kolies strongly posted on the further bank ot a ravine; these at once opened on us a heavy and well-directed fire, which was returned with effect by the Right Grenadier Company.

3. As my skirmishers advanced steadily, the enemy gave way, still keeping up a heavy fire of matchlocks, and obstinately defending every ridge and favorable position.

4. Our advance was continued as long as the men were able to fight their way (about four miles) over most difficult, indeed almost impracticable ranges of hills, and the attack, or rather pursuit, was only discontined when from fatigue and the nature of the ground we were unable to proceed further.

5. In ground such as we passed over, it was

most difficult correctly to estimate the loss of the enemy opposed to me; but from what I saw myself, I am of opinion that it could not have amounted to less than about twenty killed, and a considerable number wounded. I saw at least nine men killed, and from the nature of the ground it was impossible for me to see at many times more than perhaps one-third of my men.

6. I cannot close this report without bringing to the notice of the Commanding Officer the good conduct of all ranks under my command on this occasion; being mostly young soldiers, their steadiness under the very heavy fire kept up by the enemy was admirable, and it is to this, as well as to the steady manner in which they took advantage of every favourable cover in advancing upon and driving the enemy from their numerous strong positions, that I attribute the impunity with which we inflicted so severe a loss.

7. I would beg to bring prominently to the notice of the Commanding Officer the conduct of Jemadar Adjutant Nagoo Chowan, who accompanied me on this ocaasion, and to whose valuable assistance much of our success is due.

I have, &c.
D. J. MACDONELL, Lieutenant and Adjutant,
2nd Grenadier Regiment Native Infantry.

No. 56.

Lieutenant-Colonel Malcolm, Commanding Field Force, to the Assistant-Adjutant-General Southern Division of the Bombay Army.

Nurgoond, June 7, 1858.

SIR,

I HAVE the honor to report, for the information of the Major-General commanding the division, that the troops under my command, as per margin,* defeated the enemy in the plain between Oomergel and Nurgoond, stormed and occupied the Petta of Nurgoond, on the 1st of June, and captured and occupied the fort of Nurgoond next morning, the 2nd June, at nine o'clock A.M.

2. The first news of the outbreak at Dumel reached Kulludghee on the 27th May. 150 Southern Mahratta Horse immediately marched ; of these 30 were left at Budarmee, 70 sent to Gujjundurguer, and 40 were brought to Gudduck. Subsequently, on the 30th May, the latter were ordered to Roan. The Dharwar posts of horse, amounting to 97 sabres, were also concentrated at Gudduck, where I arrived early on the 29th, and immediately urged by telegraph the despatch of troops to Nurgoond

3. The first detachment, consisting of troops as per margin,† under the command of Captain Paget, R.A., reached Nurgoond on the morning of the 31st. I had been directed to join them with the horse, and to take command. 12 sabres of the Southern Mahratta Horse and a considerable police force were left in Gudduck.

The horse at Roan were ordered to Nurgoond —a portion by way of Yangal, and on the morning of the 31st, besides the artillery and infantry, we had 150 horse at Nurgoond.

4. The state and feeling of the country, and the almost certainty that the Nurgoond chief intended to play the Pindaree game, and plunder, as also that his troops, reported by every one at 3,000

* One 9-pounder gun and one howitzer, Royal Artillery, under Captain Paget ; two companies Her Majesty's 74th. 170 rank and file, including serjeants, under Captain Davies ; one company 28th Native Infantry, 108 rank and file, including havildars, under Lieutenant Heish ; 150 Southern Mahratta Horse, under Ressuldar Sew Pursand Sing.

† One 9-pounder, one howitzer, two companies Her Majesty's 74th, one company 28th Native Infantry.

foot and 500 horse, were likely to increase daily, —all demanded active operations. I therefore marched to Oomergul, seven miles, on the morning of the 1st June, arrived there at 6 A.M., and pitched my camp.

5. About 7 A.M., Captain Paget, Lieutenant Thomas, Superintendent of Police, myself, and some others, proceeded with 100 horse to reconnoitre the fort, distant about four miles and a half. We got up to within 500 yards of the Petta walls. The enemy drew up outside the walls, about 600 strong, mostly foot. I retired the horse by alternate troops, and went back to camp, arriving about 9 A.M.

6. At half-past 10 A.M. the horse videttes, posted above a mile from camp, reported the approach of the enemy.

7. The ground between our camp and Nurgoond was a gentle rise for about two miles, then a gentle descent of nearly a mile to a broad dry watercourse, fringed with trees, and from thence it gradually ascended for about another mile to Nurgoond

8. Ordering the force to get under arms, I went to the front, and found the enemy, mostly foot, gathering in force on the crest of the first slope.

9. The outlying picket, strengthened to about 60 sabres, was advanced sufficiently near to prevent escape; the remainder of the horse moved out, as it was got ready, in support, and the guns and infantry were ordered to move along the road to Nurgoond.

10. My object was to get the enemy to stand till the whole force got up, but in about five minutes he showed symptoms of moving off, and his main body disappeared behind the crest. The rear troops had scarcely closed up, but I directed the 60 leading sabres to advance at a trot, which

they did with great order and alacrity, under Rus-
saldars Sirdan Khan and Shumshoodeen. On our
gaining the crest, the enemy was in rapid retreat,
but he still kept his main body of two or three
hundred men well together. My leading troop,
weak as it was, dashed at them, while the other
troops, about 75 sabres in all, followed at a gallop, led on by Russaldar Sew Pursand Sing and
Woordee Major Koondojee Jadow.

11. The enemy, completely routed, spread over
the plain, and the sowars followed up and sabred
them to within 500 yards of the Petta. Those
whom we pursued down towards the watercourse
may have been about 800, but there were more
joining from the rear, and I would compute them
at not less than one thousand, while our cavalry
force was not more than 150 sabres. Their loss
was not less than 60 killed, besides wounded ; but
knots of footmen, armed with sword and matchlock, and fighting to the last, prevented our getting up to the main body, which made good a very
hurried retreat into the Petta. Only three prisoners were taken.

12. A party of 12 Mysore horse, who had accidentally joined me, also behaved most gallantly,
and their Jemadar Lokajee Kuddum was severely
wounded. I saw him and one or two of his men
(his son among the number) among the leading
men charging a band of nine of the enemy, who
would not give up their arms, but fought desperately behind some mounds.

13. This spirited action lasted till about 1 P.M.,
when our wounded (six men in all, and six horses),
were sent back with forty sabres to camp, and we
formed up in the watercourse about a mile or less
from Nurgoond.

14. The infantry and guns joined us about the
same time.

15. The enemy's horse had disappeared ; and a

false report that they had gone round to attack the camp, detained us nearly an hour, and obliged me to detach forty more horse for its protection.

16. At about 3 P.M. the whole force advanced; Captain Davies, as we neared the Petta, throwing out one of the companies of the Highlanders as skirmishers, under Lieutenant Bell, H.M. 74th, and holding his other company, with the company of the 28th Native Infantry, under Lieutenant Heish, as a reserve. At 600 yards, Captain Paget opened fire with shot and shell. which was answered from the Fort guns and a few matchlocks from the Petta, but the enemy's fire was languid, and he was seen moving in crowds to the Fort.' The guns were advanced nearer to the Petta, and the skirmishers, strengthened by half the company, 28th Native Infantry, moved close up.

17. The artillery practice was excellent; the round shot was directed chiefly against the Chief's palace and the neighbouring temple, strong buildings commanding the Petta, and the former protected by its position from the fort guns. Our shell burst among the crowds flying to the fort, and these, with the round shot and heavy rifle fire, seemed either to have driven the enemy out, or to have put down all opposition.

18. About 5 P.M. I directed Captain Davies to push forward into the Petta and occupy the Chief's palace; a party of dismounted Sowars, under Ressaldar Sew Pursand Sing, also accompanied this column, which entered from the western gateway, previously broken in by the skirmishers, and, in about three quarters of an hour, they were seen going up the steep pathway to the palace. I beg to enclose Captain Davies's report. He acknowledges his obligation to Ressaldar Sew Pursand Sing, who showed the way. His progress does not seem to have been seriously opposed, but the work was

well and rapidly done. Simultaneously with Captain Davies's advance, a small party of the 28th Native Infantry, with more dismounted Sowars, entered by the south gateway, and made their way also to the palace. The remainder of the 28th Native Infantry remained with the guns, while the horse observed the rear and flanks.

19. About half past 5 P.M., the guns were moved up to the infantry in the chief's palace; guards were placed on the gateways, and the whole place was in our possession by 6 P.M. The camp was ordered from Oomergul, and thirty horse were sent back to increase the escort.

20. The rock of Nurgoond is so extensive that any attempt to have invested it that night with my small cavalry force would have been useless. I felt also that its immediate occupation, under any circumstances, ought to be my sole object. I had serious intentions of taking further advantage of the enemy's panic, and making the attempt at once, but on consideration it seemed better to wait till the morning, as the panic would probably decrease the garrison, and our troops would be fresher.

21. The whole Petta was commanded from our position, and the fort guns could not be depressed to bear upon us. The enemy fired from the fort, but his fire did no damage, as we had good cover, and it ceased almost entirely before dark; no doubt a shot from the rifle of Private Thomas Hopkins, Her Majesty's 74th, which killed a man in the embrasures, 200 yards over our head, did much to keep the enemy quiet.

22. We bivouacked for the night; the troops had been without food since 11 A.M. of the 1st June, and the commissariat was not up till the morning of the 2nd,

23. The information gleaned from the prisoners showed that there were, at most, not more than

500 men in the fort, and I felt that I should meet
with at least not serious opposition. Four bags of
powder were prepared and carried by Privates D.
McIntosh, E. Timmins, J. Friend and A. Hamilton,
of Her Majesty's 74th, while Serjeant-Major
W. Lindsay, Royal Artillery, carried the train
powder and fuzee.

Lieutenant White, Engineers, and Lieutenant
Burn, Royal Artillery, accompanied the party; I
took command of the whole.

24. We started about 8 A.M., with the two
companies of Her Majesty's 74th, under the command of Captain Davies, and the company of the
28th Native Infantry, under Lieutenant Heish,
Ressaldar Sew Pursand Sing, with a few dismounted sowars, leading; this officer had always
urged an immediate advance; his conduct throughout the day was energetic and gallant in the
extreme, not only in action but with advice. I
give to him the chief credit for activity in the
operation.

25. It took us about half an hour to wind up the
hill to the first gate. Only one man showed himself, without arms, on the wall. Sowar Shaikh
Abdoolla, of the Southern Mahrata Horse, climbed
over the wall and unbarred the first iron-plated
gate, and we entered. We passed on to the second.
The guard-rooms were deserted; the arms and
accoutrements were hanging on the walls; the same
sowar opened the second gate in a similar way;
the third and fourth were open, and we entered the
fort; a few persons armed and disarmed fled down
the precipitous rocks on our approach, but there
was not a show of opposition. It was a matter of
congratulation and thankfulness that such a stronghold had fallen into our hands without the loss of
one life.

26. The casualties in the capture of the Petta
and fort were, one Highlander severely wounded,

and two gunners and four horses severely scorched by an explosion.

27. I am much indebted to the troops of all arms for their gallant and spirited conduct. To this alone is to be attributed our complete success and the prostration of the enemy's spirit.

28. I owe my most cordial thanks to Captain Paget, commanding Royal Artillery, for his quick and effective fire, and to Captain Davies, Her Majesty's 74th, commanding the infantry, for his prompt and spirited advance and occupation of the Petta and Chief's palace, and to both for their ready support on all occasions.

29. My obligations are especially due to Ressaldar Sew Pursand Sing to whom our immediate advance into the fort is to be mainly attributed. He is a brave and very useful officer.

30. My thanks are also due to Ressaldars Sindur Khan and Shumshoo Deen and Woordee, Major Khoondajee Jadow. It was the gallant charge of the horse, under the first two officers, which broke the enemy's spirit, and from which they never rallied.

31. I would also bring to your notice the conduct of Sowar Shaikh Abdoolah, who climbed the wall and opened the gates. I beg to assure the Major-General that his conduct was felt by all to be very fearless, and the work was considered to be one of great danger.

32. My thanks are due to Lieutenant Thomas, Superintendent, for his assistance at all times, both in the field and for intelligence of the state of the country ; Mr. Skoulding, Veterinary Surgeon, R.A., acted as my staff-officer, and gave me every assistance both in field and quarters. The force is also indebted to Mr. Gray, for his assistance in procuring us supplies and assisting our march. I would also beg to acknowledge the assistance received from Dr. Imlach, who is always at hand both in action and

quarters, not only in his own immediate capacity, but to assist in his own quiet way wherever he can be useful.

33. I have omitted to mention that all my cavalry were distributed round the fort early on the morning of the 2nd.

34. It is difficult to state the enemy's loss; it could not be less than 200, independent of those killed in the cavalry action. We took 113 prisoners (some of importance), of whom about 60 have been liberated as non-combatants; the Dewan of the Chief was found drowned in a tank in the Petta.

35 All accounts state that the enemy's force was 3,000 foot and 500 horse. I think this exaggerated, but the force has wholly dispersed, and the country is strewed with arms. The Major-General will, I trust, agree with me in considering that immediate occupation of this famous stronghold was, under any circumstances, the paramount object.

36. As Bheem Rao, of Moordurghee, considered the most active rebel, was still at large, I despatched Ressaldar Sew Pursand Sing towards Ramdoorg, in pursuit of the Nurgoondkur, immediately after the capture of the fortress; and, leaving the two companies of the Highlanders to garrison Nurgoond, under command of Captain Davies, I proceeded with the rest of the force towards Kopul.

37. The report of the capture of Kopul by Major Hughes, and death of Bheem Rao, which I heard when fifteen miles from Nurgoond, made me send back the guns. At Gudduck this news was authenticated, and the capture of the Nurgoondkur by Mr. Souter, was also officially reported to me.

38. Several important arrests have also been made, and I may congratulate the Major-General

on the complete frustration of the operation of the rebels, and on restored tranquillity.

39. I returned only yesterday to Nurgoond, and this report has consequently been delayed.

40. A return of ordnance and ordnance stores, captured in the fort and Petta, will be forwarded hereafter. The list is scarcely completed.

I have, &c.,

G. MALCOLM, Lieutenant-Colonel,
Commanding Field Force.

No. 57.

Captain A. Davies, commanding a detachment of the 74th Highlanders, to the Staff Officer of the Field Force.

Fort Nurgoond, June 2, 1858.

SIR,

I HAVE the honor to report to you, for the information of the Officer Commanding the Field Force, that, after receiving his orders to enter the Petta with the reserve, I joined myself to my skirmishers and entered the Petta at the west gate, from whence, driving such opponents as we met in our way, I proceeded to the foot of the eminence, on which appeared to be a fortified place; not knowing the way, however, I was much indebted to Ressaldar Sew Pursand Sing, of the S. Mharata Horse, who was there with a party of that corps, and volunteered to show me the way, by which I was enabled to seize and occupy the strong building in question.

I have, &c.,

A. DAVIES, Captain,
Commanding Detachment, 74th Highlanders.

A further list in continuation of Office Memorandum from the Military Department, dated 3rd

June, 1858, forwarded by the President of the Council of India to the Court of Directors of the East India Company, of Europeans, whether belonging to the East India Company's Service or not, who have been killed or wounded by the hands of rebels, appears in this Gazette. The names in this list were included in previous returns of casualties, &c.

At the Court at *Osborne House, Isle of Wight,* the 31st day of *July,* 1858.

PRESENT,

The QUEEN's Most Excellent Majesty in Council.

WHEREAS by an Act passed in the Session of Parliament, holden in the sixth and seventh years of Her Majesty's reign, intituled, "An Act to remove doubts as to the exercise of power and jurisdiction by Her Majesty within divers countries and places out of Her Majesty's dominions, and to render the same more effectual," it was enacted, that it was and should be lawful for Her Majesty to hold, exercise, and enjoy any power or jurisdiction which Her Majesty then had or might at any time thereafter have within any country or place out of Her Majesty's dominions in the same and as ample a manner as if Her Majesty had acquired such power or jurisdiction by the cession or conquest of territory. And whereas Her Majesty hath power and jurisdiction in the dominions of the Sublime Ottoman Porte, and the same or certain parts thereof hath or have heretofore been exercised by Her Majesty's Ambassadors, Consuls, and other officers resident within the said dominions. And whereas the right of levying hospital duties on British and Ionian merchant vessels entering the ports of the

Levant was within the powers conferred upon the late Levant Company by its charter. And whereas under and by virtue of certain rules and regulations duly made and issued by the authority of the late Levant Company and before the surrender of the charter of the said Company in the year of our Lord one thousand eight hundred and twenty-five a certain tonnage rate or duty was imposed and levied upon all British and Ionian merchant vessels entering the port of Smyrna by the British Consul at that port for the maintenance and support of the Sick Seamen's Hospital there. And whereas the said tonnage rate or duty continued to be so levied and applied as aforesaid until the year one thousand eight hundred and fifty-four. And whereas under and by virtue of a certain statute made and passed in the sixth year of the reign of His late Majesty King George the Fourth, intituled, "An Act to repeal certain Acts relating to the Governor and Company of Merchants of England trading to the Levant Seas, and the duties payable to them, and to authorize the transfer and disposal of the possessions and property of the said Governor and Company for the public service, it was enacted, that from and immediately from and after the enrolment of a certain deed or instrument therein mentioned (which deed or instrument has been since enrolled) all such rights and duties of jurisdiction and authority over His Majesty's subjects resorting to the ports of the Levant for the purpose of trade or otherwise, as were lawfully exercised and performed, or which were by certain letters patent and Acts of Parliament (therein more particularly referred to), or any of them, authorized to be exercised and performed by any Consuls or other officers appointed by the said Company, or which such Consuls or other officers lawfully exercised and performed, under and by virtue of any power or authority whatever, should from and after the enrolment of such deed or instrument as aforesaid, be and become vested in, and should be exercised and performed by such Consuls and other officers respectively, as His Majesty might be pleased to appoint for the protection of the trade of His Majesty's subjects in the ports and places respectively mentioned in the said letters patent and Acts, or any or either of them. And whereas the right of levying hospital dues on ships trading to the Levant was one of the rights theretofore exercised by the said Company and its Consuls, and the same may now be lawfully exercised and performed by Her Majesty's Consuls in and throughout the dominions of the Sublime Ottoman Porte. And whereas it was considered expedient to provide for the establishment, support, and maintenance of British hospitals for sick seamen coming in British or Ionian merchant-vessels, within the dominions of the Sublime Ottoman Porte. And whereas by an Order in Council, dated the third day of July, one thousand eight hundred and fifty-four, it was ordered that it should be lawful for Her Majesty's Consuls residing within the said dominions, and they were thereby authorized to levy upon all British or Ionian merchant-vessels which might enter any of the ports within their respective jurisdictions, a tonnage-duty or dues, not exceeding one penny per ton on each vessel; and they were thereby authorized, directed, and required to apply all the said duty or dues, and all moneys raised or received by them on account thereof for and towards the establishment, maintenance, and support of British hospitals for sick seamen coming in British or Ionian vessels within the said dominions. And whereas the said tonnage-duty ordered to be levied and raised as aforesaid is insufficient to provide for the annual expenditure of the said hospitals. And whereas it is expedient, in order to provide for the proper support and maintenance of the said hospitals, to increase the said duty in manner hereinafter mentioned. Now, therefore, under and by virtue and in pursuance of the premises, and of the said recited Acts of Parliament, and of all or any power, jurisdiction, or authority whatsoever, thereby or otherwise vested in or belonging to Her Majesty in this behalf, Her Majesty is pleased, by and with the advice of Her Privy Counc l, to order, and it is hereby ordered, that the said recited Order in Council of the third day of July, one thousand eight hundred and fifty-four, shall be, and the same is hereby revoked and rescinded; and further, that it shall be lawful for Her Majesty's Consuls residing within the said dominions, and they are hereby authorized to levy upon all British or Ionian merchant vessels, which may enter any of the ports within their respective jurisdictions, a tonnage duty or dues not exceeding 1½ per ton on each vessel, and they are hereby authorized, directed, and required to apply all the said duty or dues, and all moneys raised or received by them on account thereof, for and towards the establishment, maintenance, and support of British hospitals for sick seamen coming in British or Ionian vessels within the said dominions. And Her Majesty is pleased, by and with the like advice, to order, and it is hereby ordered that it shall be lawful for her Principal Secretary of State for Foreign Affairs, from time to time, by any writing under his hand, to make and issue, and he is hereby authorized to make and issue any such rules and regulations as to him may seem fit, with regard to the manner in which the moneys which may be so levied or received as aforesaid by the said Consuls. shall be applied or expended for the establishment, maintenance, or support of such hospitals as aforesaid. And Her.

Majesty is further pleased to order, and it is hereby further ordered, that it shall be lawful for any such Secretary of State as aforesaid, from time to time, by any rule, regulation, or order in writing under his hand, to provide for the exempting any British or Ionian merchant vessel, which may, within any period therein set forth, have once paid the said tonnage duty or dues, from all or any other or additional or subsequent payment or liability in respect thereof. And Her Majesty, by and with the like advice, is further pleased to order, and it is hereby further ordered, that it shall be lawful for any such Secretary of State as aforesaid, and he is hereby authorised from time to time, by any such rule, regulation, or order, in writing under his hand, to alter and vary the rate or amount of the tonnage duty or dues, so to be levied or paid as aforesaid, or the manner of levying or paying or receiving the same : provided always, that no such alteration or variation shall extend or operate, so as to increase or exceed the aforesaid rate or amount of tonnage duty, or dues, that is to say, $1\frac{1}{2}d.$ per ton upon each vessel. And it is hereby further ordered, that it shall be lawful for Her Majesty's Principal Secretary of State for Foreign Affairs, by any writing under his hand, from time to time to limit the extent to which any Consul-General, Consul or Vice-Consul, shall exercise jurisdiction over British subjects within the dominions of the Sublime Ottoman Porte, in the matter of or in anything relating to the said tonnage duty, or dues, anything in the present Order contained notwithstanding. And Her Majesty is by and with the like advice, pleased further to order, and it is hereby further ordered, that for the purpose of this Order the words " British merchant vessel or vessels" and " British ship or ships," shall be taken and deemed to include all or any merchant ship or vessel, being the property of any subject of Her Majesty.

And the Right Honourable the Earl of Malmesbury, one of Her Majesty's Principal Secretaries of State, is to give the necessary directions herein accordingly.

C. C. Greville.

At the Court at *Osborne House, Isle of Wight,* the 31st day of *July*, 1858.

The QUEEN'S Most Excellent Majesty in Council was pleased to approve and ratify the schemes duly prepared (as set forth in this Gazette) by the Ecclesiastical Commissioners for England—

For substituting a money payment to the Bishop of Worcester for certain estates belonging to his see.

For authorizing the sale of certain property lately forming the possessions of the prebend or rectory of Wherwell, in the county of Southampton.

Whitehall, August 9, 1858.

The Queen has been pleased to direct letters patent to be passed under the Great Seal, granting the dignity of a Baron of the United Kingdom of Great Britain and Ireland unto the Right Honourable Thomas Pemberton Leigh, and the heirs male of his body lawfully begotten, by the name, style, and title of Baron Kingsdown, of Kingsdown, in the county of Kent.

Whitehall, August 10, 1858.

The Queen has been pleased to direct letters patent to be passed under the Great Seal, appointing:

Rear-Admiral James Hope, C.B. ;

Major-General Sir John Mark Frederic Smith;
William Schaw Lindsay, Esq.;
Captain John Washington, R.N., Hydrographer
of the Admiralty;
Captain Bartholomew James Sulivan, R.N.,
C.B.;
Captain James Vetch, R.E.; and
John Coode, Esq.;

to be Her Majesty's Commissioners to complete
the inquiry recommended in the report of the
Select Committee of the House of Commons on
Harbours of Refuge.

Downing-Street, August 9, 1858.

The Queen has been pleased to appoint William
Henry Doyle, Esq., to be Assistant Justice of the
General Court for the Bahama Islands; A. L.
Inglis, Esq., to be Harbour Master and Marine
Magistrate for the Colony of Hong Kong; L. G.
Tucker, Esq., to be Stipendiary Magistrate for
the Colony of British Guiana.

Crown-Office, August 10, 1858.

MEMBER returned to serve in this present
PARLIAMENT.

Northern Division of the County of Chester.

Wilbraham Egerton, of Rostherne Hall, in the
said county, Esq., in the room of William
Tatton Egerton, Esq., who has accepted the
office of Steward of Her Majesty's Manor of
Northstead, in the county of York.

(1220).

Board of Trade, Whitehall,
August 10, 1858.

THE Right Honourable the Lords of the Committee of Privy Council for Trade and Plantations have received, through the Secretary of State for Foreign Affairs, a copy of a Despatch from Her Majesty's Chargé d'Affaires at the Hague, stating that the following ports will be opened to general trade on the 31st May, 1859, in addition to those which have been already made accessible to foreign shipping in the Dutch East India possessions, viz. :

In the Island of Java, Aujer, Bantam, Nedramaijoe, Cheribon, Tagal, Pekalougan, Rembang, Passoewean, Peobolingo, Bezoekie, Panarockan, Barijoewangie, Pangool Palzitan, Tjilatjap, and Wynkoopsbay, on the west coast of Sumatra, Natal, and Priaman, and Sampit in the south eastern portion of Borneo.

(1225.)

Board of Trade, Whitehall,
August, 10, 1858.

THE Right Honourable the Lords of the Committee of Privy Council for Trade and Plantations have received, through the Secretary of State for Foreign Affairs, a copy of a Despatch from Her Majesty's Minister at Copenhagen, transmitting the following notice which has been issued by the Danish Government, respecting a Submarine Telegraph which has been laid down in the little Belt.

NOTICE TO MARINERS.

SUBMARINE TELEGRAPH IN THE LITTLE BELT.

Notice is hereby given that a submarine tele‐graphic wire has been laid down in the Little

Belt, from the coast of Jutland, 100 fathoms west of Snoghoi Ferry-bridge, and extending to the coast of Funen, 10 fathoms to the eastward of "Kongebrolu" (King's-bridge). The position of the cable is indicated exactly by two beacons painted red and white, and erected on the southern side of the Belt, east of Kongebrolu. Of these beacons, the one standing nearest the beach has been erected over the southern termination of the wire, while the other, standing further off, shows the continuation of the direction in which the said wire has been laid down in the Belt.

All mariners passing the Little Belt, are warned not to anchor over, or in the neighbourhood of the above telegraphic wire ; and all those who either intentionally, or through negligence, shall injure the same, will be punished and held responsible for the damages done, as prescribed by law of 29th December, 1853.—Ministry of Marine, June, 30, 1858.

(Signed)   O. W. MICHELSEN
                 N. B. PETERSEN.

(1231.)

Board of Trade, Whitehall,
August 10, 1858.

THE Right Honourable the Lords of the Committee of Privy Council for Trade and Plantations have received, through the Secretary of State for Foreign Affairs, a copy of a Despatch from Her Majesty's Ambassador at Constantinople, reporting that the Porte has decided to allow perfect freedom of trade in salt, and has issued orders to the effect that henceforward that article is to be traded in with the same freedom as all other articles, whether for purposes of internal trade or exportation.

Admiralty, August 9, 1858.

In consideration of the services performed by Commander Thomas Saumarez, at the capture of the Forts, at the Mouth of the Pei Ho, as recorded in the Supplement to the London Gazette of the 27th July, 1858, Commander Saumarez, has been promoted to the rank of Captain, from the date of the Gazette.

Commissions signed by the Lord Lieutenant of the West Riding of the County of York, *and of the City and County of the City of* York.

West York Rifle Regiment of Militia.

Ensign Richard Hewley Graham to be Lieutenant, vice Clayton, resigned.   Dated 23rd July, 1858.

Commissions signed by the Lord Lieutenant of the County of Worcester.

Queen's Own Regiment of Worcestershire Yeomanry Cavalry.

William George Throckmorton, Gent., to be Cornet.

MEMORANDUM.

Queen's Own Regiment of Worcestershire Yeomanry Cavalry.

Her Majesty has been pleased to accept the resignation of the Commission held in this Regiment by Captain William F. Taylor.

Commissions signed by the Lord Lieutenant of the County of Worcester.

Queen's Own Regiment of Worcestershire Yeomanry Cavalry.

Lieutenant Ferdinando Dudley Sea Smith to be Captain, vice Taylor, resigned,

Cornet James Kerr Moilliett to be Lieutenant, vice Smith, promoted.

Worcestershire Regiment of Militia.

Richard John Griffiths, Gent., to be Captain, vice Frederick Clifton, deceased.

Commission signed by the Lord Lieutenant of the County of Lincoln.

Royal North Lincoln Militia.

George Tomline, Esq, M.P., to be Honorary Colonel of the Royal North Lincoln Militia. Dated 4th August, 1858.

RESIGNATIONS.

2nd Regiment of the Royal Surrey Militia.

H. E. Legge, Paymaster.

1st Regiment of the Royal Surrey Militia.

Ensign Edward Henry Saunders.

FROM THE

LONDON GAZETTE of AUGUST 13, 1858.

AT the Court at *Osborne House, Isle of Wight,* the 31st day of *July,* 1858.

The QUEEN'S Most Excellent Majesty in Council was pleased to approve and consent to certain bye-laws submitted (as set forth in this Gazette) by the corporation of the Trinity House in Kingston-upon-Hull, in accordance with the provisions of the " Merchant Shipping Act, 1854, ' with respect to pilotage by masters and mates of ships in the districts of the said corporation.

At the Court at *Osborne House, Isle of Wight*, the
31st day of *July*, 1858.

The QUEEN'S Most Excellent Majesty in
Council was pleased to approve a representation
duly prepared (as set forth in this Gazette) by the
Ecclesiastical Commissioners for England—

As to the assignment of a consolidated chapelry
to the consecrated church of the Holy Trinity,
situate at the Lickey, in the parish of Bromsgrove,
in the county and diocese of Worcester, to be
named "The Consolidated Chapelry of the Lickey."

At the Court at *Osborne House, Isle of Wight*,
the 31st day of *July*, 1858.

The QUEEN'S Most Excellent Majesty in
Council was pleased to approve and ratify the
schemes duly prepared (as set forth in this Gazette)
by the Ecclesiastical Commissioners for England—

For making better provision for the cure of
souls in certain parishes and districts.

For constituting a separate district for spiritual
purposes to comprise certain portions of the ancient
chapelry of Meltham, the chapelry district of South
Crosland, and the particular district of Saint
James, Meltham Mills, in the townships of Mel·
tham and South Crosland, in the parish of Almond-
bury, in the county of York and diocese of Ripon,
to be named "The District of Helme."

For setting out and constituting districts for
spiritual purposes, and annexing such districts to
the consecrated Churches of All Souls, Ancoats;
Saint Matthias, Salford; Saint Philip, Salford;
Christ Church, Salford; Saint Bartholomew, Salford; Saint Matthew, Manchester; Saint Peter,
Manchester; Saint Thomas, Old Trafford; Saint

Paul, Hulme; and Christ Church, Moss Side; respectively situate within the original limits of the parish of Manchester, in the county of Lancaster and diocese of Manchester.

For constituting a separate district for spiritual purposes out of the parish of Llanddeniolen, in the county of Carnarvon, and in the diocese of Bangor, to be named "The District of Llandinorwig."

Foreign-Office, August 9, 1858.

The Queen has been pleased to approve of Mr. Alexander Henderson as Consul at Londonderry, and of Mr. John G. Barr as Consul at Melbourne, for the United States of America.

The Queen has also been pleased to approve of Mr. Thomas Hampden Mullens as Consul in the Mauritius for His Majesty the King of Denmark.

The Queen has also been pleased to approve of Mr. Louis T. Power as Consul at Gibraltar for His Majesty the King of Hanover.

The Queen has also been pleased to approve of Don José de Aguilar as Consul at Hong Kong for Her Majesty the Queen of Spain.

Whitehall, August 11, 1858.

The Right Honourable Spencer Horatio Walpole, one of Her Majesty's Principal Secretaries of State, has appointed Henry Longridge, Esq., to be an Inspector of Coal Mines, in the room of Herbert Francis Mackworth, Esq., deceased.

(1232.)

Board of Trade, Whitehall, August 12, 1858.

THE Right Honourable the Lords of the Committee of Privy Council for Trade and Plantations have received, through the Secretary of State for Foreign Affairs, a copy of a Despatch from Her Majesty's Consular Agent at Rome, reporting that all vessels arriving at Civita Vecchia, from Malta and Marseilles, will be subjected to quarantine.

(1242.)

Board of Trade, Whitehall,
August 12, 1858.

THE Right Honourable the Lords of the Committee of Privy Council for Trade and Plantations have received, through the Secretary of State for Foreign Affairs, a copy of a Despatch from Her Majesty's Consul, at Genoa, enclosing copy of an Order of the Board of Health of that Port, containing the following regulations respecting quarantine :

All vessels arriving from the coast of Tripoli will be subjected to a quarantine of fifteen days, to commence from the discharge, for purification, of any susceptible cargo which might be on board; and all vessels arriving from the above-mentioned coast, and having had sickness on board during their voyage will be subjected to such further extension of the above quarantine as the authorities may deem proper.

Vessels arriving from the coasts of Tunis, Egypt, or Syria, will be subjected to a quarantine of five days, to commence from the discharge of any susceptible cargo on board, or, if having had sickness on board during the voyage, to a quarantine of not less than fifteen days.

Vessels arriving from Malta, without having touched at any intermediate port, or without having obtained free pratique at any intermediate port at which they may have touched, will be subject to five days' quarantine, or, if having had sickness, &c., on board during the passage, to a quarantine of fifteen days, or more, as may seem fit to the authorities. Such vessels having obtained free pratique at intermediate ports will be subject to quarantine according to circumstances.

Vessels arriving from Algiers, Morocco, Candia, Salonica, and the Asiatic shores of the Turkish Empire, will be subject to the visit of a medical officer, and such measures as may be necessary, previous to their admission to free pratique.

(1251.)

Board of Trade, Whitehall,
August 12, 1858.

THE Right Honourable the Lords of the Committee of Privy Council for Trade and Plantations have received, through the Secretary of State for Foreign Affairs, a copy of a Despatch from Her Majesty's Consul-General at Venice, stating that all vessels arriving at Austrian ports from the coast of Tripoli, will be considered as having foul bills of health, and subjected to quarantine accordingly ; and that all vessels arriving at the said ports from the coasts of Northern Africa, including Egypt and Syria, and from the Island of Malta, will be subjected to a quarantine of observation of six days; it being requisite, however, that they should be furnished with clean bills of health, properly attested by the Consulate of an European power, otherwise the period of quarantine will be extended to seven days: also that suspected merchandize will require to undergo a quarantine of ten days, after being opened in the Lazaretto ; and that pratique will be refused in all suspected cases.

War-Office, Pall-Mall,
13th August, 1858.

2nd Regiment of Dragoon Guards, Captain and Brevet-Major W. H. Seymour to be Major,

without purchase, vice Price, deceased. Dated
13th May, 1858.

Lieutenant P. A. W. Carnegy to be Captain,
without purchase, vice Seymour. Dated 13th
May, 1858.

Cornet William Jones Thomas to be Lieutenant,
without purchase, vice Carnegy. Dated 13th
May, 1858.

3rd Dragoon Guards, Edwin Brett, Gent., to
be Cornet, without purchase, vice Gifford, appointed to the 1st Dragoon Guards. Dated
13th August, 1858.

4th Light Dragoons, James Edward Bradshaw,
Gent., to be Cornet, without purchase, vice
Davies, appointed to the 6th Dragoons. Dated
13th August, 1858.

Assistant-Surgeon John Charles Campbell, M B.,
from the Staff, to be Assistant-Surgeon, vice
Carte, about to be appointed Physician and
Surgeon to the Royal Hospital, Kilmainham.
Dated 13th August, 1858.

6th Dragoons, Henry Albert Reade Revell, Gent.,
to be Cornet, without purchase, vice Billing,
whose transfer from 13th Light Dragoons, as
stated in the Gazette of the 27th July, 1858,
has been cancelled. Dated 13th August, 1858.

William Valentine King, Gent., to be Cornet,
without purchase, vice Beaumont, whose transfer from 4th Dragoon Guards was cancelled in
Gazette of 6th August, 1858. Dated 14th
August, 1858.

7th Light Dragoons, Ensign Herbert Owen
Johnes, from the 56th Foot, to be Cornet, without purchase, vice Bankes, deceased. Dated
13th-August, 1858.

18th Light Dragoons, Surgeon Edward Scott
Docker, from the 7th Foot, to be Surgeon, vice
Mapleton, appointed to the Staff. Dated 13th
August, 1858.

Military Train.

To be Ensigns, without purchase.

Cornet Fergus McKenzie, from half-pay, late Land Transport Corps, vice Morris, appointed to the 75th Foot. Date 13th August, 1858.

Cornet Thomas Churcher, from half-pay, late Land Transport Corps. Dated 13th August, 1858.

Royal Regiment of Artillery, Captain and Brevet-Major Edward Moubray, from temporary half-pay, to be a Supernumerary Captain. Dated 21st July, 1858.

The date of the appointment of Assistant Surgeons Alexander Dudgeon Gulland and Eugene Francis O'Leary, from the Staff to the Royal Artillery, has been altered from 28th May to 27th May, 1858.

Scots Fusilier Guards, Lieutenant and Captain and Brevet-Major Francis Baring to be Captain and Lieutenant-Colonel, by purchase, vice Montgomery, who retires. Dated 13th August, 1858.

5th Foot, William Bevington Knox, Gent., to be Ensign, without purchase, vice Fremantle, appointed to the Rifle Brigade. Dated 13th August, 1858.

6th Foot, Captain John William Preston, from the 76th Foot, to be Captain, vice Waldy, who exchanges. Dated 13th August, 1858.

7th Foot, Ensign Hardinge Giffard Follett to be Lieutenant, by purchase, vice Butler, who retires. Dated 13th August, 1858.

Staff-Surgeon of the Second Class Edward William Thomas Mandeville to be Surgeon, vice Docker, appointed to the 18th Light Dragoons. Dated 13th August, 1858.

10th *Foot*, Captain Douglas Ernest Mnaners, from half-pay Unattached, to be Captain, vice Hamilton, promoted, without purchase, to an Unattached Majority. Dated 13th August, 1858.

20th *Foot*, Lieutenant Charles K. Chatfield to be Instructor of Musketry. Dated 2nd August, 1858.

42nd *Foot*, Ensign William James to be Lieutenant, without purchase, vice Bramley, killed in action. Dated 16th April, 1858.

45th *Foot*, Henry Hodson Hooke, Gent., to be Ensign, without purchase. Dated 13th August, 1858.

55th *Foot*, Ensign Thomas Dunn to be Adjutant, vice Lieutenant Williams, who resigns the Adjutancy only. Dated 13th August, 1858.

60th *Foot*, Serjeant-Major Robert Duncan to be Quartermaster, vice Campbell, deceased. Dated 13th August, 1858.

Assistant-Surgeon James Doran, M.D., from the Staff, to be Assistant-Surgeon. Dated 13th August, 1858.

66th *Foot*, Charles Tennant Wallace, Gent., to be Ensign, without purchase, vice Bent, promoted in the 4th Foot. Dated 13th August, 1858.

73rd *Foot*, Lieutenant Philip Gibaut to be Adjutant, vice Godfrey, promoted. Dated 2nd June, 1858.

76th *Foot*, Captain Edward G. Waldy, from 6th Foot, to be Captain, vice Preston, who exchanges. Dated 13th August, 1858.

90th *Foot*, Oscar William de Thoren, Gent., to be Ensign, without purchase, vice Gordon, deceased. Dated 13th August, 1858.

91st *Foot*, Lieutenant Lloyd Henry Thomas to be Captain, without purchase, vice Brevet-Lieutenant-Colonel E. W. C. Wright, promoted in a Depôt Battalion. Dated 13th August, 1858.

Ensign Edward Kelly Obbard to be Lieutenant, without purchase, vice Thomas. Dated 13th August, 1858.

Serjeant-Major William Grant, to be Ensign without purchase, vice Obbard. Dated 13th August, 1858.

100*th Foot*, William Palmer Clarke, Gent., to be Ensign, without purchase. Dated 13th August, 1858.

2*nd West India Regiment*, Serjeant-Major Henry Lowry to be Ensign, without purchase, vice Lewis, promoted in the 21st Foot. Dated 13th August, 1858.

Ceylon Rifle Regiment, Francis Daniell, Gent., to be Ensign, without purchase, vice Walker, promoted. Dated 13th August, 1858.

St. Helena Regiment, Edward Drummond Hay, Gent., to be Ensign, without purchase, vice Furnell, promoted. Dated 13th August, 1858.

DEPOT BATTALIONS.

To be Majors.

Major P. Robertson, from half-pay Unattached. Dated 13th August, 1858.

Major F. G. T. Deshon, from half-pay Unattached. Dated 13th August, 1858.

Major W. Warry, from half-pay Unattached. Dated 13th August, 1858.

Major H. Rowlands, from half-pay Unattached. Dated 13th August, 1858.

Major G. E. Brown-Westhead, from half-pay Unattached. Dated 13th August, 1858.

Major F. C. Elton, from half-pay Unattached. Dated 13th August, 1858.

Major R. Inglis, from half-pay Unattached. Dated 13th August, 1858.

Major F. E. Drewe, from half-pay Unattached. Dated 13th August, 1858.

UNATTACHED.

Lieutenant N. Goddard, from 35th Foot, to be Captain, by purchase. Dated 13th August, 1858.

HOSPITAL STAFF.

Surgeon Henry Mapleton, M.D., from the 18th Light Dragoons, to be Staff-Surgeon of the Second Class. Dated 13th August, 1858.

The appointment of Acting-Assistant-Surgeon J. B. Jardine to bear date 14th July, 1858, and not 23rd July, 1858, as previously stated.

BREVET.

Brevet-Lieutenant-Colonel Patrick Leonard Mc-Dougall, Major, half-pay Canadian Rifles, Commandant of the Staff College, to be Colonel to the Army. Dated 17th July, 1858.

Brevet-Major James Palmer, retired full-pay 3rd West India Regiment, to be Lieutenant-Colonel in the Army, the rank being honorary only. Dated 13th August, 1858.

Lieutenant-Colonel Arthur Thomas Phillpotts, of the Royal Artillery, having completed three years' service in the rank of Lieutenant-Colonel, to be Colonel in the Army, under the Royal Warrant of 3rd November, 1854. Dated 13th August, 1858.

Major-General C. G. Falconar, Colonel 73rd Foot, to be Lieutenant-General in succession to General Lord Clyde, G.C.B., placed on the Fixed Establishment of Generals. Dated 20th July, 1858.

The undermentioned promotions to take place consequent on the death of Lieutenant-General Sir Frederick Ashworth, Colonel 44th Foot, on 1st August, 1858 :

Major-General Alexander Fisher Macintosh, Colonel 90th Foot, to be Lieutenant-General. Dated 2nd August, 1858.

Major-General T. Harte Franks, K.C.B., the Senior Supernumerary, promoted for distinguished service, to be placed on the Fixed Establishment of Major-Generals. Dated 2nd August, 1858.

Brevet-Lieutenant-Colonel John Knight Jauncey, half-pay, as Major Unattached, to be Colonel. Dated 2nd August, 1858.

Brevet-Major John Home Purves, half-pay, as Captain Unattached, to be Lieutenant-Colonel. Dated 2nd August, 1858.

Captain Charles Fanshawe, Royal Engineers, to be Major. Dated 2nd August, 1858.

To be Majors in the Army.

Captain C. J. W. Norman, 72nd Foot. Dated 20th July, 1858.

Captain Arthur J. Nixon, Rifle Brigade. Dated 20th July, 1858.

Captain Martin Dillon, Rifle Brigade. Dated 20th July, 1858.

The undermentioned Gentlemen Cadets of the East India Company's Service, at present doing duty at the Royal Engineer Establishment at Chatham, with the rank of Ensign, to have the local and temporary rank of Lieutenant, while employed at that establisment :

John Herschel. Dated 13th August, 1858.

Isaac Peat Westmorland. Dated 13th August, 1858.

Robert Claude Daubug. Dated 13th August, 1858.

Hastings Macsween. Dated 13th August, 1858.

Arthur Charles Padday. Dated 13th August, 1858.

Thomas Freeman Dowden. Dated 13th August, 1858.

Oliver Beauchamp Coventry St. John. Dated 13th August, 1858.

Augustus Le Mesurier. Dated 13th August, 1858.

David Henry Trail. Dated 13th August, 1858.

Arthur Herbert Bagge. Dated 13th August, 1858.

William Coningham. Dated 13th August, 1858.

Frank Robertson. Dated 13th August, 1858.

William Merriman. Dated 13th August, 1858.

Julius Moxon. Dated 13th August, 1858.

Keith Alexander Jopp. Dated 13th August, 1858.

Henry Ravenshaw Thuillier. Dated 13th August, 1858.

Alexander John William Cumming. Dated 13th August, 1858.

Thomas Claridge Manderson. Dated 13th August, 1858.

Alexander Francis Baillie. Dated 13th August, 1858.

Alexander Jerome Filgate. Dated 13th August, 1858.

Lewis Conway Gordon. Dated 13th August, 1858.

James Browne. Dated 13th August, 1858.

Charles Mont. Dated 13th August, 1858.

Henry Herbert Lee. Dated 13th August, 1858.

Alexander Reginald Seton. Dated 13th August, 1858.

Thomas Tupper Carter. Dated 13th August, 1858.

Henry Meredith Vibart. Dated 13th August, 1858.

Lewes Gower Stewart. Dated 13th August, 1858.

Walter Malcolm. Roberts. Dated 13th August, 1858.

MEMORANDUM.

Captain John Wallace Colquitt, upon half-pay 34th Foot, has been permitted to retire from the Service, by the sale of his Commission, he being about to become a Settler in Canada. Dated 13th August, 1858.

Commission signed by the Lord Lieutenant of the Tower Hamlets.

King's Own Light Infantry Regiment of Militia.

Captain George Kitson to be Major. Dated 20th July, 1858.

Commissions signed by the Lord Lieutenant of the County of Monmouth.

Royal Monmouthshire Militia.

Captain John Selwyn Payne to be Major. Dated 9th August, 1858.

Lieutenant John Griffith Wheeley to be Captain, vice Payne, promoted. Dated 9th August, 1858.

Ensign John Zamoiski to be Lieutenant, vice Wheeley, promoted. Dated 9th August, 1858.

Commissions signed by the Vice Lieutenant of the County of Lincoln.

Royal North Lincoln Militia.

Captain the Honourable William John Monson to be Major. Dated 6th August, 1858.

Lieutenant William Longstaffe to be Captain, vice the Hon. Captain Monson promoted. Dated 6th August, 1858.

Commissions signed by the Lord Lieutenant of the County of Stafford.

1st Regiment of King's Own Staffordshire Militia.

Hercules Akerman, Gent., to be Ensign. Dated 6th August, 1858.
John Alexander William Fabie Wilson, Gent., to be Ensign. Dated 6th August, 1858.
David Dowie, Gent., to be Ensign. Dated 6th August, 1858.

Commission signed by the Lord Lieutenant of the North Riding of Yorkshire.

North York Rifle Regiment of Militia.

Henry Cradock, Gent., to be Lieutenant, vice Charles Paget retired. Dated 7th August, 1858.

Commission signed by the Lord Lieutenant of the County of Warwick.

Warwickshire Militia 2nd Regiment.

Captain William Reader to be Major, vice Sir Theophilus W. Biddulph, Bart., resigned. Dated 6th August, 1858.

Commissions signed by the Lord Lieutenant of the County of Kent.

East Kent Regiment of Militia.

Lieutenant George Shirley Maxwell to be Captain, vice Young, resigned. Dated 30th July, 1858.
Ensign George Francis Simmons (formerly Carlyon) to be Lieutenant, vice Maxwell, promoted. Dated 30th July, 1858.

Commission signed by the Lord Lieutenant of the County of Northumberland.

Northumberland Regiment of Militia Artillery.

Henry Hope Nettlefold, Gent., to be Surgeon. Dated 9th August, 1858.

FROM THE

LONDON GAZETTE of AUGUST 17, 1858.

Whitehall, August 17, 1858.

THE Right Honourable Spencer Horatio Walpole has received the following Despatch from the Earl of Malmesbury, dated at Potsdam, the 13th of August, 1858.

Sir,   *Potsdam, August 13, 1858.*

HER Majesty the Queen and the Prince Consort, attended by the Lady Macdonald and Miss Cavendish, and by Sir C. Phipps, Sir J. Clarke, and Colonel Hood and Captain Duplat, left Gravesend in the royal yacht on Tuesday, at 10 A.M., and arrived here safely last night at 10 o'clock.

The royal yacht anchored above Flushing, at 8 P.M., on the 10th, and Her Majesty slept the following night at Dusseldorf. The King of the Belgians met the Queen at Malines, and accompanied Her Majesty as far as Verviers. The Prince of Prussia joined Her Majesty at Aix, and remained with Her Majesty during the rest of the journey. Lord Bloomfield and Mr. Gordon also joined the train. The Queen dined with the

Prince of Hohenzollern on the 11th, at Dusseldorf, which was brilliantly illuminated.

Yesterday Her Majesty stopped to dine with the King and Queen of Hanover, at three o'clock. At Magdeburg Prince Frederick of Prussia met Her Majesty at the Vwildparc Station. Her Majesty had the satisfaction of finding the Princess Royal waiting Her arrival. Her Majesty and the Prince Consort are now residing at the Château of Babelsburg, with Prince Frederic of Prussia and the Princess Royal. Notwithstanding the extraordinary heat of the weather, and long journeys, the last of which was of fifteen hours' duration, Her Majesty remains in perfect health.

From Antwerp to Potsdam, wherever the train stopped, immense crowds were assembled, who evinced by every kind of demonstration, their sincere respect for the Queen of Great Britain.

I have, &c.,

MALMESBURY.

The Right Hon. S. H. Walpole, M.P.,
&c., &c., &c.

NOTIFICATION.

WHEREAS there was concluded at Monte Video, on the 23rd of June, 1857, between the Governments of Great Britain, France, and the Oriental Republic of Uruguay, an Agreement, providing for the settlement, by means of a Mixed Commission, of certain claims of British and French subjects upon the Republic, of which Agreement the following is a translation :

ACT.

His Excellency Don Joaquin Requena, Minister for Foreign Affairs, and Mr. Edward

Thornton and Mr. Martin Maillefer, Chargés d'Affaires of England and France, having met in the Foreign Office, for the purpose of conferring a second time upon the means of establishing the Mixed Commission to settle the claims of English and French subjects on account of losses suffered during the war; the above-mentioned Gentlemen agreed to adopt, as they did adopt, the following bases.

I.

The claims of English and French subjects on account of losses suffered during the war, to which the law, sanctioned on the 14th of July, 1853, refers, shall be definitively settled, with respect to their justification and amount, by a Mixed Commission, having the character of arbitrator.

II.

This Commission shall be composed of four persons, two on the part of the Government of the Republic, whom they shall name, and two on the part of the claimants, named by the Governments of England and France, or by their Agents duly authorized.

The Judge of Finance of the Republic shall preside over the said Commission, but without a deliberative vote.

III.

The presentation of the claims shall be made before the Mixed Commission, and the proceedings for their justification shall be executed by the Judge of Finance, in the presence of the arbiters.

IV.

The legal documents being concluded, they shall be submitted to the sentence of the Mixed Commission, who shall decide without appeal.

V.

The decision shall be given by majority of votes, and in case the votes be equally divided, a fifth person shall decide, who shall be drawn by lot from a list of eight persons, four Oriental citizens, and four Englishmen and Frenchmen, named beforehand, in the same way as the arbitrators.

VI.

The claims shall be presented in the term of ninety days for persons residing in the territory of the Republic, and of a hundred and eighty days for those who may be abroad, counting from the day on which the Mixed Commission shall publicly announce their installation. This term ended, no claim shall be admitted, the right of claiming being annulled.

VII.

The amount of the indemnities which the Mixed Commission shall have admitted as proved, shall be acknowledged by the Government of the Republic as National Debt, the extinction of which shall be settled by a special Convention.

In witness whereof the above-mentioned Gentlemen agreed to conclude the present Act, in three identical copies, which they signed and sealed accordingly in Monte Video the twenty-third day of June, one thousand eight hundred and fifty-seven.

(Signed)

(L.S.) JOAQUIN REQUENA.

(L.S.) EDW. THORNTON,
Chargé d'Affaires of Her Britannic
Majesty.

(L.S.) M. MAILLEFER,
Le Chargé d'Affaires de Sa Majesté
l'Empereur des Français.

Notice is hereby given, for the information of all persons concerned, that the Mixed Commission appointed in pursuance of the foregoing Agreement, was installed at Monte Video on the 23rd of June, 1858 ; and that, consequently, claims of persons residing within the territory of the Republic will be admitted up to the 21st of September next, and claims of persons beyond that territory up to the 20th of December next.

Foreign-Office, August 14, 1858.

India Board, *August* 17, 1858.

THE following papers have been received at the East India House :—

No. 1.

Brigadier Wheler, Commanding Saugor District, to the Adjutant-General of the Army.

Head-Quarters, Saugor,
Sir, *April* 18, 1858.

I HAVE the honor to forward a letter from Major Hampton, commanding 31st Native Infantry, dated Marowra, 16th instant, transmitting a report from Captain Finch, of an attack made by him on some Bundela rebels at Patna in the hills near Mooltan.

Just at the time these rebels were known to have collected two guns, and the head-quarters 3rd Irregular Cavalry (which had been sent to aid in the taking of   ) were ordered to return to Saugor to Major Hampton, he took the opportunity to attack the rebels at Putna, which is a mile off the road.

The service seems to have been satisfactorily carried out.

I have, &c.
F. WHELER, Brigadier,
Commanding Saugor District.

No. 2.

Major Hampton to Major Lamb, Assistant Adjutant-General, Saugor District.

Camp, Murowra, April 16, 1858

SIR, No. 68.

IN continuation of my letter, No. 62, of the 14th instant, I have the honor to forward the report of Captain Finch, 31st Regiment Native Infantry, detailing the particulars of the attack on the position held by rebels at the village of Putna, for the information of Brigadier Wheler, commanding the Saugor District.

2. In submitting this report to the Brigadier, I shall feel obliged by your bringing to his favorable notice the satisfactory manner in which Captain Finch and the detachment under his command have performed the service in which they have been employed.

I have, &c.
W. P. HAMPTON, Major,
Commanding 31st Regiment N.I.

No. 3.

Captain Finch, Commanding Detachment, to Major Hampton, Camp Brigadier.

SIR, Camp Bugnas, April 15, 1858.

AGREEABLY to instructions, I marched at 10 o'clock A.M. yesterday to Putna with detachment as per margin,* and arrived there at about 7 o'clock A.M., and found that, instead of Putna being a loop-holed house, it was a strong fort on the extreme end of a precipitous hill of about half a mile in length. I found both hill and fort strongly occupied by five or six hundred matchlock men, and as I had no battering-guns,

* 2 6-pounder guns, 4 European sergeants of artillery, 150 sepoys 31st Regiment N.I., 18 sepoys Bhopul Force, 22 sowars 3rd Irregular Cavalry.

I did not expect I should have been able to take the fort. I consequently determined to crown the heights, and drive the enemy into the fort and jungle.

I opened fire with round shot and shrapnel into large bodies of rebels on both fort and hill for upwards of an hour and a half, and in the meantime had sent off two parties of about 60 sepoys in each to crown the height and take the enemy in flank and rear, and it gives me the greatest pleasure to state that the behaviour of these men, led by Lieutenant Fellowes and Jemadar Ramdun Puttuck, is beyond all praise.

The enemy, finding themselves commanded and out-flanked, and likely to be cut off, retreated as we advanced, and evacuated the fort, leaving behind them quantities of baggage and provisions.

I am happy to say that we had not a single casualty, and that the enemy suffered severely, but I can make no correct estimate of their loss in consequence of the dense jungle into which they carried their killed and wounded.

I marched with the detachment to Mundunpore the same evening (having marched during the day upwards of 30 miles), and made the guns over to Captain Mayne to escort to Saugor as per orders.

I have, &c.

H. FINCH, Captain,
Commanding Detachment.

No. 4.

GENERAL ORDERS BY THE PRESIDENT OF THE COUNCIL OF INDIA IN COUNCIL.

Fort William, June 4, 1858.

No. 867 of 1858.

Captain L. Barrow, late Commanding Volunteer Cavalry, having brought to notice that the name of Captain W. J. Hicks, 22nd Native Infantry, was inadvertently omitted in his letter, No. 7, dated 15th December, 1857, published in the Extraordinary Gazette of the 30th December, 1857*, the Honorable the President of the Council of India in Council desires to rectify that omission, and directs that the name of that Officer be added to the list of names published in the margin of Captain Barrow's letter above referred to. Order books to be corrected accordingly.

F. D. ATKINSON, Major, Officiating Secretary to the Government of India, in the Military Department.

Crown-Office, August 13, 1858.

MEMBER returned to serve in the present
PARLIAMENT.

County of Devon.

Southern Division.

Samuel Trehawke Kekewich, of Peamore, in the county of Devon, Esq., in the room of Sir John Buller Yarde Buller, Bart., who has accepted the office of Steward of Her Majesty's Manor of Hempholme.

(1243.)

Board of Trade, Whitehall,
August 14, 1858.

The Right Honourable the Lords of the Committee of Privy Council for Trade and Plantations have received, through the Secretary of State for Foreign Affairs, a copy of a Despatch from Her Majesty's Acting Consul at Saint Vincent, Cape de Verde Islands, reporting that by a recent order of the Finance Committee of those Islands, foreign currency will bear the following values :

* G. G. O. No. 1666, 30th December, 1857.

GOLD.		Milreis.	Reis.
Doubloons ...	Spanish, Peruvian, Chilian, Bolivian, Mexican, Buenos Ayres, Equator, and Central America, and New Granada	14	600
Half Doubloons ...	Ditto ...	7	300
Quarter Doubloons ...	Ditto ...	3	650
Eagles of 10 dollars ...	United States of America...	9	200
Half Eagles ...	Ditto	4	600
Peças ...	Brazilian ...	8	000
Half Peças ...	Ditto ...	4	000
Coins of R 4$000 ...	Ditto ...	4	500
Sovereigns ...	English ...	4	500
Half Sovereigns ...	Ditto ...	2	250
SILVER.			
Dollars ...	Spanish (pillar dollars and others), Chilian, Peruvian, Bolivian, United States, America, Mexican, Brazilian, Buenos Ayres, and Columbian	...	920
Five Franc Pieces ...	French ...	...	860

(1244.)

Board of Trade, Whitehall,
August 14, 1858.

The Right Honourable the Lords of the Committee of Privy Council for Trade and Plantations have received, through the Secretary of State for Foreign Affairs, a copy of a Despatch from Her Majesty's Consul-General at Leipzig, reporting that the duties upon the importation into the States of the German Customs Union, of the undermentioned kinds of Sugar, are renewed, without alteration, from the 1st September next :

Loaf, Candy, Lump, Raw, and Powdered Sugar, and Raw Sugar for refining :

also, that the duty upon the importation of Molasses has been fixed at three dollars (9s.) per centum.

(1258)

Board of Trade, Whitehall,
August 17, 1858.

THE Right Honourable the Lords of the Committee of Privy Council for Trade and Plantations have received, through the Secretary of State for Foreign Affairs, a copy of a Despatch from Her Majesty's Consul in Rhodes, reporting that vessels arriving at that place from Tripoli will be required to undergo the same quarantine as in cases of plague.

(1265.)

Board of Trade, Whitehall,
August 17, 1858.

THE Right Honourable the Lords of the Committee of Privy Council for Trade and Plantations have received a Despatch from Her Majesty's Consul at Cagliari, stating that the following Quarantine Regulations will be enforced on vessels arriving in the Sardinian States from the coasts of the regencies of Tripoli and Tunis, from Malta,

Algeria, Morocco, Candia, Salonica, and the Syrian Coasts of the Ottoman Empire.

1. All vessels arriving from the territory of the regency of Tripoli, on the coast of Barbary, whatever may be the nature of the bill of health which accompanies them, are to be subjected to fifteen days' quarantine, to commence from the discharge of the susceptible goods they have on board into a Lazaretto of the Sardinian States, where they are to be disinfected and purified.

The above mentioned arrivals where aggravating circumstances of sickness or death having occurred on their passage, to a quarantine extended beyond the fifteen days, according to the results of the interrogatory.

2. All vessels arriving from the regency of Tunis, Egypt, and Syria, without the occurrence of aggravating circumstances on the passage, to five days' quarantine after discharging the susceptible goods on board into a lazaretto of the State.

With aggravating circumstances the quarantine is not to be of less than fifteen days' duration, or more according to the results of the interrogatory.

3 Vessels arriving from Malta, whether they have or have not touched at any port on their way without taking pratique, to be subjected to five days' quarantine, after discharging their susceptible goods into a lazaretto in the States. With aggravating circumstances on the passage, such vessels to be subjected to a quarantine of rigour of fifteen days, which may be extended beyond that period, according to the results of the interrogatory.

Such vessels as have been admitted to pratique at intermediate ports to be subjected to particular measures on their arrival, more or less rigorous according to circumstances.

4. All vessels arriving in the Sardinian States from Algeria, Morocco, Candia, Salonica, and the Asiatic Coasts of the Ottoman Empire, are subjected to medical visits, to rigorous sanitary measures, it being reserved to decide upon each arrival as to the greater or less time to expire previous to being admitted to free pratique.

(1274)

Board of Trade, Whitehall,
August 17, 1858.

The Right Honourable the Lords of the Committee of Privy Council for Trade and Plantations have received, through the Secretary of State for Foreign Affairs, a copy of a Despatch from Her Majesty's Acting Consul at Carthagena, reporting that that place ceased to be a Free Port on the 9th instant.

(1275)

Board of Trade, Whitehall,
August 17, 1858.

The Right Honourable the Lords of the Committee of Privy Council for Trade and Plantations have received, through the Secretary of State for the Colonies, a copy of a Despatch from the Lord High Commissioner of the Ionian Islands, stating that he has placed the Island of Corfu in free pratique with the Ionian Islands, and that the Governments of Greece and Naples have placed those Islands in free pratique with their respective dominions.

(1283.)

Board of Trade, Whitehall,
August 17, 1858.

THE Right Honourable the Lords of the Committee of Privy Council for Trade and Plantations have received a Despatch from Her Majesty's

Consul-General in Cuba, stating that a Notification had been issued by the Captain-General of Cuba, that, on and after the 1st of August (instant), the Port of Guantanamo, in that island, would be open to foreign commerce.

Admiralty, 14th August, 1858.

Her Majesty having been pleased, by Her Order in Council, of the 31st July, 1858, to approve of Rear-Admiral Sir Henry John Leeke, C.B., K.H., being transferred in his proper seniority from the Reserved to the Active List of Flag Officers of Her Majesty's Fleet, the name of Sir Henry John Leeke, C.B., K.H., has this day been placed on the list of Rear-Admirals of the Red Squadron of Her Majesty's Fleet, with seniority of 15th April, 1854, accordingly.

Commissions signed by the Lord Lieutenant of the County of Somerset.

West Somerset Regiment of Yeomanry Cavalry.

Henry Acland Fownes Luttrell, Esq., to be Major. vice Browne, resigned. Dated 7th August, 1858.

Lieutenant Stucley Lucas to be Captain, vice Carew, resigned. Dated August 7th, 1858.

Richard Axford, Gent., to be Assistant-Surgeon, vice Sewell, appointed Cornet. Dated August 7th, 1858.

Commission signed by the Lord Lieutenant of the County of Southampton.

Hampshire Regiment of Militia.

James Nicol, Esq., Adjutant, to serve with the rank of Captain, from the 8th May, 1857. Dated 12th August, 1858.

Commission signed by the Lord Lieutenant of the County of Suffolk.

West Suffolk Regiment of Militia.

Lieutenant William Julius Marshall, Gent., to be Captain, vice Ross, promoted. Dated 7th August, 1858.

TREASURY WARRANT.

WHEREAS by an Act of Parliament passed in the fourth year of the reign of Her present Majesty, intituled "An Act for the regulation of the duties of postage," power is given to the Commissioners of Her Majesty's Treasury from time to time, by Warrant under their hands, to alter and fix any of the rates of British postage or inland postage payable by law on the transmission by the post of foreign or colonial letters or newspapers, or of any other printed papers, and to subject the same to rates of postage according to the weight thereof, and a scale of weight to be contained in such Warrant, and from time to time by Warrant as aforesaid, to alter or repeal any such altered rates, and make and establish any new or other rates in lieu thereof, and from time to time by Warrant as aforesaid, to appoint at what time the rates which may be payable are to be paid.

And whereas by another Act of Parliament, passed in the eleventh year of the reign of Her present Majesty, intituled "An Act for giving further facilities for the transmission of letters by post, and for the regulating the duties of postage thereon, and for other purposes relating to the Post Office," further powers are given to the Commissioners of Her Majesty's Treasury, and power is also given to the Postmaster-General (amongst other things) to collect and receive the foreign and

colonial postage charged or chargeable on any
letters sent by the post, and also with the consent
of the Commissioners of Her Majesty's Treasury,
to require the postage, British, colonial, or foreign,
of any letters sent by the post to be prepaid, either
in money or in stamps, as he might think fit, on
the same being put into the Post Office; and also
with such consent, to abolish or restrict the prepayment in money of postage on letters sent by
the post, either altogether or on certain letters, and
to require the prepayment thereof to be in stamps;
and also to refuse to receive or send by the post
any letters tendered contrary to any regulations
thereby made; and power is also given to the
Postmaster-General and any officer of the Post Office
to detain any letters which should be posted or
sent by the post contrary to the regulations therein
mentioned, and to open such letters, and either to
return them to the senders thereof or to forward
them to the places of their destination, charged in
either case with such rates of postage as the Postmaster-General, with the consent of the Commissioners of Her Majesty's Treasury, should from
time to time direct.

And whereas the Commissioners of Her Majesty's Treasury have by divers Warrants under
their hands fixed, made, and established certain
rates of British postage payable on the transmission by the post of certain colonial letters therein
respectively mentioned.

And whereas the Commissioners of Her Majesty's Treasury, by a certain other Warrant under
their hands, bearing date the 15th day of January,
1858, did make regulations for the prepayment of
the several rates of postage payable on letters
posted in the United Kingdom, addressed to any
of the colonies therein mentioned, and on letters
posted in any of such colonies addressed to the
United Kingdom.

And whereas it is expedient to extend the provisions of the said last-mentioned Warrant to letters posted in the United Kingdom addressed to the East Indies, and to letters posted in the East Indies addressed to the United Kingdom.

Now we, the Commissioners of Her Majesty's Treasury, in exercise of the powers reserved to us in and by the said hereinbefore recited Acts, or either of them, and of all other powers enabling us in this behalf, do by this present Warrant under the hands of two of us the said Commissioners, by the authority of the Statute in that case made and provided, order and direct as follows; that is to say:

1. On every letter posted in the United Kingdom, addressed to the East Indies, and on every letter posted in the East Indies addressed to the United Kingdom, the postage thereof shall be paid at the time of the same being posted.

2. If any letter shall be posted in the United Kingdom, addressed to the East Indies, without any postage having been paid thereon, or having thereon or affixed thereto a postage stamp or stamps, the value of which shall be less in amount than the single rate of postage to which such letter, if not exceeding half an ounce in weight, would be liable under the regulations in force relating thereto, every such letter shall be detained and opened, and shall be either returned or given up to the sender thereof.

3. If any letter shall be posted in the United Kingdom, addressed to the East Indies, having thereon or affixed thereto a postage stamp or stamps, the value of which shall be less in amount than the rate of postage to which such letter would be liable under or by virtue of the regulations in force relating thereto, but equal in amount to the single rate of postage chargeable on any such letter, if not exceeding half an ounce in weight, every

such letter shall be forwarded charged with the amount of the difference between the value of such stamp or stamps so being thereon or affixed thereto and the postage to which it would have been liable if the postage had been paid when posted, together, with a further and additional rate of postage of sixpence; and if any letter shall be posted in the East Indies addressed to the United Kingdom and the postage paid thereon shall be less in amount than the rate of postage to which such packet, would be liable under and by virtue of the regulations in force relating thereto, but equal in amount to the single rate of postage chargeable on any such letter if not exceeding half an ounce in weight, every such last-mentioned letter shall be forwarded charged with the amount of the difference between the postage paid thereon and the postage to which it would have been liable if the postage had been paid when posted together with the further and additional rate of postage of sixpence.

4. The term "East Indies" used in this Warrant shall be construed to mean every port or place in Asia within the limits of the Charter of the East India Company (China, Ceylon, the Mauritius, Java, Borneo, and Australia excepted); and the several other terms and expressions used in this Warrant shall be construed to have the like meaning in all respects as they would have had if inserted in the said Act passed in the fourth year of the reign of Her present Majesty.

5. The Commissioners for the time being of Her Majesty's Treasury may by Warrant under their hands duly made at any time hereafter alter, repeal, or revoke any of the orders, directions, or regulations hereby made, and may make and establish any new or other orders, directions, or regulations in lieu thereof.

6. This Warrant shall come into operation on the first day of September, 1858.

> Whitehall, Treasury Chambers, the thirteenth day of August, 1858.
>
> > *Henry Whitmore,*
> > *Thomas Edward Taylor.*

FROM THE

LONDON GAZETTE of AUGUST 20, 1858.

War-Office, August 18, 1858.

THE Queen has been graciously pleased to give orders for the appointment of Captain Adolphus Slade, R.N., C.B., Vice-Admiral in the Ottoman Navy, to be an Honorary Member of the Military Division of the Second Class, or Knights Commanders, of the Most Honourable Order of the Bath.

Foreign-Office, August 18, 1858.

The Queen has been pleased to approve of Don Enrique de Vedia as Consul at Liverpool for Her Royal Highness the Duchess Regent of Parma.

(1269.)

> *Board of Trade, Whitehall,*
> > *August* 19, 1858.

The Right Honourable the Lords of the Committee of Privy Council for Trade and Plantations have received, through the Secretary of State for Foreign Affairs, a copy of a Despatch from Her Majesty's Consul at Lagos, reporting that he has concluded an agreement with the King and principal Chiefs of Abeokuta, and the Presidents of the Trading Corporations of that town, by which the monopoly hitherto enjoyed by the latter, of the trade of Lagos, Abeokuta, and the towns on the coast, has been abandoned.

(1288.)

Board of Trade, Whitehall,
August 19, 1858.

The Right Honourable the Lords of the Committee of Privy Council for Trade and Plantations have received, through the Secretary of State for Foreign Affairs, a copy of a Despatch from Her Majesty's Consul at Stockholm, reporting that by a recent Swedish Order, all hides, hoofs, and other portions of cattle not certified to be imported from countries other than those in the Gulf of Finland and the Baltic Sea, between Hango and Lubec, will be required to be kept free from contact with live animals, and susceptible articles of a similar nature, also they will be required to be separately warehoused and purified with lime or otherwise before delivery.

(1290.)

Board of Trade, Whitehall,
August 20, 1858.

The Right Honourable the Lords of the Committee of Privy Council for Trade and Plantations have received through the Secretary of State for Foreign Affairs, a copy of a Despatch from Her Majesty's Minister at Lisbon, enclosing the following regulations respecting vessels coming from ports in the Regency of Tripoli and Lower Egypt.

1. The port of Bengazi is considered infected with "Oriental Pest," and all the other ports of the Regency of Tripoli and of Lower Egypt.

. 2. All arrivals from the ports *infected* with Pest will be subjected to a rigorous quarantine of twelve days, and those from ports *suspected* of the same disease, to a quarantine of observation of eight days.

3. The *day* for quarantine is 24 hours complete, and will be counted from the hour of the vessel's arrival in port.

4. The said arrivals will only be admitted in such ports as contain an accredited lazaretto.

———————

(1291.)

Board of Trade, Whitehall,
August 20, 1858.

The Right Honourable the Lords of the Committee of Privy Council for Trade and Plantations have received, through the Secretary of State for Foreign Affairs, a copy of a Despatch from Her Majesty's Minister at Lisbon, reporting that the Portuguese Board of Health have notified that the port of Buenos Ayres is considered clean, and the port of New Orleans infected with yellow fever.

———————

(1293.)

Board of Trade, Whitehall,
August 20, 1858.

The Right Honourable the Lords of the Committee of Privy Council for Trade and Plantations have received, through the Secretary of State for Foreign Affairs, a copy of a Despatch from Her Majesty's Consul at Costa Rica, reporting that provisions of all descriptions may be imported into that place, free of duty, for a period of two years from the 9th of June last.

(1294.)

Board of Trade, Whitehall,
August 19, 1858.

The Right Honourable the Lords of the Committee of Privy Council for Trade and Plantations have received, through the Secretary of State for Foreign Affairs, a copy of a Despatch from Her Majesty's Acting Consul at Panama, inclosing a copy of a law recently passed by the Congress of New Granada, and containing an article by which the ports of the islands of the Confederation, both on the Pacific and Atlantic sides, are closed to foreign trade, the port of San Andreas, in the island of that name being excepted from the above regulation.

Commission signed by the Lord Lieutenant of the
County of Lancaster.

1st Regiment of Duke of Lancaster's Own Militia.

Louis Robert James Versturme, Esq., late a Captain in Her Majesty's 27th Regiment of Foot, to be Captain. Dated 6th August, 1858.

TREASURY WARRANT.

WHEREAS by an Act of Parliament, passed in the fourth year of the reign of Her present Majesty, intituled " An Act for the regulation of the duties of postage," power is given to the Commissioners of Her Majesty's Treasury from time to time, by Warrant under their hands, to alter and fix any of the rates of British postage or inland postage payable by law on the transmission by the post of foreign or colonial letters or newspapers, or of any other printed papers, and to subject the same to rates of postage, according to the weight thereof and a scale of weight to be contained in such Warrant, and fron time to time, by Warrant as aforesaid, to alter or repeal any such altered rates, and make and establish any new or other rates in lieu thereof, and from time to time, by Warrant as aforesaid, to appoint at what time the rates which may be payable are to be paid.

And whereas by another Act of Parliament, passed in the eleventh year of the reign of Her present Majesty, intituled "An Act for giving further facilities for the transmission of letters by post, and for the regulating the duties of postage thereon, and for other purposes relating to the Post Office," further powers are given to the Commissioners of Her Majesty's Treasury, and power is also given to the Postmaster-General (amongst other things) to collect and receive the foreign and colonial postage charged or chargeable on any letters sent by the post, and also with the consent of the Commissioners of Her Majesty's Treasury, to require the postage, British, colonial, or foreign, of any letters sent by the post to be prepaid, either in money or in stamps, as he might think fit, on the same being put into the Post Office, and also with such consent to abolish or restrict the prepayment in money of postage on letters sent by the post, either altogether or on certain letters, and to require the prepayment thereof to be in stamps, and also to refuse to receive or send by the post any letters tendered contrary to any regulations thereby made, and power is also given to the Postmaster-General, and any officer of the Post Office to detain any letters, which should be posted, or sent by the post, contrary to the regulations therein mentioned, and to open such letters, and either to return them to the senders thereof, or to forward them to the places of their destination, charged in either case with such rates of postage as the Postmaster-General, with the consent of the Commissioners of Her Majesty's Treasury should, from time to time, direct.

And whereas the Commissioners of Her Majesty's Treasury have, by divers Warrants under their hands, fixed, made, and established, certain rates of British postage, payable on the transmission by the post of certain colonial letters therein respectively mentioned.

And whereas the Commissioners cf Her Majesty's Treasury, by a certain other Warrant under their hands, bearing date the 15th day of January, 1858, did make regulations for the prepayment of the several rates of postage payable on letters posted in the United Kingdom, addressed to any of the colonies therein mentioned, and on letters posted in any of such colonies addressed to the United Kingdom.

And whereas it is expedient to extend the provisions of the said last-mentioned Warrant to letters posted in the United Kingdom, addressed to Barbadoes, Trinidad, and Saint Helena, and to letters posted in such colonies addressed to the United Kingdom.

Now we, the Commissioners of Her Majesty's Treasury, in exercise of the powers reserved to us in and by the said hereinbefore recited Acts, or either of them, and of all other powers enabling us in this behalf, do by this present Warrant, under the hands of two of us the said Commissioners, by the authority of the Statute in that case made and provided, order and direct as follows ; that is to say :

1. On every letter posted in the United Kingdom, addressed to Barbadoes, Trinidad, and Saint Helena, and on every letter posted in Barbadoes, Trinidad, and Saint Helena, addressed to the

United Kingdom, the postage thereof shall be paid at the time of the same being posted.

2. If any letter shall be posted in the United Kingdom, addressed to Barbadoes, Trinidad, or Saint Helena, without any postage having been paid thereon, or having thereon, or affixed thereto, a postage stamp or stamps, the value of which shall be less in amount than the single rate of postage to which such letter, if not exceeding half an ounce in weight, would be liable, under the regulations in force relating thereto, every such letter shall be detained and opened, and shall be either returned, or given up to the sender thereof.

3. If any letter shall be posted in the United Kingdom, addressed to Barbadoes, Trinidad, or Saint Helena, having thereon, or affixed thereto, a postage stamp or stamps the value of which shall be less in amount than the rate of postage to which such letter would be liable, under or by virtue of the regulations in force relating thereto; but equal in amount to the single rate of postage chargeable on any such letter, if not exceeding half an ounce in weight, every such letter shall be forwarded, charged with the amount of the difference between the value of such stamp or stamps so being thereon, or affixed thereto, and the postage to which it would have been liable if the postage had been paid when posted, together with a further and additional rate of postage of sixpence. And if any letter shall be posted in Barbadoes, Trinidad, or Saint Helena, addressed to the United Kingdom, and the postage paid thereon shall be less in amount than the rate of postage to which such packet would be liable, under and by virtue of the regulations in force relating thereto, but equal in amount to the single rate of postage chargeable on any such letter if not exceeding half an ounce in weight, every such last-mentioned

letter shall be forwarded charged with the amount of the difference between the postage paid thereon and the postage to which it would have been liable if the postage had been paid when posted, together with the further and additional rate of postage of sixpence.

4. The several terms and expressions used in this Warrant shall be construed to have the like meaning in all respects as they would have had if inserted in the said Act passed in the fourth year of the reign of Her present Majesty.

5. The Commissioners for the time being of Her Majesty's Treasury may, by Warrant under their hands duly made, at any time hereafter alter, repeal, or revoke any of the orders, directions, or regulations hereby made, and may make and establish any new or other orders, directions, or regulations in lieu thereof.

6. This Warrant shall come into operation on the first day of October, 1858.

Whitehall, Treasury Chambers, the six teenth day of August, 1858.

Henry Whitmore.
H. G. Lennox.

FROM THE

LONDON GAZETTE of AUGUST 24, 1858.

Admiralty, August 23, 1858.

DESPATCHES, of which the following are copies, have been received by the Lords Commissioners of the Admiralty from Captain Sotheby, C.B., of Her Majesty's ship Pearl, commanding a Naval Brigade in India.

SIR, *Camp, Bustee, June 22, 1858.*

I HAVE the honour to acquaint you, for the information of the Lords Commissioners of the Admiralty, that a portion of the Naval Brigade,* under charge of Lieutenant Turnour, and the Marines under Lieutenant Pym, R.M., were engaged in a very creditable affair on the 9th instant, in driving the enemy out of Amorha, where one party was posted in the village, and the other in a long belt of bamboo jungle, and a large house at the entrance; and I beg to recommend both these active Officers, then suffering from sickness, to their Lordships' notice, with the accompanying report.

Mr. Foot, Midshipman, was also present with the guns.

I have, &c.,
E. S. SOTHEBY, Captain, R.N.,
Commanding Pearl's Naval Brigade.
The Secretary of the Admiralty.

SIR *Camp Bustee, June 11, 1858.*

I HAVE the honour to report for your information, that while employed on detached service, between the dates of 24th May and 11th June, the force, as per margin,† under command of Major Cox, of the 13th Light Infantry, the following engagement took place on the 9th instant. Information having reached us that the rebels, in force under Mahomet Hussein, were at Amorha, a village five or six miles off, arrangements were made for attacking them. Accordingly having divided our force into two columns, the largest

* Fifty-three Naval Brigade, two 12-pr. howitzers, one 24-pr. rocket.

† 200 13th Light Infantry; 2 Troops Madras Cavalry; 2 Troops Bengal Cavalry; 2 guns (Pearl's), 20 seamen, 1 rocket, 8 seamen, 3 officers, 20 marines; 20 Seikhs.

commanded by Major Cox and the other, to which I was attached, by Major Richardson, of the Bengal Yeomanry Cavalry, we left the camp at 2 A. M. and marched along the road leading through the village. When within a mile of the place, we received a heavy fire from their skirmishers; these were immediately attacked and driven in by the Marines, under Lieutenant Pym, while the guns threw shell and shot at their main body, which, after quarter of an hour's firing, retreated into the Banee's house and jungle. There they were met and driven off by the other column under Major Cox; the enemy then retreated towards Belwah, and were pursued four miles by the cavalry, who succeeded in cutting up a considerable number. The force having halted to refresh the men, then returned to Hurreah.

I have, &c.

N. E. B. TURNOUR, Lieut. H.M.S. Pearl,
In command of Naval Detachment.

To Captain E. Sotheby, R.N.,
Pearl's Naval Brigade, Bustee.

SIR, *Camp Bustee, June 25, 1858.*

I HAVE the honour to acquaint you, for the information of my Lords Commissioners of the Admiralty, that the force, as per margin,* left Captangunge on the 18th instant, at 3 A.M., to attack a body of rebels from 3,500 to 4,000 strong, including 900 sepoys, under Mahomed Hussein, posted in, and entrenched about, the village of Hurreah, eight miles in our front.

* Pearl's Naval Brigade 111; 13th Light Infantry 145; Seikhs 50; Bengal Yeomanry Cavalry 130; 6th Madras Cavalry 100; one 24-pr. rocket, and two 12-pr. howitzers horsed. Naval Brigade.

One 9-pr. gun; one 24-pr. howitzer bullock guns, Bengal Artillery.

On approaching within 1¼ miles of the bridge at 6·30, we discovered the enemy's skirmishers thrown across the river, screened in some thick bamboo jungle, villages, topes, and a considerable number in ambush in a dry nullah. Our skirmishers, consisting of 70 of the Pearl's Naval Brigade, and a Company of Her Majesty's 13th Light Infantry, supported by our 2-horsed 12-pounder howitzers, immediately advanced on our left, and by their quick fire drove them in ; following the enemy over the river (which they forded above their waists), they turned their right flank; our guns, after shelling and clearing out the village, galloped over the bridge, rejoined the skirmishers, and broke their centre, drove the rebels from tope to tope whenever they attempted to stand, and pursued them for about four miles. From the quick and well-directed fire, and apparent confusion in the enemy's ranks, they must have suffered very severely from our shells and rifles.

The remainder of the force had in the mean time been engaged on the right, where the rebels obstinately held the jungle, but were finally driven out and over the river. The heat was most intense, and as the troops had been under arms for nearly seven hours, at 10 o'clock we halted and all firing ceased.

I am thankful to say we had only six wounded, whereas the enemy is reported to have lost 200, with all their baggage and a quantity of ammunition.

Mahomet Hussein has since fled to the jungle, and his force is reported to be entirely dispersed, the Sepoys having crossed the Gogra to Fyzabad.

Lieutenant Turnour, assisted by Mr. T. M. Maquay, Acting Mate, was in charge of the guns, and Mr. A. W. Ingles, Acting Mate, with Mr.

Herbert H. Edwards, Midshipman, commanded the skirmishers, and Serjeant-Major Argent the Marines, to all of whom I am much indebted for their zealous conduct, as also the rest of the men, whose conduct at all times has been most exemplary, especially Alexander Wilson, Coxswain of the launch ; and I must beg you will have the goodness to draw the attention of their lordships that this is the 10th time the Pearl's Naval Brigade has been in action in India during nine months.

I have, &c.,
E. S. SOTHEBY, Captain, R.N.,
Commanding Pearl's Naval Brigade.

To the Secretary of the Admiralty.

Foreign-Office, June 26, 1858,

The Queen has been graciously pleased to appoint Captain Sir Henry Huntley, Knt., R.N., to be Her Majesty's Consul at Loanda.

War-Office, 23rd August, 1858,

The Queen has been graciously pleased to signify Her intention to confer the Decoration of the Victoria Cross on the undermentioned Officer and Non-Commissioned Officers, who have been recommended to Her Majesty for that Decoration on account of Acts of Bravery performed by them in India, as recorded against their several names ; viz. :

66th (Goorkha) Bengal Native Infantry.

Lieutenant John Adam Tytler. – On the attacking parties approaching the enemy's position under a heavy fire of round shot, grape, and musketry, on the occasion of the Action at Choorpoorah, on

1858.   9 L

the 10th February last, Lieutenant Tytler dashed on horseback ahead of all, and alone, up to the enemy's guns, where he remained engaged hand to hand, until they were carried by us; and where he was shot through the left arm, had a spear wound in his chest, and a ball through the right sleeve of his coat. (Letter from Captain C. C. G. Ross, Commanding 66th (Goorkha) Regiment, to Captain Brownlow, Major of Brigade, Kemaon Field Force.) — Date of Act of Bravery, 10th February, 1858.

37th Bengal Native Infantry.

Serjeant - Major M. Rosamond. — This Non-Commissioned Officer volunteered to accompany Lieutenant-Colonel Spottiswoode, Commanding the 37th Regiment of Bengal Native Infantry, to the right of the Lines, in order to set them on fire, with the view of driving out the Sepoys, on the occasion of the outbreak at Benares, on the evening of the 4th of June, 1857; and also volunteered, with Serjeant-Major Gill, of the Loodiana Regiment, to bring off Captain Brown, Pension Paymaster, his wife and infant, and also some others, from a detached Bungalow, into the Barracks. His conduct was highly meritorious, and he has been since promoted.—Date of Act of Bravery, 4th June, 1857.

Loodiana Regiment.

Serjeant-Major Peter Gill.—This Non-Commissioned Officer also conducted himself with gallantry at Benares, on the night of the 4th of June, 1857. He volunteered, with Serjeant-Major Rosamond, of the 37th Regiment of Bengal Native Infantry, to bring in Captain Brown, Pension Paymaster, and his family, from a detached Bungalow to the Barracks, as above recorded, and saved the life of the Quartermaster-Sergeant of the 25th Regiment of Bengal Native Infantry, in the early part of the evening, by cutting off the head of the Sepoy who had just bayonetted him. Serjeant-Major Gill states, that on the same night he faced a Guard of 27 men, with only a Serjeant's sword; and it is also represented that he twice saved the life of Major Barrett, 27th Regiment of Bengal Native Infantry, when attacked by Sepoys of his own Regiment.—Date of Act of Bravery, 4th June, 1857.

42nd Regiment.

Colour-Serjeant William Gardner.—For his conspicuous and gallant conduct on the morning of the 5th of May last, in having saved the life of Lieutenant-Colonel Cameron, his Commanding Officer, who during the Action at Bareilly on that day, had been knocked from his horse, when three Fanatics rushed upon him. Colour-Serjeant Gardner ran out, and in a moment bayonetted two of them, and was in the act of attacking the third, when he was shot down by another soldier of the Regiment. (Letter from Captain Macpherson, 42nd Regiment, to Lieutenant-Colonel Cameron, Commanding that Regiment.)—Date of Act of Bravery, 5th May, 1858.

War-Office, Pall-Mall,
24th August, 1858.

44th Regiment of Foot.

Major-General Thomas Reed, C.B., to be Colonel, vice Lieutenant-General Sir Frederick Ashworth, deceased. Dated 2nd August, 1858.

War-Office, Pall-Mall,
24th August, 1858.

4th Regiment of Dragoon Guards, Cornet John Bosworth Smith Marriott, from the 1st Dragoons, to be Cornet, vice Du Cane, appointed to the 2nd Dragoons. Dated 24th August, 1858.

1st Dragoons, John Bosworth Smith Marriott, Gent., to be Cornet, by purchase, vice Crozier, who retires. Dated 24th August, 1858.

3rd Light Dragoons, Lieutenant William Morrison Bell to be Captain, by purchase, vice Dettmar, who retires. Dated 24th August, 1858.

Cornet Henry Henzell Unett to be Lieutenant, by purchase, vice Bell. Dated 24th August, 1858.

Troop Serjeant-Major Henry Higgins to be Cornet, without purchase, vice Nettles, appointed Quartermaster. Dated 24th August, 1858.

Edward Arthur Gore, Gent., to be Cornet, by purchase, vice Unett. Dated 25th August, 1858.

4th Light Dragoons, Cornet Arthur Watson De Capell Brooke to be Lieutenant, without purchase. Dated 24th August, 1858.

Conwy Grenville Hercules Rowley, Gent., to be Cornet, without purchase. Dated 24th August, 1858.

6th Dragoons, Cornet Robert John Garnett to be Lieutenant, by purchase, vice Wetherall, promoted. Dated 24th August, 1858.

Paymaster Maurice Hartland Mahon, from the 13th Foot, to be Paymaster, vice Marshall, who retires upon half-pay as Quartermaster. Dated 24th August, 1858.

10*th Light Dragoons*, Captain the Honourable Augustus H. A. Anson, from the 84th Foot, to be Captain, without purchase, vice Cowell, promoted in the 6th Dragoons. Dated 24th August, 1858.

13*th Light Dragoons*, Lieutenant Thomas Price Gratrex to be Captain, by purchase, vice Smith, who retires. Dated 24th August, 1858.

14*th Light Dragoons*, Edward Williams Pritchard, Gent., to be Cornet, without purchase, in succession to Lieutenant Leith, promoted in 6th Dragoons. Dated 24th August, 1858.

Royal Artillery, Colonel Poole Vallancey England to be Major-General, vice Dundas, deceased. Dated 9th August, 1858.

Brevet-Colonel John William Ormsby to be Colonel, vice England, promoted. Dated 9th August, 1858.

Brevet-Major Henry L. Gardiner to be Lieutenant-Colonel, vice Ormsby. Dated 9th August, 1858.

Supernumerary Captain and Brevet-Major Henry Rogers to be Captain, vice Gardiner. Dated 9th August, 1858.

Royal Engineers, Brevet-Colonel Benjamin Spicer Stehelin to be Colonel, vice Ward, promoted Major-General. Dated 12th August, 1858.

Brevet-Major John Summerfield Hawkins to be Lieutenant-Colonel, vice Stehelin. Dated 12th August, 1858.

Second Captain Gwavas Speedwell Tilly to be Captain, vice Hawkins. Dated 12th August, 1858.

Lieutenant William Crossman to be Second Captain, vice Tilly. Dated 12th August, 1858.

1st Regiment of Foot.

To be Ensigns, by purchase.

William Stewart Thorburn, Gent., vice Shanly, promoted. Dated 24th August, 1858.

Nathaniel Stevenson, Gent., vice Logan, promoted. Dated 25th August, 1858.

4th Foot, Richard Uniacke Bayly, Gent., to be Ensign, by purchase, vice Chinn, promoted. Dated 24th August, 1858.

5th Foot, Ensign Francis Sterling Brown Holt to be Lieutenant, by purchase, vice Kingsley, who retires. Dated 24th August, 1858.

8th Foot, Captain James Johnston to be Major, without purchase, vice Wheatstone, retired upon full-pay. Dated 24th August, 1858.

Captain Charles Henry Martin, from half-pay Unattached, to be Captain, vice Johnston, promoted. Dated 24th August, 1858.

9th Foot, Ensign Spencer Lynne to be Lieutenant, by purchase, vice Agnew, who retires. Dated 24th August, 1858.

Nathaniel Forte, Gent., to be Ensign, by purchase, vice Lynne, promoted. Dated 24th August, 1858.

11th Foot, Lieutenant Richard Hotham to be Captain, by purchase, vice Travers, who retires. Dated 24th August, 1858.

Ensign and Adjutant Alexander Miller Arthur to be Lieutenant, by purchase, vice Hotham. Dated 24th August, 1858,

Ensign Frederick James S. Whiteside to be Instructor of Musketry. Dated 8th June, 1858.

13th Foot, Matthew John Bell, Gent., to be

Ensign, by purchase, vice Bridges, who retires. Dated 24th August, 1858.

15th Foot, Lieutenant R. T. P. Cuthbert to be Captain, by purchase, vice Christie, who retires. Dated 24th August, 1858.

Ensign and Adjutant John Macdonald to have the rank of Lieutenant. Dated 24th August, 1858.

Ensign John Burdon to be Lieutenant, by purchase, vice Cuthbert. Dated 24th August, 1858.

16th Foot, Lieutenant H. Stewart Cochrane, from the 86th Foot, to be Captain, without purchase. Dated 24th August, 1858.

23rd Foot, Lieutenant Luke O'Connor to be Captain, without purchase. Dated 24th August, 1858.

29th Foot, Elsden Peter Henry Everard, Gent., to be Ensign, by purchase, vice Bomford, promoted. Dated 24th August, 1858.

35th Foot, Ensign Frederick B. Gipps, from the 15th Foot, to be Ensign. Dated 24th August, 1858.

William Poste, Gent., to be Ensign, without purchase. Dated 24th August, 1858.

40th Foot, Ensign Thomas Ormsby Johnston to be Adjutant, vice Lieutenant Richards, promoted. Dated 24th August, 1858.

Staff-Surgeon of the Second Class Henry Frederic Robertson to be Surgeon, vice Adolphus Collings, M.D., placed upon half-pay. Dated 24th August, 1858.

43rd Foot, Lieutenant William Stewart Richardson to be Captain, by purchase, vice Elliott, who retires. Dated 24th August, 1858.

Ensign Henry Charles Talbot to be Lieutenant,

by purchase, vice Richardson. Dated 24th August, 1858.

44*th Foot*, Lieutenant George Ingham to be Adjutant, vice Ensign Francis O'Neill, who resigns the Adjutancy only. Dated 18th June, 1858.

45*th Foot*, Lieutenant Henry Lucas to be Captain, by purchase, vice Coxon, appointed to a Depôt Battalion. Dated 24th August, 1858.

Ensign Henry B. Hayward to be Lieutenant, by purchase, vice Lucas. Dated 24th August, 1858.

46*th Foot*, Lieutenant Richard Coote to be Captain, by purchase, vice Lluellyn, who retires. Dated 24th August, 1858.

49*th Foot*, Thomas Cowper Hincks, Gent., to be Ensign, by purchase, vice Christian, who retires. Dated 24th August, 1858.

52*nd Foot*, Assistant-Surgeon Alexander Thorburn, McGowan, M.D., from the Staff, to be Assistant-Surgeon, vice Ingham, promoted on the Staff. Dated 24th August, 1858.

54*th Foot*, Ensign Lancelot K. Edwards to be Lieutenant, without purchase, vice Houston, promoted in 4th Foot. Dated 30th March, 1858.

Lieutenant Joseph Willam Hughes to be Adjutant, vice Houston, promoted in the 4th Foot. Dated 21st June, 1858.

58*th Foot*, Thomas Egerton Jones, Gent., to be Ensign, by purchase. Dated 24th August, 1858.

60*th Foot*, Charles Pierson Cramer, Gent.. to be Ensign, by purchase, vice King, promoted. Dated 24th August, 1858.

61*st Foot*, John Cockle, Gent., to be Ensign, by purchase. Dated 24th August, 1858.

71*st Foot*, Henry Brooke Wilson, Gent., to be Ensign, by purchase, vice Harris, promoted. Dated 24th August, 1858.

74*th Foot*, Edward Bradby, Gent., to be Ensign, by purchase, in succession to Lieutenant W. J. Bell, promoted in 9th Foot. Dated 24th August, 1858.

77*th Foot*, Major and Brevet-Lieutenant-Colonel T. J. Deverell to be Lieutenant-Colonel, without purchase. Dated 24th August, 1858.

Captain Henry Kent to be Major, without purchase, vice Deverell. Dated 24th August, 1858.

Lieutenant T. P. Harvey to be Captain, without purchase, vice Kent. Dated 24th August, 1858.

Ensign H. S. Weigall to be Lieutenant, without purchase, vice Harvey. Dated 24th August, 1858.

Assistant-Surgeon Thomas Norton Hoysted, from the Staff, to be Assistant-Surgeon. Dated 24th August, 1858.

79*th Foot*, Lieutenant Douglas Wimberley to be Adjutant, vice James Young, who resigns the Adjutancy only. Dated 18th June, 1858.

84*th Foot*, Lieutenant John Penton to be Captain, without purchase, vice the Honourable A. H. A. Anson, appointed to 10th Light Dragoons. Dated 24th August, 1858.

Ensign Henry Shawe Jones to be Lieutenant, without purchase, vice Penton. Dated 24th August, 1858.

89*th Foot*, Lieutenant Richard Edward Beck to be Captain, without purchase, vice Morris, deceased. Dated 10th August, 1858.

Ensign Alexander Dixon Grier to be Lieutenant, without purchase, vice Beck. Dated 10th August, 1858

3rd *West India Regiment*, Lieutenant William John Russwurm to be Captain, without purchase, vice Palmer, retired on full-pay. Dated 13th August, 1858.

Ensign Ebenezer Rogers to be Lieutenant, without purchase, vice Russwurm. Dated 13th August, 1858.

Ceylon Rifle Regiment. The Christian names of Ensign Daniell are *Frederick* Francis.

DEPOT BATTALIONS.

Major Dawson Cornelius Greene, from half-pay Unattached, to be Major. Dated 24th August, 1858.

Major Cam Sykes, from half-pay Unattached, to be Major. Dated 24th August, 1858.

Captain and Adjutant Frederick B. Tritton to be Major, by purchase, vice Wing, who retires. Dated 24th August, 1858.

Captain George Stacpole Coxon, from the 45th Foot, to be Adjutant, vice Tritton, promoted. Dated 24th August, 1858.

HOSPITAL STAFF.

Assistant-Surgeon William James Ingham, from the 52nd Foot, to be Staff-Surgeon of the 2nd Class, vice Mandeville, appointed to the 7th Foot. Dated 24th August, 1858.

Assistant Staff-Surgeon Francis Holton, M. B., to be Staff-Surgeon of the Second Class, vice Robertson, appointed to the 40th Foot. Dated 24th August, 1858.

To be Assistant-Surgeons to the Forces.

Joseph Edward O'Loughlin, Gent., vice Gulland, appointed to the Royal Artillery. Dated 5th August, 1858.

James Henry Jeffcoat, Gent., vice O'Leary, appointed to the Royal Artillery. Dated 5th August, 1858.

Frederic Murray Chalk, Gent., vice Woodfull, appointed to the Royal Artillery. Dated 5th August, 1858.

Francis Roberts Hogg, M.D., vice Hardinge, appointed to the Royal Artillery. Dated 5th August, 1858.

John Mackenzie, M.D., vice Daltera, appointed to the Royal Artillery. Dated 5th August, 1858.

John Walsh, Gent., vice Catton, appointed to the 35th Foot. Dated 5th August, 1858.

Wallace Lindsay, Gent., vice Tate, appointed to the Royal Artillery. Dated 5th August, 1858.

John Davidge, Gent., vice Prescott, appointed to the Royal Artillery. Dated 5th August, 1858.

John Kinahan, Gent., vice Hoffman, promoted on the Staff. Dated 5th August, 1858.

William Carberry, Gent., vice Marshall, appointed to the 2nd Foot. Dated 5th August, 1858.

James George Stewart Mathison, Gent., vice Boutflower, appointed to the Cape Mounted Rifles. Dated 5th August, 1858.

Samuel Halliday Macartney, Gent., vice Colahan, appointed to the 24th Foot. Dated 5th August, 1858.

Samuel Argent, Gent., vice Gibson, appointed to the 12th Light Dragoons. Dated 5th August, 1858.

Samuel Archer, Gent, vice Reid, appointed to the 54th Foot. Dated 5th August, 1858.

James Wilson, M.B., vice Wall, appointed to the 64th Foot. Dated 5th August, 1858.

Walter Crisp, Gent., vice Madden, appointed to the 69th Foot. Dated 5th August, 1858.

To be Acting Assistant-Surgeons.

William Castledine Tucker, M.D., vice Young,

who resigns his appointment. Dated 14th August, 1858.

Charles Dycer, M.D., vice Bowden, who resigns his appointment. Dated 24th August, 1858.

BREVET.

Brevet-Colonel John Gordon, on Retired Full-pay List of the Royal Artillery, to be Major-General, he having been senior on the Effective List, at the date of his retirement, to Colonel England. Dated 9th August, 1858.

Major-General Griffith George Lewis, C.B., of the Royal Engineers, to be Lieutenant-General, vice Sir Charles F. Smith, K.C.B., deceased. Dated 12th August, 1858.

Colonel William Cuthbert Ward, of the Royal Engineers, to be Major-General, vice Lewis. Dated 12th August, 1858.

Brevet-Colonel George Elliot, retired full-pay of the Royal Marines, to have the honorary rank of Major-General. Dated 24th August, 1858.

Brevet-Colonel William Bookey Langford, retired full-pay of the Royal Marines, to have the honorary rank of Major-General. Dated 24th August, 1858.

Captain Walter Welsford Lillicrap, retired full-pay of the Royal Marines, to have the honorary rank of Major. Dated 24th August, 1858.

Lieutenant-Colonel Arthur John Reynell — Pack, half-pay, 7th Foot (Assistant Quartermaster-General, Ireland), having completed three years' actual service in the rank of Lieutenant-Colonel, to be promoted to be Colonel in the Army under the Royal Warrant of 6th October, 1854. Dated 16th August, 1858.

Admiralty, S.W., 11th August, 1858.

Corps of Royal Marines.

Gentlemen Cadets Francis Edmund Begbie and George Harrie Thom Colwell to be Second Lieutenants.

Commission signed by the Queen.

Shropshire Militia.

Kenneth Robert Murchison, late Lieutenant 58th Regiment, to be Adjutant, vice Pardey, retired, Dated 7th August, 1858.

Commission signed by the Queen.

Royal Aberdeenshire Highlanders.

Edward Alleyne Dawes, Esq., late Captain 97th Foot, to be Adjutant, from 15th April, 1858.

Commission signed by the Lord Lieutenant of the West Riding of the County of York, and of the City and County of the City of York.

George Skirrow Beecroft, Esq., M.P., to be Deputy Lieutenant. Dated 4th August, 1858.

Commission signed by the Lord Lieutenant of the County of Aberdeen.

Royal Aberdeenshire Highlanders.

Adjutant Edward Alleyne Dawes, late Captain, 97th Foot, to serve with the rank of Captain.

Commission signed by the Lord Lieutenant of the County of Denbigh.

Royal Rifle Regiment of Denbighshire Militia.

Hugh Robert Hughes, Gent., to be Ensign. Dated 16th August, 1858.

Commissions signed by the Lord Lieutenant of the County of Stafford.

3rd Regiment of King's Own Staffordshire Militia.

Lieutenant Francis William Bott to be Captain, vice Bagot, resigned. Dated 12th August, 1858.

Ensign the Honourable Alexander Victor Paget, commonly called Lord Alexander Victor Paget, to be Lieutenant, vice Bott, promoted. Dated 17th August, 1858.

Alexander William Radford, Gent., to be Ensign. Dated 14th August, 1858.

Commissions signed by the Lord Lieutenant of the County of Warwick.

Warwickshire Militia.

2nd Regiment.

Lieutenant George William Plevins to be Captain, vice Reader, promoted. Dated 13th August, 1858.

Ensign James Taylor Hyatt to be Lieutenant vice Plevins, promoted. Dated 13th August, 1858.

Henry Robert Grimes, Gent., to be Ensign, vice Percival Richards, promoted. Dated 13th August, 1858.

William Taylor Miller, Gent., to be Ensign, vice Malcolm Ronalds, promoted. Dated 13th August, 1858.

Commission signed by the Vice Lieutenant of the County of Lincoln.

Royal North Lincoln Militia.

James Ward, Esq., to be Captain, vice the Lord Worsley, resigned. Dated 14th August, 1858.

Henry Metcalfe, Gent., to be Lieutenant, vice William Longstaffe, promoted. Dated 14th August, 1858.

Royal South Lincoln Militia.

William Grinfield Ostler, Gent., to be Lieutenant, vice Edward Jackson Fitzsimmons, promoted. Dated 13th August, 1858.

Commission signed by the Lord Lieutenant of the County of Flint.

Royal Flintshire Militia.

Lieutenant William Fry Foster to be Captain, vice Philips, retired.

Commissions signed by the Lord Lieutenant of the County of Wilts.

Royal Wiltshire Militia.

Thomas Holman, Gent., to be Ensign, vice Bevan, resigned. Dated 4th August, 1858.

Edward Thomas Burr, Gent., to be Ensign, vice Blennerhassett, promoted. Dated 13th August, 1858.

Commission signed by the Lord Lieutenant of the County of Nottingham.

Royal Sherwood Foresters or Nottinghamshire Regiment of Militia.

William Blucher Dolton, Esq., M.D., to be Assistant-Surgeon, vice Nettlefold, resigned. Dated 12th August, 1858.

FROM THE

LONDON GAZETTE of AUGUST 27, 1858.

Foreign-Office, August 25, 1858.

THE Queen has been pleased to approve of Mr. James B. Hayne as Consul at Turk's Island for the United States of America.

The Queen has also been pleased to approve of Mr. J. M. Vanderspar to be Consul at Point de Galle for His Majesty the King of the Belgians.

Foreign-Office, August 27, 1858.

The Queen has been pleased to approve of Mr. Benjamin Isaac as Consul in London for the Republic of New Granada.

The Queen has also been pleased to approve of Mr. George William Jones as Vice-Consul at Newport (Monmouthshire), for His Royal Highness the Grand Duke of Mecklenburgh Schwerin.

Whitehall, August 27, 1858.

The Queen has been pleased to present the Reverend Sidney Henry Widdrington, M.A., to the vicarage of Saint Michael, in the city of Coventry, and diocese of Worcester, void by the resignation of the Reverend John Brownrigge Collisson.

The Queen has also been pleased to present the Reverend John Alexander MacRae to the church and parish of North Uist, in the presbytery of

North Uist, void by the death of the Reverend Finlay MacRae.

Whitehall, August 13, 1858.

The Queen has been pleased to grant unto George-Lindsay Anthony, of Westbourne-terrace, in the parish of Paddington, in the county of Middlesex, Esquire, late a Cornet in the 2nd Light Dragoons, British German Legion, Her royal licence and authority that he and his issue may, in compliance with a direction contained in the last will and testament of Sir John Wilson, late of Westbourne-terrace aforesaid, Knight Commander of the Most Honourable Order of the Bath, General of Her Majesty's Forces and Colonel of the 11th (North Devon) Regiment of Foot, deceased, take and henceforth use the surname of Wilson, in addition to, and after that of, Anthony, and that he and they may bear the arms of Wilson ; such arms being first duly exemplified according to the laws of arms, and recorded in the Herald's office, otherwise the said royal licence and permission to be void and of none effect :

And to command that the said royal concession and declaration be registered in Her Majesty's College of Arms.

(1330.)

Board of Trade, Whitehall,
August 26, 1858.

The Right Honourable the Lords of the Committee of Privy Council for Trade and Plantations have received, through the Secretary of State for

1858.   9 M

Foreign Affairs, a copy of a Despatch from Her Majesty's Consul at Kertch, reporting that all foreign vessels entering that port will be subjected to a quarantine of six days, unless provided with a clean bill of health by the Russian Consular Officer at the port of departure, as well as a similar bill from the Russian Consular Officer at each port at which vessels may have touched during their voyage.

(1244.)

Board of Trade, Whitehall,
August 27, 1858.

The concluding paragraph of the notice which appeared in the Gazette of the 17th instant, respecting the alteration of duties on the importation of Sugar into the States of the German Customs Union, should read " 3 dollars (9*s.*) per centner," instead of " 3 dollars (9*s.*) per centum."

Commission signed by the Queen.

Dumfries, Roxburgh, and Selkirk Regiment of Militia.

Michael Moriarty, Gent., to be Quartermaster from 23rd July, 1858. Dated 29th July, 1858.

Commission signed by the Lord Lieutenant of the County of Cambridge.

Cambridgeshire Militia.

Joshua Brenton, Gent., to be Ensign, vice Edward Muriel Martin, promoted. Dated 16th August, 1858.

Commission signed by the Lord Lieutenant of the County of Warwick.

Warwickshire Militia.

2nd Regiment.

Ensign George Goodwin Norris to be Lieutenant, vice Cragg, resigned. Dated 16th August, 1858.

Commission signed by the Vice Lieutenant of the County of Lincoln.

Royal North Lincoln Militia.

Ensign Robert Waller to be Lieutenant, vice James Ward, promoted. Dated 17th August, 1858.

Commission signed by the Lord Lieutenant of the County of Pembroke.

Royal Pembrokeshire Artillery Regiment of Militia.

Henry Lyons Walcott, Gent., to be First Lieutenant, vice John Brogdon Labarte, resigned. Dated 11th August, 1858.

War-Office, Pall-Mall, S.W., August 27, 1858.

From the Nominal Lists of Casualties in the Army serving in India, received by the Secretary of State for War.

In Action near Jugdespore, June 4, 1858.

Captain Peter John Macdonald, 2nd Battalion, Military Train, severely wounded.

Serjeant Patrick McEmaney, 2nd Battalion, Military Train, severely wounded.

In Action at Nawabgunge, June 13, 1858.

Captain C. C. Fraser, 7th Hussars, severely wounded.

Lieutenant R. Topham, 7th Hussars, slightly wounded.

Cornet and Adjutant J. Mould, 7th Hussars, slightly wounded.

Lieutenant Hugh Lawton, 2nd Battalion Rifle Brigade, severely wounded.

FROM THE

LONDON GAZETTE of AUGUST 31, 1858.

India Board, August 30, 1858.

THE following papers have been received at the East India House :—

No. 1.

GENERAL ORDERS BY THE GOVERNOR GENERAL OF INDIA.

Military Department, Allahabad, June 5, 1858.

No. 198 of 1858.

THE Right Honorable the Governor-General is pleased to direct the publication of the following despatch from the Deputy Adjutant-General of the Army, No. 373 A, dated 31st May, 1858, forwarding one from Major-General Sir H. Rose, K.C.B., enclosing a report from Major R. H. Gall, of Her Majesty's 14th Light Dragoons, of his capture of the Fort of Loharee, on the 2nd ultimo.

The Governor-General desires to express his entire approval of the gallant conduct of the officers

and men engaged under Major Gall in this affair,
and his cordial appreciation of the merits of Major
Gall himself, both in the present affair, and on all
occasions in which he has been employed.

No. 2.

*The Deputy Adjutant-General of the Army, to the
Secretary to the Government of India.*

*Head-Quarters, Camp, Futtehgurh,
May, 31, 1858.*

SIR, No. 373 A.

BY desire of the Commander-in-Chief, I have
the honor to transmit, for the information of the
Right Honorable the Governor-General, a copy of a
despatch* from Major-General Sir H. Rose, K.C.B.,
dated 17th instant, enclosing a report from Major
R. H. Gall, of Her Majesty's 14th Light Dragoons,
of his capture of the Fort of Loharee, on the 2nd
idem.

2. His Excellency heartily concurs in the praise
bestowed by the Major-General upon Major Gall,
and the officers and men engaged in this gallant
affair.

I have, &c.,
H. W. NORMAN, Major,
Deputy Adjutant-General of the Army.

No. 3.

No. 213 of 1858.

THE Right Honorable the Governor-General is
pleased to direct the publication of the following
despatch from the Assistant Adjutant-General of
the Army, dated the 3rd instant, forwarding one
from Brigadier-General Walpole, C.B., command-

* London Gazette, July 28, 1858, p. 3543.

ing in Rohilcund and Kumaon, submitting reports
from Captain Browne, 2nd Punjaub Cavalry,
giving an account of the operations which he found
it necessary to undertake against a band of rebels,
under Nizam Allie Khan, in the district of
Bareilly.

R. J. H. BIRCH, Colonel,
Secretary Government of India, Military Department, with the Governor-General.

No. 4.

*Brigadier-General R. Walpole, C.B., Command-
ing in Rohilcund and Kumaon, to the Chief of
the Staff, Bareilly, May 29th, 1858.*

SIR,   No. 25.

WITH reference to my despatch of the 24th
instant, acquainting you, for the information of
His Excellency the Commander-in-Chief, that I
had directed a force of cavalry and infantry to
proceed to Buheree, for the purpose of bringing to
Bareilly, the Rohilcund Horse under Captain
Crossman, I have the honor herewith to transmit
copies of reports from Captain Browne, 2nd Punjaub Cavalry, who commanded the detachment,
giving an account of the operations which he found
it necessary to undertake against the band of rebels
in that district.

2. Captain Browne returned to Bareilly this
morning, and reports that the band above alluded
to have dispersed, and that their leader, Nizam
Allie Khan, has taken refuge in the Rampoor
territory.

3. The day after Captain Browne left Bareilly,
Mr. Alexander received a communication from
Captain Crossman, stating that he had changed
his mind, and intended to march *viâ* Moradabad,
and not by Buheree ; upon the receipt of which I

sent to Captain Browne, to acquaint him with
this change in Captain Crossman's intentions, and
directed him to return to Bareilly by the route
already furnished to him, without waiting at
Buheree.

4. I feel sure that the march of this force has
had a beneficial effect, and that confidence in the
Government has been in a great measure restored
in those parts.

5. I have every reason to be well satisfied with
Captain Browne, who appears to have acted with
judgment and discretion.

I have, &c.,
R. WALPOLE, Brigadier-General,
Commanding in Rohilcund and Kumaon.

P.S.—Since writing the above, Mr Alexander
has heard that Nizam Allie Khan has fled with a
few followers to the eastward, in the direction of
the Terai.

No. 5.

*Captain S. Browne, Commanding 2nd Punjaub
Cavalry and Detachment, to the Assistant Adjutant-General, Rohilcund Division, Bareilly.*

Camp, Kuthura, May 25, 1858.

Sir,

I HAVE the honor to submit the following
report, for the information of the Brigadier-General
Commanding.

This morning, on arrival at Durunnia, where I
had proposed halting for the day, information was
brought to Mr. Low, Civil Service, who accompanied the detachment, that Nizam Allie Khan
had attacked and burnt the Thannah at Rickah,

killing and wounding some of the Burkundauzes
and Ryots, and that he was at that moment encamped at Mohunpoor, some 4 miles distant, on
the direct road to Buheree, with some 300 cavalry
and infantry.

I at once decided on moving off and attacking
him, after giving the men and horses an hour's rest
after the march of 18 miles.

I accordingly marched again at 9-30 a.m. On
arrival at Kuthura, I left the baggage there under
a small guard. From this place Mohunpoor was
visible, and the villagers stated that a portion of
Nizam Allie Khan's Force had moved to destroy
another village, and that the remainder was still
at Mohunpoor. Mohunpoor contained the usual
native Gurrie, a small loop-holed enclosure, with a
ditch some 7 feet wide and 5 deep, recently
repaired.

I made my arrangements accordingly, directing
Lieutenant Hoggan to advance in skirmishing
order with one company, the remainder in support,
and behind them again one troop of cavalry, under
Lieutenant Warde, who was instructed, when our
infantry gained a footing in the village, to move
off to the right, and take up a position there;
The remainder of the cavalry I kept on the left,
where I considered their services would be principally required.

The infantry at once entered the village, meeting
with some opposition, but gradually driving the
enemy before them, and setting fire to the village.
It now became evident that but very few of Nizam
Allie Khan's force had remained at Mohunpoor,
and only a few sowars and some 30 infantry were
in the village, the remainder having, some two
hours previously, gone off on a looting expedition
to another village some 3 miles distant.

Being well aware, that the Gurrie would be impracticable to the small force under my command, and without guns, I had desired Lieutenant Hoggan to avoid it ; simply clearing the village, and driving out those who could not shelter themselves in the Gurrie was my object, hoping that the cavalry might have an opportunity of cutting them up. In this I was disappointed, owing to the instant flight of the few cavalry, who were in the village, the desperation of a few of their infantry who fought well, and the remainder taking refuge in the Gurrie. When the infantry came up to the gurrie, ascertaining that there was not the most remote chance of effecting an entrance, I ordered them to move off to the left, and form up on the cavalry.

Just at this moment, Nizam Allie Khan appeared in the field, with the remainder of his force, some 100 or so cavalry, and about 150 infantry, and moved down with the intention of attacking me. I formed up the cavalry to receive them. He advanced and took possession of a village on a rising mound. Some few sowars showed themselves through the village in my front, and pulled up there. A little delay and a flight of dust on the Rickah and Sheregurh directions, showed me that Nizam Allie Khan thought "discretion the better part of valour." A pursuit was hopeless ; the more so, considering the distance we had already come, the length of time men and horses had been accoutred, and the heat and fatigue all had undergone.

I regret to add, that Lieutenant Hoggan, Commanding the Detachment of 17th Punjaub Infantry, was severely wounded. He has my thanks for his endeavours on the occasion of the attack on the village.

To Mr. Low, Civil Service, I am indebted for the excellent information he procured for me, and his making himself useful in the field.

I have omitted to mention above, that the loss of the enemy in the village was about 20 killed.
I enclose a casualty return.

I have, &c.,

SAM. BROWNE, Captain,
Commanding 2nd Punjaub Cavalry and
Detachment.

No. 6.

Casualty Return of the Detachment under Command of Captain S. Browne, in the Action at Mohunpoor, on the 25th May, 1858.

Camp Kuthura, May 25, 1858.

2nd Punjaub Cavalry—1 private and 1 horse, wounded.

17th Punjaub Infantry—2 sepoys, 1 kahar, killed; 1 European officer, 3 native officers, 1 non-commissioned officer, 2 privates, wounded.

Total—2 sepoys, 1 kahar, killed; 1 European officer, 3 native officers, 1 non-commissioned officer, 3 privates, 1 horse, wounded.

Lieutenant Hoggan, 17th Punjaub Infantry, severely wounded.

SAM. BROWNE.

No. 7.

Captain S. Browne, Commanding 2nd Punjaub Cavalry and Detachment, to the Assistant Adjutant-General, Rohilcund Division, Bareilly.

Camp, Buheree, May 26, 1858,
9 A.M.

SIR,

IN continuation of my report of yesterday, I have the honour to state, that information was conveyed to me of the evacuation of the little Gurrie in the village I attacked yesterday, and in

it this morning were found 10 dead of the enemy.
The Gurrie was made over to the charge of one
Mohun Sing, a friendly Zemindar, who occupied
it with some of his followers.

Nizam Allie Khan yesterday made for Jawum,
about a mile on the Bareilly side of Buheree; he
remained there a short time only, and then continued his flight towards Sheregurh. Reports received this morning state, that he has now left
Sheregurh, and that a number of his followers
have deserted him, some 50 horsemen only remaining with him. I trust this may prove correct.
The informants are the Hindoo population of the
villages round about, who have been much op-
pressed by Nizam Allie Khan's plundering parties.

Captain Crossman, with the Rohilcund Horse,
has not arrived, nor can I obtain any information
whatever regarding him. I have to-day again
addressed that officer by cossid, informing him of
my arrival here, and that I will halt here to-
morrow in the hope of his arrival; but, that,
should he not arrive, or I obtain no authentic
intelligence regarding him, it was not my intention
to delay here any longer, but to move towards Bareilly by the route furnished me.

As my object in coming out here was to escort
Captain Crossman's party into Bareilly, I trust
that the Brigadier-General will approve of the
course I intend adopting in halting one day, with
the view of carrying out the purpose for which I
was detached; but at the same time I do not consider I should be justified in remaining out here
any longer.

I have, &c.,

SAM. BROWNE, Captain,

Commanding Detachment.

P.S.—4 P.M.—Since the above was written, Mr.
Low informs me, that Nizam Allie Khan is at

Budouree raising followers. Budouree is some five miles distant, nearly north-west of this.

No. 8.

Captain S. Browne, Commanding 2nd Punjaub Cavalry and Detachment, to the Assistant Adjutant General, Rohilcund Division, Bareilly.

SIR,   *Camp, Sheregurh, May* 27, 1858.

I HAVE the honour to acknowledge the receipt of your letter No. 19, dated 26th instant.

Yesterday, some few hours after the despatch of my letter, I had ascertained from a cossid, and from some travellers from Huldwanee, that Captain Crossman had that morning marched for Kala Doongee, which being the first march by the Moradabad road, I determined on not remaining another day at Buheree, and accordingly this morning marched here.

I am glad to be able to state, that the attack on the village of Mohunpoor has had an excellent effect. Nizam Allie Khan's followers have dispersed; the band is broken up ; Nizam Allie Khan himself has fled to the Nawab of Rampore's district.

To-morrow morning I will proceed to Chahee.

I have, &c.,

SAM. BROWNE, Captain,
Commanding Detachment.

No. 9.

GENERAL ORDERS BY THE RIGHT HONORABLE THE GOVERNOR-GENERAL OF INDIA.

Military Department,
Allahabad, June 16, 1858.

No. 217 of 1858.

THE Right Honorable the Governor-General is pleased to direct the publication of the following despatch from the Assistant Adjutant-General of the Army, dated 10th June, 1858, forwarding one from Brigadier-General Sir E. Lugard, K.C.B., Commanding Azimgurh Field Force, reporting the operations of his force, since the 14th ultimo, the date of his last report.

No. 10.

Brigadier-General Sir E. Lugard, K.O.B., Commanding Azimgurh Field Force, to the Chief of the Staff.

SIR,   *Camp, Jugdespore, May* 27, 1858.

I HAVE the honor to report to you, for the information of his Excellency the Commander-in-Chief, the following operations of the force under my command since the 14th instant, the date of my last report.

2. On the 16th, I despatched a party under the command of Major Lightfoot, 84th Foot, to burn the house of Hurkissen Sing and the village of Buradhee, in which it was situated; the village of Uraila, the inhabitants of which had aided the rebels and evinced an inimical spirit, was destroyed at the same time.

3. On the 18th, I moved out against the rebels, who had established themselves at Metahi, where Ummer Sing had a large house, about two miles from Jugdespore. On our approach, the rebels opened fire from the two 12-pounder howitzers they captured from the Arrah party on the 23rd ultimo, and showed in great force; but so soon as the line of infantry advanced, they retired into the jungle, carrying away their guns; upon which I destroyed the house and village, and returned to camp; the loss of the rebels must have been severe, as the fire from the battery guns, under Lieutenants Campbell and Bradford, was very good. My own

casualties were small, as shown by the accompanying return.

4. On the 20th, Mr. Burrows, railway contractor, commenced, at my desire, cutting down the jungle in the vicinity of Jugdespore, so as to obtain a broad clear road through it, in the direction of Arrah, and, fearing that the rebels might creep up and fire upon the workmen, who, if once struck, would no doubt abandon the work altogether, I sent my horse artillery and cavalry, under Lieutenant-Colonel Robertson, Military Train, round to the south-west of Duleeppoor, where the main body of the rebels were established, to endeavour to divert their attention. In a few hours, receiving a report from the Lieutenant-Colonel that the enemy were following him into the open country in great numbers, I hastened from camp with a few companies of the 10th Foot, the battery guns, and some cavalry, direct upon Metahi, in the hope of getting between them and the jungle; in this I partially succeeded and inflicted severe punishment upon them. I regret, however, that Lieutenant Dawson, Military Train, was killed, and Lieutenant Maxwell, Royal Horse Artillery, with Serjeant H. Robinson, Royal Horse Artillery, and Private B. McGuire, 10th Foot, were wounded in this skirmish.

5. From the operation of the 20th instant, it seemed to me that, by a combined movement upon the rebels, I might possibly crush them, and capture their 2 guns, which they prized greatly, and invariably withdrew so rapidly into the jungle when we advanced, that there was little chance of taking them by any direct attack.

6. It was my earnest wish to have had a small force to co-operate with me from the south, but as Colonel Corfield had declared his inability to assist me in any way, I decided upon making a final

assault upon the rebels on the 26th instant with my own force.

7. My plan was to endeavour to draw the enemy out from the jungle, as I did on the 20th, then to make a feeble attack upon them at Metahi, so as to occupy them without actually driving them in, whilst a body of infantry moved down through the thick jungle direct from Jugdespore, and came upon their rear.

8. This, I am happy to say, succeeded almost beyond my expectation, and resulted in the capture of the 2 howitzers, 2 elephants, and the complete dispersion of the rebels.

9. The horse artillery and cavalry under Lieu-nenant-Colonel Riddell, Royal Artillery, left camp as soon as day broke, and moved round to the south-west of Duleeppoor, attracting the attention of the rebels, who evidently expected an attack, and made their arrangements accordingly.

10. Eight companies of the 10th Foot, under the direction of Brigadier Douglas, C.B., were formed in the jungle close to Jugdespore post, pre-pared to move down when I should send the order; and the remainder of the troops available, consisting of two companies 10th Foot, five companies 84th Foot, 100 of Rattray's Sikhs, Punjaub sappers, with 4 battery guns (Cotter's) under Lieu-tenant Campbell, and some cavalry, I moved direct upon Metahi, leaving the camp in charge of a party of the 84th Foot, with some Sikh sowars under Captain Creagh, and the post at Jugdespore with a company of the Madras Rifles, under Captain Bolton.

11. Major Carr, whom I had moved from Arrah to the east side of the jungle, I reinforced with another company of the 84th Foot, and 50 Sikh cavalry, and directed to patrol along, and watch the Eastern limit of the jungle.

12. The movement upon Metahi apparently

convinced the rebels that the attack was to be the same as on the 20th, and they lined the same banks, and took up the same position as before. I now directed Brigadier Douglas' column to move down, and so soon as I ascertained they had penetrated the jungle as far as where I was, without the enemy perceiving it, I advanced my skirmishers, and the rebels most fortunately fired their howitzers, and thus showed us their exact position.

13. A cheer and a rapid rush settled the affair : the guns were secured by the Grenadier Company of the 84th Foot, whilst the 10th pursued the rebels through the jungle south, down to Chitowrah, and through the dense jungle to the west of that place, scattering them, and driving them completely out into the open county, at a distance, however, of several miles from where the artillery had been posted. Two elephants were captured, and many rebel sepoys killed in this rapid pursuit, which nothing but the excitement of the chase, and the high spirit and powers of endurance of the soldiers enabled them to carry out. The greater proportion, however, at last dropped, thoroughly exhausted, and it was some hours before they could move to camp, then distant some seven miles.

14. I am happy to say no casualty occurred in my force.

15. I take this opportunity of bringing to the notice of his Excellency, as I promised in a former report, the excellent conduct of the troops under my command, from the 29th March, the date of our quitting Lucknow, and throughout these operations; the work has been most arduous, but the spirit and cheerfulness of the soldiers have never failed. The whole of the troops named in the margin,* with their respective commanding officers,

* 3 guns, E. Troop, Royal Horse Artillery, under Major Michell ; A Company, 3rd Battalion Madras Artillery, with 6 guns, under Major Cotter ; Heavy Ordnance, under

have earned my warmest thanks, and merit his Excellency's approbation.

16. To Brigadier Douglas, C.B., I feel much indebted for the zealous manner in which he has invariably carried out all my instructions. I am also much indebted to Lieutenant-Colonel Riddell, commanding the artillery, for his able and indefatigable assistance, as well as to the several officers commanding the regiments and detachments before named.

17. Of the merits of the divisional and personal staff of this force, I cannot speak too highly, or recommend them in sufficiently strong terms to the notice of his Excellency.

18. Lieutenant-Colonel Longden, Chief of my Staff, Major Sir H. M. Havelock, Bart., Deputy Assistant Adjutant-General, and Captain Wilkinson, Deputy Assistant Quartermaster-General have aided me in every possible manner, with untiring zeal and energy. Lieutenant McNeill, my Aide-de-Camp, with Captain Middleton, extra Aide-de-Camp, (latterly also Deputy Judge Advocate-General to the Force,) deserve my best thanks; they are both very intelligent and active staff officers, and have rendered me much assistance ; the exertions of Captain Stevenson, Brigade-Major,

Captains Thring and Waller ; 2nd Battalion, Military Train, under Lieutenant-Colonel Robertson ; Detachment 6th Madras Cavalry, under Captain Douglas ; 3rd Seikh Cavalry, under Lieutenant Pearse and Lieutenant Jennings, Lieutenant Beadon (now in command) ; 12th Irregular Cavalry, under Sirdar Bahadoor Mahomed Bux ; 10th Foot, under Lieutenant-Colonel Fenwick and Captain Norman ; 34th Foot, under Lieutenant-Colonel Kelly ; 84th Foot, under Major Lightfoot ; Madras Rifles (2 Companies), under Major Carr ; Detachment 4th Company Royal Engineers, under Lieutenant Keith, Royal Engineers ; Punjaub Pioneers, under Lieutenant Fulford, Bengal Engineers ; Detachment of Rattray's Seikhs, under Subadar Nehal Shing.

have been most indefatigable, as have been those of Major Turner, Adjutant, Royal Artillery, and Captain Young, Royal Artillery, Commissary of Ordnance : with the Commissariat Officers, Captain Roberts, Captain Holland and Lieutenant Bates, I have been well satisfied, as also with Captain Creagh, Postmaster, lately in charge of the Military Chest.

19. I beg most especially to recommend to his Excellency's notice, Doctor Gordon, Surgeon of the 10th Foot, and Senior Medical Officer in charge of this force ; his exertions have been untiring ; though at times suffering from sickness, he never quitted his post, but continued his valuable superintendence ; I feel more indebted to him than I can express. To the other Medical Officers of the force also much credit is due.

20. It affords me much pleasure to bring to the notice of his Excellency, Serjeant Edward Connor, 10th Foot, who has performed the duties of Deputy Provost and Deputy Baggage-Master to this Force, with a zeal and untiring energy that could not be surpassed. A more trustworthy, intelligent, and hard-working public servant, or a braver soldier does not exist.

21. I have also to record my best thanks to Mr. Macdonell, Civil Service, who has accompanied my camp in this district as Special Commissioner ; to Mr. Madocks, Civil Service, Collector of Behar ; and to Mr. Charles Kelly, Railway Engineer, for the very valuable assistance they have given me.

I have, &c.
EDWARD LUGARD, Brigadier-General,
Commanding Azimgurh Field Force.

No. 14.

From the Nominal Return of Casualties in the Azimgurh Field Force, under Command of Brigadier-General Sir Edward Lugard, K.C.B., in the Skirmish near the Village of Chowbeypore, on the 20th of May, 1858.

Camp, Jugdespore, May 20, 1858.

Lieutenant Stuart S. M. Maxwell, E Troop Royal Horse Artillery, May 20, 1858, slight gun-shot wound in the right knee.

Serjeant Henry Robinson, E Troop Royal Horse Artillery, May 20, slight gun-shot wound in the back.

Lieutenant William H. Dawson, 2nd Battalion Military Train, May 20, killed.

No. 17.

No. 218 of 1858.

THE Right Honorable the Governor-General is pleased to direct the publication of the following despatch, from the Assistant Adjutant-General of the Army, dated 9th June, 1858, forwarding one from Brigadier-General J. Jones, C.B., commanding Shahjehanpore Field Force, reporting his operations against Mohumdee, from the 24th to 26th May inclusive.

No. 18.

Brigadier-General J. Jones, C.B., Commanding Shahjehanpore Field Force, to the Deputy Adjutant-General of the Army.

Camp, Shajehanpore,

SIR, **June 1, 1858.**

THE Shahjehanpore Field Force crossed the river by the bridge of boats during the night of

9 N 2

the 23rd, and formed in order of battle in front of the village of Loodipore.

At daylight the force advanced, and found the enemy in position at the fort of Burnai.

The following was the order in which the troops advanced :—The heavy guns along the road in the centre ; First brigade on the right, consisting of the 79th Highlanders and 1st Seikhs, supported by Her Majesty's 82nd Regiment ; Captain Hammond's Battery, the Carabiniers, and Captain Lind's Horse being on the right flank ; 2nd Brigade on the left of the heavy guns, composed of the 60th Royal Rifles and 1st Punjaub Rifles, supported by the 64th Regiment ; Lieutenant-Colonel Tombs Troop Horse Artillery, 9th Lancers, and Captain Cureton's Cavalry on the left flank.

The Sappers and Miners were in rear of the heavy guns, and Captain Austen's Battery in support.

The enemy opened their guns in quick succession, and for a few minutes their fire was heavy ; but the effect produced by our 24-pounders was soon seen ; the enemy withdrew his bullock guns at once, continuing the fire with the guns he had horsed. As the line advanced, these also were withdrawn, and the fort was entered without any attempt at a stand.

The force rapidly continued its advance, the right bringing right shoulders forward, the Carabiniers and Captain Hammond's Battery at the trot.

When in pursuit of the enemy, one of the ammunition waggons of Captain Hammond's battery accidentally exploded, when, I regret to say, three men were killed.

I was particularly anxious that the left should push on with still greater rapidity, but the enemy seemed to be equally aware of the necessity of checking us here. He threw masses of cavalry round our flank, and a few of his horsemen were found ready to charge when any opportunity offered

The Mooltanee Regiment of Cavalry were charged by a large body under cover of a tope of trees ; about thirty of them were enabled to get into the rear of the regiment, whilst some galloped up to the front, and discharged their carbines.

Those who had got into the rear of the regiment were cut to pieces, when Captain Cureton dashed at the body in his front, broke, and pursued them to some distance, killing the commandant of cavalry and another officer of rank.

The pursuit was kept up by the infantry for a few miles, when they were obliged to halt, and was continued by the light field guns and cavalry to a considerable distance ; but the overpowering heat of the sun rendered it advisable to place the European portion of the troops under cover as soon as possible.

I encamped six miles beyond the fort of Burnai, which I caused to be blown up, one damaged gun being there taken.

Early on the 25th, I was close to Mohumdee. The enemy's cavalry were seen formed on the road. I ordered up the light guns, 9th Lancers, and Captain Cureton's Cavalry, but a few rounds from Captain Austen's Battery dispersed the party.

The town and fort were found to be evacuated, and they were immediately occupied.

Under the superintendence of that able officer of engineers, Captain Drummond, they were soon destroyed. One damaged gun was taken in the fort, and four were found concealed in a neighbouring garden.

The enemy had commenced his retreat from Mohumdee, about noon on the 24th ; his families and valuables had been carried far into the jungles that skirt the north-eastern portion of Oude.

The cavalry was employed, during the 26th, in clearing the country in the direction of the enemy's retreat, and to the right and left of Mohumdee. One party of Mooltanee Cavalry, under Lieutenant B. Williams, discovered a fort in which was found a large quantity of gunpowder, which was used in blowing it up ; 3 guns were dug up there, and a large number of gun carriages evidently manufactured at Futtygurh. Three other guns were discovered in a village close at hand ; several of the villages round were burnt, and, after completely scouring the country, the force returned to Shahjehanpore, which it reached on the morning of the 29th.

I have the honor to enclose a list of casualties, and a return of the ordnance captured.

The troops behaved admirably ; for two days the heat was excessive, and, notwithstanding every possible precaution, I regret to say that, on the 24th and 25th the loss of European troops by stroke of the sun amounted to twenty-seven.

I am much indebted to Brigadier Hagard, commanding Cavalry Brigade ; Lieutenant-Colonel Tombs, C.B., command Artillery Division ; Brigadier Taylor, C.B., commanding 1st Infantry Brigade ; and Brigadier Coke, C.B., commanding 2nd Infantry Brigade ; also to the several officers commanding regiments and detachments of the force.

My staff as usual afforded me every assistance in carrying out my orders.

I have, &c.
JOHN JONES, Brigadier-General,
Commanding Shahjehanpore Field Force.

No. 19.

Return of Killed and Wounded which took place in the Shahjehanpore Field Force, in Action with the Enemy, during the Operations against Mohumdee, from the 24th to the 26th of May, inclusive.

Camp, Shahjehanpore, May 31, 1858.

Mooltanee Regiment of Cavalry—2 rank and file, killed ; 2 non-commissioned officers, 10 rank and file, 10 horses, wounded ; 1 horse, missing.

Artillery Division—3 rank and file, killed.

Total—3 European rank and file, 2 native rank and file, killed ; 2 native non-commissioned officers, 10 native rank and file, and 10 horses, wounded ; 1 horse, missing.

JOHN JONES, Brigadier-General,
Commanding Shahjehanpore Field Force.

No. 20.

Return of Ordnance Captured by the Shahjehanpore Field Force, under Command of Brigadier-General Jones, C.B., from the 24th to the 27th of May, inclusive.

Camp, Mohumdee, May 28, 1858.

No. 1, 9-pounder brass gun, weight 15 cwt., foreign manufacture.

No. 2, 9-pounder brass gun, weight 10 cwt., foreign manufacture, burst in pieces.

No. 2, 6-pounder brass gun, weight 9 cwt., foreign manufacture, burst in pieces.

No. 1, 5-pounder brass gun, weight 8 cwt., foreign manufacture, quite new.

No. 1, 3-pounder brass gun, weight 4 cwt., foreign manufacture, quite new.

No. 1, 2-pounder brass gun, weight 2 cwt., foreign manufacture, quite new,

No. 4, 1-pounder and under, brass gun, weight 2 qrs., foreign manufacture, quite new.

No. 1, 6-pounder iron gun, weight 10 cwt., foreign manufacture, rifle bore.

No. 2, 1-pounder and under, iron gun, weight 2 qrs., foreign manufacture, rifle bore.

Several component parts of gun carriages, wheels, trail beams, &c., were found buried in the Fort of Kheejooriah, near Mohumdee, also four wall-pieces.

> TODD BROWN, Lieutenant,
> Commissary of Ordnance.

At the Court at *Osborne House, Isle of Wight,* the 31st day of *July*, 1858.

The QUEEN'S Most Excellent Majesty in Council was pleased to approve and ratify the schemes duly prepared (as set forth in this Gazette) by the Ecclesiastical Commissioners for England—

For effecting an exchange of the patronage of the rectory of All Saints, Southampton, in the county of Southampton, and in the diocese of Winchester, for the patronage of the rectory of Bramdean, in the same county and diocese.

For improving the Precincts of the Cathedral Church of Hereford.

Also, representations duly prepared by the said Commissioners as to the assignment of District Chapelries to—

The consecrated church of Saint Matthew, situate at Bayswater, in the parish of Saint James, Paddington, in the county of Middlesex, and in the diocese of London.

The consecrated church of Saint Margaret, situate in Collier-street, in the parish of Yalding, in the county of Kent, and in the diocese of Canterbury.

Also, a scheme duly prepared as aforesaid, for authorizing the sale of certain property formerly belonging to the prebend of Ferring, in the cathedral church of Chichester, and now vested in the said Commissioners.

Also a representation, duly prepared as aforesaid, as to the assignment of a district chapelry to the consecrated church of Saint Stephen, situate at Willington, in the parish of Brancepeth, in the county of Durham, and in the diocese of Durham.

Whitehall, August 30, 1858.

The Queen has been pleased to direct letters patent to be passed under the Great Seal, granting the dignity of a Knight of the United Kingdom of Great Britain and Ireland unto Frederic Hughes, Esq., late a Captain in the 7th Regiment of Madras Light Cavalry.

(1526.)

Board of Trade, Whitehall,
August 30, 1858.

The Right Honourable the Lords of the Committee of Privy Council for Trade and Plantations have received, through the Secretary of State for Foreign Affairs, a copy of a Despatch from Her Majesty's Minister, at Lisbon, reporting that the Board of Health of that capital has issued an Edict, declaring the port of Ferrol to be infected with yellow fever, and that the other ports of the province of Corunna are considered as suspected. Her Majesty's Minister at Lisbon further reports, that another edict of the same Board declares the port of Alexandria to be considered infected with

the plague, and the port of Gibraltar to be suspected.

War-Office, Pall-Mall,
31st August, 1858.

2nd Regiment of Dragoon Guards, Brevet-Major
Cook Synge Hutchinson to be Major, by pur-
chase, vice Keene, who retires. Dated 31st
August, 1858.

Lieutenant George Eden Jarvis to be Captain, by
purchase, vice Hutchinson. Dated 31st August,
1858.

2nd Dragoons, Surgeon Augustus Purefoy Lockwood, from the 8th Hussars, to be Surgeon,
vice Llewelyn who exchanges. Dated 31st
August, 1858.

4th Light Dragoons, Serjeant-Major James William Kelly to be Cornet, without purchase, vice
Brooke promoted. Dated 31st August, 1858.

8th Light Dragoons, Cornet Thomas Richards to
be Lieutenant, without purchase, vice Reilly,
killed in action. Dated 18th June, 1858.

Regimental Serjeant-Major John Pickworth to be
Riding Master. Dated 31st August, 1858.

Surgeon Jenkin Homfray Llewelyn, from the
2nd Dragoons to be Surgeon, vice Lockwood,
who exchanges. Dated 31st August, 1858.

15th Light Dragoons, Lieutenant William Henry
Horne to be Captain by purchase, vice Lord
W. C. M. D. Scott, who retires. Dated 31st
August, 1858.

16th Light Dragoons, Walter P. Bagenal, Gent.,
to be Cornet, without purchase, vice Atkinson,
promoted. Dated 31st August, 1858.

Military Train, Lieutenant Robert M. Hornby,
from the 99th Foot, to be Captain, by purchase,
vice Brevet-Major Wood, who retires. Dated
31st August, 1858.

1st Regiment of Foot. The promotion of Lieutenant-Colonel A. B. Montgomery, C.B., to be Colonel in the Army, as stated in the Gazette of the 28th May, 1858, to be antedated to 18th January, 1858.

7th Foot, Brevet-Major Frederick Ernest Appleyard to be Major, by purchase, vice Gilley, who retires. Dated 31st August, 1858.

Morris James Fawcett, Gent., to be Ensign, by purchase, vice Follett, promoted. Dated 31st August, 1858.

10th Foot, Lieutenant George C. Bartholomew to be Captain, by purchase, vice Milner, who retires. Dated 31st August, 1858.

Ensign P. W. Matthews to be Lieutenant, by purchase, vice Bartholomew. Dated 31st August, 1858.

13th Foot.

To be Captains, without purchase.

Lieutenant Samuel Head, from 24th Foot. Dated 31st August, 1858.

Lieutenant John Peyton, from 87th Foot. Dated 31st August, 1858.

Lieutenant A. C. Bogle, from 78th Foot. Dated 31st August, 1858.

To be Lieutenants, without purchase.

Ensign W. S. Cunninghame. Dated 31st August, 1858.

Ensign George Turville. Dated 31st August, 1858.

Ensign A. G. Wynen. Dated 31st August, 1858.

Ensign E. Bolger. Dated 31st August, 1858.

14th Foot, Ensign Francis Fox Robinson has been superseded, being absent without leave. Dated 31st August, 1858.

15th Foot.

To be Ensigns, by purchase.

Charles Clifton Tabor, Gent., vice Burdon, promoted. Dated 31st August, 1858.

Charles Samuel Chapman, Gent., vice Heaton, promoted. Dated 31st August, 1858.

20th Foot, Lieutenant John Carden to be Captain, by purchase, vice Hewett, who retires. Dated 31st August, 1858.

21st Foot, George Henry Shuttleworth, Esq., to be Paymaster. Dated 31st August, 1858.

22nd Foot. The Commission of Quartermaster George Wohlmann to be antedated to 5th March, 1858.

24th Foot, Lieutenant Charles O'L. L. Prendergast, from the 3rd West India Regiment, to be Lieutenant, vice J. Scott, who exchanges. 31st August, 1853.

30th Foot, Ensign Henry F. Morewood to be Lieutenant, without purchase, vice G. H. Sanders, who retires upon half-pay. Dated 31st August, 1858.

39th Foot, Ensign C. Francis Oldfield to be Lieutenant, by purchase, vice Arbuckle, who retires. Dated 31st August, 1858.

Francis Ernest Kerr, Gent., to be Ensign, by purchase, vice Oldfield. Dated 31st August, 1858.

43rd Foot, Joseph Hogarth, Gent., to be Ensign, by purchase, vice Talbot, promoted. Dated 31st August, 1858.

46th Foot, Major Arthur George Vesey to be Lieutenant-Colonel, without purchase. Dated 31st August, 1858.

Brevet-Major Algernon Robert Garrett to be

Major, without purchase, vice Vesey. Dated 31st August, 1858.

Lieutenant Thomas John Barlow Connell to be Captain, without purchase, vice Garrett. Dated 31st August, 1858.

Ensign Vesey Daly to be Lieutenant, without purchase, vice Connell. Dated 31st August, 1858.

Ensign Allan Joshua Kentish to be Lieutenant, by purchase, vice Coote promoted. Dated 31st August, 1858.

48th *Foot*, Assistant-Surgeon Jean Valleton de Boissiere, from the Staff, to be Assistant-Surgeon, vice Hemphill, appointed to the 66th Foot. Dated 31st August, 1858.

49th *Foot*, Ensign Frederick Platt Blackmore to be Lieutenant, by purchase, vice Maule, who retires. Dated 31st August, 1858.

William John Gillespie, Gent., to be Ensign, by purchase, vice Blackmore. Dated 31st August, 1858.

Lieutenant Robert Hall Spratt to be Instructor of Musketry, vice Chaplin, retired. Dated 17th August, 1858.

54th *Foot*, Ensign M. W. E. Gosset to be Lieutenant, by purchase, vice Edwards, whose promotion by purchase on the 13th July, 1858, has been cancelled. Dated 31st August, 1858.

Ensign Charles Samuel Chapman, from the 15th Foot, to be Ensign, vice Gosset. Dated 31st August, 1858.

60th *Foot*, Edward Digby O'Rorke, Gent., to be Ensign, by purchase, vice Heathcote, promoted. Dated 31st August, 1858.

64th *Foot*, Henry Frederick Scobell, Gent, to be Ensign, by purchase, vice George Thompson, who resigns. Dated 31st August, 1858.

65th *Foot*, Staff-Surgeon of the Second Class

Thomas Esmonde White, M.D., to be Surgeon, vice Marshall, who exchanges. Dated 31st August, 1858.

79*th Foot*, Ensign G. W. Coventry, from the 84th Foot, to be Ensign, vice Simpson, who exchanges. Dated 31st August, 1858.

84*th Foot*, Ensign James M. Thomas Simpson, from the 79th Foot, to be Ensign, vice Coventry, who exchanges. Dated 31st August, 1858.

91*st Foot*, Brevet-Lieutenant-Colonel B. E. M. Gordon to be Lieutenant-Colonel, without purchase. Dated 31st August, 1858.
Brevet-Major Henry J. Savage to be Major, without purchase, vice Gordon. Dated 31st August, 1858.
Lieutenant Alexander C. Bruce to be Captain, without purchase, vice Savage. Dated 31st August, 1858.
Ensign Robert Powell Jones to be Lieutenant, without purchase, vice Bruce. Dated 31st August, 1858.

2*nd West India Regiment*, Ensign A. E. Pierson has been permitted to resign his Commission. Dated 31st August, 1858.

3*rd West India Regiment*, Lieutenant James Bligh Scott, from the 24th Foot, to be Lieutenant, vice Prendergast, who exchanges. Dated 31st August, 1858.

RECRUITING DISTRICT.

Brevet-Colonel David Russell, C.B., from the 84th Foot, to be Inspecting Field Officer, vice Brevet-Colonel Kelly, deceased. Dated 31st August, 1858.

HOSPITAL STAFF.

Staff-Surgeon of the First Class, with local rank, Thomas Patrick Matthew to be Staff-Surgeon of the First Class. Dated 31st August, 1858.

Surgeon Thornton Marshall, from the 65th Foot to be Staff-Surgeon, of the Second Class, vice White, who exchanges. Dated 31st August, 1858.

To be Acting Assistant-Surgeons.

John Goodrick Cambell, Gent. Dated 18th August, 1858.

George Palatiano, M.D. Dated 18th August, 1858.

Thomas Henderson Somerville, Gent. Dated 18th August, 1858.

Thomas Howell, Gent. Dated 18th August, 1858.

Thomas Lightfoot, Gent. 20th August, 1858.

Acting Assistant-Surgeon Richard Robinson Alderson has been permitted to resign his appointment. Dated 31st August, 1858.

MEMORANDUM.

The second Christian name of Quartermaster John Croker, on half-pay 6th Foot, is *Charles.*

Commission signed by the Lord Lieutenant of the County of Lancaster.

The Duke of Lancaster's Own Regiment of Yeomanry Cavalry.

Adjutant Charlie Berkeley Molyneux to be Captain, and to serve with the rank of Captain from the date of his Adjutant's Commission, vizt., the 11th day of December, 1856. Dated 20th August, 1858.

Commissions signed by the Lord Lieutenant of the County of Oxford.

Oxfordshire Regiment of Militia.

Lieutenant William Frederick Raitt to be Captain, vice Cole, resigned. Dated 27th August, 1858, Ensign Henry Olivier Lloyd to be Lieutenant, vice Raitt, promoted. Dated 28th August, 1858.

Commission signed by the Lord Lieutenant of the County Palatine of Chester.

2nd Regiment of Royal Cheshire Militia.

Walter Alexander James Wakeman, Gent., to be Ensign, vice J. D. Barnes, resigned. Dated 20th August, 1858.

RESIGNATION.

Lieutenant James Broff Byers.

1st Regiment of Royal Cheshire Militia.

RESIGNATION.

Captain Archibald Edmund Bromwich.

TREASURY WARRANT.

WHEREAS by an Act of Parliament, passed in the fourth year of the reign of Her present Majesty, intituled " An Act for the regulation of the duties of postage," power is given to the Commissioners of Her Majesty's Treasury from time to time, by Warrant under their hands, to alter and to fix any of the rates of British postage or inland postage, payable by law, on the transmission by the post of foreign or colonial letters or newspapers, or of any other printed papers, and to subject the same to rates of postage according to the weight thereof, and a scale of weight to be contained in such Warrant, and from time to time, by Warrant as aforesaid, to alter or repeal any such altered rates, and make and establish any new or other rates in lieu thereof, and from time to time, by Warrant as aforesaid, to appoint at what time the rates which may be payable are to be paid.

And whereas further powers are given to the Commissioners of Her Majesty's Treasury by another Act of Parliament, passed in the eleventh year of the reign of Her present Majesty, intituled "An Act for giving further facilities for the transmission of letters by post, and for the regulating the duties of postage thereon, and for other purposes relating to the Post-office."

And whereas the Commissioners of Her Majesty's Treasury, by a certain Warrant under their hands, bearing date the 13th day of August, 1858, did order and direct, that on every letter posted in the United Kingdom addressed to the East Indies, and on every letter posted in the East Indies addressed to the United Kingdom, the postage thereof should be paid at the time of the same being posted; and that if any letter should be posted in the United Kingdom, addressed to the East Indies, without any postage having been paid thereon, or having thereon or affixed thereto a postage stamp or stamps, the value of which shall be less in amount than the single rate of postage to which such letter, if not exceeding half an ounce in weight, would be liable under the regulations in force relating thereto, every such letter should be detained and opened, and should be either returned or given up to the sender thereof.

And whereas it is expedient that a further

regulation should be made as to the letters here-inafter mentioned.

Now we, the Commissioners of Her Majesty's Treasury, in exercise of the powers reserved to us in and by the said hereinbefore recited Acts, or either of them, and of all other powers enabling us in this behalf, do by this present Warrant, under the hands of two of us the said Commissioners, by the authority of the statute in that case made and provided, order and direct as follows; that is to say:

1. If any letter shall be posted in the United Kingdom, addressed to the East Indies, without any postage having been paid thereon, or having thereon or affixed thereto a postage stamp or stamps, the value of which shall be less in amount than the single rate of postage to which such letter, if not exceeding half an ounce in weight, would be liable under the regulations in force relating thereto, every such letter shall, until the 31st day of December, 1858, inclusive, be forwarded charged with the amount of the postage to which it would have been liable if the postage had been paid when posted, together with the further and additional rate of postage of sixpence; and from and after the said 31st day of December, 1858, every such letter instead of being forwarded shall be detained and opened, and be either returned or given up to the sender thereof, as directed by the said recited Warrant of the 13th day of August, 1858.

2. The several terms and expressions used in this Warrant shall be construed to have the like meaning in all respects as they would have had if inserted in the said recited Warrant of the 13th day of August, 1858.

3. The Commissioners for the time being of Her Majesty's Treasury may by Warrant, under

their hands, duly made at any time hereafter, alter, repeal, or revoke any of the orders, directions, or regulations hereby made, and may make and establish any new or other orders, directions, or regulations, in lieu thereof.

4. This Warrant shall come into operation on the first day of September, 1858.

> Whitehall, Treasury Chambers, the twenty-seventh day of August, one thousand eight hundred and fifty-eight.
>
> *Henry G. Lennox.*
> *Henry Whitmore.*

FROM THE

LONDON GAZETTE of SEPTEMBER 3, 1858.

AT the Court at *Osborne House, Isle of Wight,* the 2nd day of *September,* 1858.

PRESENT,

The QUEEN's Most Excellent Majesty in Council.

HER Majesty having been pleased to appoint the Right Honourable Edward Henry Stanley (commonly called Lord Stanley), to be one of Her Majesty's Principal Secretaries of State, he was this day, by Her Majesty's command, sworn one of Her Majesty's Principal Secretaries of State accordingly.

IT is this day ordered by Her Majesty in Council that the Parliament, which stands prorogued to Tuesday the nineteenth day of October next, be further prorogued to Thursday the eighteenth day of November next.

At the Court at *Osborne House, Isle of Wight,* the 2nd day of *September,* 1858.

The QUEEN'S Most Excellent Majesty in Council was pleased to order, upon a petition from the Justices of the Peace of the county of Wilts, in quarter sessions assembled at Warminster, on the twenty-ninth day of June last, that Westbury shall be a polling place for the southern division of the said county of Wilts.

At the Court at *Osborne House, Isle of Wight,* the 2nd day of *September,* 1858.

The QUEEN'S Most Excellent Majesty in Council was pleased to order that the time for the discontinuance of burials in the churchyards and burial-grounds undermentioned be postponed as follows, viz.:

In the churchyard of the parish of CLAYBROOK, from the first of October next to the first of June, one thousand eight hundred and fifty-nine; in the churchyard of the parish of GILLINGHAM, Kent, from the first of September, instant, to the first of January, one thousand eight hundred and fifty-nine; in the churchyard of MELBOURNE, Derbyshire, in the Friends Burial-Ground, in the New Jerusalem Chapel Burial-ground, and in the Baptist Chapel Burial-ground, in that parish, from the first of September instant, to the first of May, one thousand eight hundred and fifty-nine; in the new portion of the churchyard at All Saints, NEWMARKET, and in the new burial-ground in St. Mary's Parish in that town, from the first of August to the first of November, one thousand eight hundred and fifty-eight; in the churchyard of the parish of SELBY, from the first of September to the first of November, one thousand eight hundred and fifty-eight; in the parish churchyard and Vicarage Croft, in St. Andrew's Churchyard, in the burial-grounds of the Baptist, Zion, and Salem Chapels, and in the Old Friends' Burial-ground, all in WAKEFIELD, from the first of November next, to the first of May, one thousand eight hundred and fifty-nine.

And whereas by an Order in Council of the eighth of June, one thousand eight hundred and fifty-four, burials were directed wholly to cease in the churchyard of All Saints, Chorlton, in MANCHESTER, from and after the first of March, one thousand eight hundred and fifty-six, and the said Order was varied by an Order of the twenty-seventh of August, one thousand eight hundred and fifty-seven, and it seems fit that the same be again varied; now, therefore, Her Majesty, by and with the advice of Her Privy Council, is pleased to order, and it is hereby ordered, that interments in All Saints Churchyard, Chorlton, in Manchester, be discontinued from and after the first day of July, one thousand eight hundred and fifty-nine; and forthwith, except in now existing private vaults and brick graves, in which each coffin shall be embedded in charcoal, and separately entombed in an air-tight manner, and except in private family graves in which no coffin shall be buried within a foot of any other coffin, or four feet of the surface of the ground; and it is further ordered, that none be buried in any grave or vault except widowers, widows, parents, children, brothers or sisters of those already interred therein, and that the entire surface of the ground, not occupied by stones or walks, be covered with soil, and a living vegetation maintained.

And whereas by an Order in Council of the

eighteenth of October, one thousand eight hundred and fifty-four, burials were directed to be discontinued from and after the first of June then next, in the churchyard of St. Edmund, SALISBURY, except as was therein excepted, and such time was afterwards postponed to the first of February, one thousand eight hundred and fifty-eight, and it seems fit that the said Order be varied ; now, therefore, Her Majesty, by and with the advice aforesaid, is pleased to order, and it is hereby ordered, that interment in the said churchyard of St. Edmund, Salisbury, be discontinued, except for the burial of the widowers, widows, parents, and unmarried children, of those already buried in now existing catacombs, vaults, and walled graves, in which each coffin shall be imbedded in charcoal, and separately entombed in an air-tight manner, and in family graves not less than five feet deep, which can be opened without the exposure of human remains.

At the Court at *Osborne House, Isle of Wight,* the 2nd day of *September,* 1858.

The QUEEN'S Most Excellent Majesty in Council was pleased to order that the representations made by the Right Honourable Spencer Horatio Walpole, one of Her Majesty's Principal Secretaries of State (as set forth in this Gazette), that no new burial-ground should be opened in any of the undermentioned parishes without the previous approval of one of Her Majesty's Principal Secretaries of State, and that interments in the same should be discontinued, with the following modifications :

GATESHEAD.—Forthwith in the *churchyards* of. *St. Edmund* and *St. Cuthberts, Gateshead,*

except so far as is compatible with the observance of the regulations for new burial-grounds,
omitting No. 3. LEDBURY.—Forthwith in the
parish church, and also in the *churchyard*, and
Baptist Burial - ground, Ledbury, except in
graves not less than five feet deep which can
be opened without the disturbance of remains,
—and that no grave be dug within three yards
of any dwelling. HORTON, NORTHUMBERLAND.
—In the *parish churchyard* on the first day of
November, one thousand eight hundred and
fifty-eight, except in graves and vaults which
are free from water, no graves to be less than
five feet deep, and no remains to be disturbed,
and that the churchyard be properly drained.
STAINDROPE.—Forthwith in the *parish church*
of *Staindrop;* and also in the *churchyard,* except in that part which is to the north of the
church, on and after the first day of March,
one thousand eight hundred and fifty-nine.
COLCHESTER, ST. BOTOLPH's.—Forthwith in
the *Garrison Burial-ground,* except so far as
they may be conducted in accordance with the
7th Official Regulation for Burial-grounds.
ROCHDALE.—Forthwith in the *parish church* of
Rochdale. WHALLEY.—Forthwith wholly in
the *church* of *Haslingden*, and also in such part
of the *churchyard* as is within three yards of
any dwelling, and in the rest of the churchyard,
except so far as is compatible with the observance of the regulations for new burial-grounds,
numbers 5, 6, 7 and 8; and that in the *Inde-*
pendent, Wesleyan and *Baptist Burial-grounds,*
in *Haslingden*, interment be discontinued, except in graves never previously opened, and
existing family graves which can be opened not
less than five feet deep without exposure of
remains, and family vaults or walled graves in

which each coffin shall be embedded in charcoal, and separately entombed in an airtight manner.

should be taken into consideration by a Committee of the Lords of Her Majesty's Most Honourable Privy Council, on the sixteenth day of October next.

At the Court at *Osborne House, Isle of Wight*, the 2nd day of *September*, 1858.

The QUEEN'S Most Excellent Majesty in Council was pleased to order, that a petition of the Local Board of Health for the district of HECKMONDWICKE, in the West Riding of the county of York, established under " The Public Health Act, 1848," praying that Her Majesty would be pleased to order that the said Local Board of Health may be a burial board for the district of such local board, should be taken into consideration by a Committee of the Lords of Her Majesty's Most Honourable Privy Council, on the fifteenth day of October next.

At the Court at *Osborne House, Isle of Wight*, the 2nd day of *September*, 1858.

The QUEEN'S Most Excellent Majesty in Council was pleased to order, with reference to the representations of the Right Honourable Spencer Horatio Walpole, one of Her Majesty's Principal Secretaries of State, that the church-wardens or such other person as may have the care of the vaults under the church of Saint Margaret, Westminster, do adopt ,or cause to be adopted, the following measures in respect of such vaults, viz.:

That all the coffins deposited in the vaults beneath the church of Saint Margaret, Westminster, be completely covered with fresh soil, mixed with powdered charcoal, or with McDougall's disinfecting powder, and entombed by concrete, brick, or stone work in an air-tight manner, and the vaults lime-washed, their entrances from the church closed by brick or stone work, and ventilating shafts constructed, and that the work be executed under the superintendence of Mr. Holland, Inspector of Burial-grounds.

Council Office, Whitehall, September 2, 1858.

This Gazette contains an Ordinance made by the Master and Fellows of Pembroke College, in the University of Oxford, under the provisions of the Act passed in the 19th and 20th years of Her Majesty's reign, intituled " An Act to amend the Act of the seventeenth and eighteenth years of Her Majesty, concerning the University of Oxford and the College of Saint Mary, Winchester," to amend an Ordinance made by the Oxford University Commissioners, under the 17th and 18th Vict. cap. 81, in relation to Pembroke College aforesaid, dated the 19th of February, 1857, and approved by an Order in Council of the 25th of June following; and whereas the said ordinance was, on the 9th of June last, approved by the said Commissioners, and has been this day laid before Her Majesty in Council, the same is published in pursuance of the said Acts.

War-Office, 3rd September, 1858.

The Queen has been graciously pleased to signify Her intention to confer the decoration of the Victoria Cross on the undermentioned Officer and Soldier, who have been recommended to Her

Majesty for that decoration on account of Acts of Bravery performed by them in India, as recorded against their respective names; viz.:

4th Bengal Native Infantry.

Lieutenant (now Captain) Frederick Robertson Aikman.—This Officer, Commanding the 3rd Sikh Cavalry on the advanced Picquet, with one hundred of his men, having obtained information, just as the Force marched on the morning of the 1st of March last, of the proximity, three miles off the high road, of a body of 500 Rebel Infantry, 200 Horse, and 2 Guns, under Moosahib Ali Chuckbdar, attacked and utterly routed them, cutting up more than 100 men, capturing two guns, and driving the survivors into, and over, the Goomtee. This feat was performed under every disadvantage of broken ground, and partially under the flanking fire of an adjoining Fort. Lieutenant Aikman received a severe sabre cut in the face in a personal encounter with several of the enemy. Date of Act of Bravery, 1st March, 1858.

Bengal Horse Artillery.

Gunner William Connolly.—This Soldier is recommended for the Victoria Cross for his gallantry in Action with the Enemy, at Jhelum, on the 7th of July, 1857. Lieutenant Cookes, Bengal Horse Artillery, reports, that " about daybreak on that " day, I advanced my half Troop at a gallop, " and engaged the Enemy within easy musket " range. The Sponge-man of one of my Guns " having been shot during the advance, Gunner " Connolly assumed the duties of 2nd Sponge-man, " and he had barely assisted in two discharges of " his Gun, when a musket-ball, through the left " thigh, felled him to the ground; nothing daunted

"by pain and loss of blood, he was endeavouring
"to resume his post, when I ordered a movement
"in retirement, and though severely wounded, he
"was mounted on his horse in the Gun-team, and
"rode to the next position which the Guns took
"up, and manfully declined going to the rear when
"the necessity of his so doing was represented to
"him. About eleven o'clock, A.M., when the Guns
"were still in Action, the same Gunner, whilst
"sponging, was again knocked down by a musket-
"ball striking him on the hip, thereby causing
"great faintness and partial unconsciousness, for
"the pain appeared excessive, and the blood
"flowed fast. On seeing this, I gave directions
"for his removal out of Action; but this brave
"man hearing me, staggered to his feet, and said,
"'No, Sir, I'll not go there, whilst I can work
"'here,' and shortly afterwards he again resumed
"his post as Sponge-man. "Late in the afternoon
"of the same day, my three Guns were engaged
"at one hundred yards from the Walls of a Village
"with the defenders, viz., the 14th Native In-
"fantry—Mutineers—amidst a storm of bullets
"which did great execution. Gunner Connolly,
"though suffering severely from his two pre-
"vious wounds, was wielding his sponge with an
"energy and courage which attracted the admi-
"ration of his comrades, and while cheerfully en-
"couraging a wounded man to hasten in bringing
"up the ammunition, a musket-ball tore through
"the muscles of his right leg; but with the most
"undaunted bravery he struggled on; and not till
"he had loaded six times, did this man give way,
"when, through loss of blood, he fell in my arms,
"and I placed him on a waggon, which shortly
"afterwards bore him in a state of unconscious-
"ness from the fight." Date of Act of Bravery,
7th July, 1857.

War-Office, September 3, 1858.

The Queen has been graciously pleased to give orders for the appointment of Lord Bloomfield, K.C.B., Her Majesty's Envoy Extraordinary and Minister Plenipotentiary to the King of Prussia, to be an Ordinary Member of the Civil Division of the First Class, or Knights Grand Cross, of the Most Honourable Order of the Bath.

Downing-Street, September 3, 1858.

The Queen has been pleased to appoint James Douglas, Esq. (Governor and Commander-in-Chief of Vancouver's Island), to be Governor and Commander-in-Chief, in and over the colony of British Columbia and its dependencies.

Her Majesty has also been pleased to appoint Matthew Baillie Begbie, Esq., to be Judge in the said colony.

NOTICE TO MARINERS.

THE Lords of the Committee of Privy Council for Trade have received, through the Secretary of State for Foreign Affairs, copy of a Notice, issued by the Netherlands Minister of Marine, descriptive of a Bell-Beacon, recently placed near the Schouwen Bank, in the North Sea. A translation is subjoined.

(Translation.)

A bell-beacon, constructed of iron, in the form of a boat, painted black, has recently been moored in the North Sea, near the N.E. end of the " Schouwen Bank."

On the mast are fixed two triangles of trellis-work (*treillages*) one placed fore and aft, and the other athwart-ships, and painted with horizontal stripes, white and black alternately.

One of the black stripes bears the inscription " Schouwen-Bank," and one of the white stripes " W. Schouwen, Z. O. misw."

At the mast-head are two black wings of elliptical form, crossing at right angles, between which is suspended a large bell, the loud and deep sound of which serves as a warning at night, and in foggy weather.

The height of the whole is more than 7 metres, or about 20 feet above the level of the sea, and will be visible in clear weather at a distance of about 2 geographical leagues, or 8 English miles.

The beacon is moored in 26 metres, about $12\frac{1}{2}$ fathoms, at ordinary low water, in latitude 51° 47' N., and longitude 3° 27' E. (Greenwich).

The bearings (magnetic) are as follows :
Schouwen revolving light, S.E.
West-Kasselle Light S. by W. $\frac{3}{4}$ W.

(Dated) The Hague 17th August, 1858.

(Signed)   J. S. LOTSIJ,
Minister of Marine.

***

Commission signed by the Lord Lieutenant of the County of Sussex.

James Graham Domville, Esq., to be Deputy-Lieutenant. Dated 26th August, 1858.

Commission signed by the Lord Lieutenant of the County of Essex.

William Michael Tufnell, Esq., to be Deputy Lieutenant. Dated 23rd July, 1858.

Commission signed by the Lord Lieutenant of the County of Lincoln.

Royal North Lincoln Militia.

Richard Ellison, Esq., to be Lieutenant-Colonel Commandant, vice Colonel George Tomline, M P., appointed Honorary Colonel.

Commission signed by the Lord Lieutenant of the County of Lanark.

1st Royal Lanarkshire Militia.

George Johnston Gossling, Gent., to be Ensign, vice Townley, resigned. Dated 23rd August, 1858.

Commissions signed by the Lord Lieutenant of the County of Middlesex.

5th or Royal Elthorne Light Infantry Regiment of Middlesex Militia.

Ensign Joseph Balderson to be Lieutenant, vice Seaton, resigned. Dated 12th August, 1858.

D'ovley William Battley, Gent., to be Ensign, vice, Nash, promoted. Dated 12th August, 1858.

Commission signed by the Lord Lieutenant of the County of Cornwall.

Cornwall Rangers Militia.

Ensign Edward Saint Aubyn to be Lieutenant, vice Ernest Frederick Peel, resigned. Dated 28th August, 1858.

RESIGNATION.

Lieutenant John Borlase has resigned his Commission.

Commission signed by the Lord Lieutenant of the County of Southampton.

Hampshire Regiment of Militia.

The Honourable Oliver George Lambert, late Lieutenant in the 12th Regiment, to be Captain, vice Captain Thomas Buckner Henry Valentine, resigned. Dated 28th August, 1858.

George Francis Birch, Esq., late Captain in the West Middlesex Militia, to be Captain, vice Captain Henry Augustus Brander, deceased. Dated 28th August, 1858.

Edmund William Crofts, Esq., late Captain in the 23rd Royal Welsh Fusiliers, to be Captain. Dated 28th August, 1858.

Poplar Union.—Parish of Saint Mary Stratford-le-Bow.

An order of the Poor Law Commissioners, to the Churchwardens and Overseers of the Poor of the parish of Saint Mary Stratford-le-Bow, in the county of Middlesex, and to all others whom it may concern, dated the 25th August, 1858, directs that so much of the Act 13 and 14 Vic. cap. 57, as relates to the providing of a room or suitable buildings for the purpose of holding vestry or other meetings for the transaction of any business of, or relating to, the said parish of Saint Mary Stratford-le-Bow shall forthwith be applied and put in force within such parish.

3152

FROM THE

LONDON GAZETTE of *SEPTEMBER* 7, 1858.

AT the Court at *Osborne House, Isle of Wight,* the 2nd day of *September,* 1858.

The QUEEN'S Most Excellent Majesty in Council was pleased under the provisions of the 410th section of the "Merchant Shipping Act, 1854," to fix the dues to be paid in respect of two new lighthouses, at High Whitby, on the coast of Yorkshire, as set forth in this Gazette.

At the Court at *Usborne House, Isle of Wight,* the 2nd day of *September,* 1858.

PRESENT,

The QUEEN's Most Excellent Majesty in Council.

WHEREAS by "The Middlesbrough Improvement Act, 1856," it is enacted that when the burgesses entered on the burgess roll of the borough, shall exceed one thousand three hundred in number, it shall be lawful for the council, with the consent and approbation of one of Her Majesty's Principal Secretaries of State, to declare that after a time, to be specified in a resolution to be passed by the council for that purpose, the council shall consist of a mayor, six aldermen, and eighteen councillors, and that the borough shall be divided into three wards, and with the like consent to appoint a barrister to divide the borough into three wards, and to set out within the period of one calendar month after the date of his or their appointment, the extent, limit, and boundary lines of such wards, and what portions of the borough shall be included therein respectively, but so, nevertheless, that no ward shall, at the time of such division, contain less than three hundred burgesses, and the barrister setting out such wards shall apportion among such wards the eighteen councillors of the borough, and in assigning the number of councillors to each ward, the said barrister shall, as far as in his judgment he may deem it to be practicable, have regard as well to the number of persons rated to the relief of the poor in such ward as to the aggregate amount of the sums at which all the said persons shall be so rated : Provided always, that the number of councillors assigned to each ward shall be a number divisible by three, and a copy of the particulars of such division into wards, and of the number of councillors so assigned to each ward, shall be signed by the barrister who made the same, and forthwith transmitted to one of Her Majesty's Principal Secretaries of State, and subject to the approval of Her Majesty by the advice of Her Privy Council, shall be published in the London Gazette, and another copy of such particulars shall be delivered to the town clerk of the borough, to be by him safely kept among the public documents of the borough ; and the borough shall, after such publication, be deemed to be divided into wards accordingly ; and the number of councillors so assigned to each ward of the borough shall, after such publication as aforesaid, be the number of councillors to be elected in such ward, and shall so continue until the same shall be altered by the authority of Parliament.

And whereas, John Robert Davison, Esquire, the barrister appointed by the council of the said borough of Middlesbrough, under the provisions of the said recited Act, has made an Award, bearing date the eleventh day of August, one thousand eight hundred and fifty-eight, dividing the said borough into three wards, and allotting the number of councillors to each, and the same has been transmitted to the Right Honourable Spencer Horatio Walpole, one of Her Majesty's Principal Secretaries of State:

Now, therefore, Her Majesty, having taken the said Award (copy whereof is set forth in this Gazette), into consideration, is pleased, by and with the advice of Her Privy Council, to declare, and doth hereby declare, Her approval of the same; and Her Majesty is further pleased to direct, that the said Award, together with this Order, be published in the London Gazette, in pursuance of the said Act.

At the Court at *Osborne House, Isle of Wight*, the 31st day of *July*, 1858.

The QUEEN'S Most Excellent Majesty in Council was pleased to approve a representation duly prepared (as set forth in this Gazette) by the Ecclesiastical Commissioners for England, as to the assignment of a consolidated chapelry to the consecrated church of Saint Peter, situate at New Bolingbroke, in the parish of Bolingbroke, in the county and diocese of Lincoln.

Also a representation for altering the boundaries of the new parish of Saint John, Bradford, in the county of York, and in the diocese of Ripon.

Also to approve and ratify the several schemes duly prepared (as set forth in this Gazette) by the said Ecclesiastical Commissioners for England,—

For constituting a separate district for spiritual purposes out of the parishes of Ware and Great

Amwell, in the county of Hertford, and in the diocese of Rochester, to be named the District of Christ Church, Ware.

For the alteration and improvement of the episcopal house of residence at Cuddesden, in the county of Oxford, belonging to the see of Oxford.

For constituting a separate district for spiritual purposes, to comprise certain portions of the parishes of Saint Leonard, Bromley, Saint Anne, Limehouse, and All Saints, Poplar, respectively, and of the new parish of Trinity, Mile End Old Town, all in the county of Middlesex and diocese of London, to be named, The District of Saint Paul, Stepney.

War-Office, September 6, 1858.

The Queen has been graciously pleased to give orders for the appointment of Richard Madox Bromley, Esq., C.B., Accountant-General of the Navy, and of Thomas Tassell Grant, Esq., late Comptroller of the Victualling and Transport Services of the Navy, to be Ordinary Members of the Civil Division of the Second Class, or Knights Commanders, of the Most Honourable Order of the Bath; and of James Ormiston M'William, Esq., M.D., Surgeon in the Royal Navy, to be an Ordinary Member of the Civil Division of the Third Class, or Companions, of the said Most Honourable Order.

Foreign-Office, September 7, 1858.

The Queen has been pleased to approve of Mr. Peter Taysen as Vice-Consul at Leith for His Royal Highness the Grand Duke of Mecklenburgh Schwerin.

(1374.)

Board of Trade, Whitehall,
September 6, 1858.

The Right Honourable the Lords of the Committee of Privy Council for Trade and Plantations have received, through the Secretary of State for the Colonies, a copy of a Despatch from the Governor of Malta, reporting that the Board of Health at Valetta has established a quarantine of twenty-one days for ships and passengers, and twenty-eight days for suspected goods, arriving from Alexandria ; also, that vessels arriving from Gibraltar, will be subject to a quarantine of fifteen days, and that vessels coming from Algiers, and ports of the Regency of Tunis, will be subject to five days' quarantine of observation. The Board of Health have further recommended that rags imported from infected places be rejected from the lazaretto of Malta.

(1380.)

Board of Trade, Whitehall,
September 6, 1858.

The Right Honourable the Lords of the Committee of Privy Council for Trade and Plantations have received, through the Secretary of State for Foreign Affairs, a copy of a Despatch from Her Majesty's Minister at Lisbon, enclosing copy of a Royal Portuguese Decree prolonging for three years the import duty upon honey, treacle, and molasses, of foreign production, and entered at the Custom-house of Funchal in the Island of Madeira.

War-Office, Pall-Mall,
7th September, 1858.

2nd *Regiment of Dragoon Guards,* Cornet Frederick Greatorex, from the 15th Light

Dragoons, to be Cornet, vice Thomas, promoted. Dated 7th September, 1858.

5th Dragoon Guards, Lieutenant T. L. Hampton to be Captain, by purchase, vice Halford, who retires. Dated 7th September, 1858.

Cornet Thomas Duffield to be Lieutenant, by purchase, vice Hampton. Dated 7th September, 1858.

4th Light Dragoons, Theophilus Gist, Gent., to be Cornet, by purchase, vice Clark, promoted. Dated 7th September, 1858.

6th Dragoons, Serjeant Joseph Malone to be Riding Master. Dated 7th September, 1858.

8th Light Dragoons, Cornet William Norris Franklyn, from the 4th Light Dragoons, to be Cornet, vice Richards, promoted. Dated 7th September, 1858.

10th Light Dragoons, Lieutenant John Fife to be Captain, by purchase, vice Townley, who retires. Dated 7th September, 1858.

13th Light Dragoons, Cornet Arthur James Billing to be Lieutenant, by purchase, vice Gratrex, promoted. Dated 7th September, 1858.

15th Light Dragoons, Cornet Thomas Marsh Horsfall to be Lieutenant, by purchase, vice Horne, promoted. Dated 7th September, 1858.

16th Light Dragoons, Cornet Thomas Brown to be Riding Master, from Cornet. Dated 7th September, 1858.

Royal Artillery. The surname of the Staff Assistant-Surgeon, appointed on the 28th May last, is *d'Altera,* and not *Daltera* as previously stated.

Royal Engineers, Lieutenant-General Edward Fanshawe, C.B., to be Colonel-Commandant, vice Sir C. F. Smith, K.C.B., deceased. Dated 12th August, 1858.

Second Captain and Brevet-Lieutenant-Colonel

Edward Stanton, C.B., to be Captain, vice Simmons, placed on the Seconded List. Dated 20th August, 1858.

Lieutenant Willoughby Digby Marsh to be Second Captain, vice Stanton. Dated 20th August, 1858.

1*st Regiment of Foot.* The Commission of Lieutenant J. J. Heywood, as Adjutant, to bear date 20*th April,* 1858, in lieu of 4*th June,* 1858.

4th Foot.

To be Ensigns, without purchase.

George Augustus Sweny, Gent., vice Smith, promoted. Dated 7th September, 1858.

William Harry Stone, Gent., vice Rynd, promoted. Dated 8th September, 1858.

Charles Cartwright Sayce, Gent. Dated 9th September, 1858.

5*th Foot,* Lieutenant Robert Moore to be Captain, by purchase, vice O'Brien, who retires. Dated 7th September, 1858.

Ensign Gersham Herrick to be Lieutenant, by purchase, vice Moore. Dated 7th September, 1858.

9*th Foot,* Lieutenant William Crosbie Harvey to be Captain, by purchase, vice Rogers, who retires. Dated 7th September, 1858.

Ensign C. T. Coote to be Lieutenant, by purchase, vice Harvey. Dated 7th September, 1858.

Edward William Forester Leighton, Gent., to be Ensign, by purchase, vice Coote. Dated 7th September, 1858.

To be Ensigns, without purchase.

Zachary Stanley Bayly, Gent., vice Chadwick, promoted. Dated 8th September, 1858.

Arthur Frederick Piercy Cosens, Gent., vice Aplin, promoted. Dated 9th September, 1858.

Assistant-Surgeon James Henry Jeffcoat, from the Staff, to be Assistant-Surgeon. Dated 7th September, 1858.

11th *Foot*, Major Arthur Charles Lowe, from half-pay Unattached, to be Major, repaying the difference, vice E. L. Blosse, who exchanges. Dated 7th September, 1858.

Captain and. Brevet-Lieutenant-Colonel A. H. L. Wyatt to be Major, by purchase, vice Lowe, who retires. Dated 7th September, 1858.

Lieutenant Thomas Hill to be Captain, by purchase, vice Wyatt. Dated 7th September, 1858.

Ensign W. G. Byron, from the 38th Foot, to be Lieutenant, by purchase, vice Hill. Dated 7th September, 1858.

Lieutenant John Frederick Trotter, from the 1st West India Regiment, to be Lieutenant. Dated 8th September, 1858.

13th *Foot*, Captain William Milnes, from half pay 7th Foot, to be Captain. Dated 7th September, 1858.

Lieutenant George Henry Cobham to be Captain, by purchase, vice Milnes, who retires. Dated 7th September, 1858.

Ensign Thomas Yardley to be Lieutenant, by purchase, vice Cobham. Dated 7th September, 1858.

15th *Foot*, Edward Cuthbert Ward, Gent., to be Ensign, without purchase, vice Chapman, appointed to the 54th Foot. Dated 7th September, 1858.

Assistant-Surgeon Frederic Murray Chalk, from the Staff, to be Assistant-Surgeon. Dated 7th September, 1858.

16th *Foot*, Lieutenant Somerville G. C. Hogge to

be Captain, by purchase, vice Hill, who retires. Dated 6th September, 1858.

To be Captains. without purchase.

Lieutenant George Augustus Ferris, from the 29th Foot. Dated 7th September, 1858.

Lieutenant W. L. Ingles, from the 74th Foot. Dated 7th September, 1858.

Lieutenant Edward Woolhouse, from the 84th Foot. Dated 7th September, 1858.

To be Lieutenants, without purchase.

Ensign Aubrey P. Powys, from the 63rd Foot. Dated 7th September, 1858.

Ensign Henry Arthur Crane, from the 62nd Foot. Dated 7th September, 1858.

Ensign Charles H. Newbatt, from the 10th Foot. Dated 7th September, 1858.

Ensign Frederick Grant, from the 10th Foot. Dated 7th September, 1858.

17*th Foot*, Lieutenant Edward John Lees to be Captain, by purchase, vice FitzGerald, who retires. Dated 7th September, 1858.

Ensign G. F. Fawcett to be Lieutenant, by purchase, vice Lees. Dated 7th September, 1858.

18*th Foot*, Lieutenant R. W. E. Dawson to be Adjutant. Dated 7th September, 1858.

19*th Foot*, Serjeant Charles Usherwood to be Quartermaster, vice Rawding, deceased. Dated 7th September, 1858.

20*th Foot*, Lieutenant John James S. O'Neill to be Captain, without purchase, vice Parkinson, deceased. Dated 3rd June, 1858.

Ensign Robert Blount to be Lieutenant, without purchase, vice O'Neill. Dated 3rd June, 1858.

Ensign F. G. Horn to be Lieutenant, without purchase, vice Blount, whose promotion on the

15th June, 1858, has been cancelled. Dated 15th June, 1858.

22nd Foot. George Robert Henry Daubeney, Gent., to be Ensign, by purchase, vice Trotter, appointed to the 39th Foot. Dated 7th September, 1858.

23rd Foot, Captain George Marryat, from half-pay Unattached, to be Captain. Dated 6th September, 1858.

Lieutenant Charles G. Blane to be Captain, by purchase, vice Marryat, who retires. Dated 6th September, 1858.

Lieutenant John Geddes, from the 76th Foot, to be Captain, without purchase. Dated 7th September, 1858.

Lieutenant Edward Armstrong, from the 75th Foot, to be Captain, without purchase. Dated 7th September, 1858.

Ensign G. F. Russell Colt to be Lientenant, without purchase. Dated 7th September, 1858.

24th Foot, Ensign Arthur W. FitzMaurice to be Lieutenant, without purchase, vice Head, promoted in the 13th Foot. Dated 7th September, 1858.

29th Foot, Ensign Alfred Godfrey Black to be Lieutenant, without purchase, vice Ferris, promoted in the 16th Foot. Dated 7th September, 1858.

30th Foot, Lieutenant Charles John Hampton, from the 56th Foot, to be Lieutenant, vice M. B. Feild, who exchanges. Dated 7th September, 1858.

Serjeant-Major Richard Nagle to be Ensign, without purchase, vice Morewood, promoted. Dated 7th September, 1858.

32nd Foot, David Bond, Gent., to be Ensign, by purchase, vice Smith, promoted in 19th Foot. Dated 7th September, 1858.

Assistant-Surgeon William Boyd to be Surgeon, for eminent services throughout the whole siege of Lucknow, vice Scott, promoted to Staff-Surgeon First Class. Dated 7th September, 1858.

35*th Foot*, Ensign and Adjutant Robert Hill Ross, to be Lieutenant, by purchase, vice Goddard, promoted, by purchase, to an Unattached Company. Dated 7th September, 1858.

William Trocke, Gent., to be Ensign, by purchase, vice Ross. Dated 7th September, 1858.

43*rd Foot*, Robert Mercer Tod, Gent., to be Ensign, by purchase, in succession to Lieutenant Trydell, promoted in the 22nd Foot. Dated 7th September, 1858.

44*th Foot*, Francis Glasse Marshall, Gent., to be Ensign, by purchase, vice Matthews, who has retired. Dated 7th September, 1858.

46*th Foot*, Henry Boscawen Scott, Gent., to be Ensign, by purchase, vice Kentish, promoted. Dated 7th September, 1858.

Joshua E. C. C. Lindesay, Gent., to be Ensign, without purchase, vice Daly, promoted. Dated 8th September, 1858.

56*th Foot*, Lieutenant Meyrick Beaufoy Feild, from the 30th Foot, to be Lieutenant, vice Hampton, who exchanges. Dated 7th September, 1858.

70*th Foot*. The Commission of Lieutenant G. R. Greaves, as Adjutant, to bear date the 8*th*, and not 18*th* May, 1858, as stated in the Gazette of 16th July last.

73*rd Foot*, Ensign William Henry Samuel Pigott to be Lieutenant, without purchase, vice the Honourable C. R. M. Ward, died at sea. Dated 9th July, 1858.

Ensign H. D'O. Farrington to be Lieutenant, without purchase, vice A. A. Young, superseded, for being absent without leave. Dated 10th July, 1858.

Bolton James Alfred Monsell, Gent., to be Ensign, without purchase, vice Pigott, promoted. Dated 7th September, 1858.

75*th Foot*, Ensign Bentinck L. Cumberland to be Lieutenant, without purchase, vice Armstrong, promoted in the 23rd Foot. Dated 7th September, 1858.

Ensign Frederick Francis Daniell, from the Ceylon Rifle Regiment, to be Ensign, vice Cumberland. Dated 7th September, 1858.

76*th Foot*, Ensign W. McDonell Clarke to be Lieutenant, without purchase, vice Geddes, promoted in the 23rd Foot. Dated 7th September, 1858.

82*nd Foot*, Ensign E. S. Lock to be Lieutenant, without purchase, vice Douglas, deceased. Dated 20th January, 1858.

84*th Foot*, Ensign George Benjamin Wolseley to be Lieutenant, without purchase, vice Woolhouse, promoted in the 16th Foot. Dated 7th September, 1858.

86*th Foot*, Ensign Charles Henry Jackson, from the 14th Foot, to be Ensign, in succession to Lieutenant Lewis, promoted in the 19th Foot. Dated 7th September, 1858.

Ensign F. G. Marshall, from the 44th Foot, to be Ensign in succession to Lieutenant Jerome, promoted in 19th Foot. Dated 7th September, 1858.

87*th Foot*, Ensign B. D'Urban Musgrave to be Lieutenant, without purchase, vice Peyton, promoted in the 18th Foot. Dated 7th September, 1858.

John Hooker Vowell, Gent., to be Ensign, without purchase, vice Musgrave. Dated 7th September, 1858.

91*st Foot*, Henry Coesar Kemm, Gent., to be Ensign, without purchase, vice Jones, promoted. Dated 7th September, 1858.

93*rd Foot*, Captain Edward Welch has been permitted to resign the appointment of Regimental Instructor of Musketry, in consequence of a severe wound received at Lucknow. Dated 7th September, 1858.

98*th Foot*. The Commission of Lieutenant E. F. Gregory as Adjutant to bear date 8th May, 1858, in lieu of 6th August, 1858.

99*th Foot*, Ensign E. C. Johnson to be Lieutenant, by purchase, vice Hornby, promoted in the Military Train. Dated 7th September, 1858.

Philip Homar ffolliott, Gent., to be Ensign, by purchase, vice Bond, promoted. Dated 7th September, 1858.

Rifle Brigade, Lieutenant Stewart Smyth Windham to be Captain, without purchase. Dated 7th September, 1858.

To be Lieutenants, without purchase.

Ensign William Steward Travers. Dated 11th May, 1858.

Ensign William George Swinhoe, vice Windham. Dated 7th September, 1858.

Ensign James Edward Vaughan. Dated 7th September, 1858.

Ensign Frederick William Marsh Chalmers. Dated 7th September, 1858.

To be Lieutenants, by purchase.

Ensign A. B. G. S. Hill, vice Tryon, promoted. Dated 7th September, 1858.

Ensign Arthur Ruck Keene, vice Thomas, who retires. Dated 7th September, 1858.

Lieutenant David Alexander Jordan to be Adju-

'tant, vice Singer, promoted. Dated 25th June, 1858.

1st *West India Regiment,* Ensign Thomas George Mawe to be Lieutenant, without purchase, vice Trotter, appointed to the 11th Foot. Dated 8th September, 1858.

Ceylon Rifle Regiment Michael Joseph Tighe, Gent., to be Ensign, without purchase, vice Hunter, promoted. Dated 7th September, 1858.

HOSPITAL STAFF.

Surgeon Charles Scott, M.D., from the 32nd Foot, to be Staff Surgeon of the First Class, for eminent Services throughout the whole siege of Lucknow. Dated 7th September, 1858.

To be Acting Assistant-Surgeons.

Frederick O'Conor, Gent. Dated 26th August, 1858.

Frederick Skinner, Gent. Dated 26th August, 1858.

BREVET.

Major Arthur Charles Lowe, 11th Foot, to be Lieutenant-Colonel in the Army. Dated 11th November, 1851.

Brevet-Lieutenant-Colonel Arthur Charles Lowe, 11th Foot, to be Colonel in the Army. Dated 15th March, 1858.

Captain George Marryat, 23rd Foot, to be Major in the Army. Dated 23rd November, 1841.

Brevet-Major George Marryat, 23rd Foot, to be Lieutenant-Colonel in the Army. Dated 11th November, 1851.

Brevet-Major William Spring, retired full-pay (late Fort Major, Edinburgh Castle), to be Lieutenant-Colonel in the Army, the rank being honorary only. Dated 7th September, 1858.

The promotion to the Brevet Rank of Colonel, conferred on Lieutenant-Colonel J. D. Johnstone, C.B., 33rd Foot, in the Gazette of 15th June last, to bear date *9th March*, 1858, instead of *2nd June*, 1858, as previously stated.

Lieutenant-Colonel William Bethel Gardner, Royal Artillery, having completed three years' service in his present rank, to be a Colonel in the Army under the Royal Warrant of 3rd November, 1854. Dated 1st September, 1858.

To be Lieutenant-Colonels in the Army.

Major William Kier Stuart, 86th Foot. Dated 20th July, 1858.

Major John William Cox, 13th Foot. Dated 20th July, 1858.

Major Thomas G. A. Oakes, 12th Light Dragoons. Dated 20th July, 1858.

To be Majors in the Army.

Captain Alfred Picton Bowlby, 64th Foot. Dated 24th March, 1858.

Captain Richard Buckley Prettejohn, 14th Light Dragoons. Dated 20th July, 1858.

Captain J. De Montmorency M. Prior, 12th Light Dragoons. Dated 20th July, 1858.

Captain Hugh Maurice Jones, 13th Foot. Dated 20th July, 1858.

Captain Arthur Need, 14th Light Dragoons. Dated 20th July, 1858.

Captain Charles Darby, 86th Foot. Dated 20th July, 1858.

Captain James Leith, 6th Dragoons. Dated 20th July, 1858.

The following promotions to take place in succession to Colonel P. V. England, of the Royal Artillery, promoted to be Major-General, vice

Major-General W. B. Dundas, C.B., Royal Artillery, deceased :

Lieutenant-Colonel Charles Robert Raitt, half-pay Unattached, to be Colonel. Dated 9th August, 1858.

Major L. C. Bourchier, 75th Foot, to be Lieutenant-Colonel. Dated 9th August, 1858.

Captain Thomas Fenwick, Royal Engineers, to be Major. Dated 9th August, 1858.

The following promotions to take place in succession to Colonel W. C. Ward, of the Royal Engineers, promoted to be Major-General, in succession to Lieutenant-General Sir C. F. Smith, K.C.B., deceased :

Lieutenant-Colonel George Hankey Smith, 73rd Foot, to be Colonel. Dated 12th August, 1858.

Major Thomas White, 49th Foot, to be Lieutenant-Colonel. Dated 12th August, 1858.

Captain Spencer Westmacott, Royal Engineers, to be Major. Dated 12th August, 1858.

Commission signed by the Lord Lieutenant of the County of Carnarvon.

Royal Carnarvonshire Militia.

Major John MacDonald, late Lieutenant-Colonel of Her Majesty's 5th Regiment of Foot, to be Lieutenant-Colonel Commandant, vice the Honourable Edward Gordon Douglas Pennant, resigned, but who retains the honorary rank of Colonel.

Commission signed by the Lord Lieutenant of the County of Hertford.

Hertfordshire Militia.

Richard Cumberlege, Gent., to be Ensign. Dated 1st September, 1858.

*Commission signed by the Lord Lieutenant of the
County Palatine of* Chester.

2nd Regiment of Royal Cheshire Militia.

William John St. Aubyn, Gent., to be Ensign,
vice R. P. Gale, resigned. Dated 30th
August, 1858.

*Commission signed by the Lord Lieutenant of the
County of* Warwick.

Warwickshire Militia.

1st Regiment.

Lieutenant William George Fetherston to be
Captain, vice Patullo, deceased. Dated 28th
August, 1858.

*Commissions signed by the Lord Lieutenant of the
County of* Cambridge.

Cambridgeshire Militia.

George King, Gent., to be Ensign. Dated 1st
September, 1858.

Charles Hurrell, Gent., to be Ensign. Dated 1st
September, 1858.

TREASURY WARRANT.

WHEREAS by an Act passed in the fourth
year of the reign of Her present Majesty, intituled
" An Act for the regulation of the duties of postage," power is given to the Commissioners of Her
Majesty's Treasury, by Warrant under their
hands, to alter and fix any of the rates of British
postage or inland postage, payable by law, on the
transmission by the post of foreign or colonial
letters or newspapers, and to subject the same to
rates of postage according to the weight thereof,
and a scale of weight to be contained in such

Warrant, and from time to time, by Warrant as aforesaid, to alter or repeal any such altered rates, and to make and establish any new or other rates in lieu thereof, and from time to time, by Warrant as aforesaid, to appoint at what time the rates, which may be payable are to be paid.

And whereas further powers are given to the Commissioners of Her Majesty's Treasury by another Act of Parliament, passed in the eighth year of the reign of Her present Majesty, intituled " An Act for the better regulation of colonial posts."

And whereas it is expedient to make regulations for the transmission by the post, within Gibraltar, of the letters hereinafter mentioned.

Now we, the Commissioners of Her Majesty's Treasury, in exercise of the powers vested in us in and by the before mentioned Acts, or either of them, and of all other powers enabling us in this behalf, do by this Warrant, under the hands of two of us the said Commissioners, by the authority of the statute in that case made and provided, order, direct, and declare as follows ; that is to say :

On every letter not exceeding half an ounce in weight, posted in Gibraltar, and transmitted by the post, addressed to a place within that colony, there shall be charged and taken a uniform rate of postage of one penny.

On every letter exceeding half an ounce in weight, posted in Gibraltar, and transmitted by the post addressed to a place within that colony, there shall be charged, taken, and paid, progressive and additional rates of postage as follows ; that is to say :

On every such letter exceeding half an ounce in weight, and not exceeding one ounce in weight, two rates of postage.

On every such letter exceeding one ounce, and not exceeding two ounces in weight, four rates of postage.

On every such letter exceeding two ounces, and not exceeding three ounces in weight, six rates of postage.

On every such letter exceeding three ounces, and not exceeding four ounces in weight, eight rates of postage.

And for every ounce in weight above the weight of four ounces, there shall be charged and taken two additional rates of postage, and every fraction of an ounce above the weight of four ounces shall be charged as one additional ounce, and each progressive and additional rate chargeable under this clause shall be estimated and charged at the sum which any such letter would be charged with under this Warrant, if not exceeding half an ounce in weight.

The postage of all such letters as aforesaid shall in every case be paid at the time of the same being posted, not in money, but by being duly stamped with the proper postage stamp or stamps affixed thereto, which stamp or stamps shall in every case be affixed or appear on the outside of every such letter, near the address or direction, and shall be of the value or amount of the postage-duty payable thereon, under or by virtue of this Warrant.

If any letter (whatever may be the weight thereof), sent, or tendered, or delivered, in order to be sent by the post under the provisions of this Warrant, shall be posted without having thereon or affixed thereto, any postage stamp, or having thereon or affixed thereto, a stamp or stamps, the value of which shall be less in amount than the rate of postage to which such letter would be liable under the provisions of this Warrant, every such letter shall be forwarded, charged in the first mentioned case with the full amount of postage to which such letter would be liable as aforesaid, together with the further and additional rate of one penny, and charged in the second mentioned case with the amount of the difference between the value of such stamp or stamps so being thereon, or affixed thereto, and the postage to which such letter would be liable as aforesaid, together with the further and additional rate of one penny.

The rates of postage chargeable on letters transmitted by the post under the provisions of this Warrant, shall be in lieu of any rates of postage now chargeable by law thereon.

The several terms and expressions used in this Warrant shall be construed to have the like meaning in all respects as they would have had if inserted in the said Act passed in the fourth year of the reign of Her present Majesty.

The Commissioners for the time being of Her Majesty's Treasury may by Warrant, under their hands, duly made at any time hereafter, alter, repeal, or revoke any of the rates of postage hereby fixed or altered, or any of the orders, directions, regulations and conditions hereby made, and may make and establish any new or other rates, orders, directions, regulations and conditions in lieu thereof, and from time to time appoint at what time the rates which may be payable are to be paid.

This Warrant shall come into operation on the first day of October, 1858.

Whitehall, Treasury Chambers, the first day of September, one thousand eight hundred and fifty-eight.

Henry Whitmore.
H. G. Lennox.

TREASURY WARRANT.

WHEREAS by an Act of Parliament, passed in the fourth year of the reign of Her present Majesty, intituled "An Act for the regulation of the duties of postage," power is given to the Commissioners of Her Majesty's Treasury from time to time, by Warrant under their hands, to alter and fix any of the rates of British postage payable by law on the transmission by the post of foreign or colonial letters or newspapers, or of any other printed papers, and to subject the same to rates of postage according to the weight thereof, and a scale of weight to be contained in such Warrant.

And whereas further powers are given to the Commissioners of Her Majesty's Treasury by another Act of Parliament, passed in the eleventh year of the reign of Her present Majesty, intituled "An Act for giving further facilities for the transmission of letters by post, and for the regulating the duties of postage thereon, and for other purposes relating to the Post Office."

And whereas certain powers are also given to the Commissioners of Her Majesty's Treasury by another Act of Parliament, passed in the eighteenth year of the reign of Her present Majesty, intituled "An Act to amend the laws relating to the stamp duties on newspapers, and to provide for the transmission by post of printed periodical publications."

And whereas a Treaty hath been lately entered into between Her Majesty and the Queen of Spain for regulating the communications by post between their respective dominions, and it is expedient for the better carrying out of the same that certain regulations should be made in the manner hereinafter mentioned.

Now we, the Commissioners of Her Majesty's Treasury, in exercise of the powers reserved to us

in and by the said hereinbefore-recited Acts and
every of them, and of all other powers enabling us
in this behalf, do by this Warrant, under the
hands of two of us the said Commissioners. by the
authority of the statute in that case made and
provided, order, direct, and declare, as follows :

1. On every letter, not exceeding one quarter
of an ounce in weight, posted in the United Kingdom, addressed to Spain or the Balearic or the
Canary Islands, and on every letter, not exceeding
one quarter of an ounce in weight, posted in Spain
or the Balearic or the Canary Islands, addressed to
the United Kingdom, transmitted by the post, viâ
France, or direct by packet-boat between the
United Kingdom and any place in Spain or the
Balearic or the Canary Islands, there shall be
charged and taken an uniform rate of postage. of
sixpence.

2. On every letter not exceeding one quarter of
an ounce in weight, posted in any of Her Majesty's colonies or any foreign country, addressed
to 'Spain or the Balearic or Canary Islands, transmitted through the United Kingdom, there shall
be charged and taken for the conveyance of every
such letter from any part of the United Kingdom
to Spain or the Balearic or Canary Islands,
whether viâ France, or direct by packet-boat, an
uniform rate of postage of sixpence.

3. All such letters so transmitted as hereinbefore in the first and second clauses of this
Warrant mentioned, if exceeding one quarter of
an ounce in weight, shall be subject to the several
further and additional and progressive rates of
postage hereinafter mentioned ; that is to say :

On every letter so transmitted, if exceeding one
quarter of an ounce in weight and not exceeding one half of an ounce in weight there shall
be charged, taken, and paid, two rates of
postage.

And on every letter so transmitted, if exceeding one half of an ounce and not exceeding three quarters of an ounce in weight, three rates of postage.

And on every letter so tansmitted, if exceeding three quarters of an ounce, and not exceeding one ounce in weight, four rates of postage.

And for every additional quarter of an ounce in weight, of any letter so transmitted respectively as aforesaid, above the weight of one ounce, there shall be charged, taken, and paid, one additional rate of postage; and every fractional part of such additional quarter of an ounce shall be charged as an additional quarter of an ounce in weight; and each progressive and additional rate, chargeable under this clause, shall be estimated and charged at the sum which any such letter would be charged with under this Warrant, if not exceedingd one quarter of an ounce in weight.

4. On letters posted in Spain or the Balearic or the Canary Islands, addressed to any of Her Majesty's colonies or any foreign country, transmitted by the post from Spain or the Balearic or the Canary Islands, to Her Majesty's colonies or any foreign country, without passing through the United Kingdom, the sea conveyance of which shall be by British packet-boat there shall be charged and taken a British postage of two shillings for every ounce weight thereof.

5. On letters posted in Spain or the Balearic or the Canary Islands, addressed to any of Her Majesty's colonies or any foreign country, transmitted by the post from Spain or the Balearic or Canary Islands to any of Her Majesty's colonies or any foreign country, through the United Kingdom, the conveyance from Spain or the Balearic or Canary Islands to the United Kingdom being viâ France,

or direct by packet-boat, there shall be charged and taken a British postage of two shillings for every ounce weight thereof.

6. On letters transmitted by British packet-boat between one port in Spain and another port in Spain there shall be charged and taken a British postage of two shillings for every ounce weight thereof.

7. On letters posted in Spain or the Balearic or Canary Islands, addressed to the Philippine Islands, or posted in the Philippine Islands, addressed to Spain or the Balearic or Canary Islands, which may be conveyed between Malta or Gibraltar and Hong Kong, by British packet-boats in the Mediterranean and Indian Ocean, there shall be charged and taken a British postage of two shillings for every ounce weight thereof.

8. On every letter not exceeding half an ounce in weight, posted in the United Kingdom, addressed to Cuba, and on every letter not exceeding half an ounce in weight, posted in Cuba, addressed to the United Kingdom, and respectively transmitted between Cuba and the United Kingdom by British packet-boat, there shall be charged and taken a British rate of postage of one shilling and sixpence.

9. On every letter not exceeding half an ounce in weight. transmitted by the post between Cuba and any of Her Majesty's colonies, or any foreign countries (France and foreign countries through France, Spain, and the Balearic and Canary Islands excepted) through the United Kingdom, there shall be charged and taken the rates of British postage following ; that is to say :

For the conveyance of every such letter between Cuba and the United Kingdom, a rate of one shilling and sixpence, and for the conveyance of every such letter between the port in the United Kingdom of the departure or arrival of the packet or ship conveying the same, and the colony or foreign country to or from which the same shall be forwarded, such a further or additional rate of postage as shall from time to time be charged and payable for British postage on letters posted or delivered at the port in the United Kingdom of the departure or arrival of the packet or ship conveying the same, and transmitted direct between such port and any such colony or foreign country : Provided that in all cases where such additional rate includes both inland and sea services, there shall be deducted from the said rate of one shilling and sixpence in this clause mentioned the sum of one penny in respect of the inland conveyance of every such letter sent through the United Kingdom.

10. On every letter not exceeding half an ounce in weight, posted in any of Her Majesty's colonies, or any foreign country, addressed to Spain, or the Balearic or Canary Islands, transmitted by the post without passing through the United Kingdom, the sea conveyance of which shall be by British packet boat, there shall be charged and taken a British rate of fourpence.

11. On every letter not exceeding half an ounce in weight, posted in any of Her Majesty's colonies or any foreign country, addressed to Spain, or the Balearic or Canary Islands, transmitted through the United Kingdom, there shall be charged and taken over and above the uniform rate of postage mentioned in the second clause of this Warrant for the conveyance from any part of the United Kingdom to Spain, or the Balearic or Canary Islands, such a further or additional rate of British postage for the conveyance of every such letter from any of Her Majesty's colonies or any foreign country to the port in the United Kingdom of the arrival of the packet or ship conveying the same as shall from time to time be charged and payable for

British postage on letters not exceeding half an ounce in weight, delivered at the port in the United Kingdom of the arrival of the packet or ship conveying the same, and transmitted direct to such port from any such colony or foreign country : Provided that in all cases in which such additional rate includes both inland and sea services, there shall be deducted therefrom the sum of one penny in respect of the inland conveyance under this clause of every such letter sent through the United Kingdom.

12. All such respective letters so transmitted as hereinbefore in the eighth, ninth, tenth, and eleventh clauses of this Warrant mentioned, if exceeding half an ounce in weight, shall be subject to the several further and additional and progressive rates of postage hereinafter mentioned; that is to say :

On every such letter, if exceeding half an ounce in weight and not exceeding one ounce in weight, there shall be charged, taken, and paid, two rates of postage.

And on every such letter, if exceeding one ounce and not exceeding two ounces in weight, four rates of postage.

And on every such letter, if exceeding two ounces, and not exceeding three ounces in weight, six rates of postage.

And for every additional ounce in weight of any such letter above the weight of three ounces, there shall be charged, taken, and paid, two additional rates of postage, and every fractional part of such additional ounce shall be charged as an additional ounce in weight, and each progressive and additional rate chargeable under this clause shall be estimated and charged at the sum which any such letter would be charged with under this Warrant, if not exceeding half an ounce in weight.

13. Every letter, whatever may be the weight of it, posted in Spain, addressed to Gibraltar, and sent by the post to Gibraltar otherwise than by sea shall be chargeable with a British rate of one penny.

14. If any letter transmitted by the post under the first clause of this Warrant shall be posted without any postage being paid thereon, either in money or by postage stamps, there shall be charged and paid on the delivery of every such letter a postage of double the amount that would have been payable on such letter had the postage thereon been paid when posted ; and if any letter transmitted by the post under the first clause of this Warrant shall be posted with a postage paid thereon, less than the sum of sixpence, there shall be charged and paid on the delivery of every such last-mentioned letter the full double postage to which it shall be liable under the provisions of this Warrant, without giving credit for any postage that may have been paid thereon ; and if any letter transmitted under the first clause of this Warrant shall be posted with a postage paid thereon, either in money or by postage stamps, less in amount than the sum chargeable under this Warrant, but equal in amount to the sum of sixpence, there shall be charged and paid on the delivery of every such last-mentioned letter double the amount of the difference between the postage so prepaid and the postage which should have been prepaid under the provisions of this Warrant.

15. The postage of every letter posted in the United Kingdom under the eighth clause of this Warrant, addressed to Cuba, shall be paid at the time of the letter being posted, and if any such letter shall be posted in the United Kingdom without any postage being paid thereon, or with a postage paid thereon less in amount than the sum chargeable under this Warrant, every such letter shall

and may be detained and opened, and shall be returned or given up to the sender thereof.

16. Registered letters may be transmitted by the post under the authority of this Warrant upon the payment of such additional charge or rates of postage, or otherwise, as the Postmaster-General may from time to time direct or appoint : Provided that all rates of postage and additional charges or rates, from time to time payable thereupon, shall be prepaid, and that no payment shall be made thereupon on the delivery of any such registered letters.

17. Nothing herein contained shall be construed in anywise to annul, prejudice, or affect any of the exemptions and privileges granted by the said recited Act, passed in the fourth year of the reign of Her present Majesty, or to annul, prejudice, or affect any of the privileges which seamen and soldiers employed in Her Majesty's service, and seamen and soldiers employed in the service of the East India Company, are now by law entitled to of sending and receiving by the post letters not exceeding half an ounce in weight, subject to the regulations and restrictions in respect of the same.

18. All packets consisting of printed British newspapers posted in the United Kingdom, addressed to Spain, or the Balearic or the Canary Islands, may be transmitted by the post from the United Kingdom to Spain, or the Balearic, or the Canary Islands, either viâ France or direct by packet boat, all which respective packets shall be transmitted in conformity with, and under and subject to, the several regulations, orders, directions, and conditions hereinafter mentioned and contained relating thereto ; and on every such packet, if not exceeding four ounces in weight there shall be charged, taken, and paid for the

transmission thereof as aforesaid, the uniform single rate of postage of two pence.

19. All packets consisting of printed papers. (other than British newspapers) posted in the United Kingdom, addressed to Spain, or the Balearic, or the Canary Islands, may be transmitted by the post from the United Kingdom to Spain, or the Balearic or the Canary Islands, either viâ France, or direct by packet boat, which respective packets shall be transmitted in conformity with, and under and subject to, the several regulations, orders, directions, and conditions hereinafter mentioned and contained relating thereto; and on every such packet, if not exceeding four ounces in weight, there shall be charged, taken, and paid for the transmission thereof as aforesaid, the uniform single rate of postage of four pence.

20. All such respective packets transmitted under the 18th and 19th clauses of this Warrant hereinbefore respectively contained shall be subject to the several progressive and additional rates of postage hereinafter mentioned; that is to say:

On every such packet, if exceeding four ounces in weight, and not exceeding eight ounces in weight, two rates of postage.

And on every such packet, if exceeding eight ounces in weight, and not exceeding one pound in weight, four rates of postage.

And on every such packet, if exceeding one pound and not exceeding one pound and the half of another pound in weight, six rates of postage.

And on every such packet, if exceeding one pound and the half of another pound, and not exceeding two pounds in weight, eight rates of postage.

And for every additional half of a pound in

weight of any such packet above the weight of two pounds. there shall be charged, taken, and paid two additional rates of postage ; and every fractional part of such additional half of a pound in weight shall be charged as an additional half of a pound in weight ; and each progressive and additional rate chargeable under this clause shall be estimated and charged at the sum which any such packet would be charged with under this Warrant, if not exceeding four ounces in weight.

21. All packets consisting of printed newspapers, whether British, colonial, or foreign, and all other printed papers posted in any of Her Majesty's colonies or any foreign country, addressed to Spain, or the Balearic or the Canary Islands, may be transmitted by the post from Her Majesty's colonies or any foreign country to Spain, or the Balearic or the Canary Islands, through the United Kingdom, either viâ France, or direct by packet boat, which respective packets shall be transmitted in conformity with, and under and subject to, the several regulations, orders, directions, and conditions hereinafter mentioned and contained relating thereto ; and on every such packet, if not exceeding two ounces in weight, there shall be charged, taken, and paid, for the transmission thereof as aforesaid, the uniform single rate of three pence.

And on every such packet exceeding two ounces in weight, there shall be charged, taken, and paid progressive and additional rates of postage as follows ; that is to say :

On every such packet, if exceeding two ounces in weight and not exceeding four ounces in weight, two rates of postage.

And on every such packet, if exceeding four ounces and not exceeding one half of a pound in weight, four rates of postage.

And on every such packet, if exceeding one half of a pound and not exceeding one pound in weight, eight rates of postage.

And on every such packet, if exceeding one pound and not exceeding one pound and the half of another pound in weight, twelve rates of postage.

And on every such packet, if exceeding one pound and the half of another pound and not exceeding two pounds in weight, sixteen rates of postage.

And for every additional half of a pound in weight, of any such packet above the weight of two pounds, there shall be charged, taken, and paid four additional rates of postage, and every fractional part of such additional half of a pound in weight shall be charged as an additional half of a pound in weight, and each progressive and additional rate chargeable under this clause shall be estimated and charged at the sum which any such packet would be charged with under this Warrant if not exceeding two ounces in weight.

22. Every packet which shall be transmitted by the post under the 18th, 19th, 20th, and 21st clauses of this Warrant shall be so transmitted in conformity with, and under and subject to, the several regulations, orders, directions, and conditions hereinafter contained ; that is to say :

Every packet shall be sent in a cover open at the ends, or in any other manner which will admit of an examination of its contents.

It shall contain no enclosure, nor any writing, signs, or mark, either within or without, other than the name and address of the person to whom it is sent, the printed title of the publication, and the printed name and address of the publisher, or of the vendor.

Every British newspaper which shall be posted
in the United Kingdom under the provisions
of this Warrant shall be printed and published
at intervals not exceeding thirty-one days,
between any two consecutive numbers or
parts of such publication, and the same shall
be registered by the proprietor or printer
thereof at the General Post Office, in London,
and shall be posted within fifteen days from
the date of its publication, and the title and
date of the newspaper shall be printed at the
top of every page thereof.

No packet transmitted by the post under this
Warrant, which in length, or breadth, or width
shall exceed the dimensions of two feet, shall
be forwarded by the post under the provisions aforesaid.

Every packet transmitted by the post under the
18th and 19th clauses of this Warrant, and
posted in the United Kingdom, shall be put into
the Post-office at such hours in the day, and
under all such regulations as the Postmaster-
General may appoint, and the postage thereof
shall be paid at the time of the same being
posted by the proper postage stamp or stamps
being affixed thereto, which stamp or stamps
shall in every case be affixed or appear on
the outside of every such packet, near the
address or direction, and shall be of the value
or amount of the postage duty payable thereon, under or by virtue of this Warrant ; and
upon every such packet which shall be posted
in Spain, the Balearic or the Canary Islands,
the postage thereof, with any transit rate payable thereon, shall be paid at the time of the
same being posted.

23. If any packet transmitted by the post under
the 18th, 19th, 20th, and 21st clauses of this
Warrant, be sent otherwise than in conformity

with the conditions and regulations established by, or under the 22nd clause of this Warrant, the same shall and may be detained and opened, and at the option of the Postmaster-General, shall be either returned or given up to the sender thereof, or be given up to the person to whom the same shall be addressed, or be forwarded to the place of its destination and any such packet ; on being so returned, given up, or forwarded, shall be chargeable with any rates of postage the Postmaster-General may think fit, not exceeding the rates that would be chargeable on such packet as an unpaid letter.

24. All packets consisting of printed newspapers and other printed papers posted in Spain, or the Balearic or Canary Islands, addressed to the United Kingdom, may be transmitted by the post to the United Kingdom, either viâ France, or direct by packet-boat, at the rates of postage hereinafter mentioned (that is to say,) if viâ France, at the rate of fivepence for every British pound net weight thereof, and if direct by packet-boat, at the rate of tenpence for every British pound net weight thereof.

25. All packets consisting of printed newspapers and other printed papers posted in Spain, or the Balearic or Canary Islands, addressed to any of Her Majesty's colonies or any foreign country, or posted in any foreign country, addressed to Spain, or the Balearic or Canary Islands, may be respectively transmitted by the post through the United Kingdom, the conveyance between Spain, or the Balearic or Canary Islands, and the United Kingdom being viâ France, or direct by packet-boat, and all such respective packets shall be charged, and chargeable with a rate of postage of tenpence for every British pound net weight thereof.

26. All packets consisting of printed newspapers and other printed papers posted in Spain, or the Balearic or Canary Islands, addressed to any of

Her Majesty's colonies, or any foreign country, or posted in any foreign country addressed to Spain, or the Balearic or Canary Islands, may be respectively transmitted by the post otherwise than through the United Kingdom, the sea conveyance being by British packet boats, and all such respective packets shall be charged and chargeable with a rate of postage of five pence for every British pound net weight thereof.

27. All packets consisting of printed newspapers and other printed papers posted in Spain, or the Balearic or Canary Islands, addressed to the Philippine Islands, or posted in the Philippine Islands, addressed to Spain, or the Balearic or Canary Islands, which may be conveyed between Malta or Gibraltar and Hong Kong by British packet boats in the Mediterranean and Indian Ocean shall be charged with a British postage of five pence for every British pound net weight thereof.

28. The respective letters and packets transmitted by the post under the provisions of this Warrant shall be subject to the several orders, directions, regulations, and rates of postage respectively contained in a certain Warrant of the Commissioners of Her Majesty's Treasury, under the hands of two of the said Commissioners, bearing date the 19th day of February, 1855, relating to redirected rates of postage upon letters and packets, which shall be redirected and again forwarded by the post.

29. The rates of postage chargeable on letters, printed newspapers, and other printed papers, transmitted by the post, under the provisions of this Warrant, shall be in lieu of any rates of British postage now chargeable by law thereon ; and as to the postage to be collected and received on letters transmitted under the provisions of this Warrant from Spain, or the Balearic or Canary Islands, addressed to the United Kingdom, two

reals de vellan shall be considered equivalent to the sum of sixpence sterling.

30. The term "packet boat" used in this Warrant shall include the conveyance by any British or Spanish packet boat, and the term "printed papers" in this Warrant used shall for the purpose of this Warrant mean and comprise all printed papers of every kind other than newspapers, whether such papers be printed or lithographed, and whether plain, or illustrated with prints, drawings, maps, or music (provided such illustrations form part of the same publication), and the several other terms and expressions used in this Warrant shall be construed to have the like meaning in all respects as they would have had if inserted in the said Act passed in the fourth year of the reign of Her present Majesty.

31. The Commissioners for the time being of Her Majesty's Treasury may, by Warrant under their hands, or the hands of any two of them, at any time hereafter alter, repeal, or revoke any of the rates of postage hereby fixed or altered, or any of the orders, directions, regulations, and conditions hereby made, and may make and establish any new or other rates, orders, directions, regulations, and conditions in lieu thereof, and from time to time appoint at what time the rates which may be payable are to be paid.

This Warrant shall come into operation on the first day of October, 1858.

Whitehall, Treasury Chambers, the sixth day of September, one thousand eight hundred and fifty-eight.

H. G. Lennox.
Henry Whitmore.

Christchurch Union.—Christchurch Parish.

An order of the Poor Law Commissioners dated the 30th August, 1858, to the Churchwardens and Overseers of the Poor of the Parish of Christchurch, in the county of Southampton, and to all other whom it may concern (as set forth in this Gazette), directs that so much of the Act 13th and 14th Vic. cap. 57, as relates to the appointment of a Vestry Clerk, shall forthwith be applied to, and be put in force within the said Parish of Christchurch.

———————

FROM THE

LONDON GAZETTE of SEPTEMBER 10, 1858.

NOTIFICATION.

WHEREAS there was concluded between Her Majesty and the Emperor of Brazil, on the 2nd day of June, 1858, a Convention in the following terms, for the settlement of outstanding claims, by means of a Mixed Commission:

WHEREAS claims have at various times since the date of the Declaration of Independence of the Brazilian Empire been made upon the Government of Her Britannic Majesty on the part of Corporations, Companies, and private individuals, subjects of His Majesty the Emperor of Brazil, and upon the Government of His Majesty the Emperor of Brazil on the part of Corporations, Companies, and private individuals, subjects of Her Britannic Majesty; and whereas some of such claims are still pending, or are still considered by either of the two Governments to remain un-

settled; Her Majesty the Queen of the United
Kingdom of Great Britain and Ireland, and His
Majesty the Emperor of Brazil, being of opinion
that the settlement of all such claims will contri-
bute much to the maintenance of the friendly
feelings which subsist between the two countries,
have resolved to make arrangements for that purpose by means of a Convention, and have named
as their Plenipotentaries to confer and agree
thereupon, that is to say:

Her Majesty the Queen of the United Kingdom
of Great Britain and Ireland, the Honourable
Peter Campbell Scarlett, Companion of the Most
Honourable Order of the Bath, and Her Britannic
Majesty's Envoy Extraordinary and Minister
Plenipotentiary to the Court of Rio de Janeiro,
&c., &c., &c.

And His Majesty the Emperor of Brazil, the
Most Illustrious and Most Excellent Sergio
Teixeira de Macedo, Member of His Council,
holding rank as His Envoy Extraordinary and
Minister Plenipotentiary, Great Cross of the
Order of the Rose, and of that of Christ of Por-
tugal, Commander of the Orders of St. Gregory
Magnus, of St. Maurice and St. Lazarus, and of
the Imperial Angelic and Constantinian Order of
St. George, Member of the Chamber of Deputies,
&c., &c., &c.

Who, having communicated to each other their
respective full powers, found in good and due
form, have agreed as follows :—

ARTICLE I.

The High Contracting Parties agree that all
claims on the part of Corporations, Companies, or
private individuals, subjects of Her Britannic
Majesty, upon the Government of His Majesty
the Emperor of Brazil, and all claims on the part

of Corporations, Companies, or private individuals, subjects of His Majesty the Emperor of Brazil, upon the Government of Her Britannic Majesty, which may have been presented to either Government for its interposition with the other since the date of the Declaration of Independence of the Brazilian Empire, and which yet remain unsettled, or are considered to be still unsettled, by either of the two Governments, as well as any other such claims which may be presented within the time specified in Article III hereinafter, shall be referred to two Commissioners, to be appointed in the following manner ; that is to say : one Commissioner shall be named by Her Britannic Majesty, and one by His Majesty the Emperor of Brazil.

Her Britannic Majesty and His Majesty the Emperor of Brazil, respectively, shall appoint a Secretary to the Commission, who shall be empowered to act as Commissioner in case of the temporary incapacity or absence of the Commissioner of his Government, and also in case of the death, definite absence, or incapacity of the said Commissioner, or in the event of his omitting or ceasing to act as such, until the appointment of, and assumption of his duties by, another Commissioner in the place or stead of the said Commissioner.

In the case of the death, or definite absence, or incapacity of the Commissioner on either side, or in the event of the Commissioner on either side omitting or ceasing to act as such, Her Britannic Majesty, or His Majesty the Emperor of Brazil, respectively, shall forthwith name another person to act as Commissioner, in the place or stead of the Commissioner originally named.

In case of the Secretary on either side being appointed permanently Commissioner, Her Britannic Majesty or His Majesty the Emperor of Brazil, respectively, shall forthwith name another person to be Secretary in the place or stead of the Secretary originally named.

The Commissioners shall meet at Rio de Janeiro, at the earliest convenient period after they shall have been named, and shall, before proceeding to any business, make and subscribe a solemn declaration that they will impartially and carefully examine and decide, to the best of their judgment, and according to justice and equity, without fear, favour, or affection to their own country, upon all such claims as shall be laid before them on the part of the Governments of Her Britannic Majesty and His Majesty the Emperor of Brazil, respectively ; and such declaration shall be entered on the record of their proceedings.

The Secretary on either side, when called upon to act as Commissioner for the first time, and before proceeding to act as such, shall make and subscribe a similar declaration, which shall be entered in like manner as aforesaid.

The Commissioners shall, before proceeding to any other business, name a third person to act as an Arbitrator or Umpire, in any case or cases on which they may themselves differ in opinion.

If they should not be able to agree upon the selection of such a person, the Commissioner on either side shall name a person ; and in each and every case in which the Commissioners may differ in opinion as to the decision which they ought to give, it shall be determined by lot which of the two persons so named shall be Arbitrator or Umpire in that particular case.

The person so to be chosen to be Arbitrator or Umpire shall, before proceeding to act as such in any case, make and subscribe a solemn Declaration, in a form similar to that which shall have already been made and subscribed by the Commissioners, which Declaration shall be entered on the record of their proceedings.

In the event of the death, absence, or incapacity of such person, or of his omitting, or declining, or ceasing to act as such Arbitrator or Umpire, another and different person shall be named as aforesaid to act as such Arbitrator or Umpire in the place or stead of the person so originally named as aforesaid, and shall make and subscribe such Declaration as aforesaid.

ARTICLE II.

The Commissioners shall then forthwith proceed to the investigation of the claims which shall be presented to their notice.

They shall investigate and decide upon such claims in such order and in such manner as they may think proper, but upon such evidence or information only as shall be furnished by or on behalf of the respective Governments.

They shall be bound to receive and peruse all written or printed documents or statements which may be presented to them by or on behalf of the respective Governments, in support of or in answer to any claim, and to hear, if required, one person on each side on behalf of each Government, as counsel or agent for such Government, on each and every separate claim.

Should they fail to agree in opinion upon any individual claim, they shall call to their assistance the Arbitrator or Umpire whom they have agreed to name, or who may be determined by lot, as the case may be; and such Arbitrator or Umpire, after having examined the evidence adduced for and against the claim, and after having heard, if required, one person on each side as aforesaid, and consulted with the Commissioners, shall decide thereupon finally, and without appeal.

The decision of the Commissioners, and of the Arbitrator or Umpire, shall be given upon each claim in writing, and shall be signed by them respectively.

It shall be competent for each Government to name one person to attend the Commission as agent on its behalf, to present and support claims, and to answer claims made upon it, and to represent it generally in all matters connected with the investigation and decision thereof.

Her Majesty the Queen of Great Britain and Ireland, and His Majesty the Emperor of Brazil, hereby solemnly and sincerely engage to consider the decision of the Commissioners, or of the Arbitrator or Umpire, as the case may be, as absolutely final and conclusive upon each claim decided upon by them or him respectively, and to give full effect to such decisions without any objection, evasion, or delay whatsoever.

ARTICLE III.

Every claim shall be presented to the Commission within twelve months from the day of its first meeting, unless in any case where reasons for delay shall be established to the satisfaction of the Commission, or of the Arbitrator or Umpire in the event of the Commissioners differing in opinion thereupon ; and then and in any such case, the period for presenting the claim may be extended to any time not exceeding six months longer.

The Commissioners shall be bound, under this Convention, to hold, for the consideration of the claims, at least eight sittings in each month, from the date of their first sitting until the completion of their labours.

The Commissioners shall be bound to examine

and decide upon every claim within two years from the day of their first meeting, unless on account of some unforeseen and unavoidable suspension of the sittings, the two Governments may mutually agree to extend the time.

The Arbitrator or Umpire shall be bound to come to a final decision on any claim within fifteen days from the time of such claim being submitted to his consideration, unless the Commissioners consider a more extended period absolutely necessary.

It shall be competent for the Commissioners, or for the Arbitrator or Umpire if they differ, to decide in each case whether any claim has or has not been duly made, preferred, or laid before the Commission, either wholly or to any and what extent, according to the true intent and meaning of this Convention.

ARTICLE IV.

All sums of money which may be awarded by the Commission, or by the Arbitrator or Umpire, on account of any claim, shall be paid by the one Government to the other, as the case may be, within twelve months after the date of the decision, without interest, and without any deduction save as specified in Article VI hereinafter.

ARTICLE V.

The High Contracting Parties engage to consider the result of the proceedings of this Commission as a full, perfect, and final settlement of every claim upon either Government, arising out of any transaction of a date prior to the exchange of the ratifications of the present Convention; and further engage that every such claim, whether or not the same may have been presented to the notice of, made, preferred, or laid before the said Commission, shall, from and after the conclusion of the proceedings of the said Commission, be considered and treated as finally settled, barred, and thenceforth inadmissible.

ARTICLE VI.

The Commissioners and the Arbitrator or Umpire, with the assistance of the Secretaries, shall keep an accurate record and correct minutes or notes of all their proceedings, with the dates thereof, and shall appoint and employ a Clerk, if necessary, to assist them in the transaction of the business which may come before them.

Each Government shall pay to its Commissioner an amount of salary not exceeding six contos of reis, or six hundred and seventy-five pounds sterling a year, which amount shall be the same for both Governments.

Each Government shall pay to its Secretary an amount of salary not exceeding three contos, or three hundred and thirty-seven pounds ten shillings sterling a year, which amount shall be the same for both Governments.

The Secretary on either side, when acting as Commissioner, shall receive the same amount of salary a year as that paid to the Commissioner; it being understood that his salary as Secretary shall lapse during that time.

The amount of salary to be paid to the Arbitrator or Umpire shall be the same, in proportion to the time he may be occupied, as the amount paid a year to a Commissioner under this Convention.

The salary of the Clerk, if one is appointed, shall not exceed the sum of two contos, or two hundred and twenty-five pounds sterling a year.

The whole expenses of the Commission, including contingent expenses, shall be defrayed by a rateable deduction on the amount of the sums awarded by the Commissioners, or by the Arbitrator or Umpire, as the case may be; provided always that such deduction shall not exceed the rate of five per cent. on the sums so awarded.

The deficiency, if any, shall be defrayed by the two Governments.

ARTICLE VII.

The present Convention shall be ratified by Her Britannic Majesty, and by His Majesty the Emperor of Brazil; and the ratifications shall be exchanged at London as soon as may be within six months from the date hereof.

In witness whereof the respective Plenipotentiaries have signed the same, and have affixed thereto the seals of their arms.

Done at Rio de Janeiro, the second day of June, in the year of our Lord one thousand eight hundred and fifty-eight.

(L.S.)   P. CAMPBELL SCARLETT.
(L.S.)   SERGIO T. DE MACEDO.

And whereas the ratifications of the said Convention were exchanged at London, on the 9th instant; and whereas Commissioners on the part of Her Majesty and of the Emperor of Brazil are about to meet at Rio de Janeiro for the purpose of carrying out the stipulations of such Convention:

Notice is hereby given, that all persons, subjects of Her Majesty, who may have claims to prefer upon the Government of Brazil, must, in conformity with the provisions of the said Convention, transmit to Her Majesty's Principal Secretary of State for Foreign Affairs, or to Her Majesty's Minister at the Court of Brazil, in sufficient time to be laid before the Commissioners within twelve months of the day of their first meeting (of which day notice will hereafter be given), the particulars of their claims, together with the requisite evidence or information in support thereof.

Foreign Office, September, 10, 1858.

At the Court at *Osborne House, Isle of Wight,* the 2nd day of *September,* 1858.

The QUEEN'S Most Excellent Majesty in Council was pleased to approve a representation duly prepared (as set forth in this Gazette) by the Ecclesiastical Commissioners for England, as to the assignment of a district chapelry to the consecrated church of Saint John, situate at Studley, in the district parish of the Holy Trinity, Trowbridge, in the county of Wilts, and in the diocese of Salisbury.

Also to approve and ratify a scheme duly prepared by the said Commissiouers,—

For constituting a separate district for spiritual purposes out of the chapelry of Saint Margaret, in the parish of Saint Oswald, Durham, in the county and diocese of Durham, to be named The District of Saint Cuthbert, Durham.

Osborne, September 2, 1858.

The Queen was this day pleased to confer the honour of Knighthood upon John William Fisher, Esq., Chief Surgeon to the Metropolitan Police.

(1389.)

Board of Trade, Whitehall,
September 8, 1858.

The Right Honourable the Lords of the Committee of Privy Council for Trade and Plantations hereby call the attention of Masters and Owners of British Vessels trading with French ports, to the Notice which appeared in the London Gazette of the 23rd July last, relative to their being provided with correct manifests of cargo, as neglect to comply with the prescribed regulations may subject them to heavy penalties.

War-Office, Pall-Mall,
10th September, 1858.

3rd Regiment of Light Dragoons, Lieutenant Henry Fawcett to be Captain, by purchase, vice Surtees, who retires. Dated 10th September, 1858.

5th Light Dragoons, Boyle Vandeleur, Gent., to be Cornet, without purchase, vice FitzSimon, appointed to the 6th Dragoons. Dated 10th September, 1858.

13th Light Dragoons, Cornet Richard William Renshaw, from the 2nd Dragoon Guards, to be Lieutenant, by purchase, vice Southwell, who has retired. Dated 10th September, 1858.

8th Regiment of Foot, Assistant-Surgeon Joseph Edward O'Loughlin, from the Staff, to be Assistant-Surgeon. Dated 10th September, 1858.

9th Foot, Captain J. Baillie, from Adjutant of a Depôt Battalion, to be Captain, vice O'Shea, who exchanges. Dated 10th September, 1858.

10th Foot, Gentleman Cadet Thomas H. Powell, from the Royal Military College, to be Ensign, without purchase, vice Newbatt, promoted in the 16th Foot. Dated 10th September, 1858.

17th Foot.
To be Captains, without purchase,
Captain Norris Goddard, from half-pay Unattached. Dated 10th September, 1858.

Lieutenant Oates Joseph Travers, from the 70th Foot. Dated 10th September, 1858.

Lieutenant Francis Horatio Gee, from the 87th Foot. Dated 10th September, 1858.

Lieutenant the Honourable S. R. H. Ward, from the 72nd Foot. Dated 10th September, 1858.

To be Lieutenants, without purchase.

Ensign C. Bunbury, from the 63rd Foot. Dated 10th September, 1858.

Ensign J. E. W. Hussey, from the 39th Foot. Dated 10th September, 1858.

Ensign G. A. Crickitt, from the 62nd Foot. Dated 10th September, 1858.

Ensign H. T. Sheppard, from the 48th Foot. Dated 10th September, 1858.

The Commission of Lieutenant F. J. Berkeley, as Adjutant, to be antedated to the 3rd May, 1858.

18th Foot.

To be Captains, without purchase.

Captain Simeon Charles Lousada, from half-pay 9th Foot, vice Adams, removed to the 20th Foot. Dated 10th September, 1858.

Captain Edward Abbot Anderson, from half-pay Unattached. Dated 10th September, 1858.

Lieutenant William Crozier, from the 70th Foot. Dated 10th September, 1858.

Lieutenant George S. Hallowes, from the 25th Foot. Dated 10th September, 1858.

Lieutenant James Tarrant Ring. Dated 10th September, 1858.

To be Lieutenants, without purchase.

Ensign J. W. Home, from the 34th Foot. Dated 10th September, 1858.

Ensign J. A. J. Briggs, from the 44th Foot. Dated 10th September, 1858.

Ensign W. H. Thomas, from the 33rd Foot. Dated 10th September, 1858.

Ensign W. O. Bourke, from the 10th Foot. Dated 10th September, 1858.

Ensign E. T. Evans, from the 25th Foot. Dated 10th September, 1858.

Ensign R. W. Beachey, from the 76th Foot. Dated 10th September, 1858.

Ensign Thomas Watt, vice Ring. Dated 10th September, 1858.

20th Foot.

To be Captains, without purchase.

Captain A. N. Adams, from the 18th Foot. Dated 10th September, 1858.

Lieutenant George L. W. D. Flamstead, from the 52nd Foot. Dated 10th September, 1858.

Lieutenant Henry Evans Quin, from the 29th Foot. Dated 10th September, 1858.

Lieutenant Patrick Geraghty. Dated 10th September, 1858.

To be Lieutenants, without purchase.

Ensign H. P. Chapman, from the 38th Foot. Dated 10th September, 1858.

Ensign F. Fox, from the 88th Foot. Dated 10th September, 1858.

Ensign H. Archdall, from the 39th Foot. Dated 10th September, 1858.

Ensign F. Wright, from the 56th Foot. Dated 10th September, 1858.

Ensign H. F. G. Webster, from the 44th Foot. Dated 10th September, 1858.

Ensign A. W. Gilley, from the 34th Foot. Dated 10th September, 1858.

Ensign N. X. Gwynne, from the 41st Foot. Dated 10th September, 1858.

Ensign F. Mansel, vice Geraghty. Dated 10th September, 1858.

Ensign John Aldridge to be Lieutenant, by purchase, vice Rochfort, promoted. Dated 10th September, 1858.

21st Foot.

To be Captains, without purchase.

Captain the Honourable William Leopold Talbot, from half-pay 9th Foot. Dated 10th September, 1858.

Lieutenant George Frederick Gildea, from the 69th Foot. Dated 10th September, 1858.

Lieutenant A. W. P. Weekes, from the 78th Foot. Dated 10th September, 1858.

Lieutenant Alexander Walker, from the 45th Foot. Dated 10th September, 1858.

To be Lieutenants, without purchase.

Ensign William Blennerhasset, from the 39th Foot. Dated 10th September, 1858.

Ensign J. A. O. Carnegy, from the 63rd Foot. Dated 10th September, 1858.

Ensign George O'Connell, from the 36th Foot. Dated 10th September, 1858.

The date of Mr. Shuttleworth's appointment as Paymaster, to be antedated to the 8th June, 1858.

23rd Foot, Ensign Eugene Mervin Roe, from the Royal Wiltshire Militia, to be Ensign, without purchase, vice Colt, promoted. Dated 10th September, 1858.

24th Foot.

To be Captains, without purchase.

Captain Robert George Jephson, from half-pay 68th Foot. Dated 10th September, 1858.

Lieutenant F. D. Wyatt, from the 74th Foot.
Dated 10th September, 1858.

Lieutenant Charles Hunter, from the 81st Foot.
Dated 10th September, 1858.

Lieutenant James Tennent Tovey. Dated 10th
September, 1858.

To be Lieutenants, without purchase.

Ensign C. R. King, from the 50th Foot. Dated
10th September, 1858.

Ensign John Foot, from the 88th Foot. Dated
10th September, 1858.

Ensign A. C. Hallowes, from the 38th Foot.
Dated 10th September, 1858.

Ensign R. N. Surplice, from the 56th Foot.
Dated 10th September, 1858.

Ensign D. W. Balfour Ogilvy, from the 34th
Foot. Dated 10th September, 1858.

Ensign G. C. Ross, vice Tovey. Dated 10th
September, 1858.

26*th Foot,* Assistant-Surgeon John Davidge, from
the Staff, to be Assistant-Surgeon, vice Cullen,
appointed to the Staff. Dated 10th September,
1858.

38*th Foot,* William Drummond Pringle, Gent.,
to be Ensign, without purchase, vice Mallet,
deceased. Dated 10th September, 1858.

40*th Foot,* Captain W. L. Murphy, from half-pay
Unattached, to be Captain, vice Michael E.
Smith, who exchanges. Dated 10th September,
1858.

42*nd Foot,* The Honourable Henry Thomas Fraser
to be Ensign, by purchase, vice James, promoted. Dated 10th September, 1858.

47*th Foot,* Dudley North, Gent., to be Ensign,
by purchase, vice Tisdall, promoted in the 15th
Foot. Dated 10th September, 1858.

48*th Foot*, Assistant-Surgeon John Gordan Grant, from the Staff, to be Assistant-Surgeon. Dated 10th September, 1858.

61*st Foot.* The second Christian name of Ensign Cockle, appointed, by purchase, on the 24th August, 1858, is *Robert.*

62*nd Foot*, Ensign Arthur Lloyd Reade to be Lieutenant, by purchase, vice Hume, who retires. Dated 10th September, 1858.

65*th Foot.*

For Richard Oliffe Richmond, Gent., to be Ensign, without purchase, vice *Butler, whose appointment, as stated in the Gazette of the 16th March*, 1858, has been cancelled, which appeared in the Gazette of 2nd July last.

Read, Richard Oliffe Richmond, Gent., to be Ensign, without purchase, vice *Henry Butler, whose appointment, as stated in the Gazette of the 17th November*, 1857 has been cancelled.

67*th Foot*, Assistant - Surgeon James George Stewart Mathison, from the Staff, to be Assistant-Surgeon. Dated 10th September, 1858.

78*th Foot*, Ensign Alexander Ewing to be Lieutenant, without purchase, vice Bogle, promoted in the 13th Foot. Dated 10th September, 1858.

Serjeant-Major James Hart to be Ensign, without purchase, vice Ewing. Dated 10th September, 1858.

84*th Foot*, Major Charles F. Seymour to be Lieutenant-Colonel, without purchase, vice Brevet-Colonel David Russell, C.B., appointed Inspecting Field Officer of a Recruiting District. Dated 10th September, 1858.

Captain Spier Hughes to be Major, without purchase, vice Seymour. Dated 10th September, 1858.

Lieutenant Robert Torrens Pratt to be Captain, without purchase, vice Hughes. Dated 10th September, 1858.

Ensign Charles Thomas Horan to be Lieutenant, without purchase, vice Pratt. Dated 10th September, 1858.

Ensign John Hunter Knox, from the 94th Foot, to be Ensign, vice Wolseley, promoted. Dated 10th September, 1858.

91*st Foot.* The appointment of William Gamul Edwards, Gent., to an Ensigncy, by purchase, as stated in the Gazette of the 30th July, 1858, has been cancelled.

94*th Foot,* Ensign Edward Logan Stehelin, from the 16th Foot, to be Ensign, vice Knox, appointed to the 84th Foot. Dated 10th September, 1858.

97*th Foot,* Quartermaster-Serjeant Peter Lawless to be Ensign, without purchase, vice Slator, deceased. Dated 10th September, 1858.

99*th Foot,* Assistant-Surgeon Samuel Halliday Macartney, from the Staff, to be Assistant-Surgeon. Dated 10th September, 1858.

Rifle Brigade, Captain George Stavely Hill, from half-pay Unattached, to be Captain. Dated 10th September, 1858.

Lieutenant William Trevor Rooper to be Captain, by purchase, vice Hill, who retires. Dated 10th September, 1858.

Ensign A. H. T. H. Somerset to be Lieutenant, by purchase, vice Rooper. Dated 10th September, 1858.

2nd West India Regiment, Lieutenant W. Cooke O'Shaughnessy to be Adjutant, vice Jones. promoted. Dated 10th July, 1858.

DEPOT BATTALION.

Major the Honourable Daniel Greville Finch, from half-pay Unattached, to be Major. Dated 10th September, 1858.

Major Herbert Russell Manners, from half-pay Unattached, to be Major, vice Sykes, whose appointment from half-pay, as stated in the Gazette of the 24th August, 1858, has been cancelled. Dated 10th September, 1858.

Captain Rodney P. O'Shea, from the 9th Foot, to be Adjutant, vice Baillie, who exchanges. Dated 10th September, 1858.

STAFF.

Brevet-Colonel Edward Rowley Hill, from the 63rd Foot, to be Deputy Adjutant-General to the Forces serving in the Windward and Leeward Islands, vice George, whose term of service on the Staff has expired. Dated 10th September, 1858.

UNATTACHED.

Major and Brevet-Colonel James R. Brunker, on half-pay 15th Foot, late Deputy Adjutant-General in Ceylon, to be Lieutenant-Colonel, without purchase. Dated 24th August, 1858.

Major and Brevet-Colonel F. Darley George, on half-pay 22nd Foot, late Deputy Adjutant-General in the Windward and Leeward Islands, to be Lieutenant-Colonel, without purchase. Dated 10th September, 1858.

HOSPITAL STAFF.

Assistant-Surgeon William Fleming Cullen, from the 26th Foot, to be Assistant-Surgeon to the Forces, vice Peppin, appointed to the 2nd Foot. Dated 10th September, 1858,

BREVET.

The undermentioned promotions to take place consequent upon the death of Lieutenant-General Archibald Money, C.B., K.C., Colonel of the 2nd Dragoons, on the 25th August, 1858 :

Major-General Beaumont Lord Hotham, Lieutenant-Colonel on half-pay Unattached, to have the rank of Lieutenant-General. Dated 26th August, 1858.

Major-General Joseph Paterson, Colonel Commandant, 60th Foot, to be Lieutenant-General. Dated 26th August, 1858.

Brevet-Colonel Marcus J. Slade, from half-pay as Lieutenant-Colonel, 4th Foot, to be Major-General. Dated 26th August, 1858.

Brevet-Lieutenant-Colonel Guy Clarke, on half-pay as Major Unattached, to be Colonel. Dated 26th August, 1858.

Brevet-Major Adolphus F. Bond, on half-pay Royal Staff Corps, Staff Officer of Pensioners, to be Lieutenant-Colonel. Dated 26th August, 1858.

Captain William Collier Menzies, Royal Engineers, to be Major. Dated 26th August, 1858.

Captain George Stavely Hill, Rifle Brigade, to be Major in the Army. Dated 9th November, 1846.

Brevet-Major George Stavely Hill, Rifle Brigade, to be Lieutenant-Colonel in the Army. Dated 20th June, 1854.

The undermentioned Officers, having completed three years' actual service in the rank of Lieutenant-Colonel, to be promoted to be Colonels in the Army, under the Royal Warrant of the 6th October, 1854 :

Lieutenant-Colonel John Alfred Street, C.B., of a Depôt Battalion. Dated 11th August, 1858.

Lieutenant-Colonel. Francis Pym Harding, C.B., 22nd Foot. Dated 9th September, 1858.

The Commission as Brevet-Colonel of Lieutenant-Colonel Arthur Lowry Cole, C.B., 17th Foot, to be antedated to the 9th March, 1858.

The undermentioned promotions to take place in the Indian Military Forces of Her Majesty, consequent on the death of Major-Generals Frederick Parkinson Lester, Bombay Artillery, on 3rd July, 1858 ; James Henderson Dunsterville, Bombay Infantry, on 12th July, 1858 ; Charles Evans, Bombay Infantry, on 19th July, 1858 ; and Lieutenant-General John Anderson, Madras Infantry, on 22nd July, 1858 ;

Major-General Duncan Gordon Scott, Bengal Infantry, to be Lieutenant-General. Dated 23rd July, 1858.

To be Major-Generals.

Colonel George Campbell, Bengal Artillery. Dated 4th July, 1858.

Colonel Peter Innes, Bengal Infantry. Dated 18th July, 1858.

Colonel Alexander William Lawrence. Madras Light Cavalry. Dated 20th July, 1858.

Colonel Sir Frederick Abbott, C.B., Lieutenant-Governor of the Military College, at Addiscombe, late of Bengal Engineers. Dated 23rd July, 1858.

Colonel John Fowler Bradford, C.B., Bengal Light Cavalry. Dated 23rd July, 1858.

The Commission of Major-General Thomas Polwhele, Bengal Infantry, to bear date 1st May, 1858, and that of Major-General Richard James Holwell Birch, C.B., Bengal Infantry, to bear date 4th May, 1858.

Commission signed by the Lord Lieutenant of the County of Forfar.

Lieutenant-Colonel Charles Brown Constable, H.E.I.C.S., to be Deputy Lieutenant. Dated 2nd September, 1858.

Commissions signed by the Lord Lieutenant of the County Palatine of Lancaster.

2nd Regiment of the Duke of Lancaster's Own Militia.

Lieutenant Le Gendre Starkie to be Captain, vice Stanley, resigned. Dated 4th September, 1858.

3rd Regiment of the Duke of Lancaster's Own Militia.

Lieutenant Robert Furey to be Captain, vice Monk, resigned. Dated 4th September, 1858.

Lieutenant Philip Haughton Whittaker to be Captain, vice Ayrton, deceased. Dated 4th September, 1858.

Ensign William Turner to be Lieutenant, vice Furey, promoted. Dated 4th September, 1858.

Ensign Thomas James Eccles to be Lieutenant, vice Whittaker, promoted. Dated 4th September, 1858.

Ensign William Fitch Storey to be Lieutenant, vice Cunliffe, resigned. Dated 4th September, 1858.

4th or Duke of Lancaster's Own (Light Infantry) Regiment of Royal Lancashire Militia.

Henry William Coyne, Gent., to be Ensign, vice Betham, promoted. Dated 4th September, 1858.

6th Regiment of Royal Lancashire Militia.

Herbert Buchanan, Gent., to be Lieutenant. Dated 4th September, 1858.

*Commission signed by the Lord Lieutenant of the
County of* Hereford.

Herefordshire Regiment of Militia.

Francis William Layng to be Ensign, in the place
of Thomas Milward Bennett, promoted. Dated
3rd September, 1858.

*Commission signed by the Lord Lieutenant of the
County of* Denbigh.

Denbighshire Yeomanry Cavalry.

Alexander Reid, Esq., to be Captain, vice Whalley,
resigned. Dated 1st September, 1858.

*Commissions signed by the Lord Lieutenant of the
County of* Devon.

*Exeter and South Devon Volunteer Rifle
Battalion.*

James Thorne George to be Lieutenant. Dated
8th May, 1858.
William Henry Rodway to be Ensign. Dated
8th May, 1858.

*Commission signed by the Lord Lieutenant of the
County of* Sussex.

*Light Infantry Battalion of the Royal Sussex
Militia.*

Thomas Jones Sherwood, Gent., to be Ensign,
vice Geneste, resigned. Dated 31st August,
1858.

*Commission signed by the Lord Lieutenant of the
County of* Essex.

The Essex Rifles.

Christopher Brice Wilkinson, Esq., late Captain
in the 68th Light Infantry, to be Major, vice
Kelly, promoted. Dated 6th September, 1858.

Commission signed by the Lord Lieutenant of the County of Kent.

East Kent Regiment of Militia.

Dominick Gore Daly, Gent., late Lieutenant 3rd Jagers, to be Ensign, vice Monypenny, promoted. Dated 30th July, 1858.

TREASURY WARRANT.

WHEREAS by an Act of Parliament, passed in the fourth year of the reign of Her present Majesty, intituled " An Act for the regulation of the duties of postage," power is given to the Commissioners of Her Majesty's Treasury, from time to time, by Warrant under their hands, to alter and fix any of the rates of British postage or inland postage, payable by law, on the transmission by the post of foreign or colonial letters or newspapers, or of any other printed papers, and to subject the same to rates of postage according to the weight thereof, and a scale of weight to be contained in such Warrant, and, from time to time, by Warrant as aforesaid, to alter or repeal any such altered rates, and make and establish any new or other rates in lieu thereof, and, from time to time, to appoint at what time the rates which may be payable are to be paid.

And whereas further powers are given to the Commissioners of Her Majesty's Treasury by another Act of Parliament, passed in the eleventh year of the reign of Her present Majesty, intituled " An Act for giving further facilities for the transmission of letters by post, and for the regulating the duties of postage thereon, and for other purposes relating to the Post-office."

And whereas the Commissioners of Her Majesty's Treasury, by a certain Warrant under their hands, bearing date the 16th day of August, 1858, did order and direct that, on any letter posted in the United Kingdom, addressed to Barbadoes, Trinidad, and Saint Helena, and on every letter posted in Barbadoes, Trinidad, and Saint Helena, addressed to the United Kingdom, the postage thereof should be paid at the time of the same being posted, and that if any letter should be posted in the United Kingdom, addressed to Barbadoes, Trinidad, or Saint Helena, without any postage having been paid thereon, or having thereon or affixed thereto a postage stamp or stamps, the value of which shall be less in amount than the single rate of postage to which such letter if not exceeding half an ounce in weight would be liable under the regulations in force relating thereto, every such letter should be detained and opened and should be either returned or given up to the sender thereof.

And whereas it is expedient that a further regulation should be made as to the letters hereinafter mentioned.

Now we, the Commissioners of Her Majesty's Treasury, in exercise of the powers reserved to us in and by the said hereinbefore recited Acts, or either of them, and of all other powers enabling us in this behalf, do by this present Warrant, under the hands of two of us the said Commissioners, by the authority of the Statute in that case made and provided, order and direct as follows ; that is to say :

1. If any letter shall be posted in the United Kingdom, addressed to Barbadoes, Trinidad, or Saint Helena, without any postage having been paid thereon, or having thereon, or affixed thereto, a postage stamp or stamps, the value of which shall be less in amount than the single rate of postage to which such letter if not exceeding half

an ounce in weight would be liable, under the regulations in force relating thereto, every such letter shall until the 31st day of December, 1858, inclusive, be forwarded, charged with the amount of the postage to which it would have been liable .if the postage had been paid when posted, together with the further and additional rate of postage of sixpence ; and from and after the said 31st day of December, 1858, every such letter instead of being forwarded, shall be detained and opened, and be either returned or given up to the sender thereof, as directed by the said recited Warrant of the 16th day of August, 1858.

2. The several terms and expressions used in this Warrant, shall be construed to have the like meaning in all respects as they would have had if inserted in the said Act, passed in the fourth year of the reign of Her present Majesty.

3. The Commissioners for the time being of .Her. Majesty's Treasury, may by Warrant, under their hands, duly made at any time hereafter, alter repeal or revoke, any of the orders, directions, or regulations hereby made, and may make and establish any new or other orders, directions, or regulations, in lieu thereof.

4. This Warrant shall come into operation on the first day of October, 1858.

Whitehall, Treasury Chambers, the sixth day of September, 1858.

H. G. Lennox.
Henry Whitmore,

FROM THE

LONDON GAZETTE of SEPTEMBER 14, 1858.

Leeds, September 7, 1858.

THE Queen was this day pleased to confer the honour of Knighthood upon Peter Fairbairn, of Woodsley House, in the county of York, Esq., Mayor of the borough of Leeds.

(6393.)

Board of Trade, Whitehall, September 13, 1858.

The Right Honourable the Lords of the Committee of Privy Council for Trade and Plantations have received, through the Secretary of State for Foreign Affairs, a copy of a Despatch from Her Majesty's Consul at Lisbon, enclosing copy of a Portuguese Royal Decree, reducing for a period not to exceed the end of May, 1859, the import duty on foreign rice, to 600 reis, per 100 lbs. weight, and permitting during a similar period the free importation into the kingdom of Portugal of grain of all kinds and of all sorts of leguminous seeds.

1338.

Board of Trade, Whitehall, September 2, 1858.

The Right Honourable the Lords of the Committee of Privy Council for Trade and Plantations have received, through the Secretary of State for

Foreign Affairs, a copy of a Despatch from Her Majesty's Consul-General at Hamburg, announcing that the Government of that State has issued a notification exempting the undermentioned articles from the transit dues of ¼ schilling per centner, hitherto levied on them by the Governments of Hamburg and Lubec, on the Berlin and Hamburg Railway.

(1338.)

Law or business documents.
Agaric.
Antimony.
Arsenic.
Ashes: potash, soda, and other kind of ashes.
Carbonate of natron (ashphaltum, bitumen), Judaicum or glutinous bitumen.
Oysters.
Live trees and shrubs.
Bamboo, Indian reeds or canes, and other rough reeds, not manufactured.
Yellow amber.
Brooms and rubbers (unless comprised under the article "brushes.")
Castoreum.
Pumice stone.
Lead in pigs, blocks and moulds, old lead for remelting, and old sheet lead.
Black lead.
Flowers and flower plants.
Bulbs and roots of flowers.
Blood.
Bloodstone or hœmotiles.
Beans.
Bole, white and red and terra sigillata.
Borax, raw or refined.
Tanners' bark or tan.
Brown, red, or Spanish brown manganese.

Printed books, with the prints which belong to them, bound or unbound.

Brushwood.

Butter.

Cadmium.

Camphor.

Cements of all kinds.

Maps and charts.

Cologne earth, white.

Corals.

Reeds for thatching.

Slates for roofing.

Tiles.

Dung and artificial manure ; also, for example, patent manure, not being animal, &c., except white saltpetre, sulphated ammonia, and similar goods.

Plaster in powder, when certified as intended to be used only for manure.

Precious stones.

Acorns.

Rough ice (natural).

Pig iron (raw).

Bar iron of all kinds, iron rails.

Elephants' teeth, or ivory.

Packages, old, or used casks, cases, trunks, chests, bags, or sacks, and old wicker flasks, empty.

Peas.

Clay, such as pipe clay, marl, English clay, China clay, fuller's earth, sugar clay, and other kinds of clay, argil and marl, unless coming in under the class of colours.

Ore, not melted, of all kinds.

Dye woods.

Quills.

Feathers for beds, and down.

Feldspar, not pulverized.

Skins, curried or not curried, without exception, such as fur skins, calf or sheep skins, cordover, morocco, &c.

Amadou, not prepared.

Whalebone, whalefins, whalebone not split.

Fresh fish and salted herrings.

Flax, dressed or undressed.

Meat, fresh and salted.

Flagstones.

Flores cassiæ (cassia buds).

Float wood (wood to be used, instead of cork, as floats for fishing nets).

Veneers.

Galls.

Calamine.

Fresh pot-herbs, also whortle-berries, or bilberries, strawberries, raspberries, gooseberries, hips, fresh grapes, horseradish, and onions.

Gut.

Pictures, as well as engravings, lithographs, and stenographs.

Gypsum, calcined.

Figures and statues in plaster.

Plaster, stone.

Globes.

Bronze or bell-metal.

Gold, in bars, and for remelting.

Peeled, shelled, or milled barley, and groats made of grain which is free from transit duty.

Hair of all kinds, including bristles, hair, and wool of pigs.

Hair, curled or crisped, is liable to duty.

Hemp, dressed or undressed.

Oil of hemp.

Isinglass.

Hay.

Wood of all kinds.

Wood for the·use of Apothecaries.

Charcoal.

Ox and cow horns (or horns of black cattle), as well as horn tips.

Leeches.

Lime.

Limestone.

Teasles.

Potatoes.

Bones.

Valonia.

Osiers, peeled or unpeeled.

Cork.

Grain, buckwheat, barley, oats, maize, rye, wheat, vetches.

Waste of grain, groats, as forage for cattle, bran, straw, chaff, and other waste of grain (offal).

Crabs' eyes.

Chalk stone, and chalk in powder.

Objects of art, such as statues, busts, bas-reliefs.

Copper—rose copper (Garkupfer), not forged or prepared by rollers, and copper in sheets for coining.

Lentils.

Rags.

Malt.

Manna.

Muscovy glass.

Mats, used.

Bricks.

Medals.

Meerschaum.

Flour or meal, made of grain which is free from transit duty.

Brass, unwrought (not forged and not prepared by rollers).

Metals, unwrought (bronze and other alloys of

metal similar to brass), not forged and not prepared by rollers,

Milk.

Minerals and objects of natural history, such as earths, stones, or ores, plants and fruits, shells, insects, birds, and other animals, stuffed or preserved in spirits of wine, for cabinets of natural history or scientific collections.

Models of all kinds.

Shells.

Music, manuscript or printed.

Oil cake.

Opium.

Paper, cuttings and shavings, and waste of paper of all kinds.

Pitch.

Pearls (real).

Mother of pearl (rough or in shells).

Platina (unwrought).

Patterns or samples of no value.

Puzzolano.

Quicksilver.

Wheelwrights' work.

Seeds—hemp, flax, colza, and other seeds of all kinds, as well as seeds for the use of apothecaries, for example, fennel seed (carraway and aniseed are liable to duty).

Salt (except medicinal salt).

Slates and slate pencils.

Turtles.

Tortoise-shell.

Sumach.

Emery.

Ropemakers' work, including hemp, nets, and fishing-nets.

Silver in bars and for remelting.

Boards for Binders, Shoemakers, Publishers ;
as well as split twigs.

Cantharides.

Bacon.

Blubber, liver, and fat, for train oil.

Steatite.

Staves, or stave wood.

Stones of all kinds.

Coals of all kinds, as well as coke and cinders.

Straw, and straw cut or chopped.

Tallow.

Seaweed, for packing and stuffing.

Cordage.

Assafœtida.

Tar and tar water.

Living animals of all kinds.

Wooden hoops.

Turf.

Tripoli.

Berries or seeds of juniper.

Juniper poles.

Wax.

Vehicles of all kinds, as well as railway carriages and tenders, locomotives are liable to
duty. Detached parts of such vehicles and
railway carriages (and dismounted vehicles
and railway carriages) are liable to duty, unless they can be considered as Wheelwrights'
work.

Spermaceti, and oil of spermaceti.

Walrus skins (of the seahorse or seacow).

Teeth of the walrus.

Lees of wine.

Sediment of wine (in a dry state).

Wool of all kinds.

Pounded brick, or brick powder.

Zinc, raw, not wrought or in cakes ; tin, raw,
unwrought and rasped tin.

Clothes and baggage of travellers.

Household furniture and implements which
have been used, if they are transported in
consequence of a change of residence,
clothes, or garments, that have been worn
transported according to the judgment of
the Custom House Officers, as travellers'
baggage, without its being necessary for
the owner to accompany them.

War-Office, Pall-Mall,
14th September, 1858.

2nd Regiment of Dragoons.

Lieutenant-General Arthur W. M. Lord Sandys,
from the 7th Dragoon Guards, to be Colonel,
vice Lieutenant-General Archibald Money,
C.B., K.C., deceased. Dated 26th August,
1858.

7th Regiment of Dragoon Guards.

Major-General Michael White, C.B., to be
Colonel, vice Lieutenant-General Lord Sandys,
transferred to the Colonelcy of the 2nd Dragoons. Dated 26th August, 1858.

Admiralty, 8th September, 1858.

Corps of Royal Marines.

The following promotions have taken place,
under Her Majesty's Order in Council of the 13th
September, 1854, in consequence of the death of
General Thomas Adams Parke, C.B., on the
Field Establishment of General Officers of the
Royal Marines, viz. :

Lieutenant-General John Rawlins Coryton to be
General.

Major-General James Irwin Willes to be Lieutenant-General, vice Coryton, promoted.

Colonel-Commandant John Tatton Brown to be Major-General, vice Willes, promoted.

Admiralty, 8th September, 1858.

Corps of Royal Marines.

Colonel Second-Commandant Anthony Blaxland Stransham to be Colonel-Commandant, vice Brown, promoted.

Lieutenant-Colonel and Brevet-Colonel Fielding Alexander Campbell to be Colonel Second Commandant, vice Stransham, promoted.

Captain and Brevet-Major Joseph Oates Travers to be Lieutenant-Colonel, vice Campbell, promoted.

First Lieutenant Richard Turberville Ansell to be Captain, vice Travers, promoted.

Second Lieutenant Andrew William Douglas Smith to be First Lieutenant, vice Ansell, promoted.

Commission signed by Field-Marshal His Royal Highness the Prince Consort, Warden of the Stannaries, *in the Counties of* Cornwall *and* Devon.

Royal Cornwall and Devon Miners Regiment of Militia.

John Borlase, Gent., to be First Lieutenant. Dated 2nd September, 1858.

Commission signed by the Lord Lieutenant of the Counties of Westmorland *and* Cumberland.

Westmorland and Cumberland Regiment of Yeomanry Cavalry.

Matthew Benson Harrison, Esq., to be Captain, vice Wilson, resigned. Dated 6th September, 1858.

Commission signed by the Lord Lieutenant of the County of Sussex.

Artillery Battalion of the Royal Sussex Militia.

Second Lieutenant Jonathan Darby to be First Lieutenant, vice 'W. W. M. Walker, resigned. Dated 1st September, 1858.

Commission signed by the Lord Lieutenant of the County of Lanark.

2nd Royal Lanarkshire Militia.

John Floyd, Esq., to be Captain, vice J. G. Campbell, resigned. Dated 26th August, 1858.

Commission signed by the Lord Lieutenant of the County of Gloucester, *and of the City and County of the City of* Gloucester, *and of the City and County of the City of* Bristol.

Royal South Gloucester Light Infantry Regiment of Militia.

John Carrington, Gent., to be Ensign, vice Tucker, resigned. Dated 10th September, 1858.

Commission signed by the Lord Lieutenant of the County of Southampton.

Hampshire Regiment of Militia.

Peter Wright Breton, Esq., late Captain in the 38th Regiment, to be Captain. Dated 9th September, 1858.

Commission signed by the Lord Lieutenant of the County of Lincoln.

Royal North Lincoln Militia.

John Woulfe Keogh, Gent., to be Ensign, vice Rambant, resigned. Dated 8th September, 1858.

FROM THE

LONDON GAZETTE of SEPTEMBER 17, 1858.

Indian-Office, September 17, 1858.

THE Secretary of State for India has received the following papers :

No. 1.

Brigadier-General G. H. MacGregor, C.B., Military Commissioner, to the Secretary to Government.

Camp, Maharajpoor, March 28, 1853.

SIR, · No. 197.

IN forwarding, for the information of the Right Honorable the Governor-General in Council, the accompanying copy of a report from Major Walsh, in military charge of a brigade of Goorkhas, giving an account of the operations which resulted in the storm and capture of Charbagh, I have the honor to bring to the favourable notice of his Lordship in Council the gallant conduct of the men and officers mentioned by Major Walsh, especially of Brigadier Junga Dooje and Colonel Sri Kishoon.

2. To General Dhere Shumshere, the youngest brother of Maharajah Jung Bahadoor, who commanded the force detached on this duty, my best thanks and those of the Government are due, for the excellent service rendered by him.

3. To Major Walsh also great credit is due for the successful issue of the operations of that day.

I have, &c.

G. H. MACGREGOR,

Brigadier-General and Military Commissioner.

No. 2.

Major C. G. Walsh, in Military Charge of 2nd Brigade, 2nd Division, Goorkha Force, to Captain MacAndrew, Military Secretary.

Camp, Lucknow, March 13, 1858.

SIR,

I HAVE the honor to report, for the information of the Military Commissioner, Brigadier-General Macgregor, C.B., that the 2nd Brigade, of which I am in military charge, moved under the orders of General Dhere Shumshere to the village situated north-east of the Charbagh yesterday morning.

On arriving in the village, we were informed that an attempt had been made to carry the Charbagh the previous evening, and had nearly succeeded. On this, General Dhere Shumshere requested me to ascertain if the village, lying a short distance to our west, was occupied. I accordingly proceeded, accompanied by Lieutenant Robertson and Serjeants Hone and Volkers, of the Artillery, and Fourah Sing, my orderly, and found the village unoccupied, and, under cover of it, passed into a garden adjacent to the Charbagh. We then returned to the General, who directed the Singanath Regiment to proceed by that route to the attack of the Charbagh, whilst he held two regiments in reserve. We effected an entrance without any loss, but had not proceeded many paces before a heavy fire of musketry, grape, and round shot was opened on us, which retarded our advance. The senior Goorkha officer suggested the advisability of bringing up the guns to open on the enemy, which, after some delay, occasioned by the difficulty of making an opening in the wall, was effected; the Goorkhas immediately resumed the advance, and I had every expectation of success crowning our efforts, when Lieutenant Sankey, of the Engineers, arrived, and informed me that it had been determined to enfilade the works on the opposite side of the canal, which would ensure the fall of the Charbagh without the necessity of any further active operations against it. The troops were accordingly withdrawn, and the enemy did not venture to molest them in their retreat. Our loss, as far as I have been able to ascertain, amounted to eleven men, of whom one was killed and ten were wounded.

My best thanks are due to Lieutenants Robertson and Gibb for their valuable assistance.

I am deeply indebted to General Dhere Shumshere for the prompt support he gave me throughout the operation. The enduring fortitude with which the officers and men of the Jungernath Regiment sustained a heavy fire without flinching was very creditable to them.

The cordial assistance rendered me by Brigadier Junge Doje and Colonel Sri Kishoon, of the Jungernath Regiment, was a source of great gratification to me.

> I have, &c.
> C. G. WALSH, Major,
> In Military Charge, 2nd Brigade,
> 2nd Division.

No. 3.

Brigadier-General J. Jones, C.B., Commanding Shahjehanpore Field Force, to the Chief of the Staff.

> *Shahjehanpore, June 3, 1858.*

Sir,

I HAVE the honor to forward herewith, for the information of his Excellency the Commander-in-Chief, a despatch from Brigadier Taylor, C.B., detailing the operations at Shahahad of the force under his command.

Brigadier Taylor, C.B., has captured two guns, and dispersed the rebels assembled at Shahabad; the successful manner in which he has carried out my instructions have elicited my entire approbation.

In forwarding this last depatch, I beg to return my sincere thanks to the officers, non-commissioned officers, and men of all branches of the service, for their ready co-operation and the cheerful endurance with which they have invariably sustained the fatigues of forced and continuous marches, during a most trying season of the year, in the Rohilcund campaigns since the formation of the Shahjehanpore Field Force.

From Lieutenant-Colonel Tombs, C.B., commanding Artillery, Brigadier C. Hagart, commanding Cavalry Brigade, Brigadier R. C. H. Taylor, C.B., commanding 1st Infantry Brigade, and from that indefatiguable officer, Brigadier Coke, C.B., whose name I have so frequently had occasion to mention in my despatches, I have received much valuable assistance.

To the officers commanding the several regiments and corps composing the field force, Major Le Mesurier, commanding 3rd company 14th battalion Royal Artillery; Lieutenant Wilson, commanding 2nd troop 1st brigade Bengal Horse Artillery; Captain H. Hammond, commanding No. 14 Light Field Battery; Captain A. G. Austen, commanding 1st company 1st battalion Bengal Artillery; Lieutenant J. W. Stubbs, commanding 4th company 4th battalion Bengal Artillery; Captain S. R. J. Coles, commanding 9th Royal Lancers; Major R. Bickerstaff, commanding wing 6th Dragoon Guards; Major T. R. Palmer, commanding 1st battalion 60th Royal Rifles, a battalion that has rendered itself conspicuous throughout the campaign, as much by its uniform good conduct as by its dashing courage in presence of the enemy; to Lieutenant-Colonel Bingham, commanding 64th Regiment; Major Butt, commanding 79th Highlanders; Lieutenant-Colonel Watson, commanding 82nd Regiment; Captain F. W. Lambert, commanding 1st Punjaub Infantry; Major Gordon, commanding 1st Seikh Infantry; Captain Ouseley, commanding 22nd Punjaub Infantry; and to Lieutenant Beville, commanding wing, Belooch battalion, I am much indebted for the efficient manner in which they have commanded their regiments on all occasions.

I beg most respectfully to bring to the notice of his Excellency the Commander-in-Chief the names of Captain C. Cureton, of the Mooltan Regiment of Cavalry, and Captain Drummond, Field Engineer. Captain Cureton, from the day the Roorkee field force crossed the Ganges, has on every occasion shown himself to be a first-rate leader of irregular cavalry. I need only instance his conduct at Nageena. Not only as an officer of cavalry has he been of the greatest advantage to me, but, from the important intelligence he was enabled to obtain, and from the reliance I felt I could place on his information, at times when all other sources failed, his services have been invaluable.

In Captain Drummond, Field Engineer, I have found an officer whose knowledge of his profession enabled me to carry out with success many undertakings, and his energy and zeal cannot be surpassed.

Brigadier Taylor, C.B., speaks in high terms of Lieutenant Hudson, his Brigade Major, and Lieutenant T. P. Campbell, his orderly officer; also of Captain J. Maguire, commanding 1st battalion 60th Rifles, and the several officers commanding the regiments and corps composing his force.

The officers serving on the staff of the field force, Major Muter, Deputy Assistant Adjutant-General, Captain Tedlie, Deputy Assistant-Quartermaster-General, Lieutenant Deedes, aide-de-camp, and Lieutenant J. H. Tyler, orderly officer, have been to me, in their respective departments, everything that I could wish.

Surgeon J. H. K. Innes, Field Surgeon, and Captain Carter, officiating Sub-Assistant Commissary-General, are also entitled to my best thanks, for their zeal and able assistance.

I beg leave to forward herewith a nominal roll of officers of the staff, and officers commanding regiments and corps of the Roorkee field force, from its crossing the Ganges at Kunkhul, on the 17th April, until its being broken up on the 7th May, after its occupation of Bareilly on the 6th May. I also forward a nominal roll of officers of the staff and officers commanding regiments and corps of the Shahjehanpore field force from its formation on the 7th May to the present date.

I have further to state, in conclusion, for the information of his Excellency the Commander-in-Chief, that the Shahjehanpore field force will be broken up from to-morrow inclusive, and, in compliance with orders received, I assume command of the brigade at Shahjehanpore.

I have, &c.

JOHN JONES, Brigadier-General,
Commanding Shahjehanpore.

No. 4

Nominal Roll of Officers of the Staff and Officers Commanding Regiments and Corps of the Roorkee Field Force, under Brigadier-General Jones, C.B., employed during the Campaign in Rohilcund.

DIVISIONAL STAFF.

Brigadier-General John Jones, C.B., 1st battalion 60th Royal Rifles, commanding Field Force.

Major D. D. Muter, 1st battalion 60th Royal Rifles, Deputy Assistant Adjutant-General.

Captain W. Tedlie, 1st battalion 60th Royal Rifles, Deputy Assistant Quartermaster-General.

Lieutenant H. G. Deedes, 1st battalion 60th Royal Rifles, Aide-de-Camp.

Lieutenant J. H. Tyler, 20th Native Infantry, extra Aide-de-Camp.

Captain C. Need, 7th Native Infantry, Baggage Master.

Surgeon J. H. K. Innes, 1st battalion 60th Royal Rifles, Field Force Surgeon.

Captain J. W. Carter, 54th Native Infantry, Officiating Sub-Assistant Commissary-General.

Captain H. Drummond, Engineers, Field Engineer.

Lieutenant H. A. Brownlow, Engineers, Assistant Field Engineer.

ARTILLERY.

Captain A. G. Austen, commanding 1st company 1st battalion Artillery.

Lieutenant J. W. Stubbs, 6th battalion 3rd brigade commanding Heavy Field Battery.

ENGINEERS.

Lieutenant W. Jeffreys, Engineers, commanding 2nd Company Sappers and Miners.

CAVALRY.

Captain S. Bott, commanding squadron 6th Dragoon Guards.

Captain C. Cureton, commanding Mooltanee Regiment of Cavalry.

Lieutenant W. Smith, commanding detachment Pathan Horse.

INFANTRY BRIGADE.

Brigadier J. Coke, C.B., commanding.

Captain H. C. Anderson, Major of Brigade.

Major F. R. Palmer, commanding 1st battalion 60th Royal Rifles.

Captain F. W. Lambert, commanding 1st Punjaub Infantry.

Major S. Gordon, commanding 1st Seikh Infantry.

Captain Larkins, commanding 17th Punjaub Infantry.

W. TEDLIE, Captain,
Officiating Deputy Assistant Adjutant-General.

J. JONES, Brigadier-General,
Commanding Roorkee Field Force.

No. 5.

Nominal Roll of Officers of the Staff, and Officers Commanding Regiments and Corps of the Shahjehanpore Field Force, under Brigadier- General John Jones, C.B., employed during the Campaign in Rohilcund.

DIVISIONAL STAFF.

Brigadier-General John Jones, C.B., 1st Battalion 60th Royal Rifles, commanding Field Force.

Major D. D. Muter, 1st Battalion 60th Royal Rifles, Deputy Assistant Adjutant-General.

Captain W. Tedlie, 1st Battalion 60th Royal Rifles, Deputy Assistant Quartermaster-General.

Lieutenant H. G. Deedes, 1st Battalion 60th Royal Rifles, Aide-de-camp.

Lieutenant J. H. Tyler, 20th Native Infantry, Extra Aide-de-camp.

Captain C. Need, 7th Native Infantry, Baggage-Master.

Surgeon J. H. K. Innes, 1st Battalion 60th Royal Rifles, Field Force Surgeon.

Captain J. W. Carter, 54th Native Infantry, Officiating Sub-Assistant Commissary-General.

Captain H. Drummond, Engineers, Field Engineer.

Lieutenant H. A. Brownlow, Engineers, Assistant Field Engineer.

ARTILLERY.

Lieutenant-Colonel H. Tombs, C.B., commanding Artillery Division.

Captain A. Bunny, Artillery Division Staff.

Major Le Mesurier, commanding 3rd Company, 14th Battalion of Royal Artillery.

Lieutenant W. Wilson, commanding 2nd Troop, 1st Brigade, Bengal Horse Artillery.

Captain H. Hammond, commanding No. 14, Light Field Battery.

Captain A. G. Austen, commanding 1st Company, 1st Battalion, Artillery.

Lieutenant J. W. Stubbs, commanding 4th Company, 4th Battalion, Artillery.

Lieutenant Tod Brown, Commissary of Ordnance.

Lieutenant J. R. Pearson, Deputy Commissary of Ordnance.

Captain C. Cookworthy, commanding 4th Company, 6th Battalion, Bengal Artillery, attached to Siege Train.

ENGINEERS.

Lieutenant P. Murray, Engineers, commanding 3rd Company Sappers and Miners.

Lieutenant W. Jeffreys, Engineers, commanding 2nd Company Sappers and Miners.

CAVALRY BRIGADE.

Brigadier C. Hagart, commanding Brigade.

Major H. A. Sarel, Major of Brigade.

Lieutenant A. W. Gore, Orderly Officer.

Captain A. R. J. Coles, commanding 9th Royal Lancers.

Major R. Bickerstaff, commanding wing 6th Dragoon Guards.

Captain C. Cureton, commanding Mooltanee Regiment of Cavalry.

Lieutenant J. B. Lind, commanding Mooltanee Horse.

——————————————— commanding Detachment 17th Punjaub Cavalry.

——————————————— commanding Pathan Horse.

1st Infantry Brigade.

Brigadier W. M. Taylor, C.B., commanding.

Lieutenant J. Hudson, Major of Brigade.

Lieutenant F. P. Campbell, Orderly Officer.

Major T. B. Butt, commanding 79th Highlanders.

Lieutenant-Colonel G. W. P. Bingham, commanding Her Majesty's 64th Regiment.

Lieutenant-Colonel D. Watson, commanding Her Majesty's 82nd Regiment.

Lieutenant H. Beville, commanding wing Belooch Battalion.

2nd Infantry Brigade.

Brigadier J. Coke, C.B., commanding.

Captain H. C. Anderson, Major of Brigade.

Major F. R. Palmer, commanding 1st Battalion 60th Royal Rifles.

Captain F. W. Lambert, commanding 1st Punjaub Infantry.

Major S. Gordon, commanding 17th Punjaub Infantry,

Captain R. Ouseley, commanding 22nd Punjaub Infantry.

W. TEDLIE, Captain,
Deputy Assistant Adjutant-General.

JOHN JONES, Brigadier-General,
Commanding Shahjehanpore Field Force.

No. 6.

Lieutenant-Colonel W. M. Taylor, C.B., Commanding Brigade, to the Assistant. Adjutant-General, Shahjehanpore Field Fore.

SIR,   Camp Shahjehanpore. June 2, 1858.

I HAVE the honour to report for the information of Brigadier-General Jones, C.B., that in compliance with his instructions, I marched with the force, as per margin,* under my command, on the evening of the 31st ultimo, about six o'clock from Shahjehanpore *en route* for Shahabad. The force halted and bivouacked a mile beyond Badshanugger, about eight miles, and resumed its march at two o'clock A.M., arriving before the town of Shahabad shortly after daylight. On the edge of a tope of trees outside the west side of the town, the enemy shewed a force of cavalry, about 150 or 200 strong, with 2 guns ; upon the column advancing towards the position, the enemy opened fire upon us, throwing several shot with precision, but fortunately without causing any casualty. I immediately sent Lieutenant-Colonel Tombs, with half of his troop, to the right front, supported by a troop of carabineers and a party of the Mooltanee Horse, under Captain Cureton. Lieutenant-Colonel Tombs advanced his guns to within about 600 yards of the enemy's, and opened fire upon them with great rapidity. Such was the precision of his fire that, after a very few rounds, one of the enemy's guns was struck and dismounted, and, the cavalry beginning to show signs of confusion, Lieutenant-Colonel Tombs advanced rapidly, when all the horsemen took to

* Colonel Tombs's Troop, Horse Artillery ; 1 Squadron of Carabineers; Cureton's Mooltanee Horse; a Wing Her Majesty's 60th Rifles ; a Wing Her Majesty's 82nd Regiment ; 22nd Regiment Punjaub Native Infantry ; Detail of Sappers and Miners ; 1 18-pounder gun: 1 8-pounder howitzer ; 1 8-pounder mortar ; 2 cohorn mortars.

flight, and 2 brass guns (a descriptive return of which is enclosed) were taken possession of by him. The whole line in the meantime had been advancing, and I now pushed forward 3 companies of the 60th Rifles, and an equal number of the 82nd in skirmishing order, and entered the city, leaving the heavy guns outside, protected by the 22nd Punjaub Native Infantry. At the same time, I ordered 3 guns of Lieutenant-Colonel Tombs's troop of horse artillery with a squadron of Mooltanee Horse, and a troop of carabineers, to work round the left of the town, whilst the remainder of the Mooltanee Horse circled round by the right. The city, however, was unoccupied, and totally deserted by the inhabitants. Having passed right through the town to the opposite side, from whence a commanding view of the surrounding country was obtained from high ground, and having ascertained that no force of the enemy was in sight, I retired the force back through the town, and sent in a detachment of engineers, under Lieutenant Jeffreys, together with the 22nd Punjaub Native Infantry, under Captain Ouseley, to burn and destroy the buildings, according to the instructions received from the Brigadier-General. During the course of the day his desire was fully carried out. About twelve of the largest and most important buildings were blown up, and the whole town set fire to in several places. Having accomplished the object of the expedition, the force marched at 7 o'clock yesterday evening, halted near Badshanugger for four hours during the night, and returned to camp at Shahjehanpore at 6 o'clock this morning. I am happy to say only two casualties occurred in the force, one man of the 60th Rifles wounded by musket shot, and one conductor of the engineer park slightly burnt by an explosion of gunpowder. Of the enemy a few sowars were cut up by the Mooltanee Horse, and a few matchlockmen were killed by the skirmishers going through the town.

To all the officers commanding corps and detachments, Lieutenant-Colonel Tombs, Horse Artillery, Major Bickerstaff, Carabineers, Captain Cureton, Mooltanee Horse, Lieutenant Stubbs, Heavy Battery, Captain Maguire, 60th Rifles, Lieutenant-Colonel Watson, 82nd Regiment, Captain Ouseley, 22nd Punjaub Native Infantry, and Lieutenant Jeffreys, Engineers, my thanks are due for the cordial assistance I received from them; more especially am I indebted to Lieutenant-Colonel Tombs, C.B., and Captain Cureton, whose experience and advice were of great use to me.

Lieutenant Hudson, 64th, Brigade Major, acted with great intelligence and zeal, and Lieutenant F. P. Campbell, 79th Highlanders, acting as my Orderly Officer, performed his duties entirely to my satisfaction.

I have, &c.

W. M. TAYLOR, Lieutenant-Colonel,
79th Highlanders,
Commanding Brigade.

No. 9.

Major-General Sir Hugh Rose, K.C.B, Commanding Central India Field Force, to the Adjutant-General of the Army, Poona.

SIR,   *Camp Goolowlee, May* 24, 1858.

I HAVE the honor to report to you, for the information of his Excellency the Commander-in-chief, that the approach of Brigadier Smith's brigade from Rajpootana to Goonah, having secured Jhansi from attack by Kotah and Bundlecund rebels, I recalled Lieutenant-Colonel Lowth commanding Her Majesty's 86th Regiment, whom I had detached with a column to watch the road from Jhansi to Goonah, and I marched with the 1st Brigade of my force from Jhansi, on the 25th ultimo, on Calpee.

I was still with the wing of the 3rd Bombay Light Cavalry, which I had sent to Goonah, to reinforce the right wing of Her Majesty's 71st Highland Light Infantry, on their march to join me, as, encumbered with a very large convoy of Treasure, and all sorts of stores, they had to cross the Sind river at a very difficult ghat, and I was not certain that they might not be exposed to a treacherous attack from the late Chandairee garrison, and other Bundelas, who, as already reported, had made an incursion on the Jhansi and Goonah road, acting, it was clear, in concert with the Kotah Rebels, to the north of the Indore and Goonah road

I left at Jhansi, for its garrison, the force, forming part of the 2nd Brigade detailed in the margin.* I left there, also, Brigadier Steuart, with the remainder of his brigade with orders to bring up to me the 71st Regiment, and two troops of the 3rd Bombay Light Cavalry.

I joined Major Gall's Force, at Pooch, sixteen miles from Koonch, on the 1st of May. I had the honor to report on the 17th instant the movements of this officer's moveable column, as well as those of Major Orr's Field Force.

I received information from Sir Robert Hamilton and Major Gall, whom I had detached along the road from Jhansi to Calpee, with a flying column, to watch the enemy, and obtain information of •

* Head Quarter Wing, 3rd European Regiment; 8 Companies 24th Bomoay Native Infantry; 100 Hydrabad Cavalry; 3 guns late Bhopal Artillery; half-Company Bombay Sappers and Miners.

their movements, that the Sepoy garrison of Calpee, of all arms, reinforced by five hundred Vilaities, under the Ranee of Jhansi, cavalry from Kotah, and guns and troops from disaffected Rajahs, the whole under the command of Tantia Topee, had occupied Koonch, and thrown up intrenchments, which they had armed, to defend the roads to the town from Jhansi ; and that they were determined to make a vigorous opposition at Koonch, to my advance against Calpee. All the accounts agreed that the rebels were strong in cavalry, mutineers of Bengal, regular and irregular cavalry.

Koonch is an open town ; but it is difficult to attack because it is surrounded by woods, gardens and temples, with high walls round them, every one of which is a defence.

I had directed Major Orr to do his utmost to prevent the Rajahs of Banpore and Shahgur, and any body of Rebels crossing the Betwa, and doubling back southwards. The two Rajahs, for the purpose of carrying out this very manœuvre, separated from the rebels of Koonch, and drove the troops of the Rajah of Goorserai, who held Kotra, commanding a ford across the Betwa, to the south bank of the river.

Major Orr crossed the Betwa, engaged the Rajahs, drove them from their position at Kotra, and took one of their guns; but he states that it was impossible to cut off the retreat of the Rajahs, who, whilst Major Orr was attacking one part of their force, retired precipitately with the remainder some distance down the river, when they crossed at a ford, and took the road southwards, carriage and supplies being furnished by the treacherous Rajah of Signee. Major Orr, by my direction, marched to Koonch.

As nothing puts the rebels out so much as turning their flank or defences, and as the excessive heat of the day rendered it advisable that I should not undertake a long operation against Koonch, much less a siege, I made a flank march with my whole force, to the north-west; my left, the 1st Brigade, resting its left flank on the village of Nagupoora; my centre, the 2nd Brigade, under Brigadier Steuart, was in the village of Chomair; my right, Major Orr's force, in front of the village of Oomree.

This position threatened seriously the enemy's line of retreat from Koonch to Calpee; and it exposed the north-west of the town, which was not protected by intrenchments, to attack.

I gave the order that, as soon as the three columns had taken up the positions which I have mentioned, they were to advance against the town, and each effect a lodgment in it.

When we came within sight of Koonch, we perceived videttes, and strong pickets of the enemy's cavalry outside the wood. They conformed to our flank movement, and posted themselves nearly opposite to Nagupoora.

A few rounds of shrapnel from Captain Lightfoot's guns emptied some of their saddles, and they disappeared into the wood. The rebel infantry now showed in force behind a long wall to our front, and in the wood to the left of it.

I had marched the 1st brigade a distance of fourteen miles from Loharee that morning, for the purpose of surprising the enemy by the flank movement, and not giving them time to alter their plan of defence. To rest and refresh the men, I ordered their dinners to be cooked for them, and in the mean time battered the wall with the two 18-pounders, and the 8-inch howitzer.

The half-troop of horse artillery, advancing diagonally to their left, shelled the infantry to the left of the wall; the enemy in return shelled the troop, and the siege guns, from a battery to our

right. Two of our guns were turned on the battery,
and soon silenced it.

Lieutenant-Colonel Gall, Her Majesty's 14th
Light Dragoons, galloped gallantly into the wood
to reconnoitre, the enemy, although he was in easy
musket range of them, did not fire at him because
the shelling from the horse artillery had caused
confusion in their ranks; he ascertained that the
infantry to the left had retreated further into the
wood, having in their rear a large body of cavalry;
that the siege guns had driven the enemy from
the cover of the wall, but that, some way in rear
of it, was posted a large body of infantry, with
elephants.

I determined to drive the enemy out of the
wood, gardens, and temples which surround Koonch,
and then to storm the town, including a dilapidated
mud fort, on a rising ground, a strong position,
which was opposite, and to the right of the 1st
brigade.

Once in possession of this position in the town,
the enemy on our left and in our front would be
cut off from the rest of their force, in the entrenchments on our right, which would be forced to retreat to the plain on the other side of the town,
pursued by the 2nd Brigade and Major Orr's force,
the 1st Brigade passing through the town, and
pressing the enemy, with whom they had been
engaged.

I effected this operation by throwing the left
wing of Her Majesty's 86th Regiment, under Major
Steuart, and the whole of the 25th Bombay Native
Infantry, under Lieutenant-Colonel Robertson,
into skirmishing order, the 86th on the left, the
25th on the right, their flanks supported by the
half-troop horse artillery, and a troop of Her Majesty's 14th Light Dragoons, and Captain Ommanney s battery, and two troops of the 14th Dragoons.

I left Captain Woollcombe's battery, one troop

14th Light Dragoons, and right wing 86th Regiment in second line in reserve, under the command of Lieutenant-Colonel Lowth. The rapidity and precision with which this formation was simultaneously made, must have surprised the sepoys. The 25th skirmishers charged into the woods, temples, and walled gardens, and occupied them under a fire of musketry and artillery, from the battery on our right, which reopened its fire ; and, after the guns of the Royal Artillery under Captain Field had effectually cannonaded the houses in the streets of Koonch, in their front, took them also. I expressed to Lieutenant-Colonel Robertson and the 25th, on the ground, my approbation of the gallantry with which they had gained this important position.

The 86th Regiment, covered by the three horse artillery guns, under Captain Lightfoot, who, throughout the day, made the most of this arm, and the troop 14th Light Dragoons, made a circuit to their left, took all the obstacles to their front, and then bringing their left shoulders forward, advanced, despite an artillery and musketry fire, through the whole north part of the town, and took the fort. The manner in which the 86th, ably led by Major Steuart, performed this movement, which completed the cutting of the enemy's line in two, adds another claim to the obligation I owe this regiment for their very distinguished conduct on all occasions in the field.

Just as the 86th and myself with the 25th were about to enter the town, Brigadier Steuart, commanding the 1st Brigade, observed that a large number of rebel infantry, strongly posted in cultivated ground, threatened the right of the line of attack of his brigade ; he moved up Captain Field's guns, with Captains Thomson's and Gordon's troops of Her Majesty's 14th Light Dragoons, and a troop

of the 3rd Regiment Hyderabad Cavalry, to dislodge them. The enemy held the position obstinately, and it was not until a portion of the
infantry, 2nd Brigade, moved down on them, from
another direction, that they retreated, when Captain
Gordon, whom I beg to recommend to his Excellency for his conduct on this occasion, with his
troop, and the cavalry above mentioned, charged
and broke the mass, cutting up several of them ;
topes of trees favored the escape of the remainder.

The 2nd Brigade, under Brigadier Steuart,
owing to some misconception on his part, did not
effect a lodgement in the town, but, moving round
the south of it, their artillery and cavalry joined
in the pursuit.

I have the honor to enclose a copy of Major Orr's
report, which shows that he did his utmost to carry
out my orders.

The enemy's line of defence being now cut in
two, and their left completely turned, they retired
in masses from Koonch to the extensive plains intersected by heavy ploughed land, stretching
towards Orai and Calpee, forming an irregular and
very long line, five or six deep in some places,
covered by skirmishers at close distances, who, at
intervals, were in groups or small masses, a mode
of skirmishing peculiar to Indians, these groups
act as a sort of bastion to the line of skirmishers.

The 1st Brigade made their way through the
town, as quickly as its narrow and winding streets
would allow them, and reached the plains in pursuit of the enemy.

But the infantry had already suffered so much
during the morning's sun (twelve men of the weak
wing of Her Majesty's 71st having died from sun
stroke,) that it would have been an heartless, and
imprudent sacrifice of invaluable infantry to pursue
with that arm. They were therefore halted, as

well as were the infantry of the 2nd Brigade, and Major Orr's force, which had advanced through the wood, round the town, to the plains.

The cavalry of both brigades, and of Major Orr's force (except a party which I had left to watch the Jaloun road and my rear), the troop of Horse Artillery, Captain Field's guns, and the four guns of No. 18 Light Field Battery, went in pursuit.

If, on the one hand, the enemy had retired from Koonch with too great precipitation on the other, it is fair to say that they commenced their retreat across the plain with resolution and intelligence. The line of skirmishers fought well to protect the retreat of the main body, observing the rules of Light Infantry drill. When charged, they threw aside their muskets, and fought desperately with their swords

The pursuit was commenced by Captains McMahon's squadron, and Blyth's troop of Her Majesty's 14th Light Dragoons charging, the first the right, and the latter the left of the enemy's skirmishers. A piece of very heavy plough caused a check in the pace, under a heavy fire, of Captain McMahon's squadron, but the deep ground was not broad, the squadron got through it, Captain McMahon leading the way, and cut to pieces the enemy, who fought fiercely to the last. Captain McMahon received three sabre wounds, but he continued the pursuit to the last. I beg to recommend him for his gallant conduct, and his unvarying zeal and attention to his duties.

On the centre, the Horse Artillery opened a hot fire on, and the cavalry charged, the skirmishers. The enemy now threw back the extreme right of their skirmishers so as to enfilade our line of pursuit. I directed Captain Prettyjohn to form line to the left, charge and cut off the enfilading skirmishers, which he did effectually. This officer, on

the horses of his own troop being knocked up,
placed himself with well-timed zeal at the head of
a troop with fresh horses, which was without an
officer, and continued with them the pursuit to the
end. I beg to submit his name to the favorable
consideration of his Excellency, as well as the
names of Captain Blyth, Her Majesty's 14th Light
Dragoons ; and Captain Abbott, Commanding 3rd
Regiment Hydrabad Cavalry, who each very gallantly charged and captured a gun from the retreating enemy under a heavy fire. In the course of
the pursuit, more guns and ammunition were captured by the cavalry.

Captain Field, with the four 9-pounders of Captain Ommanney's battery of Royal Artillery, notwithstanding the heavy plough he had frequently
to go over, and the weight of his guns, continued
to turn them to good account. and kept up well
with them to the close of the pursuit.

The greater part of the enemy's line of skirmishers being killed, the remainder driven in, and
the rebel artillery captured, the main body, the first
line, got into confusion, lost their nerve, and
crowded into the road of Calpee, a long and help-
less column of runaways; the Horse Artillery and
cavalry were now so beat by sun and fatigue, that
they were reduced to a walk; the guns were only
able to rake the column in all its depth with round
shot and shell, but could not approach sufficiently
close to give it grape. The cavalry on their part
had only strength to reach the numerous stragglers
who could not keep up with the enemy.

On reaching some woods and broken ground
about a village, seven or eight miles from Koonch,
profiting by this cover, they sought safety from
attack by breaking into a scattered flight across
the country.

The scorching rays of the sun, and the pace at
which they retreated, told even on the sepoys ;

several fell dead on the road, struck by apoplexy, many, exhausted, threw away their arms ; whilst others to quench their thirst, rushed to the wells, although our cavalry were upon them.

But the sun, fatigue, and scarcity of water, told still more on my artillery and cavalry, a great part of whom were Europeans, and had been marching or engaged for sixteen hours. The commanding officers of artillery and cavalry having on our arrival at the village reported to me that they were not longer able to pursue, I halted, and having watered the horses as well as I could, marched them back at sunset to Koonch.

The enemy must have lost about five or six hundred men in the action and pursuit; and, according to their own account, the 52nd Bengal Native Infantry, or "Heuryki Pultun," which covered the retreat, was nearly destroyed. Nine guns, and quantities of good English ammunition and stores, furnished to the late Gwalior Contingent, were taken.

The defeat at Koonch gave rise to animosities and mistrust in the rebel army. The infantry sepoys accused their brother mutineers of the cavalry with having pusilanimously abandoned them ; and all three arms brought the same charge against their general, Tantia Topee, who had disappeared at Koonch, as rapidly as he had done at Betwa, leaving to its fate at the most critical moment the force which he had called into existence under the pompous title of "The Army of the Peishwa."

The velaities also were charged with not having exhibited at Koonch the stern courage on which they pride themselves ; they were accused with having left the field too soon, and their excuse, that they had felt it their duty to escort the Ranee of Jhansi to a place of safety, was not held to be a military one. It was said that the destruction of velaities at Jhansi had made their countrymen less anxious than usual to try the fate of war. These various causes created confusion in the councils of the Calpee mutineers; my immediate advance towards that fortress made matters worse; a panic seized the sepoys in Calpee, as well as those retreating towards it; they commenced to take different lines of retreat; and I was assured, on good authority, that at one time there were only eleven sepoys in the town and fort. The unexpected arrival of the Nawab of Banda with a large force of good sepoy cavalry, mutineers, some guns, and infantry; and his energetic exertions, backed up by those of the Ranee of Jhansi, produced one of those sudden changes from despair to confidence which mark the Indian character.

Their leaders again exhorted the sepoys, as I learnt from an intercepted letter, "to hold to the last Calpee, their only arsenal, and to win their right to paradise by exterminating the infidel English." The rebels returned to Calpee and its environs, reoccupying the strong position in the labyrinth of ravines which surround it, and in the entrenchments which they had thrown up and armed to arrest my advance; a few miles in front of the Chowrasse (eighty-four) Temples, which extended two or three miles from Calpee, they had already cut deep trenches across the road near the entrenchments, and in several other places, which were serious obstacles, because the ravines on each side of the road rendered it very difficult to turn them.

When driven out of the entrenchments, the rebels could fall back on the eighty-four temples, built, as well as the walls round them, of most solid masonry; the network of ravines afforded them a third; the town of Calpee a fourth; another chain of ravines, between the town and the fort, a fifth; and, finally, the fort, a sixth and last line of defence.

The fort of Calpee is wretched, as a fortification; but, as a position, it is unusually strong, being protected on all sides by ravines, to its front by five lines of defence, and to its rear by the Jumna, from which rises the precipitous rock on which it stands.

Besides the officers previously mentioned in this despatch, I beg leave to bring to your Excellency's favorable notice, two officers who have lately joined my force, Colonel Wetherall, Chief of the Staff, and Captain Cockburn, of Her Majesty's 43rd Regiment, my Acting Aide-de-Camp. Colonel Wetherall, at Koonch, and since he joined my force, has given me all the assistance which was expected from his coolness, valuable experience, and excellent judgment.

Sickness had deprived me of the services of some of my staff, amongst others of that of Captain Macdonald, Assistant Quartermaster - General, who, although unable to stand from illness, would, with the never-failing devotion which characterises him, have taken part in the combat, if I had not ordered him back to his bed ; but Captain H. H. A. Wood, Assistant Adjutant-General, and Captain Cockburn, made up amply for the deficiency by their intelligence and unwearied zeal under fire.

Lieutenant Baigrie, Acting Deputy-Assistant Quartermaster-General, and Lieutenant Lyster, 72nd (late) Bengal Native Infantry, my interpreter, deserve also to be specially mentioned ; the former was severely wounded by a sword cut, which all but severed two fingers from his hand; notwithstanding, he gallantly continued during the action to discharge his duties with as much efficiency as before.

I had sent Lieutenant Lyster with an order for the cavalry to charge ; on his way, he came across a group of some thirty sepoy skirmishers ; singlehanded he charged, in view of the pursuing force, cut his way through, and broke them ; his horse was severely wounded. This is the second time that I have had the honor to mention this officer for gallant conduct in the field. The exertions of Dr. Arnott, Superintending-Surgeon, to take care of the sick and wounded, and to supply the field and other hospitals with medical comforts and requisites, are as unwearied as they are successful. I ought before now to have mentioned the conduct of Dr. Vaughan, Staff-Surgeon, at the Pass of Muddinpore, where, on account of the paucity of officers, he gallantly led a party of the Hydrabad Contingent Infantry, who cleared a difficult position of the enemy. The great heat of the sun, and the numerous casualties caused unfortunately by it, called into play all the zeal and devotion of the medical department of my force, shewing how eagerly the members of it go into danger when duty calls them there. Dr. Stack, of Her Majesty's 86th Regiment, was killed in the streets of Jhansi, in giving his first cares to a wounded man in the conflict.

Brigadier Stuart, C.B., Commanding 1st Brigade, reports that his best thanks are due to the officers of his staff ; Captain Fenwick, Field Engineer ; Captain Coley, Major of Brigade ; Captain Bacon, Deputy Assistant Quartermaster-General ; Lieutenant Henry, Deputy-Assistant Commissary-General, and Staff-Surgeon Mackenzie ; also to Captain Lightfoot, Commanding 1st Troop Horse Artillery ; Major Gall, Commanding Left Wing Her Majesty's 14th Light Dragoons ; Captain Abbott, Commanding 3rd Regiment Hydrabad Cavalry ; Captain Field, Commanding No. 6 Field Battery, Royal Artillery ; Lieutenant Strutt, Commanding No. 4 Light Field Battery, Bombay Artillery ; Lieutenant Edwardes, Assistant Field Engineer ; and Lieutenant Gosset, Commanding 21st Company Royal Engineers ; Lieutenant-Colonel

Lowth, Commanding 86th Regiment ; aud Major Robertson. Commanding 25th Regiment Bombay Native Infantry.

Brigadier Steuart, C.B., Commanding 2nd Brigade, mentions that his staff, Captain Todd, Major of Brigade, and Captain Leckie, Deputy Assistant - Quartermaster - General, afforded him every assistance.

I beg also to bring to his Excellency's notice the officers named in Major Orr's despatch.

I have, &c.,

H. ROSE, Major-General,
Commanding Central India Field Force.

No. 10.

Major W. A. Orr, commanding Field Force, Hyderabad Contingent, to the Chief of the Staff, Central India Field Force.

Sir,　　　　　Camp Etowra, May 14, 1858.

I HAVE the honor to forward the subjoined report, for submission to the Major-General-Commanding, of the part taken by the field force, Hyderabad Contingent, under my command, as per margin,* in the action at Koonch, fought with the rebel forces under Tantia Topee, on the 7th instant.

2. I received, during the night of the 6th instant, the instructions transmitted to me by you, directing me to move from my encampment at Aite towards my left flank, and, proceeding by

* 1st Cavalry, Hyderabad Contingent, 182 sabres, Lieutenant Dowker, commanding ; 4th Cavalry, Hyderabad Contingent, 137 sabres, Captain Murray, commanding ; 1st Company Artillery, 2 6-pounder guns ; 2nd Company Artillery. 3 6-pounder guns ; 4th Company Artillery, 2 12-pounder howitzers, 2 5½-inch mortars ; Captain Douglas commanding ; Left Wing 3rd Infantry, 333 bayonets. Lieutenant Macquoid, commanding ; 5th Infantry, 241 bayonets, Captain Hore commanding.

Bappojee and Sonnow, align my force by its left, with the right of the 2nd Brigade, which I should find resting on the village of Oomree. I marched during the night, and early the next morning (the 7th), opened a communication with Brigadier Steuart, commanding 2nd Brigade. From Sunnow I advanced to Purrayta, took possession of the small village of Daree, about a quarter of a mile in front, and occupied it with a strong picquet of cavalry and infantry.

3. About eight o'clock the enemy appeared in force on my right flank. A large body of cavalry, supported by infantry, moving steadily down towards Daree, apparently advancing with much determination, and having opened fire from a battery mounting two or three guns, one of them of considerable calibre, I moved forward my line, and a few rounds from the guns forced the enemy back to their original position.

4. Having received the Major-General's orders to take ground to the left, I moved in that direction to the front of the village of Oomree, from which I advanced direct upon Koonch. In my immediate front were some gardens and walled enclosures held in force by the enemy, and from which a heavy fire was directed upon our line. The artillery, under Captain Douglas, advanced, and, its fire having silenced that of the rebels, I ordered the gardens and enclosures to be seized by the infantry. This was very gallantly effected by a detachment of the 5th Infantry, consisting of two companies, under command of Lieutenant Partridge, 23rd Bengal Native Infantry, doing duty 5th Infantry Hyderabad Contingent, a very promising young officer, and the enemy were very quickly driven out ; at the same time, I directed the whole of the cavalry, under command of Captain Murray and Lieutenant Dowker, to move to the right and charge the enemy's horsemen, who

had all this time been threatening our flank. This service was promptly and effectually performed, the horsemen being driven quite off the field at this point, and forced back within the line of their supports of infantry, occupying several deep ravines and broken ground, and from the shelter of which a heavy fire was directed. The enemy's guns at the same time opened with round shot and shrapnel. The cavalry were subsequently joined by one squadron of Her Majesty's 14th Light Dragoons, and two Horse Artillery guns, the whole commanded by Major Scudamore, and they retained possession of the ground they had gained until the general advance, when they also followed the enemy in pursuit.

5. The artillery had meanwhile advanced so far as to bring it completely within range of the enemy's guns from two batteries, and they were thus enabled to open upon it a double fire of round shot, shell, and shrapnel, from the effects of which several casualties occurred. The rebel infantry also, being strongly reinforced, again suddenly came forward with a rush in great numbers, and forced back the detachments holding the garden. I was about to advance once more at this point, when I learnt that the Major-General, with the 1st Brigade, had forced the enemy's positions, and was in possession of the fort and town. The whole force now advanced. The enemy was driven from the enclosures he held, and, joining in the retreat of his main body, proceeded in the direction of the Orai road. I moved forward with the cavalry portion of the force under my command, and joined with Her Majesty's 14th Dragoons, the Horse Artillery, and Horse Field Battery, in the pursuit, which continued for about eight miles, cutting up a great many of the fugitive rebels, consisting almost entirely of sepoys of the mutineer corps of the Gwalior Contingent and Bengal

Army. The great start obtained by the enemy
before the fact of their retreating became known,
the extraordinary great heat of the day, and the
utter want of water, and the exhaustion of both
men and horses from these two causes, all combined
to make the loss of the enemy—heavy though it
was—less so than it would otherwise have proved.
The force returned to camp at 8 P.M., having been
since 2 A.M. under arms and in the saddle.

6. My best thanks are due to the undermentioned officers for the gallant, zealous, and efficient
aid they afforded me throughout the day, and at
all other times, and if I beg to bring their names to
the favorable notice of the Major-General.

Captain Douglas, Bengal Artillery, commanding
Artillery Field Force, Hyderabad Contingent;

Captain G. Hare, commanding 5th Infantry,
Hyderabad Contingent.

Captain W. Murray, commanding 4th Cavalry.

Lieutenant H. C. Dowker, commanding 1st
Cavalry.

Lieutenant R. Q. Macquoid, Adjutant 5th Infantry, commanding Left Wing 3rd Infantry.

Lieutenant E. W. Dun, second in command 4th
Cavalry.

Lieutenant H. Fraser, Adjutant 4th Cavalry, and
Staff Officer Field Force.

Lieutenant Westmacott, 23rd Bengal Native Infantry, and doing duty 4th Cavalry.

Lieutenant Johnson, Adjutant 1st Cavalry.

Lieutenant Partridge, 23rd Bengal Native Infantry, and doing duty 5th Infantry.

Surgeon J. H. Orr, 4th Cavalry Hyderabad Contingent, and Senior Surgeon Field Force.

Assistant-Surgeon Sanderson, 1st Cavalry.

Assistant-Surgeon Burn, 5th Infantry.

7. I beg to forward casualty rolls both in men
and horses.   I have, &c.,

W. A. ORR, Major, Com. Field Force.

From the *Nominal Roll of Officers and Men of the Central India Field Force Killed, Wounded, and Sunstruck, in the Action with the Insurgents, at Koonch, on the 7th of May,* 1858.

1st Brigade.

Lieutenant Baigrie, Depnty-Assistant Quartermaster-General, Staff, May 7, 1858, severely wounded.

Line-Serjeant Charles H. Wilson, May 7, killed.

Colour-Serjeant Charles Hawkins, 21st Campany Royal Engineers, May 7, severely wounded.

S. S. Major Samuel Whitaker, Left Wing H.M.'s 14th Light Dragoons, May 7, severely wounded.

Lieutenant P. P. P. Fenwick, 25th Bombay N.I., May 7, sunstroke.

2nd Brigade.

Captain W. McMahon, H.M.'s 14th Light Dragoons, May 7, wounded severely by sword cut in right hand and leg.

Captain H. Need, H.M.'s 14th Light Dragoons, May 7, sunstroke.

Lieutenant H. H. J. C. Travers, H.M.'s 14th Light Dragoons, May 7, sunstroke.

Serjeant-Major — Holloway, H.M.'s 14th Light Dragoons, May 7, sunstroke, died 16th May.

Paymaster-Serjeant R. Sexton, H.M.'s 14th Light Dragoons, May 7, sunstroke.

Serjeant Stephen Sweeny, H.M.'s 14th Light Dragoons, May 7, sunstroke.

Sarjeant-Major J. Fisher, H.M.'s 14th Light Dragoons, May 7, sunstroke.

Colour-Serjeant Robert Bank, H.M.'s 71st Regiment Highland Light Jnfantry, May 7, sunstroke.

Colour-Serjeant Stephen McGill, H.M.'s 71st Regiment Highland Light Infantry, May 7, sunstroke.

Serjeant Alexander Ross, H.M.'s 71st Regiment Highland Light Infantry, May 7, sunstroke.

Abstract.

1st Brigade.

Staff—1 officer, wounded ; 1 non-commissioned officer, killed.

Royal Engineers—1 rank and file, sunstroke.

Left Wing H.M.'s 14th Light Dragoons—5 non-commissioned officers and rank and file, wounded.

3rd Cavalry Hyderabad Contingent—2 rank and file, wounded.

H.M.'s 86th Regiment—1 rank and file, wounded ; 3 rank and file, sunstroke.

25th Regiment Native Infantry—2 rank and file, sunstroke.

2nd Brigade.

H.M.'s 14th Light Dragoons—1 officer wounded ; 4 non-commissioned officers and rank and file, killed ; 13 non-commissioned officers and rank and file, wounded ; 2 officers, 16 rank and file, sunstroke ; 3 horses, killed ; 6 horses, wounded ; 4 horses, missing.

71st Highland Light Infantry—1 rank and file, wounded ; 19 rank and file, sunstroke.

3rd European Regiment — 2 rank and file, wounded ; 1 rank and file, sunstroke.

24th Regiment Bombay Native Infantry—1 officer, 1 rank and file, sunstroke.

Total—2 officers, wounded ; 5 non-commissioned officers and rank and file, killed ; 24 non-commissioned officers and rank and

file, wounded ; 3 officers, 43 rank and file,
sunstroke ; 3 horses, killed ; 6 horses,
wounded ; 4 horses, missing

H. H. A. WOOD, Captain,
Assistant Adjutant-General,
Central India Field Force.

No. 15.
GENERAL ORDERS BY THE GOVERNOR-
GENERAL OF INDIA.
Allhabad, June 30, 1858.
No. 238 of 1858.

THE Right Honorable the Governor-General is
pleased to direct the publication of the following
letter from Brigadier Wood, C.B., commanding at
Allahabad, No. 520, of 11th June, 1858, forwarding one from the officer commanding the post
of Soraon, submitting a report of the operations
of a detachment under the command of Lieutenant Aynsley, 6th Madras Light Cavalry, against
a body of rebels headed by a Beni Bahadoor
Sing.

No. 16.
*Brigadier D. E. Wood, C.B., Commanding at
Allahabad, to the Chief of the Staff.*
No. 520.
SIR, *Allahabad, June* 11, 1858.

I HAVE the honor to forward a despatch
from Lieutenant-Colonel Whistler, commanding
the post of Soraon, with inclosures, detailing the
operations of a detachment of troops under the
immediate command of Lieutenant Aynsley, 6th
Madras Light Cavalry, who successfully encountered a force of rebels far superior in numbers,

and by the ability he displayed in his disposition, and the bravery and determination of the 6th Madras Cavalry, he was enabled to destroy and capture a great many.

> I have, &c.,
> D. E. WOOD, Brigadier,
> Commanding at Allahabad.

No. 17.

Lieutenant-Colonel J. Whistler, Commanding Field Detachment, to the Major of Brigade.

No. 55.

Camp Soraon, Allahabad, June 11, 1858.

SIR,

I HAVE the honor to report, for the information of the Brigadier Commanding, that on the receipt of your letter No. 514, at 8 P.M., on the 9th instant, I immediately gave orders for a party, as per margin,* under command of Lieutenant Aynsley, 6th Madras Cavalry (being the only native troops available, the heat being too great to detach Europeans) to march at midnight, to attack a party of rebels at Kurnaipore, about 12 miles south-east of this, said to be about 1,000, and headed by the rebel Beni Bahadoor Sing. The expedition appears to have been very ably and most successfully carried out, and the detachment 6th Madras Cavalry behaved admirably, and with great zeal and gallantry against an enemy more than five times their number, who fought desperately, first firing their matchlocks, and then defending themselves with swords. The report of Lieutenant

* 6th Madras Cavalry, 74 sabres; Seikhs, 30; Police Levy, 67.

Aynsley, who commanded the detachment, I beg
to inclose for submission to the Brigadier.
I have, &c.,
J. WHISTLER, Lieutenant-Colonel,
Commanding Field Detachment.

No. 18.

*Lieutenant G. H. M. Aynsley, 6th Madras Ca-
valry, to the Station Staff Officer, Soraon.*

SIR,   *Camp Soraon, June* 10, 1858.

I HAVE the honor to state, for the information of the Officer Commanding, that this morning,
a little after 12 o'clock, I proceeded, according to
my instructions, with the force noted in the
margin,* to Kurnaipore (distant from this about
14 miles to the eastward, and one of the residences
of Beni Bahadoor Sing), for the purpose of attacking
the rebels congregated there.

I arrived near the place at sunrise, and sent
one troop round to the south of the village, which
had the effect of making the rebels think we were
going to attack on that side, and they accordingly, to the number of about 500 well armed
men, marched out, as I wished, towards the
north, in good order, with a strong advance and
rear guard.

Being joined by the troop I had detached, I
advanced with the squadron to the attack of the
main body, which was completely successful. The
enemy attempted to stand the charge, but in vain;
he was instantly broken, 31 of his men were
counted dead on the field (and many more must
have been killed, but I had not time to go over all
the ground,) and 11 prisoners were taken. The
slaughter would have been greater, but every

* 6th Madras Cavalry, 74 sabres; Seikhs, 30; Police
Levy, 67.

individual fought with desperation, discharging and throwing away his musket or matchlock, and fighting with his sword. My men were thus scattered over the country in hand to hand fights, and my own charger being so weak from loss of blood from a sword-cut, that I was obliged to dismount, I was unable to carry on the pursuit as far as I could have wished.

The conduct of all ranks gave me the greatest gratification, and I desire to bring to the particular notice of the Commanding Officer the gallant way in which, without having any support at hand, and opposed to a force so immensely superior in numbers, standing firmly to receive them, they rushed to the charge, shouting " deen, deen," more especially when it is considered that this is the first time they have ever been called on to charge a determined enemy, many of whom were Sepoys. Where all did their duty so well, it would be invidious to mention names.

I have brought in 30 matchlocks and 5 muskets and 11 swords, found on the field ; many more were scattered about, but, as I wished to return as soon as possible, to save the troops from the sun, I was unable to collect them.

I am sorry to report that Havildar Gholam Mohedeen was killed, one trooper had his arm broken, and one farrier was wounded. One horse was killed, one missing, and two wounded.

After the action was over, I returned to Kerama, remained there during the heat of the day, and returned to camp in the evening.

I have said nothing of the infantry in this report, as they were unfortunately unable to take part in the action, but I was much pleased with the steady way in which they advanced to the attack of Kurnaipore under Lieutenant Sawers, before it was found to be evacuated.

I have the honor to forward Lieutenant Sawers's report.

I have, &c.,

G. H. M. AYNSLEY, Lieutenant,
6th Madras Cavalry.

No. 19.

Lieutenant John L. Sawers, Adjutant, Police Military Levy, to Lieutenant G. H. M. Aynsley, 6th Madras Cavalry.

Fort Soraon, June 11, 1858.

SIR,   No. 1.

I HAVE the honor herewith to forward a report of the proceedings of the infantry force placed under my orders, at the village of Kurnaipore yesterday. The force, as per margin,* was made over by you to me on our arriving at Kurnaipore, where the sepoys in the service of the rebel Beni Bahadoor Sing were found collected in force.

According to your instructions, I took ny men to the north of the village, that having been represented by you to be the weakest point for an attack

When proceeding to carry out your orders, I was met by a villager, who reported that the enemy, to the number of 500, were collected in a grove of trees about 200 yards in advance of the intended point of attack. I at once communicated with you; when we were talking together, your trumpeter called your attention to a body of infantry moving off in regular order from the said grove.

Your orders were to follow the cavalry; this I

---

* Seikhs belonging to the Ferozepore Regiment of all ranks, 23; 1st Seikh Volunteer Regiment, 7; Police Levy, 67; total, 97.

did, halting for some time in the grove, in the chance of cutting off any of the enemy that might try to double back, and gain the entrenchment they had so shortly before evacuated. Seeing that none of them returned, I pushed my men towards the fight as fast I could, and joined you about a mile ahead. A large garden lay to our right. This I searched, but sáw no one, so returned to the village of Kurnaipore, which was found to be quite destroyed by fire, and deserted by its inhabitants.

In conclusion, I beg to bring to your notice the conduct of the new Police Levy, who quite emulated the Seikh soldiers in their anxiety to reach the front, where the cavalry were skirmishing, and had they had an opportunity, I doubt not they would have acquitted themselves with credit.

I have &c.,

JOHN L. SAWYERS, Lieutenant,
Adjutant, Police Military Levy.

No. 20.

Nominal List of Casualties in the Field Detachment under the Command of Lieutenant-Colonel J. Whistler, in the cavalry combat at Kurnaipore, on the 10th June, 1858.

Camp Soraon, June 11, 1858.

Havildar Gholam Mohedeen Khan, killed.
Farrier Francis Antony, severe musket-shot.
1 horse killed.
1 horse missing.
2 horses wounded.
Private Shaik Bram, arm broke.

J. WHISTLER, Lieutenant-Colonel,
Commanding Field Detachment.

3259

No. 21.

No. 239 of 1858.

THE Right Honorable the Governor-General is pleased to direct the publication of the following despatch from Brigadier-General Sir E. Lugard, K.C.B., Commanding Azimgurh Field Force, dated 14th June, 1858, inclosing a report from Brigadier Douglas of his operations and arrangements for intercepting the enemy in the vicinity of Buxar.

No. 22.

Brigadier-General Sir E. Lugard, K.C.B., Commanding Azimgurgh Field Force, to the Chief of the Staff.

Army Head Quarters, Camp Narainpoor, June 14, 1858.

Sir,

AFTER despatching my letter of yesterday's date, I received the accompanying Official Report from Brigadier Douglas, which I herewith beg to forward.

To show the rapidity and secrecy with which the rebels conduct their movements, I beg to state that in order to guard against the return of any party from the West towards the jungles without my getting timely intelligence, so that I might intercept them, I posted at Roop-Sagur, a village 13 miles to my south-west, on the track taken by the rebels in their flight, Captain Rattray with his Seikh battalion, who again threw forward scouts some miles in the same direction, and constantly had parties patrolling to the different villages; but in spite of every precaution, the rebel force were at Medneepore, within 4 miles of him, before he could communicate with me, and passed on towards the jungle the same night. Every endea-

vour to obtain information from the people of the
district has proved vain; scarcely ever has any
intelligence been given to us until the time has
passed when advantage could be taken of it.

EDWARD LUGARD, Brigadier-General,
Commanding Azimgurh Field Force.

P.S. 5 P.M., 14th June.—A report has just
reached me that the rebels made for the Soane towards Beta, or Nonone, at day-break this morning,
with intention of crossing the river. I have
despatched scouts to ascertain the truth of this,
and will report to-morrow.·

I moved my camp to this side (east) of Jugdespore this morning, in order, if possible, to check
any movement of this kind.

EDWARD LUGARD.

No. 23.

Brigadier John Douglas to the Chief of the Staff.

Azimgurh Field Force, Camp Buxar,
June 12, 1858.

SIR,

I HAVE the honor to state, for the information of Brigadier-General Sir Edward Lugard,
K.C.B., that according to his instructions I proceeded on the evening of the 7th instant, with a
force as per margin,* *en route* to Buxar. I arrived
at Shahpoor at 11 P.M., and bivouacked; 8th,
mrrched to Saumgunge, 12 miles, and encamped.
Two men of the 84th died from sun-stroke this
day. 9th. Marched to Buxar, 14 miles, and encamped. 10. Understanding that the rebels occupied the village of Ghamur, I advanced to attack
them; at 3 miles from Buxar, crossed the Sarro-
nuddy by a plank bridge; when within a mile of

* 3 guns Royal Horse Artillery; 3 troops Military Train·
1 troop 4th Madras Cavalry; Her Majesty's 84th Regiment.

the Korumnassa river, I received information that a body of the enemy had crossed to this side of the river. I sént forward the cavalry and horse artillery, under command of Major Mitchell, Royal Horse Artillery ; the artillery advanced to the river side, marked by the cavalry, and discovered the enemy, who had re-crossed the river, in a tope at some 500 yards ; they fired about twelve rounds, dispersed and killed several of the enemy. The river not being fordable, and there being no bridge, the cavalry and artillery returned to the main body ; the force then proceeded to Chawsa, 9 miles from Buxar, and encamped ; during the afternoon a bridge of boats was thrown across the Korumnassa, by Captain Wilkinson, Deputy Assistant Quartermaster-General, and a guard sent over for its protection. 11th. No certain information of the enemy's movements could be obtained ; crossed the river at 4 A.M., and advanced through Barra to Ghamur ; a thick tope of trees surrounds the village ; at about 1,200 yards distance, a number of people were seen in the tope ; two companies of the 84th advanced in skirmishing order and drove them off. I then moved to the rear of and round the village, sending skirmishers through it, but could not discover the enemy ; the accounts of his movements were very conflicting. I sent the cavalry and artillery forward to Sheopoor Ghaut, to intercept them if they were crossing the river, having heard that the main body had taken that direction ; but they did not see them   I heard afterwards that they had gone south and south-west. I burned the villages of Ghamur and Barra, re-crossed the Korumnassa and encamped near Chawsa. Three men of the Royal Horse Artillery died during the night from the effects of the sun, and 1 man of the 84th, 1 horse, and 1 trooper of Rattray's Seikhs were slightly wounded while burning the villages ; the detachment of this regiment joined me on my marching out of Buxar. The heat during the operations was intense, and the troops suffered much, particularly the 84th Regiment, who have now been thirteen months in the field. I consider this regiment at present to be quite unfit for active service ; the men have no positive disease, but they are so exhausted that they can neither eat nor sleep. 12th. I returned to Buxar, and encamped. In the village of Ghamur, 45 brood mares belonging to Government were recovered and handed over to Mr. Jackson, of the stud establishment here, who accompanied the force. In conclusion, I beg to state that I have every reason to be satisfied with the way in which all did their duty. I have, &c.,

JOHN DOUGLAS, Brigadier.

No. 24.
No. 241 of 1858.

THE Right Honorable the Governor-General is pleased to direct the publication of the following despatch, from Colonel Millar, commanding Nagpore Irregular Force, dated 2nd June, 1858, detailing the operations of the Kamptee Moveable Column, late under his command, from August, 1857, to January, 1858.

No. 25.

Colonel Millar, 33rd Regiment, Madras Native Infantry, late in Command of the Kamptee Moveable Column, to Major-General Sir W. R. Mansfield, K.C.B., Chief of the Staff of his Excellency the Commander-in-chief in India.

Kamptee, June 2, 1858.

SIR, No. 106.

I DO myself the honor of laying before you the following circumstances, for the favorable consideration of his Excellency the Commander-in-chief in India.

It will be remembered, that at the commencement of the mutinies, a small moveable column as per margin,* was organized from the Nagpore force for service in the Saugor and Nerbudda territories.

This column reached Jubbulpore, on the 21st August, 1857, and was there joined by two companies of the 28th Regiment Madras Native Infantry, and two companies of the Bengal 52nd Regiment Native Infantry. The whole then proceeded towards Saugor ; but in consequence of the incessant rain, and the almost impassable state of the roads and rivers, did not reach Dumoh till the 30th August.

Dumoh, which was garrisoned by about 300 of the 31st Bengal Native Infantry, two companies of the 42nd Bengal Native Infantry, and about 120 of the 3rd Bengal Irregular Cavalry, with two 6-pounder guns, had been for some time hard pressed by the rebels and mutineers, but who at once withdrew on the approach of the column. I however found it necessary to send out large detachments against several petty chiefs in the neighbourhood before advancing upon Saugor, vide marked A. and B.

On the 7th September, I was obliged, in consequence of very alarming accounts from Jubbulpore, to detach two guns of the European Battery of artillery, one troop of the 4th Light Cavalry, and three companies of the 33rd Madras Native Infantry, for the protection of that station. This detachment, under the command of Captain Tot-

* D Company, 3rd Battalion Madras Artillery ; 65 rank and file (Europeans), with 6 guns ; 3rd squadron 4th Regiment, Madras Light Cavalry, 92 sabres ; Head Quarters 33rd Regiment Madras Native Infantry, 425 rank and file ; Rifle Company, 1st Regiment Nagpore Irregular Infantry, 91 rank and file.

tenham, of the 4th Light Cavalry, reached Jubbulpore in ample time to secure the safety of that
important station, which would otherwise have
been destroyed.

With my force thus reduced, it was hardly possible to effect much, but I still persisted in my
attempt to relieve Saugor, and had got as far as
the right bank of the Sonar river on the 8th September, when my further progress was arrested by
the intelligence, that the Dinapore mutineers were
menacing the Rewah territories, and might come
down upon Jubbulpore.

The aspect of affairs was at this time very un-
promising, the Rewah Rajah having intimated to
Lieutenant Osborne, the political agent at his
Court, his inability to protect him ; we therefore
return to Dumoh, around which the rebels had
again collected, but who fled at our approach.

About midnight on the 19th September, an express arrived, conveying the intelligence of the
mutineers of the 50th and 52nd Regiments Bengal
Native Infantry, at Nagode and Jubbulpore. It
now became imperatively necessary for us to return at once to Jubbulpore, and before doing so to
disarm the two companies of the 52nd Bengal
Native Infantry, which was accomplished early
next morning, without bloodshed, notwithstanding
that the muskets of the 52nd were loaded at the
time, they having just returned from a dour.

On the 21st September, the column was en route
to Jubbulpore, having brought away with it a lac
and 20,000 rupees from the Government Treasury,
a considerable quantity or ammunition, and the
arms of disarmed party of the 52nd.

On the 27th September, the column, while passing through a dense jungle near Kuttungunj, about
twenty-five miles from Jubbulpore, was attacked
by the mutineers of the 52nd Regiment Bengal
Native Infantry, and a large body of rebels, who,

after a brisk skirmish, were completely repulsed, vide marked C.

This I believe was the first time that Madras sepoys had been called upon to act against the mutineers, and it was highly gratifying to find, that there was no sympathy whatever between the men of the two armies.

The column reached Jubbulpore with all the treasure, etc., on the 1st October

From this period till the end of January, the column was employed in protecting Jubbulpore, and the neighbouring district, and parties of greater or less strength, were continually obliged to be sent out to drive back the rebels, the whole country being up in arms against us.

In one of these skirmishes, the brave and talented Major Jenkins, of the Quartermaster-General's department, was shot dead while leading on his men in an attack upon the rebels near Kuttungunj, vide enclosure marked D.

On another occasion, Captain Tottenham, of the 4th Madras Light Cavalry, was mortally wounded, while pursuing at the head of his troop, some rebels near Ghosulpore, vide enclosure E.

I beg here to acknowledge my obligations to Major Erskine, Commissioner of the Jubbulpore and Saugor territories, who accompanied the column, and was present during the encounter with the mutineers at Kuttungunj, and without whose energetic assistance in procuring elephants and supplies, it would have been impossible for the column to have made any forward movement during the very heavy monsoon in which its operations were conducted.

Although it did not fall to the lot of this column to see any severe fighting, yet it was continually engaged in sharp skirmishes with the rebels, in all of which it was uniformly successful, and in addition to which, the men were subjected to great hardships and privations, in consequence of long and continued marches in the midst of an exceedingly heavy monsoon, over roads, the state of which may be imagined when I mention, that the battery of artillery was seventy-six hours in accomplishing a march of eleven miles with the aid of numerous elephants.

In conclusion, I beg to draw attention to the fact, that on the occasion of the mutiny of the 52nd Bengal Native Infantry the preservation of Jubbulpore, together with the extensive public buildings, treasure, etc., was owing to the presence of Captain Tottenham's detachment, and the firm attitude he then assumed.

Moreover, the advance of the column to Damoh saved that station, and the lives of the Europeans there, as also the Government Treasure, and induced the Shahgurh Rajah to release Lieutenant Gordon and the other Europeans he had detained in confinement for nearly three months.

I have, &c.

J. MILLAR, Lieutenant-colonel, Brevet-Colonel 33rd Regiment Madras Native Infantry, lately commanding the Kamptee Moveable Column.

No. 26.

Major W. G. P. Jenkins, Assistant Quartermaster-General, Nagpore Force, to Colonel J. Millar, Commanding Nagpore Moveable Column.

September 19, 1857.

No. 68.

SIR,

I HAVE the honour to inform you, that on the morning of the 17th instant, I proceeded agreeably to your orders, with the force as per margin,* for the purpose of collecting grain from certain rebel villages.

2. On arriving with a reconnoitering party at Nursinghur, I found that the fort was a very strong stone-built place, with a wet ditch, and well covered with gardens and stone enclosures. The fort was occupied by about 250 matchlockmen.

3. Behind the fort runs the Sonar river, having a very deep and difficult ford immediately behind the fort, and another pretty good ford about half a mile lower down.

4. Finding that the enemy were so strongly posted, I extended a portion of the infantry to cut them off from the lower ford, and brought the guns into position for throwing shrapnel.

5. Before, however, a shot could be fired from the guns, the enemy suddenly retired, and advancing the infantry at a run, we came on the enemy retreating in confusion across the upper ford.

6. The river at this ford is about 250 yards wide, the stones were exceedingly slippery, the water at one place so deep as to oblige men to swim, and the current was running with great force.

7. The enemy had to make their way across the above difficult ford, under a heavy and continuous fire, poured in by our men from the bank above ; and the panic was so great, that hardly a shot was fired in return.

8. Upwards of 30 prisoners were taken in the fort and town, 13 of whom were hung at Nursinghur by the civil authorities, and the remainder brought into Dumoh.

* One troop 4th Light Cavalry; two guns ; two Companies 33rd Madras Native Infantry ; two Companies 52nd Bengal Native Infantry.

9. On the morning of the 18th, Lieutenant Nembhard, the deputy commissioner of the district, received a report from Busseah (a village under the hills about 10 miles south-east of Nursinghur) informing him that during the previous night, the enemy had fled in great disorder through the place, and given out that they had lost 50 men killed in the river : and on hearing this, a number of rebels, who had for some time occupied Busseah, fled with them to the hills.

10. Captain Ludlow, Field Engineer, having demolished the outer works of the fort, and partly filled up the ditch, the detachment, agreeably to your instructions, returned to camp this day.

I have, &c.,

W. G. P. JENKINS, Major,
Assistant-Quartermaster-General
Nagpore Force.

No. 27.

Brevet-Colonel J. Millar, Commanding Nagpore Moveable Column, to the Adjutant-General of the Army, Fort St. George.

Camp Dumoh, September 3, 1857.

SIR.   No. 42.

I HAVE the honor to report, for the information of his Excellency the Commander-in-chief, that, at the request of the Commissioner of the Saugor and Nerbudda territories, a party, as per margin,*

* 3rd Squadron 4th Madras Light Cavalry, under Capt. Tottenham ; ½ Battery of D. Company 3rd Battalion Artillery, with three guns under Captain James; two Companies 33rd Madras Native Infantry, under Captain Applegate; two Companies 52nd Bengal Native Infantry, under Lieutenant Oakes; Rifle Company 1st Nagpore Irregular Infantry, under Lieutenant Pereira; 1 Squadron 3rd Bengal Irregular Cavalry, under Lieutenant Sutherland; Captain Harrison, A.S.O. of the Detachment; Captain Ludlow, Field Engineer.

under my command, marched without tents or baggage against Balacote, fifteen miles distant, a large village with an old fort on a neighbouring hill, and the residence of a rajah of the Lodhee caste, named Surroop Sing, who had assisted with his followers in the attack upon Damoh, and been very active in plundering the neighbouring village.

2. The detachment marched from camp at 3½ A M. on the 1st instant, and arrived within a mile of the place at about 11 A.M. The last four miles was up a steep and rugged ghat, and through a dense jungle, which extended to within a few hundred yards of the place.

3. At about a mile from the village, I observed a small open valley leading down towards the right, by which I ordered the cavalry to proceed and endeavour to surround the village, and cut off the retreat of the rebels. When the infantry approached to within about three-quarters of a mile from the town, the enemy opened a brisk fire upon them, but were speedily driven in by the 33rd and 52nd, who advanced in skirmishing order and vied with each other in pushing forward, and would have entered the place, but I thought it prudent to halt them out of reach of fire till the guns which were close in the rear came up, and, from a height which commanded the town, fired a few rounds into it, when I allowed the infantry to go on, who entered the town, but found it completely evacuated, and most of the property removed.

4. I regret to say that, in the skirmish in the jungle, three men of the 33rd were wounded, one of whom has since died. I was unable to ascertain what loss was sustained by the enemy, on account of the thickness of the jungle; there was, however, one of the enemy killed in the evening by a party sent out to clear the immediate neighbourhood of the town previous to my picquets being posted.

5. I have much pleasure in expressing my satisfaction at the manner in which the whole of the troops employed behaved; the Artillery deserve great credit for the rapidity with which they brought up their guns over an almost impassable road.

6. The detachment, after having destroyed and set fire to the village, returned to camp the next day by a different road, destroying one of the enemy's recently deserted villages en route.

7. I beg to enclose the doctor's return of casualties.

I have, &c.,
J. MILLAR, Brevet-Colonel,
Commanding Nagpore Moveable Column.

No. 28.

Lieutenant-Colonel J. Millar, Commanding Kamptee Moveable Column, to the Adjutant-General of the Army, Fort St. George.

Camp Kuttunghee, September 28, 1857.

SIR,   No. 69.

I HAVE the honor to report, for the information of his Excellency the Commander-in-chief, that, thanks be to God, the Kamptee Moveable Column gained a complete and decisive victory over the mutineers of the 52nd Bengal Native Infantry, numbering about 500 rank and file, and 1,000 insurgent matchlock-men, on the 27th September, 1857.

The 52nd Regiment Bengal Native Infantry, having mutinied at Jubbulpore, it was decided that the town and district of Dumoh should be abandoned by regular troops, and that the moveable column under my command, strength as per

margin*, having disarmed the detachment of the
Bengal 52nd Native Infantry serving with the
column, and taking with it the Dumoh treasure,
amounting to upwards of a lakh of rupees, and the
arms and ammunition of the disarmed men, should
retire to defend Jubbulpore.

The column left Dumoh on the 21st instant, and,
after having been delayed in crossing the Nowtah
river for three days, reached Singrampoor on the
evening of the 26th September, where intelligence.
was received that the mutineers 52nd Regiment,
numbering about 500 rank and file, had taken up
a position at Kanee on the west of the Heran river,
about twelve miles below Kuttunghee.

As there was a probability that the mutineers.
might seize and destroy the boats on the Heran, at
Kuttunghee, on the road to Jubbulpore, I despatched, at 2 A.M. on the 27th instant, a party
under Lieutenant Watson, strength as per margin†,
to secure the boats above referred to.   This part
was accompanied by Major Jenkins, Assistant
Quartermaster-General.   At 5 A.M. on the 27th,
just as the column was preparing to march, two
troopers galloped into camp, with the intelligence
that the advanced party had been surprised by the
52nd Mutineers, that the two officers had been
killed, and the party retreating on our camp.   I
forthwith gave the order to march, and pushed on
through a jungle country with a party, and took
possession of the village of Gobra, about three

---

* 4th Madras Light Cavalry, 42 ránk and file, under
Lieutenant Burnet ; D Company 3rd Battalion Madras
Artillery, 4 guns, under Captain James and Lieutenant
Caine ; 28th Madras Native Infantry, 105 rank and file,
under Captain Yates ; 33rd Madras Native Infantry, 238
rank and file, under Lieutenant Benwell ; Rifle Company
Nagpore Light Infantry, 81 rank and file, under Lieutenant
Pereira.

† One Company 33rd Madras Native Infantry ; twelve
Troopers, 4th Madras Light Cavalry.

miles in advance of Singrampoor, and which commands the mouth of the pass, and to the north of which the ground is open. I waited there a short time for the guns and main body to join here. Shortly after the guns came up, the 52nd Bengal Native Infantry were seen marching along the road in column of sections : two guns were fired into them, on which they left the road and advanced against us in the jungle, on both sides, accompanied by the matchlock-men. As the position the guns at first took up was too much exposed to fire from the jungle, and the enemy were evidently endeavouring to steal round our flanks, I retired about 200 yards close to the village, and took up a more favorable position, where the ground was a little more open. I kept the guns on the road, occupied the village and the jungle right and left with my infantry, and posted the cavalry in rear of the left, where the ground was open. After a brisk fire, which lasted for about half an hour, the enemy were driven back. The baggage having now closed up, I placed the treasure, guarded by the 33rd, in rear of the guns, threw out a strong body of skirmishers from the 33rd on the right, a little in front of the leading gun, and another line of skirmishers from the 28th and 33rd on the left, leaving one company of the 28th with the park and the rifles to protect the baggage and rear. In this order, we advanced slowly through three or four miles of very jungly country, driving the enemy before us, and halting occasionally to give them a few rounds from our guns.

Ou reaching the open country near Kuttunghee, I pushed on the cavalry to feel for the enemy, who were discovered making off up the hills with their baggage in rear of the town. From the nature of the ground the cavalry could not follow them, and, before the infantry arrived, the greater number had effected their escape. The rifles and parties from the 28th and 33rd, however, succeeded in killing some, and taking a few prisoners on the hill, and also in the town, who were afterwards hanged.

On our approaching Kuttunghee, we were agreeably surprised by Major Jenkins and Lieutenant Watson riding up to the column ; they had succeeded in cutting their way through the ambuscade in the dark, and had concealed themselves on the hills until the advance of the column enabled them to rejoin us. Lieutenant Watson, I regret, was wounded on the cheek by a musket ball, and knocked off his horse ; his escape was most miraculous. Major Jenkins's charger had two bullets through him, and is not likely to survive.

At the entrance to the town, was found lying on the public road, the body of Captain MacGregor, of the 52nd Regiment Bengal Native Infantry, with his throat cut, a shot in his breast, and a bayonet wound in his body, whom the mutineers having made prisoner on the occasion of their mutiny, had murdered at 3 A.M. before they proceeded to attack us.

My movements during the above operations were much hampered by having to keep an eye on the 120 disarmed men of the 52nd Bengal Native Infantry, who accompanied the column, and by the treasure, large amount of baggage, and people returning with us from Dumoh.

The whole force behaved well, and proved incontestably that the Madras sepoy has no sympathy with the Bengal mutineers.

The cavalry were very forward in pursuit of the enemy, and followed them up the side of the hill, capturing some of their baggage.

The Rifle Company of the 1st Irregular Infantry, were very active in ascending the hill, and captured a colour havildar of the 52nd Bengal Native Infantry, who was one of the chief ringleaders of the mutiny. I enclose Lieutenant Pereira's report on this subject, and beg to inform you, that the commissioner has promoted the havildar therein mentioned to jemadar, and that I have promoted the two sepoys to havildars.

I feel much indebted to all the Eurpoean officers; and the conduct of the European gunners was most exemplary.

I beg to add, that I received every assistance from Captain Ludlow, Field Engineer; and from Captain Harrison, Officiating Sub-Assistant Commissary-General, who acted as my staff; and from Captain Pinkney, 34th Regiment Madras Native Infantry, Deputy Commissioner, who was constantly with me, and whose knowledge of the localities enabled him to be of great service.

I enclose a medical return of casualties.

I have, &c.,

J. MILLAR, Lieutenant-Colonel,
Commanding Kamptee Moveable Column.

No. 29.

From the Nominal List of Killed and Wounded in the Action on the 27th September, 1857.

33rd Regiment, M.N.I.

Lieutenant H. Watson, wounded slightly.

No. 30.

Colonel Munsey, Commanding Kamptee Moveable Column, to the Assistant Adjutant-General, Nagpore Force, Kamptee.

Camp Jubbulpore, November 15, 1857.

SIR,   No. 195.

IT is with much regret I have the honor to report, for the information of the Brigadier Commanding Nagpore Force, the death of Brevet-

Major W. P. Jenkins, Assistant Quartermaster-General, Nagpore Force; this officer was killed in a skirmish with some Bondailiah rebels near Kuttunghee yesterday afternoon.

I beg to enclose the copy of a report made on the subject by Lieutenant Oakes, 52nd Bengal Native Infantry, who is attached to the moveable column, and accompanied the detachment under the command of the late Major Jenkins.

I have. &c.,

T. A. A. MUNSEY, Colonel,
Commanding Kamptee Moveable Column.

No. 31.

Lieutenant Richard Oakes, commanding Detachment, to the Brigadier commanding Kamptee Moveable Column, Jubbulpore.

Camp, *Kuttunghee, November* 14, 1857.

SIR,

IT is with deep regret I have to report the death of Major Jenkins, who was killed this afternoon in a skirmish with the Boondelas near the village of Enotah, about four miles from Kuttunghee.

About half-past 12 P.M. information was received that a party of Boondelas were looting a village about Rukreeta, two miles from camp; Major Jenkins ordered a party consisting of half a troop of cavalry under Lieutenant Burnett, 4th Light Cavalry, and 50 rank and file of the 33rd Regiment Madras Native Infantry, under Lieu-Oakes, 52nd Native Infantry, to march immediately against them. The cavalry proceeded in advance, accompanied by Major Jenkins and Captain Pinkney, Sessions Judge, and, on their arrival at Rukreeta, found that the enemy had evacuated it and retreated to Enotah, to which place Major Jenkins followed them, and placed videttes to prevent their further retreat. On arrival of the infantry, Major Jenkins directed me to advance in skirmishing order, through a jowarree field at the back of the village. The rebels, on seeing us approach, succeeded, owing to the jungly nature of the ground, in making their escape to a hill in the vicinity. We followed them, and, on reaching the summit, Major Jenkins fell, mortally wounded by a matchlock ball. After driving the enemy off the hill I returned to the village and burnt it.

I am happy to say that there were no other casualties on our side.

On the part of the rebels we counted twelve killed, and brought in nine prisoners.

I shall remain encamped at Kuttunghee, waiting your further orders.

I have, &c.,
RICHARD OAKES, Lieutenant,
Commanding Detachment.

No. 32.

Lieutenant C. S. Stewart, 5th Troop 4th Regiment Light Cavalry, to the Brigade Major, Nagpore Moveable Column, Jubbulpore.

Camp, Jubbulpore, November 11, 1857.

SIR,

I HAVE the honor to state, for the information of the officer commanding Nagpore Moveable Column, that Captain Tottenham, having been ordered to take the 5th troop 4th Madras Light Cavalry, on special service to Ghosulpore, marched on the morning of the 7th instant. On getting news at Pownalghur, the 1st stage, that Ghosulpore was being looted, we galloped on, but arrived too late, as the looters had all left and gone away to the right of the road, in which direction we followed, and after some time caught sight of nearly 1000 people running towards a village called Ramkaria (they were about one mile or so from the village, we were more than three). We went after them, but, owing to the bad nature of the ground, they reached the village before we got up to them. We followed them into the village, but nobody was to be seen ; at last a man pointed out the Rajah's house as one likely to conceal men. We burst open the door and searched the house thoroughly, but could find nobody; at last Captain Tottenham, who was on foot, walked up to another door of the house to break it open, when four or five shots were fired through the door, and from the balcony above, at Captain Tottenham, who ran to his horse, mounted, and called on me to take the troop out of the village, which I did afterwards. We had to go back to fetch Captain Tottenham, who had fainted on account of a wound, which I then for the first time learnt he had received in the middle of a village. I then posted the troop in small parties to watch the village all round, which they did till sunset, when I withdrew them as there were too few men with me to surround so large a village so as to prevent anybody getting away in the dark. I am unable to say, whether there were many people concealed in the village Ramkaria, or whether they ran through it to the jungles on the other side. We killed seven or eight men, and took eighteen prisoners, one of whom died of wounds ; the rest were hanged.

I have, &c.,

C. S. STEWART, Lieutenant,

5th troop, 4th Regiment Light Cavalry.

No. 33.

Brevet-Major R. S. Sullivan, commanding De-
tachment Kamptee Moveable Column, to Major
Jenkins, Assistant - Quartermaster - General,
Nagpore Force, Jubbulpore.

SIR, Camp, Ghosulpore, Nov. 7th, 1857.
I HAVE the honor to report, for the information of the officer commanding the column,
that, finding it impossible to push on the Dawk
further than Kylwanah, where we arrived on the
evening of the 4th (it being reported that the
rebels were in force on the road in the neighbourhood of Jokai, and that the 52nd mutineers were
also in our immediate vicinity), I deemed it prudent
to retire on the evening of the 5th to Moorwanah.

On the morning of the 6th, the detachment
had just resumed its march, and had only advanced about 400 yards, when we were surprised
by a heavy fire upon us from two guns, ginjals
and matchlocks. As soon as the guns could be
got into position, we returned the fire with both
our pieces, but unfortunately the axle tree of one
of our guns broke down at the second round. Some
delay ensued of course in effecting the repairs,
which were accomplished in the most admirable
and cool manner by Lieutenant Lane and his artillery men under fire.

Seeing the enemy making attempts to surround
us, I ordered the squadron of cavalry to attack
the enemy by a flank movement from my left,
and the infantry to accomplish a similar movement along the road to the right. This was done
to my most perfect satisfaction. The cavalry,
previously on the right rear of the guns, passed
in rear of them, crossed the road, and, after getting through two most difficult ravines, at a given
signal from Lieutenant Lane of two guns in rapid
succession, charged and captured one of the ene-

my's guns, which was turned on them as soon as they perceived the flank movement. Moving onwards, they sabred about 30 of the rebels, three of whom fell under Lieutenant Clerk's sword. The 33rd Native Infantry, entering the village, bayonetted several, and came on the second gun, which had been disabled and withdrawn before the cavalry charge.

In this engagement, we lost one Gun Lascar killed, one naique and two privates 4th Light Cavalry, severely wounded, and one private 33rd Native Infantry, and one grass-cutter 4th Light Cavalry, also severely wounded; Lieutenant Clerk received a slight graze from a sword.

The enemy are reported to have numbered from 1500 to 2000 men, with a fair proportion of matchlock-men, 60 of them were counted dead upon the field, and it is impossible to calculate the number of the wounded.

I cannot extol too highly the cool and gallant manner in which Lieutenant Lane and the Artillery under him worked their one gun and repaired the other, under a heavy fire of both grape and round shot. The squadron of the 4th with Lieutenant Clerk, also did their work most gallantly; and Lieutenant New with the infantry entered the village in the most spirited manner, and, along with some of the gunners, cleared the village most effectually.

My thanks are also due to Lieutenant Dick, 52nd Bengal Native Infantry, attached to the infantry, and to Assistant-Surgeon Adam for his great attention to the wounded men.

I beg to enclose a return of casualties. The guns captured are brass guns of small calibre.

I have, &c.,
R. S. SULLIVAN, Brevet-Major,
Commanding Detachment Kamptee
Moveable Column.

No. 34.

Return of Casualties in the engagement at Moor-wanah, on the morning of the 6th November.

CAVALRY.

1 naique, $\left.\right\}$ Severely wounded.
2 privates,
1 camp-follower (grass-cutter) severely.

ARTILLERY.

1 Gun Lascar killed.

INFANTRY. 33RD MADRAS NATIVE INFANTRY.
1 private severely wounded.

HUNTER ADAM,
Assistant-Surgeon in medical charge.

No. 35.

Brevet-Colonel J. Millar, commanding Detachment Kamptee Moveable Column, to the Brigade-Major, Kamptee Moveable Column, Jubbulpore.

Dated Camp, Patun, December 27, 1857.

SIR,

IN continuation of my report of yesterday's date, I have the honor to state, for the information of the Brigadier commanding, that I marched out this morning at 6 A.M. to attack the rebels on the Konee Pass, and did not return till near 4 P.M. this afternoon.

2. There appeared to be about 1,000 of the rebels on the brow and sides of the hill, with an advanced picquet about a third of the way up the hill, where they had made a stone breastwork, behind which was a small gun.

3. After crossing the river I extended the grenadier and light companies of the 33rd Regiment Native Infantry, which covered the advance of

the guns; the latter were unlimbered in a convenient position, and a few rounds of shrapnel and grape from the guns soon cleared the way for the advance of the skirmishers, who advanced up the hill without any check.

4. The artillery under Lieutenant Lane did excellent service in turning the enemy out of the side and from the brow of the hill, but were unable to ascend it, owing to the number of loose boulders and slabs of stone on the ghat. I therefore left them at the bottom with one company of infantry for their protection.

5. As soon as the skirmishers had reached the top of the ghat, which was covered with very thick jungle, I directed Captain Macintire to ascend with part of the cavalry and pursue the enemy as far as possible, which service was performed in the most satisfactory manner, the sowars ascending a pass over ground at a pace which I should have deemed utterly impossible for any cavalry to have accomplished. They cut down and captured six rebels to my knowledge.

6 The whole party then was formed up and advanced without opposition about three miles over a very rocky and difficult country, covered for the most part with thick jungle. As there was no water near, and as everything, including the guns, was below the ghat, I deemed it better then to return to our old camping ground, the pass being held for us during the night by a friendly thakoor.

7. The skirmishers were commanded by Lieutenant Dun and Watson, supported by Lieutenant Pearson with the E company, and advanced up the hill (especially the light company) in very gallant style, as the jungle was thick and the rebels in large numbers.

8. To Captain Baldwin, the Deputy-Commis-

sioner, my best thanks are due for the very gallant style in which he led his Burkundauze up the hill, as well as for the general assistance he rendered.

9, About seven of the rebels we know to have been killed, and it is probable that many more were knocked over by the artillery, and carried off before we got up.

10. To morrow I propose to make another dour after the rebels.

I have, &c.,

J. MILLAR, Brevet-Colonel,
Commanding Detachment Kamptee
Moveable Column.

P.S.—Six prisoners taken in arms have been hanged. No casualties on our side at all.

STRENGTH OF THE DETACHMENT ENGAGED.

Head Quarters and one troop 2nd Cavalry Hyderabad Contingent, two guns D Company Madras Artillery, Head Quarters and 300 rank and file, 33rd Regiment Madras Native Infantry.

No. 36.

Captain and Brevet-Major G. A. Harrison, Kamptee Moveable Column, to Colonel Millar, commanding 33rd Madras Native Infantry, Detachment Kamptee Moveable Column, Patun.

Camp, Jubbulpore, December 28, 1857.

SIR,   No. 334.

I HAVE had the honor of receiving and laying before Brigadier Lawrence your letters of 26th and 29th instant, and am directed to convey his approbation of the conduct of the Field Detachment under your command, as reported by you. The Brigadier congratulates you on the good service you have done without loss on our

side, and he begs you will express his thanks to
Captain Macintire, commanding 2nd Cavalry Hyderabad Contingent, and all the officers and men
of your detachment.

2. The Brigadier requests you will convey to
Lieutenant Baldwin, Deputy Commissioner, his
best thanks for the assistance he has rendered you
as reported in your letter.

3. I am instructed to inform you that copies of
your reports, together with this letter, will be
forwarded for the information of his Excellency
the Commander-in-Chief.

4. The Brigadier having learned that there is
water to be procured a little in advance of where
you proceeded on to the table land above the
Konee Ghaut, he begs that you will, if possible,
advance and entirely dislodge the rebels from
the neighbourhood, but it is left to your own discretion how far you follow them up, it being
desirable that you should return to this station
as soon as possible, as the troops under your
command are required.

1 have, &c.,

G. A. HARRISON,

Captain and Brigade Major, Kamptee
Moveable Column.

No. 37.

No. 242 of 1858.

THE Right Honorable the Governor-General
is pleased to direct the publication of the following letter from the Adjutant-General of the
Army, No. 431 A, dated 23rd June, 1858, enclosing a despatch from Major-General Sir J.
Hope Grant, K.C.B., giving the details of a most
successful action near Nowabgunge on the 13th
instant.

9 Z 2

The Governor-General entirely concurs in the commendation bestowed by his Excellency the Commander-in-Chief on Major-General Sir J. Hope Grant on this occasion.

No. 38.

The Adjutant-General of the Army to the Secretary to the Government of India, Military Department, with the Governor-General.

Head Quarters, Allahabad, June 23, 1858.

No. 431 A.

SIR,

BY desire of the Commander-in-Chief, I have the honor to forward, for submission to the Right Honorable the Governor-General, the enclosed despatch, dated the 17th instant, from Major-General Sir J. Hope Grant, K.C.B., commanding Lucknow Field Force, giving the details of a most successful action, in which 16,000 rebels were signally defeated near Nowabgunge, on the 13th idem.

2. I am directed to request you will inform his Lordship that the Major-General's operations upon this occasion appear to his Excellency to have been conducted throughout with the greatest skill and prudence, and to deserve high approval.

3. The return of the despatch is requested, when no longer required.

I have, &c.,
W. MAYHEW, Lieutenant-Colonel,
Adjutant-General of the Army.

No. 39.

Major-General J. Hope Grant, commanding Lucknow Field Force, to the Deputy Adjutant-General of the Army.

Head Quarters, Camp Nowabgunge,
June 17, 1858.

SIR,   No. 104.

I HAVE the honor to report to you, for the information of his Excellency the Commander-in-Chief that, on the morning of the 12th instant, I arrived with the column as per margin,* at Chinhut, where a garrison column had been stationed under command of Colonel Purnell, during my absence to the south of Lucknow. At this place I ascertained that a large force of rebels, amounting to some 16,000, with a good many guns, had taken up a position along a nullah in the neighbourhood of Nowabgunge, 12 miles miles from Chinhut.

I determined to start at night, though there was no moon, and to get close to this nullah before daybreak. I accordingly directed all baggage and supplies to be left at Chinhut, under charge of Colonel Purnell, and formed up my column along the Fyzabad road, at eleven o'clock P.M. The nullah ran across this road about four miles from Nowabgunge, over which there was an old stone bridge, but knowing that there was a large jungle about three miles to the north of the town, I determined to cross at a ford, or rather causeway, which lay about two miles above the bridge, that

---

* DETAIL.—Artillery: One troop Horse Artillery; two Light Field Batteries. Cavalry: Her Majesty's 2nd Dragoon Guards (two squadrons); Her Majesty's 7th Hussars; 1st Seikh Infantry Cavalry (one squadron); one troop Mounted Police; Hodson's Horse. Infantry: 2nd Battalion Rifle Brigade; 3rd ditto ditto; 5th Punjaub Rifles; detail of Engineers and Sappers.

I might get between the enemy and this jungle. We got off soon after eleven o'clock, and the whole march was performed with the greatest regularity, though a great part of the way was across country.

The advanced guard arrived within about a quarter of a mile of the nullah, which ran along the front of the enemy's position, about half an hour before day-break on the morning of the 13th.

The column was halted, and the men had some refreshment.

As soon as it was light the force advanced towards the ford, which was defended by a body of the enemy, strongly posted in topes of trees and ravines, supported by three guns.

Three Horse Artillery guns of Captain Mackinnon's troop, and Captain Johnson's battery were immediately got into position to cover the passage of the advanced guard. The enemy's guns were soon silenced, and one of them turned over, and the advance, consisting of two horse artillery guns, under Lieutenant McLeod, two squadrons of cavalry, under Captain Stisted, 7th Hussars, and Lieutenant Prendergast, Wale's Horse, and 200 Infantry under Major Oxenden, immediately crossed and took up a position on the other side.

Our two guns opened fire, and the Rifles, advancing in gallant style, in skirmishing order, under a heavy fire, soon drove the enemy from his first position.

The remaining guns of the Horse Artillery, Captain Johnson's Battery, and a portion of the cavalry, immediately followed, and I at once advanced, at a trot, against what appeared to be the centre of the enemy's position. As soon as the dust cleared off, the enemy were to be seen all round, and their guns opened in my front, and on both flanks.

The troop of Horse Artillery immediately got into action to the front, and Captain Johnson's Battery, supported by two squadrons, 2nd Dragoon Guards, under Major Seymour, I sent to engage the enemy on my left, where they were in very considerable force.

About this time a large body of the enemy, cavalry and infantry, and two guns, moved round to my right rear, in the direction of the ford, expecting, no doubt, to find my baggage crossing; but Hodson's Horse, under Major Daly, C.B., a squadron of the Police Horse under Lieutenant Hill, and the 3rd Battalion of the Rifle Brigade under Lieutenant Colonel Glyn, had just crossed, and were ready to receive them. This body of cavalry and two companies of the Rifles, under the command of Captain Atherley, formed line to the right and advanced against them. Major Carleton's Battery, which was following, had some difficulty in crossing the ford, but, as soon as he got two guns across, he brought them up to the support of Major Daly.

Here the enemy offered considerable opposition. The Rifles charged them twice with the sword, cutting up many.

Major Daly detached 100 cavalry, under Lieutenant Mecham, and Lieutenant the Honourable J. Fraser, to act upon their left, while he with the remainder of his cavalry, charged them in front. Lieutenant Mecham led his men on gallantly over broken ground, and was severely wounded.

The remainder of Major Carleton's battery was brought up by Lieutenant Percival, into a good position on the right, and in time to open with considerable effect on the enemy as they retired.

Meanwhile, Captain Mackinnon's Troop Horse Artillery, supported by the 7th Hussars, under the command of Major Sir W. Russell, was hotly en-

gaged to the front and left ; as also Captain Johnson's battery, which was on my extreme left. The
enemy in my front having been driven back,
Mackinnon's troop changed front to the left, and
the troop and battery advanced, supported by the
cavalry, and the remainder of the 3rd Battalion
Rifle Brigade, which had come up under the command of Lieutenant-Colonel Glyn. The enemy
here also were driven from their position after a
sharp cannonade.

The action on my proper right having commenced again with great vigour, I proceeded in
that direction, leaving Colonel Hagart to superin-
tend the troops on the left. On arriving at this
point, I found a large number of Gazzies, with two
guns, had come out on the open plain, and attacked
Hodson's Horse with two guns of Major Carleton's battery, which covered my rear. I immediately ordered up the other four guns under the
command of Lieutenant Percival, and two squadrons of the 7th Hussars, under command of
Major Sir W. Russell, and opened grape upon this
force within 300 or 400 yards with terrible effect.
But the rebels made the most determined resistance, and two men, in the midst of a shower of
grape, brought forward two green standards, which
they planted in the ground beside their guns, and
rallied their men. Captain Atherley's two companies of the 3rd Battalion Rifle Brigade at this
moment, advanced to the attack, which obliged
the rebels to move off. The cavalry then got between them and the guns, and the 7th Hussars,
led gallantly by Major Sir W. Russell, supported
by Hodson's Horse, under Major Daly, C.B.,
swept through them twice, killing every man. I
must here mention the gallant conduct of two
officers of the 7th Hussars, Captain Bushe and
Captain Fraser. The latter I myself saw surrounded by the enemy, and fighting his way gal-

lantly through them all; he was severely wounded in the hand.

About this time, Brigadier Horsford advanced with the 5th Punjaub Infantry, under Major Vaughan, being joined by the two companies of the Rifles, under Captain Atherley, and two of Major Carleton's guns, under Lieutenant Percival, and proceeded against a body of the enemy, which had taken up a position on their extreme proper left, in a large tope of trees, having two guns in position. Brigadier Horsford advanced steadily in skirmishing order, under a sharp cannonade from the enemy's guns, which were well served and supported by large bodies of infantry.

The enemy was soon pressed, they retired their guns some distance, and then re-opened them, but in a few minutes they were carried in gallant style, without the aid of any cavalry. This closed the action on my left, front, and right.

The enemy having, at the commencement of the action, detached a large force which seriously threatened our rear, Brigadier Horsford sent the 2nd Battalion Rifle Brigade to hold them in check. This duty was ably performed by Lieutenant-Colonel Hill. The advance of the enemy was not only checked, but they were forced to retire with considerable loss.

I trust, through the mercy of God, this severe blow to the rebels, will be the means of quieting all this part of the country.

I beg that the under-mentioned officers' names may be laid before his Excellency the Commander-in-Chief.

Brigadier Horsford, I am much indebted to for the very excellent way in which he led on the infantry, and for the support he gives me upon all occasions.

To Colonel Hagart I am also much indebted.

He has been most active, zealous, and attentive to all the duties entrusted to him.

Lieutenant-Colonel Hill, who, with his battalion, so gallantly and successfully protected our rear, a most important service.

Lieutenant-Colonel Glyn, a most excellent officer, and whose battalion, the third, behaved so well, being actively employed during the whole day.

Major Carleton, commanding the Artillery, to whose activity and zeal in getting his guns into action, I am much indebted.

Major Sir W. Russell, whose gallantry in leading the charge of the 7th Hussars, is deserving of my highest praise.

Major Vaughan, commanding 5th Punjaub Rifles, who commanded his regiment to my entire satisfaction, who, supported by two companies of the Rifles, captured two guns, and whose name I inadvertently left out in my despatch from Barree on the 24th April last, when he was well deserving of mention.

Major Daly, to whom I am greatly indebted for his excellent conduct in the field, and for the good information he brought me.

To Captain Mackinnon, commanding troop Bengal Horse Artillery, and Captain Johnson, commanding battery Royal Artillery, I am also indebted for their excellent services.

Captains Bushe and Fraser, of the 7th Hussars, who commanded the two squadrons in the charge above mentioned, and whose gallantry in leading their men, was most conspicuous.

Major Seymour, commanding two squadrons 2nd Dragoon Guards, and Captains Aytoun and Stisted, 7th Hussars, all detached with guns, performed their duty much to my satisfaction.

Lieutenant Prendergast, commanding detachment Wale's Horse, also detached with guns, on this, as on all former occasions, proved himself an excellent and intelligent officer.

I beg to bring to his Excellency's notice, the efficient manner in which Captain the Honourable J. Fiennes, 7th Hussars, has conducted the duties of Major of Brigade of Cavalry in the Field. On this occasion he was most active and zealous, as also Cornet the Honorable W. Harbord, 7th Hussars, who was Colonel Hagart's Orderly Officer for the day.

Brigadier Horsford speaks in the highest terms of his Staff, viz.

Major Mallon, 75th Regiment, Major of Brigade, who had his horse killed under him, and Lieutenant Ramsbottom, Rifle Brigade, his Orderly Officer.

Lieutenant and Adjutant Baker, Hodson's Horse, is particularly mentioned by Major Daly, for his gallantry. Lieutenant Hill, commanding detachment of Mounted Police.

Lieutenant Mecham, Hodson's Horse, who was severely wounded in leading his squadron to the charge.

I beg also to mention the services of Lieutenant Percival, Bengal Artillery, second in command of Major Carleton's Battery.

Also Lieutenant Smart, Adjutant, Royal Artillery, and Lieutenant Strange, Quartermaster, Royal Artillery, and Lieutenant Wynn, commanding detachment of Engineers.

I beg also to bring to his Excellency's notice my personal and divisional Staff, viz. :—

Captain the Honourable A. Anson, 84th Regiment, Aide-de-Camp, who had his horse wounded.

Major Hamilton, 9th Lancers, Deputy Assistant-Adjutant General ; Major Wolseley, Deputy Assistant-Quartermaster-General, from whom I have received great assistance on all occasions.

Dr. Fraser, Senior Surgeon, who deserves my approbation for his zeal and attention to the sick; Dr. Lynch, 7th Hussars, Division Surgeon; and Lieutenant Graham, Deputy Assistant-Commissary-General, a most active and intelligent officer, and whose name I inadvertently omitted to mention in my despatch from Barree, on the 24th April last.

I have to bring to notice the conduct of Private Same Shaw, of the 3rd Battalion Rifle Brigade, who is recommended by his commanding officer for the Victoria Cross.

An armed rebel had been seen to enter a tope of trees; some officers and men ran into the tope in pursuit of him. This man was a Ghazee. Private Shaw drew his short sword and with that weapon rushed single-handed on the Ghazee. Shaw received a severe tulwar wound, but after a desperate struggle he killed the man.

I trust his Excellency will allow me to recommend this man for the Victoria Cross, and that he will approve of my having issued a Division Order stating that I have done so.

I would now report the good and gallant conduct of Resseldar Man Sing, and Jemadar Hussain Ali, both of Hodson's Horse: the former came to the assistance of Lieutenant Baker, and was severely wounded, the latter dismounted, and sword in hand, cut up some gunners who remained with their guns.

The return of guns captured (nine), I enclose.

From all the information which I can obtain, the enemy must have left between five and six hundred dead bodies on the field, and their wounded must have been very numerous.

My casualty return has already been forwarded.

In conclusion, I beg to point out, that the troops were under arms from 10 P.M. on the 12th until 9 A.M. on the 13th; during a most oppressive night they made a march of ten miles, and in the morning fought an action of three hours' duration. All officers and soldiers did their utmost, and their exertions deserve high praise.

I have, &c.

J. HOPE GRANT, Major-General,
Commanding Lucknow Field Force.

No. 41.

List of Officers Wounded.

Captain C. C. Fraser, 7th Queen's Own Hussars, severely wounded.

Lieutenant R. Topham, 7th Queen's Own Hussars, slight contusion.

Cornet and Adjutant J. Mould, 7th Queen's Own Hussars, slightly wounded.

Lieutenant Mecham, Hodson's Horse, severely wounded.

Lieutenant the Hon. F. Frazer, Hodson's Horse, Slightly wounded.

Lieutenant Hugh Lawton, 2nd Battalion Rifle Brigade, severely wounded.

No. 43.

No. 243 of 1858.

THE Right Honorable the Governor-General is pleased to direct the publication of the following letter, from the Assistant Adjutant-General of the Army No. 408 A, dated the 9th June 1858, enclosing a despatch from Major-General Sir Hugh Rose, K.C.B., commanding Central India Field Force, reporting the details of an action with the rebel army under Tantia Topee near Jhansie, during the siege of that fortress.

The Governor-General cordially concurs with his Excellency the Commander-in-Chief, in the unqualified approbation he has expressed of the conduct of the officers and men concerned in this action, and in his admiration of the brilliant charge made by Captain Need, at the head of a troop of Her Majesty's 14th Light Dragoons.

No. 44.

The Assistant Adjutant-General of the Army, to the Secretary to the Government of India.

Camp Poora, June 9, 1858.

SIR,   No. 408A.

I AM desired by the Commander-in-Chief to forward for submission to the Right Honorable the Governor-General, the enclosed copy* of a despatch, dated 30th April last (which has only now reached head-quarters), from Major-General Sir H. Rose, K.C.B., commanding Central India Field Force, reporting the details of an action fought on the 1st idem, with the rebel army under Tantia Topee, on the river Betwa near Jhansie.

2. The operations of the troops engaged upon this occasion, appear to his Excellency to have been conducted with the highest skill and vigour ; and the behaviour of all concerned merits his unqualified satisfaction.

3. Sir Colin Campbell cannot, however, refrain from drawing his lordship's attention to the gallant and successful charge made by a troop of Her Majesty's 14th Light Dragoons, under Captain Need ; and, indeed, to the services of all those especially named by the Major-General and Brigadier Stuart.

I have, &c.,
D. M. STEWART, Major,
Assistant Adjutant-General of the Army.

* See London Gazette of Aug. 14, 1858.

No. 45.

Allahabad, July 1, 1858.

No. 244 of 1858.

THE Right Honorable the Governor-General is pleased to publish the following despatch from Major-General Sir Hugh Rose, K.C.B., commanding Central India Field Force, bringing to notice the names of certain officers inadvertently omitted in his despatch, published in the General Orders of the Governor-General, No. 174, dated 31st May last, detailing the operations against, and the capture of, the fort and town of Jhansie.

No. 46.

Major-General Sir Hugh Rose, K.C.B., commanding Central India Field Force, to the Chief of the Staff.

Camp Soopowlie, June 14, 1858.

SIR,

IN my despatch, detailing the operations against, and the capture of, the fort and town of Jhansie, the names of several officers of the force under my command were inadvertently omitted, whose services I should have acknowledged ; I have now the honor to request you to bring them to the notice of his Excellency the Commander-in-Chief.

The name of Captain Abbott, commanding 3rd Hydrabad Cavalry, although mentioned more than once in the despatch, is omitted in the list of officers in command of corps. Captain Abbott, at the commencement of operations, was placed by me in command of the whole of the cavalry of the Hyderabad contingent, engaged in the investment of the fort and town.

The name of Captain Montriou, commanding

24th Regiment Bombay Native Infantry, was also omitted in the same list.

Captain Scott, Military Paymaster, Captain Ashburner, Deputy Judge-Advocate-General, and Captain Gordon, Assistant Commissary-General to the force, have each, in their several departments, performed their duties to my entire satisfaction. To the two first, I have been indebted more than once for assistance volunteered in the field.

I have, &c.,

HUGH ROSE, Major-General,

Commanding Central India Field Force.

No. 47.

No. 245 of 1858.

THE Right Honorable the Governor-General is pleased to direct the publication of the following despatch, from Brigadier Rowcroft, commanding Sarun Field Force, dated 12th June, 1858, submitting a report from Major Cox, Her Majesty's 13th Light Infantry, of a successful attack on a strong position of the enemy at Amorah, on the 9th inst.

No. 48.

Brigadier F. Rowcroft, commanding Sarun Field Force, to the Deputy Adjutant-General of the Army.

Camp Bustee, June 12, 1858.

SIR, No. 324.

I HAVE the honor to forward, enclosed, a report from Major Cox, Her Majesty's 13th Light Infantry, commanding a detachment sent out from the Field Force under my command, on the 30th ultimo, relative to his successful attack on the

enemy's strong position at Amorah, on the 9th
instant, for submission to his Excellency the Commander-in-Chief.

2. On the 29th ultimo, I received from the
commissioner, Mr. Wingfield, an urgent requisition for a strong detachment to proceed to Bansee,
about 32 miles to the north of this; the late
Nazim Mahomed Hoossen having suddenly arrived there, with a rebel force of some 3,000 or
4,000 men, and 6 guns, driving out the Bansee
Rajah, who, with his family and adherents, fled to
Sunnowlee, to a fort about 12 miles north of
Bansee, in the jungle, where the Nazim followed
him and besieged the fort. I immediately ordered
a detachment as per margin,* half of my force, as
much as I could venture to spare, with reference
to the enemy lying in my front to the west and to
the south, under the command of Major Cox, Her
Majesty's 13th Light Infantry to march the next
morning, the 30th ultimo, at 2 o'clock for Bansee,
the Commissioner accompanying the detachment,
to make it in three marches, that the third into
Bansee might be short, to enable the troops to
arrive fresh for any work required of them in
action. I divided my force with reluctance, but
the case was urgent.

3. On the 31st ultimo, about 8 A.M., the Teh-
seeldar and Thannadar of Captaingunge, with some
200 irregular matchlock-men, hurried into Bustee,

* One squadron Bengal Yeomanry Cavalry, 10 officers
and 93 rank and file; one squadron 6th Madras Cavalry,
3 officers and 90 rank and file; detachment 4th company
5th battalion Artillery, with one 9-pounder and one 24-
pounder howitzer, one officer and 16 rank and file; detachment Naval Brigade with two 12-pounder mountain train
howitzers and one 24-pounder rocket tube, 2 officers and
26 rank and file; detachment of Her Majesty's 13th Light
Infantry, 8 officers and 203 rank and file; detachment
Bengal Police Battalion, 1 native officer and 20 rank and
file.

reporting that about 600 sepoys and other rebels, with 2 guns, had advanced on Captaingunge, 12 miles to the west of this, from Amorah, and that a greater force was coming on behind. To prevent the rebels holding on at Captaingunge, and having time to increase their numbers, and probably attack me here, I immediately ordered the headquarters of the field force, with the two remaining 12-pounder howitzers of the Naval Brigade, to march for Captaingunge, at 7 o'clock the same evening, so as to arrive there about 11 o'clock, and have a few hours' rest before attacking the enemy at daybreak, the cavalry to push on at 4 P.M., under Captain Clerk, 4th Madras Cavalry, to be at Captaingunge before dark, for information, and to keep the enemy in check. All baggage, stores, ammunition, and tents were ordered to be collected at 5 P.M. in the hospital compound, for I could barely spare 50 men as a guard to remain behind for their protection.

4. The enemy probably heard of our preparations to advance on them, for about 6 P.M. I received reports that the rebels had retreated in the middle of the day, having plundered the place, burnt down the lines of the irregulars and the bazaar, and trying to burn the gateway of the brick teseel, a stronghold for treasure, and calculated to hold about 150 or 200 men. The order for the march of the troops was countermanded, and the camps re-pitched, and orders sent out to the cavalry to push on at daybreak, four or five miles beyond Captaingunge, to see the enemy well cleared off, and then return to Bustee.

5. Major Cox's detachment reached Bansee on the 1st instant, and, as they approached the place, the Nazim getting information of it, he immediately gave up the siege of the Rajah's fort, retired a few miles towards Bansee, and made a precipitate retreat with his force towards the north-

west. The Bansee Rajah returned the same evening. Major Cox pursued for two marches towards
Doomuriagunge, by the south bank of the river
Raptee, and the Bansee Rajah was to move and
co-operate on the north side, but his aid was not
very great or efficient. They came up with the
enemy's rear guard, and ten of them were cut up
by a party of cavalry, Bengal yeomanry, and 6th
Madras Light Cavalry, sent out under Lieutenant
Percival, Bengal Yeomanry Cavalry.

6. The detachment then moved, turning down
towards the south-west, by the Bahnpore Thanna
road, to Hurryah, about six miles west of Captaingunge, where they arrived on the 8th instant, and
were reinforced by 90 rank and file, Her Majesty's
13th Light Infantry, 20 Royal Marines, and 40
Madras Light Cavalry, which I had sent on to
Captaingunge to hold that post, and placing them
at the disposal of Major Cox, if he called them up
for an attack of the enemy at Amorah, which was
successfully carried into effect on the 9th instant,
as detailed in Major Cox's report.

7. I beg to express my best thanks to Major
Cox, and my full satisfaction with the careful
manner my instructions were carried out, and for
the judgment and ability shown by Major Cox, in
carrying out so successfully the service confided to
him.

8. The officers and troops of all arms went
through their fatigues at this hot and most trying
season of the year, with their usual cheerfulness
and readiness.

9. I beg to offer my best and cordial thanks to
Mr. Wingfield, the Commissioner, for his valuable
assistance to Major Cox, and for the daily information he communicated to me, and the Deputy
Magistrate, Shekh Kairoodeen, who accompanied
the Commissioner, and afforded all the active aid
in his power.

10. I beg to recommend to the most favourable notice of his Excellency, Sir Colin Campbell, all engaged in the operations herein detailed.

11. The Nazim Mahomed Hoossen is reported to-day to be at Sirooampore, about six miles north of Amorah.

12. Brigadier-General Sir E. Lugard not having yet assumed command of the Dinapore division, I beg to forward this despatch direct to army head-quarters.

I have, &c.,

F. ROWCROFT, Brigadier,

Commanding Sarun Field Force.

No. 49.

Major J. W. Cox, commanding Detachment, to the Brigade-Major, Sarun Field Force.

Camp Henyah, June 9, 1858.

SIR,

I HAVE the honor to report, for the information of Brigadier Rowcroft, that the force under my command attacked and drove the enemy from two strong positions at Amora this morning.

From the information I received, it appeared that in number about 1,000, almost all rebel sepoys, occupied the Ranee's house and adjacent buildings at Amorah, round which an earthwork had been constructed. Here they had the principal part of their force with 2 guns; they also occupied our old fortifications on the Bustee road, which they had repaired and improved; here also they had 2 guns, so placed as to command the approach and sweep the bridge about 700 yards distant.

From having been for some time encamped in the neighbourhood, I was aware of the difficulties of a direct attack, especially on the Ranee's house, as the usual road to that place passes close to an extensive bamboo jungle. I therefore made arrangements to attack them from another direction, and during the night had a putte constructed, which, crossing the river Ramburka at a ford, would bring us to Amorah by the Gaighat road.

Having struck the tents and packed the baggage, I left them on the ground under a sufficient guard, and marched by this route at $2\frac{1}{2}$ A.M., with 250 of the 13th Light Infantry, 85 of the Bengal Yeomanry Cavalry, and 6th Madras Cavalry, under Captain Vine, 6th Madras Cavalry, and 2 Foot Artillery guns, and sent Major Richardson on the direct road with the remainder of the cavalry, 88 in number, two 12-pounder howitzers of the Naval Bridge, and 55 infantry, with instructions to consider his as a false attack, not to pass the river, while the fort was occupied by the enemy, but to open fire on it from his side of the bridge.

The party under Major Richardson came in contact with some of the enemy's picquets, who were strongly posted along the edge of a nullah'; this delayed his advance, and obliged him to take up a position to keep them in check; meanwhile, the column under my command, coming unexpectedly on the enemy's flank and rear, quickly drove him out of his position near the Ranee's house.

I pursued him with infantry skirmishers, and the fire of Lieutenant Welch's guns, and sent the cavalry after them round the jungle, while I cleared it with a company of the 13th Light Infantry, in extended order, and pushed the column through the village towards our old fortification.

Such, however, was the consternation caused

by the simultaneous advance of our two columns, that they also speedily evacuated this strong post, and made a most hurried retreat towards Belwah. As soon as I found the fort was evacuated, I again sent the squadron under Captain Vine in pursuit; the sepoys, however, broke up into several small bodies, which made for different villages, so that although the pursuit was continued for four miles and Captain Vine charged whenever an opportunity offered, he was only able here to cut off 15 or 20 sepoys, the number of the enemy found killed on the ground during the day being 30 or 40 men.

The positions being both completely carried, and the enemy in full flight, I returned to Hurriah, with most of the force, leaving the Madras Cavalry, and one troop of the Bengal Yeomanry Cavalry, to cover the destruction of the houses, &c., recently occupied by the enemy. The infantry and artillery were back in camp before 8·30 A.M., having marched fourteen miles, and been upwards of an hour in action. I beg to enclose a list of our casualties on this occasion.

I have, &c.
F. ROWCROFT, Brigadier,
Commanding Detachment.

No. 50.

From the Return of Casualties in the Field Force under Command of Major Cox, Her Majesty's 13th Light Infantry, in the Engagement at Amorah.

June 9, 1858.

Lieutenant A. R. J. Ellis, Bengal Yeomanry Cavalry, severely wounded, sword cut on right arm.

No. 51.

Allahabad, July 3, 1858.

No. 250 of 1858.

THE Right Honorable the Governor-General is pleased to direct the publication of the following despatch from Brigadier-General R. Walpole, C.B., commanding the Rohilcund Division, forwarding a communication from Brigadier Coke, C.B., reporting the movements of the rebels in the Budaon District, and of the measures adopted by him to intercept them.

No. 52.

Brigadier-General R. Walpole C.B., Commanding the Rohilcund Division, to the Chief of the Staff.

Bareilly, June 6, 1858.

SIR, No. 32.

WITH reference to my communication, acquainting you, for the information of his Excellency the Commander-in-Chief, that the Tantia Rao, or some other rajah, had crossed the Ganges from the Doab near Oosaith, and transmitting copy of letter from Mr. Alexander, upon this subject, and copy of instructions to Brigadier Coke, directing him, in consequence, to proceed to the Budaon district, instead of to Phillebheet ; I have the honor herewith to transmit copy of communication from Brigadier Coke respecting his march.

It appears from information received, that the rebel force left the neighbourhood of Jatee, on the 31st ultimo.

I have sent the left wing 42nd Highlanders, squadron of carabineers, and Lieutenant Caddell's heavy field battery to Budaon, all under Lieutenant-Colonel Wilkinson, from whence they will proceed to Moradabad, under Brigadier Coke ; and I have instructed Brigadier Coke to leave at Budaon, the Seikh Irregular Infantry, and detachment 17th Irregular Cavalry.

I directed Major Cary, Deputy Assistant-Quartermaster-General, to accompany the troops under Lieutenant-Colonel Wilkinson, as far as Budaon.

I have been in communication with Lieutenant Chesney, Engineers, at Moradabad, and I am in hopes, that cover for the European part of Brigadier Coke's force, will be ready by the time he arrives at that station. The hospital accommodation was to have been completed about the 10th.

The rebels who were at Islamnugger, have been defeated by the troops of the Nawab of Rampoor, and their guns taken. It is stated, that they are now dispersed.

I have, &c.,

R. WALPOLE, Brigadier-General, Commanding Rohilcund Division.

No. 53.

Brigadier John Coke, C.B., Commanding Infantry Brigade, to the Deputy-Assistant Adjutant-General, Rohilcund Division.

Camp, Oosaith, June 4, 1858.

Sir,   No. 82.

IN continuation of my letter, No. 79, dated Shahjehanpore, 31st May, I have the honor to report, for the information of the Major-General commanding, my arrival at this place.

2. On reaching Burrie Mathana, on the 1st of June, I received intelligence that the rebels were in the jungle, on the banks of the Ramgunga, in the vicinity of Kundurria Ghat. On my approaching the Ramgunga, this was confirmed by the report of a traveller, who said he had seen

their force on the 1st of June in the forest. I
sent off intelligence to Captain Beville, commanding at Jeellalabad, to which place he had marched
with a wing of the Belooch regiment and 2 guns
from Shajehanpore, on the night of the 31st May.
I received his reply after crossing the Ramgunga,
to the effect that, shortly after his arrival at Jeellalabad, on the 1st of June, the rebels had crossed
the Ramgunga, near the fort of Jeellalabad, and
had passed in considerable force, with a number
of elephants, about three miles south of the fort,
and were proceeding towards Palee. Captain
Beville's guns drawn by bullocks, having marched
twenty miles that night, were not in a condition
to move, and, as he had only a wing of his regiment and no cavalry, of which the enemy had a
considerable number, he could not leave the fort
in pursuit of them. Captain Beville, with a
few horsemen, followed the enemy, to ascertain
which road they took, and found that they were
making for Palee.

3. Yesterday, on my way towards Budaon, I
received intelligence, that more of the rebels were
passing the Ganges near Soorujpore, on which I
moved down from Myaoon to this place, and found
that the enemy had not crossed. It is stated
that there are considerable numbers of them on
the other side of the Ganges about Eta.

4. I have this day halted here to rest the men
and cattle, the long marches having knocked up
the latter. I have sent out the cavalry, about
eight miles towards Soorujpore on the banks of
the Ganges, to obtain, lf possible, correct information regarding the rebels. Should they not be in
that vicinity, I shall march to-morrow to "Kuk-
rala," and the next day, 6th instant, to Budaon.

I have, &c.
JOHN COKE, Lieutenant-Colonel,
Commanding Infantry Brigade.

No. 54.

No. 251 of 1858.

THE Right Honorable the Governor-General is pleased to direct the publication of the following letter from the Resident at Hyderabad, No. 85, dated the 9th ultimo, forwarding copies of despatches from Major J. E. Hughes, reporting his successful operations in the re-capture of the fort of Copal, which had been seized by a body of rebels under Beem Row Dessaye.

No. 55.

Lieutenant-Colonel C. Davidson, Resident at Hyderabad, to Colonel Birch, C.B., Secretary to the Government of India, Military Department, with the Governor-General.

Hyderabad Residency, June 9, 1858.

SIR, No. 85.

I HAVE the honor to transmit, for the information of the Right Honorable the Governor-General of India, the despatches noted in the margin,* relative to the re-capture of the fort of Copal, seized by Beem Row Dessaye, with a body of rebels from the Zillah of Dharwar, in the southern Mahratta country.

I have, &c.

C. DAVIDSON,
Resident.

* 1. From Major Hughes, commanding Field Force, to the Military Secretary, dated June 1, 1858. 2. From Major Hughes, commanding Field Force, to the Military Secretary, dated June 2, 1858. 3. From Major Hughes, commanding Field Force, to the Military Secretary, dated June 4, 1858. 4. From the Military Secretary to Major Hughes, No. 568, dated June 5, 1858.

No. 56.

*J. E. Hughes, Major, Commanding Field Force,
to the Military Secretary, Residency Hyderabad.*

SIR,   *Camp, Copal, June 1, 1858.*
    I HAVE the honor to report to you, for the
information of the Resident, that I was ordered on
the 28th of May, 1858, to proceed with a field
force from Bellary against rebel Beem Row and
his followers in your territories. Hearing that
they had surrounded Copal, I immediately
marched to that place from Hospet, which I
reached at break of day yesterday, and halted
close to the fort unperceived by the enemy, by
taking a circuitous route ; and, having ascertained
for certain that the fort was held by Beem Row
and the rebels, I proceeded to surround as much
of the fort as I was enabled with the infantry and
Mysore Horse, on which the rebels opened fire on
us, and have continued doing so up to the present
time, which is occasionally returned by the infantry. The fort appears to be excessively strong
with a lofty citadel, and I am therefore awaiting
the arrival of the artillery, which I sent round by a
route different to the one by which I came,
escorted by a sub-division of the 47th Regiment
Native Infantry. The rebels appear to have only
3 guns from which they can fire. I am informed
by Tehsildar Bodun Khan, who was not in the
fort when they seized it, that Beem Row's followers amount to about 400.
    A small force from Lingsoogoor under the com-
mand of Lieutenant Pedler, has just arrived in
camp. The fort I have entirely surrounded, and
am now commencing to take it. My artillery has
also arrived.
                        I have, &c.
                J. E. HUGHES, Major,
                    Commanding Field Force.

No. 57.

J. E. Hughes, Major, to the Military Secretary, Residency Hyderabad.

Sir,   Camp Copal, June 1, 1858.

I HAVE the honor to report, for the information of the Resident that I arrived at Copal on the 30th May, 1858, as reported in my letter, dated 31st May, 1858. On the following morning, at four o'clock, a small force under the command of Lieutenant Pedler, accompanied by Lieutenant Taylor, Deputy Commissioner, arrived in camp, when I despatched a letter to Beem Row, recommending him to allow all the villagers and families of Copal to evacuate the town, and that three hours would be allowed for that purpose, at the expiration of which time, having received no reply, my guns were placed in position, and action commenced by shelling, and endeavouring to make a breach. I had previously disposed of the infantry and cavalry of Lingsoogoor, to strengthen my chain of picquets and sentries. At twelve o'clock noon, as I was preparing a portion of the 74th Highlanders, under Captain Menzies, and a company of the 47th Regiment Native Infantry, under Captain Rutherford, to storm the lower forts, signals were shown from the Pettah that the rebels were retreating to the citadel. The storming party immediately rushed forward, and entered the fort by the breach (that was partly made) and gateway, which was opened by the townsmen, and pursued and attacked the rebels, following them up towards the citadel, till the passage of the storming party was stopped by a strong gate. Up to this time about 100 of the rebels had fallen, including the chief Beem Row, and Keuchema Gowd. During this time, I brought round the 2 guns, under Lieutenant Gloag, to a point below the citadel, to cut off the retreat of the rebels, and prevent their gaining the uppermost bastions. Shortly after this, a message was sent to me, from Captains Menzies and Rutherford, to send up powder and a bag, to blow open the gate. When proceeding to join them with the powder, the rebels who had gained the inside of the gate, offered to surrender, and by three o'clock we had gained entire possession of the fort and town, and have taken, up to the present time, 150 prisoners. The 74th Highlanders and 47th Regiment Native Infantry, vied with each other in the pursuit. A portion of the rebels attempted to escape to the right of the fort by a breach, but were driven back by a sub-division of the Hyderabad Contingent. Their escape was entirely cut off. I had guarded every point; the chain of cavalry picquets and sentries completely surrounded the fort and range of hills at the back, for a distance of about seven miles. The infantry I had placed on the left of the fort and Pettah, advanced after the storming party had entered the breach. Had it not been for the great assistance rendered to me by every officer and man, I never could have accomplished what has been effected, namely, the complete annihilation of Beem Row and his followers; a few may have escaped, but I have as yet heard of none. I am happy to add that, in the attack, only one serjeant, six privates of Her Majesty's 74th Highlanders, and a duffadar of the Mysore Horse were wounded, a return of which I beg leave to enclose; none were killed. I have been unable to ascertain by whose hand Beem Row fell, on whose head a Government reward of 5,000 rupees was placed; he fell between gateways amongst others, and, being so hotly pursued by the infantry, I am informed by the officers, who were present that it was impossible to discover who actually shot him, so many muskets being levelled at the time.

Great assistance has been rendered to me by Lieutenant Taylor, Deputy Commissioner, Raichore Doab. I have, &c.,

J. E. HUGHES, Major,
Commanding Field Force.

No. 58.

J. E. Hughes, Major, Commanding Field Force, to the Military Secretary, Hyderabad Residency.

SIR,   *Camp Copal, June 4, 1858.*

I HAVE the honor to report to you, for the information of the Resident, that 77 prisoners, rebels in arms against Government, have been, by sentence of a General Court-Martial, executed, and that I have 100 more under trial.

2. Having received information from Mr. Collett, the Assistant Collector of Bellary, of yesterday's date, stating that Nurgoond is in our possession, and the chief supposed to have fled towards Copal, pursued by Colonel Malcolm; in consequence of this, I have disposed 4 ressallahs of the Mysore Horse, 2 of which to Kookunnoor, and 2 to Yelburgah, and I have also sent out spies in other directions. All perfectly quiet round Copal.   I have, &c.

J. E. HUGHES, Major,
Commanding Field Force.

No. 59.

The Military Secretary, Resident at Hyderabad, to Major Hughes, Commanding Moveable . Column, Copauldroog, Hyderabad Residency.

June 5, 1858.

SIR,   No. 568.

THE Resident has learnt the re-capture of the fortress of Copauldroog, by the troops under your command, and has directed me to convey his thanks for the rapidity of your advance, and the opportune important assistance you have thus afforded.

2. He begs me also to congratulate you, and the officers and men under your command, on the successful storm of the fortress, and the gallantry of their conduct. I have, &c.

S. C. BRIGGS, Major,
Military Secretary.

No. 60.
Allahabad, July 6, 1858.
No. 254 of 1858.

THE Right Honorable the Governor-General is pleased to direct the publication of the following despatch from Brigadier Sir T. Seaton, K.C.B., commanding Futtehgurh District, No. 655 dated June 4, 1858, forwarding reports from Colonel Riddell, commanding Mynpoorie Moveable Column, detailing his operations in the Etawah District.

No. 61.

Brigadier Sir T. Seaton, K.C.B., commanding Futtehghur District, to Major H. W. Norman, Deputy Adjutant-General of the Army.

Fort Futtehgurh, June 4, 1858.

SIR, No. 655.

I HAVE the honor to forward, for submission to his Excellency the Commander-in-chief, the accompanying reports from Colonel Riddell, Commanding the Mynpoorie Moveable Column, detailing his operations in the Etawah district, for securing boats for the use of Sir Hugh Rose's force.

All seems to have been managed with great

prudence and judgment, and I would beg to bring to the particular notice of his Excellency, Lieutenant Sheriff's account of his expedition by water to collect and bring down the boats.

I have, &c.,
T. SEATON, Brigadier,
Commanding Futtehgurh District.

No. 62.

Colonel Wm. Riddell, Commanding Mynpoorie Moveable Column, to the Major of Brigade, Futtehgurh.

Camp Oreyah, May 30, 1858.

SIR,   No. 44.

I HAVE the honor to forward herewith a report, dated 29th instant (with three enclosures from Captain and Brevet-Major C. E. Walcott, Royal Artillery, Captain A. Pond, 3rd European Regiment, and Lieutenant W. Sherriff, of the 2nd Punjaub Infantry), to the address of Brigadier Sir T. Seaton, K.C.B., commanding the Futtehgurh district, detailing the services of the Mynpoorie Moveable Column, in the Etawah district, from the 9th to the 28th instant, which I beg may be submitted to the Brigadier with my request that, should he deem the services performed to be of sufficient importance, he will do me the favor of transmitting the papers for the information of his Excellency the Commander-in-chief and of Government.

I have, &c.,
WM. RIDDELL, Colonel,
Commanding Mynpoorie Moveable Column.

No. 63.

Colonel W. Riddell, Commanding Mynpoorie Moveable Column, to Brigadier Sir T. Seaton, K.C.B., Commanding the Futtehgurh District.

Camp Oreyah, May 29, 1858.

SIR,

YOUR instructions, dated Futtehgurh, the 7th instant, directing me to march to Oreyah, collect the boats on the Jumna, and construct a bridge at Sheregurh Ghaut, for the purpose of taking ammunition, &c., across to the Central India Field Force, under Sir Hugh Rose, K.C.B., having reached me at Etawah on the forenoon of the 8th instant, and a reinforcement of 100 recruits of the 3rd Bengal European Regiment, having joined the Mynpoorie Moveable Column the same morning, I at once placed myself in communication with Mr. Hume, the collector, and made arrangements for an immediate move.

2. On the morning of the 9th instant, my force as detailed in the margin,* marched to Bukewar, where I was joined by the collector with the civil establishments, &c., a portion of the Etawah Yeomanry Levies, consisting of 200 horse, 150 foot, and 4 guns (one a 12-pounder carronade, and the rest small pieces, of native manufacture, carrying about a 3-pound ball).

3. In the course of the day, I ascertained that the band of insurgents, who, for some days past, had been in possession at Anuntram (a village six miles in advance of my present camp), had entirely broken up, and retired in different directions, principally towards Oreyah and Aianah, a small

---

* Two 9-pounder guns, with detail of No. 7 Company, 14th Battalion, No. 4 Field Battery, Royal Artillery, 44 men ; Head-quarters 5 Companies 3rd European Regiment, 444 men ; detachment of the 2nd Punjaub Infantry, 117 men ; Alexander's Hf̄rse, 217 sabres,

fort belonging to Roop Sing, a noted rebel and one of their leaders. I accordingly decided on halting here for a day or two, until arrangements could be completed for floating down the boats.

4. To assist Mr. Hume, and conduct the river part of the expedition, I detached the following morning (10th instant), Lieutenant J. P. Sherriff with his Seiks, and the Etawah Local Troops and two small guns to the village of Naugaon, at which point it was proposed to collect the boats from Etawah downwards.

5. On the 12th instant Major Macpherson, Resident at Gwalior, reached my camp, *en route* to join Sir R. Hamilton at Calpee, and next morning the force marched to Ajeetmul, and Lieutenant W. Sherriff having reported all to be ready for an onward movement, the following morning (14th instant), I again marched to Nowadah, a village in the immediate vicinity of the little fort of Aianah, for the twofold purpose of reconnoitring and covering the passage of the boats.

6. On approaching our halting ground, I directed Lieutenant W. H. Furnell to make a detour to our right, with a squadron of Alexander's Horse, and ascertain the nature of the ground about Aianah, now in full view and not above a mile and-a-half off. As he neared the village, the rebels showed in considerable numbers, and opened a brisk fire on him, but without doing any mischief, whereupon he rejoined the force, and our camp was immediately formed.

7. The heat during the forenoon and throughout the day was most intense and extremely trying, and several cases of sun-stroke occurred ; one of them, Lieutenant and Adjutant R. Thompson, of the 3rd European Regiment, terminated fatally after three hours' illness. Before midday, I heard that the rebels had evacuated Aianah, and in the evening I sent Captain A. Pond, with 100 men of the

3rd European Regiment, to take possession of the place and adopt measures for its destruction. Major C. E. Walcott, Royal Artillery, accompanied the party, and afforded his valuable aid in driving two mines under the Zemindar's house, and under one of the bastions. This party returned next morning, having accomplished the object desired, and destroyed the village and fort of the insurgents.

8. Information having again reached me from Lieutenant W. Sherriff, that the river expedition was successfully progressing, I resumed my march on the morning of the 16th instant, reaching Oreyah by sunrise. The accounts given me by the local authorities and townspeople about the rebel bands, who have now so long been infesting this locality, were most vague and unsatisfactory, tending, however, to lead me to believe, that they had all gone across the river ; but, doubting the truth of their statements, and hearing that a few armed men had been seen by our advance guard lurking about the encamping ground just before we came up, I sent off Lieutenant W. H. Furnell, with a party of Alexander's Horse, to feel his way in the direction of the river, whilst our camp was being pitched. As he approached some broken ground about half a mile to our right front, and in the immediate vicinity of the village of Rampoor, the rebels showed themselves by firing on his party, and shortly afterwards they advanced in greater numbers with a few horsemen from the cover of some topes, creeping along over the broken ground. Lieutenant W. H. Furnell then withdrew his sowars, and I ordered the force to get under arms.

9. As the enemy appeared to grow somewhat bolder, I sent forward Major C. E. Walcott, with his two 9-pounder Royal Artillery guns, and two companies of the 3rd European Regiment under

Captain A. Pond, with a squadron of Alexander's
Horse, to drive them back, and act as circumstances might require; and I herewith append the
reports of these officers, showing how ably and
judiciously these orders were carried out. I regret
having to record, that it was during this part of
the operations that Lieutenant W. H. Furnell, in
command of Alexander's Horse was very dangerously wounded by a sepoy, who fired at him from
a few yards' distance, whilst gallantly charging a
small knot of infantry, well ahead of his men; and
Lieutenant H. Chapman, doing duty with Alexander's Horse, who accompanied Lieutenant W.
H Furnell in this charge, had his horse severely
wounded in two places by musket shots. I subsequently threw forward a third company of Europeans, to occupy the village in our front, on ascertaining that Major E. C. Walcott and Captain
A. Pond had succeeded in driving the enemy
across the river, which they had fully effected by
1 P.M.

10. In the meantime, I received a communication from Major the Honorable T. Bourke, Her
Majesty's 88th Regiment, in command of a detachment from Colonel Maxwell's column, informing
me of his being within a short march of Oreyah,
and soon afterwards Lieutenant Angelo reached
my camp with his Towana Horse, having been
sent over by Major the Honorable T. Bourke on
hearing our guns opon. I immediately sent word
to Major the Honorable T. Bourke, requesting
him to move up to Oreyah in the cool of the evening, and at 5 P.M., I changed my camp close down
to the river's bank, so as to secure complete possession of the Sheregurh Ghaut. Major the
Honorable T. Bourke reached Oreyah soon after
dusk, and formed his camp between Oreyah and
the village of Rampoor, which stands on the verge
of the ravines.

11. The enemy took up a position on the opposite bank of the river about 1,200 yards distant, in a village and a small tope of trees, planting their three small guns in the ruins of a small bungalow, from which they kept up a random fire at intervals, until the afternoon of the 17th instant, when they suddenly withdrew their guns, and retired some two miles on the village and fort of Bhudeh.·

12. On the evening of the 17th instant, Lieutenant J. P. Sherriff reached the ghaut with his fleet of boats, and I herewith forward his report of the river portion of the expedition, and to which I beg to call particular attention, as I consider the manner in which this duty has been performed reflects the highest credit on all engaged in it.

13. Deeming it advisable to destroy the village of Sheregurh, and a number of huts erected by the rebels on the opposite bank as a sort of standing camp, I sent over the Seikhs and 100 of Mr. Hume's Levies, under Lieutenant W. Sherriff, on the morning of the 18th instant, supported by a party of 100 Europeans, under Lieutenant H. B. Blake, to effect this object, which was completely carried out, notwithstanding that the rebels assembled in considerable force, and brought out two of their guns from the Ghurree of Bhudeh. Having taken up a position on the high cliff on this bank of the river, I watched the whole operation ; and on observing that the rebels were advancing in great numbers, and gradually drawing round our detachment, I sounded the recall, on which Lieutenant Sherriff withdrew his men slowly, and with the greatest regularity, and the party re-embarked and returned to this bank. We had one European Sergeant (Serjeant-Major Edmonds, of the Etawah Local Artillery), one sepoy, and a regimental bheestie, slightly wounded.

14. On this occasion, I calculated that the rebels

mustered at least from 1,000 to 1,200 footmen, many of them armed and accoutred as sepoys, about 100 cavalry and horsemen, and two guns; and as far as I can ascertain, were under the direction of Lallpoorie Gosain, an adherent of the Nana, aided by the Chief of Bhudeh, and Roop Sing of Aianah; they took up their former position immediately opposite to us, but the greater part of their force returned again to Bhudeh, on finding we had no intention of making any further movement on their side of the river. Nevertheless, they recommenced firing at intervals from their guns, and to take random shots with their rifles, and large heavy matchlocks, without the slightest injury to us.

15. On the 20th instant, I ordered Major the Honorable T. Bourke to rejoin Colonel Maxwell, C.B., now before Calpee on this side of the river, the latter officer having written to me urgently, requesting that the detachment might be allowed to return, their services being greatly needed to work his mortar batteries, &c.

16. Thus matters continued till the forenoon of the 24th, when suddenly the enemy again withdrew their guns, and entirely disappeared, there not being apparently a scout left as a look out. This somewhat unexpected movement was, however, fully explained by the receipt, that evening, of the intelligence of the occupation of Calpee, by Sir Hugh Rose, on the preceding day, an event of which they no doubt got intimation some hours earlier.

17. Sir Hugh Rose's instructions for the disposal of the boats having reached me through Colonel Maxwell, C.B., on the morning of the 28th, I immediately entered into communication with Mr. Hume, and arrangements were at once made for their being sent down to Calpee, under charge of the local police. The boats left Sheregurh

Ghaut the same afternoon, and this morning I formed my camp in the vicinity of Oreyah.

18. Having thus completed the special duty entrusted to me, I have only to record my entire satisfaction with the conduct of all the troops composing my force. Their cheerful endurance of the fatigues and exposures to which they have been necessarily subjected has never flagged, and every officer and soldier has vied one with another in the performance of the trying duties which the nature of the service called for.

19. I would beg particularly to call attention to the services of Captain and Brevet-Major C. E. Walcott, commanding detail of Royal Artillery; to Captain A. Pond, 3rd European Regiment; to Lieutenant J. P. Sherriff, in command of detachment of 2nd Punjaub Infantry, and Lieutenant W. H. Furnell, of Alexander's Horse, who succeeded to the command of that corps on the departure of Captain W. R. E. Alexander, on Medical Certificate. Captain Pond is a first-rate officer, and, being my second in command in the 3rd European Regiment, and the only officer with the force above the rank of subaltern, except Captain and Brevet-Major Walcott, his services have been most onerous, and I beg to recommend his services to favorable notice. Lieutenant C. F. Sharpe, of the 72nd Regiment Native Infantry, and Acting-Quartermaster of the 3rd European Regiment, has acted throughout as my Detachment Staff and Orderly Officer, and has proved himself an efficient Staff Officer.

20. The services of Surgeon A. W. Crozier, F.R.C.S., of the 3rd European Regiment, and Senior Medical Officer of the force, have been most valuable, and, owing to his unremitting attention to the sick, no less than to his judicious sanatory precautions, I attribute in a great measure the almost perfect immunity from sickness, which we

have been mercifully permitted to enjoy during the last two months.

21. In conclusion, I have now only to record my sense of the assistance I have at all times received from Mr. Hume, whose local experience and complete knowledge of the district of which he is the Magistrate and the Collector, has been of the greatest service to me.

I have, &c.,

WM. RIDDELL, Colonel,
Commanding Mynpoorie Moveable Column.

No. 64.

Major C. E. Walcott, Royal Artillery, to Colonel Riddell, 3rd European Regiment, Commanding Mynpoorie Moveable Column.

Sir,   *Sheregurh Ghaut, May* 17, 1858.

IN obedience to your orders on the morning of the 16th instant, in consequence of the enemy showing themselves in force, about three quarters of a mile from our camp, and engaging a party of Alexander's Horse, who had been sent to reconnoitre, I advanced with my two guns, supported by a party of the 3rd European Regiment under Captain Pond. I opened on the enemy at about 600 yards, and drove them into the village (they had only one small gun, a 3-pounder), and then went to support Lieutenant Furnell and his cavalry, who were engaged on my left, where it was now evident the chief part of the enemy were having the ravines to retire through.

Captain Pond extended his men in skirmishing order, and, after a few rounds from my guns, the enemy retreated, Captain Pond following; and I advanced with my two guns along the high ground on my right, with a few Europeans for my support; this brought me in the road in rear of the

village, which Lieutenant Wimberley, whom I had
sent with a few men, found clear of the enemy.

I advanced along the road, passed a ditch and
strong parapet across it, and approached a second
village which the enemy evacuated on our approach. They had evidently intended defending
this position, as there was a strong parapet completely commanding the road. Captain Pond here
rejoined me, and we determined to drive the
enemy across the river, and obtain possession of
the ghaut.

Another company having arrived, that I had
requested you to send me, and not liking to take
my guns into the unknown ravines. I left them
and the company to hold the village, and proceeded,
with Captain Pond and the original company,
towards the ghaut.

The heights were crowned by parties on each
side, and we advanced down the road; the enemy
fled, and, when we arrived at the ghaut, we found
them crossing in great confusion. A few horses
and some baggage were captured at the water's
edge.

Captain Pond returned to report our success.
The enemy numbered some 500 or 600, chiefly
sepoys; 25 or 30 were found killed.

I regret to say Lieutenant Furnell, of Alexander's Horse, was dangerously wounded. I particularly noticed his gallantry in charging, with
Lieutenant Chapman and one sowar, a body of 80
or 90 of the enemy. Captain Pond's coolness and
judgment was conspicuous.

No casualties in the Royal Artillery.

   I have, &c.,

    C. E. WALCOTT, Major,

      Royal Artillery

No. 65.

Captain A. Pond, 3rd European Regiment, to Colonel Riddell, Commanding 3rd European Regiment, and Mynpoorie Moveable Column.

SIR, Camp, *Sheregurh Ghaut, May* 17, 1858.

I HAVE the honor to report that, agreeably to instructions received from you on the morning of the 16th, I proceeded in command of two companies, accompanying two guns, Royal Artillery, under Major Walcott.

As soon as the guns came into action, I sent Lieutenant E. B. Wimberley with a party to skirmish through the ravines, and feel his way in advance of the guns on the right of the road, while I took another party down the ravines on the left of the road, and threw out a party of twenty-five men, principally Enfield riflemen, under Lieutenant Hood, still further on my left, to prevent the rebels from turning our left flank : thus we advanced, driving the enemy through and out of the ravines, past the first two villages, and took possession of the last village, " Descullee," standing on a height in the midst of the ravines, and where the enemy had evidently intended making a stand, as we found they had thrown up an entrenchment, planted a stockade, and cut a trench across the road.

At this point, whence the road winds down at a rapid slope towards the ghaut, Major Walcott halted the guns, and another company of the 3rd moved up in support ; a strong picquet was left in the village, to command the ravines and guard the guns, and the remainder pushed on in pursuit.

I detailed parties on either height of the road to skirmish down to the ghaut, while Major Walcott and myself with the main party, advanced down the road to the water's edge. On coming within sight of the river, we saw the enemy, to the

number of 600, crossing with the greatest precipi-
tancy, leaving a quantity of their baggage and
several of their horses on this side the river, while
the enemy fired upon us from a village on the
other side of the river.

We took possession of the ghaut, and placed a
picquet well under cover and commanding the
ghaut : by one o'clock P.M., we were complete
masters of the position.

The heat throughout the day, and especially in
the ravines, was very great, and I regret to say
several men fell down with sun-stroke, but the
men bore up manfully and behaved admirably. A
number of the enemy were killed in different parts
of the ravines ; it is impossible to calculate the
number with any accuracy ; but, from my own
observations, and that of others who were skirmishing in the ravines, it may be set down at
twenty-five or thirty killed, several of them
sepoys.

I have, &c.,

A. POND, Captain,
3rd European Regiment.

No. 66.

*Lieutenant J. P. Sherriff, in command of the Jumna
Expedition, to Colonel Riddell, Commanding
Mynpoorie Moveable Column.*

SIR,   *Camp, Sheregurh, May* 18, 1858.

ON the evening of the 9th May, when at Bukewar, I was directed to proceed with a force, as per
margin,* to support the magistrate of Etawah, in
collecting boats for a bridge to be made at Sheregurh Ghaut, and in conveying them thither.

2. On the morning of the 10th, I marched to

* 110 2nd Punjaub Infantry; 50 Alexander's Horse;
150 Etawah Local Horse; 150 Etawah Local Infantry;
two 3-pounder guns, Etawah Local Battery.

Nundgaon, which was evacuated by the rebel
Rajah Nirunjun Sing, on our approach ; only one
shot was fired at us. We took here a quantity of
native ammunition, and one very large wall piece.

3. On the 11th, with Messrs. Hume and Maconochie, and thirty riflemen, I proceeded to the
Koondurea Ghaut, and, though the enemy fired
pretty smartly on us at first, succeeded in raising
and bringing over two boats that they had sunk
on the other side.

4. On the evening of the 12th, the boats sent
for by the magistrate having arrived from Etawah,
the detachment of Alexander's Horse returned to
your camp, the whole of our guns and infantry
were embarked ; and, the local horse a little in
advance on the left bank, and infantry skirmishers
thrown out on both banks, we started in the
evening for Dulleep Nugger. The enemy fired at
us from the right bank pretty nearly the whole
night ; but, kept in check by the skirmishers, did
no harm, and we then proceeded steadily down the
river, only halting to raise and bring on boats (for
we found them all sunk), till about ten o'clock on
the morning of the 16th, when we neared Beejhulpore with a train of thirty-two boats : as all the
villages on the right, and many of those on the
left bank were hostile to us, it was only by the
greatest care in keeping the boats together that
we proceeded thus far without accident.

5. Before reaching Beejhulpore, we had received
information that the heights commanding that
ghaut were occupied by the enemy in force, with
guns, and having reconnoitred the place, and ascertained that it was impossible for the boats to pass
without doing so, I determined to attack. I arranged for the boats with the guns to proceed down
the river to support the land attacks, which consisted of three parties, one under Sergeant Purcell
of about fifty of the local infantry, who were

nearest the river (and therefore on the left of my line), a second under a havildar of the 2nd Punjaub Infantry with sixteen men, who occupied the centre, and the 3rd under myself, consisting of sixty-four of my detachment; with these latter, I forced the rear of the enemy's position, while the other two parties kept them engaged in flank. The place was very strong and some of the sepoys fought desperately, but my men were not to be repulsed, and the place was carried, some seventy sepoys killed, five small guns (one 4, two 3 and two 1-pounders), two immense wall-pieces, and a great quantity of ammunition captured, and the enemy utterly dispersed in about two hours. I may add that a party of about forty sepoys crossed on to the left bank early in the affair, and attacked the cavalry, but were held in check by these, till a small party of eleven of my own men and twenty of the new levies, whom I sent over to support, reached and drove them back again. I had one sowar severely, two sepoys very slightly wounded, and one horse was killed. Mr. Hume and Sergeant Purcell both fainted from the extreme heat and exertions to which we were all exposed in the ravines. Further details of the affair are given in the magistrate's narrative, a copy of which I annex.

6. On the 17th we again started and reached Sheregurh safely, with thirty-five boats.

7. The whole operation has been one of considerable difficulty and danger, and has entailed a very great deal of bodily labour, exposure, and privation on both men and officers, while the affair at Beejhulpore Silawa was, notwithstanding the enemy's great superiority in numbers and position, so entirely successful, and reflects so much credit on the men, that I trust you may consider it, worthy of being brought to the notice of his Excellency the Commander-in-chief.

8. I cannot conclude without acknowledging the cordial support and assistance that I have received from first to last from Messrs. Hume and Maconochie, the civil authorities, who, from the nature of the expedition, shared equally in all its dangers, and on whom, of course, the whole of the non-military portion of the arrangements devolved.

9. To Dr. Sheetz, who was exposed in a like manner, my best thanks are also due for his conspicuous kindness and attention to all of us.

10. Sergeants Edmonde and Purcell, of the Etawah Local Artillery and Infantry, behaved admirably, and will, I hope, receive due notice.

I have, &c.,

J. F. SHERRIFF, Lieutenant,
Commanding Jumna Expedition

No. 67.

Narrative.

Sunday, May 16, 1858

IT was too late last night to communicate to Colonel Riddell the intelligence we had heard, as he was to march for Oreyah at 2 A.M., so we had to make up our minds to trust to ourselves alone to force our way. At daylight we started; but, there being absolutely no current, and the wind being dead against us, it was eleven o'clock before we neared Beejhulpore. As usual, our local horse, with the camels, &c., was a little in advance on the left bank, and, when we were still some half mile off the enemy's main position, which was in Silawa (a village of the Jugummunpore Illaqua, opposite Beejhulpore) they, the cavalry, drew up in front of it. We halted to reconnoitre; the enemy at once opened with guns and musketry on the cavalry, and with musketry on us, a party of their skirmishers having crept up along the cliffs of the right bank close to us. We had ascertained

that the force opposite us consisted of between 200
and 300 regular sepoys with a crowd of bundook-
chees ; that they were mostly posted in an almost
inaccessible village by the river bank entirely
commanding the channel, though they had also
several outlying moorchas defending the approaches, and that they had five guns in position,
and a number of immense wall-pieces. Lieutenant
Sherriff determined (as it was impossible to get the
boats down without doing so) to attempt to drive
the enemy out of their position, strong as it was.
We, therefore, leaving seventy of the new levies
and twenty-four artillerymen to guard the boats,
landed on the right bank, and at once threw out a
few skirmishers, who occupied the heights in our
immediate proximity. In the mean time, the
enemy crossed about forty sepoys lower down
opposite their main position, who attacked the
cavalry; one-half of the latter fell back on the boats
covering the camels, our riding horses, &c.; the
other half wheeled right and left, fell back and
advanced, and kept them in check, till we sent
twelve of the seikhs and about twenty of the new
levies to support them, and these very soon drove
the sepoys back across the river with a loss of
eleven men. Whilst this was taking place, Lieutenant Sherriff, myself, and Sergeant Purcell, with
the rest of the force, viz., eighty of the 2nd Punjaub Infantry, and fifty of the new levies, advanced
in skirmishing order along the river bank, and the
heights crowning the bank. Lieutenant Sherriff's
arrangements were admirable, and he so led us,
that, after driving the enemy from crag after crag
and morcha after morcha, he and his men forced
the rear of the main position while the attention of
the enemy was engaged in front by the new levies;
some of the sepoys fought desperately (Lieutenant
Sheriff killed a havildar in hand to hand fight), but
they were soon overpowered, and the main body

fled in utter confusion, leaving guns, wall-pieces, papers, plunder, &c. While we were engaged on land, Mr. Maconochie, Dr. Sheetz, and Sergeant Edmonds brought up the boats also, to a certain extent diverting the enemy's attention ; but the attack of the infantry was so rapidly made good, that our two light guns on board the boats never had occasion to open, as Lieutenant Sherriff had arranged that they should, in support of the land attack. The whole operation was most successful, great as the disadvantages were with which we had to contend. The victory was complete, the whole force behaved admirably, but the men of the 2nd Punjaub Infantry especially displayed the greatest gallantry, and a havildar of my new levies distinguished himself much. About seventy sepoys were killed, whereas we had only one sowar and two sepoys wounded, and one horse killed. We found six boats in the neighbourhood destroyed and three uninjured, of which we took possession. The heat in the ravines was inexpressible. Both Sergeant Purcell and myself fainted, and the whole force were so exhausted by their exertions, that we were obliged to halt for the night where we were.

A. O. HUME.

No. 68.

No. 255 of 1858.

THE Right Honorable the Governor-General is pleased to direct the publication of the following letter from the Commissioner in Nagpore, forwarding one from the Deputy-Commissioner of the Chanda District, submitting a report from Lieutenant Nuttall, Adjutant 2nd Regiment Irregular Infantry, detailing the operations of the detachment of that regiment, and of a party of the Moolkee Horse under his command, up to the date on which they were brought on the strength of the Chanda Field Force.

R. J. H. BIRCH, Colonel,
Secretary to the Government of India, Military Department, with the Governor-General.

No. 69.

George Plowden, Esquire, Commissioner of Nagpore, to Colonel R. J. H. Birch, C.B., Secretary to the Government of India, Military Department, with the Governor-General, Allahabad.

Nagpore, Commissioner's Office,
17th June, 1858.

SIR, No. 44.

I HAVE the honor to forward a copy of a letter, No. 81, dated the 14th instant, from the Deputy-Commissioner of the Chanda District, giving cover to one, No. 1, (without date) from Lieutenant Nuttall, the Adjutant of the 2nd Regiment of Irregular Infantry, furnishing a detailed account of the separate operations of the detachment of that regiment, and of a party of the Moolkee Horse under his command, up to the date on which they were brought on the strength of the Chanda Feld Force, under Captain Shakespear.

2 The Right Honorable the Governor-General will perceive that both Captain Crichton and Lieutenant Nuttall bear the highest testimony to the willingness, endurance, and gallantry, both of the infantry and the Moolkee Horse.

3. It appears to me that this praise is entirely supported by the account given of the operations, and that Lieutenant Nuttall is himself entitled to

1858. 10 C

much commendation for the intelligent and spirited manner in which he conducted the operations.

I have, &c.,

GEORGE PLOWDEN,

Commissioner.

No. 70.

Captain W. H. Crichton, Officiating Deputy-Commissioner, Chanda, to George Plowden, Esq., Commissioner of Nagpore.

Chanda, June 14, 1858.

SIR,   No. 81.

I HAVE the honor to forward copy of a letter from Lieutenant Nuttall, Commanding the detachment of the 2nd Regiment Nagpore Irregular Infantry, which was out with me quelling the disturbances in the Ghote and Arpeillee Zemindaree, and I take the opporunity of bringing to your favorable notice the hearty co-operation I have received from Lieutenant Nuttall, as well as the excellent conduct of all ranks composing his detachment. Indeed, I cannot speak too highly of their willingness on every occasion.

2. The party who manned the guns deserve especial mention; they reached Tarsa, a distance of 48 miles, on the 3rd day after leaving Chanda; the bullocks, like the men, were unaccustomed to moving a gun about, and, to make matters worse, all the drivers had absconded; however, from the zeal and activity of the Sepoys, who took the place of the drivers, feeding and taking care of the bullocks, &c., &c., the gun and ammunition waggon were moved about from place to place over bad roads, with a steady regularity which did the men much credit.

I have, &c.,

W. H. CRICHTON, Officiating Deputy-Commissioner.

3331

No. 71.

Lieutenant Nuttall to Captain Crichton, the Officiating Deputy-Commissioner, Chanda District.

SIR,

I HAVE now the honor to forward, for your information, a detailed account of the work done by the detachment under my command from the morning of the 26th April, 1858, the day I joined your camp, up to the 20th May, 1858, the day the force under the command of Captain Shakespear arrived.

Having joined your camp at Tarsa on the morning of the 26th April, 1858, with the detachment strength as per margin,* along with a small hospital and bazar establishment, I, the same evening, at your request, detached guards, strength as per margin, to the villages of Dhabba, Seonee, and Nandgaon, and moved my camp along with that of your own to the village of Ashtee, situated on the eastern bank of the Wein Gunga river ; at daylight, on the following morning, I started along with you *en route* to the village of Arpeillee, with the rifle company as an advanced guard, leaving the Grenadier Company to escort the baggage a short distance in rear, as also No. 6 Company as the rear guard. After proceeding about 6 miles, and close to the village of Bemunpett, 4 sowars, who were riding about 30 yards at the head of the detachment, came suddenly on a band of 200 armed men, lying down behind the wooded bund of a tank ; they opened fire on the sowars, who galloped back to me, and reported the circumstance. On this, I halted the Rifle Company to allow of the Grenadier Company

* 3 subadars, 3 jemadars, 18 havildars, 18 naiques, 3 drummers, 3 fifers, and 300 privates. Dhabba: 1 havildar, 1 naique, and 12 privates. Seonee : 1 naique and 6 privates. Nandgaon : 1 havildar, 1 naique, and 12 privates.

10 C 2

joining us, which it did almost immediately. I then extended the right sub-division of the Rifle Company as skirmishers, and, with the left sub-division and Grenadier Company as supports, advanced on the bund ; on our nearing the bund of the tank, a smart fire was opened on the skirmishers by the insurgents, who were under cover of the trees on the bund of the tank ; on getting within about 20 yards of the bund, I charged the same with the skirmishers, who topped it with a cheer ; the insurgents fled in every direction, leaving behind them a bag of gunpowder, 2 daggers, 3 spears, some clothes, cooking utensils, as also a packet of letters. I followed them up for some distance through the dense jungle bordering the tank ; but they broke and dispersed in every direction, and, although we scoured the jungle, yet could find no trace of them, so I closed the skirmishers on the supports, and, bringing all the things they had abandoned with me, I rejoined you at the village of Bemunpett.

On my rejoining you, after your having perused the letters I had seized, you informed me that, from the contents of the letters, as also from the information you had received regarding two or three other strong parties being in the vicinity of the river bank. you deemed it advisable to return to our old encamping ground at Tarsa, so as to be able to protect the frontier of your districts. I accordingly did so, and again encamped at Tarsa, the men having been under arms for upwards of 9 hours. On your informing me, the following morning, that, from the reports you had received, you considered the rebels mustered about 1,000 or 1,200 men, as also that there were two mud-forts, one at Arpeillee, and the other at Ghote, as also that the insurgents had several wall-pieces with them, I brought to your notice the advisability of having a gun brought out from Chanda, as also a

reinforcement of another company of infantry, so
as to be able to establish such a strong line of posts
along the frontier, that it would be impossible
for the rebels to enter your district. The following morning, viz., the 23rd April, I started
with two full companies at 4 o'clock A.M., and
visited the villages of Nandgaon, `Kownserrie,
and Kurrowlie, but did not fall in with any of
the rebels.

On the 30th April, 1st and 2nd of May, not
having received any more information as to the
exact whereabouts of the rebels, with the exception of sending a patrol up and down the river,
remained inactive, but, on the evening of the
same day, the gun, with a complete company
of infantry, both of which left Chanda on the
30th April, having arrived, I, the following
morning, viz., 3rd May, established a strong line
of posts at the villages of Nandgaon, Dhabba, and
Tarsa, which, with a detachment sent from Chanda
to Chummoorsee, strength as per margin*, in
my opinion, quite protected the frontier of the
Chanda district, facing the rebel zemindaree. On the
evening of the same day, crossed the river with
the gun` and the remainder of the detachment,
as also your own camp. Shortly after the men
had piled arms, a very severe storm of wind and
rain came on, which, in a quarter of an hour, had
turned the black cotton soil into a sea of mud;
as the men had no tents, and as the old encamping ground was only a coss distant, we both of
us thought it the best plan to return to our old
encamping ground at Tarsa, which I did; but,
although it was only a coss, yet I did not get in

---

* Nandgaon: 1 jemadar, 2 havildars, 2 naiques, 30 privates. Dhabba: 1 jemadar, 1 havildar, 2 naiques, 30 privates. Tarsa: 1 jemadar, 4 havildars, 3 naiques, 52 privates. Chammoorsee: 1 subadar, 1 jemadar, 5 havildars,
4 naiques, 70 privates.

with the gun until quarter past 1 o'clock A.M., it having continued raining the whole time. The men were on this occasion upwards of nine hours under arms.

Halted on the 4th May, to give the men a rest; and early on the morning of the 5th May, again moved across the river to the village of Ashtee along with your own camp, and with the same detachment as I moved across the river on the evening of the 3rd May.

On the morning of the 6th, moved our camps to Kownserrie, and on the following morning at daylight, leaving our camps standing under charge, of a strong guard, moved on to the village of Arpeillie, the residence of one of the rebel zemindars. On nearing the village, expecting opposition, I threw the grenadier company out in skirmishing order, and with the rifle company as supports, and gun in the centre, advanced on the village, passed through the village and mud fort, the other side of which came in view of the bund of a tank distant from the village about 500 yards. Several armed men were seen evidently watching our movements. On seeing this, I doubled down with the grenadier company to the right corner of the bund, intending to take them in flank. On their seeing me do this, they retreated in a body at the double through the dense jungles. Previously to this, I had directed the Quartermaster-Sergeant, who was with the gun, in the event of his seeing a body of armed men, to open upon them. He, seeing these men, mustering, as far as he could judge, about 100, coming down towards his left, opened fire at about 400 yards, and gave them four rounds, but apparently to no effect, as they were immediately lost in the dense jungles. As I was advancing with the skirmishers at the double, I observed a man making the best of his way for the thick jungle, galloped

up with four or five sepoys and made him prisoner, and, on handing him over to you, he proved
to be one of the dewans of the rebel zemindar
Yenkut Rao. This man, after being seized, pointed
out two ghurries in the jungle, which he said
contained his property; in one of these a matchlock with some powder was found. After scouring the jungle for some distance in the vicinity of
the tank, and not being able to obtain any trace
of where the armed men had gone to, I closed the
skirmishers and returned to the village, where I
rejoined you; and, after burning the zemindar's
village to the ground, as we were returning to
Kownserrie, several shots were fired at the detachment. On this occurring, I wheeled a company forward into line to the flank the shots came
from. After extending, entered the jungle for
some distance, but all to no use, from the extreme
denseness of the jungle, as nothing could be seen
of them at all. I closed the men, and resumed my
march back to Kownserrie, which place I reached
at 7 o'clock P.M., the men having been under arms
for upwards of 14 hours, during which period they
traversed about 30 miles of jungly tract of country, in which a great scarcity of water was experienced.

Halted at Kownserrie on the 8th May, to give
the men a rest, and, on the following morning,
moved with our camps to the village of Jamri.

On the morning of the 10th May, moved at daylight on the village of Ghote, the chief residence of
the other rebel zemindar. As, from the reports
you had received, much opposition was expected,
the detachment marched in the following order,
ready at any moment to come into action. As an
advanced guard, the Grenadier company along
with 30 men of the Rifle company, after which
came the gun, then the baggage, escorted by about
60 men of the Rifle company, and last of all a rear

guard of 60 men under command of a native commissioned officer ; on nearing the village, and at a distance of about 200 yards from the same, fire was opened on the detachment from a hill a short distance off the road, on our right flank, in which hill the insurgents had a small wall-piece in position, as also a large body of matchlock-men, posted amongst the rocks and jungle, whilst at the same time a heavy fire of matchlocks was kept up from the village to our front, in one corner of which was a large mud fort; on my getting clear of the jungle, and seeing the positions the insurgents occupied, I determined first to attack and gain possession of the fort. Accordingly, I extended the Grenadier company in skirmishing order, at the same time making the quartermaster-serjeant open fire from the gun with round shot on the hill. I then advanced on the fort, which the Grenadier company carried with a rush, the insurgents flying in every direction. I pursued them through the jungle, but they would not stand, and dispersed in every direction amongst the dense jungle. In the meantime, at the second round, the carriage of the gun broke down, and the gun was thus rendered useless. On this occurring, Subabar Ali Mahomed mounted the hill to the right of the road with a sub-division of No. 6 company, the insurgents fleeing and dispersing in every direction. The affair altogether lasted for about an hour ; no one killed on our side ; only a horse of the Moolkee Rissallah wounded. On the side of the insurgents, three men killed, and others reported wounded. The small loss of life on the side of the insurgents I attribute to the excellent cover they were in, as also their retreating so rapidly, as it was a case, after they were driven from the fort and village, of their firing and retiring through dense jungles, every foot of which they were acquainted with. On searching the village, numbers of swords, matchlocks, spears, bows and arrows, &c., were found.

On my rejoining you, it was just 1 o'clock, the men having been upwards of 9 hours under arms, during which period they had marched 10 miles, at the end of which they had engaged and driven the insurgents from two strong positions. The insurgents in this affair mustered between 600 and 700 men. The same evening I started at 5 P.M., with 100 men, and visited several villages in the vicinity of Ghote, from which villages, during the afternoon, shots had been fired at some camp-followers, but I found them quite deserted.

Halted on the 11th May, to get the gun repaired. Early in the morning, taking 150 men with me, searched several villages, but found them entirely deserted. During the course of the day, two prisoners were brought in, who were found to have arms in their posseesion, and I accordingly handed them over to you for punishment, having burned the villages of Ghote to the ground; and, as you urged the necessity of making a demonstration in the Chummoorsee direction. I accordingly marched with your camp to that place, on the morning of the 12th May, and halted there for five days; again, on the evening of the 18th May, marched to Ghote, halted there the 19th May, and, on the following morning, was joined by Captain Shakespear, and was that same day brought on the strength of his force. I cannot close this without bearing testimony to the willingness, endurance, and gallantry of the infantry under my command, a party of which served the gun in the most able manner; as also to the gallant conduct of the party of Moolkee Horse, who accompanied me throughout these operations, and who made themselves useful in many ways.

I regret this report has not reached you sooner;

but, from constantly moving about, I have been delayed in sending it in.

I have, &c.,

JOHN NUTTALL, Lieutenant,

Commanding Detachment 2nd Regiment Nagpore Irregular Force, on Field Service.

War-Office, Pall-Mall,

17th September, 1858.

2nd Regiment of Life Guards, Lieutenant R. D. Barré Cuninghame, from the 4th Dragoon Guards, to be Cornet and Sub-Lieutenant, by purchase, vice Wynne promoted. Dated 17th September, 1858.

2nd Dragoon Guards, Major William Henry Seymour to be Lieutenant-Colonel, without purchase, vice Brevet-Colonel Campbell, deceased. Dated 7th July, 1858.

Major C. S. Hutchinson to be Major, without purchase, vice Seymour. Dated 7th July, 1858.

Captain Henry Miles Stapylton to be Major, by purchase, vice Hutchinson, whose promotion by purchase on the 31st August, 1858, has been cancelled. Dated 17th September, 1858.

Lieutenant Robert Blair to be Captain, without purchase, vice Hutchinson. Dated 7th July, 1858.

Cornet Francis O'Beirne to be Lieutenant, without purchase, vice Blair. Dated 7th July, 1858.

4th Dragoon Guards, Cornet Robert James Wright to be Lieutenant, by purchase, vice Cuninghame, appointed to the 2nd Life Guards. Dated 17th September, 1858.

9th Light Dragoons, Oliver Ormerod, Gent., to be Cornet, without purchase, in succession to Lieutenant A. S. Jones, promoted in the 18th Light Dragoons. Dated 17th September, 1858.

13th Light Dragoons, William Gore, Gent., to be Cornet, without purchase, vice Keyworth, promoted. Dated 17th September, 1858.

16th Light Dragoons, Cornet George Ludlow Lopes has been permitted to retire from the service by the sale of his Commission. Dated 17th September, 1858

Military Train, Paymaster George W. Macquarie, from the 99th Foot, to be Paymaster, vice Thomas, who exchanges. Dated 17th September, 1858.

3rd Regiment of Foot, Major Thomas Henry Somerville to be Lieutenant-Colonel, without purchase. Dated 17th September, 1858.

Captain Walter Pownall to be Major, without purchase, vice Somerville. Dated 17th September, 1858.

Lieutenant Talbot Ashley Cox to be Captain, without purchase, vice Pownall. Dated 17th September, 1858.

Assistant-Surgeon John Henry Beath, M.D., from the Staff, to be Assistant-Surgeon. Dated 17th September, 1858.

4th Foot, John William Goddard Telfer, Gent., to be Ensign, without purchase. Dated 17th September, 1858.

8th Foot, Brevet-Colonel Edward Harris Greathed, C.B., to be Lieutenant-Colonel, without purchase, vice Brevet-Colonel Hartley, deceased. Dated 26th June, 1858.

Captain James Johnston to be Major, without purchase, vice Greathed. Dated 26th June, 1858.

Brevet-Major A. C. Robertson to be Major, without purchase, vice Johnston, whose promotion on the 24th August, 1858, has been cancelled. Dated 24th August, 1858.

Lieutenant F. B. McCrea to be Captain, without purchase, vice Johnston. Dated 26th June, 1858.

Ensign J. E. W. Black to be Lieutenant, without purchase, vice McCrea. Dated 26th June, 1858.

Ensign A. G. Westby to be Lieutenant, without purchase, vice Black, whose promotion on the 30th July, 1858, has been cancelled. Dated 30th July, 1858.

9th Foot, Ellsworth Fursdon, Gent., to be Ensign, without purchase. Dated 17th September, 1858.

15th Foot, Alexander Herbert Arthur Smith, Gent., to be Ensign, without purchase, vice Gipps, appointed to the 35th Foot. Dated 17th September, 1858.

16th Foot, Charles Platt, Gent., to be Ensign, by purchase, vice Stehelin, appointed to the 94th Foot. Dated 17th September, 1858.

17th Foot, Oliver John Bradford, Gent., to be Ensign, by purchase, vice Fawcett, promoted. Dated 17th September, 1858.

Lambart Francis Wilson Dwyer, Gent., to be Ensign, without purchase, vice Mosse, promoted. Dated 17th September, 1858.

18th Foot, Captain H. J. Haydock, from the 90th Foot, to be Captain, vice McGrigor, who exchanges. Dated 2nd July, 1858.

26th Foot, Lieutenant G. W. Northey to be Instructor of Musketry. Dated 1st August, 1858.

28th Foot, Brevet - Lieutenant - Colonel Percy Archer Butler to be Lieutenant-Colonel, without purchase. Dated 17th September, 1858.

Brevet-Major William Roberts to be Major, without purchase, vice Butler. Dated 17th September, 1858.

Lieutenant Thomas Sutton Kirkpatrick to be Captain, without purchase, vice Roberts. Dated 17th September, 1858.

Ensign Mark Farley Wade to be Lieutenant, without purchase, vice Kirkpatrick. Dated 17th September, 1858.

Assistant-Surgeon William Gerard Don, M.D., from the Staff, to be Assistant-Surgeon. Dated 17th September, 1858.

29*th Foot*, Ensign Kenrick Verulam Bacon to be Lieutenant, without purchase, vice Quin, promoted in the 20th Foot. Dated 17th September, 1858.

34*th Foot*, John MacCarthy O'Leary, Gent., to be Ensign, by purchase, vice Wood, promoted. Dated 17th September, 1858.

39*th Foot*. Ensign O. J. Bradford, from the 17th Foot, to be Ensign, vice Hussey, promoted in the 17th Foot. Dated 17th September, 1858.

Lieutenant Augustus Frederic Raper to be Adjutant, vice T. W. Bennett, who resigns the Adjutancy only. Dated 17th September, 1858.

40*th Foot*, Edward Stack, Gent., to be Ensign, without purchase. Dated 17th September, 1858.

43*rd Foot*, John McNeill, Gent., to be Ensign, by purchase, vice Blyth, promoted. Dated 17th September, 1858.

Horatio Morgan, Esq., late Captain in the Turkish Contingent, to be Paymaster, vice Joseph Denton, deceased. Dated 17th September, 1858.

45*th Foot*, Ensign C. B. Steward to be Lieutenant, without purchase, vice Walker, promoted in the 21st Foot. Dated 17th September, 1858.

Edward Browne, Gent., to be Ensign, by purchase. vice Hayward, promoted. Dated 17th
September, 1858.

46*th Foot*, Assistant-Surgeon George R. Woolhouse, from the Staff, to be Assistant-Surgeon.
Dated 17th September, 1858.

47*th Foot*, Paymaster Henry Charles Watson,
from the 67th Foot, to be Paymaster, vice
Pope, who exchanges. Dated 17th September,
1858.

48*th Foot*, Major Alfred Augustus Chapman to
be Lieutenant-Colonel, without purchase.
Dated 17th September, 1858.

51*st Foot*, Captain William' Agg to be Major, by
purchase, vice the Honourable W. S. Knox,
who retires. Dated 17th September, 1858.

Lieutenant M. C. Farrington to be Captain, with-
.out purchase, vice Goddard, deceased. Dated
23rd June, 1858.

Lieutenant Augustus Brigstocke to he Captain,
by purchase, vice Agg. Dated 17th September,
1858.

Ensign Edward Dudley Oliver to be Lieutenant,
without purchase, vice Farrington. Dated 23rd
June, 1858.

Paymaster George Henry Shuttleworth, from the
21st Foot, to be Paymaster, vice Powell, placed
on half-pay as Lieutenant of the 15th Foot.
Dated 17th September, 1858.

63*rd Foot*, Brevet-Lieutenant-Colonel Thomas
Harries to be Lieutenant-Colonel, without purchase, vice Brevet-Colonel E. R. Hill, appointed
Deputy Adjutant-General in the Windward
and Leeward Islands. Dated 17th September,
1858.

Captain Francis Douglas Grey to be Major, without purchase, vice Harries. Dated 17th September, 1858.

Lieutenant Walter S. Marson to be Captain,

without purchase, vice Grey. Dated 17th September, 1858.

67*th Foot*, Major Thomas Edmond Knox to be Lieutenant-Colonel, without purchase. Dated 17th September, 1858.

Brevet-Major John Porter to be Major, without purchase, vice Knox. Dated 17th September, 1858.

Lieutenant G. T. Horton Atchison to be Captain, without purchase, vice Porter. Dated 17th September, 1858.

Serjeant-Major Charles Preice Killeen to be Ensign, without purchase. Dated 17th September, 1858.

Ensign C. P. Killeen to be Adjutant, vice Atchison, promoted. Dated 17th September, 1858.

Paymaster John Andrew Pope, from the 47th Foot, to be Paymaster, vice Watson, who exchanges. Dated 17th September, 1858.

69*th Foot*, Ensign H. H. Bartlett to be Lieutenant, without purchase, vice Gildea, promoted in the 21st Foot. Dated 17th September, 1858.

William F. Butler, Gent., to be Ensign, without purchase, vice Bartlett. Dated 17th September, 1858.

84*th Foot*, Ensign William Charles Driberg to be Lieutenant, without purchase, vice G. P. Blake, promoted in the 100th Foot. Dated 17th September, 1858.

87*th Foot*, Ensign G. W. Marsden to be Lieutenant, without purchase, vice Gee, promoted in the 17th Foot. Dated 17th September, 1858.

John Leigh Hollest, Gent., to be Ensign, without purchase, vice Marsden. Dated 17th September, 1858.

89*th Foot*, Ensign the Honourable William Harry

Bruce Ogilvy, from the 26th Foot, to be
Ensign, vice Grier, promoted. Dated 17th
September, 1858.

James Shaw Hay, Gent., to be Ensign, without
purchase, vice Hardinge, promoted in the 22nd
Foot. Dated 17th September, 1858.

90*th* *Foot*, Captain W. T. McGrigor, from the
18th Foot, to be Captain, vice Haydock, who
exchanges. Dated 2nd July, 1858.

91*st* *Foot*, Assistant-Surgeon Hugh Mackay Macbeth, from the Staff, to be Assistant-Surgeon.
Dated 17th September, 1858.

93*rd* *Foot*, Lieutenant FitzRoy McPherson to be
Adjutant, vice McBean, promoted. Dated 2nd
July, 1858.

99*th* *Foot*, Brevet-Lieutenant-Colonel George
Marmaduke Reeves to be Lieutenant-Colonel,
without purchase. Dated 17th September,
1858.

Brevet-Major Henry James Day to be Major,
without purchase, vice Reeves. Dated 17th
September, 1858.

Lieutenant Francis Seymour Gaynor to be Captain, without purchase, vice Day. Dated 17th
September, 1858.

Ensign Augustus William Henry Atkinson to be
Lieutenant, without purchase, vice Gaynor.
Dated 17th September, 1858.

Charles Bruce Henry Somerset, Gent., to be Ensign, without purchase, vice Atkinson. Dated
17th September, 1858.

Paymaster Charles Schomberg Thomas, from the
Military Train, to be Paymaster, vice Macquarie, who exchanges. Dated 17th September, 1858.

100*th* *Foot*, Lieutenant George Pilkington Blake,
from the 84th Foot, to be Captain, without
purchase, vice Bruce, who resigns. Dated 17th
September, 1858.

Royal Malta Fencible Regiment, Paolo Bernard, Gent., to be Ensign, with local and temporary rank, vice Sedley, removed to the 1st Dragoon Guards. Dated 17th September, 1858.

HOSPITAL STAFF.

To be Assistant-Surgeons to the Forces.

Edward Acton Gibbon, Gent., vice Chester, appointed to the 74th Foot. Dated 1st September, 1858.

Charles Drelincourt Campbell, M.D., vice Reid, appointed to the 75th Foot. Dated 1st September, 1858.

Thomas Ryan, Gent., vice Holton, promoted on the Staff. Dated 1st September, 1858.

Robert Cardiff Crean, Gent., vice Sharkey, appointed to the 97th Foot. Dated 1st September, 1858.

Robert Gillespie, M.D., vice Newland, appointed to the 5th Foot. Dated 1st September, 1858.

Austin Jonas Ferguson, Gent., vice Burton, appointed to the 6th Dragoons. Dated 1st September, 1858.

James Speedy, Gent., vice Seward, appointed to the Rifle Brigade. Dated 1st September, 1858.

John McLean Marshall, Gent., vice Hoysted, appointed to the 77th Foot. Dated 1st September, 1858.

To be Acting Assistant-Surgeons.

Edmund Brown, Gent. Dated 10th September, 1858.

Henry Frederick Meadows, Gent. Dated 17th September, 1858.

1858.   10 D

BREVET.

The undermentioned Officers, having completed three years' actual service in the rank of Lieutenant-Colonel, to be promoted to be Colonels in the Army, under the Royal Warrant of the 6th October, 1854 :

Lieutenant-Colonel C. W. D. Staveley, C.B., 44th Foot. Dated 6th May, 1858.

Lieutenant-Colonel William Fenwick, C.B., 10th Foot. Dated 26th July, 1858.

The undermentioned promotion to take place in the Indian Military Forces of Her Majesty, consequent on the death of Major-General Richard Benson, C.B., Bengal Infantry, on the 26th August, 1858 :

To be Major-General.

Colonel Harry Meggs Graves, Bengal Infantry. Dated 27th August, 1858.

The undermentioned Officers of the Indian Military Forces of Her Majesty, retired upon full-pay, to have a step of honorary rank, as follows:

To be Major-Generals.

Colonel James Kilner, Bombay Engineers. Dated 21st May, 1858.

Colonel William Biddle, Madras Infantry. Dated 17th September, 1858.

To be Colonels.

Lieutenant-Colonel Robert Edward Turnour Richardson, Bengal Infantry. Dated 17th September, 1858.

Lieutenant-Colonel Samuel Landon, Bombay Infantry. Dated 17th September, 1858.

To be Lieutenant-Colonel.

Major Charles William Hodson, Madras Infantry. Dated 17th September, 1858.

To be Majors.

Captain David Lester Richardson, Bengal Infantry. Dated 17th September, 1858.

Captain John William Goad, Madras Artillery. Dated 17th September, 1858.

Captain Robert Levison James Ogilvie, Madras Infantry. Dated 17th September, 1858.

Admiralty, 8th September, 1858.

Corps of Royal Marines.

Gentleman Cadet James Samuel Derriman to be Second Lieutenant.

14th September, 1858.

Second Lieutenant William Crosbie Hesketh to be First Lieutenant, vice Hope, deceased.

Commission signed by the Queen.

Royal North Lincoln Militia.

David Davis, Gent., late of the 35th Foot, to be Quartermaster. Dated 23rd July, 1858.

Commission signed by the Lord Lieutenant of the County of Middlesex.

1st or Royal East Middlesex Regiment of Militia.

William Henry Mangles, Esq., late Captain 50th Foot, to be Captain, vice Birch, resigned. Dated 9th August, 1858.

Commission signed by the Lord Lieutenant of the County of Northumberland.

Northumberland Regiment of Militia Artillery.

John William Finch, Gent., to be First Lieutenant. Dated 8th September, 1858.

Commissions signed by Her Majesty's Commissioners of Lieutenancy of the City of London.

Regiment of Royal London Militia.

Lieutenant Arthur Cumming Thomas Barrow to be Captain, vice Charles Clement Brooke, resigned. Dated 15th September, 1858.

Lieutenant Frederick Peto to be Captain, vice Alfred Chicheley Plowden, resigned. Dated 16th September, 1858.

Lieutenant Robert Harris Hardy, late 5th Fusiliers, to be Lieutenant, vice James Stuart Tulk, resigned. Dated 15th September, 1858.

Lieutenant Richard Lee Mayhew, late East Norfolk Militia, to be Lieutenant, vice John Thomas Henry Butt, resigned. Dated 16th September, 1858.

James Johnston Brown, Gent., to be Lieutenant, vice Edward Vere Jones, promoted. Dated 17th September, 1858.

George Coulson Childs, Gent., to be Ensign, vice Alexander Renwick. Dated 15th September, 1858.

Commissions signed by Her Majesty's Commissioners of Lieutenancy of the County of Ayr.

Royal Ayrshire Rifles.

Sir James Fergusson, Bart., late Lieutenant and Captain Grenadier Guards, to be Lieutenant-Colonel, vice Sir Thomas Montgomery Cuninghame, Bart., resigned. Dated 14th September, 1858.

FROM THE

LONDON GAZETTE of SEPTEMBER 21, 1858.

Whitehall, September 21, 1858.

THE Queen has been pleased to give and grant unto Captain James Rawstorne, of the Royal Navy, Her Majesty's royal licence and permission that he may accept and wear the Imperial Order of the Medjidie, of the Fourth Class, which the Sultan hath been pleased to confer upon him, as a mark of His Imperial Majesty's approbation of his distinguished services before the enemy during the late war.

The Queen has also been pleased to give and grant unto James Vaughan Hughes, Esq., M.D., Her Majesty's royal licence and permission that he may accept and wear the Cross of a Knight of the Order of Saint Maurice and Saint Lazarus, which the King of Sardinia hath been pleased to confer upon him in testimony of His Majesty's approbation of his distinguished services before the enemy during the late war.

Downing-Street, September 18, 1858.

The Queen has been pleased to appoint the Right Reverend Dr. Rigaud, Bishop of Antigua, to be a Member of the Council for that Island ; Galvan L. Bellot, Esq., to be a Member of the Council for the Island of Dominica ; and Edwin D. Baynes and John F. Kirwan, Esqrs., to be

Members of the Council for the Island of Montserrat.

Her Majesty has also been pleased to appoint John Clements,, Esq., to be Inspector-General of Police for the Island of Barbadoes.

Indian Office, September 21, 1858.

It is hereby notified that, in compliance with the enactment contained in the eighth clause of the Act of Parliament "for the better government of India," passed in the session holden in the 21st and 22nd year of Her Majesty's reign, chapter 106, the late Court of Directors of the East India Company certified to the late Board of Commissioners for the Affairs of India, under the seal of the said Company, that they had elected—

Charles Mills, Esq.
John Shepherd, Esq.
Sir James Weir Hogg, Baronet.
Elliot Macnaghten, Esq.
Ross Donnelly Mangles, Esq.
William Joseph Eastwick, Esq., and
Henry Thoby Prinsep, Esq.
to be Members of the Council of India, established by the said Act.

It is further notified that, in compliance with the enactment aforesaid, Her Majesty has been pleased, by warrant under Her Royal Sign Manual, to appoint to be Members of such Council the following eight persons : —

Sir Henry Conyngham Montgomery, Baronet ;
Sir Frederick Currie, Baronet ;
Sir John Laird Mair Lawrence, Baronet, Knight
Grand Cross of the Civil Division of the Most
Honourable Order of the Bath ;

Sir Robert John Hussey Vivian, Major-General
of the Forces of the East India Company, and
Knight Commander of the Military Division of
the Most Honourable Order of the Bath ;
Sir Proby Thomas Cautley, formerly Colonel of
the Forces of the East India Company, and
Knight Commander of the Civil Division of the
Most Honourable Order of the Bath ;
Sir Henry Creswicke Rawlinson, formerly Lieu-
tenant-Colonel of the Forces of the East India
Company, and Knight Commander of the Civil
Division of the Most Honourable Order of the
Bath ;
John Pollard Willoughby, Esq., and
William Arbuthnot, Esq.

Board of Trade, Whitehall,
September 21, 1858.

The Right Honourable the Lords of the Committee of Privy Council for Trade and Plantations
have received, through the Secretary of State for
Foreign Affairs, a copy of a Despatch from Her
Majesty's Minister at Saint Petersburg, announcing that a quarantine of four days will be
imposed on all vessels arriving at the ports of
Soukoum Kalé, Redout Kalé, and Poti, from ports
in the Turkish dominions.

War-Office, Pall-Mall,
21st September, 1858.

Royal Engineers, Lieutenant-Colonel Edward
Frome, from the Seconded List, to be a Super-
numerary Lieutenant-Colonel. Dated 18th
August, 1858.

3352

Lieutenant John Sargent, from half-pay of the Royal Artillery, to be Paymaster in the Royal Artillery and Royal Engineers. Dated 4th September, 1858.

Admiralty, 17th September, 1858.

In consideration of the successful operations on the Pei Ho, as recorded in the Supplement to the London Gazette of the 27th July, 1858, the following promotions have this day taken place :—

Commander Charles T. Leckie,
Commander Samuel G. Cresswell,
to be Captains.

Lieutenant Alleyne Bland,
Lieutenant Ralph P. Cator,
Lieutenant Arthur T. Thrupp,
to be Commanders.

Mr. Charles Prickett, Second Master, to be Master.

Staff-Surgeon Charles A. Anderson, M.D., to be Deputy Inspector of Hospitals and Fleets.

Mr. William H. M. Arnold, Assistant-Paymaster, to be Paymaster.

And for general services during the operations in China, the following promotions have been made :

Deputy Inspector George Burn, M.D., to be Inspector of Hospitals and Fleets ; and

Mr. John T. Gabriel, Assistant-Surgeon, to be Surgeon.

Commissions signed by the Lord Lieutenant of the County of Bedford.

Bedfordshire Regiment of Militia.

Alfred - Herbert Lucas, Gent., to be Ensign. Dated 1st September, 1858.
Ensign Stephen Kent Winkworth to be Lieutenant. Dated 26th August, 1858.

Commission signed by the Lord Lieutenant of the County of Worcester.

Worcestershire Regiment of Militia.

Thomas Rainforth, Gent., to be Eusign.

Commission signed by the Lord Lieutenant of the County of Sussex.

Light Infantry Battalion of the Royal Sussex Militia.

William Batley, Gent., to be Surgeon, vice Young, resigned. Dated 14th September, 1858.

Commission signed by the Lord Lieutenant of the County of Middlesex.

2nd or Edmonton Royal Rifle Regiment of Middlesex Militia.

Lieutenant Jervoise Smith to be Captain, vice Glyn, resigned. Dated 27th August, 1858.

Commission signed by the Lord Lieutenant of the County of Monmouth.

Royal Monmouthshire Militia.

Rhys Brychan Powell, Gent., to be Ensign. Dated 17th September, 1858.

FROM THE

LONDON GAZETTE of SEPTEMBER 24, 1858.

Whitehall, September 15, 1858.

THE Queen has been pleased to give and grant unto Charles Thomas Vesey Bunbury Isaac, Esquire, Major in the 82nd Regiment of Foot, and to Vesey Thomas Bunbury Isaac, Esquire, sometime an Officer in the 82nd Regiment, younger sons of Simon Isaac, late of Dunkirk, in the Kingdom of France, and formerly of Dromore Cottage, in the county of Monaghan, deceased, and grandsons of Thomas Bunbury Isaac (formerly Thomas Bunbury), of Bloomfield and Holly-wood, in the county of Down, Esquire, also deceased, Her royal licence and authority that they may henceforth resume their paternal family surname of Bunbury only, and be called and known by the names of Charles Thomas Vesey Bunbury, and Vesey Thomas Bunbury, respectively:

And also to command that the said royal concession and declaration be recorded in Her Majesty's College of Arms, otherwise to be void and of none effect.

NOTICE.

Foreign-Office, September 24, 1858.

The Earl of Malmesbury, Her Majesty's Secretary of State for Foreign Affairs, has received a note from M. Van de Weyer, Belgian Minister at this Court, dated the 21st instant, stating that henceforward Passports granted by Her Majesty's Government to British Subjects proceeding to the continent, by way of Belgium, will not require the formality of being countersigned by any Belgian diplomatic or Consular agent in this country.

Foreign-Office, September 23, 1858.

Notice is hereby given, that the Earl of Malmesbury has appointed George Grant Francis, Esq., to be Agent at Swansea for the issue of Foreign-Office Passports.

War-Office, Pall-Mall,
24th September, 1858.

2nd Regiment of Dragoon Guards, Serjeant-Major James Russell, from the 5th Dragoon Guards, to be Riding Master, vice Kirk, deceased. Dated 24th September, 1858.

3rd Light Dragoons, Cornet Reginald Piffard to be Lieutenant, by purchase, vice Fawcett, promoted. Dated 24th September, 1858.

9th Light Dragoons, Thomas Smales, Esq., late Chief Paymaster of the Turkish Contingent, to be Paymaster, vice Ratcliff, placed upon half-pay. Dated 24th September, 1858.

Royal Artillery, Lieutenant Thomas Bland Strange to be Second Captain, vice Earle, deceased. Dated 16th September, 1858.

To be Paymasters in the Royal Artillery and Royal Engineers.

Charles Wilkinson, Gent. Dated 17th September, 1858.

Edward Gibbs, Gent. Dated 17th September, 1858.

3rd *Regiment of Foot*, Assistant-Surgeon James Wilson, M.B., from the Staff to be Assistant-Surgeon. Dated 24th September, 1858.

8th *Foot*, Lieutenant Forster Longfield to be Captain, by purchase, vice Martin, who retires. Dated 24th Se tember, 1858.

10th *Foot*, Robert Blakeney Mitchell, Gent., to be Ensign, without purchase, vice Grant, promoted in the 16th Foot. Dated 24th September, 1858.

13th *Foot*.

To be Ensigns, without purchase.

Andrew Charles Cunningham, Gent., vice Henzell, promoted. Dated 24th September, 1858.

William James Hall, Gent., vice Starr, who resigns. Dated 25th September, 1858.

16th *Foot*. The promotion of Ensign C. H. Newbatt, from the 10th Foot, to a Lieutenancy, without purchase, as stated in the Gazette of 7th September, 1858, has been cancelled.

22nd *Foot*, Ensign William Busfeild, from the 50th Foot, to be Lieutenant, without purchase. Dated 24th September, 1858.

23rd *Foot*. The second Christian name of Ensign Jones, appointed, without purchase, on the 4th June, 1858, is *Palmer*.

24th *Foot*, Ensign Hugh Backhouse Church to be Lieutenant, without purchase. Dated 24th September, 1858.

Lieutenant Robert Paterson Fox to be Adjutant. Dated 16th July, 1858.

Lieutenant A. T. Jones to be Instructor of Musketry. Dated 15th September, 1858.

28th *Foot*, Robert Burn Singer, Gent., to be Ensign, without purchase, vice Wade, promoted. Dated 24th September, 1858.

29th Foot, Robert Berkeley, Gent., to be Ensign, without purchase, vice Bacon, promoted. Dated 24th September, 1858.

30th Foot, Lieutenant Henry Corbet Singleton to be Captain, by purchase, vice Litton, who retires. Dated 24th September, 1858.

Ensign Montagu D. Stevenson to be Lieutenant, by purchase, vice Singleton. Dated 24th September, 1858.

37th Foot, Charles Edward King, Gent., to be Ensign, without purchase, vice Mason, promoted. Dated 24th September, 1858.

39th Foot, Lieutenant Edward Gatty to be Instructor of Musketry. Dated 24th August, 1858.

48th Foot, Brevet-Colonel Edward George Walpole Keppel, from half-pay Unattached, to be Major, vice Chapman, promoted. Dated 24th September, 1858.

Brevet-Major Robert Blakeney to be Major, by purchase, vice Keppel, who retires. Dated 24th September, 1858.

Lieutenant H. F. Brooke to be Captain, by purchase, vice Blakeney. Dated 24th September, 1858.

49th Foot, John Jamison Russell Russell, Gent., to be Ensign, without purchase, vice Hill, appointed to the 70th Foot. Dated 24th September, 1858.

51st Foot, Ensign Henry Steuart Tompson to be Lieutenant, by purchase, vice Brigstocke, promoted. Dated 24th September, 1858.

Arthur Shaen Carter, Gent., to be Ensign, without purchase, vice Oliver, promoted. Dated 24th September, 1858.

56th Foot, Assistant-Surgeon William Cathcart Boyd, from the Staff, to be Assistant-Surgeon;

vice Knox, promoted on the Staff. Dated 24th September, 1858.

60*th Foot*, Major W. Butler to be Lieutenant-Colonel, without purchase, vice Brevet-Colonel Spence, deceased. Dated 9th September, 1858.

Brevet-Major Sir E. F. Campbell, Bart., to be Major, without purchase, vice Butler. Dated 9th September, 1858.

Lieutenant J. Hare to be Captain, without purchase, vice Sir E. F. Campbell, Bart. Dated 9th September, 1858.

Ensign F. A. Campbell to be Lieutenant, without purchase, vice Hare. Dated 9th September, 1858.

65*th Foot*, Lieutenant John Owen Jones Priestley to be Captain, by purchase, vice Marsh, who retires. Dated 24th September, 1858.

Ensign Falcon Peter Leonard to be Lieutenant, by purchase, vice Priestley. Dated 24th September, 1858.

67*th Foot*, Lieutenant R. E. Barry to be Captain, by purchase, vice D'Arcy, who retires. Dated 24th September, 1858.

Ensign Charles William Creyke to be Lieutenant, by purchase, vice Barry. Dated 24th September, 1858.

70*th Foot*, Ensign W. H. Ralston to be Lieutenant, without purchase, vice Travers, promoted in the 17th Foot. Dated 24th September, 1858.

Ensign John Beldham to be Lieutenant, without purchase, vice Crozier, promoted in the 18th Foot. Dated 24th September, 1858.

Norman Huskisson, Gent., to be Ensign, without purchase, vice Ralston. Dated 24th September, 1858.

83*rd Foot*, Lieutenant John Sprot to be Captain,

without purchase, vice Cooper, deceased. Dated 14th July, 1858.

Lieutenant Richard Thomas Sweeny to be Captain, without purchase, vice Nott, deceased. Dated 2nd September, 1858.

Ensign Frederick Karslake to be Lieutenant, without purchase, vice Sweeny. Dated 2nd September, 1858.

88th Foot, Lieutenant Edgar Edward Austin to be Adjutant, vice Evans, who resigns the Adjutancy only. Dated 20th June, 1858.

89th Foot, Richard Nathan Hubbersty, Gent., to be Ensign, without purchase, vice Warburton, deceased. Dated 24th September, 1858.

98th Foot, Lieutenant William Henry Joseph Lance to be Instructor of Musketry, vice Griffin, appointed to act as Adjutant to an Eurasian Corps. Dated 6th July, 1858.

99th Foot, Quartermaster-Serjeant John Johnston to be Quartermaster, vice Browne, who retires on half-pay. Dated 24th September, 1858.

The second Christian name of Ensign ffolliott, appointed by purchase on the 7th September, 1858, is *Homan*, and not *Homar*, as previously stated.

100th Foot, Ensign Frederick Morris to be Instructor of Musketry. Dated 10th September, 1858.

Rifle Brigade, Ensign A. A. A. Kinloch to be Lieutenant, by purchase, vice Moore, promoted. Dated 24th September, 1858.

Ceylon Rifle Regiment, Lieutenant Charles Hamilton Roddy to be Captain, by purchase, vice Bews, who retires. Dated 24th September, 1858.

Ensign F. A. Stewart to be Lieutenant, by purchase, vice Roddy. Dated 24th September, 1858.

Frederick Chenevix Baldwin, Gent., to be Ensign, without purchase, vice Daniell, appointed to the 75th Foot. Dated 24th September, 1858.

Cape Mounted Riflemeh, Ensign Charles Henry Marillier to be Instructor of Musketry. Dated 7th September, 1858.

Royal Canadian Rifles, Captain K. M. Moffatt to be Major, by purchase, vice Seton, who retires. Dated 24th September, 1858.

HOSPITAL STAFF.

Assistant-Surgeon Francis Walter Knox, from the 56th Foot, to be Staff-Surgeon of the Second Class, vice John Grogan, M.B., placed on half-pay. Dated 24th September, 1858.

BREVET.

Lieutenant-Colonel C. Cameron Shute, of the 6th Dragoons, having completed three years' actual service in the rank of, Lieutenant-Colonel, to be Colonel in the Army under the Royal Warrant of the 6th of October, 1854. Dated 21st September, 1858.

Brevet-Lieutenant-Colonel Patrick Gordon, 11th Bengal Native Infantry, to be Colonel in the Army. Dated 20th July, 1858.

Admiralty, 11th August, 1858.

Corps of Royal Marines.

Captain and Brevet-Major Gallway Byng Payne to be Lieutenant-Colonel, vice Langford, retired on full-pay.

First Lieutenant George Bazalgette to be Captain, vice Payne, promoted.

First Lieutenant Edward Gough McCallum to be Captain, vice Lillicrap, retired on full-pay.

Second Lieutenant Henry Towry Miles Cooper to be First Lieutenant, vice Bazalgette, promoted.

Second Lieutenant Frederick Edward Molyneux St. John to be First Lieutenant, vice McCallum, promoted.

Commission signed by the Lord Lieutenant of the County of Monmouth.

Royal Monmouthshire Militia.

William Allanay, Gent., to be Ensign.

Commissions signed by the Lord Lieutenant of the County of Buckingham.

Royal Bucks King's Own Militia.

Ensign John Wood to be Lieutenant, vice Russell, deceased.

John Stratton Fuller, Gent., to be Lieutenant, vice Roworth, resigned.

FROM THE

LONDON GAZETTE of SEPTEMBER 28, 1858.

Admiralty, September 27, 1858.

WITH reference to the despatches from Rear-Admiral Sir Michael Seymour, K.C.B., the Commander-in-Chief of Her Majesty's ships and vessels on the East India station, dated the 21st May last, inserted in the supplement to the London Gazette of the 27th July, 1858, the following despatch has been also received from Sir Michael Seymour, by the Lords Commissioners of the Admiralty.

1858.   10 E

No. 179.

Coromandel, at Tientsin,
SIR, *June* 1, 1858.

OWING to the short time I had to prepare my despatches, after the capture of the forts at the mouth of the Pei-Ho, I omitted to inform the Lords Commissioners of the Admiralty that the Cormorant, the leading ship at the attack, had to force and break a heavy boom of bamboo cables drawn across the channel, upon which the fire of the enemy was concentrated ; a description of the boom is inclosed. I should also have mentioned the essential services rendered by Captain Roderick Dew, in Her Majesty's steam gun vessel Nimrod, the fire from her formidable broadside having mainly contributed to destroy a sand bag battery of nineteen guns, upsetting nearly every gun in the work.

I enclose a statement of the troops in the batteries, translated by the Rev. Mr. Martin, from muster rolls picked up in the forts, amounting to 3,200. This is independent of the large encampments of troops which were in rear of the position.

I have, &c.,
(Signed) M. SEYMOUR,
Rear-Admiral and Commander-in-Chief.
The Secretary of the Admiralty,
London.

Her Majesty's Ship Cormorant,
SIR, *River Pei-Ho, May* 21, 1858.

I HAVE the honour to inform you, that in obedience to orders received from you to examine into the size and description of the cables stretched across the rivers which the ship under your command had to force her way through, under a heavy fire from the batteries on both sides of the river, the first set of cables were 7 in number, made of 9-inch bamboo rope, and buoyed the whole way across the river with spars of about 10-inch, and moored with Chinese anchors.

The second set of cables, about 200 yards north of the first set, were of the same size and description as the first.

I have, &c.,

(Signed)   W. H. FAWCKNER,

Master Commanding Hesper.

Commander Saumarez,
Her Majesty's Ship Cormorant.

A Summary of Chinese Troops at the Southern Battery at the mouth of the Pei-Ho, from a Paper picked up on the day of the Battle.

Old Fort.—Total of all the battalions 885, distributed as follows :

Haikow Battalion	...	...	... 300
Ho Koo Battalion	...	...	... 85
Ho Kien Battalion	...	...	... 3'0
Tiëntsin Regiment	...	...	... 200

Middle Fort.—Total of all the battalions 1034, distributed as follows :

Left and Marine Battalions	...	...	300
Ho Kien, 2 Levies	...	...	197
He Kow Battalion	...	...	25
Militia Trained Band	...	...	512

Southern Fort.—Total 628, distributed as follows :

Left Battalion	...	...	... 300
Woo Kwan	...	...	... 150

(Cetera desunt.)

A roll picked up upon the north bank gives the number of troops at the North Bank Fort as 358.

10 E 2

A wounded man met with at this place gave
the total at all the batteries as 3200.
(Signed)   W. A. P. MARTIN,

At the Court at *Osborne House, Isle of Wight,*
the 31st day of *July,* 1858.

The QUEEN'S Most Excellent Majesty in
Council was pleased to approve and ratify a
scheme duly prepared (as set forth in this
Gazette), by the Ecclesiastical Commissioners
for England, —

For constituting a separate district for spiritual
purposes out of the parish of Christchurch, Spitalfields, in the county of Middlesex, and in the
diocese of London, to be named the District of
Saint Stephen, Spitalfields.   .

War-Office, September 28, 1858.

The Queen has been graciously pleased to make
and ordain a special statute of the Most Honour-
able Order of the Bath, for appointing the Earl of
Elgin and Kincardine, K.T., Her Majesty's High
Commissioner and Plenipotentiary on a Special
Mission to the Emperor of China, to be an Extra
Member of the Civil Division of the First Class,
or Knights Grand Cross, of the said Order.

Her Majesty has also been graciously pleased to
give orders for the appointment of—
 Captain William Cornwallis Aldham, R.N.,
 Captain George William Preedy, R.N., and
 The Honourable Frederick William Adolphus
  Bruce, Her Majesty's Agent and Consul-
  General in Egypt,
to be Ordinary Members of the Civil Division of
the Third Class, or Companions, of the said Most
Honourable Order.

Downing-Street, September 24, 1858.

The Queen has been pleased to appoint Philip Francis Little, and Bryan Robinson, Esqrs., to be Assistant Judges of the Supreme Court of the Island of Newfoundland; and George James Hogsett, Esq., to be Attorney-General, and John Hayward, Esq., to be Solicitor-General, for the said Island.

Her Majesty has also been pleased to appoint Charles Young, Esq., to be Attorney-General, and William Swabey, Esq., to be Registrar of Deeds and Keeper of Plans, for the Island of Prince Edward.

Whitehall, September 28, 1858.

The Queen has been pleased to present the Reverend William Mungall to the church and parish of Barr, in the presbytery and county of Ayr, vacant by the death of the Reverend James Gibson, late minister thereof.

(1449.)

Board of Trade, Whitehall,
September 27, 1858.

The Right Honourable the Lords of the Committee of Privy Council for Trade and Plantations have received, through the Secretary of State for Foreign Affairs, a copy of a Despatch from Her Majesty's Consul at Kertch, reporting that all vessels arriving from the ports of the North Coast of Africa, and from Malta, will be required to perform quarantine at Theodosia, there being no quarantine establishment at the port of Kertch.

(1450.)

Board of Trade, Whitehall,
September 27, 1858.

The Right Honourable the Lords of the Committee of Privy Council for Trade and Plantations have received, through the Secretary of State for Foreign Affairs, a copy of a Despatch from Her Majesty's Consul-General in Syria, reporting that all vessels arriving at that port from the undermentioned places will be subjected to quarantine, as follows:

	Vessels and Passengers.	Cargo.
Tripoli (Barbary), Morocco, Ceuta, Malta, and Gibraltar . .	15 days.	21 days.
Egypt	20 days.	31 days.

(1453.)

Board of Trade, Whitehall,
September 27, 1858.

The Right Honourable the Lords of the Committee of Privy Council for Trade and Plantations have received, through the Secretary of State for Foreign Affairs, a copy of a Despatch from Her Majesty's Consul at Lisbon, enclosing copy of a Portuguese Royal Decree, prolonging for three years, the period during which machinery for the manufacture of the products of the sugar cane may be imported, free from duty, into the islands of Madeira and Porto Santo.

(1456.)

Board of Trade, Whitehall,
September 27, 1858.

The Right Honourable the Lords of the Committee of Privy Council for Trade and Plantations, have received information, through the Secretary of State for Foreign Affairs, that an Official Notification has been issued by the Russian Government, warning masters of vessels visiting the southern ports of Russia, of the inconvenience to which they may expose themselves, by neglecting to be furnished with proper Consular Certificates of Health.

(1461.)
Board of Trade, Whitehall,
September 27, 1858.

The Right Honourable the Lords of the Committee of Privy Council for Trade and Plantations have received, through the Secretary of State for Foreign Affairs, a copy of a Despatch from Her Majesty's Consul at Lisbon, reporting that all vessels arriving from Brazil, and having had yellow fever on board, will be subjected to a quarantine of eight days, and will be admitted into the port of Lisbon on the condition only that eight days shall have elapsed since the cessation of the last case.

War-Office, Pall-Mall,
28th *September,* 1858.

Coldstream Regiment of Foot Guards, Andrew Spittall, M.D., to be Assistant-Surgeon, vice Phipps, deceased. Dated 28th September 1858.

Admiralty, 14th *September,* 1858.
Corps of Royal Marines.

Gentleman Cadet Edward Ellice Hill to be Second Lieutenant.

Lightning Source UK Ltd.
Milton Keynes UK
UKHW020711080119
334942UK00012B/1920/P